ATATÜRK

Patrick Kinross was educated at Balliol College, Oxford, after which he became a journalist. During World War II he was posted as intelligence officer to the Middle East and later served as press counsellor at the British Embassy in Cairo. His travels through the Levant resulted in many books, including *Within the Taurus* and *Europa Minor*. Repeated visits to Turkey led to the publication of *Atatürk* in 1964, and to *The Ottoman Centuries*, which he finished just before his death in 1976.

Also by Patrick Kinross

The Ruthless Innocent
The Orphaned Realm
Within the Taurus
Europa Minor
The Century of the Common Peer
Portrait of Greece
The Innocents at Home
The Candid Eye
Portrait of Egypt
The Windsor Years
Between Two Seas
The Ottoman Centuries

ATATÜRK
The Rebirth of a Nation

Patrick Kinross

PHOENIX

5 UPPER SAINT MARTIN'S LANE
LONDON
WC2H 9EA

A PHOENIX PAPERBACK

First published in Weidenfeld paperback in 1993
Phoenix edition published in 1995
This paperback edition published in 2001
by Phoenix Press,
a division of The Orion Publishing Group Ltd,
Orion House, 5 Upper St Martin's Lane
London WC2H 9EA

An Hachette UK company

15 17 19 20 18 16

A CIP catalogue record for this book
is available from the British Library

ISBN 978-1-8421-2599-1

The Orion Publishing Group's policy is to use papers
that are natural, renewable and recyclable products and
made from wood grown in sustainable forests. The logging
and manufacturing processes are expected to conform to
the environmental regulations of the country of origin.

Printed and bound by CPI Group
(UK) Ltd, Croydon, CR0 4YY

www.orionbooks.co.uk

To
CHRISTOPHER SYKES

CONTENTS

CONTENTS

PART TWO

THE WAR OF INDEPENDENCE

PART THREE
THE RISE OF THE TURKISH REPUBLIC

ILLUSTRATIONS

MAPS

ACKNOWLEDGEMENTS

My thanks are due in the first place to President Gürsel and the Government of the Turkish Republic for granting me access to the Presidential Archives at Çankaya, Ankara, and for otherwise assisting my researches. They are due in particular to the Ministry of Tourism and Information for facilitating visits to Atatürk's battlefields and other parts of the country and for supplying me with photographs. I must also thank Professor Enver Ziya Karal, head of the Department of the History of the Revolution at Ankara University, for his assistance in the supply of information and photographs and for his consistent encouragement.

In Britain my thanks are due to Sir Anthony Rumbold, Bt, CB, CMG, for access to the papers of his father, the late Sir Horace Rumbold, High Commissioner and Ambassador at Constantinople 1920–24; Admiral Sir Bertram Thesiger, KBE, CB, CMG, for the loan of his unpublished *Naval Memories*; Alan Moorehead for an unpublished translation of Atatürk's Gallipoli Diaries; J. D. Latham, of the University of Manchester, for his unpublished translation of Ali Fuat Cebesoy's *Moscow Memories*.

Elsewhere I have to thank the Library of Congress, Washington DC, for access to the papers of Admiral Bristol; the Foreign Affairs Division of the National Archives, Washington DC, for access to certain official records; the Widener Library, Harvard University, for access to the papers of Ambassador Grew; the Hoover Library, Stanford University, California, for access to those of Louis E. Browne; S. Hassan, of the Pakistani Information Office, Istanbul, for papers concerning the relations between the Kemalist Government and the Khilafat Committee, Bombay.

For oral information on the subject I am indebted to the following individuals:

In Turkey, General Ismet Inönü, the late Rauf Orbay (Hussein Rauf), General Ali Fuat Cebesoy (Ali Fuad), the late General Refet Bele (Refet Pasha), Tevfik Rüştü Aras, Bayan Fethi Okyar, Osman Okyar, the late Bayan Adnan Adivar (Halide Edib), Falih Rifki Atay, Kiliç Ali, Hasan Riza Soyak, Yakup Kadri Karaosmanoğlu, Bayan Ruşen Eşref Ünaydin, Dr Afetinan (Afet), Bayan Sabiha Gökçen, Hamdullah Suphi Tanriöver, the late Hasan Ali Yücel, the late Behiç Erkin, the late Fuat Bulca, the late Tevfik Biyiklioğlu, Ismail Hakki, Kâzim Özalp, Fuat Köprülü, Şakir Zümre,

Yusuf Kemal Tengirşenk, Dr Hussein Pektaş, Ahmed Adnan Saygun, Uluğ Iğdemir, Cevat Dursunoğlu, Ahmet Emin Yalman, Şevket Süreyya Aydemir, Kadri Cenani, Ahmet and Abbas Celal, Behcet Kemal Cağlar, Dr Akdes Nimet Kurat, Bayan Esma Nayman, Bayan Leyla Cambel, Bayan Şefika Urgan and Bayan Süreyya Ağaoğlu.

Elsewhere, HRH the Duke of Windsor; the late Sir Percy Loraine and Sir Knox Helm, former British Ambassadors to Turkey; M Ponsot, former French Ambassador, General Hassan Arfa, former Persian Ambassador and M Sokolnicki, former Polish Ambassador to Turkey; Lieutenant-General Nicholas Rangabe and A.A. Pallis, of Athens; Madame Dayanova and Simeon Radev, of Sofia; Captain Webb Trammell, Edward Whittall, Sami Gunzberg, of Istanbul; Lady (Charles) Townshend, Mrs Ethel McLeod-Smith, the late Sir Clifford Heathcote-Smith, Colonel J. C. Petherick, J. G. Wilson-Heathcote, J. G. Bennett, and Mrs S. F. Newcombe.

For other assistance I am indebted to Nejat Sönmez and Yusuf Mardin, now of the Turkish Embassy in London; L. T. Naslednikov and N. Todorov, of Sofia; B. T. Naslednikov, of Paris; Dr Tayyip Gökbilgin, Kemal H. Karpat, Satvet Lütfi Tozan, Reşit Safet Atabinen, Özcan Ergüder, Captain and Mrs Irfan Orga, the late Dr Ernest Altounyan, Albert Hourani, Dr Gotthard Jäschke, of Münster; Sir Hamilton Gibb, of Harvard University; Dr L. V. Thomas, of Princeton University; Dr Dankwart A. Rustow and Dr J. C. Hurewitz, of Columbia University, New York; Dr Frederick P. Latimer, of the University of Salt Lake City; Dr Walter F. Weiker, of Rutgers University; Lawrence Moore, of Ankara; Mrs John Earl Davis, of New York; M Gaston Bergery, former French Ambassador to Turkey; Sir James Bowker and Sir Bernard Burrows, former British Ambassadors to Turkey, Mr and Mrs Geoffrey Lewis, and John Hyde, of the British Consulate-General in Istanbul.

With regard to the text, I have to thank Miss Adele Dogan, Robert Rhodes James and Andrew Mango, for constructive criticism of the completed work; W. E. D. Allen for advice at an earlier stage; and Mrs Jasper Streater for helpful attention, on my behalf, to detail and general content.

Mrs St George Saunders has given me valuable assistance, by her work on English newspaper sources; Bayan Içten Erkin and Bilge Karasu, of Ankara, have helped me patiently in reading and translating from Turkish sources. Above all I must express profound gratitude to Dr Mina Urgan, Professor of Literature at Istanbul University, for her devoted industry over a long period in research, reading and translation on my behalf. Without her untiring and discerning collaboration, this book could not have taken the shape it has.

NOTE ON SPELLING

The transliteration of Turkish names into English presents problems in a book of this kind. Throughout most of the period which it covers the Arabic script prevailed in Turkey, and was transliterated into European languages in various phonetic forms. It was only in 1928 that the Latin script was introduced. But the form of it chosen was not consistently phonetic. The 'j' sound, for example, became 'c', the 'ch' sound 'ç', the 'sh' sound 'ş'. Since these are misleading to the English general reader, I have preferred in principle to adhere to the earlier and more familiar transliteration, except in the case of place-names where the new spelling coincides phonetically with the old, and of the proper names of Turks still living today (eg Celal Bayar, Tevfik Rüştü). In the case of the Gallipoli place-names I have adhered, for the convenience of readers, to the versions already familiar in English works on the campaign, even if they do not always exactly accord with the above principles. I owe apologies to Turkish readers for taking these various liberties, also for eliminating entirely the Turkish undotted 'i' from my text.

It was not until 1930 that foreigners were asked to use the Turkish versions of place-names, instead of those current abroad – eg Ankara for Angora, Izmir for Smyrna, Bursa for Brusa, Antalya for Adalia, Edirne for Adrianople. For convenience, however, I have introduced these versions at an earlier stage in the text, from the inception of the Republic at the beginning of Part III onwards.

PROLOGUE

MUSTAFA KEMAL, later Kemal Atatürk, was an outstanding soldier-statesman of the first half of the twentieth century. He differed from the dictators of his age in two significant respects: his foreign policy was based not on expansion but on retraction of frontiers; his home policy on the foundation of a political system which could survive his own time. It was in this realistic spirit that he regenerated his country, transforming the old sprawling Ottoman Empire into a compact new Turkish Republic.

Atatürk was no ordinary Turk. Fairer than most, with high cheekbones and broad-set steel-blue eyes, he was slight in build and deliberate in movement. His body radiated energy, even in repose; his cold eyes gleamed with it, all-seeing and alive with the light of his contradictory moods. Alternately outspoken and taciturn, the tension within him would now erupt into a harsh explosion of temper, now relax into an expression of urbane polished charm. Vain of his personal appearance, he dressed fastidiously, twirled up his eyebrows self-consciously, took a pride in his well-shaped hands and feet, which he liked to show off to his more intimate guests on the pretext of paddling in a pool he had made in his garden.

Vain of popular acclaim Atatürk was not. He needed it for the task he had imposed on himself, but often flouted it and was seldom deceived by it. Once, when a friend proposed a gesture to public opinion, he flashed back at him scornfully, 'I don't act for public opinion. I act for the nation and for my own satisfaction.' The two motives coincided. In so far as Atatürk was capable of love, he loved his country. His ambition, kindled by imagination, driven by a dominant nature and an inflexible will, was for power; but for power to give his people, in his own way, what he had determined, in his own mind, was best for them.

It was a restless mind, nurtured on those principles of Western civilization which had influenced Turkish liberal thought since the nineteenth century; continually refuelled by the ideas of others, which he adapted and adopted as his own; but always grounded in a common sense mistrustful of theory. In method he was pragmatic, restraining his natural impatience in order to progress 'step by step towards the desired goal'. The steps none the less were swift, liberal ends pursued often by illiberal means, with ruthless treatment of friends as of enemies.

Callous at times of human life, Atatürk was not personally inhuman. He knew and appreciated human beings, whether individually or in the mass, assessing their character and predicting their actions with shrewd intuition. Flexible in his methods of handling them, knowing just when to persuade, when to cajole, when to threaten, when to command, he was a master of political finesse. Convivial in his habits, he enjoyed human company, governing the country in effect from his dinner-table. He loved, in a clear resonant voice which has been compared to that of 'a masculine Sarah Bernhardt', to talk, always frankly, often long-windedly, sometimes pointedly, with a sardonic wit and an acute turn of phrase. Of Ismet Inönü, for many years his Prime Minister, he once said, 'There are fifty foxes chasing around in his belly, but none of them ever catch each other's tails.'

Atatürk enhanced the life around him. He relished and responded openly to the admiration of women. In the anti-climax which followed his death and succession by the more conventional Inönü, a feminine admirer remarked, 'Turkey has lost her lover and must now settle down with her husband.' It was a sentiment which many of his countrymen shared.

PART ONE

THE DECLINE AND FALL OF THE OTTOMAN EMPIRE

CHAPTER ONE

BIRTH OF A MACEDONIAN

MACEDONIA, with its precipitous mountains and torrential rivers, was a land where the peoples of the Ottoman Empire met and merged and led their different lives. It was a projection in miniature of that loose but functioning organism by which the Turks had held together for five centuries a disparity of races of East and West. It lay at the centre of Turkey in Europe, the country which the Ottomans called Rumeli and which, to the Byzantine Greeks, had been 'the land of the Romans'. The Macedonians, whether Moslem or Christian or Jew, Turk, Greek, Slav, Vlach or Albanian, were a vigorous people, hardened by the discipline of their landscape and of a climate which ran to extremes, yet tempered from within and without by the civilizing influences of the West. Compounded of these contrasting elements, they were a people of fiercely individual spirit.

Mustafa Kemal was a Macedonian. The place of his birth was Salonika, the cosmopolitan port where the province had its outlet to the sea; the date of it 1881, a time of unrest when Rumeli was disintegrating into its various component parts, Christian turning against Moslem, Greek and Slav against Turk and against each other. Inspired by nationalist feeling, they sought to break free of the Empire and carve up the country between them for the respective benefit of Greece, Bulgaria and Serbia. The great powers, the rival expansionist empires of Austria-Hungary and Russia, intrigued from behind their adjoining frontiers, marking out spheres of influence, stirring up satellites, and preparing to move in when the moment was ripe. The British Empire strove to hold a balance of power, concerned not to grab territory but to secure communications with its own imperial possessions farther east. Thus at the time of Mustafa's birth the Ottoman Empire, the East succumbing to the West as the West had once succumbed to the East, was in decline and drifting towards its fall.

Hitherto the pressure against it had come from within its frontiers. But in 1877, four years before Mustafa's birth, it came from without. The

Russians, pursuing pan-Slav dreams of a drive to the Mediterranean, violated its frontiers and marched to the outskirts of Constantinople, where only the British fleet stopped them. Through the intervention of the powers a treaty was signed at San Stefano which in effect meant the dismemberment of Turkey in Europe, mainly to the advantage of an enlarged Bulgaria. But the powers had second thoughts: Britain and Austria grew alarmed at so substantial a Russian encroachment, and at the Congress of Berlin in 1878, thanks largely to the influence of Disraeli, these decisions were reversed in favour of concessions to Russia in the East. Hence Rumeli gained a last precarious lease of life, with a smaller but more turbulent Bulgaria for a neighbour and a Macedonia still simmering explosively, but still within the Ottoman Empire.

Mustafa was thus born into a restless world, beset by internal upheavals and external threats from the foreigner. He was born an Ottoman Moslem, of lower middle-class family and ostensibly Turkish stock. Whether, like most Macedonians, he had about him a touch of the hybrid – perhaps of the Slav or Albanian – can only be a matter for surmise. But as he grew up a certain 'apartness' in looks – in his colouring and the cast of his features – gave a hint of it. To the child of so mixed an environment it would seldom occur, wherever his racial loyalties lay, to enquire too exactly into his personal origins beyond that of his parentage.

Mustafa's parents were Ali Riza and his wife Zübeyde. Zübeyde was as fair as any Slav from beyond the Bulgarian frontier, with a fine white skin and eyes of a deep but clear light blue. Her family came from the lake district to the west of Salonika, in the direction of Albania, where the rough bare mountains sweep down into broad opaque stretches of water. It was a country in which, following the Turkish conquest of Macedonia and Thessaly, groups of villages had been peopled by settlers from the heart of Anatolia. Thus she liked to think that she had in her veins some of the pure fair blood of the Yuruks, those nomadic descendants of the original Turkish tribes who still survive in isolation among the Taurus mountains. Mustafa took after his mother in looks, inheriting her fair hair and blue eyes. She became his predominant influence, to which he was to react with alternate respect and a spirit of rebellion. A woman of the people, with no pretensions to be otherwise, she had a strong will and a robust peasant beauty. She was a woman of native intelligence but of scant education, who barely learned to read and write.

Ali Riza was twenty years older and a more shadowy personality than she. But as the son of an elementary school-teacher he had received some education, and this brought him a minor post as a clerk in a government office – the Customs and the administration of Pious Foundations. He never rose high in his profession, and when he sought her in marriage her family demanded a price which he could not afford.

But her brother Hussein intervened in his favour and they were married in Salonika.

Afterwards they lived in a village on the slopes of Mount Olympus, where her husband was stationed. In this richly wooded country Ali Riza, confined by his meagre Customs salary, saw all around him that fortunes were being made out of timber and decided, despite his total lack of commercial experience, to resign his post and go into the timber trade. He moved back to Salonika, where he formed a partnership with one Jafer Effendi, investing his savings in the business and, encouraged by an initial success, building a larger house for his family. It was a two-storeyed house with spacious rooms, overlooking a cobbled street and an unkempt garden behind, its projecting barred bay-windows shuttered against the fierce sun and the inquisitive neighbours.

But Ali Riza had chosen the wrong moment in history to embark on his enterprise. These mountains had for long been peopled by gangs of Greek brigands, many of them fugitives from the oppression of the Turkish beys and to some extent protectors of the local Christian peasantry. Now, following the defeat of the Turks by the Russians and the consequent weakening of provincial authority, they grew bolder in their depredations and more overtly rebellious in their aims.

Ali Riza soon fell a victim to their constant raids. They extorted money from him by threats to burn his timber. They burned it none the less. They blackmailed his labourers into deserting him. They made it impossible for him to transport his logs to the coast. He had fights with them in the forest. On the advice of the commander of the gendarmerie in Salonika, whose job was to clean up the brigands, he cut his losses and abandoned the business. Such was the measure of the decline of Turkish law and order in the Macedonian province.

Zübeyde bore her husband five children, of whom only one son, Mustafa, and a daughter, Makbule, were to grow to maturity. Ali Riza had given Mustafa his name, whispering it into his ear at birth according to custom, calling him after a brother of his own whom he had accidentally killed, spilling him out of his cradle in infancy. A negro nurse, whose forbears had once been slaves, looked after him, crooning over his cradle the old Rumeli folk-songs, compounded of Byzantine and Slav and Turkish melodies, which were to ring in his head throughout life.

Zübeyde was a pious woman, assiduous in her devotions, subscribing implicitly to the traditional beliefs of her Moslem forbears. She took pride in the fact that in her family and that of her husband there had been *Haji*, otherwise pilgrims to Mecca. She would have liked Mustafa to follow their example, to become a *hafiz* (a reciter of the Koran) or even a *hoja* (a teacher). In the meantime he must go to the clerical school, as the children of all good Moslems did, and receive an education based on the principles of the Koran.

For this once Ali Riza was able to do his son a service. Anti-clerical by bias, liberal in outlook, with a respect for the new ideas which, here in Macedonia especially, were seeping in from the West, he insisted that Mustafa should go to the private secular school of Shemsi Effendi, the first to be opened in Salonika with a modern curriculum. After some dispute an effective compromise was reached. Ali Riza appeared to give in to his wife and Mustafa was introduced with the usual religious ceremony into the school of Fatima Mollah Kadin.

> On the morning of my admission [he later recalled with some irony], I was festively attired by my mother in a white dress and a gold-threaded scarf, wound turbanwise around my head; in my hand I carried a gilded bough. Then the teacher – a *hoja* – arrived before the green bedecked door of our house, accompanied by all his scholars. After a prayer had been offered, I made an obeisance to my mother, my father and the teacher, lifting my finger-tips to my breast and forehead and kissing their hands. Then, amid the cheering of my new companions, I went in joyous procession through the streets of the city to the school, which adjoined the mosque. On our arrival there another prayer was repeated in chorus; then the teacher, taking me by the hand, led me into a bare, vaulted chamber, where the sacred word of the Koran was unfolded to me.

Thus Zübeyde's religious scruples were satisfied, and she kept face in the eyes of the neighbours. Mustafa did not unduly object to the school. But already there was germinating in him an aversion to the old Moslem customs and practices which were still universal among the Turks and to which his mother subscribed with traditional fervour. He thus took a dislike to the calligraphy lessons in the Arabic script, and to the posture in which they were studied – the children sitting cross-legged on the floor to write on their knees. Foreign children, he observed, did not write or sit like this.

One day he got up, and was ordered by the teacher to sit down but refused, protesting that this position cramped him.

'You dare to disobey me?' exclaimed the teacher.

'Yes, I dare to disobey you,' Mustafa replied.

At this the rest of the class rose and said, 'We're all going to disobey you,' and the teacher was forced into a compromise.

Shortly afterwards his father, without protest from Zübeyde, whose initial wishes had after all been met, took him away from the clerical school and sent him to that of Shemsi Effendi. Here his education proceeded satisfactorily enough.

Mustafa, with his fairer hair and his cleaner-cut features, stood out from the other boys in his looks. He developed grown-up ways, gravely watching them at their street games – dicing with knuckle-bones, gaming with fruit stones. But he never joined in. When they asked him to play leap-frog, he refused indignantly to bend down, and challenged them to jump over him in an upright position. He was aloof and proud, with a superior air, quick to resent any hint of an affront.

The busy mercantile city of Salonika, with which he now grew familiar, was to have a formative influence on his childhood and adolescence and again on his youth. Clambering up its mountainside, sprawling along the waters of its broad sluggish gulf, Salonika had long since burst from its confining Roman and Byzantine and Turkish walls to throw out quays and boulevards on a modern Western scale. Given its geography and consequent history, it could hardly help being a cosmopolitan city. Above the ruins of its fortifications, minarets and church-towers punctuated a confusion of roof-tops. Its people lived as it were in layers. From the top, from the medieval battlements cresting the ridge, the quarter of the Moslems zig-zagged downwards in a haphazard labyrinth of steep cobbled streets. At the foot of it around the harbour lived the Jews, nearly a half of the whole population, of whom an independent section, the Dönmes, had been converted to Islam. In between, the Greek quarter filled the centre of the city, while around it there spread, in various directions between the hillside and the sea, the quarters of the Bulgarians, the Armenians, the Vlachs (or gipsies) and above all the 'Franks' of all nations – the prosperous merchants and powerful consuls of Britain, France, Germany, Austria, Italy, Portugal.

Mustafa, who lived near the foot of the hillside within earshot of the Greek church bells below, thus grew to manhood used to the ways of the foreigner, whom he learnt to appraise with alertness and caution. In his teens he was to see the railway come for the first time to Salonika, and to share in some of the excitement which the snorting steel monster created. 'The century was drawing to a close,' wrote a native of the city. 'Stealthily the West was creeping in, trying to lure the East with her wonders. . . . She dangled before our dazzled eyes the witchery of her science and the miracle of her inventions. We caught a glimpse of her brilliance and timidly listened to the song of the siren. Like country folk at a banquet, we felt humble and awkward in our ways. But vaguely we sensed the coldness of her glitter and the price of her wooing.'[1]

Meanwhile Mustafa was to leave Salonika for a while. Ali Riza, his father, lost the remainder of his capital in the salt trade. He applied for readmission to the Civil Service but was rejected. He took to drinking, developed tuberculosis of the bowels and, after an illness of three years, died. Zübeyde was left badly off. So she removed Mustafa from school and took him with his sister Makbule to the country, some twenty miles inland from Salonika, where her brother Hussein managed a farm near Langaza.

Here in the red earth of the plain, dry in summer and marshy in winter,

[1] Leon Sciaky, *Farewell to Salonika.*

mixed crops flourished and animals grazed on the stubble. Bullocks drew the plough, storks prancing behind them to pick at the upturned furrow, while creaking peasant carts took the produce to market. Breathing in the smell of green things, of the earth and the moisture and the mud and the dung, Mustafa developed for the first time some feeling for the soil and for nature. He enjoyed the open-air life and adapted himself easily to odd jobs on the farm. Makbule was his close companion, a plump, outspoken, self-willed girl of coarser grain than himself, with whom he frequently quarrelled. During the day the two children would be set to watch in the fields, sitting in a hut to scare the crows off the bean crop. In the winter evenings they would sit before the farmhouse fire, roasting chestnuts from a bag by the hearth.

Life on the farm was healthy, and Mustafa grew muscular and strong. The food was plentiful and his uncle Hussein was kind. But he soon grew restless. The peasant life was not for him. His mind was awakening. He wanted urgently to learn and his education was being neglected. Among local teachers there was little choice between the Greek priest and the Moslem *hoja*, and Mustafa was sent to each in turn. But he disliked the outlandish Greek tongue and the Christian boys cold-shouldered him, wounding his pride. After a brief spell under the *hoja*, he protested, 'I won't go to school in a mosque!' Zübeyde found him a tutor, but after three days Mustafa pronounced him ignorant and refused to be taught by him. A female neighbour then offered to teach him, but he would not take lessons from a woman.

Clearly, Zübeyde realized, the time had come for him to have some form of regular schooling. She sent him back to Salonika to lodge with her sister and to attend the civil school of Kaymak Hafiz. His name meant Cream, and he was known to the boys as 'Slushy'. Mustafa did not stay there for long. One day he became involved in a general scrap and the schoolmaster, singling him out as the ringleader, beat him roughly, leaving him covered with bruises. Mustafa resented this fiercely. He refused to remain in the school and his grandmother took his side and removed him.

By now, however, he had begun to know what he really wanted to do. Vain since childhood of his personal appearance, he took an interest in his clothes and liked always to look neat. Now he began to fret at the traditional Turkish costume, the wide trousers and the cummerbund which the school-boy had to wear. It was a uniform that belonged to the past. Not so the uniform of the soldiers whom he watched with respect strutting through the streets, twirling their moustachios and rattling their swords on the cobblestones with a self-important air. He envied their panache, their authority, their assumption of superior status, their assured Turkishness in a city of foreigners.

He envied especially a neighbour's boy, named Ahmed, who attended the Military Secondary School and flaunted its uniform. His mother had returned to Salonika, and he begged her to let him go there. But she refused. If he was not to follow in the steps of the Prophet, as she had so dearly wished, then she would prefer him to become a merchant as his father had failed to be. She had the mother's fear of war and death and the interminable exiles which an Ottoman soldier's life involved – more especially if he failed, as Mustafa might well fail, to obtain a commission.

But Mustafa was not to be crossed. He confided his ambition to the father of his young neighbour, a major in the army, and contrived with his help, and without telling his mother, to sit for the entrance exam to the Military Secondary School. He worked with intense concentration. He passed it and thus faced Zübeyde with a *fait accompli*. But her signed consent still had to be obtained before he could enter the school. Looking back to his early childhood, he shrewdly recalled to his mother that his father had presented him with a sword at birth and had hung it on the wall above his cradle. That could only mean that he had wished him to be a soldier. 'I was born as a soldier,' he said, striking an attitude of heroism, 'I shall die as a soldier.'

Zübeyde began to weaken. But it was a timely dream that finally clinched her decision. In this she saw her son sitting on a golden tray on the top of a minaret. Running to the foot of the minaret, she heard a voice intoning, 'If you allow your son to go to military school, he shall remain high up here. If you do not he shall be thrown down.' Clearly she had been vouchsafed a vision of a brilliant military future for her son. She gave in, and signed the necessary document. Mustafa kissed her respectfully and she gave him her blessing. He entered the Military Secondary School in Salonika.

Mustafa was now twelve years old. After six years of educational vicissitudes at the hands of his family, he had chosen his own vocation. He had chosen it well. The officer class was the élite of the country. Its academies, subsidized by the Sultan, were nurseries of instruction, giving their pupils a grounding not only in military matters but in history, economics, philosophy. They were democratic institutions, composed of all social classes, in which it was possible to rise by ability and merit alone. Their graduates moreover, on entering the army, had the opportunity, denied to the ordinary civilian, to travel, to see the world and to learn of the ways of the remoter peoples of the far-flung Ottoman Empire.

Mustafa found his lessons easy and learned them quickly. His best and favourite subject was mathematics. He was already working on algebra problems before his companions had progressed beyond simple arithmetic. His teacher, another Mustafa, paid him the compliment of treating him as his mathematical equal. The young Mustafa thought up difficult questions for the old. One day, to distinguish between them, he followed a common Turkish custom by bestowing a second name upon his pupil. He chose that of Kemal, a word meaning, in the broadest sense, perfection; and Kemal he became for life. Sometimes the teacher would challenge any boy who claimed proficiency to stand up for interrogation before the rest. Few dared to do so, but Mustafa, refusing to admit the superiority of any teacher to himself, would rise and vindicate himself as the best of his class.

Mustafa Kemal quickly reached the rank of sergeant, or monitor, and enjoyed the superior status of pupil-teacher, expounding lessons to his class-mates in the master's absence, with the aid of a blackboard. Didactic by nature, he was at home in the teacher's role. This assumption of maturity set him apart from his schoolfellows. Here clearly was no child. He made few friends among them, seeking rather the company of senior boys. That unfamiliar fair complexion, that lone-wolf demeanour, the solemn, super-cilious, even contemptuous look in those cold blue eyes seemed to classify him as a creature of a separate species. He instinctively rebelled against authority, and his teachers found him hard to handle.

At home his relations with Zübeyde were often stormy. The solitary male in a feminine household, he despised the ways of women and resented the fatherlessness which obliged him to live among them. Then Zübeyde married again. Her second husband was Ragib, a widower of some substance, with two sons and two daughters. Mustafa was as jealous as a lover of another man in his mother's life; he was humiliated at the financial necessity which had guided her choice. But he came to terms with his stepfather, seeing that he was a good husband to his mother, and found a friend in his step-brother, an officer in the army, who gave him sound advice. The young man preached to the boy of his honour and dignity. He must never allow another to beat him. He must never bear an insult. He must resist any attempt by another man on his sexual honour. He gave him a knife to protect himself, but advised him never to use it rashly. From now onwards, how-ever, Mustafa was much away from home. For at the age of fourteen he passed out of the Secondary School and entered the Military Training School of Monastir, as a boarder.

Monastir, placed high in a broadening plain between ranges of mountains, commanded at close quarters the frontiers of Greece and Albania and, farther off, those of Serbia and Bulgaria. It thus held an important strategic position. It was the principal military centre of Macedonia, aspiring in its provincial way to some of the cosmopolitan airs and graces of Salonika. The Military School, a stuccoed building of substantial dignity, lay on the fringe of it, looking up towards a graceful mountain peak, which the Greeks called *Pelister*, or the Pigeon, from the softness of its snow-cap in winter.

Here Mustafa found himself for the first time right in the centre of strife. Turkish authority in Macedonia was continuing to disintegrate at the hands cf the Greek and Slav guerilla gangs. In this atmosphere passionate loyalties and rivalries flared up among the cadets. The school was torn by conflicting views, and had its own gang warfare of plots and intrigues and fights, leading often to bloodshed. The strongest gang was that of the cadets from Salonika, of which Mustafa Kemal was a leader, shrewdly electing, howevei, to work in the background and keep clear of the fights. A memory which still haunted him, later in life, was of awaking one night in the dormitory to see a boy standing over the bed of a comrade, one of his own gang, with a knife raised to stab him. The boy awoke just in time to snatch the knife from his assailant's hand.

Mustafa became for the first time aware of what was happening in the larger world beyond the school. The boys had been fired by heroic tales and songs and epics of the Ottoman conquest of Macedonia. Now revolt and reconquest threatened. He learned how, throughout Rumeli, Greeks and Serbs and Bulgarians were fighting to regain Turkish lands. In 1897 the Greeks launched a war of liberation in Crete, and the Turks marched against them in Rumeli. Monastir was fully mobilized. Crowds thronged the streets; soldiers were recruited to the sounds of the drum and the bagpipe. Students marched through the town, waving Turkish flags. Turkish guerillas fought to the death in the mountains around. One night Mustafa and a comrade ran away in an attempt to volunteer for the army. They were recognized and reluctantly returned to the college. But there had been kindled in the young Kemal a flame of patriotism and a fierce protective love for his country.

As the volunteers poured in from all parts of the Empire, Mustafa bemoaned his inability to join them. He had made friends at Monastir with a young poet named Ömer Naji. Together, while on vacation, they used to go to the station at Salonika to see the troop trains leave for the front. One evening they saw, among the crowd on the platform, a group of sheikhs and dervishes in flowing robes and long pointed bonnets. The dervishes seemed, as they clashed their cymbals and beat their drums and piped on their flutes in a shrill pandemonium of sound, to be in a state of fanatical ecstasy, while the people around them had caught their infection and were shrieking and wailing and fainting from hysteria. Mustafa looked on at the scene with a cold disgust. To Ömer he confessed that it made him blush with shame. There was born in him a horror of all religious fanaticism.

Mustafa grew strong in the spartan conditions of college life. He did not, however, care for sports, apart from the routine gymnastic exercises. He preferred to concentrate on his work. Mathematics were still his first concern. But his mind was opening to other interests. Ömer Naji liked to recite his poems, to which Mustafa would listen, responding to the lilt of the words as to that of the music of the Rumeli songs which he had learnt in his childhood. He lent Mustafa books to read, making him realize the existence of 'something called literature'. He became interested in poetry and even tried his hand at some verses. But his mathematics master discouraged this fancy.

Through another friend there was born in him an awareness of 'something called politics'. This was Ali Fethi, a Macedonian like himself, from the neighbouring countryside, who combined an easy charm of manner with a lively and flexible mind. Fethi was proficient in French, a subject in which Mustafa was backward. Stung by the reproaches of his French master he had begun to study the language independently on his first visit home, and he now redoubled his efforts. As his knowledge of the language improved Fethi introduced him to the works of the French political philosophers – Rousseau and Voltaire, Auguste Comte, Desmoulins, Montesquieu. Soon the two cadets were eagerly discussing the ideas of these masters which were relevant to their own country's problems.

Back at home Mustafa, no longer a child, began to taste the pleasures of Salonika, where life was various and free. Often, with a young friend related to his stepfather's family,[1] he took to frequenting the cafés at the cross-roads down by the waterfront – the Olympos, the Kristal, the Yonyo – places run for the most part by Greeks. They preferred the Yonyo, where the price of a glass of beer entitled them also to a supply of *meze*, the local *hors d'œuvres*, so ample that they did not have to put their hands in their pockets for a meal. At the others, where they sampled stronger drinks, they could only afford to buy chestnuts from the itinerant vendors, which were the cheapest fare available. This prompted Ömer Naji to the sad poetic comment, 'What is life but a dry chestnut?' But this was life *à la Franka*, preferable to life *à la Turka* in those cafés where Turkish music was played.

Seeking to see more of it, Mustafa and his friend were taken by their French teacher to a dancing-class, frequented mainly by non-Moslems, where they made a show of learning the steps of the polka and the waltz – but only with other boys, since no girls were in attendance. Girls, however, were available in the *cafés chantants* at the other end of the city. To these the elder brother of his friend introduced them. Here there were orchestras to which the girls sang and danced. There were Neapolitan songs, sung by stout Italian women. There were Arabian dances, performed with cymbals and jingling anklets by Armenian girls. The girls came to sit and to drink at their tables – no Moslems among them, but only Christians and Jews, unveiled and accessible. As they grew older they frequented the brothels. Here the unusually fair young Mustafa was so admired that women would often allow him their favours for nothing. Thus did the trend of his sexual life start to show – more sought after than seeking, but readily complying. Sentimentally he was more loved than loving, his vanity now gratified by the passionate attentions of a young girl of good family, whom he was tutoring on his vacations from Monastir.

[1] Fuat Bulca.

From the bulk of his fellows he still remained aloof. When they tried to pierce his reserve and discover his aims, he replied only, 'I am going to be somebody.' Ambition, still undirected, was already smouldering within him.

He passed his final examinations well, and on 13th March 1899 graduated to the infantry class of the War College at Harbiye, in Constantinople.

CHAPTER TWO

THE EDUCATION OF AN OFFICER

CONSTANTINOPLE, at the turn of the century, was two distinct cities. To the north of the Golden Horn rose Pera, the city of the Christians; to the south of it Stambul, the city of the Moslems. To drive across the harbour by the Galata Bridge was to pass from one world, from one period of history, to another.

Stambul, with its ridge of domes and minarets and its array of palace buildings, jutting out above Seraglio Point, was a medieval city, which had blossomed into an architectural Renaissance during the sixteenth century, but was now tumbling into picturesque decay. It was a human hive where men still swarmed and multiplied and lived as they had done for centuries past. They busied themselves in the cavernous markets and labyrinthine streets; they sought relaxation in the spacious precincts of the mosques and sacred places. But the heyday was long over; the majesty had dwindled; the splendours were those of past history. Walls crumbled and fell, paint flaked off the houses, paving-stones cracked in the courtyards, grass grew in the alleyways. The women were black-veiled phantoms, sidling along the pavements, scurrying to be home by dusk. The men sat mute on the ramshackle divans of the coffee shops, beneath the shade of the straggling vines and plane trees, stirring only at the call of the *muezzin* from the minarets, five times a day. At night Stambul, looming up above the Golden Horn, was a dead silhouette behind which the Turk lay rapt in an Oriental hush.

Pera, with its bright lights, beckoned like a siren from across the water – the city of the present. From its congested quays, lined with taverns, the streets rose vertiginously through tall narrow canyons of buildings designed in an Italianate style. Here and there a handsome double doorway led into the courtyard of an embassy or of a rich merchant's palace, more amply and gracefully built, with gardens that stepped down in terraces towards the shores of the Bosporus. Pera flaunted itself as the last word in modernity, combining what it took to be the airs and graces of the West with the garish vulgarity of the Levant. Its hotels were palaces, where ladies and gentlemen of fashion listened in palm courts to polite orchestral music. Its streets were thronged with smart carriages. Its shops purveyed the latest goods from Paris and Vienna. Entertainment abounded – theatres, music-halls, cabarets, clubs with a Frenchified décor, where the 'upper ten' played poker and retailed the gossip of the bazaar and the Palace.

Pera was the city of the foreigner, and the wealth of the Empire was in the foreigner's hands. His strength lay in the Capitulations, extra-territorial privileges which exempted him from taxes and enabled him to trade freely, to practise his own religion and to live by his own laws, regardless of the central Turkish authority. These had been granted by earlier sultans for their own advantage, at a time of Turkish expansion when they needed foreign merchants to open up western markets. But as the West in its turn expanded and Turkey declined, they had rebounded to the advantage of the foreigner, confirming him in a freedom which the Turk no longer enjoyed, creating a series of powerful foreign states within the state, and so tightening the foreign hold over the Ottoman Empire as to make the Turk feel that the foreigner's word was law and that he was no longer master of his own affairs. Thus the modern city of Pera held the ancient city of Stambul in its power.

Quick in his perceptions, he soon summed up in his mind the true nature of this 'harlot of the ages', Constantinople. To a fellow cadet, Ali Fuad, he expressed himself in no way surprised that only the early sultans of the Ottoman dynasty had ruled honestly and well. For their capitals were successively the small homogeneous cities of Brusa and Adrianople. In this mixed seething city of Constantinople, with its ancient associations and its decadent influences, their ultimate decline was inevitable. It was a place made for the enjoyment of life, not for the business of government.

Ali Fuad was to fill a gap in Mustafa's life. At first his days and nights in Constantinople, for all their distractions, had been lonely. He found himself in a strange city without friends, relations, contacts of any kind.

A.—2

In Salonika he had at least had a background of his own, however modest and restricted in character. In the world of the metropolis which now engulfed him he became acutely aware of his provincial obscurity.

Then Ali Fuad became his friend. Fuad was younger than he, but relatively old for his years. He had been brought up in Constantinople and had the poise, the self-assurance of one who was at home in the world. He came of a good family, as Mustafa was quick to appreciate. It was one of those military families which, outside the aristocratic world of the Palace with its prolific hereditary caste, fulfilled the role of an upper class and made Mustafa's own background seem humble and drab. Fuad's father, Ismail Fazil, had been a general of some standing, of whom Fuad spoke with affection and pride. Mustafa confessed, rather wistfully, that he had never known what it meant to have a father.

Fuad's family lived at Kuzgunjuk, on the Asiatic shores of the Bosporus, where the houses and gardens of the Ottoman gentry spread themselves along the water's edge. Here, one day, he brought his new friend, Mustafa. Ismail at once sensed the qualities of this fair, wiry, alert young man, with the good manners natural to the people of Salonika, and encouraged him to treat Fuad's home as his own. Mustafa, for his part, began to see him as in some sense a substitute for the father he had lost in childhood. He took to passing his weekends here with the family, among whom he soon felt at home.

He and Fuad spent much of their spare time together, exploring the widespread and infinitely various city, determined to discover all of it, and the more stimulated to do so by Ismail's suggestion that they should make a complete map of Constantinople. The two cadets would make excursions in caiques up the Bosporus and around the Sea of Marmara. One summer weekend they decided to go to Prinkipo, the largest of the Isles of the Princes, so called from the princes for whom they had been places of imprisonment and exile. The hotels were expensive, so they would camp in the pine woods which ran down into sandy bays, giving to the islands a Mediterranean air. They would take food, cooking equipment, kindling wood for a fire – above all something to drink. Mustafa suggested a case of beer, his normal drink. Fuad protested that this would be too heavy to carry and proposed instead one bottle of *raki*, the raw Turkish spirit, flavoured with aniseed, with which Mustafa was still unfamiliar. He responded at once to its stimulus and thus contracted a habit in which thereafter he freely indulged.

It was a moonlight night. Warmed by the food and the *raki*, the two youths fell into a romantic mood. They sat enraptured by the natural beauties around them – the fragrant woods, the shimmering sea, the starlit sky. Too exalted to sleep they recited poems, they exchanged dreams of love. Mustafa said, 'Fuad, you may be sure that if I had given as much attention to poetry and painting as to mathematics, you wouldn't find me now locked within the four walls of Harbiye. I would run away from the school each moonlight night, I would come here, I would write poems. At dawn, as soon as it grew light enough, I would start to paint.'

These were passing fantasies. Mustafa, after a first year at Harbiye in which his studies were often deflected by the dreams and distractions of youth, settled down in his second to serious study, developing his mind and striving to sort out the ideas which began to crowd in upon it. Military matters were still his main concern. But he was beginning to extend his range of knowledge. He still worked to improve his French, and was now able to read the French newspapers. At the same time he delved more deeply and with more comprehension into the works of the French writers, to which Fethi had introduced him at Monastir. Such subversive books were banned to the cadets, and Mustafa read them covertly at night in his dormitory, together with the literature of Namik Kemal and other Turkish liberal poets, precursors of the revolution to come, whose very names it was a mortal sin to mention.

Out of school, he and his fellow cadets held debates and practised public speaking. On Kemal's initiative they organized contests in oratory. He would choose a subject on which each was to speak for a fixed number of minutes, while he kept time with his watch. He himself, in these orations, began to display a forcible capacity for convincing his audience. But politically he was still only on the threshold of experience. His mind still wrestled with thoughts and emotions which he did not yet wholly understand. They were the growing pains of a young man's political consciousness. As it grew Kemal's personal ambition and love for his country coalesced into the realization that he himself might do something to save and redeem it.

Kemal had been born into an age in which tyrannical reaction had arrested a process of liberal advancement. Since the French Revolution, of which he now had some knowledge, the Ottoman Empire had been pursuing a chequered but continuous course from a medieval theocracy towards some form of modern constitutional state. Through the nineteenth century this trend assumed, at intervals, a concrete form, partly on the initiative of an enlightened young Sultan Abdul Mejid, who, by the *Tanzimat* decrees of 1839 and ensuing reforms of a Western kind, confirmed the rights of the subject and the obligations of the sovereign; partly under pressure from the Western powers who in 1876, concerned for the interests of their Christian minorities, induced a less progressive Sultan, Abdul Hamid, to grant a parliamentary constitution.

Socially Abdul Hamid carried on, in certain directions, the progressive traditions of modernization and reform. But politically, fearful as he was, sometimes to the point of insanity, of the forces of disruption which seemed to tnreaten his Empire from every hand, he could not for iong tolerate a democratic régime. Taking advantage of the war with Russia, he dissolved Parliament in 1877 to rule for the next generation as a despot. He established a form of police state, effectively suppressing freedom of the individual, of speech, and of the press, employing a vast regiment of secret agents, and reigning no longer from the palace on Seraglio Point, as his forbears had done, but from within the security of the twenty-foot walls of the Yildiz Palace, at a safe distance outside the city.

Sooner or later indignation against such oppression and its accompanying corruption was bound to flare up into revolt. But at first the Turkish political reformers were driven either abroad or underground. In such cities as Paris and Geneva, traditional cradles of liberty, they formed committees, sought to win the West to their cause, published propagandist literature and infiltrated it into the Ottoman Empire through the foreign post offices and similar agencies. Reform was no longer enough for them; only revolution, the deposition of the Sultan himself, would achieve their purpose.

In Constantinople the reformers had to work secretly. They worked on the same revolutionary lines. Ironically, it was Abdul Hamid's own élite that were the first thus to plot for his overthrow, the young students of those very military schools which he had built up for the protection and reinforcement of his régime. The first secret revolutionary society in the Ottoman Empire was formed by students of the Imperial Military Medical School in 1889, the centenary year of the French Revolution. In 1896 – while Mustafa Kemal was still a student at Monastir – they attempted a *coup d'état*, which failed. The ringleaders were rounded up, tried, and exiled to remote parts of the Empire. Abdul Hamid thus succeeded in postponing the revolutionary movement in Turkey for a further decade.

The political ideas of Mustafa himself rapidly assumed a more coherent shape when, in 1902, he graduated as a lieutenant to the Staff College. He began to devour history as he had previously devoured mathematics and poetry. He read all he could about the career of Napoleon, who became (with qualifications) one of his heroes. He read the works of John Stuart Mill. He caught the prevailing infection of the 'popular' ideas. He and some friends of his year formed a secret committee and started a manuscript newspaper, most of which was written by Mustafa, with a view to exposing administrative and political evils.

The Palace got wind of these activities. The director of the college was reprimanded and instructed to take action against the culprits. He entered a lecture room in the veterinary section where Mustafa and his friends were in the act of preparing an issue of the newspaper. But, being a man of lenient disposition and, like many among even the older army officers, not wholly well-disposed towards the Sultan, he chose to turn a blind eye, pretended not to have seen what the young men were doing, and imposed a mild punishment upon them – which was not even carried out – for neglecting their proper studies.

Mustafa, however, did not allow his new political interests to interfere with his military education. His mind soon had to grapple with those wider problems of strategy and tactics which a would-be staff officer must master. Far into the night he would lie wide awake in the dormitory, thoughts pounding away in his head while the other cadets slept. He would then fall asleep with the dawn, so that each morning, when the bugle blew for reveille, the officer-in-charge had to shake him until he awoke. He seemed to his comrades in a perpetual day-dream, until suddenly in class he would prove himself twice as awake as the rest, raising some awkward question with the teacher which would force them to bestir themselves and rack their brains. He developed an intense interest in guerilla warfare, and one day, with an uncanny prophetic sense, posed to the class the hypothetical problem of a revolt against the capital from the Asiatic shores of the Bosporus.

Mustafa finished his course at the Staff College in 1905, at the age of twenty-three, and was commissioned as a captain. He lodged in a house in the Bayazid quarter of Stambul, and with a few friends rented a room in the neighbouring house of an Armenian. Here they carried on with their political activities. These amounted in effect to little more than talk, the familiar outspoken criticism of the Sultan's régime, and the study of the 'forbidden books', of which they had acquired a library. Among them was a cadet who had been expelled from the school and to whom, since he had nowhere to go, they had given a room in the house. He informed against them to the Palace and, by a forged note, lured them to a neighbouring café, where they were arrested.

Mustafa, Ali Fuad, and two other newly gazetted captains were carried off to prison and interrogated singly. Mustafa at his interrogation was roughly handled. Ali Fuad, a man-of-the-world conversant with protocol, protested that, as a wearer of the Sultan's uniform, he might not be struck by any officer below the Sultan's rank – a diplomatic evasion which afterwards evoked from Mustafa a wry smile at his own inexperience. Mustafa did not feel unduly concerned as to his possible fate, though his mother Zübeyde feared the worst. He whiled away the time in prison writing verses, reading books, which were smuggled in to him, and planning what he would do when released.

The prisoners were kept in gaol for some months while a judicial enquiry was held. The director of the college counselled lenient treatment for what he maintained was little more than a youthful misdemeanour, and his counsel prevailed. The officers were released, with a view to posting away from the capital. It was decided to send them to the Second and Third Armies, at Adrianople and Salonika respectively. If they could not agree among themselves they were instructed to draw lots to decide which should go to each. But, at a sign from Mustafa, they announced immediate agreement, and the swiftness of their decision aroused suspicions of a pre-arranged plot.

Thus several officers were exiled instead to 'places from which they would not easily find a means of returning'. Mustafa and Ali Fuad were posted to the Fifth Army at Damascus, in Syria. Mustafa was resigned. 'All right,' he jested, 'let's go to this desert and found a new state there.' They sailed forthwith, and some two months later landed at the port of Beirut.

CHAPTER THREE

SERVICE IN THE FIELD

KEMAL THUS EMBARKED on the first stage of his career as a serving officer. As captain in a cavalry regiment his main duty was to instruct the other ranks, to pass on to them some of the military knowledge which he himself had acquired in the modern military schools, and which not all his fellow-officers shared. He took the task seriously and, with his taste and talent for teaching, performed it well.

Ali Fuad and he remained together until Fuad was sent on a mission to Ibn Saud, then a little-known tribal sheikh, under nominal Turkish suzerainty, in Southern Arabia. He applied for permission to take Mustafa with him, but this was refused. Thus history missed an opportunity. These two men, both destined to greatness in a similar field, were never to meet.

It was one of the tasks of the Fifth Army to control the Druses, those unruly people of cryptic ancestry, esoteric religion and fiercely independent spirit, who inhabited the black rocky country of the Hauran to the south of Damascus. They had for long resisted Turkish rule, but some ten years earlier they had been brought under control, agreeing to pay taxes in return for release from the obligation to serve in the Ottoman army outside their own territory. Periodically it became necessary to send a force to the Hauran, to quell disorders, and these were frankly regarded by the Ottoman officers as an occasion for pillage.

Kemal first had an inkling of this when he learnt, to his surprise, that his regiment had been ordered to the Hauran, and that he had not received orders to accompany it. He protested to his commanding officer that, as squadron commander, it was his duty to lead his troops. But the officer was evasive: Kemal was under training, his place was at headquarters. Kemal was angry. Clearly something was afoot which the old hands were trying to conceal from the young officers, fresh from the Staff College. With a brother officer named Müfit,[1] who had been similarly dropped from

_____
[1] Later Müfit Özdeş, a Member of Parliament in Ankara.

the expedition, he disregarded his orders and went off to join his unit, which was encamped near a Circassian village. There were no tents for them, and they slept in those of the soldiers.

Next day Kemal confronted the officer who had taken his place, and who explained that he had been detailed for 'special duty' on the operation on account of his previous experience. If, however, Kemal would promise to keep quiet about it afterwards, he would be allowed to take part. Kemal, anxious to learn the truth, gave the promise. What he learned was that it was the practice of the troops, on the pretext of collecting arrears of taxation, to extort money from the inhabitants or, in default of it, to loot their homes and villages.

Kemal refused to be party to such methods. As a conscientious young officer he preferred to control the Druses by coming to terms with them. In one village he was able to persuade the inhabitants that he and a fellow-officer had come not to rob but to help them. An understanding was immediately reached with the headman, who agreed to do what Kemal asked of him, but declared that he would never obey this Ottoman Government which sent troops to oppress and plunder his people. In another village, he arrived in time to rescue a Turkish major from a menacing situation. He harangued the villagers, who trusted his good intentions and released his brother officer.

In such ways Kemal attracted attention to himself, earning the respect of the new school of officer and the mistrust of the old. The traditional Ottoman officer took the view that, provided he did what was expected of him by his master the Sultan, he was free to reap what personal advantage he could out of his military service, with no questions asked. The idea that soldiering might be a science, to be studied in a professional spirit and with a view to improvement in training, in tactics and in modern techniques, seldom entered his head. For him, the new type of college-trained officer was an upstart, to be regarded with suspicion.

Kemal used to protest against the exaggerated operational reports which were concocted to impress headquarters in Constantinople. A certain engagement reported as a victory was not, he pointed out, a victory at all; the enemy had simply retired of his own free will. The commander mocked at his naïveté. 'You are still ignorant,' he said. 'You do not understand what our Sultan wants.'

'I may be ignorant,' he replied, 'but our Sultan should be a man clever enough to understand what types like you are really up to.'

When the time came for the officers to divide up the spoils of their raids, Kemal and Müfit were offered their share. As Müfit hesitated, Mustafa turned to him and asked, 'Do you want to be a man of today or a man of tomorrow?'

'Of course, a man of tomorrow.'

'Then you must refuse to take this money, as I have done.'

Kemal's phrase was revealing. He had begun to see his own self in perspective, as one who belonged not to the past, like these dug-outs around him, but to the future. The 'Men of Today' stood for the incompetence and corruption of an Empire in decline. It was less the moralist than the realist in Kemal that was shocked by their attitude. It was not just morally wrong; it was worse; it no longer worked. The pacification of the Druses, the salvation of the Empire, could not today be attained by mere force and rapacity and bribery; it must be sought more scientifically, by skill and diplomacy and the use of intelligence.

In another respect Damascus was to leave a deep imprint on this Man of Tomorrow. For the first time he came to know a city which lived still in the darkness of the Middle Ages. The cities with which he was familiar – Salonika, Constantinople and more recently Beirut – were cosmopolitan places, alive with the various amenities and pleasures of a modern civilization. But the holy Arab city of Damascus was a city of the dead. The narrow streets which he paced after dark were deserted and silent. Not a sound came from within the high shuttered walls of the houses. One night, to his surprise, he heard the sound of music floating out from a café. He looked in, to find it filled with Italians, workers on the Hejaz Railway, playing the mandolin, singing and dancing with their wives and their girls. As an officer in uniform he might not enter. But on an impulse he went home, changed into rough clothes, and returned to join them in their gay and uninhibited Western pleasures.

Otherwise all was dark, smelling of bigotry, repression and, beneath all, hypocrisy. Kemal began to see that the real enemy of his people was not simply the foreigner, from whom, despite his aggressive designs, they had after all something to learn. The enemy lay within their own ranks. It was the Moslem religion, which oppressed them and stunted their growth, shutting them off from the more advanced and enlightened ways of the Christian peoples. The Ottoman Empire, as he once put it, was a place where the joys of Heaven were reserved for non-Moslems, while Moslems were condemned to endure the shades of Hell.

Here in Damascus Kemal felt imprisoned. He longed to break his bars, to bring life to this moribund community. The remedy of course lay in political action. One day he was wandering in the market with two brother officers. Outside a shop they found a table and chairs and sat down. The shopkeeper greeted them – not in Arabic but in Turkish. Kemal became curious. He went into the shop, where he saw scattered on a table books in French on such subjects as philosophy, sociology and medicine. He asked the shopkeeper, 'What are you? A tradesman or a philosopher?'

'A tradesman,' he replied, 'but I like to read books – the literature of liberty.'

He then revealed that he had been a student in the Military Medical

School in Constantinople, the cradle of the revolutionary movement, but had been thrown into gaol for subversive activities and sent into exile. His name was Haji Mustafa. He invited Kemal and his friends to his house a night or so later.

Kemal went with Müfit and two other officers, all three sympathetic to his political ideas. The house was in a dark, narrow street. Haji Mustafa opened the door cautiously, holding a petrol lamp above his head to make sure of their identity before he would admit them. Inside they began to talk freely. For some time their host had been trying to form a secret political society. He had been unable to find trustworthy associates.

Kemal and two of his friends promised their support. The third said, 'I am with you in sympathy. But I have a wife and children. You must not expect active help from me.' At their request he left them alone. They talked far into the night, the young officers growing romantic in their aspirations to 'die for the Revolution'.

Kemal, the realist, brought them down to earth. 'Our aim is not to die,' he protested sharply. 'It is to carry out the Revolution, to make a reality of our ideas. We must live, to get them accepted by the people.'

Thus, in the autumn of 1906, they formed a society known as *Vatan*, the Fatherland Society. Its importance lay in the fact that it was the forerunner of a number of revolutionary cells formed from now onwards among serving officers in field formations. It was here in the field, no longer in Constantinople in the toils of the Sultan's security network, that revolution now had the best chance to develop.

Under cover of his military duties Kemal helped to found branches of the society in Jaffa, Jerusalem and Beirut. But all this was too far from home. This country was a backwater, moreover an Arab country, where no Turkish revolutionary movement had a chance of popular support. It must remain confined to army officers alone. The obvious centre for it was Macedonia, which was closer to the outside world, hence more accessible to the new ideas, and where the ubiquitous presence of the foreigner not only intensified nationalist feeling but, paradoxically, made it easier for it to operate, owing to the greater freedom of movement and the consequent weakening of palace control. Three years earlier Austria and Russia, in their efforts to introduce reforms into the province, had imposed upon the Turks a gendarmerie under foreign officers, which made it harder for the Sultan's own secret police to operate in Salonika as effectively as it did in Constantinople.

Mustafa Kemal made up his mind that, somehow or other, he must get to Salonika. The commandant of Jaffa connived at his plans for departure, ostensibly on leave, and promised to warn him if there was any comment on his absence. He left for Egypt and Piraeus, where he boarded a Greek ship for Salonika. Dressed in civilian clothes, he was met by a friend, and landed without undue interference. He went straight to his mother's house.

Zübeyde was overjoyed but disturbed to see him. How had he been so rash as to come here, contrary to the orders of our Lord the Sultan? Mustafa reassured her: 'I had to come, so I came. I shall show you what your Lord the Sultan really is. But later.' He stayed at home during the day, and in the evening went to the house of an artillery general, Shükrü Pasha, who held progressive political views and had encouraged him to come.

Shükrü was taken aback at his arrival. He explained that, in view of his position, he could give him no active help. But he would do nothing to hinder him and would look with good will on anything he chose to do. He asked only that Kemal should not compromise him. He gave the necessary promise. He went home to his mother's house. Put out by the Pasha's attitude, he lay awake half the night, undecided what to do, where to go, how to begin.

In the morning, he put on his uniform and went to headquarters. Here he saw a staff colonel, whom he had known when a student in the Military School. Mustafa reminded him of his identity and, believing him to be a patriot, revealed his predicament. The colonel devised a means by which to help him. He told him to apply for sick leave, not in the name of his unit but simply as a captain on the General Staff. He supported his application. The subterfuge worked and Kemal was granted four months' sick leave. He was thus able to remain in Salonika and to circulate freely.

None the less he felt his way carefully, disconcerted by his initial rebuff and sensing currents in the atmosphere that were not always favourable to his designs, even among officers of his own political sympathies. But by the end of these months he had succeeded in organizing a Macedonian branch of the *Vatan* society, which he had helped to found in Damascus. Its name was expanded to *Vatan ve Hürriyet* – Fatherland and Freedom; its half-dozen members included his old school friend Ömer Naji, the poet, and two officers of the staff of the Military School. They had meetings in the house of one of them, an officer of musical accomplishments, who played the flute and received them in Japanese pyjamas.

Here one evening they met to swear their first oath of allegiance to the revolutionary cause. After a number of speeches, suitably heroic in character, Kemal read out the three articles of the society, which he had jotted down on a card. After that a revolver was produced and laid on the table. The oath was to be sworn on this weapon, not on the Koran or on the honour of an officer as was the Ottoman practice. It symbolized their fidelity to the Revolution and their intention to resort to arms, if need be, to bring it about. One by one they kissed the revolver and swore. Afterwards Kemal remarked, 'This revolver is now sacred. Keep it carefully, and one day you will give it to me.'

It was known by now in Constantinople that Mustafa Kemal had left his post in Jaffa. Orders were sent to Salonika for his arrest. Warned by a ɟriend, he left in secret, and returned to Jaffa. The commandant, who had connived at his departure, met him on arrival and hurried him off to Beersheba, where a frontier force had been sent to protect Turkish claims in a dispute over the port of Akaba with the Anglo-Egyptian Government. Following an enquiry into his movements it was implied in a report to Constantinople that he had been at Beersheba for some months. The officer in Salonika was presumably another Mustafa. In the labyrinth of the Turkish bureaucracy, where records were haphazardly filed and the duplication of names caused convenient confusion, such a fiction was easy enough to sustain.

The Turks retained Akaba, and Mustafa Kemal returned to Damascus. There, bent on earning the remission of his 'exile', he behaved circumspectly. In due course he obtained his promotion to adjutant-major, and a transfer to the General Staff at Damascus. In September 1907 he was posted as he had hoped, to the Third Army in Macedonia, but on his arrival was transferred instead to the General Staff at Salonika itself.

CHAPTER FOUR

THE 'YOUNG TURK' REVOLUTION

IN MACEDONIA the sands were running out. No thinking Turk could
fail to sense that the Empire was on the brink of disintegration. 'Macedonia
for the Macedonians' was the mounting cry. Russian and Austrian agents
abounded. The Bulgarians had a powerful underground organization, a
state within a state with its own army of *komitajis* – 'committee men' who
were in fact terrorists – spreading panic and engineering continuous bomb
outrages. Security on the frontiers had vanished, as bands of Greeks,
Bulgarians, Serbians and Albanians scrapped with one another and with
the Turkish authorities. The great powers closed in, ready to dismember
the body. They had lately been joined by a 'late-comer at the feast of the
vultures', the German Empire, bent on its *Drang nach Östen*. Bismarck had
taken advantage of the fall of Disraeli, and the advent to power of Glad-
stone with his Hellenophil aversion to the 'unspeakable Turk', to supply
Abdul Hamid with a German military mission under Marshal von der Goltz,
and the Kaiser had followed up this move with a much-advertised state
visit to the Sultan.

Abdul Hamid, making shift for a policy, played all against all, foreigner
against foreigner and Turk against Turk. In Macedonia he reinforced his
team of agents, now reputed by the people of Salonika to number forty
thousand. The Christian minorities at least had foreign governments to
protect them. The Turks felt themselves to be a persecuted minority inside
their own frontiers. They looked around them in search of salvation. Only
the young Turkish officers seemed to offer it.

Thus the revolutionary movement gained in impetus and expanded with
speed, founding branches in all parts of the Empire and training groups of
propagandists whose duty it was to spread its ideas among all classes of the
population. By the end of 1907 it had outgrown Mustafa Kemal, who on
his return found himself faced with the bitter realization that his 'exile' in
Syria had effectively prevented him from becoming one of its leaders. His

own limited Fatherland and Freedom Society had been outstripped by the growth of a wider organization, which was to be known as the Committee of Union and Progress, and whose members included such leaders in embryo as Talat, then a clerk in the Post Office, and Jemal, an army colonel, both men clearly destined for power. It contained few of his friends except Ali Fethi. On the initiative of Talat the Fatherland and Freedom Society was merged within this larger group, and its name disappeared altogether.

The political atmosphere of Salonika had been conducive to secret societies ever since the early Christians of the city, converted by St Paul, had gone underground to escape the persecutions of Nero. The Committee of Union and Progress made free use of both the premises and the techniques of the Freemasons, imposing a ritual of initiation by which the aspirant was blindfolded and led into the presence of three masked strangers in cloaks, and was obliged to swear an oath, both on the sword and on the Koran, to redeem his country, to keep the secrets of the society, and to obey its orders, including the order to kill any person whom it might condemn to death. Such mumbo-jumbo went against the grain with Kemal. More especially, having initially sworn on the revolver alone, did he resent this Islamic symbolism of the new oath. For the moment, however, he had no alternative but to come to terms with the Unionists as best he could.

Instinctively they tended to dislike him, seeing him as opinionated, conceited and brash. They found pretexts to push him out of the way, taking advantage of the fact that his staff duties involved inspection of the Macedonian railways and could thus be combined with propagandist activities outside Salonika. His beat became the valley of the Vardar, up as far as Üsküb, on the fringe of the Serbian plain. Gnawed by frustration, but more and more confident in his capacity to lead, he drew together with a small group of his friends and adherents, meeting and talking and planning with them far into the night in the cafés and in the house of Zübeyde, now widowed for the second time and living with her daughter Makbule. Both became resigned to his subversive activities, and made coffee for the plotters at their nocturnal meetings.

The Revolution was ripening, but not yet entirely ripe. The international situation helped to precipitate events. King Edward VII and the Tsar Nicholas II met on a yacht in the Baltic for a series of polite talks, which were seen by the Committee as an ominous shift in British policy against Turkey. At home time was still needed to indoctrinate the officers in Thrace and Asia Minor. But speed became necessary, for Abdul Hamid began to wake up. Taking positive action, he sent commissions of enquiry to Salonika. The Committee shot at and wounded the leader of the first of them. The second resorted to conciliation and bribery.

A young major named Enver, a Committee member of no great seniority, was invited, together with others, to visit Constantinople on a promise of

promotion and hints of other rewards. He ignored the invitation and took
to the hills, where he began to organize a Resistance movement. On 4th July
1908 another officer, Major Ahmed Niyazi, an experienced guerilla warrior
of Albanian origin, followed his example, taking followers from the garrison
at Monastir. Ali Fuad, who chanced to be in the neighbourhood on Committee business, took a detachment of troops to his aid and advised him
to declare his intentions in public. Niyazi drafted a telegram to the Sultan
proclaiming open revolt. The Committee came out into the open, demanding
the restoration of the Constitution of 1876. The Sultan rushed reinforcements
from Anatolia, but their officers fraternized with the rebels.

Abdul Hamid realized that he was beaten. After two days of hesitation,
during which he is said to have consulted his astrologer, he accepted an
ultimatum from the Committee. This threatened, in default of his accession
to its demands, to dethrone him in place of his brother, and to march on
Constantinople. After an all-night sitting of his State Council he agreed to
restore the Constitution which he had violated a generation before. On
23rd July the news was proclaimed to a rejoicing Empire.

Niyazi marched with his band of faithful followers into Monastir, beneath
banners proclaiming 'Liberty, Equality, Fraternity, Justice'; but, having
little taste for politics, he soon retired to his native Albanian mountains.
Enver, on the other hand, appeared, young and solemn and triumphant,
on the balcony of the Olympos Palace Hotel in Salonika, where he was
acclaimed by a vast crowd as the political hero of the hour. He announced
to them ardently that arbitrary rule was at an end and that henceforward
all citizens, of whatever race or creed, were brothers, glorying in being
Ottomans together.

So indeed it seemed, for some days of delirious euphoria, when Moslem
hojas, Orthodox priests and Jewish rabbis embraced one another and walked
arm in arm. Turkish women tore off their veils. The gaols were thrown
open and aged political prisoners emerged, blinking at the light and
embracing their now unfamiliar relatives. Constantinople, according to
Aubrey Herbert, was 'glowing like a rose and tense with excitement'. Continuous speeches were made to the crowds, proclaiming the principles of
democracy. The magic but still meaningless word Constitution was on all
lips, seeming to portend Utopia. Thus a new era began.

Mustafa Kemal played no part in these momentous events. On the balcony
of the hotel in Salonika he was but a shadowy figure behind Enver. It was
more or less by chance that Enver had been thrown up as the revolutionary
hero. He was well enough cast for this popular role. Trim, polished, dapper
in his uniform, with well-waxed moustaches and a stiff manner of saluting,
he presented to the public the model image of the smart young Turkish
officer. His courage was beyond reproach. He would stroll nonchalantly in

front of his men under enemy fire. He was vain, basking in the plaudits of the crowd, glancing sidelong into a mirror whenever he passed one. But he was not bombastic. He was a good Moslem, who rode into battle with the Koran at his breast. He neither smoked nor drank. His private life was impeccable, just such as to appeal to the bourgeois sentiments of a revolution aimed against palace corruption and decadence. But it was, at the same time, a romantic revolution, and Enver cut the dashing romantic figure it needed.

Kemal, his opposite in almost every respect, saw him as a marionette jumped up fortuitously into the hero's role. After the scene on the balcony he walked into the Kristal Casino, to find his fellow-officers toasting the Revolution and glorifying Enver.

'What's this?' he exclaimed irritably. 'You're praising Enver all the time. Nothing but Enver! Enver! It's not good that he should be praised so much.'

An officer protested, 'Don't be jealous of Enver. He took to the mountains for the sake of freedom. Of course I'm going to praise him.'

'Naturally I'm jealous of him. I too come from a middle-class family. Don't you realize that all this praise and all these speeches will make Enver very proud, and so full of himself that in the end he will do harm to the country?' Jealous he certainly was, but with a jealousy based on an irresistible belief in his own superior capacities. Kemal was always quick to praise Enver's qualities as a soldier. But in the broader field he saw him from the start as a man inadequate to the tasks which he would be required to perform.

Difficulties indeed soon multiplied. The Young Turks, as they came to be called, were officers of unassailable patriotism, but without political experience and without, in effect, a policy. The sole aim of the Revolution was to force Abdul Hamid to his knees, and to replace his despotism with the panacea which would inevitably cure all ills – a liberal constitution. Otherwise theirs was an essentially conservative revolution. There was no ideology, no programme behind it, no understanding of the fundamental problems which confronted the Ottoman state. Imperialists in essence, blind to the new nationalist forces now at work in the modern world, the Young Turks aspired merely to conserve, if in a more liberal form, the Ottoman Empire of their forbears.

Theirs differed from previous régimes in the important respect that it was now subject to constitutional safeguards, in which all had a share; that its inhabitants were promised Union, in terms of equal rights and obligations for all races and creeds, Progress, in terms of education and economic development, and the 'Justice' that had been added to the French revolutionary slogan of 'Liberty, Fraternity and Equality'. But they were still to remain Ottomans. All that the Christian minorities were offered, in response to their yearnings for nationhood, was the privilege of becoming free citizens of a Turkish state with an alien religion.

Their reaction to this prospect was swift. The Revolution, far from arresting the disintegration of the Empire, as the Young Turks had hoped, at once accelerated it. The response was in effect a Balkan counter-revolution. Within a bare three months of the establishment of the Constitution, Bulgaria proclaimed her independence; within the same week, Austria annexed the Turkish provinces of Bosnia and Herzegovina, and Crete voted for union with Greece. Austria's act, in defiance of the Treaty of Berlin, was a unilateral breach of international law to which Sir Edward Grey attributed the ensuing 'era of European anarchy'.

Mustafa Kemal saw all too clearly the muddled course which events were taking. His criticisms of the new administration were outspoken. Night after night he would sit talking and drinking with his officer friends in those Salonika cafés which he had known since his boyhood. The Olympos and the Kristal, freed since the Revolution from all restrictions, had overflowed on to the pavements and into the streets, where their chairs and tables encroached even on the tram-lines. A new open-air café, the White Tower, had appeared at the other end of the sea-front beneath the round medieval tower which surveyed the whole sweep of the gulf and caught its evening breezes. Here the hubbub of conversation and of the street-vendors' cries clashed with the vehement clap of the pieces on the domino and backgammon boards at the crowded marble-topped tables.

Kemal's trenchant voice rose about it, reverberating clearly and emphatically around. He argued vigorously. He bore down his interrupters. He criticized the Committee openly, indiscreetly. What need was there for a Committee at all, now that the Revolution had been accomplished and a proper constitutional authority established?

This Mustafa Kemal was a nuisance. He must be sent away from Salonika on some party mission – this time farther afield than Üsküb. An opportunity now offered. There had been trouble in Tripoli since the departure of the Committee representative. At a meeting in Kemal's absence it was agreed to send him to Tripoli to investigate conditions, and to take any action on the Committee's behalf which might seem to be necessary. Confronted with the decision, he at once divined the motives behind it. He judged that Tripoli might well have been chosen by his enemies as his political, if not his actual, graveyard. But he thought it best to accept the challenge and, after drawing the necessary funds, embarked on a ship bound for the North African coast.

On the way the ship put in at a Sicilian port. He disembarked with a fellow-passenger and went for a drive in a carriage. Children in the streets mocked at their fezes, and pelted them with lemon peel. Kemal's dignity as a Turk was not affronted, as it might well have been. On the contrary, there was born in him from that moment, not resentment at the insult, but a hatred for the fez, that outworn symbol of Ottoman prestige which could so arouse the mockery of street urchins.

In Tripoli, where the Committee had not yet succeeded in establishing its authority over the Arabs and the more reactionary Ottoman elements, Kemal found a hostile atmosphere. As its representative, he had first to win over the Pasha who commanded the district. This, by a combination of threats and diplomacy over the coffee-cup, he finally succeeded in doing. Learning that Arab rebels were planning to capture him, he went boldly to the precincts of the mosque, where they had made their headquarters. After promising their leaders that his Government would take account of their grievances, he addressed the crowd in the courtyard. Greeting them as his brothers in religion he delivered them a long patriotic harangue, emphasising the power of the new régime, but insisting that it would be used only for their protection. The crowd seemed to be impressed.

But the Arab sheikh, a man with wiles of his own, sent for him and demanded, 'Who are you and what is your authority?' Kemal produced from his pocket his terms of reference from the Committee. The sheikh laughed openly and produced from his own pocket three identical papers, the credentials of three of his predecessors who had been thrown into prison on arrival.

Kemal changed his ground. 'Take the paper,' he said. 'Tear it to pieces if you like. I am a man who has no need for paper, a man who comes to talk to you with no paper at all.'

The sheikh replied, 'Then I can talk with you.' And the release of the three other prisoners was finally agreed.

Before returning to Salonika, Kemal visited Benghazi. Here he found a struggle for power between the Turkish authorities and a strong local sheikh, Mansour, who had made puppets of them, forcing them to carry out his wishes. Kemal judged that this was a case for a tougher line of action. When the sheikh called on them he took the offensive, rebuking him in menacing fashion. Then he asked the local commander to gather all his troops in their barracks for an inspection.

When the other officers protested, suspecting him of an intention to examine and find fault with them, Kemal reassured them with congratulatory words. Then he suggested that he should lead them in a short infantry exercise. To this they agreed, and Kemal briefed them: a regiment of infantry, facing Benghazi, marches to confront an enemy coming from the left. While doing so it receives orders to turn about and confront a more formidable enemy on the right.

The operation was carried out, without arousing suspicion, and the final objective proved to be the house of Sheikh Mansour, which was immediately encircled. A man with a white banner came out, offering surrender. Kemal agreed to raise the siege on condition that the sheikh came to call upon him. At this interview he expounded to him the intentions of the new régime and its policy of reform. The sheikh, producing a copy of the Koran, said to him, 'Can you swear on this Book that you will not do mischief to our Lord the Caliph?'

Kemal took the Koran, kissed it, and said, 'I honour and bless this Book. I swear on this Book and on my word of honour that, in terms of the principles laid down in it, I will do no harm to the man who is called Caliph.' Thus the sheikh, his face saved by the calming of his religious scruples, admitted political defeat. An agreement was reached by which Government and Army reaffirmed their authority, and a reasonable balance of power was restored.

Mustafa Kemal left for Salonika satisfied with the results of his mission. If only on his own valuation, he had proved himself adroit in combining the functions of soldier and diplomat.

CHAPTER FIVE

THE COUNTER-REVOLUTION

MUSTAFA KEMAL returned home from North Africa to find an uneasy political situation. The inevitable reaction was at hand. The Committee of Union and Progress had suffered an initial setback from the swift opposition of the foreigner. It was now confronted with increasing opposition at home. Its enemy Abdul Hamid still sat upon his throne, largely because the revolutionaries had not felt strong enough to depose him. Time, he judged, might well be on his side. As long as he retained the Sultanate he was bound to become a focus for such reactionary forces as survived. He could still command the loyalty of the bulk of illiterate masses, who revered him as their religious chief, no less a personage in his capacity as Caliph than the shadow of God on Earth.

The Revolution moreover had originated in Salonika; and Salonika was not the capital of the Empire. In Constantinople the Committee was less sure of its ground. From the outset the Young Turks had been divided into two conflicting groups. To the Right of them was the Committee of Union and Progress itself, favouring Union in the form of a centralized government, and tending to develop an authoritarian spirit. To the Left of them, subdivided into several groups, were the Liberals, favouring progress in terms of a decentralized régime, on more democratic principles, and with autonomous rights for the minorities. In an open trial of strength the extremists prevailed, forcibly replacing a liberal Grand Vizier, Kiamil Pasha, with a nominee of their own. This not only angered the moderates but opened the door to the latent forces of reaction.

Tension mounted, and only an incident was needed to ignite the various elements of discontent. It was duly provided one night on the Galata Bridge by the murder – supposedly at the hands of the Committee – of the insignificant editor of a liberal newspaper, and his subsequent well-staged public funeral as a martyr to the liberty of the press. The result was a counter-revolution in the name of the Holy Law of the *Sheriat* and the over-all authority of Islam for which it stood.

During the night of 12th April 1909 several units of the First Army mutinied in their barracks, bound, imprisoned or shot their officers, swarmed across the Galata Bridge, and from dawn onwards massed in the square of Santa Sophia, before the Chamber of Deputies. The procession was swelled as it advanced by other units, including even the Committee's own troops from Salonika, turning renegade, and by groups of theological students and white-turbaned *hojas* who harangued the men and inflamed their gruff, staccato cries of, 'We want the *Sheriat*! We want the Holy Law!' Clamouring for the ejection of the President of the Chamber, the abolition of the Committee, the resignation of the Government and the appointment of a new one, they swarmed into the Parliament building itself, from which the members of the Committee had fled into hiding. From the public galleries they listened, with some impatience and an occasional sarcastic interjection, to a rambling debate, the upshot of which was a decision to present their demands to the Sultan. It was not until the evening that Abdul Hamid finally made up his mind to appoint a new Grand Vizier. He chose Tevfik Pasha, a man of reasonably constitutional sympathies. At the news, given out by the new War Minister in a voice somewhat stifled by the fact that he had just suffered a slight stroke, the troops dispersed with joyous salvoes of rifle fire, happy to have held Constantinople in their power for a day.

This was not, however, to save Abdul Hamid his throne. The reaction from Salonika was sharp and swift. A meeting of the Committee decided on immediate military intervention, and entrusted Mahmud Shevket, a competent general, with the command of a striking force for the purpose. Mustafa Kemal sat silent and morose at the meeting. His achievements in Tripoli had brought him little recognition from the Committee, far less a step in promotion, and he was still only an adjutant-major of insignificant status. Bitterly, he foresaw another triumph for Enver, who had hurried back from his post as military attaché in Berlin to play his part in the operation.

For the first time, however, Kemal was given a chance to show his capacities as a staff officer. He was appointed chief of staff of a division – and at first in effect of the force itself – under Mahmud Shevket. He set to work with thoroughness and vigour to help plan the advance. It was partly on his suggestion that the force was named the Army of Liberation. Its staff work, discipline, morale and rapidity of movement were a credit to the Young Turk officers and to the German mission which had helped to train them. Within a week the army had encircled Constantinople on the landward side, establishing its headquarters at San Stefano, just outside the walls of the city, while the circle was completed to seaward by a ring of warships whose crews had declared for the Committee. A deputation from

Parliament, which came to assure Mahmud Shevket of the uselessness of his journey, met only with expressions of polite dissent.

The army had been joined by a number of prominent Committee members, including deputies who had been in hiding since the events of the previous week. Before entering the city they met with the officers in a 'National Council' to decide what to do with the Sultan. All were in favour of his deposition; a band of hot-heads called for his execution. The meeting decided on his deposition and replacement by his brother and heir apparent. The officers did not, however, show their hand publicly for fear of alarming the population of Constantinople, and perhaps causing disaffection among their own troops.

Shevket issued a proclamation, designed to tranquilize the city. It promised punishment to the mutineers and protection to the civil population. Kemal, one of whose tasks had been the drafting of Shevket's telegrams, had a hand in its composition. A naval officer named Hussein Rauf met him in the telegraph office, seeing him as a quiet young officer with a pale face and a tired expression. With a cloak over his shoulders, he was writing out orders to the dictation of Shevket, who sat in an armchair beside him. Jemal Pasha, the Minister of Marine, planning naval co-ordination, introduced them. It was a significant meeting; for Rauf was destined to become one of his closest friends and supporters.

During the night the liberating troops began to infiltrate silently into the city. After a morning of street-fighting and a siege of the two principal barracks Constantinople was theirs. A number of ringleaders were publicly hanged on the Galata Bridge. But Shevket's promise was kept, and no civilians were intentionally molested, though *The Times* correspondent was shown a corpse in the gutter which he was assured by a Greek was that of *The Times* correspondent.[1]

The Committee had determined that the deposition of the Sultan should be carried out strictly in legal form, according to the principles of the *Sheriat*. Parliament was summoned, and a reluctant Sheikh of Islam induced to promulgate a religious decree which entitled it to depose him. Thus Abdul Hamid was deposed by a unanimous vote, and a deputation was sent to Yildiz to break the news to him. The Sultan replied, 'This is kismet,' then enquired whether his life would be spared. This was a question which the delegation had not the authority to answer. In a voice of fury he cried, 'May the curse of God rest on those who have caused this calamity!' His small grandson then burst into tears, and the deputation took its leave. In the evening officers came to escort him to the station, where a special train had been prepared for his departure. On learning that his place of exile was to be Salonika, the source of all his woes, Abdul Hamid fainted into the arms of his chief eunuch.

[1] Philip Graves, *Briton and Turk*.

Meanwhile his younger brother, a timid delicate old man named Mehmed Reshad, was released from the palace where he had been imprisoned by Abdul Hamid for the past thirty years to ascend the throne in his place. Proceeding by boat down the Bosporus to the ceremony of accession he turned white with fear at the sound of gunfire. He was informed that this was the start of the traditional salute of a hundred-and-one guns, fired in his honour. But the colour came back into his cheeks only as he landed to cries of, 'Long live the Sultan!' He was proclaimed Sultan and Caliph Mehmed V.

The counter-revolution had been broken. The Committee had survived. But clearly all was not well with its conduct of affairs. Externally it had failed to resist an intensified foreign pressure. Internally it had failed to establish a securely based political structure. Kemal and a small group of brother officers in Shevket's force were convinced of the reason why. It was the association of the army with politics. These were the views of Hussein Rauf, who now again met Kemal at Shevket's headquarters and discussed the situation with him at length. Rauf was a man with a profound respect for British democratic institutions, acquired while visiting Britain in the course of his naval duties. He contended with Kemal that the Unionist leaders, instead of basing their actions on the consent of a freely elected Parliament, had based them on force, on the support of the army. This was a policy disastrous not only to the constitutional régime, whose task was to regenerate the country, but to the army itself, whose task was to protect it. The official post-mortem confirmed these views. A court of enquiry, appointed to investigate the revolt, attributed it to the fact that a number of influential officers had neglected their military duties to engage in the insidious pursuit of politics.

The ideas of Kemal and Rauf were shared by another young officer, Kiazim Karabekir, who had been expressing them even before the Revolution of 1908. Another supporter was Ismet (later Ismet Inönü), an officer of some education and a product likewise of the military schools, two years junior to Kemal, who had been impressed by his personality and had watched his career with respect. Ismet had been working for the Revolution with the Second Army in Adrianople, as Kemal had been working for it with the Third in Salonika. He had been in personal touch both with Fethi in Salonika and with one Dr Nazim who had been working on the officers in Smyrna. He had the support of another officer at his headquarters named Refet, a lively young man who had been in charge of the rail transport for the striking force. Thus there now arose in the armed forces a small but active group of patriotic young officers – Kemal, Fethi, Rauf, Ismet, Kiazim Karabekir, Refet, Ali Fuad, Tevfik Rüştü, an army doctor, and some others – who openly disapproved, not indeed of the régime, but of its methods, and who were to be regarded henceforward with growing suspicion by Enver and the Committee of Union and Progress.

Kemal had put forward their views to members of the Committee. But they refused to listen to him. They suspected his motives – not without reason in view of his own clear ambition to play both the politician and the soldier. But in fact he was not wholly disingenuous. He knew well that, at this stage in the Revolution, only the support of the army could give it the necessary cohesion and force; for no other organized parties in effect yet existed. Thus the army need not be in practice – much as it might be in theory – harmful to politics. But politics could indubitably be harmful to the army, as the recent events had proved. As a soldier and a patriot he sincerely felt this threat to its future and thus to the future of the country in its increasingly precarious position.

Three months after the 'liberation' of Constantinople the party of Union and Progress held its annual congress in Salonika. Mustafa Kemal, sitting as its delegate for Tripoli, made his first public appearance in politics, acting as spokesman for his group of companions. He attracted the momentary attention of his fellow-delegates by the unwelcome argument that, if Empire and Constitution were to be preserved, they needed not a military party but a strong army on the one hand and a strong party on the other. The officer, he argued, who tried to serve two masters, became at once a bad soldier and a bad politician. He neglected his military duties – hence the counter-revolution. He remained out of touch with the population – hence political disorders and general discontent. The country was losing both ways. For this the remedy was obvious: army officers must be called upon to decide whether to remain in the party and resign from the army, or to remain in the army and resign from the party. Then a law should be passed prohibiting officers from belonging to any political organization.

The logic of Kemal's thesis and his forceful exposition of it won him some supporters at the Congress. All he achieved, however, was the despatch of two delegates to sound out the opinion of the Second Army in Adrianople. Despite emphatic confirmation of Kemal's views to them from Ismet, his resolution failed to obtain a majority. Agreeing with its terms, a few officers withdrew from the army while others withdrew from the party. But army and party had grown so closely together that it was impossible effectively to break the connection. It obstinately prevailed at the higher levels in particular. In the previous year Enver had himself made the gesture of withdrawing from politics to become military attaché in Berlin. But he was hardly disposed to do so again just after a counter-revolution. Joint military and political power was needed to secure control of the masses, whom he now had cause to fear. Only time was to prove Kemal right, and to justify his subsequent comment, 'If my proposition had been followed many later calamities would have been avoided.'

Meanwhile the party bosses, for whom he had hitherto been merely a nuisance, now saw him as a danger, and the *komitajis* were brought into action. A party member was detailed to dispose of him and called at his office for the ostensible purpose of discussing the question which he had raised at the Congress. Kemal suspected his manner and, as he spoke to him casually, took a revolver from his drawer and laid it on the desk by his side. Then he dealt equably with the young officer's questions. The combination of Kemal's own forcible eloquence with that of the revolver drew from him the confession that he had intended to kill him, but had now changed his mind. Kemal's boast, with regard to this and two subsequent attempts, was, 'I am my own policeman.'

His policeman on the second occasion was in fact his chosen assassin. This was one Yakub Jemil, who in the past had performed similar services for the party, but who chanced to have a respect for Kemal. He not only refused the assignment but secretly warned him concerning it. Thus Kemal took extra measures for his protection while walking in the streets after dark. One night, realizing he was being followed, he retreated into a doorway with his back to the wall, and waited, gun in hand, for his would-be assailant. But the man, whom he recognized as an uncle of Enver, passed by, pretending not to see him, and Kemal let him go.

CHAPTER SIX

THE MATURING STAFF OFFICER

KEMAL NOW SUITED his actions to his principles by withdrawing from politics and immersing himself in his military duties. The Government was committed to army reforms and, with the enemy at the gates and within them, there was much to be done. Basically this was a matter of the education of other officers, most of whom had yet to learn the principles of commanding men, and the techniques of modern warfare as taught in the military schools. Kemal was attached to the Training Command of the Third Army. He plunged with energy into his allotted task of instruction. He had criticized outspokenly the out-of-date system of training which still prevailed, and in doing so had annoyed some of the older officers. Now they sat back to see how this talkative and swollen-headed young man would fare at a practical task.[1] Thanks to his aptitude for teaching his lectures soon won him the respect of his own officers. He also surprised them by the fact that, however late he had been up and talking and drinking the night before, he was usually the first to arrive at headquarters each morning.

As a patriot Kemal deeply resented the German officers whom Abdul Hamid had introduced to train the Turkish army. As a professional soldier, however, he was ready to appreciate their worth. For he respected soldiery as a science whether it was practised by his friends or by his enemies. He had indeed translated into Turkish a work by a former director of the Berlin Military Academy, General Litzmann, dealing with platoon and company combat drill, and now published part of it as a supplement to a revised Turkish Infantry Training Manual, with the addition of a preface

---

[1] He expressed to his friends his scorn for these seniors, maintaining that in this new army no officer above the rank of major was qualified to command. Jokingly, he added that if he had his way he would preserve only the register of officers up to that rank, and destroy the earlier records, so that when the colonels and upwards came for their salaries at the beginning of the month, they would be told, 'Sir, your name is not on the books. We do not know you.'

stressing the problems presented to troops through the sudden but necessary replacement of an old system of tactical instruction by a new one.

Army manœuvres, discontinued by Abdul Hamid, were now revived, and in August 1909 Kemal was attached to the army Chief of Staff for the inspection of training exercises near Köprülü. It was a military gathering such as had not been seen for years – the muster for manœuvres of a whole cavalry brigade, in the presence of the army commanders and chiefs of staff. To Kemal it was the real start of the long-desired soldier's life. One day he learned that the German Marshal von der Goltz, the respected head of the German Military Mission, was due to visit Salonika to command an exercise in the field. He resolved to prepare a scheme for him in advance. The senior officers were shocked by such presumption.

'The Marshal comes here to give us lessons,' they protested, 'not to take lessons from us.'

Kemal agreed that it was important to profit from the knowledge of so great a master of the military art. But it was just as important for the Turkish General Staff to show the Marshal that they had ideas of their own as to how their own native land should be defended. Moreover, it would be courteous to save him trouble; and in any case he was perfectly free to reject the scheme and impose his own, if he wished.

In fact the Marshal, on his arrival, was shown the scheme and decided to carry it out. The terrain chosen for the exercise was in an area unfamiliar to him, but well known to Kemal from his journeys on the railway. He kept the young officer at his side throughout the operation, and sought his advice. After hearing his final criticisms Kemal, glowing with self-confidence, became convinced that he was as good a soldier as the Marshal himself. These manœuvres in the open country became more and more frequent, and he now invariably took a lead in them. They gave him valuable experience and built up for him a military reputation out of proportion to his adjutant-major's rank.

As a tactician he would act as though he himself were conducting a battle, making his own plan of campaign, writing down in advance the orders that he would give and comparing them with those that were actually given. As a strategist he would submit plans to General Rabe, a leading German expert, studying his answers with care, and with gratification when their two minds thought alike. As an instructor, summing up the results of an exercise, he was stimulating, lucid, ruthless in analysis. He was strict with his juniors, reprimanding them for inattention to detail – for reading maps incorrectly, for failing to consult their watches, for making those minor mistakes and omissions which can lead to major disasters in warfare. He gave them the will to excel and they admired him accordingly.

But he continued to annoy senior officers – especially by his outspoken reports, written and otherwise, on staff work and military exercises. Regarding him as a theorist who might easily fail as a commander of troops in battle, they removed him from his staff post and put him in command of an infantry regiment. His rank was low for such a command and they doubtless hoped that, given this rope, he would hang himself. But he proved just as able to command troops in the field as to instruct officers at headquarters.

As the process of disintegration in Rumeli continued a revolt broke out in Albania, and here he saw active service. Mahmud Shevket took over the command and chose Kemal, whose service he had valued in the Liberation Army, as his chief of staff. It was in this campaign that he first met Colonel Fevzi Bey, another picked officer who was to become one of his group of adherents. Kemal carefully weighed up the position and drew up a tactical plan for the capture of a vital pass, which Shevket accepted and which proved so effective that it was taken, as Kemal afterwards boasted, without a single Turkish soldier 'even bleeding at the nose'. Thus the revolt was crushed and his reputation rose once more. But this merely intensified the jealousy of his rivals. It did not bring him promotion. Personal feuds riddled this close bureaucratic world of the Ottoman army; and Kemal remained an adjutant-major.

At a garrison dinner in Salonika, to celebrate the success of the operation, the German Colonel von Anderten raised his glass to the Ottoman army, which had crushed the revolt. After the toast had been drunk, Kemal rose to his feet and subjected the company to a long display of rhetoric, ironically deflating their heroics. As a Turkish officer he could not drink to so little an event as the subjection of Albania, a place within the Turkish borders. But the time would come, he assured his audience, when the Turkish not the Ottoman army would save the independence of the Turkish nation.

The Turkish army, Kemal afterwards maintained to the German colonel, would accomplish its duty only when it saved the country not simply from the enemy but from fanaticism and tyranny of thought. The real problem of Turkey was its backwardness compared with the Western world and the need to bring the Turks up to the level of contemporary civilization.

That autumn Kemal was made a member of the Turkish delegation which visited France for the manœuvres of the French army in Picardy. This was his first visit to Western Europe. He prepared for it by fitting himself out, in Salonika, with a suit of what he took to be Western clothes and a soft hat to wear when he had crossed the frontier. The officer with whom he was travelling kept on his fez, regarding it still as a symbol of Turkish prestige in these parts. But as he leaned out of the window at Belgrade a Serbian boy, selling fruit, shouted contemptuously, 'Tuh! Turkos!' Kemal's Western costume, however, was not a success. On greeting him Fethi, now military attaché in Paris, burst out laughing. 'What's this get-up?' he enquired. The suit was dark green and the hat had a jaunty Tyrolean air to it. On Fethi's advice both were at once laid aside and clothes more in line with the Parisian style procured.

In uniform Kemal and the rest wore the kalpak, the cap shaped like a fez but made of fleece instead of felt, less cylindrical in aspect, moreover brown instead of red in colour, which was now regulation headgear for Turkish officers. This singled the Turkish delegation out from the others, giving them, in the eyes of the French officers, a faintly absurd *opéra bouffe* air. Kemal soon became aware that, at the conferences which accompanied the manœuvres, he and his brother officers were not taken too seriously by the foreigners. Yet he was able to discern behind their military stylishness certain flaws in their military science. He liked to consider himself inferior to no European and it mortified him thus to be regarded askance, to be placed at a disadvantage not merely by his kalpak but by his halting French. Generally he was content to observe and absorb in a watchful, baleful silence, to form his own judgements as to the calibre of this modern Western army, the first he had seen. But at times he felt an urge to break his silence, to express ideas which he thought better than those of the rest.

One day he primed himself with cognac and, during a conference over a map on the next day's operational plan, broke out impertinently with a contradictory plan of his own, holding forth to the assembled staff officers on the need to change the agreed point of attack. They looked upon him with a certain disdain, mingled with irritation at his patronizing, hectoring manner of speech. But next day he was proved right, as a high-ranking foreign officer admitted to him: 'Your point of view was more correct than that of the others. But why,' he added in jest, 'do you wear that funny thing on your head? As long as you have it you are never going to be given credit for your views.'

At least Kemal made a good impression on the leader of his own delegation, who saw in him a clear-headed officer and listened with attention to his schemes. Back in Salonika, however, he fell into periodic moods of discouragement. There was still no talk of his promotion. Once evening he said to a friend, who had come to fetch him from his office, 'I have decided to resign from the army.' As they walked together to the White Tower, Kemal reiterated angrily, 'I can't continue with these people. I can't get on with them.' But after an hour or so of drinking and talking he had changed his mind.

Politically he felt equally frustrated. For though he had withdrawn meanwhile from an active part in the affairs of the Committee his ultimate ambition, as it had now crystallized, was for political power. At these midnight sessions in the cafés he began to boast in his cups of the day when it would be his and to confer, right and left, government posts on the friends around him. Fethi would be his Ambassador-at-large, Tevfik Rüştü his

Minister of Foreign Affairs, one friend Kiazim his Minister of War, another friend Nuri his Prime Minister. There were to be posts for all.

'But how about you yourself?'

'I shall be the man,' he answered darkly, 'who will be able to appoint you to all these posts.' Fethi, laughingly, took to calling him Mustafa the drunken Sultan.

Kemal felt in himself that he would be great. Yet he had few illusions about greatness. One night, not long after the march on Constantinople, he went into the Kristal and, finding the main café full, moved to a smoke-filled room upstairs. Here he joined some friends at a table, all drinking *raki* and beer and holding forth, with patriotic bombast, about the Revolution and the need for great men to carry it through with success. Kemal listened to their talk knowing that each dreamed of himself as the great man his country was seeking. But what were the true qualities of greatness?

'I should like to be a man like Jemal,' said one, naming the major who now dominated the party with Enver and Talat.

The others agreed. They turned to Kemal for his opinion but he refused to be drawn, giving them a cold silent look which they took, not incorrectly, for a belief in his own superior qualities. Two views emerged from the discussion which followed. One was that a man must be born great if he was to save his country. The other was that only action could achieve greatness. A man must save his country first – and even when he had done so there should be no talk of greatness. The second view was Kemal's.

A few days later he chanced to leave his office with Jemal to go in the tram to the Olympos Hotel. Jemal showed him an anonymous article from a Salonika newspaper. Kemal read it and dismissed it as mere journalistic scribbling. Jemal revealed that he had written it. This prompted Kemal to deliver him a homily on the subject of greatness. It was a short-sighted policy to seek the applause of the populace. 'Greatness consists,' he said, 'in deciding only what is necessary for the welfare of the country, and making straight for the goal. . . . In the belief that you are not great, but small and weak, and expecting no help to reach you from any quarter, you will in the end surmount all hindrances. And if any man, after that, calls you great, you will simply laugh in his face.'

This was not the kind of lecture to which Jemal was accustomed. It reflected Kemal's genuine mistrust for heroics. He was a realist, who thought in terms not of gestures but of action, thoughtfully conceived, scientifically planned and systematically executed. Too many of those whom he saw around him, and who were pretending to govern the country, were men of words, of undigested feelings and vague ideas. The Oriental mind, that of the 'men of the present', thrived on abstractions and their emotional impact. The Western mind, that of the 'men of the future', rested on practical conceptions translated into action.

It was not merely the Oriental mind but the Oriental method that aroused his mistrust. The Committee of Union and Progress, as he saw it, was not a party in the Western sense of the word. It was simply a series of decentralized committees scattered over the various provinces of the Empire, and only loosely linked together, without proper co-ordination or central control. It had no leader, only a changing series of leaders. Moreover it was saturated with the Oriental spirit of secrecy and intrigue. It was still an underground organization, which took its decisions behind closed doors with all the abracadabra of the secret society, in which conspiracy flourished, rivalry was rife in the paying off of personal scores, and power was abused through the informer, the plotter and the political assassin.

All this went thoroughly against the grain with Kemal. There was nothing he abominated more than 'political murders at street-corners'. In mind and method he was a Westerner, neither born nor made but by deep-seated instinct. He realized that only in the West was there a constructive spirit capable of moulding the societies of the future. He detested the shifts and evasions of the oblique approach to Oriental politics, the circumlocutions and imprecisions of its thought and speech. He liked to speak his mind directly, to call spades spades. His outspokenness indeed not only infuriated his enemies but, on occasion, embarrassed his friends.

Kemal differed from previous Turkish reformers in that his vision of change was, at this stage, essentially in terms not of law and administration – as that of the *Tanzimat* had been – but of politics. He wanted to change the political structure of the country, to rouse the people to a new conception of popular sovereignty, such as had been born with the French Revolution and was now growing to maturity in the various countries of Western Europe. This would take time to achieve and he understood the reason why. It lay in Islam. It was the forces of religion that would hold back democracy. Islam stood for authority not discussion, for submission not freedom of thought. The roundabout habits of mind and method which he abhorred were habits inherent in the Moslem mentality. To him political reform meant, in the first place, religious reform.

From his childhood, in defiant reaction against his mother's beliefs and devotional practices, he had been developing subconsciously into an agnostic. Now his disbelief was conscious and militant. It was shared by Fethi, whose agnosticism was sealed by an association with the Freemasons. But by both it must remain unacknowledged, except to each other. In public Kemal still had to tread warily, conforming outwardly to the traditions of Islam, mentioning the unmentionable only in the company of his most intimate friends.

For he had not only the extremists, the illiterate masses, to contend with. The bulk of his own associates, the literate élite, were still religious con-formists who had carried out their Revolution within the framework of

Islam. The reactionaries might cry against their officers as godless. But they were in fact good Moslems, to whom Kemal was the godless one. He drank, he sought to shock, he was promiscuous with women, he scorned moral principle. He was a social *arriviste* who offended against the conventions of the decent middle-class Moslems which they smugly saw themselves to be. It was for this reason, as much as for his political views and his military ambitions, that they sided against him.

None the less some of the young men of the day had begun to turn away from Islam as a political, as distinct from a religious, force. In its place was arising a new concept of nationalism, which put race before religion and saw Turks, for the first time, as Turks. Hitherto the name of Turk had been used, even among Turks themselves, as a term of contempt applicable only to the more menial strata of the Anatolian peasantry. There was even a certain conscious irony in the coining by Kemal, years later, of the patriotic phrase, 'Happy is the man who calls himself a Turk'. But now the name was acquiring a new and more noble significance. Young Turks, in their search for fresh roots, began to reach back to a racial past in the Central Asian steppes. Here, where they were Turks before they were Ottomans and Moslems, they would surely find a common social and cultural heritage on which to build a common future.

A professor of such ideas had arisen to fulfil their need. He was Ziya Gökalp, a teacher of philosophy and the new science of sociology in a secondary school in Salonika. A prominent member of the Committee of Union and Progress he had made his mark, more as an intellectual than as a practical force, in that same Party Congress of 1909 at which Kemal himself had first attracted attention. His nationalist ideas first followed the path of pan-Turanism, a movement which had grown up among the minorities in Russia as a retort to pan-Slavism, and which aspired to unite all the Turks in the world, whether within the frontiers of Turkey or beyond them. Enver, a man of misty aspirations with a vague taste for universal brotherhood, religious or social, subscribed to this thesis. But as time went on it came to seem an impractical dream and Ziya modified his ideas to a form of pan-Turkism, embracing only the Turks within the Empire itself.

This strange-looking little scholar with the shy ways, the faraway eyes, and the scar on his forehead like the sign of the Cross where, in his youth, he had tried to shoot himself in a mood of despair, struck an incongruous note among the groups of stalwart young officers drinking and talking in the Salonika cafés. But they treated his ideas with respect and began, under his influence, to develop in themselves a new sense of 'Turkishness'. There was none the less a certain difference of intellectual outlook between Ziya, who favoured a return to the pre-Moslem Turkish customs, and Kemal, who favoured those of the West. In this respect he was more in sympathy with the ideas of another intellectual of the time, Tevfik Fikret, who sought to make the Turkish reader familiar with the social and cultural life of Europe, and especially of France; and later with those of Abdullah Jevdet, who held that 'there is no second civilization; civilization means European civilization, and it must be imported with both its roses and its thorns'.

Kemal could not keep clear of politics. His circle of friends had assumed the complexion of a political splinter-group. Now he began to hold regular meetings of his regimental officers for tactical discussions. They too acquired, in the eyes of his seniors, a political significance. The agents of the Committee reported on him to Constantinople. On the instructions of Mahmud Shevket, now Minister of War, he relinquished the command of his regiment and was posted to the capital, where he was employed under close supervision in the offices of the General Staff.

But he did not remain there for long. For in the summer of 1911 the international situation took a new turn. Attention shifted from the imperialist activities of Austria and Russia in the Balkans to those of Germany, pursued hotfoot by Britain and France, on the African continent. The 'Panther's Spring' of the Germans to Agadir in Morocco, with its threat of war, led to the conclusion of a Franco-German agreement, conceding Morocco to France and a small portion of the Congo to Germany. This brought Italy on to the imperialist stage. If there was to be a scramble for North Africa she was not to be left out of it. She announced her decision to take over the neglected Turkish provinces of Tripoli and Cyrenaica, provoked a war with Turkey, and occupied Tripoli and Benghazi.

Here was a new chance for Enver to play the role of the chivalrous hero that became him so well, this time in the guise of a crusader of Islam. Tripolitania could not be allowed to go by default, as so many of the Balkan provinces and Crete had done. Too much face would thereby be lost with the Moslem world. He left for North Africa, with a fervent band of young officers, to form a defence force.

Mustafa Kemal had misgivings about the wisdom of the campaign. He was acutely aware of the greater danger to come in the Balkans. His comrades took things as they came, not seeming to grasp, as he did, that the invasion of Tripolitania was simply one more step towards the ultimate liquidation of the Ottoman Empire, and that this process could only be arrested nearer home. But he could hardly go against the tide of public feeling; to win laurels in the field might help his position in the party; and his movements were in any case hamstrung here in Constantinople under Mahmud Shevket's eye. Besides, he could not allow himself to be left behind by Enver.

He thus sailed to join him, travelling with false papers in the civilian guise of a newspaper reporter and taking with him his friend Ömer Naji, the poet, who had now blossomed into a prize orator of the Union and

A.—3

Progress Party. Rather to his embarrassment two other party members joined them, one of them Yakub Jemil, who had been his destined assassin and whose company on such an enterprise he would not himself have chosen.

Before leaving, he left his close friend and subsequent ADC, Salih (Bozok), in charge of his affairs at home, and gave him money for Zübeyde, but instructed him not to tell her, meanwhile, where he had gone. From the ship he wrote to him: 'Give my best greetings to our friends in the regiment. The drill programme which we prepared together has produced excellent results. See that they don't get tired and give up. Nothing will ever be done if they go on with their past laziness.'

CHAPTER SEVEN

THE TRIPOLITANIAN WAR

THE NORTH AFRICAN FRONT fell into two sectors – that of Tripolitania in the West, to which Fethi was hurrying from Paris; and that of Cyrenaica in the East, for which Kemal was bound. To reach it he had to pass through Egypt; and Egypt, being in the hands of Great Britain, was neutral. Turkish officers and troops were not permitted to traverse the country on their way to the war, hence Enver and the rest had to move warily to avoid identification. One day a shopkeeper with a Salonika accent enquired of Enver, 'You Enver Bey?' To this he replied coolly, 'I wish I were,' and completed his purchases without further questions.

Kemal cut a more conspicuous figure in the Cairo streets. Fair and striking, with an erect military carriage, it should have been easy enough to guess that he was a Turkish officer. He obtained an audience with the Khedive, Abbas Hilmi, who took a personal interest in his enterprise and promised him moral support. He requested extra funds and reinforcements of officers from Constantinople, and recruited locally some volunteers from among the Senussi Arabs, to send to Benghazi. He assumed the disguise of an Arab and left as soon as he could for the Western Desert, joined by two friends from Salonika who, posing as law students, had joined him at his request in Alexandria.

They reached the desert railhead in the company of three others, a Turkish gunner, an Arab interpreter and an Egyptian guide. An Egyptian officer searched the train, divulging that he had instructions to arrest five Turkish officers on board it. Kemal, realizing that their Arab disguises would not deceive the officer, revealed their identity and harangued him with an appeal to his religious sentiments. This was a Holy War, he urged, against the infidel Christians. Surely he, as a good Moslem, would not stand in the way of the will of Allah, setting himself against the principles of the Prophet and the sacred Book.

Seduced by the eloquent flow of words, the officer agreed to a compromise.

He allowed the three Turkish officers to proceed but insisted on holding their three companions while he asked for instructions. One of them could probably be passed off to his superiors as Mustafa Kemal. Next day he released all but the Turkish gunner.

The party proceeded to a camp beyond the railhead which the Egyptian 'underground' had organized with notable efficiency. Pack camels were available for them, horses, stores, water-skins – all they were likely to need except a medicine chest, and this they had brought with them. One night, after riding for a week through the heart of the desert, they reached what they took to be the frontier and put damp cloths over the mouths of the camels to stifle their barks. They pitched camp, removed their Arab clothes, put on Turkish uniforms and took their guns from their place of concealment. But a detachment of soldiers, with British and Egyptian officers, arrived and barred their progress.

Kemal again played the spokesman. This was Ottoman territory, he declared in a threatening manner. They had no business to be trespassing here. They replied that the frontier had lately been changed and that this was in fact Egyptian territory. Kemal maintained his truculent attitude and gave them an ultimatum to withdraw at once. Otherwise he and his party would fire. The British officers laughed at the discrepancy between their numbers but shrugged their shoulders and let them go. Two days later they reached the Turkish encampment on the outskirts of Tobruk.

The Italians had quickly occupied Tripoli, Benghazi and the other Libyan ports. At Tobruk, with its surrounding heights, they had made a sound defensive position. The Turks were encamped to the west of the town. They had only a small garrison force of Turkish troops and depended on the support of the Senussi Arab tribesmen, of whose loyalty, despite the efforts of Enver, they were not entirely sure. He had been distributing gold to them, arraying himself in the robes of a sheikh and inviting their homage in a finely caparisoned tent. But they remained reluctant to fight.

Kemal too, not to be outdone, donned a similar costume, which he found became him, and which he later enjoyed flaunting in the streets of Cairo. But his was a more down-to-earth military approach. Having reconnoitred the fortifications on horseback, he called a meeting of sheikhs and tribesmen. They proved a rough lot, armed for the most part with obsolete rifles and clubs. Summoning Sheikh Mebre, who controlled the rest, he addressed him as a 'brother in religion', and exhorted him to fight the Holy War against the invading infidel. He proposed a night attack on a lightly defended position, east of Tobruk. But the sheikh was not to be roused so easily. How could his people fight, he protested, with only sticks for weapons? Kemal took out a notebook and pretended to consult it. Then he said, 'Now, I realize who you are, Sheikh Mebre. They told me about you in Egypt. You are a leading spy in the pay of the Italians. I came here to talk not to Italian spies but to Arabs ready to fight for their own land. Further talk is useless. I shall give my support to other tribes, who are better armed and equipped.'

The stratagem succeeded. Next day the sheikh declared that he would launch an attack with his own tribe alone, scorning the help of the rest. After some rifles had been distributed to the tribesmen and they had learnt how to use them the attack took place at dawn, and proved successful. Some seventy guns were destroyed or captured and two hundred Italian prisoners were brought back to the Turkish camp, happy enough – as in subsequent desert campaigns – not to have to continue the fight. They were let loose in the desert to find their way home, or across the Egyptian frontier, as best they could.

It was, however, impossible to capture Tobruk, impossible indeed to do more than hold the Italians within its walls, as within the walls of the other fortresses strung out along the coast. The value of such a minor engagement to the Turks lay only in the fact that it obliged the Italians to bring in reinforcements, an operation which was impossible to prevent since they came by sea. This campaign indeed taught Kemal a military lesson which was to serve him well later, in the Gallipoli campaign. He became aware of the importance of the command of the sea, and of the impossibility of preventing the landing of enemy troops on a shore commanded by naval artillery. Turkish naval power had virtually ceased to exist. Abdul Hamid had deliberately allowed his fleet to rot to pieces, permanently at anchor in the Golden Horn. Meanwhile Turkish arms and supplies had to be run into Tripoli in a variety of precarious ways. This was the task of Hussein Rauf.

Rauf had at his disposal the cruiser *Hamidiye*, the only Turkish warship now outside the Dardanelles. She had been procured from America and was under the effective command of an engaging American adventurer named Bucknam Pasha. A former captain of the United States mercantile marine, he had sailed her across the Atlantic, following the refusal of the American authorities to detail a naval officer for the task. He was now empowered to touch a convenient percentage on each shipment of arms for which he was able to return a receipt. The arms were to be shipped to Syria then transferred in boats to the North African coast. His task was aggravated when, in the spring of 1912, the Italians occupied Rhodes and the neighbouring Dodecanese Islands.

Kemal meanwhile had transferred himself to the Turkish headquarters in Derna, alternating between there and Tobruk until the autumn of 1912. This was the first time he had served in the field at close quarters with Enver, thus his first opportunity to judge of his rival's military capacities. Kemal was quick to see Enver's limitations. He had always respected his bravery, but he now found his powers of reasoning to be disconcertingly naïve. He was prone to wishful thinking, seeing only what he wanted to see, deluding himself with dreams which had little basis in tactical or strategical reality.

To Kemal, with his hard-headed military logic, it soon became clear that this campaign had a limited scope. The Turks could not dislodge the Italians from their positions on the coast. On the other hand the Italians could not advance into a waterless hinterland held by Arabs whose support they had failed to obtain. The result was a stalemate. Any thinking staff officer could see that the maintenance of anything more than a holding force here was a drain on Turkish man-power and resources sorely required elsewhere. But Enver saw – or rather felt – things differently. He dreamed of himself, in romantic terms, as a Sultan of the Tripolitanian Arabs, with a vast expanding domain. He thus convinced himself, and in his rose-coloured reports tried to convince Constantinople, that the Italians could be dislodged from Derna and the campaign brought to a glorious conclusion. In a series of costly engagements he tried in vain to recapture it, until the ravines of the Wadi Derna were filled with corpses. A section of his officers doubted the wisdom of these tactics but dared not express their doubts. They looked instead to Kemal, whom they saw to be a commander of superior calibre.

But Kemal was in a difficult position. He realized that a breach in so small a force would have disastrous repercussions both here and at home. Open disagreement between himself and Enver must thus, at all costs, be avoided. Hence he curbed his impatience and kept the peace, maintaining relations with Enver which were reserved but polite, and trying as far as possible to curb his more reckless projects. At last he had become a full major. His promotion came through in the course of the winter. His decision to volunteer for active service had, to this extent, been rewarded. Meanwhile there had been born, in those *wadis* around Derna, a band of patriotic young officers, bent on injecting new blood into the Revolution who, as time went on, would tend increasingly to rally around Major Mustafa Kemal.

For all the tedium of the campaign, with its indecisive engagements, Kemal wrote of it in a heroic vein to his friend Salih in Constantinople:

I have no doubt that you are pleased by the fact that some of your brothers-in-arms have crossed the Mediterranean Sea, have covered distant deserts to confront an enemy based on his Fleet, and, after embracing their fellow-countrymen over here have managed to keep the enemy at bay at certain points on the coast. . . . You know that what I like best in the soldier's profession is its craftsmanship. If we have here enough opportunity and enough time to carry out all the requirements of this craft, then we shall be able to perform services which will please the country. Oh Salih, God is my witness that up to now my only aspiration in life is to be a useful element within the army! I have for long been convinced that, to safeguard the country and give happiness to the people, it is necessary first of all to prove once more to the world that our army is still the old Turkish army.

But news soon reached the officers in the field that things were not well at home. The Committee of Union and Progress was drifting into difficulties, to which the long slow drain of the war against Italy contributed. Seeking to curb opposition it dissolved Parliament and with a 'big stick election' packed a new Chamber with a vast majority of its own supporters. Thus driven underground the opposition took military shape. History repeated itself in reverse as a group of young officers took to the Rumeli hills, rebelling in the name of democracy against the despotism of the Committee, much as, four years before, the officers of the Committee had rebelled against that of the Sultan. In concert with a group of 'saviour officers' in Stambul they demanded the removal of the new Government and the restoration of a freely elected parliament. They also demanded, as Mustafa Kemal had unsuccessfully done, the withdrawal of the army from politics. Following a revolt in Albania they were able to bring down the Government and replace it with another of liberal complexion. An oath was at once imposed on all serving officers not to 'enter any political society, secret or public, nor interfere in any way whatsoever in the internal or external affairs of the State'. From Derna, Kemal wrote bitterly of the Committee's débâcle to an old comrade-in-arms, Behich (Erkin), in Salonika, recalling his own unheeded prophecies and adding, 'With time and the march of events all truths are shown and proved.'

Soon, however, the internal upheaval was to be followed by an external crisis of catastrophic proportions. In the spring of 1912, for the first and last time in their history, the Balkan peoples, with the encouragement of Russia and to the diplomatic discomfiture of Austria, smothered their differences to unite against the Turks. Serbia and Bulgaria, the one aspiring to reach the Adriatic and the other to reach the Mediterranean, signed a treaty in March 1912 which embodied a military convention aimed at Turkey. Two months later Greece joined the alliance. The iron ring around Constantinople was at last complete.

The moment had come for the *coup de grâce* to the Ottoman Empire in Europe. The King of Montenegro, who was having a flutter on the Bourse in Vienna, jumped the gun by declaring war against Turkey on 8th October 1912. Serbia, Bulgaria and Greece joined in a few days later. At the same time Turkey signed a peace with Italy and began to evacuate Tripolitania.

Mustafa Kemal left at once for home. This time he had no trouble at the Egyptian frontier. A British officer said to him, 'I know you. You're Mustafa Kemal. You may go anywhere you like in this damned country.' While in Cairo he heard of the fall of Monastir to the Serbs and of his native Salonika to the Greeks. He reached Constantinople after a roundabout journey through Italy, Austria, Hungary and Rumania.

CHAPTER EIGHT

THE BALKAN WARS

WHEN KEMAL reached Constantinople the first Balkan War was as good as over. All Rumeli was lost. In a *blitzkrieg*, lasting barely a month, the Turks had been routed on both fronts. Their collapse was due less to inferior numbers than to the virtual absence of any supply organization, and to the inability of both officers and troops to handle the modern equipment with which the Germans had furnished them.

Macedonia had gone. Mustafa Kemal's mother and sister had fled from Salonika, abandoning their home, borne away on the tide of fleeing Moslem refugees and wounded soldiers, many thousands of whom were never to reach Constantinople alive. The ex-Sultan Abdul Hamid had been hurriedly removed on a German warship, with his thirteen wives and suite, to end his days six years later in the Beylerbey Palace on the Asiatic side of the Bosporus – occupying a back room from which he could not be tormented by views of the city.

The Greek army marched into Salonika behind a detachment of kilted Evzones, to be pelted with roses by delirious crowds shouting, *'Zeto! Zeto!'* The blue-and-white Greek flag waved from the roofs and the windows. The star and crescent vanished for ever. Meanwhile, presaging a rift in the lute which was to cause a second Balkan War, the Bulgarians followed the Greeks in with a division, commandeering houses and churches and occupying a sector of the city.

Kemal was deeply affected by the loss of the place where he had spent most of his life. Meeting some brother officers in a café in Constantinople he joined them silently and reluctantly, with hardly a greeting. Then he burst out: 'How could you do this? How could you surrender that beautiful Salonika to the enemy? How could you sell it so cheaply?' He found thousands of its Moslem inhabitants massed together in the courtyards of the mosques, ragged and destitute and dying in the cruel winter weather. Eventually he found his mother and sister. Zübeyde sat rocking to and fro, suddenly aged and broken by the loss of her home. Fikriye was with them, an adopted member of the family. She was a niece of Zübeyde's late husband, whom Kemal had known as a child but who was now blooming into adolescence, with a promise of ripeness to come. Kemal found them a house and turned to his duties on the General Staff, where he was detailed to look after the defence of the Gallipoli Peninsula.

Troops from Anatolia and officers from Tripoli had strengthened the defences of the Chatalja lines before Constantinople, and the Bulgarians could advance no further. Adrianople still held out stubbornly, indifferent to hunger and bombardment. But it was the *Hamidiye* and her exploits that gave a real lift to the morale of the Turkish people. Holed in her side while bombarding Varna at the outset of the war, the 'phantom' cruiser had limped home to the Golden Horn, navigated to safety by Rauf, but hardly expected to see service again. Then the news came that she had slipped out through the Dardanelles, running the gauntlet of the Greek fleet, and was careering around the Aegean and up the Adriatic like some privateer of an earlier age, bombarding coastal towns and islands and sinking Greek transports, but in chivalrous style saving the lives of passengers and crew to put them ashore on some deserted coast. Rauf, in his gentlemanly modesty, sought no personal recognition for these exploits but insisted on giving the credit to his own sailors, who were thus collectively applauded as popular heroes.

Now the powers, having failed to prevent the war, devoted their efforts to peacemaking. The Grand Vizier, once more Kiamil Pasha, was ready enough to cede Adrianople, together with most of Thrace. This would have left Turkey in Europe reduced to Constantinople and a narrow strip of hinterland. At this moment, however, Enver returned from Africa and won over the Committee to strong action against the cession of Adrianople. As the Cabinet deliberated on the peace terms in the brocaded and gilded council chamber of the Sublime Porte, a crowd surged up to the building, with flags in their hands. Enver, who was at the head of it, ran up the marble steps, followed by Talat and others. He hurried across the vast hall to the door of the chamber. It had been opened by Nazim Pasha, the Minister of War, who bore much of the responsibility for the Turkish defeat. He greeted the deputation casually, with a cigarette hanging out of his mouth. He was shot dead by one of them, crying as he fell, 'The dogs have done for me!'

The Grand Vizier coolly remarked, 'You want the Imperial Seal, I suppose.' He handed it over and wrote out his letter of resignation. The Sultan acceded to the demand that Mahmud Shevket be appointed Grand Vizier. Shevket proceeded to the Sublime Porte and read his letter of appointment to the crowd. A *hoja* was forced to recite a prayer. The crowd dispersed. The ministers were released. Enver was on the threshold of supreme power.

Mustafa Kemal deplored this *coup d'état* and especially the manner of its execution. Though not above judicial murder, as he was later to prove, he abhorred political assassination. As a realist he saw the necessity for peace on the best available terms. But he had urged his friends in the Committee that the Government should first be forced to resign by constitutional means. Only if they refused to do so and to grant free elections should a *coup* be considered. And then it should at all costs be carried out without bloodshed. Such was the far-sighted and civilized way of dealing with crises of this sort. But only Fethi and his own group of friends heeded him.

Meanwhile the *coup* was generally popular. The country had been saved at the last moment from an ignominious surrender. The new régime hoped to save Adrianople, which the Bulgarians, now reinforced by the Serbs, were investing with a final burst of ferocity. The General Staff favoured a period of careful preparation before action was resumed. But Enver dreamed of a spectacular operation to relieve Adrianople by outflanking the Chatalja lines with an attack from the Marmara coast, and thus encircling the Bulgarian army. Though not himself in command he became the moving spirit of a new offensive.

Kemal had been appointed director of operations with the army corps on the Gallipoli Peninsula, of which Fethi was chief of staff. It was their duty to defend the Dardanelles, hence Constantinople, against a Bulgarian break-through. They were now to form the spearhead of this hazardous attack. They were strongly opposed to so speculative an operation at this crucial stage; and indeed the offensive, after an initial success, failed disastrously. Thus Adrianople surrendered to the Bulgarian army, its fall precipitated from within the walls by a Fifth Column of well-fed Greeks and Bulgars, undermining the defence of the starving Turkish garrison.

At a peace conference in London, Mahmud Shevket was forced to accept the very terms which he had previously rejected as degrading. To placate public opinion it was explained that he had ceded the city after its fall, not, as his predecessors had tried to do, while it was still holding out. Less than a fortnight later, he was driving in his car from the War Ministry to the Sublime Porte when another car drew alongside, and its occupant fired at him. Shevket was hit on the cheek. He was carried unconscious into the Sublime Porte where he died half an hour later. It was an act of reprisal for the murder of Nazim.

This deed gave Enver and the Committee of Union and Progress the pretext to force a military dictatorship on the country without further pretence at constitutional methods. They hanged the principal leaders of the opposition and established a Triumvirate, consisting of Enver, Jemal and Talat, which ruled supreme henceforward. The Young Turk Revolution, designed to defeat an autocracy, was thus to end in a party oligarchy almost as despotic as the Sultan's rule had been.

External events at once sealed its prestige. The makeshift union of the Balkan states, formed for the purpose of the war, was too artificial to survive it for long. Inevitably they started to quarrel over the division of the spoils. The result was a second Balkan War in which Bulgaria turned on the rest. The Turks marched westwards, recovering Adrianople and a large part of Eastern Thrace. As the main Turkish forces were about to enter the city in a planned operation, Enver, at the head of a detachment of cavalry, outdistanced them and entered it first, thus ensuring acclaim once more as a conquering hero.

His precipitate action angered a group of staff officers concerned with the plan of campaign, among them Fethi and Mustafa Kemal. The Governor of Adrianople brought them together with Enver, in a local landowner's house, to compose their differences. A journalist present, Falih Rifki, thus records the scene: 'A very blond young officer was sitting on a chair in front of the divan. He was handsome and very well-dressed, he had keen eyes, and he was very proud. He attracted the attention of everybody, but he did not speak much. But it was obvious that in all this he was far more important than his rank suggested.' It was his first impression of Mustafa Kemal, whom he was not to encounter again until the dark days of the First World War. He sensed that the young officer was of a different stamp to some of his fellows. He was not, he remarked, of the *komitaji* type.

Thus ended the second Balkan War. By a treaty signed at Bucharest, Greece and Serbia divided most of what Bulgaria had lost, while Turkey was confirmed in the possession of Adrianople. Enver emerged supreme. He became Minister of War. He became a Pasha. He married an Ottoman princess and lived like a prince in a palace on the Bosporus. As the debonair 'hero of freedom' grew into the all-powerful military dictator it began to be said, 'Enver Pasha has killed Enver Bey.'

Jemal was the second figure of the Triumvirate. Beneath a façade of elegant manners and a tigerish charm there lay in him a hard and ruthless energy, which combined with a cold intelligence to make of him a capable if often brutal administrator. Talat, the third figure, was the only civilian. A burly Thracian peasant, with a ruddy complexion and gipsy eyes, educated as the sole Gentile pupil in a Jewish school and afterwards entering the Post Office, he disarmed by a frankness of manner which masked a shrewd and supple mind. Only two other men played a significant part in the Government. Its figurehead was Prince Said Halim, a rich Egyptian prince of gentlemanly manners and liberal sentiments whom, as an older man, it suited the Triumvirate to co-opt meanwhile as Grand Vizier. Its *éminence grise* was Javid, a polite little Jew (a Dönme) like a cock-sparrow, from Salonika, who had charm, the gift of the gab and a quick financial brain.

When in 1913 the British general, Sir Henry Wilson, visited the scenes of the Balkan campaigns he met Enver and Jemal in Constantinople.

Neither of them impressed him by their military capacity. No more did the other officers he met. But he made one exception: 'There is a man called Mustafa Kemal,' he said, 'a young staff colonel. Watch him. He may go far.'[1] At the moment there was little sign of it. The men who ruled Turkey did not share the British general's vision.

Kemal, at the age of thirty-two – hardly younger than Enver – had made little headway either in his military or in his political career. Events were passing him by. Impatient everywhere but on the battlefield itself he had, under a régime based on personal power, scorned to conciliate those persons who could make him or mar him. He had still to learn self-control. No dissembler, no conciliator, he displayed his ambition to command, and forced on others his conviction that he was right whereas all of them were wrong. This angry young man thus spread around him a mistrust and resentment which discounted his patriotism and barred both his military and political progress.

In politics he now saw an opening through the appointment of Fethi to succeed Talat as secretary-general of the party. For a while he moved into Fethi's house and they discussed at length what should be done. Their antagonism to Enver had come to a head in the recent campaign, and their accusations against him continued both openly and by means of anonymous pamphlets. Fethi felt strongly, as Kemal did, that the time had come to rid the party of the komitajis, its Balkan terrorist instruments, but went too far in proposing a cut in the budget, by which their salaries would be stopped. Kemal warned him that such tactics would provoke the komitajis to conspire with his enemies against him. He was proved right. Feeling against the new secretary-general grew.

One day, when he was sitting at home with Kemal, Talat was announced. He took Fethi into another room and offered him the post of Minister in Sofia. Fethi thought it wise to accept. Not long afterwards Kemal was summoned by Jemal, who invited him to go to Sofia too, as military attaché for all the Balkan countries. At first he protested. But, burn as he might with frustration, he knew that he had no choice but to accept the appointment. As in 1905, on his emergence from Harbiye, this was the punishment of exile for Kemal as for Fethi.

But it was an exile that may easily have saved his life. For the komitajis were out for his blood once more, as after his first dispute with the party. And this time they might well have succeeded in their murderous assignment.

[1] *The Times*, 11th November 1938.

CHAPTER NINE

A POST IN SOFIA

LIFE IN SOFIA was a new and formative experience for Mustafa Kemal. For the first time he found himself living in a Western society. His visit to Paris had been brief, moreover occupied with military duties. Now he was introduced for the first time to the refinements of social life in a European capital. Sofia was, it is true, a mere Balkan city of no great size or distinction. But it had about it in 1913 a strong Western veneer, reflecting, in Kemal's eyes at any rate, some of that atmosphere of *douceur de vivre* which stemmed from the larger capitals of Central Europe.

Its King was the ambitious and by European reputation 'foxy' Ferdinand, a Coburg prince. In the 'eighties, under the auspices of his predecessor, the old Turkish city with its narrow tortuous streets had been razed to the ground and rebuilt in a European style, with long straight streets and spacious boulevards. Its wooded parks and gardens, laid out in the Romantic manner, suggested those of some small German capital. Its yellow stuccoed architecture, though provincial in scale, had about it an elegant rococo air. The ladies bought their clothes in Vienna and listened to Viennese music at the Opera.

When Kemal arrived in Sofia, joining Fethi as his military attaché, there was a post-war feeling in the atmosphere. The Balkan Wars were being forgiven and forgotten in a round of entertainments – *thés dansants*, dinners, receptions, balls, weekly dances at the exclusive Officers' Club where the men, handsome in their Ruritanian uniforms, at once outshone and intrigued the ladies. The Bulgarians proved anxious to fraternize with the Turks, their recent enemies. Fethi, supple in his ways and charming in his attentions to all, they saw as the Europeanized type of Turk, and he was soon a popular figure in Bulgarian society.

Kemal was always at his side, and as bachelors they often came to be invited together. Soldier-like, striking in his slim taut way, with the clipped moustache which the Young Turks had substituted for the twirling moustachios of the Sultan's officers, the young military attaché dressed well and was correct enough in his manners. But it was easy to see that he was of a different sort from his polished sophisticated friend. He liked to drink freely; he had few airs and graces; he had about him a reserve and a dark taciturnity which stamped him, in Bulgarian eyes, as the 'Turkish type of Turk'. Impressed by the social world Kemal was not yet at ease in it, and felt his way carefully. His Bulgarian accent, picked up during his service in the Balkans, was still rough. But as he persisted in frequenting Bulgarian circles it began to improve. Light on his feet, with a sense of rhythm from the songs of his Rumeli childhood, he danced well and, after a lesson or two, was adept at the waltz and the tango. At the weekly dances of the exclusive Officers' Club this brought him some success with the ladies, who responded to his interesting looks and sensed in him, behind a certain gaucherie and an absence of small-talk, a hint of the mystery man.

One night he was taken by a friend, Shakir Zümre, a Bulgarian Turk, to a gala performance at the Opera. It was a smart social occasion and the glitter and elegance of the audience made a deep impression on Kemal. In the interval he was presented to King Ferdinand, who asked him for his impressions. He could only reply, 'Wonderful!' Afterwards the two friends took a party to supper at the Grand Hotel de Bulgarie. When their guests had left Kemal poured out his enthusiasm to Shakir. This was Western civilization. There was nothing like it in Turkey. Constantinople had barely a theatre, far less an opera house. One of these days his country must enjoy these amenities.[1] His people must be introduced to the graces and refinements of European social life. It was with difficulty that Shakir, tired by the evening's entertainment, could persuade him to retire to bed.

Kemal, however, before he arrived in Sofia had not been an entire stranger to polite society. While in Constantinople he had formed a liaison with Corinne, the widow of a brother officer named Ömer Lütfü. A woman of Italian origin, with some musical talent, she kept a salon in Pera, and gave soirées for a variety of people at which he became a frequent guest. She set herself to 'groom' him for the beau monde, to give him a taste for European books and music and especially to perfect his French. In his rather stilted and ill-spelt version of the language, and occasionally in Turkish with a European script, he now began to write to her of his doings in Sofia:

I received your last letter. It gives me great pleasure to know that you think about me every day, and I thank you for giving me the news as to what we have gained as a result of the war in Africa. . . . You know that I have left the Bulgaria Hotel, where I stayed on my arrival in Sofia. Now I am living at the Splendide Palace, which has just been built. It is

---

[1] The plans for the new Ankara, fifteen years later, allowed for a large modern opera house.

a really comfortable hotel. It has bathrooms, and *femmes de chambres*, in short everything you could want, and the attractions at the hotel make it worth while to stay there. But no, no, Corinne – it isn't possible to see even one beautiful woman in Sofia. I am staying at the hotel because I can't find a proper house.

We are very friendly with Jevdet Bey. I never thought I should find him so charming and such a good friend. The night before last he took me to Madame Denigi, a Parisian lady whom he had known very well for a long time. There was a personage of importance at her house. Some Ministers and other gentlemen were playing baccarat. As I do not play we left them after a few polite greetings and some small talk. Let me tell you that I did not find this Parisian lady beautiful. I think it was she herself who asked Jevdet Bey to bring me to her house. As she said goodbye, she said to me, '*Mon Commandant*, you were not amused this evening at my house, but rest assured that I shall try to please you the next time.' But I am not so sure.

Later we went to a *Café Concert* called *Novia Amerika*. There were a lot of female singers, German, French, etc., and these ladies walked by the boxes in the hope of being invited in by gentlemen. Jevdet Bey invited two Hungarian ladies. One of them spoke German. The other, who was smaller, could not speak anything but Hungarian. I don't know why, but I didn't enjoy myself. I was bored. And, leaving the ladies alone there in the box, we left the café. When I went to bed at the hotel, it was already past midnight. . . .

Give me your news always. I embrace you with all my heart.

Corinne's reply prompted her pupil to write: 'You write that my last letter had fewer faults in spelling than you expected . . . that it must have come from the pen of another. I regard this little remark as a compliment.' Later he wrote to her in more self-revealing and high-flown terms:

How happy it makes me to think that, in spite of all your highly placed friends, you still continue to remember me, and that your continual relations with all those big hats – or, if you like, all those big vegetables – leave you a moment of respite to occupy yourself with me. . . .

I have ambitions, and even very great ones; however, they do not consist in material satisfactions like holding high places and gaining large sums of money. I seek the realization of these ambitions in the success of a great idea which, while profiting my country, will give me the keen satisfaction of a duty worthily accomplished. That has been the principle of my whole life. I acquired it while I was still quite young, and I shall continue to hold it until my dying breath.

After a while Kemal found himself a house, not far from the Legation, which he shared with Shakir. When it was ready the two friends gave a house-warming dinner for the Bulgarian Minister of Justice, serving caviar, with the best brand of *raki*, procured from Turkey, and champagne to follow. The excellence of the meal and the success of the evening came to the ears of General Kovatchev, the Minister of War, who had fought against Kemal in the second Balkan War, and who, with his Macedonian wife, had already entertained him. He made it known that he would like to be invited, with his family, to the house of the young military attaché, and another dinner was given. This started a close friendship with the Kovatchev family.

Kemal now often went to their house, where he and the general treated one another as comrades-in-arms, exchanging military reminiscences and engaging in long discussions on the art of war. He had not at first paid much attention to the general's daughter, an attractive and accomplished young girl named Dimitrina, with a slim figure and a head of dark curls. But now he slowly became aware of her, talked to her shyly and politely, and often asked her to dance when he met her at parties.

Kemal was soon invited everywhere. He was taken up by the leading hostess of Sofia, Sultana Ratcho Petrova, the wife of a general. He achieved his social apotheosis at a masked fancy-dress ball at the Palace. He had sent an orderly to Constantinople to procure for him from the museum a janissary's uniform, complete with turban and jewelled sword. Resplendent in this he created a sensation, and when the guests unmasked at midnight King Ferdinand sent for him to congratulate him, and presented him with a silver cigarette case. Many years later, when Ferdinand was in exile, Kemal returned the compliment by sending him a gold one, as a token of his respect for his gifts as a statesman.

Life in Sofia seemed good. Kemal, as his cultural standards advanced, had come across the old French tag, which he quoted in a letter to a friend:

> *La vie est brève*
> *Un peu de rêve,*
> *Un peu d'amour*
> *Et puis bonjour.*
>
> *La vie est vaine*
> *Un peu de peine,*
> *Un peu d'espoir*
> *Et puis bonsoir.*

But life in Sofia was not all social and amatory dalliance. Kemal took his duties seriously, and these, as he and Fethi saw them, were as much political as military. He made it his business to get to know the country and especially to establish contact with its influential Turkish minority. With Shakir he toured around the Turkish districts, and became impressed by the superior standard of living of his countrymen in this foreign land. In Bulgaria the Turks engaged freely and successfully in commerce, as in Turkey only foreigners were able to do. They ran their own industries at Pleven and elsewhere. Many of them had made fortunes. Their women were more emancipated than those of the Fatherland, and many had discarded the veil. Everywhere there were schools such as had yet to be introduced into Turkey itself. Kemal began to form in his mind a concrete picture of the way of life to which his own people in his own land could and must be helped to rise.

On his tours he began also to appreciate the sturdy qualities of the peasant. One day in Sofia he was sitting in a fashionable café at the hour of the *thé dansant*, listening to the orchestra, when a Bulgarian, wearing peasant clothes, came in and sat down at the next table. He called several times for the waiter, who first disregarded him and then refused to serve him. Finally the proprietor told him to leave. The peasant refused, saying, 'How dare you throw me out of this place? Bulgaria lives by my labour. Bulgaria is defended by my rifle.' A policeman was called, who took his side, and the peasant was served with tea and cakes, for which he was well able to pay. Kemal, recounting the incident afterwards, added, 'That's how I want the Turkish peasant to be. As long as the peasant is not master of the country, there can be no real progress in Turkey.' Thus germinated a Kemalist slogan of the future, 'The peasant is the master of this country.'

He now also acquired useful first-hand experience of the workings of a Parliamentary régime. Shakir was a Member of Parliament, one of the small group of seventeen Turkish deputies who had an influence out of proportion to their numbers in the confused deliberations of this multi-party Assembly, holding a balance and sometimes turning the scale with their votes. Night after night Kemal would sit in the gallery, concentrating on the debates with deep attention, studying in detail, for his own future advantage, the political tactics of a Parliament, much as he would study the military tactics of the battlefield. Here, however, he had a more direct and immediate objective. It seemed possible, through the Turkish minority, so to manipulate the political machine as to influence it in favour of his country's policy.

First the mass of the Bulgarian Turks must be roused to a spirit of national consciousness. For this purpose he controlled through the Legation two Turkish-language newspapers, which slanted news and comment in the required direction. He sent out agents to indoctrinate *hojas* and other influential members of the community, and distributed money judiciously from secret funds. In the course of these activities he found himself faced with a reactionary element, which resented the fact that both he and Fethi were often seen in the streets of Sofia wearing hats, not fezes. Such behaviour on the part of a Turkish Minister was found to be deeply shocking. This gave

Kemal the chance to launch forth boldly into speeches and discussions on a pet subject – the respective merits of the two forms of headgear.

There was another element in the country which could be won over to the Turkish side. This was a group of Macedonians who had crossed the frontier to settle here after the second Balkan War. Kemal established close relations with the Macedonian Committee and helped it with funds. Madame Kovatcheva, the wife of his friend the Minister of War, was a Macedonian, and Kemal's growing association with her young daughter Dimitrina was assumed by the local gossips to have political undertones.

In fact, it had a more romantic flavour. Kemal had never before come to know on close terms a young girl of good family and European refinement, and it was this that intrigued him in Dimitrina. His courtship came to a head at a masked ball at which he danced with her for most of the evening. At first they talked of music, to which she was devoted. But soon his conversation shifted to politics. He began to pour out, with passionate earnestness, his plans for the Westernization of Turkey, and especially for the emancipation of its womenfolk. They must discard the veil and become free to dance and consort with men, as she herself and the women in the ballroom around them were doing. They must be released from the bonds of slavery to which Moslem marriage condemned them. Dimitrina found herself swept away on the irresistible flood of his talk.

Kemal, for his part, saw her as the European wife of his desires. But he would have to ask her father for her hand in marriage; and here he risked a rebuff. Would the general, as a Christian, consent to her marrying a Moslem? He consulted with Fethi, who had himself taken a fancy to another Bulgarian girl, the daughter of General Ratcho Petrov. Tactful soundings were taken on behalf of them both, and the result was discouraging. General Petroff's reaction was instantaneous. 'I would sooner cut off my head,' he said, 'than have my daughter marry a Turk.' General Kovatchev shared his view and politely refused for his family an invitation to a ball at the Turkish Embassy. Thus Kemal and Dimitrina did not see one another again[1]

Meanwhile, as 1914 dawned, Enver and the Triumvirate had embarked on a career of swift and constructive reform. The Balkan Wars had at last awoken the Turks to a sense of national identity, and they now had a Government competent, for all its arbitrary ways, to translate this into some form of national unity.

Reforms went ahead more speedily in various home departments, but above all in the armed forces. Enver applied himself to the radical reorgan-

[1] She did not forget him, for he remained in touch with her family. Four years later, towards the end of the war, she was about to leave with her father for Constantinople, where she hoped to see him. But the collapse of the Bulgarian front prevented their visit. She later married a Bulgarian deputy, and still lives in Sofia, lately widowed.

ization of the army, Jemal to that of the navy. Enver worked with energy and a cold efficiency, introducing a radical purge of the old type of officer and promoting the new in his place.

He gained for himself a new reputation. He was no longer simply the gallant young warrior; he was the clear-headed, competent young organizer. He won praise even from Kemal himself. From Sofia he wrote to congratulate Enver on his work as Minister of War. To Tevfik Rüştü he wrote in the same strain, but criticized the incompetence of Enver's Chief of the General Staff, and declared his own readiness to serve under his rival in place of him. It was an appointment hardly likely to come his way.

There was, however, a price to be paid for this regeneration of the Turkish army. This was its increasing control by the Germans. The army reforms were carried out under the auspices of the German military mission, which was now led by General Liman von Sanders, a reliable and intelligent commander, and was invested with a high degree of executive authority over Turkish troops. German officers proliferated throughout the General Staff and the various army units, and their numbers swelled rapidly throughout 1914. Here was the culmination of that policy of 'German aid' to Turkey, which in the hands of Enver was to have catastrophic consequences for the Ottoman Empire.

For war was now imminent. On 28th June 1914 the Archduke Franz Ferdinand, the Austrian Heir Apparent, was assassinated in Sarajevo by a young student, armed and briefed by a secret Serbian terrorist organization. A month later, the Austrians declared war on Serbia, the Kaiser supported them, and the First World War had begun. Two days before, with the knowledge of only four members of the Turkish Cabinet, a secret alliance, aimed against Russia, had been agreed between Turkey and Germany. It was signed on 2nd August.

Nevertheless it was still by no means certain that Turkey would enter the war. Talat had been driven to seek the alliance in his belief that Turkey needed the support of a great power, and in his fear of isolation. For he had failed in his attempt to secure any positive guarantees from Britain and France against Russia, the hereditary enemy. Aware, however, that the Turkish army, despite Enver's reforms, still needed time to recover and build up its strength, he favoured neutrality for as long as it could possibly be maintained.

In Sofia Kemal argued strongly against Turkey's entry into the war on the German side. If Germany won the war she would make a satellite of Turkey; if she lost it Turkey would lose everything. Kemal, unlike Enver, not merely disliked and mistrusted the Germans; he was unsure of their capacity to win. His visit to Paris had convinced him that the military situation held many imponderables. The German army, it is true, was advancing swiftly on Paris. But the soldier in Kemal saw, and wrote to his friend Salih, that 'under the influence of various factors it will have to advance in a zig-zag manner, and this may have a harmful result for it. We declared mobilization without determining our aims. It will be harmful for us to maintain a large army for a long period. The outcome of this will not be certain for us or our Allies.'

On the other hand, he foresaw that if war spread Turkey could hardly stay neutral indefinitely. In this event he favoured her entry into it against Germany. In an official despatch to Enver, as Minister of War, on 16th July 1914, he had reported from his observations in Sofia that the Bulgarians were drawing together with the Austrians, hoping with Austrian aid to achieve their dreams of a great Bulgarian state. But this alone, Kemal argued, would not satisfy them. They would require also to expand eastwards, and this could only be at Turkey's expense. It would thus be dangerous for Turkey to remain inactive. The Bulgarians would doubtless try, in various ways, to win over the Turks. Being committed to no Western group it should be the policy of Turkey at this stage to lie low, maintaining an appearance of friendship with Bulgaria. But if the war were to involve her in this way, as he predicted, then 'the thing for us to do is to provoke a pretext and invade Bulgaria'. Such a policy might also further Turkey's interests in Greece.[1]

Meanwhile he lobbied his friends in Constantinople insistently, writing views to them which showed a far-sighted grasp of international realities. He even foresaw that, sooner or later, America might become involved in the struggle, and that it would in fact be the First World War. Clearly it was to the advantage of Turkey, for the present, to remain neutral and continue to build up her military strength, holding a balance between the powers and watching events until the moment arrived for a decision whether to intervene or not, and if so on which side. There was no need for hurry. For this would be a long war – of that he was convinced.

Enver, on the other hand, was convinced that it would be a short one, and that if Turkey was to reap her reward she must enter it at once. Two events helped to turn the scale in his direction. The first was the requisitioning by the British Admiralty of two cruisers built for the Turkish Government by Armstrong Whitworth, which had been paid for and were ready for delivery. Though a clause in the contract had allowed for its cancellation in the event of war, this roused indignation against Britain even among those who had favoured a pro-Allied policy.[2] The second event was the dramatic and opportune appearance in the Bosporus, with the connivance of Enver, of the *Goeben* and the *Breslau*, after running the gauntlet of the British fleet through the Mediterranean. The ships, which should have been

[1] *Çankaya Archives*, Ankara.
[2] The women of Turkey had contributed their jewels and other valuables in a public subscription to help finance the purchase.

disarmed, were instead bought by the Turkish Government and renamed the *Yavuz* and *Midilli*, while the German officers and crews remained on board, gaining popular approval by exchanging their caps for fezes.

Only an incident with the Russians was now needed to precipitate Turkey's entry into the war. Despite the opposition of the bulk of the Cabinet this was easy enough for Enver to aid and abet. The *Goeben* and the *Breslau* were sent frequently into the Black Sea 'on manœuvres', in the hope of provoking an attack. At the end of October the *Goeben* sailed up with the old *Hamidiye* and other ships, and proceeded, without warning or pretext, to bombard the Russian ports of Odessa, Sebastopol and Novorossisk. The German admiral had in his pocket a secret order from Enver: 'The Turkish fleet should gain mastery of the Black Sea by force. Seek out the Russian fleet and attack her wherever you find her, without declaration of war.'[1] In the ensuing battle a number of Russian ships were sunk. It was an act of war.

Enver pretended not to have known of the attack. Talat learned of it only after it had happened. He remarked, 'Would that I were dead! Would that the country had not been dead!' But he remained in office. Jemal received the news while playing cards in the *Cercle d'Orient*. He showed astonishment, turned pale, and swore on the head of his daughter that he knew nothing of the incident. He too remained in office.[2] Said Halim, the Grand Vizier, offered his resignation to the Sultan, who embraced him and begged him not thus to deprive him of his sole source of comfort and leave him to the mercy of incompetent men. He agreed to remain. Tears were pouring down his cheeks when the British and French Ambassadors came for their passports. Only Javid, together with three minor ministers, resigned. 'It will be our ruin,' he had said, 'even if we win.' Thus began the last phase in the decline and fall of the Ottoman Empire.

[1] Ernest Jäckh, *The Rising Crescent*.
[2] Later he argued that it was best thus to enter the war, 'rather than fall miserably under the yoke of the Russians'.

CHAPTER TEN

THE FIRST WORLD WAR

MUSTAFA KEMAL had opposed the war. But now that it was a *fait accompli* he threw himself into it with energy and in a patriotic spirit. The Germans were his natural enemies. But now that they had become his military Allies he was ready to make common cause with them so far as his patience allowed. His first task, here in Sofia, was to help bring pressure on the Bulgarians to enter the war. Aiding Fethi he worked to this end through all available channels, countering in the process a barrage of propaganda from the side of the Russians.

At dinner one evening with Madame Petrova Kemal whom, as she afterwards recalled, 'the wines had made talkative and generous', became free with his offers to General Petroff of all the territory Bulgaria had lost in the second Balkan War. She should have Adrianople; she should return to the Chatalja lines, and stay there; all the hinterland of Constantinople should be hers. His imagination carried him further, to the prophetic conception of an Asiatic Turkey, with its capital in Anatolia, looking westwards in permanent alliance with a Bulgaria embracing Turkey in Europe, and co-operating in the joint defence against the Russians of a free Constantinople. He seemed about to offer the city itself to the general when a newly arrived Turkish attaché made naïve signs of alarm to Fethi, otherwise engaged in paying compliments to Mademoiselle Petroff, the lady of his choice, at the head of the table. Fethi burst out laughing at his military attaché's lavish cessions of territory, and remarked to the general, 'Well now, what are you going to give us in compensation?'

Another task of Kemal's was to obtain arms and supplies from the Bulgarians for the support of the Turkish armies. He secured a promise of a large load of flour against cash payment, and sent Shakir Zümre to Constantinople to arrange the deal. He saw Talat, now Minister of Finance. But Talat passed him over to Javid who, though he had resigned from the post, still worked behind the scenes, giving influential advice on financial policy. Javid refused to recommend the payment. There was, he said, no money available for such a purpose. 'You seem to think,' he added, 'that this war is going on for years.'

Kemal met Shakir at the station on his return to Sofia, eager for news of his mission. When Shakir told him of Javid's refusal, he exclaimed angrily – and, as it turned out, prophetically – 'A man like that deserves to be hanged!'[1]

As the war proceeded Kemal began to fret with impatience. He was now a lieutenant-colonel, and thus entitled to a divisional command. He wrote to Enver, asking for a post in accord with his rank. But Enver replied, 'There will always be a post for you in the army, but as your retention at Sofia, as military attaché, seems especially indicated, we are leaving you there.' To this Kemal retorted that a more sacred duty called him to the front, and added, 'If you consider me unworthy to become an officer of the first rank, please tell me so openly.' To this Enver did not reply.

Kemal was indeed sounded by an emissary from Constantinople about a project of Enver to send a force of three regiments through Persia into India, with the object of stirring up a Moslem revolt against the British. Would he accept the command of such a force? Kemal recognized the proposal as one of Enver's more fanciful dreams, a disquieting sign as to how his mind, at the outset of a war, was working. He treated it with cynicism, replying, 'I am not such a hero.' For such an operation, he added, three regiments would be superfluous. Only a single officer was needed, who would raise his troops on the way. The thing, of course, was impossible. 'Had it been possible,' he drily remarked afterwards, 'I shouldn't have waited for orders. I should have gone by myself and found my troops. I should have conquered India and become an Emperor.' Instead, he replied that he intended to fight at the front in his own country.

The first few months of the war had proved disastrous for Turkey. Had her leaders been wise they would have devoted this period to a defensive strategy, conserving and building up such military strength as she had, completing the training of her forces and disposing them with forethought, waiting to see from which quarter the Allied threat would come.

But Enver would have none of this. He preferred great and romantic adventures. He saw himself in the role of an Islamic Alexander the Great, moving against Britain in quest of a new Turkish Empire in Asia. This was a dream which coincided nicely with Germany's own plans for world conquest. For its realization he decreed two immediate offensives: the first northwards against Russia, the second southwards against Egypt. The first offensive, designed to encircle the Russian forces in the Caucasus, and executed against the advice of the German commander, General Liman von Sanders, ended in total disaster. In appalling winter conditions virtually a

---

[1] Javid was hanged in Ankara, following the treason trials of 1926.

whole Turkish army was lost – a crucial force which should have been held in reserve for the defence of the east.

It was only after Enver had left on this catastrophic excursion that Kemal was given a command. He had decided to leave Sofia, despite his orders, and even talked of enlisting as an ordinary soldier. But as he was on the point of departure he received a telegram from Enver's deputy at the Ministry of War. This appointed him commander of the Nineteenth Division and instructed him to report at once to Constantinople.

Reporting at GHQ he was shown in to Enver, who had just returned from the east. He looked thin and pale.

'You are a little tired,' Kemal said to him.

'Not particularly.'

'What happened?'

'We were beaten. That's all.'

'And the general situation, how is it?'

'Very good,' replied Enver.

Not wishing to press him further, Kemal raised the question of his posting. 'I must thank you for being good enough to appoint me to the command of the division which bears the number nineteen. Where is this division – in what army or army corps?'

Enver replied vaguely, 'Oh yes. Perhaps you will be able to get more precise information from the General Staff.'

Kemal then toured the various offices of the General Staff, in search of his division – but in vain. Finally someone advised him to try the army of Liman von Sanders, whose offices were in the Ministry of War. He was shown into the office of his chief of staff, who answered him, 'We have no such division in our formation. But it is quite possible that the Third Army Corps, which is stationed at Gallipoli, may be planning to form the unit you mention. If you would care to give yourself the trouble of going there you will certainly be able to obtain all the necessary information.'

Before he went he was shown in to General von Sanders. He had not met him before, but they were already known to one another through his outspoken anti-German sentiments. The German general received him with affable courtesy, asked him when he had returned from Sofia, and enquired, 'Are the Bulgarians going to make up their minds to come into the war?'

Kemal replied that in his opinion they would not do so yet. They were waiting for one of two things to happen: either a striking German success, or the extension of the war to their own territory. This remark provoked an irritable gesture from von Sanders, who remarked with a sneer, 'Then the Bulgarians don't believe in the success of the German army?'

Kemal answered calmly, 'No.'

Von Sanders then asked him suspiciously, 'And what is your opinion?'

Kemal hesitated. As a mere commander of a division which did not yet exist how could he express an opinion? On the other hand he had for long been committing his views to paper and could hardly retract them now. Besides, for all that he might have said in public, he could not help privately sympathizing with the circumspect policy of the Bulgarians. He decided to be frank, and said briefly, 'I think the Bulgarians are right.'

Liman von Sanders rose without a word and Kemal took his leave. He left for the Gallipoli Peninsula, where his division was in the process of formation.

Meanwhile Enver was proceeding – again against the advice of von Sanders – with his second spectacular offensive. This was to be a swift descent upon the Suez Canal, with the object of ejecting the British from Egypt. The Turkish force, marching across the desert under the command of the German Colonel von Kress, took seven days to reach the Canal. But it marched by night and surprised the British. A few of its troops succeeded in crossing the Canal, but the west bank was strongly held and the defence was soon reinforced by British military and naval artillery. The Turkish force was thus forced to retire. Its incursion acted as a warning to the British, who proceeded so to build up the defence of the Canal Zone as virtually to preclude any future attack on Egypt by the Turks.

Having failed in their own two offensives the Turks were now faced with an offensive by the Allies. From the beginning of 1915 onwards it became evident, from intelligence reports of enemy naval and troop movements, that Allied forces were assembling on the islands before the Dardanelles, and that an Anglo-French attack on Constantinople, through the Narrows and across the Sea of Marmara, was imminent. The failure of the Caucasian and Egyptian campaigns had lowered morale, and the people of Constantinople began to talk despondently of the capture of the city as though it had already occurred. The Germans grew a trifle hysterical, fearing the arrival of the Russians, and began to talk of a separate peace. Turkish families began to leave for Anatolia. The Turkish Government prepared two special trains on the Asiatic side, with steam up for departure at an hour's notice, one for the Sultan and his suite and the other for the Diplomatic Corps. Abdul Hamid, now in exile in the Beylerbey Palace, was invited to accompany the Imperial family party, but refused to move, saying shrewdly to his brother the Sultan, 'If once you leave Constantinople, you will never be able to return.'

The Government had made plans to move to Eskishehir, whither the Archives of the Sublime Porte and the gold from the banks had already preceded them. Cans of petrol were stored in the police stations of Constantinople, ready to fire the city. Works of art were buried in the cellars of the museums and plans made to dynamite a number of public buildings, including Santa Sophia. When the American Ambassador protested that it should be spared, Talat replied that there were not six men in the Committee of Union and Progress who cared for anything old. 'We all like new things,' he explained.

Talat was a 'picture of desolation and defeat'. Thousands of Turks were secretly praying for an Allied victory, and the Chief of Police was sending gangs of unemployed out of the city, for fear of revolution. When in February 1915 the British navy reduced by gunfire the forts at the entrance to the Dardanelles the rumour spread around that they had levelled two whole hills. Citizens began to listen for the sound of the guns, and organized picnics on the islands in the Marmara to look out for the periscopes of enemy submarines.

Only Enver, who had kept out of the public eye since his defeat in the Caucasus, remained cool and collected. This was a faculty for which he was remarkable, never seeming ruffled or excited, conveying a sense of calm whenever he entered a room. Now he expressed his absolute conviction that the British would never succeed in forcing the Dardanelles. All this, he declared, was a 'silly panic'. The fortifications of the Straits were impregnable. Even if they proved not to be, Constantinople would be defended to the last man and would never yield to the enemy. He was carried away by a new dream, that of going down to history as the man who had exploded the legend of the invincibility of the British navy – a thing that neither Germany nor any other nation had succeeded in doing.

Enver, as events turned out, was proved right – for the wrong reasons. The British naval attack of 18th March failed to break through the Narrows. It was not followed up. The British, for a complexity of causes, decided not to proceed with the campaign until they could support their fleet with a land advance – as indeed Liman von Sanders had prophesied that they would be obliged to do. Flags were put out by order in Constantinople. But few Turks seriously believed that this was a final victory. There was hard fighting still to be done.

Enver decided to form a separate army, the Fifth, for the defence of the Dardanelles, and appointed Liman von Sanders to command it. Liman asked for a new division, the Nineteenth, and it was to the command of this that Lieutenant-Colonel Mustafa Kemal had been posted, with his headquarters at Maidos. He had just two months in which to organize his troops before the Allies attacked.

CHAPTER ELEVEN

THE GALLIPOLI LANDINGS

KEMAL KNEW the Gallipoli Peninsula from his operations against the Bulgarians in the Balkan War, when his headquarters as now was at Maidos. He had then formed strong opinions about its defence, which conflicted with those of his fellow staff officers. They maintained that any enemy could be prevented from landing on the peninsula by adequate barbed wire defences on shore. Kemal argued, on the contrary, that any enemy could land under cover of naval fire and that it would be the task of the defence to tackle him after he had done so, from defensive positions inland.

Discussing these tactics with Rauf, who as a naval officer agreed with them, he had said at the time, putting himself in the place of the enemy, 'You may have as many barbed wire defences as you like, but I can easily break them to pieces and land; and if I don't find superior forces to stop my advance on land, I can very well occupy the peninsula.' Kemal had learnt this lesson of military science during the Tripolitanian campaign, when the Italians had landed their troops under the cover of naval fire, making shore defence by the Turks impossible. This had awakened him to the inherent tactical power of naval bombardment, of which the rest of the Turkish staff, innocent of land–sea manœuvres, was now for the first time to have harsh practical experience.

Under the German command it was, as Kemal had maintained that it should be, the principle of the Turkish defence to hold the ridges – the rugged vertebrae of the peninsula – and oblige the enemy to storm them when once he had landed. Liman von Sanders, finding his six divisions scattered into small units along the coast line, grouped them together into fewer and larger concentrations inland, leaving a minimum of covering detachments on shore. The question remained, where would the enemy land? Kemal was convinced, from his knowledge of the terrain, that he would do so at two main points – Cape Helles, at the southern tip of the peninsula, where he could command the land on every side with his naval guns; and Gaba Tepe, on the western coast, whence he could most easily cross to the Narrows on the eastern coast.

But the assessment of Liman von Sanders was different. In his opinion the two likeliest points for a landing were the Asiatic coast, where he thus sent two divisions to the region of the field of Troy; and the narrow northern isthmus of the peninsula at Bulair, for which he earmarked two more. Of his remaining two, one was sent to Cape Helles, while the last, the Nineteenth, under his own direct control but under the effective command of Mustafa Kemal, was held as the main reserve of his army near Maidos, ready to move to any area, north, south or west, where the main attack might fall. This role suited Kemal, who chose as his headquarters the village of Boghali, north of the Narrows and within reach of either coast. Here he sat down to watch for the landings and prepare for the subsequent defence of the heights.

Soon after dawn on 25th April the Allied troops landed in force, as he had foreseen, on these two groups of beaches – the British at Cape Helles and the Australians and New Zealanders north of Gaba Tepe. There were besides two diversionary manœuvres – a raid by the French on the Asiatic coast and a demonstration by the Royal Naval Division at Bulair. Von Sanders fell for this second diversion. The Allies, he judged, sought to cut the narrow neck of the peninsula and so isolate the whole of his army. He thus ordered a division northwards to Bulair, away, as it proved, from the battle, and rode there with his staff, later sending his corps commander, Essad Pasha, to look after the attack in the south, but leaving him, as the day wore on, without much-needed reinforcements.

Kemal on the other hand, awoken that morning at Boghali by the naval bombardment, found himself right at the centre of gravity. The sound of the guns came from beyond the Sari Bair range, a long and often precipitous ridge which ran parallel with the western coast, rising up to three prominent crests of a thousand feet, and breaking up near the sea into subsidiary ridges scored with ravines. At once he sent a cavalry squadron up the eastern slope of the ridge to the northerly crest of Koja Chemen to reconnoitre the position. Next he received a report that a 'small enemy force' was advancing up its western slope to the southerly crest of Chunuk Bair, together with a request from the neighbouring division to send a battalion to check its advance.

Kemal saw at once what was happening. Here was no small enemy force; here was a major offensive. With his acute grasp of military essentials he knew that the Sari Bair ridge, and especially the Chunuk Bair crest, was now the key to the entire Turkish defence. Its capture would enable the enemy to dominate all sides of the peninsula. A single battalion would be totally insufficient to hold it. The whole of his division would be needed. Acting on his own responsibility and exceeding his authority as a divisional commander, he thus ordered his best regiment, the Fifty-Seventh, with a mountain battery, to advance up the ridge to the crest of Koja Chemen. As it happened the regiment was already drawn up for a field exercise planned for that day. Kemal reported what he had done to corps head-quarters then rode with an ADC and his chief medical officer to its head-quarters to hasten and lead the advance.

Kemal's decision was a bold one. He was committing the bulk of von Sanders' reserve on the basis of not very clear information as to the strength of the enemy, but only on that of his own intuitive conviction that this was the crucial attack. Had his judgement been wrong, had the enemy planned another important landing elsewhere, there would have been only one Turkish regiment left to resist it. But he was right, and in his abounding self-confidence knew it.

The Australians had indeed landed in force, not at Gaba Tepe, as they had planned and as the Turks had expected, but on a beach at Ariburnu – the 'Cape of Bees' – in more difficult country a mile to the north of it, to which an uncharted current had carried their boats. It was a place to be known as Anzac Cove. Here the Turks were unprepared for them, and despite the more formidable natural obstacles they were able to advance against only confused opposition up the western slopes of the ridge.

Up the eastern slopes the path of Kemal with his regimental officers and men, winding through strong scrubby undergrowth amid a confusion of dried-up watercourses strewn with boulders, was hard to find. Two guides, sent on ahead, lost touch with the main body and it was Kemal himself, riding at the head of a company and consulting a map and compass, who finally led the way. From Koja Chemen he looked down on the shimmering sea and the ships of the enemy scattered across it, but his view of the advance, among the broken ridges beneath, was blocked. Seeing that his men were tired from their arduous climb, he ordered their officers to give them a ten-minute break. Then he moved on himself, with a few of his staff, towards Chunuk Bair. They started to ride but, finding the terrain too rough, dismounted and proceeded on foot. Near the crest they came upon a company of men streaming down over the ridge in full retreat. They were a unit of the outpost screen, spread out to watch for the landings, which for more than three hours had been the only force to oppose the enemy.

Kemal stopped them and asked, 'What's up? Why are you running away?'

'They come, they come,' was the reply.

'Who comes?'

'Sir, the enemy. *Ingiliz, Ingiliz.*'

'Where?' he asked. They pointed down the slope to a patch of scrub, from which a line of Australians was freely advancing. They were closer to Kemal than his own troops, whom he had left behind to rest. 'Whether by logic or instinct' as he afterwards put it, he said to the retreating soldiers, 'You cannot run away from the enemy.'

They protested, 'Our ammunition is finished.'

'You have your bayonets,' he said. He commanded them to fix bayonets and to lie down on the ground. He sent an officer back to instruct his own infantrymen to come up at the double, together with any available gunners from the mountain battery. Then, as he observed, 'When our men lay down, the enemy lay down. This was the moment of time that we gained.'

It was a moment of hesitation by the Anzacs which may well have decided the fate of the peninsula. While they hesitated the Fifty-Seventh Regiment began to come up, and Kemal sent it straight into action. He rode through the forward positions, driving the troops over the slope with unwavering energy. Placing his mountain battery on the ridge, he helped to wheel its guns into position. He directed operations from the skyline with a complete disregard for his own safety. In an order of the day he wrote: 'I don't order you to attack, I order you to die. In the time it takes us to die, other troops and commanders can come and take our places.' By the end of the battle almost the whole of the Fifty-Seventh Regiment had died, charging continuously through a curtain of enemy rifle-fire to win immortality in the annals of the Turkish army.

But the Turkish fire was as deadly. Time after time it would halt the Anzacs as they surged into view over a ridge, while the mountain battery poured shrapnel upon them in an awful baptism of shell-fire, forcing them to scatter and take cover in the meagre scrub without means of retaliation. For their artillery was not yet in action, and even the naval batteries were silent, fearing to fire on their own forces on a front so confused. The confusion in this battle of sudden hand-to-hand encounters and shifting positions was indeed such that, with bullets raining from every direction, neither Turks nor Australians knew just who might prove to be an enemy and who a friend. Meanwhile Kemal, once again without authority, had ordered a second regiment – composed of Arab troops – into the line to reinforce the first. Then he rode back to corps headquarters at Maidos to report to Essad Pasha and urge upon him the necessity for an all-out attack with every man available. Essad agreed with his appreciation, approved of his actions and handed over to him the remaining regiment of the Nineteenth Division, thus putting him in command of the whole Sari Bair front.

As the afternoon wore on the Anzacs were slowly driven back, not indeed to the sea, as Kemal insistently urged, but to those coastal spurs and ridges which they had occupied early that morning. Night fell, lulling the storm of the main battle. But, in the words of the official historian, there was 'no rest for anyone on those rugged hillsides that night. Worn out with fatigue, scattered and disorganized, it was impossible for either side to make further progress. But the noise of battle continued; and with only the flash of their assailants' rifles to guide them, invaders and invaded alike kept up a continuous fire.'

Kemal himself spent the night without sleep, riding over the whole front, trying to obtain information and giving orders for the following day. Reinforcements were being landed, under cover of darkness, as he rode. But the morale of the Anzacs was shaken – by the unfamiliar shrapnel fire, by the unforeseen rigours of the terrain, by the disruption of units, which drove leaderless men back to the beach in their hundreds.

Around midnight Sir Ian Hamilton, the British Commander-in-Chief, was awoken from his sleep aboard HMS *Queen Elizabeth* by a message from General Birdwood, the Anzac commander. It was an admission of defeat and a proposal for an immediate evacuation. Hamilton wrote immediately to Birdwood that a supreme effort must be made to hold on. The southern force had established a bridgehead around Cape Helles, and should advance tomorrow, diverting pressure from Ariburnu. He added a postscript: 'You have got through the difficult business and you have only to dig, dig, dig until you are safe.' Later he wrote in his diary: 'Better to die like heroes on the enemy's ground than be butchered like sheep on the beaches like the runaway Persians at Marathon.' Such were the fruits of Kemal's leadership of the Turks that crucial day.

The Australians pulled themselves together and dug. The clink of shovels was everywhere heard on the hillside. Next morning Kemal remained on the defensive. His losses in the initial battle had been heavy; moreover he knew that the imminent danger was now in the south, at Cape Helles, where all available reserves would be needed. He resumed his attack only on receiving reinforcements from Bulair. Hamilton, from the deck of his warship, watched the operation, this time effectively countered by shell-fire from land and sea. He recalled it in his *Gallipoli Diary*:

> Under so many savage blows [he wrote], the labouring mountains brought forth Turks. Here and there advancing lines; dots moving over green patches; dots following one another across a broad red scar on the flank of Sari Bair; others following – and yet others – and others, closing in, disappearing, reappearing in close waves converging on the central and highest part of our position. The *tic-tac* of the machine-guns and the rattle of the rifles accompanied the roar of the big guns as hail, pouring down on a greenhouse, plays fast and loose amidst the peals of God's artillery. The fire slackened. The attack had ebbed away; our fellows were holding their ground. A few, very few little dots had run back over that green patch – the others had passed down into the world of darkness.

Kemal's surviving troops were exhausted and his new units were unused to the terrain. The naval bombardment had demoralized all. His force for the moment was spent. But he had driven the enemy back into a confined scrap of land along the sea-coast. Its perimeter was hard to defend; it was supplied only by a beach, exposed not only to the varying winds but also to the enemy fire; it was dominated actually and psychologically by the Turks, looking down on it unseen. Kemal had held the heights, which he had seen to be the key to the peninsula. By his flair, his sense of urgency, the sureness of his decisions and the insistence of his leadership he had, at the outset of an invasion on the lines he had predicted, saved the Turks from a defeat which might well have opened the road to Constantinople.

Like the Anzacs the Turks now dug in. On both sides the initial impetus, with its element of surprise, had waned. But Kemal, following a minor attack on the enemy on 30th April, was determined on a third counter-attack before they could land further reinforcements. Aware of the necessity to keep up the morale of his men and the spirit of leadership in his officers, he called a group of them together at his headquarters, now known as Kemalieri – Kemal's Place. They sat cross-legged around him '*à la Turka*' on the floor of his tent, and wrote on pads in the palms of their hands as he briefed them. 'I am convinced,' he instructed, 'that we must finally drive the enemy opposing us into the sea if it means the death of us all. Our position compared to the enemy's is not weak. His morale has been completely broken. He is ceaselessly digging to find himself a refuge. You saw how he ran away immediately when a few shells dropped near his trenches. . . . I am convinced that there is not one amongst the troops we command who would not rather die here than see a second chapter of our Balkan disgrace. If you feel there are such men, then let us shoot them with our own hands.'

To the troops themselves he issued an order of the day:

Every soldier who fights here with me must realize that he is in honour bound not to retreat one step. Let me remind you all that if you want to rest there may be no rest for our whole nation throughout eternity. I am sure that all our comrades agree on this, and that they will show no signs of fatigue until the enemy is finally hurled into the sea.

The section commanders were told to trust to only one thing – their soldiers' bayonets. The soldiers, as they advanced, must not stop short of the enemy trenches. They must, when it grew dark, jump right into them.

On the eve of the attack, the German Colonel Kannengiesser arrived at Kemal's headquarters to take over the command of another division – for the present inextricably confused with Kemal's own. He was impressed by this 'clear-thinking, active, quiet man, who knew what he wanted. He weighed and decided everything for himself, without looking elsewhere for support or agreement to his opinions. He spoke accordingly but little, and was always reserved and retiring without being unfriendly. He did not appear to be very strong bodily, although extremely wiry. His stubborn energy gave him apparently complete control, both of his troops and of himself.'

The attack at first went well, against a single shore battery. But Kemal had miscalculated. Aware as he had been, as a strategist, of the impossibility of preventing an enemy invasion covered by naval fire, he had underrated its tactical power once the enemy had landed. The British warships, strongly supported by the heavy artillery on shore, began to shell Kemal's positions, protected only by out-of-date mountain guns, and his onslaught immediately flagged. Attack after attack was smashed by the overwhelming superiority of their gun power, and a number of Turkish battalions broke in panic and ran. Kemal threw in all his reserves in the hope of a break-through by night. But he failed to penetrate the enemy's positions. For once, he had suffered a major tactical defeat. 'The battle,' he recorded, 'which has lasted for twenty-four hours, had caused great fatigue to our troops, and I gave an order for the attack to stop.'

Afterwards, to Rushen Eshref, who came to interview him for the press, he recounted how, at one point in the battle, faced by an attack from the enemy lines a mere ten yards away, all the men in his first trench fell. Those in the second, seeing them fall, at once took their places, knowing that they too would die, but remaining unshaken. Those who could read died with a Koran in their hands. Those who could not called upon Allah with a prayer. All were ready to go to Heaven. Therein, he declared, lay the spiritual strength of the Turkish soldier, which should make victory possible. But in down-to-earth terms the reckless and profitless sacrifice involved in such frontal attacks was leading to casualties which the Turkish army could not easily afford. Essad, Kemal's corps commander, realized that a conservation of forces was needed to meet the Helles offensive. Thus Kemal received orders to desist from further such operations.

On 18th May, however, there was another major onslaught by the Turks on the Anzac bridgehead. This time it was conceived by von Sanders himself, but with a suggestion behind it of Enver's taste for a spectacular enterprise. Kemal, as a mere divisional commander, played no part in its conception. The plan, which displayed little tactical finesse, was to fling an overwhelming force, reinforced from Helles and from the Asiatic side, against Ariburnu, and thus either to annihilate the Anzacs or to drive them once and for all into the sea. Since they had withdrawn troops from the bridgehead to reinforce Helles, they were now in a minority of one to three. But though the Turks were on top of the Anzacs, and sometimes only a few yards away from them, they were now a vulnerable target, obliged as they were to charge on prepared dug-in positions. The result was a holocaust.

The losses were so great as to prompt a truce with the enemy, that each side might bury its dead. Kemal was one of a party of officers who, to negotiate the truce, was led blindfold into the Anzac bridgehead, goose-stepped by the Australians over imaginary barbed wire entanglements to impress them with the extent of their defences, then conducted to a cave by

A.—4

the beach which was General Birdwood's dug-out. Here a cease-fire for nine hours was agreed. Pending agreement, Aubrey Herbert was held as an honoured and contented hostage by his friends in the Turkish lines.

In June Kemal was promoted full colonel. Liman von Sanders, though he found him hard to handle, fully appreciated his qualities as a divisional commander. Enver, however, still mistrusted him and was for ever seeking a pretext to find fault with his actions. He found one on a whirlwind visit to the front at the end of the month, when the friction between them flared up into a serious explosion. Kemal, reinforced by a crack Turkish regiment, had persuaded Essad to sanction an attack on a crucial Australian position whose capture, he believed, could force a withdrawal from the peninsula. Enver objected to it, accusing Kemal, not without justification, of squandering lives. But von Sanders made the peace between them and the attack took place. Partly owing to a fierce thunderstorm which combined with a demonstration of star-shells and flares by the Australians to confuse the attackers, partly owing to the death of the regimental commander before they attacked, it failed.

Kemal blamed Enver's interference for the failure. Enver, while praising Kemal's troops for their gallantry, threw aspersions on his leadership. Kemal resigned. But when Enver returned to Constantinople he was pacified by Liman and agreed to take over the command of his division once more.

But he was not content. Though he had won for his country the first round in the Gallipoli campaign he still had no say in its general direction. There were continual disputes with corps headquarters as to the extent of his command, the inadequacy of its forces, its exact delimitation with the command adjoining, which was now given to a German officer, Major Willmer. Kemal was convinced that Essad Pasha, the corps commander, did not attach enough importance to this Ariburnu area, and wrote to him of its defence problems in continual and laborious detail. Fixed singly in his mind still was the Sari Bair ridge, with its peaks of Chunuk Bair and Koja Chemen. If and when the enemy reinforced their troops and resumed the offensive, as they had openly shown their intention of doing, it would once more be the major objective. He had been convinced of its importance before, and had been proved right; he was convinced of it still.

He tried in vain to convince Essad Pasha. A key to the defence of the heights was the ravine of Sazlidere, which led directly up to Chunuk Bair, offering valuable cover to an enemy advancing over the foothills towards it. It had at first been included in his command but was now, it seemed, to form the dividing line between the two commands. Who in fact was to control so important an area, he or the German major? It was essential that this should be clarified.

Essad Pasha came down to divisional headquarters with his chief of staff, to see for himself. Kemal took them up on to the top of the ridge and gave them a lecturer's eye-view of the whole position, spread beneath and around them – the broken rocky country on either side of Sazlidere, the beach below it, the bay of Suvla and the salt lake beyond, the line of the ridge stretching north-eastwards to the summit of Koja Chemen. Rising to meet the sky, it looked from here like an unscalable slope.

The chief of staff remarked that only raiding parties could advance through such difficult country. Essad Pasha asked Kemal, 'Where will the enemy come from?' Kemal waved his hand in the direction of Ariburnu and the line of the coast as far as Suvla: 'From there.'

'Very well,' replied the Pasha, 'if he does come from there, then how will he advance?'

Kemal pointed again at Ariburnu and described a broad half circle towards Koja Chemen: 'That's how he will advance.'

The Pasha smiled and patted him on the shoulder. 'Don't worry, Bey Effendi. He can't do it.'

Kemal saw that it was useless to continue the discussion. *'Insh'allah,'* he exclaimed. 'Let's hope you are right.'

Kemal recorded the interview in his diary. In the light of what afterwards happened he underlined the passage in red ink, adding to the entry a justified comment on those who had disagreed with him, and whose inadequate measures had 'greatly endangered the military position and the fate of the country'. For the second time Kemal was right.

Meanwhile, he wrote in French to Corinne Lütfü, with whom he had been in correspondence since the start of the campaign:

Here the view is not so calm. Every day and night shrapnel and other shells burst incessantly above our heads. The shells whistle and the noise of the bombs mingles with that of the cannons. In effect, we are living an infernal life. Happily our soldiers are very brave and much more resistant than the enemy. Besides, their easy comradeship greatly facilitates the execution of my orders, which often demand death. As it happens, this leads only to two celestial results: to become a victorious Gazi or a Chehad. Do you know what this last means? To go straight away to Paradise, where the *houris*, God's most beautiful women, will come to receive them and remain permanently at their disposal. Supreme happiness!

He had a desire, he added, to read some novels to 'help soften the hard character which present events have developed in me, and to make me capable of responding to some of the good and agreeable things in life'. He asked Corinne to give a list of appropriate titles to a mutual friend in Constantinople, that he might procure him the books. They could provide some slight substitute for that charming and intelligent conversation of Corinne's, with which it was her habit to seduce all the world.

CHAPTER TWELVE

A TURKISH VICTORY

FOR THE SECOND TIME in the campaign Kemal was right, while his superiors were wrong. On 6th August the enemy launched his offensive on the very lines he had foretold to Essad. This time it was indeed the intention of the British to shift the main weight of their offensive from the Helles to the Ariburnu front. Secretly landing and effectively concealing 25,000 more men in the Anzac bridgehead, they planned a frontal assault on the Sari Bair range. One column would advance directly up the Sazlidere ravine to the west of Chunuk Bair; another, by a more northerly and circuitous route, up the valleys and over the foothills to Koja Chemen and the crests between. This dual advance was to be supported by a fresh landing at Suvla Bay, north of Anzac, of some 20,000 troops, mostly of Kitchener's 'New Army'. They in turn would advance to the northern ridge of Anafarta, linking up in an enveloping movement with the Anzacs to march to the Narrows, cut the peninsula in two, and thus isolate the bulk of the Turkish forces.

As the thunder of the preliminary barrage rolled forth over the slopes, Kemal awaited the development of the attack as he had foreseen it, in the centre. Not so, once again, Liman von Sanders, who expected it to come either on his extreme right or on his immediate left – against Bulair, where he thus ordered increased vigilance; or against the southern spurs of the Sari Bair range, where indeed in the evening the Anzacs carried out an effective diversion, drawing off the bulk of Essad Pasha's reserves. This cleared the field for the main attack, which was to take place – against even Kemal's expectations – by night. It was planned to capture the summits by dawn.

The attack began well, with a successful ruse rehearsed for some days beforehand – the naval bombardment of a line of Turkish trenches. Punctually at the same hour after dark the shells had begun to fall while searchlights raked the hillsides. As punctually the Turks had left the trenches to take cover elsewhere. But this time, as they did so, the enemy moved in, their way lit by the searchlights, and the first Turkish position was captured. Fighting followed up the Sazlidere ravine, from which the Turks, owing to the inadequate defences which Kemal had criticized, were obliged to withdraw. Thus most of their outposts were occupied by the covering forces, and the way lay open for the main assault on the crests. The outlook for the Anzacs seemed hopeful.

Though Kemal's own division was under continuous gunfire it was not at first involved in this fighting, for the main line of the enemy's two-pronged advance was over the heights to the north of the Sazlidere ravine which, together with the summits, came under the adjoining command. From his observation post on a spur which the British had named Battleship Hill he was in telephonic contact all night with this sector, and could hear continual infantry fire not only on his immediate right, beneath Chunuk Bair, but farther away to the north, from the Aghildere ravine. Sooner or later, perhaps towards dawn, he expected an attack on his own front. Thus he kept his units on the alert with a series of brief general orders. At 3.30 a.m. he signalled:

It is probable that the enemy will attack our front in the morning. The distance between us is very short. To be able to repel any sudden attacks, our troops must be wide awake and ready to use their weapons. I instruct officers to keep their men awake, and to maintain the highest degree of readiness at all times, as the delicacy of the tactical situation demands.

An hour later, after the first streak of dawn, the attack came. It had been planned to coincide with the occupation of Chunuk Bair and thus to secure the right flank of the assailants against enfilade by Kemal's division. One force was to sweep down on Battleship Hill from the crest, while the other was to move up on it from the foothills.

But, though the enemy's night advance had begun well, it soon ran into trouble. The darkness had defeated the Anzacs. One section of the first column, misled by its guides, got lost, finding itself back, after a series of fruitless ascents and descents, at its starting-point; the other section reached a shoulder of the ridge, but was unable to proceed further without it. The second column, in the Aghildere ravine to the north, had fared even worse. Similarly misled in the darkness its men, after a long confused series of marches, now lay scattered over the slopes in a state of exhaustion, well below Koja Chemen and their other objectives. The Allies had missed their opportunity of capturing the Sari Bair ridge before dawn, while it was still thinly defended and the weapon of surprise was on their side.

Nevertheless, though no converging support was now available from above, and though Kemal's defensive positions below were known to be among the strongest in the Turkish lines, the dawn attack on them went ahead. It ended in disaster, wave after wave of heroic but inexperienced Australians perishing at the hands of Kemal's men, awake and prepared as they were, in a suicidal and fruitless assault.

Meanwhile to the north the men of the new British army were landing on the beaches of Suvla Bay. Since the Turkish defences against them consisted of a mere three lightly armed battalions, under Major Willmer's command, they faced little effective resistance. But they seemed curiously reluctant to advance. Liman von Sanders, however, at last realized that here, in the centre, was the main attack. He summoned reinforcements to Suvla and Anzac from Bulair, from the Asiatic shore and from Helles, where the secondary British attack had collapsed. But for the next twenty-four hours, until they arrived, the situation of the Turks and of the Sari Bair ridge would be critical.

Kemal was fully alive to the danger. A successful enemy advance from the north-east, with so little opposition, could easily outflank his own division and might lead to a general withdrawal from the whole Ariburnu front. He kept a continuous and anxious eye on Chunuk Bair, over which he had no control. Early in the morning, when he had won his own battle, he sent his divisional reserve to picket the spur beneath it. Later Colonel Kannengiesser arrived from the south with two regiments to hold the summit. This he succeeded in doing at the cost of a serious wound in the chest, against a daylight attack from the Anzac right by troops physically weakened from three long months in the trenches.

Next day at dawn a fresh attack was launched, 'the ferocity of which', in Kemal's words, 'can hardly be described'. But the Anzacs, expecting casualties as heavy as those of the day before, were surprised to meet with no fire from the dreaded ridge above them. On storming it they found only a Turkish machine-gun crew, asleep on the crest, from which the infantry, for some unexplained reason, had gone. Thus Chunuk Bair was captured.

But their foothold was precarious. Immediately, as the sun rose, they were raked by a fierce fire from either flank – from Kemal's positions on Battleship Hill to their right, and from those on the adjoining crests of the ridge, where the assault had failed, to their left. The ground was too hard for them to dig in effectively. Most of the men on the summit were killed and only the remnants, heroically led, held on. But when darkness fell reinforcements arrived and they had a respite at least until morning.

Had they known it, the situation of the Turks was as precarious as theirs. For Kemal it had been a day of nervous anxiety and frustration. From an early hour he grasped that the Turkish defences, to the right of him, were in a state of confusion which bordered on chaos. News coming in to his head-quarters made it all too clear that no effective command existed. A typical message from an officer ran:

An attack has been ordered on Chunuk Bair. To whom should I pass this order? I am looking for the battalion commanders but cannot find them. Everything is in a muddle. The situation is serious. At least a commander should be appointed who knows the ground. We have no reports, no information. I am at a loss as to what I should do. . . .

All the units are mixed up. No officers are to be found. I am at a place where the previous regimental commander was hit. I have been given no information as to what is happening. All the officers are killed or wounded. I do not even know the name of the place where I am. I can see nothing from my observation post. I request in the name of the safety of the nation that an officer be appointed who knows the area well.

Another bewildered officer reported: 'At dawn some troops withdrew from Shahinsirt towards Chunuk Bair. They are digging in on Chunuk Bair. But it is not known whether the troops are the enemy's or ours.'

Kemal judged that they were the enemy's and sent his divisional adjutant and his ADC to reconnoitre and report. The ADC was killed. He sent the chief of the divisional staff, whose reports confirmed his own observations. A regimental commander named Nuri (later to become his ADC) got through on the field telephone from group headquarters. He said that he had been ordered by the group commander to advance on Chunuk Bair and to attack the enemy there. He had asked for information about the units in the area and about the command. But the commander, who was in a nervous state, and his chief of staff seemed reluctant or unable to give it to him. 'Please enlighten me about the situation,' he asked Kemal. 'There is no commander anywhere.'

Kemal ordered him to advance at once on Chunuk Bair, and added, 'Events will appoint a commander.'

In fact, two commanders of the division now holding the ridge had been killed one after the other, and the command had been given in quick succession to two more. Now the commander was a lieutenant-colonel with more experience of railway administration behind the lines than of action in the field, who had chanced to arrive from Constantinople, and who was in the invidious position of giving orders to staff officers of superior rank. His only idea of dealing with the crisis was to pour as many troops as possible into Chunuk Bair, regardless of plan. Kemal criticized these tactics to group headquarters and urged that something should be done. But he received only the reply that they were doing their best. He got the impression, over the telephone and from the orders he saw, that the staff had lost their heads and that officers were shifting responsibility on to others. This prompted, that evening, a solemn note in his diary: 'The weight of responsibility is heavier than death.'

The situation soon came to a head. The commander of the Anafarta

Group, as it had now been named, was Colonel Feyzi, who had arrived from Bulair with the reinforcing divisions called up by von Sanders. Kemal sent a message, begging him in the name of the country and its safety, to attract von Sanders' attention to the critical position on Chunuk Bair. Shortly afterwards the chief of staff called Kemal on the telephone, on Liman's behalf, to ask for his views. He gave them forcibly. The offensive was general. The enemy, as a result of the landings, was greatly superior. Urgent action was essential if the whole ridge were not to be lost. 'There is one moment left,' he said. 'If we lose that moment, we are faced with a general catastrophe.'

Asked what was the remedy, he replied, 'A unified command.' He went further: 'The only remedy is to put all the available troops under my command.'

The chief of staff asked ironically, 'Won't that be too many?'

'It will be too few,' Kemal replied.

Disaster threatened not merely the Sari Bair ridge but the Anafarta ridge to the north of it, on the Suvla front. Here Major Willmer's three battalions had been holding on for nearly forty-eight hours. Only British irresolution had saved them. Thanks to their corps commander, General Stopford, the British troops had spent the day bathing on the beaches instead of advancing to the hills. But this could not last. At any moment their attack might begin.

Feyzi had rashly promised von Sanders that his troops, marching from Bulair, would be ready to go into action against them at dawn that day, 8th August. But here too there was irresolution. By the afternoon they were still not ready, nor, Feyzi maintained, would they be in a fit state to attack until dawn the next day. Von Sanders angrily insisted that an evening attack was imperative. Feyzi replied that, in the opinion of his divisional commanders, this was impossible. Their men were tired and hungry, the ground was unfamiliar, the artillery was inadequate.

Liman asked him, 'You are the group commander. What do *you* say?' Feyzi replied, 'I am of the same opinion.'

Liman von Sanders promptly relieved Feyzi of his command. 'That evening,' he wrote, 'I gave command of all the troops in the Anafarta section to Colonel Mustafa Kemal Bey, commander of the 19th Division. . . . He was a leader that delighted in responsibility. . . . I had full confidence in his energy.' Kemal, in a mood of self-congratulation, moralized in his diary: 'What a fine mirror history is! Men, especially those races which are morally backward, cannot help expressing evil sentiments, even in the face of sacred causes. The actions and conduct of the participants in great historical events reveal their true moral characters.'

At last Kemal was in control of the whole front. Calmly he handed over his divisional command, first making dispositions for the renewed attack on

Chunuk Bair which would inevitably come in the morning. He issued a farewell message to the division encouraging the troops and commending their self-sacrifice. Then shortly before midnight he rode off northward over the hills to the Anafarta ridge, where the more immediate danger now lay. Anafarta had not yet seen fighting and Kemal wrote in his diary: 'For the first time in four months I was breathing air which was more or less pure and clear, because in the Ariburnu district and its neighbourhood the air we breathed was polluted by the corruption of human corpses.'

He took with him his divisional doctor, to look after him and to organize the hospital services on Anafarta where casualties were likely to be heavy. It was Kemal's third night without sleep and he was weak, not only from exhaustion but from a severe bout of malaria, which he could not shake off and for which he needed constant treatment. Haggard and drawn he had a preoccupied look in his sunken eyes. What worried him especially was the lack of information as to the strength of his own and the enemy's forces.

But beneath his outward tension there was an inward confidence. Responsibility acted on him like a tonic. No longer did he have to sit by and watch, in a growing frenzy of frustration, the errors and muddles of those whom he saw as his inferiors. He was free to act, and with his acute calculating grasp of the military position he knew, in the broad sense if not yet in detail, what action to take. He had no false optimism. He was taking over a battle already half lost by other commanders, at the expense of their lives or careers. He knew that he too might fail to save it. But with his will, his patriotism, his ambition and his belief in his own powers, he was wholly determined on victory. In a heroic vein suitable for public consumption he said afterwards, 'To assume such responsibility was no simple affair, but as I had decided not to survive the ruin of my country, I accepted the responsibility with all due pride.'

Kemal soon found signs of confusion. He came upon a divisional commander and his staff sitting idle, at this moment 'when the country was being stabbed', far away from the place where their troops were in action. He ordered them to move to the front. Reaching another headquarters he found it in darkness. There was neither a light to be seen or a sound to be heard. Everyone slept. Kemal and his party shouted. He described the scene in his diary: 'A man came out of his tent in a nightgown and answered our calls. I asked him what the place was. He said it was Major Willmer's headquarters. But he didn't seem to know much about it. I asked him to take me to his commander. But this man, who didn't know who he was, was unwilling. He merely pointed somewhere in the darkness with his hand. I forced him to take us there. He took us to the hut where Willmer was in bed. Willmer was asleep. I talked to Haydar Bey, an officer on his staff. I asked where the headquarters of the Anafarta Group was. He answered,

"Today it was here. But later" – he pointed toward the north – "it was removed somewhere in that direction." ' He mentioned the name of a place unknown to Kemal.

Anxious to lose no time he rode on in the darkness. At 1.30 a.m. he found group headquarters, where the chief of staff and his officers were awaiting him. He at once asked him where was the enemy and what was his strength? Where were his own two divisions and what was their situation? What were the last orders given to them by Group? But the chief of staff was vague in his answers. Where, Kemal then asked, was the ex-commander, Feyzi Bey? He was asleep in his tent. Kemal said that he must be awakened and confirm to him the last order he had given. The chief of staff showed him a note of an order, without signature.

'If Feyzi gave this order,' Kemal insisted, 'let him sign it.'

The chief of staff went back and forth between Feyzi and Kemal. But Feyzi refused to sign it. Kemal gave up, called a meeting of the staff officers, and asked them where were the divisions and what were their orders for the attack. They told him what they knew. One of them, a courier who had seen something of the front, was more explicit than the others. But the picture remained vague. Dawn was approaching and there was no time to probe further. Kemal issued an order, announcing that he had taken over the command, giving orders for a general attack along the whole line from one ridge to the other, and instructing his officers to inform him immediately of their positions and the measures they had taken. He sent copies of the order by the hand of two officers to the divisional commanders. He took measures for the organization of medical services and of food and other supplies, which he found to have been neglected. Then at 4.30 a.m. he rode with a few officers up to an observation post beyond the crest of Great Anafarta. From here he was to survey and direct the battle soon due to begin.

Its fate was to depend on a preliminary race, between Turks and British, for the crest of the Anafarta ridge, and especially for the summit of Tekke Tepe. Both sides had wasted two days – the Turks with more reason than the British – and were hastening to recover the lost time. While Liman von Sanders was ruthlessly changing his group commanders. Sir Ian Hamilton, less ruthless, was at least now himself on the spot before Suvla, insisting to his own reluctant divisional commanders on the occupation of Tekke Tepe by daybreak. Even a single battalion, forestalling the Turks on the crest, could provide invaluable support to the rest of the army when it advanced up to the ridge.

But it very soon got into difficulties. The commander took too long to assemble his men. They were dazed with fatigue and there was a further delay before they were ready to start. One company went ahead leaving word for the others to follow. Meanwhile the Turks were mounting the opposite slope. The going was hard through the scrub and the British company split up into scattered groups. Dawn broke and they met with a persistent fire from the Turks in front and on the flanks. Finally a handful of men reached the top of the ridge – only to be met by a detachment of Turks pouring over it from the opposite side. The Turks had won the race for Tekke Tepe by a mere half-hour.

Kemal's men swarmed down the hillside spreading slaughter and havoc among the enemy forces. Sir Ian Hamilton, watching through a telescope from the deck of his warship, described the scene:

> Very soon the shrapnel got on to those trenches of men on our left and there was something like a stampede from North to South. Looking closer we could see the enemy advancing behind their own bursting shrapnel and rolling up our line from the left on to the centre. . . . Our centre made a convulsive effort (so it seemed) to throw back the steadily advancing Turks. . . . Then about 6 a.m. the whole lot seemed suddenly to collapse: including the right! Not only did they give ground but they came back – some of them – halfway to the sea.

Over all the hillside the picture was similar. The men of Kitchener's Army broke with the cry: 'The Turks are on us!' The Turkish fire was so intense that the scrub caught alight sending them scurrying helter-skelter for safety. By midday Kemal was satisfied that the Suvla battle was won. He ordered his men to dig in. With a single incomplete division he had routed a far stronger enemy. Later he attributed his victory to the element of surprise. The enemy, advancing in small groups, had expected only slight skirmishes. But in the aggregate his skirmishers, well co-ordinated by their leaders and superior in marksmanship, had by the momentum of their downhill charge broken the enemy's morale. He expressed surprise at the hesitancy of Hamilton, unable, though present in person, to ensure the carrying out of his orders. Among Hamilton's commanders he discerned an incapacity to make decisions at the right moment, 'that fear of responsibility which leads to defeat'. General Stopford, he sardonically observed, seemed out of politeness to have been postponing the start of the battle until he himself should arrive.

Anafarta was thus secure. The Suvla offensive had failed. But the enemy had yet to be dislodged from the Sari Bair range. Here the situation on Chunuk Bair was more acute than ever. During the night a further attack had helped the Anzacs, despite only partial success, to consolidate their hold on the crest. Kemal, for whom Chunuk Bair was still the pivot of the whole campaign, at once halted the advance across the Suvla plain and ordered his two most trustworthy regiments up to the ridge for a counter-attack. They had been in action half the night and required some rest. Thus he instructed his two acting divisional commanders, 'Tonight I am going to demand great sacrifices from the troops on Chunuk Bair.

Meanwhile I ask you to find means of providing hot soup for the two infantry regiments which are proceeding to the area.'

Then he went to confer on the plan of attack with Liman von Sanders. Liman favoured a flank assault on the enemy's left, in the Aghildere region below Koja Chemen; Kemal preferred a frontal assault on Chunuk Bair itself, the immediate source of danger. If this was recaptured the enemy in Aghildere would ultimately have to retreat. Liman gave him a free hand, saying, 'You have accepted the responsibility for this action. I don't want to influence you in your plans. I only wanted to tell you, purely as an observation, what came into my mind.'

Kemal planned to direct the battle from the front line in person. In the evening he rode with his staff along the crest of the ridge towards Chunuk Bair. An enemy aircraft swooped low over their heads; his officers dispersed but he continued, with one of them, to ride down the middle of the track, and the aircraft, though it followed them, did not attack. On arrival at divisional headquarters, behind the summit, he rode through the trenches talking to officers of the various units.

He instructed them to call their men together and encourage them to fight with renewed spirit. Their morale had been shaken by the breakdown of the command. To this they attributed all their troubles. The Turkish soldier, lacking initiative, primitive in training and education, is lost without leadership and it was now his task to restore it. He ordered the Eighth Division to prepare for an attack at dawn,. reinforced by the two regiments which were on their way. But a little later the divisional commander came to see him with a staff officer, named Galib, who asked permission to put forward the views of a group of his officers. For two days they had been attacking Chunuk Bair. They had suffered heavy losses and had achieved no success. They were in a state of deep discouragement and did not believe that a new attack could succeed, even with the support of two extra regiments, of which one had in any case not yet arrived. Without it an attack might end in disaster.

Kemal knew and respected this officer. He had seen his bravery under fire. Though he was at first annoyed at the insubordinate method of his approach, he had to admit to himself that his attitude was logical enough. But, as he recorded in his diary, 'certain convictions are hard to explain in terms of logic and reason. Such are the convictions which arise from what we feel in the blood and the fiery moments of battle. What Galib had said described the situation very well. But his opinion could not make me change my mind. I had come to the conclusion that we could defeat the enemy by means of a sudden, surprise assault. To achieve this we needed more than numbers, we needed a cool and courageous command.'

He thus told the divisional commander that his decision was irrevocable and would be carried out whether the second regiment arrived or not.

He spent the night at divisional headquarters, in personal control. It was his fourth night without sleep and he was feverish and in acute physical discomfort from the malaria. But rest was impossible. Besides preparing for the attack he had to direct the Anafarta front, from which information was scanty and unreliable; and he had to sort out the tangle among his forces on the spot, continually disturbed in his tent by officers seeking lost units or commanders.

As dawn approached Kemal stood in front of the tent and looked around to make sure that all was ready. In his observation trenches, which were a mere twenty yards from the enemy, he had placed one of his fighting regiments. Into another line thirty yards behind it, as quietly as possible and under cover of darkness, he had moved two more. If the last regiment arrived in time it would be thrown into the battle as the situation demanded. The initial attack was to be totally silent. Strict orders were given that there was to be neither artillery nor rifle fire. No weapon but the bayonet must be used. Both lines would move swiftly forward on the enemy in the dark, without making a sound. The fate of the battle would depend on the surprise of those first few minutes. The next phase of it would be decided by events.

Kemal looked at his watch and saw that it was almost 4.30. In a few minutes it would be light and his men, massed close together, would be visible to the enemy. If he saw them and fired the attack would fail. Kemal ran forward. His divisional commander joined him. Together with other officers they stood before the troops. Kemal passed down the line and in a low voice instructed them, 'Soldiers, there is no doubt at all that we are going to defeat the enemy in front of you. But do not hurry. Let me go ahead first. As soon as you see me raise my whip then you will all leap forward.' He told the other officers to give their men the same signal. Then he took a few steps forward and raised his whip. Instantly the soldiers, with fixed bayonets, and the officers, with drawn swords, leapt into the darkness, as he afterwards put it, 'like lions. A moment later, the only sound which came from the enemy trenches was the heavenly cry of, "Allah! Allah!" '

The British soldiers had no time even to raise their rifles. They were overwhelmed in their trenches by sheer weight of numbers, while those in the open were swiftly annihilated. Hamilton's front line was broken. 'The ponderous mass of the enemy,' as he described it, swept over the crest and down the slopes, turning his right flank and piercing his lines below, so that his troops were driven 'clean down the hill'. It was a series of struggles 'in which generals fought in the ranks, and men dropped their scientific weapons and caught one another by the throat. . . . The Turks came on again and again, fighting magnificently, calling upon the name of God. Our men stood to it and maintained, by many a deed of daring, the old traditions of their race. There was no flinching. They died in the ranks as they stood.'

But with their artillery they gave the Turks back as good as they got.

From daylight onwards they poured shells on to Chunuk Bair, turning it, as Kemal wrote, 'into a kind of hell. From the sky came a downpour of shrapnel and iron. The heavy naval shells sank into the ground, then burst, opening huge cavities all about us. The whole of Chunuk Bair was enveloped in thick smoke and fire. Everyone waited resignedly for what fate would bring.' Few of the heroes of that first charge survived. The dead lay all over the hillside, fingers still gripping their rifles as though awaiting the order to charge. Asked by Kemal where his troops were, a commander replied, 'Here are my troops. Those who lie dead.'

Kemal stood recklessly in the line of fire giving orders and encouraging his men. At one moment a piece of shrapnel struck him in the breast. In consternation an ADC exclaimed, 'Sir, you have been hit.' Kemal put his hand over the officer's mouth, lest others hear, and said, 'Nothing of the sort.' The shrapnel had hit his breastpocket, shattering the watch inside it and leaving only a superficial flesh wound. Later he took out the watch, which he had used since his days at the Military School, and philosophized, 'Here is a watch that is worth a life.' When the battle was over, at Liman von Sanders' request, he gave it to him as a souvenir, receiving in return a handsome chronometer engraved with the von Sanders family arms.[1]

The artillery bombardment, devastating as it was to the Turks, could not save the Sari Bair ridge for the Anzacs. By 10 a.m., though scattered units fought doggedly on until the evening, the bulk of their force had been driven off it into the foothills and back to the beach-head below. On the right superior enemy forces, stranded with their flank in the air by the central attacks, had been forced to withdraw, thus justifying Kemal's argument with Liman for a frontal in preference to an outflanking attack. Sir Ian Hamilton was still sanguine enough to write: 'Well, we had Chunuk Bair in our hands the best part of two days and two nights. So far the Turks have never retaken trenches once we had fairly taken hold. Have they done so now? I hope not. . . . The Turks were well commanded: that I admit. Their Generals knew they were done unless they could quickly knock us off our Chunuk Bair. So they have done it. Never mind; never say die.'

None the less there was only one more slender hope. Chunuk Bair was lost beyond recovery. But there was still a chance of retrieving the situation at Suvla. Another attempt to capture Tekke Tepe failed. But the Turks were in a weak position at Kirech Tepe, at the north of the Anafarta line, and Liman von Sanders was seriously afraid that an attack here, before he could consolidate, might turn his right flank and envelop his army. Thus for the next ten days there was no disposition among the Turks to regard victory as certain. Kemal, strung up as he himself was, continued to keep up the pressure on his overtaxed troops, leading them still from the front

---

[1] Later when the Turkish authorities tried to recover the watch from Germany to place in a museum, they were informed that it had been stolen.

line in person. Supremely confident now that he could never be hit he led a charmed life under enemy fire such as invested him, in the eyes of his men, with the magic quality of a hero of legend. This leader of theirs had skill. He had courage. But above all he had luck.

It was told of him how once in the battle an enemy field battery opened fire on a trench where he was sitting. They had the range exactly, dropping one shell in front of the trench, then two more, each twenty yards nearer. It became mathematically certain that the fourth shell would fall just where he sat, on the edge of the trench. Urged by an officer to take cover, he replied, 'It's too late now. I can't set my men a bad example.' He continued to smoke, but his face grew perceptibly paler. The men in the trench looked paralysed with fear, as they waited for the next shell to fall. But nothing happened. Only three shells were fired, not four.

Now, in the battle of Kirech Tepe, he rode to the rear for reinforcements, which could only be brought up along the shore, between the ridge and the sea, under fire from the enemy's fleet. Here the column of troops had stopped. He was told, 'The enemy spreads death. Not even a bird can pass.' Kemal swiftly retorted, 'You can pass this way.' He ran forward himself, with his chief of staff and ADC, ordering the others to follow. They did so, running after him in single file and, despite many casualties, retrieved the position.

His own evident readiness to die made others ready to die at his orders. This also became part of his legend. During a battle a few days later for two spurs of the Anafarta ridge it became necessary to gain time for the infantry reserves to move up. Remembering the report of a *'chevaleresque'* charge which the French had made on the Asiatic shore, riding to almost certain death to cover the advance of their infantry, Kemal decided in a ruthless spirit to repeat the operation, and ordered his cavalry commander to charge. He assented, then hesitated. Kemal called him back: 'Did you understand what I said?'

'Yes, sir. . . . You ordered us to die.'

Many of them died, but their charge delayed the enemy advance and thus helped to save the vital hilltop.

But these last fierce battles of Anafarta were in fact the ebbtide of the Gallipoli campaign. Already, a week after the loss of Chunuk Bair, Sir Ian Hamilton had cabled to Kitchener announcing its failure. Not only were the Turks now superior in numbers and in reserves but they had gained for the moment a moral ascendancy over some of his new troops. As surprise would now be absent he would need close on another 100,000 men to resume the offensive. 'We are up against the main Turkish army,' he concluded, 'which is fighting bravely and is well commanded.'

The weapon of surprise had indeed twice failed the British, offset as it was by an exacting terrain, faulty planning and indecisive leadership. Instead the Turks, whom they at first underrated, had turned the weapon against them. The first surprise was the emergence, at the crucial time and place, of a Turkish commander equal if not superior in military skill to their own. The second surprise was the Turkish soldier himself. Besides a sure grasp of tactical essentials Kemal had shown a shrewd understanding of his men. He knew the psychology of the Turk, and the dogged fanatical fighting spirit of which he was capable, once he had faith in his leaders and his blood was roused; and he knew how to rouse it. Thus between them Kemal and the Turkish soldier saved the Gallipoli Peninsula. 'Seldom in history,' wrote the British official historian, 'can the exertions of a single divisional commander have exercised, on three separate occasions, so profound an influence not only on the course of a battle but, perhaps, on the fate of a campaign and even the destiny of a nation.'

Kemal afterwards declared that the battles for Chunuk Bair and Anafarta ranked among the closest in history. Nor was there any false sentiment in a remark which he made years later, on revisiting the battlefields. Asked by a companion why no great monument marked them, he replied, 'The greatest monument is Mehmedjik himself.[1] It is thanks to him that these lands have remained within the Turkish frontiers.'

Kemal could now rest and try to recover his health. He made himself tolerably comfortable, as he had the gift of doing even in battle, moving from his tent into a hut like a snug log-cabin. Members of a delegation from Constantinople were impressed by its neatness, by its atmosphere of a place built 'not for fighting but for watching the sea in peace', by the four-course meal which he served to them.

A German friend[2] found him still weak with malaria and was shocked by his ravaged appearance. But his mind was as active as ever and he plunged into a strategical discourse. He had no illusions as to the permanence of his victory. He knew, as he had known from the start, the vital importance of sea power. 'We are landlocked,' he said, 'just like the Russians. They are bound to collapse because I have locked them into the Black Sea by blockading the Dardanelles and the Bosporus. I have thus cut them off from their Allies. But we too are bound to break down, and for the very same reason. True, we sit on the fringes of the Mediterranean, the Red Sea, the Indian Ocean, but we are unable to venture out on any ocean. As a land power without sea power, we will never be able to defend our peninsula against sea powers which can bring up their land forces unchallenged.'

The months went by and the campaign grew static, relapsing into trench warfare. Kemal became convinced that the enemy was preparing to evacuate the peninsula. This was the moment, he argued, for one last Turkish attack, to destroy him before he could do so. But he could not convince his superiors. Permission for the attack was refused on the grounds that, 'We have no

[1] The Turkish 'Tommy Atkins'.
[2] Ernest Jäckh, op. cit.

forces, not even a single soldier, to waste.' He then asked to be relieved of his command in the peninsula, and von Sanders agreed to post him elsewhere. His health was in any case worse and he was in no fit state to remain. Nor was there anything left for him to do.

His friend of the Salonika days, Tevfik Rüştü, arrived on a visit to his headquarters in his capacity as a doctor. On impulse Kemal said to him, 'I'll come back with you now to Constantinople.' He had accumulated arrears of back pay and they would spend it together. Thus he left the Gallipoli Peninsula.

Ten days after his arrival in the capital he heard the news that the Allied forces had withdrawn from the peninsula, without detection or loss. Up to the end he had been right.

CHAPTER THIRTEEN

THE EASTERN FRONTS

THE BRITISH FAILURE at the Dardanelles gave a momentary psychological lift to the Turkish people. For the first time within living memory they had won a victory against a European power. Few Turks perhaps nourished the illusion that the tide of foreign pressure had been turned, that the Empire could look forward to a period of resurrection and recovery. But at least there had been a flicker of light and hope to illuminate the dark defeatist horizon. There was life in the old Turk yet. The national qualities of tenacity and courage and pride had vindicated themselves once again, as in the glorious past, here on the ridges of the Gallipoli Peninsula.

The Turks are a race who seek heroes; and a new hero had arisen to save them. No triumphal welcome, it is true, awaited Mustafa Kemal on his return to Constantinople. The exploits of this hitherto unknown young colonel were played down in the press. His name was barely mentioned. Hardly a photograph of him appeared. An interview which he gave on the campaign was suppressed by Enver.

But through that word of mouth that creates myths his name and his deeds became known to the people. The legend spread of this young Turkish warrior who knew no fear, whose life was so charmed that no bullet could kill him, who could advance immune to all hurt through a hail of fire, the naval shells of the British sailing over his head like birds. To the élite of the young generation in particular, disillusioned now by their Young Turk rulers, he was a symbol to be quietly cherished. Could this Mustafa Kemal be the national hero they craved?

Admittedly Enver, who appreciated Kemal's qualities as a soldier, had been known to refer to him as his only possible successor. But he saw no reason to precipitate the succession. He knew very well that high military rank and the title of Pasha that went with it meant prestige and authority, not only in the army itself but outside it; and Kemal knew it too. He had been promoted to full colonel in the peninsula, and a colonel, so Enver determined, he should for the present remain.

Thus Kemal, back in Constantinople, was frustrated and restless. To recover his health he lodged with his mother and sister in the house which he had found for them on their evacuation from Salonika, at Beshiktash, on the Bosporus. But he chafed at the atmosphere of feminine fuss that pervaded it. This was mitigated a little by the maturing charms of Zübeyde's adopted niece, Fikriye. The time had come all the same for him to live by himself. Meanwhile, for relaxation in a maturer and more worldly atmosphere, he sought again the company of Corinne Lütfü, with whom he had corresponded throughout the Gallipoli campaign and who encouraged him by her belief in his star.

At a musical party one evening, while she was at the piano, he had to take his leave and tiptoed silently out of the room. Corinne, who had noticed his departure, stopped short in the middle of the piece she was playing. A Turkish poet, who was one of the guests, went up to her anxiously, thinking she was ill. But she turned to the company, saying, 'Do you know who that officer is who has retired on tiptoe? He is Mustafa Kemal, someone who will become a great man and will be renowned, not merely in Turkey, but in the whole world.'

Few of those with whom Kemal had to deal seemed to think so. He had become a nuisance again, with his outspoken opinions and his blunt disconcerting ways. Seething inwardly he sought out his friends and acquaintances, hammering his convictions into the heads of any who had the patience to listen to him. The successful defence of Gallipoli had in no way blinded him to the fatal course of the war in Turkey, and its increasing misdirection by the German military mission. He wrote detailed reports to the Grand Vizier, backing up his contentions with documents. Troops and supplies were being wasted. Wrong decisions were being made. He poured out his criticisms to his friend Rauf, in the Ministry of Marine. All was the fault of Enver, who was a toy in the hands of the Germans.

The Germans, for the sake of their own interests in the west, were dragging Turkey to ruin in a war they could not win – all with Enver's acquiescence and approval. Some of the best Turkish troops, armed with equipment much needed at home, were indeed about to be sent to fight the German battles in Eastern Europe. Such units as remained, apart from mere paper organizations, consisted very largely of raw recruits, conscripted as young as sixteen, whom the officers spent most of their time in training, at the expense of all other military exercises. Arms were short; one unit, eight thousand strong, had a mere thousand rifles. Yet German officers were deceiving their own High Command into thinking that Turkey's resources were inexhaustible, and that its military situation had never been better.

To give the Government the benefit of his views and forebodings Kemal secured an appointment with the Minister of Foreign Affairs. The minister spoke with rosy optimism of the general position. Kemal disagreed with him and, speaking as one who had seen the war at close quarters, expressed his misgivings. The minister, growing irritable, suggested that he enlighten himself as to the true situation from the General Staff. Kemal, growing arrogant, retorted that, as one who had devoted his life to the military career, he knew the Turkish army and its value better than most – and certainly, he implied, better than the minister himself. He added that the only General Staff that existed was that of the German military mission, who had tried to have him expelled from the army as a rebel.

To escape from the atmosphere of Constantinople he went for a while to Sofia, where he relaxed in the company of his old friends. He left instructions with his ADC to accept, on his behalf, any reasonable posting that was offered him, and he presently received news of an appointment which was to amount once more to an exile. It was to the command of the Sixteenth Army Corps, then resting at Adrianople on withdrawal from Gallipoli but destined for transfer further afield. He rode into Adrianople at the head of an infantry division which had just arrived from the Gallipoli front, and his newly gained reputation won him cheers from the crowd. Still with the idea in his mind of hastening Bulgaria's entry into the war – for King Ferdinand was shrinking from the inevitable plunge – he took the opportunity to invite a party of Bulgarian Turkish deputies to Adrianople for a tour of inspection. He remained there for a bare six weeks. The Second Army, with his Sixteenth Army Corps, was then sent to the Russian front to help retrieve some of the débris of Enver's disastrous initial campaign. It was to reinforce the Third Army, which had been driven back in the subsequent Russian offensive, and to join with it in a counter-offensive in the summer of 1916.

Though this was a responsible command Kemal had still not received his promotion from colonel to general. This was partly due to the influence of Dr Nazim, an early evangelist of the Committee of Union and Progress, who had always mistrusted Kemal's ambitions and after the Gallipoli campaign had seen fit to warn him not to 'play the Napoleon'. 'A man like that,' Kemal exclaimed to Shakir Zümre – as he had previously exclaimed of Javid – 'deserves to be hanged.'[1] Nazim advised Enver to promote Kemal only after his safe but reluctant departure for the Caucasus. He had been there some weeks before his promotion to general, and thus at last Pasha, came through.

Soon after reaching his headquarters at Silvan, near Diyarbekir, he wrote to Corinne:

After travelling for two months over a long and tiring road which stretches

[1] Nazim, like Javid, was hanged following the Ankara treason trials in 1926.

from the West to the East, one is entitled to hope for a moment of rest, don't you think? But alas! It seems that that will only come after death. All the same, to achieve this imaginary rest, I shan't agree too easily to go to your *Bon Dieu's* Paradise.

To show her, no doubt, that he was keeping up with his reading, he quoted a passage from a work of French military history, and ended with an aphorism from Chateaubriand: 'I should like not to be born rather than be for ever forgotten.'

On arrival Kemal found chaotic conditions. The troops on the spot were the mere remnants of an army, exhausted and demoralized, rotting with disease, exploited by unscrupulous officers in league with corrupt contractors and reduced to bedrock in arms and ammunition. He telegraphed Constantinople for arms, reinforcements, medical supplies, but was hardly surprised when he received no answer. He must use his own efforts to turn the army corps into some sort of fighting shape. He was fortunate to have the assistance of a steady industrious second-in-command, Kiazim Karabekir, who had been one of his supporters in his attempt, at Salonika, to separate the army from politics.

Earlier in the year the Russians, taking tardy advantage of Enver's débâcle, had advanced into Anatolia to capture the important fortress of Erzurum, then to occupy Trebizond, the principal Turkish Black Sea port. The Turks planned their counter-offensive for the recapture of Erzurum in July. But the Second Army was not yet ready, nor had it yet established proper liaison with the Third Army. Thus the Russians forestalled them by attacking once more in force along the whole of the front, and they were obliged, after violent fighting, to withdraw still further.

Kemal, fighting with his army corps on the right flank of the Second Army, was in the thick of the battle. At one moment he and his men were involved in a hand-to-hand fight with a large force of Russian infantry amid a 'forest of bayonets' which almost surrounded them. Only by a cool head and a ruthless use of his own bayonet did he extricate himself from the fray and thus from probable capture or death. Then, on his own responsibility, he ordered a general retreat, gambling on the belief that the Russians would not follow it up. They did not and, since he was acting without orders, may thus have saved him his military career.

In the course of the retreat a Turkish soldier grumbled to him, 'What cowardly commanders are these? I was killing Russians all the way. Why do they drag us back?'

Kemal replied, 'Very good. But the battle will not be decided just by your killing Russians. This is a big army and there may be reasons for the retreat that you don't understand.'

'And who may you be?'

'I am your commanding officer.'

The soldier looked surprised and conceded, 'Oh well, that's different.' He believed that his officers had run away first, as they all too often did.

The Turks regrouped their forces. Kemal's army commander was Izzet Pasha, to whom he acted as second-in-command. A general of the old school but of liberal political ideas, Izzet had found himself in opposition successively to Abdul Hamid and (after a spell as their Minister of War) to the Committee of Union and Progress. Like Kemal he had overtly protested against Turkey's entry into the war, and from 1914 onwards had prophesied a German defeat on the grounds that the Kaiser had not the stuff in him to rule a country and command an army at the same time. He was a man of amiable countenance, bulky proportions and an irresolute disposition.

Early in August the Second Army began its counter-offensive. Kemal had so strengthened the morale of his force, following its defeat, that within five days his two divisions captured not only Bitlis but the equally important town of Mush, greatly disturbing the calculations of the Russian Command Izzet, with the rest of the Second Army, failed to match these successes on other parts of the front and the offensive petered out. Mustafa Kemal, however, could claim the only Turkish victory in a round of defeats. He was rewarded for his efforts with the medal of the Golden Sword. To Corinne Lütfü he wrote, from Diyarbekir: 'What a pleasure it is to face fire and death among those one esteems.' The letter ended, as was becoming his custom, with a French quotation. With time now on his hands he kept up his reading. 'Continuing,' he recorded in his diary, 'to read the book, *Est-il possible de renier le Dieu?*'

The troops settled down to a winter which was to be hard and bitter. Izzet's force, at the mercy of long and badly planned lines of communication, was deficient not merely in guns but in foodstuffs. Nor could an army any longer subsist here on the country, for the ironical reason that in the earlier stages of the campaign the Armenians had been massacred or deported *en masse*, leaving the land a virtual desert, without peasants to grow food or artisans to provide service. One division was reduced to a third of a ration per man and there was almost no fodder for the draft animals. Many of the troops had only their summer uniforms, with foot-rags for boots and, following blizzards, whole detachments were found in caves, dead from hunger and cold.

It was to the command of this decimated army that Kemal was promoted in the course of the winter, in succession to Izzet, who was now put in over-all command of both the Second and Third Armies. As it happened they did not have to fight a spring campaign. For in March 1917 a political event of world importance supervened – the Russian Revolution. The Caucasian front remained more or less static while the Russian armies fell slowly to pieces and finally withdrew towards Tiflis, disorganized by soldiers' committees which gave orders to the staff and deprived officers of their badges of rank.

Meanwhile this, Kemal's first army command, was notable chiefly for the fact that it brought him for the first time into intimate contact with one who was to become the closest of all his associates. He was Colonel Ismet, his chief of staff who, like Kiazim Karabekir, had backed him in his dispute with the party in Salonika. Ismet was a small silent man, slightly deaf, with a twinkle in his mild eyes, a sound slow brain and a conscientious disposition. The education and subsequent careers of the two officers had followed roughly parallel lines. While Kemal was fighting the Italians in Tripoli Ismet was dealing with an Arab revolt in the Yemen, deploring, as Kemal did, the pan-Islamic policy which tied down troops in these remote Arab regions at a time when the Balkans were threatened. Fretting here, he was able to console himself only with games of chess with Izzet Pasha, his commanding officer, and of bridge, a game which the Pasha had introduced into the officers' mess.[1] Now, on Izzet's staff once again, he had followed Kemal to the Caucasian front, stopping for two days on the way to marry, on his father's insistence, a neighbour's daughter whom he had not before seen and whom indeed he was barely to see after the ceremony was over. Thanks to the demands of the soldier's career it was not for another six years that he was able seriously to embark on a long, happy and respectable marital life.

Ismet was a man with a scholarly mind, better read than Kemal. The two shared the same radical ideas and found many opinions in common. Both saw clearly the fatal course of the war – the trench warfare in the west which was wearing the Germans down; the need, if Turkey were to be saved, for an early peace; the disastrous policy of sending Turkish troops to Europe; the deplorable state of the Turkish armies in Asia. Ismet, as a practical modern officer, was especially concerned with those problems of supply which had bedevilled the Second Army. As a 'man of the future', he realized the vital importance of railways. The Russians were ahead of the Turks in this respect. On capturing Erzurum they had immediately built a narrow gauge line to the city and beyond, linking it up with their internal supply lines. The Turks on the other hand were hamstrung, in terms of supply, by the absence of any railway line east of the Taurus.

Though Kemal and Ismet had similar views and aims, they were so opposite in temperament as to complement one another. The mind of Kemal moved swiftly and flexibly, with a grasp of broad issues, unorthodox reactions, and a capacity for making bold judgements; Ismet's mind worked within a narrower, more literal compass, slowly and deliberately, with a

---

[1] What gave him more solace was a pile of gramophone records, left behind by some British officers. These bred in him a lifelong devotion to classical music.

laborious attention to detail. Kemal was adventurous in spirit, independent in character, decisive in action; Ismet was cautious, dependent on the views of another, lacking in initiative and hesitant in making decisions. Kemal had an intuitive understanding of human behaviour and character; Ismet was an unsure judge of people, whom he treated with reserve and a certain suspicion. Where Kemal was restless, quick-tempered, temperamental, hard-drinking and promiscuous with women, Ismet was calm, stolid, patient, sober and a model family man. He was the antithesis of Kemal, hence just the assistant he needed. Ismet was in fact the born chief of staff, painstaking and loyal, to whom he could dictate his plans, confident that he would interpret them correctly and carry them out with efficiency. He became Kemal's indispensable 'shadow'.

In the army commander's mess, in this wild remote outpost of the Empire, Kemal insisted on keeping up civilized appearances. Officers had fallen into the habit of wandering into meals at all hours, loosening their tunics and keeping their kalpaks on their heads as they ate. Kemal put a stop to such unceremonious habits. Always fastidious in matters of uniform he ordered that officers should be properly dressed and observe correct behaviour. They should eat bare-headed, as European officers did. The mess, especially at times when there was a lull in the fighting, was to maintain a certain style, like the messes of Western armies. And so it did, with Kemal himself sitting at the head of the table, drinking and holding forth and drawing his officers into provocative discussions at which he liked to shine. Once, when a new wireless operator arrived at headquarters, Kemal asked him what was happening in Constantinople.

'Sad scenes, sir,' he reported. 'The old traditions are being forgotten. Everywhere our women are starting to discard the veil.'

Such scenes, Kemal decided defiantly, should be repeated here in the east. He at once organized a dance in the Officers' Club at which a few surviving Armenian ladies were provided as partners for the Turkish officers.

But Kemal, during this lull in the fighting, had other matters to preoccupy him besides reading and dancing. Back in Constantinople Yakub Jemil, who had been briefed as a *komitaji* to kill him in Salonika six years earlier, but who had since become one of his staunchest disciples, was arrested for plotting to overthrow the Government and to assassinate its leaders. The war, he argued, was lost; the country had reached the end of its resources. A new Government should be installed and Kemal should be appointed Minister of War and Deputy Commander-in-Chief in Enver's place, to negotiate a separate peace – a course of action of which he knew that Kemal was in favour.

In the course of his trial there were hints of Kemal's complicity. It was recounted that he had sent a circular telegram from Diyarbekir to other army commanders, criticizing the management of the war and the indecision of the Government, and proposing a meeting to discuss what steps should be taken. This was reported to Enver by a general, who was one of his enemies, and Kemal's cipher correspondence was thereafter tapped. Yakub Jemil was sentenced and executed while his confederates were imprisoned. To Rauf Kemal later denied the story of the telegram, attributing it to a personal grudge on the part of an enemy. As for the plot, he admitted that if it had succeeded and he had been invited to take Enver's place he might indeed have accepted. But his first action would have been to hang this Yakub Jemil.

Meanwhile neither he nor Ismet were to remain for much longer on the crumbling Russian front. There were more urgent tasks to be tackled elsewhere, notably on the Syrian front, to the south of it. Ismet was the first to be transferred to Syria, in command of an army corps. Kemal soon joined him, first still as commander of the Second Army then as commander of the important Seventh Army, now forming in Aleppo.

The British forces were pressing, both in Syria and in Mesopotamia. In March 1917, to release troops for these fronts, Enver was persuaded by the Germans to evacuate the army corps which garrisoned Medina, in the Hejaz, now a beleaguered enclave at the end of a long, highly vulnerable railway. The holy city of Mecca had already been lost to the Arabs, through the revolt of its chief, the Emir Feisal; and now the British, through Colonel T. E. Lawrence and other officers, were giving him effective support.

Enver picked on Mustafa Kemal as commander of an expedition to carry out the evacuation. It was a task which, the holy status of Medina being second only to that of Mecca, could hardly fail to bring national odium on any officer who succeeded in carrying it out. As an operation moreover it involved a grave military risk and, in face of Arab pressure, might well have led to the destruction or capture of the whole Turkish force. Kemal firmly refused the assignment; and, indeed, Fahri, the devout commander of its garrison, refused as firmly to abandon the city. Thus the plan, through which Kemal might well have ended his career at the hands of Lawrence, was dropped. Medina remained in possession of the Turks, 'sitting in trenches', as Lawrence put it, 'destroying their own power of movement by eating the transport they could no longer feed'.[1]

Now, however, Medina was thrown into the shade by a major disaster – the loss of Baghdad to the British and Indian forces. It caused widespread

[1] *Seven Pillars of Wisdom.*
Fahri continued obstinately to defend the grave of the Prophet until some time after the Armistice. Finally, in response to repeated orders from Constantinople, and to a meeting of his own staff officers, he reluctantly surrendered the city, offering his sword to the Supreme Master at the foot of the Holy of Holies and afterwards fainting away. He thus won the acclaim of all good Turkish Moslems, save those who resented the fact that he had cut down the palm trees shading the sacred tomb.

dismay throughout the Empire, and started for the first time some popular clamour against Enver. He made immediate plans to retrieve the position. The remedy was to be another of his grandiose strategical schemes, this time under the virtual command of the Germans. An army group was formed for offensive purposes, with the dramatic designation of Yildirim, otherwise 'Lightning'.[1] Its objective was to be nothing less than a spectacular march across the desert and the recapture of Baghdad from the British. And beyond Baghdad lay Persia and India, tempting attractions to von Ludendorff, who was becoming convinced that only big acquisitions of territory in the East could now save the German Empire.

There was to be an end to all pretence that the Germans were merely instructing and advising the Turkish army. This was a German army group, with a German staff and a German commander. He was Marshal von Falkenhayn, who had been replaced by von Hindenburg as Chief of the German General Staff, following his failure to reduce Verdun in the previous year, and who now sought to redeem his reputation in a glorious eastern campaign. The nucleus of Yildirim was to be the Turkish Seventh Army, and of this Mustafa Kemal, of all people, had been placed in command. When his ADC brought him the relevant telegram he was asleep in bed. He sat up, read the message, and in reply to the enquiry of the ADC, said, 'Yes. Of course I shall accept. But not for the reasons you think.' He made a rude gesture. 'I shall accept only to prevent this German commander from making a bloody offensive against Baghdad.'

Kemal knew that the recapture of Baghdad was impossible, for the same reasons that its capture had been inevitable – bad desert communications, gaps in the railway line and lack of fuel for the trains, the absence of barges on the Euphrates.[2] Von Falkenhayn knew nothing of the country, its conditions, its climate, its people. Nor did he consult those of his countrymen who knew it – the German officers of the military mission. He was stubborn, overbearing, tactless in his dealings with others, and had soon antagonized all around him, with the exception of Enver himself.

The Marshal had an idea that all Turks could be bought and injudiciously tried to bribe Kemal. Through one of his officers he offered him a present of several 'elegant little boxes', which proved to contain gold. Kemal, enjoying the comedy of the proceedings, chose to assume that the gold was intended for the expenses of his army and suggested that it be sent to the Paymaster's department. The German officer explained in some embarrassment that this was not the intention. Kemal then asked him to count the money and gave him a receipt for it, which the officer took with reluctance. Kemal lodged it with the Paymaster in return for another receipt.

---

[1] It was a name which had been applied by the Turks to Napoleon's campaign in Egypt.
[2] The trains were being fired on cotton-seed, liquorice, olive branches, vines and even camel dung.

From the outset Kemal criticized von Falkenhayn freely. In his presence, before other German officers, he poured scorn on his plans, fixing him sardonically with his cold fixed stare. In his attitude Kemal had the strong support of Jemal Pasha, who reigned over Syria with all the trappings of a monarch, and whose word until now had been law. As commander on the Palestine front Jemal vehemently opposed the Baghdad project on the same grounds as Kemal. He wanted to concentrate the available force between Aleppo and Damascus, ready to move wherever the situation might demand its support. To this Enver, at a conference in Aleppo of army commanders who included Kemal, merely replied that the campaign was decided upon, with the best German general available. 'Please don't waste time,' he added, 'in trying to make me change my mind.'

But, thanks largely to the sage advice of one of his principal staff officers, Major Franz von Papen, the Marshal began to change his own mind. After a tour of the Palestine front with von Papen he saw the danger that if the British attacked they might break through the Turkish positions, overrun Palestine and Syria and cut all lines of communication with Baghdad. He thus decided to sacrifice prestige to prudence and to postpone, for the moment, the Baghdad offensive.

As a face-saver Enver revived his pet dream of ejecting the British from Egypt. An offensive would be launched through Sinai to drive them back to the Suez Canal before they themselves could attack. The plan went ahead, despite strong opposition from Jemal, who now found himself superseded in his over-all command by von Falkenhayn. Kemal himself opposed it as strongly. Von Papen met him on his way south to Nablus with his army, 'in a fearful temper with Falkenhayn over the measures to be adopted . . . a most regrettable situation'.[1]

At that moment he was in fact on the point of resigning his command. Before doing so he wrote a long and considered report to Talat and Enver on the situation of the Ottoman Empire as he saw it in September 1917. He was helped in drafting the document by Ismet who had arrived in Aleppo, after a visit to Constantinople to take up a new army group command, and whose energy had been renewed by a delayed week's honeymoon on the salubrious slopes of Mount Olympus. Kemal argued first that the Turkish people were tired of the war:

There are no bonds left between the present Turkish Government and the people. Our 'people' are now nearly all women, disabled men and children. For all alike, the Government is the power which insistently drives them to hunger and death. The administrative machine is devoid of authority. Public life is full of anarchy. Each new step taken by the Government increases the general hatred against it. All officials accept

[1] Von Papen, *Memoirs*.

bribes and are capable of all sorts of corruption and abuse. The machinery of justice has entirely broken down. The police forces do not function. Economic life is collapsing at a formidable speed. Neither the people nor the government employees have any confidence in the future. The urge to keep alive rids even the best and most honest people of every sort of sacred feeling. If the war lasts much longer the whole structure of the Government and the dynasty, decrepit in all its parts, may suddenly fall to pieces.

He then went into some detail to show the weakness of the Turkish army. Most formations were at one-fifth of their proper strength. One of the divisions of the Seventh Army, sent at full strength from Constantinople, consisted of men so weak that fifty per cent of them could not stand on their feet. The best-organized divisions were losing half their numbers by desertion and sickness before they reached the front.

Kemal propounded the military strategy needed to meet this situation:

It must be wholly defensive, aimed at saving the life of every soldier possible. We should not hand over a single man for foreign Governments' purposes. No Germans should be employed in the service of Turkey. What is left of the Turkish army must not be senselessly endangered for the personal ambitions of a Falkenhayn. The Germans should not be given the opportunity to prolong this war to the point of reducing Turkey to the position of a colony in disguise.

Kemal's objective was the restoration of the command to Jemal. All Turkish forces should be recalled from Europe to help defend Syria against the forthcoming British offensive. The whole front should then be placed under the orders of 'an Ottoman Moslem commander', to whom von Falkenhayn, if it were necessary to use him, should be subordinate. He himself would be prepared to serve in such a chain of command, though it meant loss of rank. Unless this were agreed, he begged to be relieved of his command of the Seventh Army.

Both Enver and von Falkenhayn tried to persuade Kemal to change his mind. But he remained adamant. Thus Enver had little alternative but to accept his resignation. This was awkward for him. Kemal was unlikely to keep quiet about it and might well cause trouble at home. Von Falkenhayn talked of disciplinary action. To save appearances Kemal was posted back to his command of the Second Army in Diyarbekir. But he refused the posting. The General Staff finally compromised by granting him a month's leave.

Having fought and lost his battle for him, Kemal considered that Jemal too ought to resign. He replied that he was thinking of doing so, but preferred to await Enver's imminent arrival in Damascus. When Enver arrived

Jemal submitted to his persuasive entreaties and to those of his own pro-vincial officials, and decided to remain at his post. Before relinquishing his command Kemal remembered the boxes of gold with which the Marshal had tried to buy his compliance. He handed them over to his successor in exchange for a receipt, then insisted on exchanging this for the original receipt which he had sent to von Falkenhayn. He sent his two ADCs to the Marshal with the message: 'Your money is lodged here, but the signature of Mustafa Kemal, which is infinitely more valuable, cannot remain in your possession.' Von Falkenhayn at first denied all knowledge of the money, and declared that the receipt was not on his files. But when Kemal persisted, with veiled threats to expose the transaction, the receipt was handed over.

Kemal now found that he had not the money for his train fare back to Constantinople. He told his ADC to sell his dozen horses. There were no offers in the market for fear that the horses would be requisitioned by the army. But Jemal, aware that they were good horses, bought them off him, and he was able to take the train for Constantinople. None the less he remained angry with Jemal for his refusal to resign with him. It was Rauf who finally reconciled them, on Jemal's arrival in the city, over a dinner at the Pera Palace Hotel. Kemal was further mollified when Jemal sent him a message, saying that he had re-sold the horses for more than twice what he had paid for them, and asking him where he should send the balance. It was a payment which, as the outright purchaser of the horses, he was under no obligation to make. Kemal expressed gratification at the gesture. The money would be useful to him in Constantinople now that he was without a command and supposedly in disgrace.

He left his mother's house, as he had for some time wanted to do, and moved to the Pera Palace Hotel, where he would be freer. He seethed with impatience and a burning conviction as to what should be done. At all costs he must persuade the more influential of his countrymen that the war was lost and must be brought to a conclusion by a separate peace. In this view he had the strong support of Fethi, who was a leader of the Opposition, such as it was, and a few other friends. One of these was Rauf, who kept a watchful eye over Kemal, trying to steer him clear of political intrigue which might land him in trouble. He was for ever giving him brotherly lectures on the need for discretion and patience and self-control.

In the general atmosphere of discontent there was indeed scope for intrigue. Kemal and Fethi found some willing listeners in high quarters who wanted, as they did, to end the war. A friend of Kemal in the War Office sounded him as to whether, if a new military Cabinet were formed to make peace, he would be willing to serve in it. He divulged to him that Enver, without the knowledge of his colleagues, had recruited a secret military force to forestall or resist any such move. Kemal and Fethi passed on this information confidentially to Talat, who was not himself happy as to the course of events. He extracted an admission from Enver that such a force existed, but an assurance that it would not be used against any Cabinet of which he, Talat, was a member.

Enver, meanwhile, continued to look upon Kemal with suspicion. Hoping to allay this Rauf, once again the peacemaker, brought the two men together over a luncheon at the Pera Palace Hotel. Kemal behaved well throughout the meal, as Enver admitted to Rauf at the end of it. He added only, echoing with unconscious irony Kemal's own protests seven years earlier: 'But I won't have him bringing politics into the army!' One day Enver summoned him and invited him – repaying him in his own previous coin – to withdraw from the army and enter Parliament. Kemal retorted that he had no desire to become a deputy, and no intention of withdrawing from the army. He knew very well that the deputy of today was a mere civil servant, and that the army was the only source of power.

Meanwhile events in Syria soon gave support to Kemal's main argument. To his secret satisfaction, since he had forecast its failure, the famous 'Lightning' operation failed to materialize. Forestalling it, Allenby's forces attacked on the Sinai front. Von Falkenhayn, far from being able to launch an offensive, was inadequately prepared even to meet this thrust. The line was soon broken by an attack, not against Gaza on the coast, as the Turks had expected, but on the Beersheba front inland. They had been deceived by the successful ruse of a British staff officer on 'reconnaissance' who, pursued from a Turkish outpost, dropped a haversack with papers ingeniously contrived to suggest that the Beersheba attack was no more than a feint. Driven back by a ferocious artillery bombardment they failed to bring up their reserves in time to form an effective second line of defence.

Lloyd George had asked Allenby to capture Jerusalem as a Christmas present for the British nation. He did so. He thus dealt one last grievous blow at the morale of the Turks. After the loss of Mecca and Baghdad, Jerusalem was their third great holy city to fall to the enemy. 1917 had been a year of catastrophe for the Ottoman Empire.

CHAPTER FOURTEEN

A VISIT TO GERMANY

AS EVENTS TURNED OUT, Kemal was now to have the chance of seeing for himself how the situation in Germany stood. In December 1917 the Kaiser invited the Sultan to pay him a visit at the German Imperial Head-quarters. Since he was clearly incapable of making the journey it was decided that his younger brother and Heir Apparent, Prince Vahid-ed-Din, should go in his place. Enver, seeing a good opportunity to get rid of Kemal for a spell, invited him to accompany the Prince as a member of his suite. He accepted the invitation.

Mustafa Kemal, the Republican, the rebel, had always poured scorn on the Palace and all that it stood for. But if it could be made to serve his own purposes so much the better. A contact of this kind with the future Sultan might well be of value. The journey besides would give him a good oppor-tunity to spy out the nakedness of the German land. Enver doubtless cal-culated that it might have the reverse effect.

Before leaving he was received by the Prince. The audience took place in a drawing-room, filled with men in morning-coats. Presently another man in a morning-coat came in and sat down at the end of the sofa. He was, it emerged, the Prince – a lean man in his fifties, with drooping shoulders, a long bony face and a prominent nose.

Kemal took in the subsequent proceedings with an observant and cynical eye. 'This man,' he afterwards recounted, 'first of all shut his eyes, appearing to be absorbed in a deep meditation. Some time afterwards he raised his eyelids and deigned to pronounce these words: "I am flattered and pleased to make your acquaintance." He then shut his eyes again. I was preparing to answer these courteous words when I saw that this man was again lost in reverie. I hesitated whether to answer or not but decided to wait until he had recovered his powers of speech. After a while he opened his eyes again and said: "We are going to travel, are we not?" ' Kemal replied that this was indeed so. In the carriage, driving away from the Palace, he exchanged bitter reflections with his companion on the lot of a country which was doomed to have such a being as its sovereign.

Kemal suggested to a member of the Palace staff that, since this was a military visit, the Prince should wear uniform. On arrival at the station he observed that he was wearing civilian clothes. The Prince had taken offence because his rank as Heir Apparent had been reduced from that of divisional general to that of brigadier. Thus he preferred to travel as a civilian. 'In reality,' Kemal subsequently remarked, 'he was worthy of no military rank whatsoever.' At the station the Prince walked past the guard of honour, raising his hands inappropriately to his forehead in an Oriental gesture of salute. Before the train left Kemal suggested to him that he should greet the crowd from the window. Was this really necessary the Prince enquired? On being advised that it was, he obeyed.

As the train proceeded across the plains of Thrace Vahid-ed-Din invited Kemal to his own compartment. This time he received him with his eyes open. He made a little speech, excusing himself for the fact that he had only just learnt of his identity, adding that he knew him well by repute for his successful campaigns in Gallipoli, and was pleased and honoured to have him as a travelling companion. 'I am one of your greatest admirers,' he said. Kemal immediately decided that the Prince was after all a man of intelligence. His strange behaviour in the Palace could no doubt be ascribed to its inhibiting influences; now that he was free of them his real qualities would emerge. Here, Kemal began to imagine, was a man who might be stimulated to action in his interests and those of the country. During subsequent talks on the journey he worked assiduously to indoctrinate the Prince on his own view of the course of events.

The party arrived at the small town where the Kaiser had established his General Headquarters. The Kaiser, standing on a daïs at the end of an imposing hall, was there in person to welcome the Prince, flanked by von Hindenburg, von Ludendorff and all his General Staff. They embraced one another and exchanged a few polite words. The Prince then presented his suite. When Kemal's turn came the Kaiser, one hand lodged in a Napoleonic pose between the buttons of his tunic, stretched out the other to him with a loud exclamation: 'Sixteenth Army Corps! Anafarta!' The company turned towards Kemal, who remained momentarily silent. The Kaiser repeated, in German, 'Are you not the Mustafa Kemal who commanded the Sixteenth Army Corps and held Anafarta?' Kemal, in his best French, replied that this was so.

Comfortably installed in the hotel which served as the Imperial Headquarters the Prince, accompanied by Kemal, paid official calls on von Hindenburg and von Ludendorff. In von Hindenburg's office, contrary to protocol in so formal an interview, the Marshal delivered to the Prince, and through him to the Turkish people, an optimistic assessment of the war situation. The Prince expressed thanks for this consoling pronouncement. Kemal, whose own ideas on the war situation were less sanguine, preferred to assume that the Marshal's words were dictated merely by courtesy.

Von Ludendorff was equally affable and reassuring. He explained his reasons for confidence, and remarked especially on the brilliant offensive just launched against the Allied armies on the western front. At this Kemal could not keep silent. Knowing something of the offensive and well aware that von Ludendorff was exploiting it as a means of raising the morale of German people and impressing their Allies, he asked him bluntly, 'What eventual line is the offensive likely to reach?'

Taken aback by so direct a question von Ludendorff reflected a moment then looked at Kemal and replied evasively, 'As far as we are concerned, we are carrying out our offensive. We shall see how events develop.'

Kemal retorted, 'To assess the effects of this offensive I don't consider it necessary to await events or a final result. Because, in fact, the new offensive is only a partial offensive.' Von Ludendorff looked at him narrowly but gave him no answer.

By now he had established a frank enough relationship with Vahid-ed-Din, who listened to his discourses with apparent attention and seemed to respond to his views. Never favourably disposed to the Committee of Union and Progress the Prince confessed his antipathy to Talat and Enver, and his belief that they were harming the country. Talking to him in his hotel room one day, Kemal tried to persuade him that it was useless to put about among the Turkish people, as the High Command was doing, the idea that, thanks to the support of the German armies, their sacrifices would be rewarded with ultimate victory. Had not von Ludendorff implied that the fate of the war was being left in the hands of the Almighty? Kemal spoke forcibly and his words seemed to meet with the Prince's approval.

At that moment they heard a clamour throughout the hotel, with shouts of, 'The Kaiser! The Kaiser!' The Emperor had come to pay his respects to the Sultan's Heir Apparent. Very much the gentleman, the Kaiser spoke warmly of the faithful and devoted Ottoman state and its value as an ally to Germany. He stressed that Enver Pasha was accomplishing his task with a sense of the high importance of the alliance, and added that the German High Command and General Staff had unlimited confidence in this eminent officer. To this discourse the Prince, using the circumlocutions which he considered proper to the occasion, replied through his interpreter:

'The words which your Majesty has just pronounced on the subject of the fidelity and loyalty of Turkey towards Germany, and on your hope that the Allies of the Empire will soon see the realization of their desires, have produced in me, whose duty it is to think of the future of my country, a feeling of joy and consolation. But, setting aside reflections that may be inspired by an examination of the general situation, I feel the need for

A.—5

enlightenment on a particular point: the blows which are being struck at the very heart of Turkey do not slacken; they are falling more strongly all the time. If this goes on for much longer Turkey will be annihilated. I have not been fortunate enough to notice among your declarations any assurances which permit me to hope that these blows will be counteracted: perhaps you will be kind enough to throw some light on this point, which may reassure me a little.'

The Kaiser rose stiffly to his feet. He realized, he said, that certain people were trying to sow trouble in the Prince's mind. 'But now that I, the Emperor of Germany, have spoken to you of the future and of our coming success, do you still, can you still have any doubts?' The Prince replied that his anxieties were not entirely at rest. The Kaiser remained standing, making it clear that he wished to leave.

At a dinner given by the Kaiser, Kemal found himself seated on the right of von Ludendorff. He was bursting to talk and argue with these imposing German commanders about the course of the war, the subject which filled his thoughts. But von Ludendorff refused to be drawn. Von Hindenburg after dinner was more talkative. He remarked that the situation in Syria had been restored; that during the last few days a new cavalry division had been sent to the front there. Kemal knew that he was simply repeating the reports of the local German commanders. The division in question was one for which he himself had asked many months before, for the reinforcement of Yildirim. It proved to be in so weak a state that its horses had to be put out to grass and fed before they were fit for service. Some time later he asked whether the division was ready, and was told to expect nothing from it. After giving these details to von Hindenburg he continued:

'I fear that what I say does not agree with the reports that you are receiving, but I can assure you that they are the truth. The situation has not been restored in Syria, believe me.' Emboldened by the lavish potions of champagne which he had drunk at dinner, Kemal added, 'Apart from this, Marshal, you are launching at the moment an important offensive. But I do not think that you have much belief in it. Will you tell me, for my ear alone, just what aim and objective you feel sure of achieving by it?'

Kemal hardly expected him to answer the question. He summed up von Hindenburg afterwards as 'a man whose eyes seemed to see to the heart of things and whose tongue knew the value of silence'. The Marshal rose and said merely, 'Excellency may I offer you a cigarette?'

The Heir Apparent and his party were conducted to various sectors of the western front, chosen with a view to impressing them and inspiring their confidence. Thanks to personal reconnaissance by Kemal, disregarding the prescribed programme and interrogating officers in the field, they did not succeed in doing so. After a visit to Krupp's they proceeded to Berlin, where they were the guests of the Kaiser at the Adlon Hotel. After so long a period of tension at his royal master's side, Kemal sought relaxation in the night life of the city, drinking and dancing and seeking women in its cabarets and *nachtlokals*. Drinking too freely one evening at the Embassy, with the Turkish Ambassador, he let his tongue run loose with denunciations of Talat and Enver, of all the Germans in Turkey, of the scenes of prostitution in the streets of Berlin at this critical time in the war. He walked out into the street, straight into the arms of a prostitute, from whom the Ambassador, with some trouble, detached him, taking him back to his hotel and seeing him safely to bed.

One day in the Adlon, when they were alone together, the Prince turned to Kemal and asked, 'What ought I to do?'

Kemal replied, 'We know our Ottoman history. It embodies many vicissitudes such as inspire you, and with good reason, with fear and anxiety. I am going to propose to you something with the promise that, if you accept it, I shall link my life to yours. Will you allow me?'

'Speak.'

'You are not yet Sultan. But you have been able to see that in Germany the Emperor, the Crown Prince and other princes all have a job to do. Why do you stand aside from public affairs?'

'What can I do?'

'Ask for the command of an army as soon as you get back to Constantinople. I shall be your chief of staff.'

'The command of which army?'

'The Fifth.' This was the army whose task it was to defend the Straits.

Vahid-ed-Din objected: 'They will not give it to me.'

'Ask for it all the same.'

'We shall think about it when we get back to Constantinople,' was the Prince's guarded reply.

Passing through Sofia, on the return journey, Kemal was met at the station by Shakir Zümre and other friends. He said to them, 'Germany has lost the war.' Back in Constantinople he continued, with redoubled urgency, his campaign for a separate peace. But he was frustrated by again falling ill. The kidney trouble which had dogged him for a number of years, and which may have been aggravated by an early bout of venereal disease, was now giving him considerable pain.[1] His doctors thus sent him to Vienna to consult a specialist, who treated him for a month in a cottage hospital outside the city. Then they sent him to Carlsbad to recuperate. Shakir, who had joined his train at Sofia, kept him company.

[1] In his youth Kemal had contracted gonorrhea, which was inadequately treated and caused complications later. Despite rumours put about by his enemies he never suffered from syphilis.

This enforced rest gave him the opportunity to resume his reading and to sort out his ideas on the possible future of his country. He kept a daily diary, in French, in which he clarified his political views. He enjoyed a flirtation with an Austrian girl, who fell in love with him – or so he afterwards boasted to his friends – and seemed to have marital designs on him. To discourage these he told her that he had a fiancée at home. She appeared upset and asked who she was. He answered lightly, 'My country.' When she looked puzzled he explained in a heroic vein, 'I am a soldier. I am obliged to love my country and to live with her until the end of my life.'

One day, early in July 1918, a friend came to see him with the news that the Sultan had died and that Vahid-ed-Din had succeeded to the throne. Kemal's immediate reaction was a feeling of annoyance that he was not in Constantinople. All he could do was to send a telegram of congratulation to the new Sultan, which was duly acknowledged.

Vahid-ed-Din mounted the throne with misgiving. To the Sheikh of Islam he confessed that he was not prepared for the post. 'I am at a loss,' he said. 'Pray for me.' Driving to his enthronement with Enver he complained of rheumatism. On arrival he asked for his stick. But it had been left behind. 'What a catastrophe!' he lamented. They were his first words on entering his Palace – words ominous for the future of his reign.

Kemal, in Carlsbad, was encouraged by the news that Izzet Pasha, with whom he had served on the eastern front, had been given the high post of Adjutant-General, in effect military adviser and chief of staff to the new Sultan. Since Izzet had no love for the Committee of Union and Progress his appointment might be said to encroach, in an encouraging fashion, on Enver's domain. In response to telegrams from his ADC, recommending his immediate return to Constantinople, Kemal left Carlsbad at the end of the month, but was delayed *en route* at Vienna by a severe attack of that Spanish influenza which was already beginning to decimate Europe. On his eventual arrival Izzet came to see him in his apartment at the Pera Palace, and suggested that he renew his contact with Vahid-ed-Din, now Sultan Mehmed VI. They discussed the prospects of orientating the Sultan towards their ideas on the grave state of the war. With Izzet's agreement Kemal applied for an audience, which was granted.

The new Sultan received him amicably and seemed to treat him as he had done before. With his permission Kemal reiterated his previous views, now suggesting that the Sultan should personally assume the supreme command of the army, and appoint him, Kemal, his chief of staff.

But Vahid-ed-Din reverted to the demeanour he had shown at their first meeting. He closed his eyes. After a while he opened them and asked, 'Are there other military leaders who share your ideas?'

'There are.'

'We shall think about it.' The audience ended. A few days later he was

summoned to another audience, together with Izzet. But this time the
Sultan was even more circumspect. Only generalities were discussed.
Undeterred, Kemal applied for a third audience. But this time Vahid-ed-Din
forestalled his representations.

'Pasha,' he said, 'I am under the obligation, above all things, to feed the
population of Constantinople. This population is hungry. Until we can find
a remedy for this state of affairs all other measures will be vain.'

Kemal replied, 'Your reflections are proper. But the steps required to feed
the population of Constantinople need not prevent your Majesty from
taking those firm and urgent measures which the safety of the country
demands. Any effort to ensure public security involves the proper functioning
of the whole machine. If the whole does not function one cannot expect
even partial results from its mechanism. I am convinced that what I say is
true. Perhaps your Majesty will not approve of my attitude, but I feel
compelled to state that the first act of the new Sultan should be to assert
his power. As long as that power – the power which safeguards the country,
the nation and all the Allies – remains in the hands of others, you will only
be Sultan in name.'

Kemal realized that he had spoken too freely. The Sultan, in the course
of his reply, used the phrase, 'I have discussed with their Excellencies Talat
and Enver Pasha what requires to be done.' He closed his eyes once more,
and gave his hand to Kemal in silence.

Kemal realized that the Sultan had been won over by his enemies. None
the less, in his capacity as an army commander, he continued to put in a
formal appearance at the weekly ceremony of the *Selamlik* in the Yildiz
Palace. One Friday he found himself there in the ante-room with Enver,
Izzet and a number of 'old school' generals from the Balkan Wars. After
the prayer, he was told that the Sultan wanted to see him in his private
drawing-room.

'Is he alone?' Kemal asked.

'No. There are one or two German generals with him.'

Vahid-ed-Din presented Kemal to the generals saying, 'This is a commander whom I much appreciate and in whom I have great confidence.'

When they had sat down he continued: 'I have appointed you army commander in Syria. The operations there have assumed great importance.
It is necessary for you to go there. And I must ask you this: do not let
these regions fall into the hands of the enemy. I have no doubt that you
will acquit yourself brilliantly in the task I confide in you. You must take
up your post at once.' Signing the order, he turned to the German generals
and said, 'This man will be able to do what I say.'

Ostensibly a mark of great favour had been conferred on Kemal. He did
not see it as such. He felt like saying to the Sultan, 'Your Majesty, you are
giving me a duty which other generals, already on the spot, have been

charged to carry to a conclusion. You consider putting me over their heads as commander? If so, I submit willingly to this order, which honours me greatly. But have you understood the nature of the problem? You are sending me to command an army whose command I resigned some time ago and, to tell the truth, an army which has since been defeated, like all the others on this front. How in these circumstances is it possible for me to carry out the task which you assign to me?'

But he knew he could say nothing. He took his leave and returned to the ante-room. Here Enver came towards him with a smile on his lips. Kemal exclaimed to him, 'Bravo! I congratulate you. You have won the day.' Then, in more earnest tones, he added, 'My friend, I want at least to talk to you of certain essential questions. As far as I know and understand it, our army, our strength, our position in Syria exists only in name. In sending me there you have taken a fine revenge. You have also done something quite contrary to the proper practice. You have made the Sultan give me a personal order.'

Enver and the Turkish general beside him laughed. The rest of the company looked indifferent. In a corner of the room a group of veterans from the Balkan Wars were engaged in an animated discussion. One of them was saying, 'There is nothing to be done with these Turkish soldiers. They are cattle, who only know how to run away. I don't envy anyone who has to command such a senseless herd.'

Overhearing the conversation Kemal intervened angrily: 'Pasha, I am a soldier too. I also have had a command in this army. The Turkish soldier does not run away. He does not know what flight means. If you happen to have seen him turning tail it is certainly because his commander has fled himself. It is unjust of you to make the Turkish soldier bear the shame of your own flight.'

The Pasha, not knowing Kemal – or pretending not to do so – was silent for a moment, then turned to his companions and asked, 'Who is this man?' There was a whispered reply and Kemal took his leave in silence.

Rauf saw him off from Haydar Pasha station. Kemal told him of the audience. Then, just before the train left, he whispered in his ear, 'Keep in touch with Fethi. Follow the situation closely.' Rauf delivered him a final rebuke: 'As long as I keep my military post, I have absolutely decided not to get mixed up in political matters. I have known Fethi since the Constitution, but do not find it right to join him politically.' The train drew out of the station *en route* for the south-east.

CHAPTER FIFTEEN

THE TURKISH DEFEAT

MUSTAFA KEMAL arrived in Palestine, to resume his command of the Seventh Army, a month before the final offensive, planned to eliminate Turkey, once and for all, from the war. Von Falkenhayn had gone. Liman von Sanders had succeeded him as commander of the army group. Kemal found his own army in an even more depleted and exhausted state than he had feared. Enver had given him not merely unwarranted predictions but incorrect figures. Three Turkish armies held a line from west to east, two (the Eighth and Seventh) between the coast and the River Jordan, and the third (the Fourth) to the east of it. But they were mere skeletons of armies, with no reserves to supply them. Before leaving Constantinople, Kemal had urged that what remained of these units should be combined into a single compact force under a unified command. But the proposal was cynically discounted as a move to further his own personal ambitions. Now after a long and thorough tour of inspection of the central sector of the front, from his head-quarters at Nablus, he reached the conclusion that the battle was lost in advance.

Many troops had been in the line for six months without relief. The traditional Turkish fighting spirit had been undermined for want of a bare minimum of rations. Reinforcements had been arriving depleted by large-scale desertions *en route*. And now there would be no more reinforcements, for a second front had been opened. Enver and the Germans had chosen this moment of acute national peril to launch a new force into the Caucasus, in pursuit of the disintegrating Russian armies and of the old pan-Islamic, pan-Germanic dream of an Asiatic Empire. A regiment destined for one of Kemal's divisions arrived minus its commander and staff, for they had been transferred to the Caucasian front without warning or replacement. One of its two battalions deserted in a body, in response to propaganda by Arab agents of the British which described the situation of the Turkish armies as hopeless.

Early in September Kemal wrote to a doctor friend: 'Syria deserves pity. There is no governor, no commander. There is a lot of British propaganda. The British secret service is active everywhere. The population hates the Government and looks forward to the arrival of the British. The enemy is strong in men and transport. We are like a thread of cotton before them. The British now think that they will defeat us by their propaganda, rather than by fighting. Every day from their aircraft they throw more leaflets than bombs, always referring to "Enver and his gang. . . ." '

This was part of the softening-up process in preparation for the 'strategical masterpiece' which General Allenby, with an over-all two-to-one superiority and an overwhelming advantage in cavalry and air support, was about to inflict upon the remains of the Turkish army. His plan was bold and simple. He would break through the Turkish front line with his infantry, then strike with his cavalry to the rear of it at the three points from which the three armies drew their main supplies. If all went swiftly and without mishap he had hopes not merely of defeating these armies but of destroying them altogether. The initial break-through was to be along the coast, against the Eighth Army, but the Turks were to be deceived into expecting it inland, against the Seventh – an exact reversal of the tactics which he had employed in the previous campaign.

The deception was so elaborately planned as to include the taking-over and preparation of a hotel in Jerusalem as a false GHQ, the throwing of new bridges over the Jordan, the pitching of new camps in its valley and the manning of them with fifteen thousand dummy horses made of canvas, for which mule-drawn sleighs raised clouds of dust at intervals to suggest that they were trotting down to drink in the Jordan. Meanwhile the real attacking force was moved by night from the hills to the coastal plain and concealed without tents in the olive woods and orange groves, doubling itself without even the local inhabitants becoming aware of any change in its numbers.

The deception succeeded. The day before the offensive the Turks still had no inkling of the enemy's coastal concentrations and were concentrating their own forces to meet an attack up the Jordan valley, where Kemal was in command. On the previous day an Indian deserter from the British forces had divulged to the Turks the date, hour and direction of the attack. But only Kemal seems to have paid any serious attention to his report. On receiving it he immediately got up from his bed, where he was lying in pain from a recurrence of his kidney complaint. He called a meeting of his staff, then dictated an order, based on the assumption that the enemy would attack in the early morning of 19th September. Taking no chances as to the intended direction he detailed the measures to be taken by his various units. Liman von Sanders, to whom a copy of the order was sent for information, discounted Kemal's prediction of the date but replied that there was no harm in taking precautions.

On the night of 18th September Kemal telephoned to his two army corps commanders – his two friends, Ismet and Ali Fuad – to ensure that they had taken the necessary steps. They had barely answered him when he heard the first roar of the British artillery bombardment – fifteen minutes of sudden and intense fire by every available gun, followed by a barrage which moved as fast as a hundred yards a minute.

It soon became clear that, after a preliminary skirmish on his own front, the main blow was falling not here in the centre but away on the right, as the deserter had foreshadowed. It fell on the Eighth Army, which was too stunned and surprised to resist it. Soon the Turks were swarming northwards in hopeless confusion, across the plain of Megiddo where, as Allenby well knew, decisive battles had been fought since the beginning of history. His infantry pursued them, his cavalry wheeled eastwards to cut off their main line of retreat. Their communications were disrupted by effective bombing. Thus Liman von Sanders knew nothing of the extent of the rout until twenty-four hours later, when enemy cavalry, after a night ride, surprised his headquarters at Nazareth, while he still lay in bed, and almost succeeded in capturing him together with his whole General Staff.

The swift encircling movements of Allenby's cavalry were soon effectively closing the net around the Turkish armies. What he had done was, as Wavell described it, to push open by the handle 'a wide and heavy door of which the hinges were in the foothills and the handle by the coast'. Kemal's Seventh Army was on the hinge. Its right wing was cut to pieces or captured. Holding the remainder together he stood firm for as long as he could, to prevent the infection of the defeat on the right from spreading. He realized that it was vital to prevent the enemy from passing east of the Jordan, where the Fourth Army was already being harassed by the Arab legions of Feisal and Lawrence in an endeavour to cut the only remaining Turkish line of retreat. With its aid the enemy was momentarily contained, and Kemal ordered the retreat in the direction of the Jordan, keeping in touch as far as possible with the remnants of the army on his right and with that on his left.

Passing through Nablus, their former headquarters, his troops found an indifferent, silent population. Elsewhere the Arab villagers had dressed up in festive clothes, ready to welcome the enemy. The Turks retreated step by step and in good enough order, checking the attacks of the British here and there, despite inferior numbers, compelling them to halt and make fresh dispositions. Given adequate reserves they might have held the position; but no reserves existed.

There were heavy losses from air attack, which had a paralysing effect on the morale of the Turkish forces. But Kemal, by ruthless and determined leadership, still contrived to keep a portion of his army in being and, after a week of hazards and hardships, had transported it across the Jordan, free of the enemy's net. Ismet, bringing up the rear with his army corps, found that the attacks were now coming from the north, not the south. The British were fast moving southwards to prevent his troops from crossing the Jordan. Already the valley was strewn with the shattered remnants of Yildirim and its equipment. Ismet, destroying his transport, setting his horses to swim, trying to keep his divisions in some sort of order, waded across with his men in a strong current under enemy fire, with the water above their waists. The German colonel accompanying him was worried because the photograph in his pocket, of his wife and daughter, had become wet. But Ismet consoled him with the thought that this was an augury of happiness, since they were now baptized in Jordan water.

At Ajlun – beneath the walls of the Transjordan fortress from which the more redoubtable Saladin had persistently prevented the Latin Crusaders from crossing the Jordan – he found Kemal, sick and in pain. Neither he nor Ismet could tell just what was happening or was likely to happen. Already the Fourth Army was retreating across tracts of waterless desert towards Damascus. Would von Sanders make a stand before the city? From here it was impossible to know. They moved on next day across the mountains to Dera'a, harried by Arab villagers, who nevertheless dispersed when they turned and fought back. Here they received orders to retreat towards Damascus and Kemal ordered the Seventh Army to assemble to the south of it at Kiswe.

He entered Damascus alone, with a small personal escort, leaving his troops to catch up with him and rest. Familiar as he was with it from his earlier soldiering days he was quick to sense among the inhabitants a cold hostility to the Turks. Feisal's Sherifian flag hung from the windows. Armed Arab bands were roaming the streets, drunk with excitement, diverting themselves with equestrian *fantasias* and firing salvoes of cartridges into the air. The city was evidently doomed. Returning to Kiswe he found orders from von Sanders to hand over his troops to the commander of the Fourth Army and to proceed to Rayak, there to rally and command a mixed group of units salvaged from various parts of the front.

Von Sanders had indeed planned to defend Damascus, but the general confusion and exhaustion of the troops, the lack of liaison and the unforeseen speed of the advance forced him to abandon the plan. It was at Homs, farther north, that he now hoped to re-group his fugitive forces, under the protection of a line running from the valley of the Barada across the plain of Rayak, which might also serve to protect Beirut. Thus the Emir Feisal triumphantly entered Damascus, preceded a day or so earlier by Colonel Lawrence, for whom the women of the city tore off their veils and leaned screaming with laughter through their lattices, splashing him with bath dippers of scent as he drove through the streets in his open Rolls-Royce.

As the Arab troops marched in Kemal was on his way to Rayak. He met

Liman von Sanders at the headquarters of the German Asia Korps. The German colonel in command ordered each of them a glass of cold beer. While they drank he proceeded over a map to illustrate, for the benefit of his new commander, the excellent situation, in spite of everything, of his excellent force.

When he had finished, Kemal asked Liman, 'Is this officer under my orders?'

'Yes.'

'In that case, Colonel, would you be kind enough to tell me where your troops are, what is their strength and their position?'

The colonel, taken aback, said, 'I can't yet give you a definite answer. The movements of the troops make the situation a little confused.'

Kemal replied, 'Colonel, my country is at stake. Those whose task it is to defend it can't be content with approximations. I have at this moment to take decisions. Can you tell me what I may count on from you?'

After reflecting for a moment the colonel told the truth: 'I must admit, sir, that I have no force on which we can count.'

'Which means that I have before me a colonel with his staff, and nothing else?'

'That is so.'

'Then let us go to our headquarters.'

Kemal's headquarters was at Rayak and Liman's at Baalbek. As far as he could see the only troops left in the neighbourhood were scattered bands which had lost their units and were quite demoralized. He instructed the officers he could trust to assemble the men and organize them into units. He was informed that certain senior officers had passed northwards on horseback; the general who had been ordered to defend Damascus had left the city; the commander of one army corps had surrendered and bolted to Beirut.

That evening he realized that there no longer existed any authority on any front or in any unit. The time had come for him to take the situation into his own hands. Exceeding his powers he issued an order that all his forces were to make for the north – those in the area of Damascus, under Ismet, and those in the area of Baalbek, under Ali Fuad. This order, which he communicated, for information, to Liman von Sanders, now at Homs, laid him open to serious censure. For it envisaged a drastic burning of boats and a further retreat on a major scale. But Kemal trusted his own judgement, confident that he would be able to justify his action.

Von Sanders had already ordered the evacuation of Rayak, no longer tenable since the British were now on the road north of Damascus. Kemal fired the railway station, amid shots from the populace, and demolished its installations and waterworks. When his last troops were gathered in he proceeded to Baalbek. Here he confirmed his order to Ali Fuad. At night he went on to Homs by train. Here he confronted von Sanders and put it to him forcibly that his decision was, in the circumstances, the only one possible. Von Sanders agreed with him.

'What you say,' he admitted, 'is true. But I, after all, am only a foreigner. I cannot take such a decision. Only the masters of the country can do so.' He realized that this involved the abandonment to the enemy, without resistance, of almost the whole of the treasured Turkish province of Syria.

In his most masterful manner Kemal replied, 'In that case, the orders will be executed.'

Together they went to see the Turkish chief of staff, who was ill. He too agreed with Kemal. Their decision was to move all surviving forces to Aleppo, a hundred and twenty miles north, in the extreme corner of Syria, and there to reorganize them pending a further decision. It was von Sanders who issued the final order. But it was in effect Mustafa Kemal who from now onwards commanded. Ironically, the unified command of the three armies, for which he had pressed at the outset, had materialized now that they had virtually ceased to exist. But at least by his efforts some sort of a Turkish force could now be kept in being.

Thus Allenby's war of movement, a 'lightning' operation if ever there was one, came to a temporary halt. He boldly decided to press forward with a small force which could not yet be supported by the rest of his army. But Kemal, with a safe distance between them, had won a respite to collect his scattered forces and prepare a defence of Turkish territory. Torrid heat paralysed the city of Aleppo, and the military traffic threw up thick yellow clouds of dust which choked the streets. Kemal formed committees of reorganization, under his two corps commanders, Ali Fuad and Ismet. Two new divisions were gradually assembled, one of them at Katina, commanding the mountain roads to the north and to the west, leading down to the port of Alexandretta. Von Sanders transferred the greater part of his staff beyond the port to Adana and presently followed himself, thus virtually retiring from the scene of battle.

Soon after his arrival in Aleppo Kemal went down once more with the kidney complaint which had troubled him throughout the retreat. He lay under treatment in the Armenian hospital, using the nurses' sitting-room for conferences with the generals and the local authorities, and impressing the doctors with the stamina which had enabled him to fight the disease. Meanwhile an advanced detachment of British armoured cars, after an engagement with a Turkish rearguard, had drawn near to the city and called upon the Turks to surrender. They refused to do so. Two days were then spent by the British forces reconnoitring the defences until their supporting troops arrived. For a while Arabs occupied the citadel and government building. Kemal, in bed and in pain once more, heard firing in the street

outside the Baron Hotel where he was staying. He went to the balcony to
see what was happening. There was a confused uproar. A crowd of Arabs
was trying to break into the hotel, past a group of panic-stricken Turkish
soldiers, in search of the Pasha and his staff. Kemal went down and, wielding
his riding crop, drove a group of them out of the lobby. The commander
of the garrison then handed him a report which he was too paralysed with
fear to read. Kemal looked through it calmly. It stated that the city was
under attack.

The crowd then saw him emerge on to the terrace of the hotel, a slim
grey-eyed assured figure, in impeccable uniform, with a cigarette between
his lips. Quietly and without fuss he gave certain orders. Then he strolled
down the street. Sardonically he observed that certain inhabitants of Aleppo,
whom he aspired to defend, were throwing grenades at him from the rooftops. Soon his men, whom he had taken the precaution of stationing nearby,
moved swiftly down the streets and dispersed the Arabs with a rain of
machine-gun fire, leaving corpses strewn over the pavements. They had
soon restored order throughout the city.

But the time had come to evacuate Aleppo. Apart from Allenby's
imminent advance there was a danger of a landing in the rear at Alexandretta. Calling for his car Kemal drove around the city, giving the
necessary orders to those concerned. Then he drove back to the hotel. That
evening the rearguard was withdrawn from the south of the city to create
the impression of a complete retreat. In fact the main force was withdrawn
only to its north-western outskirts.

An English nurse, one of two who had been marooned throughout the
war in the hospital which Kemal had just left, described the 'day of excitement' which followed:

At 6 a.m. firing was going on all over the city, it seemed to rain bullets,
and quite impossible to put one's head outside a door or go on the
balcony: the Arabs were stationed in the streets letting off their guns at
random. Many houses were looted of everything the Arabs could carry
off, even to cooking and washing utensils; we watched them break into a
house on the opposite side to us and load up their horses with bedding,
pillows and all kinds of articles obtainable. At 8 a.m. the Hedjazi Arab
troops forerunning our own army entered the city, shouting, singing,
galloping their horses, swaying in the saddles, wielding their swords and
guns in the air and carrying their banner: we knew that the English were
not far from us, and at 9 a.m. we had the great joy of seeing our helmeted
men gliding through the city on armoured cars. Our feeling of thankful-
ness knew no bounds, we hoisted our Union Jack, to the cheers of
outsiders, and away over the hills facing our hospital was to be seen a
moving black streak getting nearer and nearer, until our cavalry were

also in the city; after half an hour's halt they passed out to the north side of the city to take position, but unfortunately the Turks were in wait, and an attack took place, where some of our men lost their lives and many were wounded.[1]

This was the first of a series of rearguard actions in which Kemal's army, repeatedly attacked but never defeated, withdrew to a line on the heights behind the city, obliging the British to call up reinforcements from Damascus. For the first time it was defending, not Arab territory, but the soil of Turkey itself, of which this was the natural frontier.

The end, however, was not far off, as Kemal well knew. The Ottoman Empire was an empire no longer. The Balkan Wars had deprived it of Turkey in Europe; now the World War had deprived it of all its Arab provinces. Kemal, though he smarted at the thought of defeat, did not regret this; in a sense he had always foreseen it. It brought nearer his vision of a new Turkish nation, surgically freed from the canker of its outlying limbs to regenerate itself as a compact healthy body rooted in the good earth of its forbears. Syria, the land of the foreigner, had gone. But Anatolia, the heart-land of the Turk, still survived and must continue to survive. It was there, behind this range of mountains, that both the past and the future of his country lay.

[1] Sister Ethel Curry (Mrs E. McLeod Smith). In *Nurses' League Journal*.

CHAPTER SIXTEEN

THE ARMISTICE

THIS VISION, however, had yet to be realized. The danger meanwhile was acute. Throughout the retreat from Homs and during the subsequent days in Aleppo, Kemal had been turning over and over in his mind the political implications of the defeat which he knew to be imminent. Had Turkey made peace independently of Germany in the previous year, as he had repeatedly urged, she might have earned such treatment from the Allies as to ensure at least an honourable survival. But now he saw that her very existence would be threatened. How was this threat to be confronted?

The Cabinet was expected to resign at any moment. It was imperative to sue for peace but impossible for Talat, exhausted and now discredited, to do so. There must be a new Government, and in Kemal's view the person to lead it was Izzet Pasha. He had opposed the war; he was a man of moderate but patriotic political views; he had consistently worked against the Committee of Union and Progress, and was favourably inclined to the Nationalists.

Kemal telegraphed accordingly to the Sultan, through his principal ADC. 'The situation,' he urged, 'is extremely serious. Our troops are becoming more and more demoralized. . . . Not only is our army threatened but the future of our State is at stake. I therefore urge that . . . peace be brought about at any cost.' The ADC was invited to put this view before the Sultan and to urge him to entrust Izzet with the formation of a Cabinet. Its members, he frankly proposed, should include Fethi, Rauf and himself, Mustafa Kemal, as Minister of War, hence Deputy Commander-in-Chief. 'This Cabinet,' he concluded, 'should immediately get in touch with the Allies and sign an Armistice which will cease military operations.'

In Constantinople events were already moving in this direction. Talat had returned from a visit to Germany. On the station platform at Sofia he was greeted with the news that the Bulgarian front had broken and that King Ferdinand was suing for an Armistice preparatory to his own abdication. Turkey was thus menaced from the west as from the east.

Constantinople itself now lay wide open to attack from Allied forces based as near home as Salonika. The bazaars began to buzz with rumours of the imminent entry into the city of the hated French General Franchet d'Espérey, a man bent, it was believed, on turning it into a French capital and enslaving its Turkish inhabitants.

As soon as he returned Talat offered his resignation to the Sultan who, after an initial refusal, accepted it. Soon afterwards, with Enver and Jemal, he fled across the Black Sea in a German warship. Talat proceeded to Germany, where he was to be shot dead by a vindictive Armenian three years later. Enver and Jemal found an eventual refuge in Russia, where no less violent deaths awaited them. In due course the Union and Progress party held a last convention, at which it admitted its guilt and decided on its own dissolution.

After the aged Tevfik Pasha, a perennial stopgap, had failed to form a Cabinet, the post was offered to Izzet Pasha who, as urged by Kemal and his friends, agreed to do so in the spirit of a soldier obeying an order from his Commander-in-Chief. It would be his policy, he declared, to seek peace on the Wilson Principles.

Rauf pressed Izzet to make Kemal either Minister of War or Chief of the General Staff. But he preferred for the moment to keep both posts in his own hands. Kemal, he argued, was still needed in the field; he could take over the War Ministry later, when peace was achieved. Meanwhile he made Ismet Under-Secretary of War, while Rauf became Minister of Marine and Fethi Minister of the Interior. Despite Kemal's absence it was the first Cabinet with effective Nationalist representation. Its immediate task was to seek an Armistice.

Unofficial British overtures had previously been made to Talat through Colonel S. F. Newcombe, one of Lawrence's officers, who had been taken prisoner in Palestine and brought by the Turks to Brusa, escaping thence to Constantinople with the aid of a girl (destined to become his wife) who was a native of the city. As a British staff officer he was able to give the Turks some idea as to the terms which his countrymen might accept, and offered them his services as an intermediary. He repeated the offer to Izzet's Government, but now suggested a more senior officer for the role – General Sir Charles Townshend, the British commander of the abortive defence of Kut, in the Baghdad campaign, who was now a respected prisoner of the Turks on the island of Prinkipo. The general, through Rauf, then proposed to Izzet his own intervention with the British authorities for peace talks. Izzet had no choice but to sue for an Armistice, and this was as good a channel as any.

He thus sent for the general and granted him his liberty. After speaking of his admiration and feeling of friendship for Britain, he deplored as a crime his country's entry into the current war on the opposing side. If

England would cease operations immediately, he continued, Turkey would be prepared to give autonomy to all the Arab provinces now in Allied possession, provided her political independence was respected in the other occupied territories and in the rest of the country. Rauf followed up this interview by a visit to the general on Prinkipo. He expressed a hope that the terms would respect Turkey's military honour. 'We are not,' he said, 'Bulgarians. . . . Let England do things quietly and trust Turkey as a gentleman.' General Townshend was conveyed to the island of Tenedos, whence he crossed in a Turkish naval tug to Mytilene. Here he was met by a British naval officer in a launch. The following dialogue took place between them:

'Who are you?'

'General Townshend.'

'Good God! I am glad to see you, sir.'

'I am once more under the British flag.'[1]

On 24th October 1918, Izzet was informed that the British Government was ready to negotiate for an Armistice, and had delegated Admiral Calthorpe[2] for the purpose. It was suggested privately by Townshend that Rauf should be a member of the Turkish delegation. Izzet called a Cabinet meeting then went to report to the Sultan. The Sultan declared that he wished his brother-in-law, Damad Ferid, to head the delegation.

Izzet was taken aback by this extraordinary proposal, delivered as it was in tones of imperial authority. He received it at first in silence; then he exclaimed, 'But he is mad!' Damad Ferid was a personage of no account but for the fact that he was married to the Sultan's sister, Princess Mediha. The marriage had been contracted on the death of her first husband, in response to an order by Sultan Abdul Hamid that a husband should be found for her between the ages of thirty and forty, who was of good family, and had never seen the face of a woman. Fulfilling these requirements Ferid was brought back from London, where he was an obscure First Secretary in the Turkish Embassy, and the union was solemnized. Later he sent his wife to Abdul Hamid to beg from him the post of Ambassador in London. But the Sultan replied, 'Sister, London is not a school. It is a most important Embassy. Only those who have real political capacities and experience can be appointed.' Ferid, thus snubbed, returned to his house, from which he had not been seen to emerge for thirty years.

This was the man whom Abdul Hamid's brother now proposed as negotiator of an Armistice for his country.[3] Izzet replied that he must consult his

---

[1] *My Mesopotamian Campaign.*

[2] Later Admiral of the Fleet Sir Somerset Gough-Calthorpe, GCB, GCMG.

[3] If necessary, he is said to have promised, he would go to England, see King George V, whose father King Edward VII he had known during his service in London, and ask him as a favour to restore to Turkey all the Ottoman territories lost since 1914.

Cabinet. The Sultan agreed, but Damad Ferid must accompany him to the Sublime Porte to receive the Cabinet's instructions. Izzet left Damad Ferid in the ante-room and went into the Cabinet room to report to his colleagues. At first nobody spoke. Then an explosion from Rauf broke the silence. As he saw the move the Sultan feared that he might be forced by the Allies to abdicate. The choice of his own brother-in-law as delegate, a man known and by repute well liked in Britain, might dissuade them from such a course. Rauf conceded that this was a natural impulse from a man who sought only to save his own throne. But did the Sultan seriously believe, at this crucial moment in his country's history, that his Government was less capable of defending its rights than a half-wit? Izzet and the rest of the Cabinet supported him and a message was sent out to Damad Ferid that he need wait no longer. The Sultan was obliged to accept the decision. Rauf himself was chosen as delegate in Damad Ferid's place. He proceeded with his delegation to the island of Lemnos where HMS *Agamemnon*, the temporary flagship of Admiral Calthorpe, was anchored off Mudros.

The negotiations were conducted on board in a gentlemanly atmosphere. They lasted for thirty-six hours. They covered only military and naval clauses. Rauf loyally contested them point by point. Admiral Calthorpe, as one sailor to another, was conciliatory. Within twenty-four hours initial agreement had been reached, subject to confirmation from Constantinople. The main provisions demanded by the British were the opening of the Dardanelles and the Bosporus; the Allied occupation of all important strategic points; the demobilization of the Turkish army apart from troops needed to police frontiers and keep internal order; the surrender of all Turkish garrisons in the occupied territories – but not, in specific terms, the surrender of its arms. The Turks proved sensitive to any suggestion of interference with their internal affairs, and were especially concerned lest these terms involve the occupation of Constantinople. But they were assured that there was no question of this unless they themselves failed to maintain order and it became necessary for the Allies to protect their own subjects.

In the middle of the conference there came a sharp request from the French that they be represented, through Admiral Amet, their man on the spot. This was refused on the grounds that the Turks were accredited to the British delegation only. Lately the French had concluded an armistice with the Bulgarians without consulting the British. The main reason, however, for now excluding them was the fear of delay through their insistence on reference to Paris. This was obviated by a high level approach to Clemenceau, who agreed in advance to the British terms and to the proposal that a British admiral should command in the Bosporus.

Thus the Armistice was signed on 30th October, with compliments all round, and an accompanying unofficial letter from Admiral Calthorpe, interpreting and amplifying some of its terms. Calthorpe remarked after

signature, 'By signing this Armistice I hope we shall put an end to this
bloodshed which has been going on for so many years.' He shook Rauf by
the hand and confirmed his 'ardent desire' for friendly Anglo-Turkish relations. He assured him that Britain was always loyal to her signature and
turned to his staff, who confirmed the assurance. Every clause would be
carefully and meticulously respected. Rauf, in replying, expressed a hope
that Britain would now send to Turkey a representative of the highest
attainments, since he was anxious that Great Britain should occupy an
'unrivalled position' in the country.

Kemal, when he received the news of the Armistice and the order to
cease fire, was still resisting with his forces in the hills behind Aleppo. 'In
the fighting of the last few days,' wrote Liman von Sanders, 'the army held
high the honour of its arms.' Thus, after four long disastrous years of war,
Kemal emerged from the general carnage as the only Turkish commander
without a defeat to his name.

The Armistice, for Kemal, was not an end. It was a beginning. Undefeated
in battle he was more than ever undefeated in spirit. There would now be
peace of a kind. But he knew that a just peace would have to be fought for,
and that the struggle would be hard and long. He began to envisage himself
as a leader in this struggle.

Just how this would happen he could not yet foresee. For the moment he
was devoured by frustration. He deeply resented Izzet's refusal to appoint
him Minister of War and was not mollified by his promise that they would
work together 'after the peace'. A critical interim period must elapse during
which he felt capable of rendering valuable services to his country. As for
the period that followed, there would be others more suited than he to
become Minister of War. He continued to agitate for the post. He sent an
emissary to Rauf, begging him to press his claims further. But Rauf had
to reply that there was nothing to be done for the moment. He bombarded
Izzet with insubordinate telegrams. When Izzet appointed a new Chief of
the General Staff, he protested that he would refuse to obey him.

Meanwhile, he had received orders to take over the command of the
army group from Liman von Sanders. He immediately hurried to its headquarters at Adana. The German general received him with his usual punctilious reserve. But there was a note of sincere regret in his voice as he said his
farewells.

'Your Excellency,' he said, 'I have known you at close quarters when
you were commanding at the front, at Ariburnu and the Anafartas. To tell
the truth, there have been certain vicissitudes and incidents between us;
but when all is said and done they have only helped us to know one another
better. I think we have become sincere friends. Today, at the moment when
I am obliged to leave Turkey, I confide the armies under my orders to an

officer whom I have been in a position to appreciate ever since my arrival in this country. In this general catastrophe how can one help feeling a great weight of sorrow? Only one thing consoles me: the thought that I am leaving the command with you. From this moment onwards, it is you who are the master: I am your guest.'

Moved by his words, Kemal said simply, 'Let us sit down.' They lit cigarettes. At Kemal's request von Sanders ordered two cups of coffee. They sat and drank them in silence, facing one another and reflecting on the past and the future. That night the sky over Adana was lit by flames from the dumps of material which the Germans had fired. At a farewell party of German and Turkish officers, a German general paid a tribute to their mutual companionship in arms, concluding, 'We are defeated. All is over for us now.' Kemal, in his own speech of farewell, concluded, 'The war may be over for our Allies, but the war which concerns us, for our own independence, begins from this moment.'

Despite his rebuff from Izzet, it was with a certain elation that Kemal thus took over the post of commander of all the troops in Southern Turkey. Now that the war was over such a command might not seem to offer him serious scope. Demobilization, under the Armistice terms, was imminent. On the other hand it gave him a political advantage. It put him for the first time in direct official touch with the Constantinople Government. Since it was a Government favourably disposed to him in principle, he should now at least be able to make himself heard and perhaps influence policy. His enemies were gone; his friends were in power. At long last he saw a prospect of achieving those political ambitions which had eluded him throughout the past decade.

In the military field too there was something to be done. For the time being at least he had two armies directly under him, the Second and the Seventh, whose ostensible task under the Armistice was to patrol the frontier. Handing it over meanwhile to Ali Fuad, he set to work at once to ensure that it should be no mere local token army but an effective national defence force. He reassembled and regrouped his units, dispersing forces to stations in the interior, transferring arms, ammunition and stores to places of safety, and giving the necessary directions to the commanders concerned. These he sorted out and selected with care, removing a number of officers who did not share his militant views. He established a close liaison with the neighbouring Sixth Army at Mosul, on whose support he hoped to be able to count for an unbroken defence line. Whatever might happen in the immediate future he could at least preserve the nucleus of a self-contained force which, at a later stage, might contribute to the defence not merely of the southern frontier of Turkey but of Turkey as a whole.

Of what was germinating in his mind there were already some signs. Before the Armistice he had chanced to meet one Ali Jenani on his way from the capital to Aintab to see to his family. Already, Ali told him, the town was being plundered, and when the army retired to Adana its inhabitants would be at the enemy's mercy. He planned to evacuate his family to some safer place. Kemal said to him, 'Are there no men left in the country? You should find some way of defending yourselves.'

'But how? With what?'

'Organize yourselves. Recruit a national force. I will give you the necessary arms.'

His loyal officers were enjoined to 'get ready, in groups, for guerilla fighting'. Irregular bands must be formed to resist enemy encroachment on the territory of Turkey itself. With an eye on the future he doled out arms to various possible centres of resistance in the interior, such as Aintab and Marash, to be stored in secret until the time came to make use of them.

For the moment his task was to fight, without quarter, the terms of the Armistice itself. He saw it as an unconditional surrender, and worse. Here were Turks promising to help the enemy to take over their own country. He determined to convince the Cabinet that, in giving in to all the demands of the powers, they would see Turkey occupied from one end to the other, until the moment arrived at which the enemy would be forming the Cabinet itself. 'One did not need to be a sorcerer to see that,' he said later.

Kemal thus embarked on an impatient interchange of telegrams with Izzet, in which a number of pertinent queries were raised. He was especially concerned about the clause demanding the withdrawal of all Turkish garrisons from Syria. Where, by this definition, was the frontier of Syria? Did it follow the line of the mountains behind Aleppo, the long-accepted northern boundary of the Ottoman province of Syria? Or was it to be prolonged down into Cilicia, to include the port of Alexandretta? The enemy were now claiming that its garrison, the Seventh Army, was stationed in Syria, hence liable to surrender.

It was clear to Kemal that here was an ambiguity which the British were deliberately exploiting. 'It is my sincere and frank opinion,' he wrote, 'that if we demobilize our troops and give in to everything the British want, without taking steps to end misunderstandings and false interpretations of the Armistice, it will be impossible for us to put any sort of brake on Britain's covetous designs.'

Izzet replied that the Armistice did not give the British the right to occupy Alexandretta. Since, however, the railways to the south, with their bridges, had been destroyed during the Turkish retreat, there was a verbal gentleman's agreement that they should be allowed to use the port and the road to Aleppo for the transport of their wounded and supplies to their forces. But the port and city of Alexandretta were to remain under Turkish control. Kemal was requested to inform the British commander accordingly.

In an urgent reply marked 'Penalty of death for delay', Kemal persisted in his objections, arguing that the British armies had access to ample food supplies in Aleppo itself and in the surrounding districts, and that their real purpose was to occupy Alexandretta and thus cut the retreat of the Seventh Army and force it to surrender. He confessed that he did not hold with all this gentlemanly procedure. He was therefore not prepared to pass on Izzet's communication to the English commander. He went further. 'I have,' he wrote, 'given orders that any British attempt to land troops, on any pretext, at Alexandretta shall be opposed by force.' Since, he added, he felt unable to suit his actions to the official views of the High Command, he begged to be relieved of his command as soon as possible.

Izzet replied sharply that this order of his was totally contrary to the policy and interests of the State, and instructed him to cancel it forthwith. Certainly there had been mistakes in the interpretation and execution of the Armistice terms. 'But if, in spite of all this,' he continued, 'we have accepted these unfavourable demands it is not from lack of foresight but as a result of our total defeat. The State is taking diplomatic steps to deal with the present situation and hopes that they will be crowned with success. I sincerely believe that, at this difficult time, I can confidently rely on your handling of these measures and negotiations which are of the highest importance to the future of the State. Since, however, the situation is too critical to admit of argument or delay, the instructions we give to our armies must be carried out to the letter.' He added that Kemal's army group was now to be dissolved as such, and to be reduced to the Seventh Army alone.

Having made his gesture of defiance and protest, Kemal drafted a conciliatory reply. He expressed the hope that the Almighty would smile upon Izzet's political efforts, and gave assurances of his loyalty to him and to the country. His misgivings, however, were wholly justified by events. Izzet was being sorely pressed by the British. Rauf, mindful of their undertakings to honour their signature, was protesting about this to Calthorpe, and Calthorpe, mindful of them too, was protesting to London. The gentlemanly atmosphere which the two old sailors had achieved on the decks of HMS *Agamemnon* was dissipating all too quickly in Whitehall. The old soldiers and the old politicians, for once but not for long in concord, had a more ruthless approach to the Armistice. They were determined to read into it and take out of it just what suited them. Alexandretta was one strategic point they wanted; another was Mosul, as indeed Kemal had been quick to observe in one of his telegrams.

When the Armistice was signed, the British troops, pursuing the Turks up the Tigris, were still forty miles south of Mosul. On the instructions of the War Cabinet they pushed on and entered it three days later. The commanding general demanded the surrender of the city and the Sixth Army which garrisoned it. Rauf protested that the occupation was contrary to the terms of the Armistice as interpreted to him by Calthorpe. 'The Turkish Government,' he added, 'are sure the Commander-in-Chief will keep his word.'

The admiral hoped he could be as sure. He telegraphed to London, upholding Rauf's point of view as reflecting his own. But the War Office was adamant, pointing out that on the Turkish General Staff map Mosul figured in Mesopotamia, not Turkey. Calthorpe had to yield. Thus the evacuation of Mosul, and the surrender of its arms, was ordered. Izzet, in his acknowledgement of the order, hastened, a shade obsequiously, to assure the admiral that he had received his telegram at 8.00 p.m. and had passed on his own orders to Mosul 'at nearly the same hour'.

With Alexandretta the story was similar. Calthorpe was overruled by London, as Kemal was overruled by Izzet. The British Government demanded the cession of Alexandretta, within a stated time, to General Allenby, who would otherwise resort to force. Izzet again gave in, and the Seventh Army was forced to withdraw. For this drastic move by the British he implied that the blame lay with the stiff and discourteous attitude of the Turkish commander towards their requests. 'In the higher interests of the country,' he instructed, 'it is essential that we remember how weak we are, and that we be circumspect in our words and actions, without, none the less, demeaning ourselves too far.'

Kemal hotly contested Izzet's implication, and insisted: 'I know very well just how weak and powerless we are. That does not alter my conviction that we must decide upon a limit to the sacrifices which the State is obliged to accept. Otherwise if we ourselves, completely defeated in a war fought to a finish at Germany's side, help the British to secure the advantages which they are already preparing to get without us, we shall be adding a very sombre page to the history of the Ottomans in general and of the present Government in particular.'

The Seventh Army was none the less abolished, and Kemal was left with a single army corps on which to build his hopes for a national defence force.

CHAPTER SEVENTEEN

THE SULTAN DISSOLVES PARLIAMENT

CONSTANTINOPLE, under Allied 'protection', was listless, defeatist, fraught with a sense of doom. 'They'll do to us whatever they want,' was the general foreboding. It was to be a cold, dark winter. There was no coal to be had. The trams were not running, the Bosporus steamers were few and far between. The main streets were lit dimly, the side streets not at all, so that criminals prospered and no citizen would stir out at night without a pistol in his pocket.[1] The police were scarce, moreover corrupt and universally mistrusted. Profiteering was shameless, the currency valueless, the prices of foodstuffs exorbitantly high. Turks shut themselves up in their houses, emerging, shadows of themselves, only to buy bread, perhaps at half a crown a loaf. Some even pretended they were not Turks at all, shed their fezes and tried to get jobs with the Allied forces which had moved into the city.

Greeks, on the other hand, swaggered through the streets, jostling the Turks to the wall. They flaunted the blue-and-white flag from their head-quarters and expected the Turks to salute it, driving them to slink down the side streets to avoid the disgrace. One day a panic rumour spread through Stamboul: 'They are putting the bells into Santa Sophia.' A Moslem crowd surged in hysterical waves up to the mosque, to breathe again when they found the Turkish troops still guarding the courtyard.

Towards the middle of November the Allies moved in. With formal pomp and ceremony Admiral Calthorpe led a sixteen-mile convoy of British and other Allied warships through the Dardanelles and into the Bosporus. Here they anchored off the Golden Horn, so closely congested that the water could scarcely be seen between their decks. It was another black day for the Turks when General Franchet d'Espérey made a triumphal entry into the city at the head of his troops, riding without reins on a white horse, and thus aspiring to lay the spectre of Fatih, the Moslem Conqueror of

[1] 'If you see me in the dark never greet me,' was a typical counsel from one friend to another. 'Something might happen.'

Byzantium, who had done the same. Soon the French were established in Stambul, the British across the water in Pera, the Italians up the Bosporus. Technically they did not 'occupy' the city since the Turks retained, at least in theory, political and administrative control. But to the average Turk it was an occupation in all but name.

The political situation was intricate. The flight of the members of the Triumvirate had caused a crisis in Parliament. The deputies of the party of Union and Progress, seeking to save their own skins and conveniently forgetting their collective responsibility for Turkey's entry into the war, now turned on the former ministers and demanded their trial. Three of Izzet's own ministers, formerly involved with the party, were attacked with them: Javid, his Minister of Finance, who had in fact resigned from the Cabinet over the declaration of war; the Sheikh of Islam, who had approved it; and Fethi, who had been secretary-general of the party in 1913.

This situation was now exploited by the Sultan as a means of establishing his own personal power. He sent Ahmed Riza, the President of the Senate, to Izzet, requesting the resignation of the three ministers or, alternatively, that of the Cabinet and the formation of a new one in which they would not be included. Izzet refused, putting forward, with the backing of Fethi and Rauf, the constitutional argument that the Sultan had the right only to give opinions, not to make demands, that he had no personal responsibility but could only respect the collective responsibility of his ministers.

In his frank way Rauf took the opportunity to give the Sultan a warning, when summoned to report to him on the Armistice terms and on Calthorpe's accompanying unofficial letter. Calthorpe, he explained, had promised that there would be no full occupation of Constantinople unless law and order broke down and the lives of Allied subjects were endangered. Just such disorders might now arise from the fact that Damad Ferid, a man known only as a relative of the Sultan, was making mischief against his Government, accusing it of plotting massacres of Greeks, and thus creating disunity and conflict. Rauf went on to refer with telling emphasis to the unrest in Bulgaria and Austria since the Armistice, which had brought only misfortune to their rulers.

At this the Sultan grew excited. His hands began to tremble and his cigarette fell from its holder, to be picked up by his chamberlain and placed in an ashtray. He disclaimed any sympathy with his relative's opinions. Then he stood up, indicating that the audience was over. He looked at Rauf with a glance full of meaning, and said with some harshness, 'Sir, we have a nation here that is a herd of sheep. It has to have a shepherd. I am that shepherd.'

Rauf said nothing, but lifted his right hand in a reluctant salute and departed. It was all too evident that the Sultan, in the role of shepherd, meant to herd his sheep together and lead them into the fold of the Allies.

Next day he reported to the Cabinet. Izzet was sick. Moreover, a fighter by profession on the battlefield, he was a fighter only up to a certain point in the political arena. Least of all was he equipped by either temperament or tradition for a fight against his legitimate sovereign. At this moment, with the Allied fleets on the Bosporus, he considered it important to preserve unity and avoid any political crisis. Even if the Sultan gave in on this issue there would be further such conflicts in the future. His only course, as he saw it, was to resign with his Cabinet, on the grounds of the Sultan's unconstitutional attitude. His other ministers had little choice but to agree.

The Sultan accepted their resignation. Taking leave of Izzet, he remarked, 'I am ill. I can't look out of the window. I hate to see them.' He nodded towards the ships in the Bosporus. Thus was to end, after little more than a month in office, the last Ottoman Government which genuinely sought to establish, in the country's real interest, a democratic and liberal régime.

One last bid was made to retrieve the position. It was animated largely by Mustafa Kemal who, in a fighting spirit, at once took the train from Adana to Constantinople. His arrival in the city coincided with that of the British fleet. The spectacle angered him, but prompted the philosophic reflection, 'As they have come, so they shall go.'

With Rauf he went directly to see Izzet and set to work to argue him out of his decision. The Sultan had replaced him with the reluctant Tevfik Pasha, overriding his complaint that he was for ever being called in as Grand Vizier, to clear up the mess made by others. But his appointment had still to be confirmed by Parliament. Kemal therefore persuaded Izzet to accept nomination again and to form a new Cabinet of a stronger and more Nationalist complexion. Rauf, after some hesitation, supported him. Together they drafted out a ministerial list in which Kemal's own name was at last prominent. They then mobilized all their resources to achieve, by assiduous lobbying of deputies, the defeat in Parliament of the vote of confidence in Tevfik.

This was Kemal's first direct experience of Parliament and its ways. Changing into civilian clothes he circulated actively in the lobbies and committee rooms. Many members, he found, were hostile to Tevfik but preferred to vote for him rather than risk a dissolution of Parliament. They would thus at least gain time. Kemal, with his more realistic sense, argued that a dissolution was inevitable whichever way they voted, and could be used to gain time for Izzet. Through Fethi he was enabled to address a meeting of members. He put forward his views to them with eloquence and force, urging them to vote their lack of confidence in Tevfik, whatever might follow. They listened with interest and apparent sympathy to this young victorious general, with the compelling eyes and the confident voice, so neat in his civilian clothes, so emphatic and frank in his speech. Some gave him definite promises and, when the division bell rang, expressed hopes of a successful outcome.

Kemal found a place in the gallery and watched the proceedings. The vote was taken, the ballot was counted, the President announced the result. It showed a large majority for Tevfik Pasha's Cabinet. Kemal confessed himself taken aback. An appreciable number of members seemed to have accepted his proposal. As a soldier, thus a stranger to Parliamentary life, he confessed his surprise at the fickle nature of their opinions. Unsure of their position, and mistrustful of the military element, they had preferred the line of least resistance.

Kemal interpreted the vote as the defeat of the national will. Only the will of the Sultan now reigned. Here he saw his one remaining chance. He applied for an immediate audience, for the purpose, as he put it, of explaining frankly to the Sultan what measures the situation demanded. After a delay of some days he was bidden to the *Selamlik*. Vahid-ed-Din took the initiative. 'I am convinced,' he said, 'that the commanders and other officers of the army respect you greatly. Can you give me a guarantee that they will take no action against me?' This point-blank question took Kemal by surprise. On reflection he said, 'Has your Majesty specific knowledge of any army movement directed against the throne?'

Vahid-ed-Din shut his eyes. Then he repeated his question.

Kemal replied, 'I must explain that I have only been in Constantinople for a few days, and I am not very familiar with the situation, but I do not consider that there can be any motive for the commanders and officers of the army to set themselves against your Majesty. Accordingly I can assure you that you have nothing to fear.'

The Sultan put on a solemn expression and said, 'I am not speaking only of today, but of tomorrow as well.'

The Sultan, Kemal judged, had decided on a policy which might displease the army, and was sounding him as to his reactions towards it. This being so, he could hardly press his own proposals without compromising himself and his cause. Vahid-ed-Din had effectively muzzled him. Kemal thus kept silent, and the Sultan, reopening his eyes, concluded, 'You are an intelligent officer, and I am sure you will know how to enlighten and calm your comrades.'

The audience, though little enough had emerged from it, had lasted an hour. On reappearing in the ante-room, Kemal thus received significant and questioning looks. Ironically, it was generally believed that he had promised the Sultan the support of the army for a dissolution of Parliament, as a prelude to a régime in which he and his military friends would predominate. He could have hoped for nothing better. But the Sultan's decision was otherwise. He did indeed plan to dissolve Parliament. His motive in doing so, however, was to please not the army but the Allies. The Sultan had elected to throw in his lot with the occupying powers.

Kemal, since it no longer suited his purposes, now came out in strong opposition to the dissolution of Parliament. He had a platform in Fethi's newspaper *Mimber* and now, posing as a champion of constitutional practice, he warned his countrymen of the dangers that threatened them. A dissolution would leave the Government free to do what it wanted; and what it wanted was co-operation with the enemy:

> Let us remember that the symbol of the Constitution of the Ottoman nation today is Parliament. The constituencies of its present members are still in a state of emergency, which rules out new elections. This alone should show us the madness of dissolving Parliament. It is essential that the present Government, which will decide on the peace terms, should have the support of the deputies.

But the Sultan was determined to rid himself of 'this cursed Parliament'. In consultation with Tevfik and his legal advisers, he found a pretext for doing so among the various contradictory articles of the Constitution. The dissolution, by right of Article 7, was proclaimed in a *firman* read out in the Chamber by the Minister of the Interior. It caused considerable hubbub. Members cried out in protest, started to speak all at once and in shrill contradiction of each other. Many protested against the Sultan's action. But since most of them had backed the vote of confidence in Tevfik they were not on strong ground. Thus the *firman* was executed. The deputies dispersed.

The Sultan, true in his own pale fashion to the tradition of his brother Abdul Hamid, had for the moment vanquished the forces of democracy.

CHAPTER EIGHTEEN

THE PARTITION OF TURKEY?

WHAT, under the auspices of its Sultan, was now to become of the relics of the Ottoman Empire? The Peace Conference, assembling in Paris in January 1919, aspired to decide its destiny. The Turks, in applying for an Armistice, had notified President Wilson that they were ready to treat for peace on the basis of his Fourteen Points – namely the principle of consent. Lord Curzon, the British Foreign Secretary, now produced, in a memorandum to the Cabinet, a solution based, as he saw it, on this principle. It allowed the right of self-determination not merely to the Arabs and Armenians – the subject races of the Empire – but to the Turks themselves. Besides an independent Arabia and Armenia there should be an independent Turkish state, confined, as it had been in the past, within the boundaries of Asia Minor, and with its capital at Angora or Brusa. Only thus, Lord Curzon foresaw, could the aspirations of the Turks be satisfied in such a way as to forestall a Nationalist outbreak.

On the other hand, Curzon wanted to remove the Turks altogether from Europe, where they had been for centuries 'a source of distraction, intrigue and corruption . . . of unmitigated evil to everybody concerned'. Thus they should be deprived of Constantinople and the Straits, which should be entrusted to the League of Nations. This was a solution which, at this psychological moment, might well have been accepted by a weak Turkish Government.

It was not, however, accepted by the British Government. For Lloyd George, with whom Curzon was in perennial conflict, had different ideas. These arose from the need to keep in harmony with the other Allies, France and Italy, on other more vital problems. With his ignorance of the Middle East and indifference to its problems, he saw Turkey not as a living organism with a past and a present and aspirations for a future, but simply as a space on the map, a convenient repository from which other powers might be compensated and other concessions obtained in return.

Here the British Government was already committed to four secret agreements, contracted during the war as bribes or rewards to her Allies for entering it. Under these the Entente powers now planned, in effect, to carve up Turkey in Asia just as the Central Powers and their satellites had carved up Turkey in Europe during the Balkan Wars. The first allowed Constantinople, Eastern Thrace, and the Straits to the Russians, in return for a British sphere of influence in Persia. This was no longer in force since the Soviet Government had renounced all such Tsarist claims. The second – the Sykes-Picot agreement – partitioned the greater part of the Arab world between France and Britain, allowing Mesopotamia to the British and Syria and Cilicia to the French. The third and fourth allowed the Italians a still larger portion of Asia Minor, namely the province of Adalia, to the west of Cilicia, the Dodecanese Islands, and the port of Smyrna, with much of its hinterland. This would have left almost the whole length of the Mediterranean and Aegean coasts of Asia Minor, together with a substantial share of the interior, in the hands of France and Italy. It would have reduced the Turkish state to a few provinces in Anatolia, with access to the Black Sea coast but only a single outlet to the Aegean.

But the crucial – and, it turned out, fatal – element in this scheme for dismemberment was the mounting ambition of the Greeks. As an inducement to come into the war, Sir Edward Grey had, early in 1915, offered Greece 'large concessions on the coast of Asia Minor'. These were in principle accepted by Venizelos, her Premier, who began to play with the traditional 'Grand Idea' of 'a really big Greece, to include practically all the regions in which the influence of Hellenism has been paramount throughout the ages'. But a neutralist policy prevailed, Venizelos resigned, and it was not until 1917, when he returned to power on the expulsion of King Constantine by the Allies, that Greece in fact came into the war.

As soon as it was over he approached Lloyd George with a Greek claim to the whole Aegean coast of Asia Minor and much of its hinterland – a territory already promised to the Italians. He based this largely on the ethnical argument that the Greek population formed a majority in the area. Similar arguments applied to the Greeks of Pontus, in the Black Sea mountains. Venizelos thus invoked those principles of self-determination on which the peace was to be based. Two months later, in fluent French, and with an 'engaging appearance of frankness', he put his case before the Supreme Council of the Peace Conference in Paris.

To Lloyd George, who considered Venizelos 'the greatest statesman Greece had thrown up since the days of Pericles', such a demand seemed both fair and expedient. The Greeks could serve Britain's interests by replacing the Turks as the protectors of her imperial communications with India. Thus, despite Lord Curzon and the Foreign Office, who preferred to compensate the Greeks in Thrace; despite doubts from the generals as to the military feasibility of Greek penetration inland; despite the claims of the Italians, which he brushed aside; despite the opposition, on the very grounds of self-determination which Venizelos had invoked, of President Wilson – despite all these powerful factors, Lloyd George resolved to give his whole-hearted support to the claims of the Greeks in Asia Minor.

Such was the trend of the peace terms which the Allies were planning to impose on the Turks, and which the Sultan was prepared to facilitate; such were the prospects that confronted Kemal as he settled down in Constantinople on his return from Cilicia – a general out of a job. Irked by the restrictions of his mother's household he rented a tall roomy house for himself in the district of Shishli. Here he was able to enjoy visits from his cousin Fikriye, now divorced from an Egyptian husband to whom the family had married her off. His interest in her had been aroused largely by her own evident feelings towards him, her hero-worship turning to love. Now, free in his own house from the disapproving presence of Zübeyde, she shed all inhibitions, and a close intimacy developed between them.

After the dissolution of Parliament a sense of defeat weighed on Kemal and his friends. Pessimism infected them; frustration confined them. Rauf became pained and disillusioned at the ungentlemanly actions of his friends the British, and hardened against them. Fethi, in his Opposition newspaper, launched a campaign against Tevfik, whose Cabinet, at this moment when a strong Government was needed, he denounced as nothing but a silent spectator of the country's catastrophe. Kemal invested some of his savings in the paper, and worked with Fethi in its offices, hoping to influence opinion by his anonymous pen.

In the large room on the first floor of his house in Shishli the three friends talked and plotted to find a way out for their country. They formed in effect a secret revolutionary committee, whose aim was to force the resignation of the Government, to form a new one, if necessary to dethrone the Sultan. But one at least of their confederates found Kemal too extreme. He feared the risk involved and the committee was disbanded. Maybe, after all, revolution was not the answer, for any attempt at it would immediately be suppressed by the Allies.

Perhaps, it occurred to Kemal, something could be achieved through the Allies themselves. With his compelling presence and his immaculate uniform, emblazoned with medals and with the insignia of an ADC to the Sultan, he was already a conspicuous figure in the Pera Palace Hotel, its mock-Oriental marble halls now teeming with officers in the occupying forces and in the Inter-Allied High Commission. He attracted their curiosity as soon as it became known that he was the hero of the Dardanelles. At first he chose to keep his distance.

But now he began to see that some contact with the Allies might serve his designs. They were, after all, in virtual control of the country. The French had landed in Alexandretta and were pressing forward into Cilicia. The Italians were about to land at Adalia, thence likewise to penetrate inland. The British had control officers scattered over Turkey from Thrace to the Caucasus, supervising demobilization and disarmament. The Sultan was in power, and unlikely to give Kemal a post of any consequence in the dwindling Turkish army. For what he sought – and this was just such a national resurgence as Curzon feared – any position of authority was better than none. Might he not obtain some post from the Allies themselves – preferably the British, who had no ultimate territorial designs on the country? Power obtained under their auspices, now that they had come, might well be turned into other and more patriotic channels once they had gone.

Deciding to sound them out indirectly, he chose as intermediary a British correspondent of repute, G. Ward Price, of the *Daily Mail*. Through the manager of the Pera Palace Hotel, he sent the correspondent an invitation to take coffee with him. After consulting the responsible colonel in the Intelligence Branch of the General Staff, Mr Ward Price accepted. He found Kemal not in uniform but in a frock-coat and fez. He struck him as handsome and virile, restrained in gestures, quiet and deliberate in voice. He was accompanied by his friend Refet.

Kemal confessed to him that his country had joined the wrong side in the war. The Turks should never have quarrelled with the British. They had done so as a result of Enver's pressure. They had lost – and now they must pay heavily. Anatolia was to be divided. Kemal was anxious that the French should be kept out of the country. A British administration would be less unpopular.

'If the British,' he said, 'are going to assume the responsibility for Anatolia, they will need the co-operation of experienced Turkish governors to work under them. What I want to know is the proper quarter to which I can offer my services in that capacity.'

Ward Price gave the staff colonel an account of the interview. He dismissed it as unimportant, remarking, 'There will be a lot of these Turkish generals looking for jobs before long.'

The Italians, on the other hand, took the initiative with direct overtures towards Kemal. Count Sforza, the Italian High Commissioner, was implacably opposed to Lloyd George's support of the Greeks. While committed to a united front on the policy of partitioning Turkey, he was crafty enough to re-insure, in the event of its probable failure, with the Nationalist movement, whose leaders impressed him as 'sincerely conscious of a force of their own'.

One of his emissaries sounded Kemal and Fethi on the prospects of their forming a Nationalist government. Two others – Turkish journalists favourable to the Italian cause – dangled an offer of armed support for a military

Resistance against the Greeks behind Smyrna, under Kemal's command. When the ground had been prepared, Kemal was invited to meet Count Sforza himself. The Count made it clear to him that whatever he did he could rely on Italian support. 'You may be sure,' he said, 'that, if you are in trouble, this Embassy is at your disposal.' Kemal was reserved in his reply. But he was astute enough to see that Italian support might be of use to him if and when his schemes matured.

Meanwhile, Allenby had paid a whirlwind visit to Constantinople from Palestine. Certain Turkish generals were showing reluctance to disband their forces according to his interpretation of the Armistice terms. Allenby summoned the Ministers of War and of Foreign Affairs and, without giving them the chance to negotiate, read them out a list of demands, which included the removal of the chief offender, the commander of the Sixth Army on the Mosul front. Having achieved his objective within five minutes, Allenby returned at once to Palestine and the offending army commander, on his return to Constantinople, was arrested by the British authorities.

Soon after Allenby's visit – and, he judged, as a result of it – Kemal was notified by the War Ministry of a reduction in his status as an army commander. He was deprived of his privileges as an ADC to the Sultan. His official car was withdrawn from him, and his salary reduced. He was offered no less a command than that of the Sixth Army, which was to be disbanded following its commander's recall. He instantly refused it. He was thus, more than ever, on the shelf.

At the end of February 1919 the Sultan changed his Government. He judged that the moment had come for the scheme which he had planned from the start. He released Tevfik, who had tried several times to resign, and made his own despised brother-in-law, Damad Ferid, Grand Vizier. It was Ferid's first official post since that of First Secretary in the Foreign Service thirty years before. To the patriotic Turk he was a nonentity, a man devoid of capacity. But to the British Ferid, with his reassuring Western appearance, his drooping moustaches, his veneer of European culture and his polite pompous manners, was 'a typical Turkish gentleman'. He was just the puppet they needed.

Determined to wipe out opposition his first action was to launch a new wave of arrests. He did so with the backing of the British authorities, who had begun to deport political and military suspects to Malta. Already Tevfik, in response to foreign demands, had imprisoned the remaining members of the Unionist Government. Now Ferid's Ministry of the Interior embarked on a further purge, using summary methods of trial by court martial. Fethi was singled out as one of his victims. A pre-war secretary-general of the party, he had been unjustly blamed by his enemies, as a post-war Minister of the Interior, for allowing the escape of Enver, Talat and Jemal. Kemal got wind of the fact that he was likely to be arrested and urged him not to return home. Fethi, in his casual way, made light of the warning. Ferid, he said, had assured him that he was in no danger. But he was arrested that night when he returned to his house.

Kemal contrived to pay him a visit in the War Ministry prison, feeling like a prisoner himself in its grim surroundings, taking the precaution to shake hands with the *gendarmes* he met on the staircase. For they might well, as he drily observed, be of use to him if he himself were arrested. He found his friends on the top floor, in cells facing each other along a dark narrow passage. Here were ministers, politicians, journalists, public men of importance – all treated as war criminals. As he opened the doors of the cells, they gathered around him, eager to talk. Prince Said Halim was among them, the Grand Vizier of the early war years. With Fethi, Kemal went up on to the roof, where they walked and talked. But Kemal felt they were being spied upon, and thought it prudent not to stay for too long.

He began to fear for his own security, starting a little at each ring at the doorbell, late at night. A newspaper enquired why, with the Unionists under arrest, Mustafa Kemal and Rauf were still 'walking about freely in Pera, swinging their arms'. Kemal cultivated his Italian contacts, suspecting that if he were known to be under Count Sforza's protection the British might hesitate to order his arrest.

Indignation at the arrests helped to stir national feelings, and a number of vague political groups, of a liberal complexion, gathered together in a house in the old quarter of Stambul, with the aspiration of uniting in some kind of a 'National Congress'. They did little, however, but talk. Kemal and Rauf, with their more positive views and plans, trod circumspectly among them. They found goodwill enough. But few, even among their own supporters, proved capable of translating it into concrete ideas, far less into plans of action, while many, demoralized by the irksome conditions of the Allied occupation, were preoccupied mainly with their personal interests and rivalries.

The solution clearly lay elsewhere. A possible way to it was shown by Ali Fuad, who returned on sick-leave from Cilicia, following the demobilization of the Seventh Army. On arrival he went straight to see Kemal at the house in Shishli, and spent the night there, as he was to spend many nights during the next few weeks. Kemal appeared in a dressing-gown, for he had been lying ill in bed, this time with ear trouble. He took Fuad into his bedroom, where piles of newspapers lay by the bedside. He put him into an armchair and himself sat on the bed. They talked, then dined, then talked again for half the night.

Fuad gave him gloomy accounts of the general insecurity and administrative paralysis throughout Anatolia. The local administration was inert and inefficient. There was no unity between the local political parties. Kemal frowned and said, 'Not good at all.' To both it was clear that the

Allies were bent on occupying most of the country and that the Government lacked both the capacity and the will to resist them. The Allies were hastening demobilization and the collection of arms. Efficient men were being dismissed from the administration and from the army on the grounds that they were Union and Progress supporters, and were being replaced by yesmen, ready to submit to the Allies. The only solution was a movement of national Resistance, for which they drew up a programme.

It could be realized only in one of two ways – from without, by forcing the Government to resign, or from within, by introducing into the Ministry of War and the Ministry of the Interior partisans of the Resistance. The first having proved impossible, it was now time to try the second. Kemal himself, of course, should be Minister of War. A suitable candidate for the Ministry of Interior would be Mehmed Ali, a friend of Fuad and his family and an influential figure in Damad Ferid's coalition. Through such as he, they might be able to achieve their designs by a process not of revolution but of infiltration.

Fuad spoke of Kemal to Mehmed Ali, who already knew of him by repute as an intelligent, energetic and patriotic young officer. On being reassured that he was not a Union and Progress man, he said that it would be an honour to meet him, and a dinner was arranged at Ali Fuad's home on the Asiatic shores of the Bosporus. Mehmed Ali explained that he was out for a Government in which his own group, which was gaining in influence, predominated. He feared however that the key portfolios of the Ministry of War and of the Interior would be given to men personally trusted by Damad Ferid. Thus the process of bringing new Nationalist blood into the régime had its difficulties.

Kemal discreetly cultivated contacts among the Cabinet ministers. Some, knowing him to have been an opponent of Talat and Enver, showed signs of wanting to win him over. One of them was Avni Pasha, the Minister of Marine, who showed however no disposition to overthrow the Government. Another was Ahmed Riza, the President of the Senate, who was exploiting his influence with the Sultan in the hope of succeeding Damad Ferid. At a secret rendezvous with Kemal he discussed the idea of forming some kind of a national *bloc*. But Kemal remained cautious and non-committal; and indeed nothing came of Ahmed Riza's intrigues. Damad Ferid remained firmly in power.

Clearly it was not going to be easy to undermine the Government from within. The key to the situation lay in Anatolia itself; the problem was how to get there. Ali Fuad's period of leave was now over, and the time came for him to rejoin his army corps, the only remaining unit of Kemal's former army. With Kemal, whom he still regarded as his commander, he agreed to transfer his headquarters northwards to Angora, a central position suited to become the pivot of any Resistance. At the moment it was difficult to do so, since the Italians controlled the railway. But if necessary he would march his troops there. He urged Kemal to join him.

With Rauf, they had a last dinner together in Shishli. They spoke of the Resistance as though it were a hard fact rather than a vague aspiration. It would not be easy for Rauf, as a naval officer, to get to Anatolia. But he was prepared to resign his commission to do so. As for Kemal, he would do all he could to secure a post for himself in Anatolia with sufficient authority. If nothing materialized, he would pass there of his own accord.

Rauf applied to the Minister of Marine for his release from the navy. He was summoned by Damad Ferid, whom he visited wearing civilian clothes. Ferid asked him to change his decision. Rauf spoke to him openly. If the Government continued on its present track, he declared, the army would rebel against it. He dwelt on the plight of the demobilized troops. The Government was contracted to send them home, but did not do so. They were left stranded without shelter or food. They were to be seen begging from the foreigners in the streets of the city. These men, who had fought for their country through fire and bloodshed, were now condemned to a state of misery worse than death. All this would lead to rebellion.

Unused to such glimpses of reality, Ferid muttered, 'How's that? What's this?'

Rauf continued, 'I only tell you what I have seen with my own eyes. I have seen all the revolutions which have taken place in this country, before the Constitution and since. . . . As a man who knows these things I tell you that there is bound to be a rebellion. I don't want to take part in that rebellion as a member of the forces. . . . I want to get rid of all official titles and privileges and be free to act on my own responsibility.'

Ferid looked at him in blank amazement. He could only say, 'Very well, sir.' Rauf's resignation from the navy took effect.

Kemal invited Ismet to the house in Shishli, where they greeted one another as old friends. Ismet was working in the War Ministry, in an Under-Secretary's post, preparing material for the Peace Conference and hoping to be sent to Paris as a member of the Turkish delegation. He greeted Kemal with a twinkle, saying, 'What's the news? What are you up to?'

In reply Kemal brought out a map of Turkey. Ismet, the trained staff officer, instinctively brought out a pair of compasses. Kemal asked his advice as to the best way to reach Anatolia. What would be the appropriate district to choose from which to organize some kind of Resistance?

Ismet looked at him with an air of gay anticipation. 'Then you have made up your mind?'

'We won't talk about that yet,' said Kemal.

Ismet sat over the map, in thoughtful silence. He then got up and said cautiously, 'There are many ways of getting there, many districts.' He added, smiling, 'When are you going to tell me what you are going to do?'

'When the right time comes,' was the reply.

Kemal was not a man to make a decision of this kind in a hurry. The gamble was a big one; much was at stake. The situation must be coolly examined, from all angles. Time was still needed to lay his plans, to convince his associates, to stiffen their resolve, to clarify in his and their minds the ideological basis on which any resistance must be based. Many people still clung to hopes of a solution through the Sultan's Government, the Allies, the Almighty, or some alternative source. Opinion must evolve and events develop to the point at which it became clear that there was no other way out but resistance.

Then Kiazim Karabekir Pasha arrived from Thrace, where he had been commanding the remnants of an army corps. Heavy and staunch and slow, militarily a fighter of the old Turkish stamp, but politically a convinced and obstinate democrat, Kiazim had been second-in-command to Kemal in the Caucasian campaign. He now visited him in Shishli before returning to the east to take over the command of the Fifteenth Army Corps, which was all that remained of the demobilized army on the Caucasian front. He urged upon Kemal his belief that the salvation of Turkey lay there, in the eastern provinces.

He himself was trusted and liked in those regions, where he had seen so much of his war service. His army was strong, and the people were behind it. All that was needed was positive and vigorous leadership. Kemal must at all costs secure for himself a command in Anatolia. Other patriotic young officers must follow him, officially or otherwise. Once there, he must come to the east. Having laid the foundations of a national Government there, he could return to rally the west, leaving Kiazim in charge in Erzurum. If Kemal could not contrive to come, then Kiazim proposed that he should act on his own. Kemal agreed with his ideas. He promised that he would try to reach him at Erzurum. Kiazim promised that he would prepare the ground for his arrival.

For a revolutionary the outlook in Anatolia was beginning to look hopeful. The spirit of resistance, it became evident, was far more positive here in the interior than in Constantinople. There had been, since December 1918, a spontaneous germination of local Nationalist groups, describing themselves as Defence of Rights Associations, or Anti-Annexation Societies. These were at their strongest in those parts of the country where the foreign threat was most direct. They were strong in Thrace and in Smyrna, in opposition to the Greeks; in Cilicia, where the French had recruited an Armenian legion to help them occupy the country; above all here in the east, where the Allies were projecting an artificial Armenian state, and where moreover the inhabitants were a fighting race, imbued with a lively spirit of independence. It was Kiazim's plan, which Kemal approved, to draw these various eastern groups together, as a basis for a national Government.

Kiazim's visit had been encouraging, even decisive. Kemal was now sure of the support of two Anatolian armies, one in the centre and now one in the east. But one question still remained unanswered. How was he to reach Anatolia? The answer was to be provided, unexpectedly, by the Allies themselves.

CHAPTER NINETEEN

PLANS FOR RESISTANCE

AS SEEN BY the Allies, the unoccupied parts of Anatolia were drifting perilously close to anarchy. Law and order in many districts had in effect ceased to exist. Gangs of brigands held the country to ransom, as they had done in Macedonia before the Balkan Wars. They terrorised the population, ambushed and robbed peaceable travellers, committed murders and barbarous atrocities.

To meet this situation the Allies, short of occupying the whole country as, despite Turkish fears, they had neither the desire nor the means to do, had to rely on the co-operation of the Turkish authorities. They realized that they might well lose this co-operation when the peace terms, inevitably unfavourable to Turkey, were announced. Haunted by memories of a Balkan past they feared massacres, on a large scale, of the Anatolian Christians.

The situation around Smyrna, where the Italians were setting the Turks against the Greeks in pursuit of their own territorial claims, was to some extent covered by the admonitory presence in the harbour of two British warships. The situation behind the port of Samsun, on the Black Sea, where the Greeks had pretensions to establish an independent state of Pontus, was assessed in a report from the local British commander. It was despatched by the High Commission to Damad Ferid, with a demand that his government take instant steps to curb the outrageous Turkish attacks on Greek villages, and to re-establish law and order. This was, they urged, an imperative duty to humanity. They implied that if the Government failed to perform it the Allied forces would be obliged to intervene themselves. Damad Ferid took immediate alarm and sent for his Acting Minister of the Interior. This, as it now happily chanced, was Mehmed Ali, with whom Kemal and Ali Fuad had lately conferred, and who had kept in touch with him since, seeking ways to further Kemal's interests. Here now was his chance.

Damad Ferid asked for his advice as to what should be done. Mehmed

Ali replied that it was clear, from the British report, that the situation could no longer be controlled from Constantinople; nor was the local administration equipped to cope with it. The solution, he suggested, was to send an energetic young officer, whom the Government could trust, to Samsun. His task would be to combine the civil and military elements into an organization strong enough to restore law and order, and thus reassure the British authorities. Damad Ferid asked for the name of a suitable officer. Mehmed Ali suggested Mustafa Kemal.

Damad Ferid hesitated. He had grounds for suspicion about Kemal. On the other hand this might prove a good opportunity to get him safely out of the way. Before deciding, he said, he would like to investigate Kemal's record and to see for himself what kind of a man he was. Mehmed Ali brought the two men together over dinner at the *Cercle d'Orient*, and Kemal took care to make a good impression.

Shortly afterwards he was summoned by the Minister of War, Shakir Pasha, who said that the Grand Vizier thought him a suitable person to go to Anatolia and report on the situation between Turks and Greeks. Kemal replied without hesitation, 'I shall be pleased to go. But is that to be my only duty?'

'Yes, that is what we have decided.'

'Good. But you will allow me to suggest that my appointment should be given proper form. I don't want to trouble you with this. Shall I discuss it with the Chief of the General Staff?'

'Certainly,' the Minister replied. 'Do it that way.'

The Chief of the General Staff at this time was his old friend Fevzi, who had succeeded him, and whom he had later succeeded, in command of the Seventh Army in Syria. But Fevzi was sick. Thus Kemal went instead to the Deputy Chief of the General Staff. Here luck was with him, for this officer, Diyarbekirli Kiazim, was also a friend, and a neighbour in Shishli, to whom he had often confided his ideas.

Kiazim knew nothing of this appointment until Kemal walked into his office. Reading the expression in his eyes he enquired, with a laugh, 'What's up?' Kemal replied that Kiazim's superiors had invented a job for him, as a pretext to get him out of the way. This suited his purposes nicely. Let Kiazim now confirm with the minister just what was required of him. Then together they would work out the details.

Kiazim returned with a directive, instructing Kemal not merely to punish the Turks who were attacking the Greeks around Samsun, but also to disband the various Nationalist organizations in the neighbourhood. Kemal exclaimed, 'Splendid! Now take pen and paper.'

Together they concocted such terms of reference as would give him the maximum scope. Kemal's post was to be that of an Inspector. The main point at issue was the extent of his authority. He must be in a position to give orders throughout Anatolia. Let two articles be inserted, giving him the command of all troops east of Samsun, and the right to issue instructions to provincial governors.

Kiazim raised his eyebrows, then laughed again, and said, 'It is our duty. We shall do our best.' He drew up a draft, which they read over together next day, making corrections and additions.

Then he said doubtfully, 'Don't you think these powers are too far-reaching, Pasha? I'm afraid the minister won't accept them.'

'Well, if he won't sign the paper, persuade him to seal it.'

Kiazim took the document to the minister, who was not feeling well. He said, 'Read it aloud. I shall listen.'

While he was reading, the minister said, 'You have not created an inspectorate of the Ninth Army but an inspectorate which will extend over the whole of Anatolia. What does this mean?'

Kiazim explained that this was normal procedure. Part of the task of an Inspector was to maintain contact with the civil administration in districts beyond his own. If the title Inspector-General of Anatolia were used, it would be nothing new. The Minister was clearly reluctant to sign. Finally he looked up at Kiazim with a smile, took his seal and threw it across to him, saying, 'My signature is unnecessary. Take this, and seal it yourself.'

On hearing this, Kemal insisted on making some additions to the document. These Kiazim inserted – with a mock protest that they were not in the instructions read out to the minister. Two clean copies were then made, and he sealed them with the minister's seal, giving one to Kemal with the jest, 'Pasha, are you trying to get me put in a sack?'

The instructions covered the restoration of law and order and an enquiry into the causes of the present disturbances; the confiscation and storage of all arms and ammunition; disbandment of all groups under unofficial army protection, and the prohibition of further recruitment and distribution of arms. For these purposes Kemal was given command of two army corps, with direct authority over five provinces, and indirect authority over five others which were instructed to 'take his demands into careful consideration'. Two other provinces were added later, by a verbal understanding with the Ministers of War and the Interior.

As he left the War Ministry, with this brief safely in his pocket, Kemal found himself biting his lips with excitement at his 'indescribable luck'. The men he had thought to be his enemies had played, in all apparent innocence, into his hands. 'I felt,' he said afterwards, 'as if a cage had been opened, and as if I were a bird ready to open my wings and fly through the sky.'

With Rauf he hastened to see Fethi, who was still in prison, to tell him the news. The director of the prison received him with a great show of respect. He was an officer who owed a debt of gratitude to Kemal. He said to him, 'Pasha, we've got the news. It is said you are going to Anatolia. The moment you order it, I will let out all the prisoners you wish, and join you there, with them.'

This time Kemal was able to see Fethi in private. Speaking more freely than before, he confided to him the plans which had been revolving in his head and which now at last he had the chance to carry out. He would form and lead a national Revolutionary army. He would establish a Parliament in Anatolia, based on the will of the people. He would not return to Constantinople until he had achieved his objectives.

The terms of his mission still required Cabinet approval. There was a danger that some minister might question the extent of his powers. Mehmed Ali found a means of circumventing this. He caught Damad Ferid in a relaxed mood over the card-table at the *Cercle d'Orient* and secured his signature to the document. When the other ministers saw this, he calculated, they would not dare protest. Among them there was indeed only one dubious voice, that of the Sheikh of Islam. 'I can see in that man's eyes,' he is reputed to have said, 'that he means to abolish the Caliphate and all religion.' His appointment, none the less, received the approval of the Cabinet and the seal of the Sultan on the last day of April 1919.

Damad Ferid, his eyes drooping behind gold-rimmed glasses, received Kemal. He confirmed that he had given him full authority, and added, 'You may communicate all your wishes to me directly. You may be sure that they will be carried out without delay.' Kemal was taken to see Mehmed Ali, who turned to congratulate the Minister of War on his choice. He too gave authority to Kemal to communicate with him direct. The chain of communication was thus complete.

Kemal now began to select his staff, which was to consist of some twenty officers. He visited Ismet, and invited him to command one of his two army corps – the Third – at Sivas, acting as opposite number to Ali Fuad, in command of the Twentieth, destined for Angora. But it was too soon for Ismet to take such a plunge. The exact course of Kemal's venture, as he saw it, was still problematical. Even he could not foresee, until he reached Anatolia, just how it would develop. Ismet, patriot though he was, lacked the temperament and the capacities for so speculative an enterprise. He was cautious by nature, moreover essentially a military man, used to cut-and-dried situations. Kemal's initial problems would be largely political; he would be dealing with a fluid situation. For the moment Ismet, or so he himself argued, might be of more use to him as a listening-post here in Constantinople, where he was well ensconced in the War Ministry and had friends at court. It was still possible too that he might be sent as a delegate to the Peace Conference, where he could hold a watching brief for the Nationalists, diagnose the attitude of the Allies, and learn a few tricks of the diplomatic trade. He could join Kemal later.

Instead Kemal selected Colonel Refet as his army corps commander. Refet was as old an associate as his five other stalwarts, Ismet, Rauf, Fethi, Ali Fuad and Kiazim Karabekir. Kemal had known him since the earliest revolutionary days in Salonika. More recently he had been commander of the gendarmerie in Constantinople, and Kemal had talked to him of his plans for overthrowing the régime, here at the source. Small in stature and dandyish in costume, Refet was alive in his movements and quick in his mind, with a French culture and an impish irreverent humour. His panache as a cavalry officer was matched by a carefree gallantry of manner, with which he charmed his way through many an awkward situation.

Finally there was Rauf, the loyal sailor and unquestioning patriot, staunchly devoted to the liberal principles of the Western world and, ironically enough, to the institutions and traditions of Britain, the present enemy. It was decided that he should travel as a civilian through Western Anatolia, starting in the country around Smyrna, to study the situation and collect information about the various Nationalist groups. He would thus proceed to Ali Fuad's headquarters in Angora, and get in touch with Kemal from there.

While Kemal was laying his plans for Samsun, in the north, Lloyd George and Venizelos were planning their own course of action for Smyrna and this western region. Lord Curzon, now deputizing for Mr Balfour at the Foreign Office, watched the situation in Turkey with growing concern. Towards the end of March he voiced his apprehensions in a memorandum to the Cabinet, warning them of the dangers of a revival of Turkish resistance, owing to the delays at the Peace Conference and the apparent decline in the Allied will to victory. It was upon a picture of Allied indecision and disillusion that 'the Old Turk, who still hopes to re-establish the former régime, and the Young Turk, who means to cheat us, if he can, of the spoils of victory look out from the crumbling watch-towers of Stambul'.

Only a group of his adherents in the Foreign Office heeded him. And now the Supreme Council was proposing to cede Smyrna and its hinterland to Greece. Curzon launched another memorandum. How could the Greeks, 'who cannot keep order five miles outside the gates of Salonika', be trusted to administer so important a part of Asia Minor? When it was realized, he argued, 'that the fugitives are to be kicked from pillar to post and that there is to be practically no Turkish Empire and probably no Caliphate at all', Moslem passions might easily 'burst into savage frenzy' throughout the Eastern world.

None of this had any effect on Lloyd George who, when the Italians walked out of the Supreme Council on the issue of Fiume, seized the chance of clinching his Greek designs. He won over President Wilson to the side of Greece, against the advice of his own Turkish experts; Clemenceau was otherwise preoccupied and raised no objections; and early in May the three decided that the Greeks should be permitted to occupy Smyrna. The Italians, on their return to the Council, registered a formal if reluctant acceptance. Venizelos could thus plead that he was acting under a mandate from the four great powers. But he went, as Winston Churchill remarked, 'as readily as a duck would swim'.[1]

On 15th May, despite all warnings and protests, twenty thousand Greek troops began to land at Smyrna, advanced inland up the railway and, in Churchill's words, 'set up their standards of invasion and conquest in Asia Minor'. By a slip in co-ordination the Allied High Commission in Con-stantinople had not yet received official news of the landings. The report was brought to them in session. It caused as much consternation as though it had been a *coup d'état*. Count Sforza could not trust himself to speak, but rushed from the room, banging the door behind him. The Italians retaliated at once by landing troops, without consulting the Allies, in the zone to the south, which was theirs by secret treaty.

The governor of Smyrna had received notice of the landings from the Allied naval authorities. He proposed to resist, with the few Turkish troops which still remained under arms, and telegraphed accordingly to Con-stantinople. Fevzi, the Chief of the General Staff, had previously urged that any such incursion should be met by force. Now, however, his minister, without consulting him, gave orders against resistance, on the grounds that the landings accorded with the terms of the Armistice. At this Fevzi resigned.

The Greeks thus entered Smyrna as though on parade, shouting 'Long Live Venizelos!' They stacked their arms, and some danced around the stacks, in celebration. The Greek civilian population swept along the streets, crying curses on the Moslems. A stray shot was fired, which led to inter-mittent firing and bloodshed. The Turkish troops hoisted the white flag and, with their officers, were marched down to the waterfront to a troop-ship with their hands above their heads, while a mob of civilians jeered at them, struck at them with clubs and tore at their fezes. A Turkish colonel, who refused to take off his fez and stamp on it, was shot and killed. The governor was arrested and similarly marched off to the quay, at the point of the bayonet, together with other notables, dragged from their houses.

The Greek troops then got out of hand and some hundreds of Turks were killed. Their bodies were thrown over the sea-wall into the harbour. Admiral Calthorpe had to intervene, virtually ordering the Greek admiral to take charge on shore. A group of Turkish Nationalist officers held a meeting of protest, in favour of the Wilson principles and thus against any form of annexation, in the Jewish cemetery in the centre of the city. They received no support from the Turkish authorities, and dispersed for the most part into the interior to organize centres of resistance. The Greek

[1] *The World Crisis: The Aftermath.*

forces meanwhile advanced inland up the two broad river valleys of the Gediz and the Menderes – the classical Hermus and Meander – towards the cities of Manisa and Aydin.

Constantinople was dismayed at the news. But it was a dismay stiffened by deep indignation, which gave sudden reality to the Nationalist movement. Occupation by the great powers could be accepted as an inevitable evil; but occupation by the Greeks, insolent and disloyal subjects for a century past, was an affront which no patriotic Turk could endure. Here was just the spark that was needed to inflame the fighting spirit of the Turks once more. Fifty thousand people gathered in the great square before the Mosque of Sultan Ahmed. Many of them carried black flags, while a black drapery was lowered behind the speakers, symbolically enshrouding the red-and-white flags of the star and the crescent around. A woman in black, her face unveiled, delivered a passionate oration, addressing the crowd with the words, 'Brothers, sisters, countrymen, Moslems: when the night is darkest and seems eternal, the light of dawn is nearest.'

She was Halide Edib, one of the few Turkish women in politics, who was destined to become an active force in the new Revolution. Her feelings at this moment reflected those of countless others. 'After I learned about the details of the Smyrna occupation,' she wrote afterwards, '. . . I hardly opened my mouth on any subject except when it concerned the sacred struggle which was to be. Turkey was to be cleared of murderers, the so-called civilizing Greek armies . . . I suddenly ceased to exist as an individual. I worked, wrote and lived as a unit of that magnificent national madness.' Lord Curzon was proved to have been right.

The news of the landings reduced the Sultan to tears. Leaning on the arm of his cousin Abdul Mejid as he left a meeting of his Council, he said to him, 'Look, I am weeping like a woman.' Kemal heard it at the Sublime Porte, where, on the eve of his departure, he chanced to be conferring with Mehmed Ali and a group of ministers.

'By God, what an impertinence!' Mehmed Ali exclaimed. 'Have you heard? The Greeks are landing in Smyrna.'

'Has that happened too?' Kemal asked. He was stirred, but not altogether surprised. The press had been foreshadowing such a move for some days. He looked around at the fussed, astonished faces of the ministers, and coolly enquired, 'What do you mean to do?'

'We are going to protest,' was the helpless answer.

'All right. But do you think your protest will make the Greeks or the British retire?'

They shrugged their shoulders. 'What else can we do?'

'There are perhaps more definite measures that might be taken.'

'What, for example?'

He did not express his thoughts, but suggested, 'You can come and join me.' He turned to the Minister of Marine, and asked, 'Is my boat ready to leave for Anatolia?'

'It has been ready for some days. The *Bandirma* – at your orders.'

He would leave next day. His ADC drafted an order to the captain, which the minister signed. Kemal left the ministers to their dazed deliberations.

On the previous evening, before the news of the landings arrived, he had dined with Damad Ferid and Jevad, who had succeeded Fevzi as Chief of the General Staff. Ferid seemed worried. He had reason to be, for the British, through Ryan,[1] their First Dragoman, had expressed doubts to him regarding the wisdom of the inspectorate scheme, though Kemal's own name still meant little to them. Ferid had reassured them. But he now asked Kemal, 'Can you show me on the map the exact extent of your command?'

With a gesture of studied vagueness, Kemal put his hand over a province or two on the map, and said, 'I'm not quite sure. Perhaps a small area like this.' He exchanged glances with Jevad, who supported him. He strolled away with an air of indifference. The Grand Vizier seemed relieved.

As they left the dinner Jevad asked, 'Are you going to do something, Kemal?'

'Yes, Pasha, I am going to do something,' was his reply.

Next day he proceeded to the Yildiz Palace, where Vahid-ed-Din received him in audience. 'My Pasha,' he said. 'So far you have done great services to the State. All this is past history. Forget it. The services you will now render are more important than all the rest. Pasha, you can save the ountry.'

Kemal concluded that the Sultan meant to say, 'We are powerless. The only way we can save the country is to submit ourselves to the will of those who rule Constantinople.'

He said to the Sultan, 'Have no fear. I have understood Your Majesty's point of view. . . . I shall not for a moment forget your orders.'

The Sultan wished him success and he was presented with a gold watch, engraved with the imperial cipher.

For Kemal all was now in order. Back at the War Ministry, Fevzi was handing over his duties to Jevad, confident that he would carry them on in the same spirit. Bending over a map on the table, he pointed at Constantinople and thundered, 'I don't understand. We are surrendering the whole country in order to be comfortable in this one spot. This is madness.'

Jevad seemed to agree. Kemal said to Fevzi, 'You are right. I am going to Anatolia in order to prove that you are right. I see no need for us to talk at great length. I expect only one thing from you. You must help me.'

'Of course I will. You may be sure of it.'

[1] Later Sir Andrew Ryan, KBE, CMG.

Kemal turned to Jevad, 'And you too, especially. For yours is now the responsible post. Shall we be able to work together?'

'Of course.'

Kemal then asked him, 'Will you at once order the Twentieth Army Corps, now at Ulukishla, to march to Angora. Don't let them be transported by train.'

'I shall give the necessary orders.' He gave him also his secret cipher, with which to communicate with him in person.[1]

Only some last-minute action by the British could now prevent Kemal's departure. The granting of visas for himself and his large staff had indeed been queried a week before by a junior British Liaison Officer in the War Ministry, Captain J. G. Bennett. Reading through the list he was struck by its high-powered military calibre. In the absence of his superior officer, he took it across to GHQ to ask for instructions, suggesting to the staff officer on duty that this looked more like a war-making than a peace-making mission. He was told to wait while the British High Commission was consulted. After about an hour, he was called in and instructed to grant the visas. 'Mustafa Kemal Pasha,' he was told, 'has the complete confidence of the Sultan.' The visa, signed by the British authorities, was thus now safely in Kemal's possession.[2]

He paid a last visit to Fethi in prison. After they had said goodbye, Fethi's fellow-prisoners realized that something was up. He was nervous, preoccupied, replying to their questions with polite evasions. He preferred not to talk, and lay down on his bed with his face to the wall, as though to sleep.

But finally he confided to his neighbour, Yunus Nadi, that Kemal was leaving tomorrow and that for the next three days, waiting for the news of his safe arrival, he would not sleep. The British, it was true, seemed unaware of the real situation. But one or two of their officers were intelligent enough, and might try to prevent him from landing, or pursue him once they found he was gone.

'These are our birth-pangs,' said Fethi. 'But we must not attract the attention of the others. We must not discuss them even here.'[3]

Kemal spent his last evening in Constantinople with his mother and sister at her house in Beshiktash. They squatted on cushions around a Turkish tray by his mother's bedside, while he told them of his imminent

[1] Certain protagonists of the Sultan claim that at this time he was pursuing an ambivalent policy, openly supporting Damad Ferid on the one hand but secretly reinsuring with the Nationalists on the other. He used to discuss such matters with his dentist, Dr Sami Gunzberg (whom he nicknamed Dish Pasha, otherwise Tooth Pasha). To him, after Kemal's success, he put forward, in the presence of Ali Riza, a later Grand Vizier, the dubious pretension that he had sent Kemal to Anatolia when all else had failed, hoping to save at least the heart of his country.

[2] J. G. Bennett, *Witness*.

[3] Later Fethi was deported to Malta.

departure on an 'important mission', he could not tell them where. It would be some days before they had news of him. To achieve his object he must be easy in his mind, he must not feel that they were worrying about him or had worries of their own. He had money in the bank on which they might draw freely, whether with his own seal or theirs.

Zübeyde grew faint at the news, then prayed for his safety and success. Makbule expressed her bewilderment. In the past he had gone off to the wars, and they knew he was fighting. But this time it was hard to grasp where he was going and why. Kemal could only tell her not to worry. Next day Zübeyde came to Shishli to bid him goodbye. When he had gone, she consoled Makbule with the proud injunction that, as the sister of a soldier, she must never weep for her brother, must never show sorrow to a stranger. Then they settled down to wait, perhaps for many days, for the ring at the telephone which would tell them of his safe arrival at his new destination.

The *Bandirma* lay at the quayside, a small British-built cargo boat bought from a Greek. Rauf accompanied him there, then left him, so that Mehmed Ali, who was coming to see him off, should not see them together. He himself was to leave secretly, with four friends, a week later.

Refet, recruited at short notice, had no visa from the Allies. This did not disconcert so resourceful an officer. He came down to the quay without badges of rank, ostensibly to embark a dozen horses which his brother had bought for him. He saw them on board and remained there, hiding among the horses, until the ship was safely out of the Bosporus.

She sailed on the evening of 16th May. Kemal was nervous that the British might try to sink the ship, or to arrest him *en route*. Rauf had thought it unlikely. Had they any such intention they would have prevented his departure. Refet too scorned his fears. But Kemal was taking no chances. The ship looked unseaworthy, her compass was inaccurate, her captain seemed inexperienced. Kemal ordered him to alter his course and sail close inshore, where it would be possible to disembark in a hurry if an Allied ship threatened.

The British authorities meanwhile had awoken, belatedly, to the imminence of Kemal's departure and its possible implications. Wyndham Deedes, military attaché to the High Commission, was hurriedly sent down to the Sublime Porte at midnight to warn the Grand Vizier. But Ferid leant back in his chair, put the tips of his fingers together, and said slowly, 'You are too late, Excellency; the bird has flown.'[1]

No steps however were taken to intercept the ship, which anchored off Samsun in rough weather on 19th May 1919.[2] Boats came out from the

---

[1] Later Brig.-Gen. Sir Wyndham Deedes, CMG, DSO. Quoted by John Presland, *Deedes Bey*.

[2] When Kemal, in later years, was asked the date of his birth, he liked to reply 'May 19, 1919'.

beach to row the new Inspector-General and his staff officers ashore. He landed on one of the rickety wooden jetties, striking out through the shallow water, which were the small port's apology for a quay. He was received by three officers, with a small detachment of troops, and by two local notables. They took him to a house, the property of a Greek, which he requisitioned as his headquarters. A few hundred yards down the dusty street one French and two British control officers were installed in the local bank.

Thus, four days after the Greeks had set up their standard of conquest on the shores of the Aegean, Kemal set up his standard of liberation on the shores of the Black Sea. The battle for Anatolia was about to begin. A new chapter had been opened in the history of the Turkish people.

PART TWO

THE WAR OF INDEPENDENCE

CHAPTER TWENTY

THE START OF THE STRUGGLE

THE MUSTAFA KEMAL who now embarked on the crucial phase of his own and his country's career was a seasoned and self-confident campaigner, two years short of forty, who had proved himself as a soldier in fourteen years of hard service. He had now to prove himself also as a politician and statesman. The challenge which he had sought, through those smouldering years of frustration, at last confronted him, bold and exacting and clear.

Kemal had lately grown stronger in build, his face had filled out and showed traces of lines, his hair and moustache had dulled in colour. But his skin was as clear, his gaze as alert, his responses as swift as those of a younger man. With his erect bearing and his cleanly cut features, Mustafa Kemal had the lines of the soldier. But latent within him was the hint of an extra dimension, of a singularity of tempo and rhythm and scale which outranged the companions around him. Strangely, for all his slightness of frame, he seemed bigger, for all his slowness of stride he seemed quicker than they. Already the grey complexion and the broad high cheekbones, the long feminine hands with their spatulate fingers and quick changing movements, set him apart from the rest.

But it was above all through those eyes, pale and stern and unblinking, that this other element in Kemal was reflected. Wide-set beneath the broad brow and the eyebrows that curled upwards like whiskers, they gleamed with a cold steady challenging light, for ever fixing, observing, reflecting, appraising, moreover uncannily capable of swivelling two ways at once so that they seemed to see both upwards and downwards, before and behind. With these eyes, with his massive head and his lithe assured limbs, he had the look of a restless tiger. In a more military idiom, he combined in his person the hardness and coldness but also the flexibility of steel, suggesting, with his high-strung nervous tension, a coil flexed and ready to spring.

It was this 'extra dimension' in Kemal that his friends needed and valued at this initial stage of the national struggle which they all had at heart. In mind he was always one leap ahead of them, in action one degree more decisive. He had just those qualities of leadership which they severally lacked. Rauf was a man of principle but deficient in imagination; Kiazim Karabekir was loyal but inflexible; Refet was brave but impulsive; Ali Fuad was adroit but lacked intellect. All were patriots, practical soldiers, men of common sense and intelligence. But among them only Kemal had the necessary over-all grasp both of internal and external affairs, that peculiar compound of intuition and reason, resilience and energy and above all will-power, required to carry such a hazardous enterprise to a successful conclusion.

With a lucidity of vision amounting almost to clairvoyance, he saw his ultimate objective and the intermediate steps that must be taken to reach it. With his insight into the personal psychology of both enemy and friend, he sensed the obstacles, both political and military, which would stand in his way and for which tactics would have to be devised. The realist in him knew that the struggle would be long and must be planned in patient stages, to be revealed not in advance but by a careful process of timing in relation to circumstances and to the current climate of feeling. The intellectual side of him knew that it was to be won by the force, not merely of guns but of an idea, which must be sown and cultivated in the minds of the people. The achievement of all this would demand an intense concentration, a superhuman effort of will, the kind of elemental driving force which Kemal alone possessed.

The spirit which fired it was a passionate ambition overriding all else. But it was the ambition of a patriot, bound up with what he saw to be his country's interests. Power for its own sake, for the sake of glory, did not interest Kemal. He sought it solely for the purpose of realizing his own radical and constructive ideas for the future of Turkey. In human terms, Kemal was a man without love in his nature. He understood people. But he did not love them. He had little time for women, except to distract him. He enjoyed the comradeship of his men friends and remained loyal to those who did not aspire to compete with him – old brothers-in-arms, young ADCs.

But with equals and would-be equals there was always a wariness behind his approach. With his present associates this was sharpened by the feeling that they too had an extra dimension, which he himself lacked, less definable than his own. This derived from their several social backgrounds. Rauf came of good Caucasian stock; Ali Fuad of a military family respected for some generations; Refet's forbears had been independent landowning beys, in the Danube valley. All, in an English idiom, ranked as 'gentlemen', armed with the assurance of an inherited prestige, an easy integrity and a natural habit of leadership.

Kemal, for all those refinements which smoothed his rough edges, came of an insignificant middle-class family and knew it. Far from pretending otherwise, he exploited his more plebeian origins to shock and defy, to assert his personality and flaunt his power, to override the conventions of his social superiors.

They, for their part, regarded him more with respect than with love. Rauf, the idealist, saw him as the man for the moment but not necessarily for the future; Ali Fuad, tougher and less concerned with political principles, took him for granted as one man of action and one old comrade takes another; Refet, appreciating his gifts but suspecting his motives, treated him with less respect than the others. All, however, had one quality in common. They had a deep and genuine love for their country.

In Kemal this derived from a pride in its destiny, nourished in boyhood; from a sense of shame at its visible decline at the hands of the foreigner and of its own decadent rulers. This feeling was rooted in a certain earthiness of spirit and love of the soil – the mountains and valleys of Rumeli, the wide-open spaces of Anatolia – for which he had fought and was about to fight again. It was animated above all by a knowledge of the men who had fought with him. Kemal saw the Turkish people without illusion. He knew that they were dour, conservative, fatalistic, slow in mind and initiative. But he knew also that they were stubborn, patient, capable of endurance; a race of fighters ruthless in battle, responsive to leadership and ready to die to order.

The peasantry of Anatolia had been neglected and despised by their Ottoman rulers. Yet it was they who gave the Empire its backbone; and it was through them that Kemal and his friends now aspired to save what remained of it. Instinct told him that the spark in them might still be rekindled for the defence of that soil to which inheritance and possession gave a half-sacred quality, and for the rescue of that nation which, after six centuries of empire, still inspired them with pride and an obstinate sense of freedom, war-weary and demoralized as they were. It was being said that even God himself could not move them to fight again. Could a Mustafa Kemal hope to succeed in a task thus surpassing the powers of the Almighty?

He started with one great advantage. The Allied occupation of Smyrna was an unhoped-for asset, to exploit to the full. But the people of Anatolia must first be roused to an awareness of its facts and implications. At Samsun he found that they were scantily informed about the landings. Thus one of his first actions, making use of the excellent telegraph network which Abdul Hamid had installed to perfect his espionage system, was to send out instructions to the various civil and military authorities within his jurisdiction, to stage mass-meetings of protest and to bombard the Sublime Porte and the foreign representatives with telegrams appealing for national justice. In Samsun itself he arranged for meetings to be addressed in the principal mosque, to rouse the people to a spirit of resistance. In the military field

Kemal established rapid liaison with all the Turkish army units surviving in Anatolia and Thrace; in the political field he began to form links between the various Defence of Rights groups and, far from disbanding them, as he had been ordered, to form new ones.

Meanwhile, in a series of telegrams to the War Ministry, he kept up, as he had done from Adana at the time of the Armistice, a running fire of complaint against the British. They had reinforced their troops in the area, without notifying the Turkish authorities; they were planning to move more units into the interior, in defiance of the Armistice terms; they were aiding and abetting the Greek partisans, who sought further Allied occupation and the creation of a Greek state of Pontus.

Back in Constantinople, the British now became alarmed. Having awoken to the danger too late to prevent Kemal's departure, the Commander-in-Chief, Sir George Milne,[1] now firmly requested the War Ministry to recall him. The War Minister at first replied that Kemal's presence in Anatolia would be a calming rather than a disturbing influence. The Cabinet met, however, to discuss a compromise proposal for the limitation of his authority, for in fact they shared some of Milne's misgivings. They were increasingly concerned at the disdainful and disrespectful tone of Kemal's telegrams, which seemed to imply their ignorance of the Anatolian situation and his determination to handle it in his own way, not consulting them in advance, but merely informing them afterwards. When they were read out to the ministers, the Unionist sympathizers smiled in a knowing way, while all looked at Damad Ferid. 'The Inspector,' he remarked, 'almost seems to be scolding us. He writes as though to say "We know what we are doing, and you may mind your own business." ' The Cabinet thus decided on his recall and informed Milne accordingly.

The Inspector meanwhile – and the people of Samsun knew him only as such, for he had not yet chosen to advertise his identity as the hero of Gallipoli – felt restricted in his actions here on the coast. The British control officers were too close for his comfort. Already Refet had shown alarm at the indiscretion of his pronouncements and propagandist activities. Requiring to act freely Kemal, after a week in Samsun, moved his head-quarters fifty miles inland to Havza. He did so on the pretext that he wished to take advantage of its thermal springs, since he had been ill in Samsun with a recurrence of his kidney disease.

Thus his small band of officers set off up the road which climbed by rough and serpentine stages to the great Anatolian plateau. Four thousand feet above the sea, it spread for a thousand miles from Mount Ararat and the frontiers of Persia and Russia in the east to Eskishehir and the mountains of the Marmara and the Aegean in the west. The Yeshilirmak (the Green River) curled away beneath them, down towards the shore, as they

[1] Later Field-Marshal Lord Milne of Salonika, GCB, GCMG, DSO.

drove up into a landscape of ripening maize and wheat-fields and patches of deciduous forest. They passed through villages of sagging mud-brick houses, those of the Turks punctuated with a minaret, those of the Greeks with a dome. Kemal's antiquated open car broke down several times during the journey. Finally, with two companions, he left it and walked up the road. Here in the hills there was fresh air to breathe and the fruitful earth to smell, and as the officers responded to the freedom of their surroundings, they found themselves humming a romantic Swedish song of misty hilltops and trees and birds and silver flowing rivers:

> 'Let us march, friends!
> Let our voice be heard by the earth, by the sky,
>   by the water,
> Let the hard ground moan from the harsh tramp
>   of our feet.'

It was to become a song of the Revolution, to be sung by a growing band of companions right across Anatolia, and eventually – its foreign origin forgotten – to be enshrined as a 'theme song' of the youth of the Turkish Republic.

Havza was in the thick of the Greek guerilla warfare. During the war the Greek villagers had made trouble, causing the Government to deport groups of them to the east. Afterwards they had remained quiet until the Armistice. But now a political organization, formed to press for the state of Pontus, was stirring them to rebellion once more, largely under the leadership of a Greek bishop. Kemal was told how gangs of black-clad bandits, their belts bristling with cartridges, were terrorizing the Turkish population, robbing and killing them on the roads, burning their villages, kidnapping their prominent citizens, lying in wait to ambush their soldiers – much as they had done in Macedonia in the days of his youth. Against this the Turks could do little since the British, much as they might complain to them of the lack of law and order, were confiscating their arms under the terms of the Armistice, but allowing the Greeks to keep theirs.

Havza and the surrounding villages thus provided a fruitful field for the start of a Resistance movement. Receiving the local notables at his headquarters Kemal, whose identity as the hero of Gallipoli had now become known, declaimed to them against the invading foreigners: 'They do not seek to kill us. They seek to bury us alive in our graves. Now we are on the edge of the pit. But if we stir ourselves to a final effort, we may still be saved.' He then left them to confer among themselves. In his methodical military fashion he drew up a long questionnaire for the mayor, requesting a comprehensive report on such matters as the relative population in the area of Moslems and Christians and their respective political attitudes; the nature of the conflict between them and the steps taken to deal with it. He demanded a dossier concerning the identity of the leading Turkish inhabitants and their behaviour and character. Did the people owe taxes and, if so, how much? What were the stocks of the army? How much transport was available? It was by such thorough and practical attention to detail, wherever he now went, that Kemal informed himself, for his revolutionary purposes, of the state of the country.

Meanwhile, at two successive meetings from which he chose to remain absent, the leading citizens decided of their own accord on a policy of resistance, forming as its foundation a branch of the Defence of Rights Association. Following a crowded service in the mosque, with prayers for success, a mass meeting was held in the small square of the town. Careful still not to seem directly involved, Kemal watched it from a window at his headquarters, sending his officers into the crowd to test the popular reaction. The speakers insisted that the country was in danger; thus all Moslems must be armed, lest they die beneath the feet of the enemy. An oath was sworn to this effect, in religious terms. Kemal had established the first active cell of resistance, the prototype of others that were to proliferate during the next few months in different parts of the country.

In the region of Smyrna the resistance had been swift, inspired largely by individual officers. The Turks had established a loose front linking together the various Resistance groups, until forced to retire to a line laid down by the Allies – the Milne Line – through the War Ministry in Constantinople. But the other groups continued to wage guerilla warfare in the mountains. When Rauf arrived in the neighbourhood from Constantinople he found his countrymen thoroughly roused. The bandit chiefs came to him, lawless men known by the local designation of Efe, whose bands had been fighting the Ottoman Government since pre-war days. They now rejoiced at the chance to go into battle once more, this time against their rivals, the Greeks. One of them, Demirji Mehmed Efe, assured Rauf that his followers were rallying to him 'as innocently as lambs', asking for orders and declaring, 'It is for today that our mothers gave birth to us.'

For Kemal, the time had now come to move on from Havza. British troops were stationed a mere twenty miles up the road at Merzifon, and reports of the open-air meeting in Havza had reached them. Moreover, its people had made them look foolish by capturing a consignment of some tens of thousands of rifle bolts, confiscated from the Turkish forces in the east, and despatched all across Anatolia by a convoy of baggage animals to the port of Samsun. A band of Turkish patriots surprised the convoy, hid the rifle bolts in a local warehouse, and sold the animals to raise funds for the Resistance. Foreseeing a stiffer British attitude, Kemal moved on to the remoter and more important city of Amasya, whose inhabitants had sent him a deputation declaring their loyalty.

He thus said goodbye to the people of Havza, dressed now in civilian clothes as a symbol of the fact that this was not merely a military but a civil Resistance, and with a procession of them walked to the bridge outside the city, where his car awaited him. As he was giving last instructions to the mayor, two cars drew up, carrying Americans from the college at Merzifon. The mayor lowered his voicé and advised Kemal to do the same. But with defiant indiscretion he talked even louder. 'We have nothing to hide,' he declared. 'Let them all hear. We have gone too far in this to draw back.'

Kemal had a mind, as he had an eye, which could see in several directions at once. While he looked inwards on Anatolia, he had at the same time been looking outwards on the world. Since the Armistice, Turkey's only hope had seemed to rest on President Wilson and his Fourteen Points. A Wilsonian League, composed of intellectuals, had drafted a proposal for a period of American aid and a guaranteed peace to assist Turkish recovery. Now, as a counter to the threat of partition, an alternative idea, born in Paris, was gaining ground in Constantinople – that of a mandate over Turkey or a part of it by America, Britain, or some other power.

On 14th May, at that meeting of the Supreme Council which had ordered the occupation of Smyrna, President Wilson agreed to consider the accept-ance of a mandate over Armenia, Constantinople and the Straits. On 26th May, Damad Ferid announced his decision 'to put Turkey under the pro-tective assistance of one of the great powers'. This provoked an immediate protest from Kemal. Early in June, Ferid was given the opportunity to state his country's case at the Peace Conference, and a Government delega-tion – from which Ismet, to his disappointment, was excluded – left in a French cruiser for Marseilles and Paris. Kemal reacted at once to the news of his forthcoming departure. He sent out to his group of commanders and governors a strongly worded circular, stressing the national rights. Insisting on complete independence and the safeguarding of the interests of the Turkish majority on Turkish soil, he attacked especially the acceptance by Damad Ferid of the principle of Armenian autonomy and the proposal for a British protectorate elsewhere.

Two days later he received the order from the Minister of War to return to Constantinople. He disobeyed this and all such subsequent orders. The time had come to muster his friends and proceed to serious action. A tele-gram arrived from Ali Fuad, who had reached Angora with the Twentieth Army Corps. He announced that Rauf – whom he described mysteriously as 'a certain person whom you know' – had arrived there after his tour of the south-west and suggested a rendezvous at some point between their two headquarters. Kemal replied that he could not himself move from the Havza region, owing to shortage of petrol. Instead he asked them to find their way to Havza, suggesting that they should travel in disguise and not divulge their names. Their party thus set out in horse-carriages on a six-day journey over primitive roads, seldom stopping and doing their best to look inconspicuous. They followed Kemal to Amasya.

This was a place well fitted to become the cradle of a Nationalist Revolution. Throughout a long and distinguished history it had shown a consistent spirit of independence. Saved from the Mongol occupation, it had been for a while the Ottoman capital and after the capture of Constantinople the tradition persisted that the heir to the Sultanate should receive his education in Amasya and serve as its governor. Thus Amasya preserved a high status and felt that it had something to teach Constantinople.

As Kemal approached it the mountains rose up abruptly before him. Ahead, as he passed through its orchards, green and warm and fertile as those of Damascus, their ridges closed in on the narrowing valley of the Yeshilirmak. Bold and rugged, pitted with the tombs of the Pontus kings and crowned with an ancient fortress, they formed a precipitous gorge in which to clamp the city to the banks of the green-flowing river. It was a place isolated in its atmosphere from the outside world, but the centre of a world of its own; a Moslem city as holy in its aspect as Brusa, with its wealth of mosques and tombs and religious buildings, but free in its remoteness and its pure Islamic traditions from the domination of the Sultanate and its crippling reactionary influence. It was a city, as Kemal had expected and soon confirmed, which looked to the future, not to the past.

Already, in its mountains, a stalwart Moslem dignitary had recruited a force of Turkish volunteers, to fight against the Greek partisans, under their Orthodox bishop. He at once came out openly for Kemal, and preached for his cause in the mosque. Kemal himself delivered a speech to the citizens, announcing the start of a national Resistance on three separate fronts – in the west against the Greeks behind Smyrna; in the south against the French and their Armenian collaborators from Adana; in the east against the Armenians from Erzurum. 'Citizens of Amasya,' he declaimed, 'what are you waiting for? . . . If the enemy tries to land in Samsun, we must pull on our peasant shoes, we must withdraw to the mountains, we must defend the country to the last rock. If it is the will of God that we be defeated, we must set fire to all our homes, to all our property; we must lay the country in ruins and leave it an empty desert. Citizens of Amasya, let us all together swear an oath that we shall do this.' The citizens declared that they awaited his orders.

It was the holy men who proved to be his strongest adherents. For the first time he was to receive public and official support from a powerful religious authority. Among the civil population he had support from a more questionable source – the local adherents of the party of Union and Progress. During the Resistance he was to be wary of encouraging the cooperation of the Unionists, of whom he had a chronic mistrust. But often he had little choice, since in many districts it was they who had formed its original nucleus, and since there were, after all, genuine patriots among them.

So the Kemalist Revolution was born. The four friends who had planned it in Constantinople now met together, here in Amasya, to draft its 'Declaration of Independence'. Ali Fuad and Rauf were the first to arrive. Refet was to join them next day. Kiazim Karabekir was informed of their arrival by telegram. Kemal now disclosed his intentions.

The ground had been prepared, so he explained to his friends, by a close-knit liaison with the various civil and military authorities and with the Defence of Rights organizations. There was an encouraging response; the idea of a Resistance was growing. The time had now come to give it a corporate identity. He had thus decided to convene immediately a National Congress at Sivas. Situated high on the rim of the plateau, some hundred and fifty miles to the east and a similar distance from the sea, it was 'by all odds the safest place in Anatolia'. He had drafted a circular, calling upon delegates from each province to proceed there at once and, if necessary, incognito. His friends approved the circular. Meanwhile, he told them, a preliminary Congress of delegates from the eastern provinces would meet at Erzurum, a further two hundred and eighty miles to the east. This had in fact been summoned by Kiazim Karabekir, before his own arrival in Anatolia.

Next day he submitted a declaration for approval and signature by Rauf, Ali Fuad and Refet. The independence of the country, it asserted, was in danger. The capital was under Allied occupation and the Government subject to foreign control, hence incapable of governing. The nation must save itself by its own will-power. Its resolve to resist foreign domination had been proved by the rise of the numerous defence organizations. These must now be co-ordinated into a central national body, capable of judging the nation's needs and voicing its demands, free from outside influence and control. Hence the Congress at Sivas. The place and date of it would be kept secret meanwhile.

It was clear to all that the declaration went further than the mere organization of the defence of the country. It envisaged the possible formation, by the Sivas Congress, of a national Government, independent of Constantinople. Ali Fuad accepted this without hesitation, and signed. Rauf, after a moment's reflection, signed also. Refet, whose late arrival had caused him to miss their earlier discussions, seemed reluctant at first to commit himself so far. But Ali Fuad overcame his doubts, and he added his own swift flourish of a signature. The band of four friends thus made history with a 'Sacred Alliance' which sealed the first concerted plan in the Turkish struggle for independence.

When they had signed it they telegraphed its contents to Kiazim Karabekir and to Mersinli Jemal, the army commander in Konya. Both gave it their approval, thus extending its range from here in the north to the east and to the south. Following the signature, a call to arms was declaimed after the Friday prayer in the mosque.

From Constantinople, the new Minister of the Interior, Ali Kemal – who had unfortunately replaced Kemal's ally, Mehmed Ali – now issued a circular of his own. Following Mustafa Kemal's refusal to return to the city, he directed that no one must in future have official correspondence with him and that his orders must not be obeyed. Thus from now onwards Kemal must clearly expect attempts by the Sublime Porte to apprehend or dispose of him.

He received warnings of probable trouble at Sivas, where he intended to stop on his way to the Erzurum Congress. He left secretly one morning at daybreak, accompanied only by Rauf and his *aides*, but instructing a detachment of troops to follow and to try to keep in touch with him. Emerging from the Amasya gorge, he drove up the broadening valley of the Yeshilir-mak, where the peasants were gathering in the harvest, to Tokat, a town similarly crowned by a rock-bound fortress. Here he took over the telegraph office and ensured that his arrival was not announced to Sivas. He called together a group of local notables to whom he made a rousing speech. 'If we have no weapons to fight with,' he declaimed to them, 'we shall fight with our teeth and our nails.' Before leaving for Sivas, six hours' journey away, he drafted a telegram to its governor, announcing his arrival, but ordering it to be sent only six hours after his departure.

He hoped thus to take him by surprise. For a plot was afoot, at the instigation of the Sultan's Government, to arrest Kemal in Sivas, prevent the Congress, and thus nip the national movement in the bud. For this purpose a certain Ali Galib, a retired staff colonel, had been sent to Sivas from Constantinople, ostensibly proceeding as governor to the neighbouring province of Erzinjan. He had bills posted on the walls, proclaiming Kemal 'a dangerous man, a mutineer, a traitor', and urged the governor, Reshid Pasha, to arrest him in terms of the order of the Ministry of the Interior. The governor was hesitant; so were his associates. They were still debating as Kemal drew near to the city.

His road wound up successively over two mountain barriers until it reached the plateau itself. At the top of the second pass – the Pass of the Pines – Kemal stopped at a spring to drink some water. A driver at his side started to fill a cup for him. But Kemal restrained him sáying, '*Dur Baba.* Stop Father. I prefer to use my hands.' The driver was to pass into Anatolian folklore with the sanctified nickname of Dur Baba.

Beyond the last ridge Kemal at last breathed the high dry air of the plateau. The sea and its marginal barrier of mountains were behind him. Before and around him a wide tawny prairie, broken only by hazy insubstantial hills, spread away to remote horizons. Here was his battleground.

On this roof of the world, to which the Turks had trekked centuries earlier from the central Asian steppes, was their new destiny now to be decided. Driving along the banks of another broad river, this time the Kizilirmak, or Red River, he reached the outskirts of Sivas.

The governor hurried out to greet him and tried to delay his entry. But Kemal politely manœuvred him into his open car in place of Rauf, and made him sit by his side, for all to see as he drove towards the city. By this time the news of his arrival had spread, and they were greeted at the gates by a detachment of troops under arms and by an interested crowd, lining both sides of the road. Their welcome effectively forestalled any attempt to arrest him and ensured Reshid's subsequent if qualified loyalty.

Instead Kemal turned the tables by arresting Ali Galib, who appeared before him to be upbraided and then treated to a long harangue, elucidating the principles of the Resistance and branding him as a traitor to his country. That night, Ali Galib thought it prudent to revisit him and declare his good intentions. As Kemal recorded, he 'tried by all kinds of sophistries to convince me that I ought not to judge from appearances that were so deceptive'. He pretended that he had stopped at Sivas to meet Kemal and place himself under his orders. 'I must admit,' Kemal said drily, 'that he managed to keep me busy till the morning.'

That morning he left for the east in his antiquated motor-car, on the long weary week's journey across the plateau, with many stops for information and instruction on the way, towards Erzurum.

CHAPTER TWENTY-ONE

THE ERZURUM CONGRESS

ERZURUM was the 'capital' of eastern Turkey. A rough grey city of the Anatolian plateau, placed where its mountain barriers converge in the direction of the Persian and Transcaucasian frontiers, it had been an early citadel, on their incursion into the country, of the Seljuk Turks, and was thus embellished with buildings combining martial strength with civilized grace. Always a military stronghold it had served in more recent centuries as a bastion of Turkish defence against a series of Russian invasions.

Here Kiazim Karabekir, the fifth of the founders of the Revolution, had salvaged from the remnants of Enver's last Caucasian army a force which was stronger than any surviving in other parts of the country. Kiazim had become the 'father figure' of this eastern region, ruling it benevolently and nurturing its independent spirit, which had been roused by the threat to incorporate it in a greater Armenia. It was a region depopulated and devastated, beyond all others, by the war, by the ebb and flow in the fighting which had accompanied the Russian advance and retreat, by the consequent expulsions of Turks by Armenians and Armenians by Turks, by the 'scorched earth' policy which had destroyed the crops and had reduced the herds to a fraction of their former strength. The population was down to a mere ten per cent. of its pre-war numbers. Disease had been rife, food was still scarce, but for eggs and black bread. For want of glasses the people were drinking their tea out of sawn-off bottles.

Kiazim, with his paternal and charitable instincts, had personally adopted more than a thousand orphan boys, between the ages of four and fourteen, whom he dressed in a para-military uniform and to whom his officers gave a form of military training. He established schools to give them an elementary education and to teach them useful trades. Since his own hobby was music, and he liked in his leisure hours to play the violin, he gave them also musical instruction, together with training in arts and crafts. The children knew him as 'Pasha Baba' – Father Pasha – and so trusted and revered him that he was able to control them with a minimum of punishment and to encourage them to develop as free individuals.

Colonel A. Rawlinson, who had arrived in Erzurum, on an official mission, to investigate the prospects of creating an independent Armenia, and to organize the surrender of arms, was so impressed by these educational activities that he wrote, 'If this is going on throughout the whole country, the Turk of the future, with his natural gifts of courage and endurance, will become a power in the East, if not in the West also, that will presently have to be reckoned with in a very different spirit from that adopted by the European Powers at their post-war conferences hitherto.' He admired the Pasha's intelligence, his conscientiousness, his mastery of every branch of his profession. He was 'the most genuine example of a first-class Turkish officer that it has ever been my good fortune to meet'.

The colonel, with the ostensible co-operation of Kiazim, was as conscientious in his efforts to inspect armaments, military stores, arsenals, fortifications and army muster-rolls and pay-sheets, with a view to completing demobilization and reducing arms to the level allowed by the Armistice. His main task was to confiscate breech-blocks of guns and breech-bolts of rifles, and to send them across the frontier by the railway into Transcaucasia, where two English divisions were stationed.

But his progress was slow, owing to 'a suspiciously large number of accidents on the railway'. These were engineered by Kiazim's men, who had the additional habit of holding up trains and unloading their cargoes on to mules and into horse-wagons to carry them away. When the railway was out of action – once for months at a time – he had to organize camel caravans across the mountains to the port of Trebizond. One day his men found a hidden artillery park, with forty modern guns and their ammunition which, the Turks explained, had been 'overlooked'. There were many other such caches which they failed to find, including stores buried by loyal Russians just before the Revolution.

Colonel Rawlinson soon realized that Kiazim had no intention of surrendering his arms. Kiazim replied to all his enquiries with polite evasions and ambiguities. The two soldiers fenced amicably enough with one another. Once Rawlinson asked Kiazim, with a menacing air, 'Do you know how many dreadnoughts the British have?' Kiazim replied, 'The Turk never fears.' This was the title of a spirited march of which the Pasha had composed the words and music, and which was later to become a theme song of the War of Independence. 'Every Turk,' he continued, 'is a dreadnought in himself. How can millions of dreadnoughts be taken under a mandate?' Rawlinson said, 'Your coffee is excellent. May I have another cup?'

On hearing the news of the occupation of Smyrna, Kiazim, who had a talent not merely for music but for drama, at once wrote a play on the

A —7

subject, a patriotic tragedy which was performed in public by a cast of officers and teachers. He also set to work to organize a Congress at Erzurum of the various Defence of Rights groups, aimed against the parallel Allied threat to this region.

Kiazim had a specific object in planning this Congress. As an officer of the traditional stamp, he had a rigid sense of duty and a deeply ingrained respect for superior authority. When sounded by the leading local Nationalist leaders as to what he would do if ordered to evacuate Erzurum, he had replied that it was his duty as a soldier to obey orders. But 'above the order of the Government', he added, 'there is the superior will which is that of the nation. If there is a national desire, expressed by its representatives, I will obey it and resist the invasion.' The Congress would thus equip him with the legal pretext to act as he had resolved to do.

Kiazim accorded Kemal a ceremonious welcome, designed to give him a much-needed confidence in the loyalty of this eastern province. For he felt far from sure of his position. For the past few days he had been bombarded, at each place *en route*, with telegrams from Constantinople, from the Palace and the War Ministry, repeatedly pressing him to resign his command and return. For in fact, despite the circular of the Minister of the Interior, he had not yet been officially dismissed. The British, he was told, were concerned as to his activities. Let him accept an exchange posting until the situation clarified and peace was agreed. To these injunctions he replied in the negative.

At Erzurum the bombardment came to a head with a series of 'conversations' over the telegraph with the Sultan's chamberlain, in which commands gave place to entreaties. In pleading tones the chamberlain declared that he himself was jealous of Kemal, because of the Sultan's great love for him. If he came to Constantinople his life and future would be guaranteed. If he did not care to do so, then let him remain in Anatolia on leave. Such was the wish of the Sultan. Kemal answered courteously, stressed his loyalty and devotion to His Majesty, but persisted in his refusal to relinquish his post.

It became clear nevertheless that his dismissal was imminent. Rauf and Kiazim both urged that he should forestall this by resigning of his own accord, not merely from his post but from the army. This would create a better impression on public opinion. Refet, from Sivas, had expressed the same view, on the grounds that resignation from the army would preclude his recall to the capital. Kiazim assured Kemal that he personally would respect him more as an ordinary individual than as an Army Inspector.

But Kemal hesitated. For what he planned to do he realized that the prestige of an official position was important. 'It is a fool's belief,' he once said, 'that people like their leaders only with ideals. They want them dressed in the pomp of power and invested with the insignia of their office.' His military rank had meant everything to him since he first contrived, as a boy, to enter the Military School in Salonika. It had given him a sense of security and purpose which, with his family background, he had previously lacked. Now he became nervous, depressed, uneasy as to the extent of his power and support if he lost it. His inner self-confidence seemed suddenly to waver.

But finally he agreed with his friends that resignation was inevitable. He sent a telegram to the Minister of War and another to the Sultan, resigning both his post and his commission in the army. They were crossed by another, from Constantinople, which dismissed him from both. In announcing his resignation to the people of the Erzurum province, he declared that henceforward he would fight as an individual 'for the achievement of our sacred national purpose'. Rauf declared, more specifically, that he would fight at his side 'until the safety of the Sultanate and Caliphate are definitely secured'.

Next day, after they had gone through the official telegrams together and Kemal had ordered coffee, his chief of staff, Colonel Kiazim Dirik, got up and said quietly to him, 'Pasha, you have resigned from the army. Henceforward I cannot keep my post with you. With your permission, I shall ask Kiazim Karabekir Pasha to assign me to a military duty. To whom shall I deliver these documents?'

Kemal turned pale. He was so shaken by Kiazim's words that he could only say, 'Is that so, sir? All right, sir. You can hand over these documents to Hüsrev Bey.' He gave him leave to go.

Kiazim Dirik strode out of the room with an air of bravado. Kemal sank into an armchair, in deep dejection. Presently he said to Rauf, 'Do you see, Rauf? Wasn't I right? Do you see how important it is to have an official post and rank? The attitude of this man, who has worked with me so earnestly, shows that my point of view was correct. . . . I have known him for a long time, very intimately, and I have never seen him so disturbed.'

Rauf tried to reassure him. His resignation from the army would not diminish his prestige and influence. 'It is better,' he said, 'that we should get rid of these weaker elements before our struggle begins.'

Kemal replied, 'You may be right in your feelings, but in practical terms you are wrong. Let us hope that this is not the first of other such actions.' He added with an air of unaccustomed pessimism, 'There is only one thing for you and me to do. We shall have to retire to some safe place where we shan't be ground underfoot.'

Rauf disagreed. Kemal's prestige would, on the contrary, be enhanced by his resignation. Kiazim Karabekir had fastened on him as the only man capable of leading them, and his affection and respect for him had increased rather than otherwise.

But Kemal had fallen into the depths of despondency. 'Let us hope so,' he said. Then he burst out, 'God curse this American mandate, or whatever it is! Let them accept it as soon as possible, so that the country may get free of this chaos!'

The ADC came into the room and said that Kiazim Karabekir Pasha wanted to see him. There was a lost look in Kemal's eyes. He knew that the Ministry of War had offered his post to Kiazim. He feared that after all he might now accept it. Smiling bitterly he said to Rauf, 'You see, I was right.' He told the ADC to admit the Pasha.

Kiazim entered the room with the air of an officer who confronts his superior. He greeted Kemal with official respect, standing at attention and saluting. He said, 'I have brought you the respects of my officers and men. You are still our honoured commander, as you were in the past. I have brought your official carriage and cavalry escort. We are, all of us, at your orders, Pasha.'

Kemal swayed a little, overcome with emotion. He rubbed his eyes, as though awaking from a dream. Then he walked up to Kiazim and hugged him, kissing him on both cheeks, thanking him many times over. Rauf had not seen him thus moved since, after the Battle of Anafarta, he had said to him, 'Thank heaven, we have saved Stambul.' His position was now assured, his confidence restored. He had the army of the east securely behind him. He began, with redoubled energy, to telegraph orders throughout the country, signed for form's sake by Kiazim Karabekir.

A few days later he was able to joke when another officer, seeing him no longer in uniform but in breeches and a hacking-jacket, showed reluctance to obey him. Kemal firmly rebuked him, saying, 'It was not the uniform with the epaulettes and the stars that gave you the orders. It was Mustafa Kemal who gave you the orders, and he is still here in front of you. So take down this order and carry it out at once.' The officer did so. Telling the story later, Kemal said, 'I thought to myself, "Suppose he presses a bell now, calls in two soldiers and has me arrested, what then?" '

As soon as his resignation was known Kemal was elected chairman of the executive committee of the Erzurum branch of the Defence of Rights Association, with Rauf as vice-chairman. But as to his participation in the forthcoming Congress there were obstacles still to be overcome. Its delegates were a mixed cross-section of merchants, farmers, lawyers, journalists, *hojas*, Kurdish sheikhs and Laz chieftains from the various eastern provinces. They regarded it as largely a local affair, designed to strengthen the hand of the civil and military administration, to organize the secret storage of arms and their recovery from the British control officers, and to discuss the protection of their homes and property against the threat from Armenia. It was true that this general from the west had expressed himself publicly against the creation of an Armenian state. All the same, he was not one of them. They knew only his reputation; and this aroused misgivings.

Some were members of the former Union and Progress Party, and thus looked upon him as an enemy. Others saw in him despotic ambitions, noting that even after his dismissal from the army he had been seen still wearing full uniform and the cordon of the Sultan's ADC – a choice of costume not wholly due, as his protagonists claimed, to the limitations of his travelling wardrobe. Others again suspected him of designs on the Sultanate. They had moreover heard tales of his drinking habits.

Eventually, however, the prestige and influence of Kiazim turned the scale. He was able to convince the doubters that Kemal, having sacrificed everything to the Nationalist cause, had earned their trust and must now have their support. He should not merely be admitted as a delegate, but elected president of the Congress.

Two delegates thus gave up their seats to Kemal and to Rauf. The Congress opened a fortnight late, on the eleventh anniversary of the 1908 Constitution, with a large picnic, given by Kiazim, at which his officers and orphan children gave moving theatrical performances. Coincident with its opening Damad Ferid issued an order throughout the country to prevent all such assemblies, 'held under the pretence that they are parliamentary sittings'. It was held in an Armenian schoolhouse and lasted a fortnight. At its first session, despite some opposition, the delegates elected Mustafa Kemal as their president. He had an official position once more, but as a civilian, a status he now symbolized by donning a frock-coat borrowed from the governor of Erzurum. When asked, years later, what he would have done if the delegates had failed to elect him, Kemal boasted without hesitation, 'I should have called a new Congress.'

From Havza and Amasya, Kemal had launched a military Resistance; from Erzurum he was now to launch its political counterpart. In his opening speech to the Congress he laid down the twin principles which were to become the foundations of the revolutionary programme. One was the rights of the nation; the other was the will of the people. The one was to be achieved by the formation of a Government based on the other. He spoke of the 'dark and tragic dangers' that surrounded them, of 'the undaunted spirit that inspires the national movement and which, like an electric flash, penetrates even to the remotest parts of our country'. The resolution of the Turkish nation to be master of its own destiny could spring only from Anatolia. Moreover, it could spring only from the people's will.

Kemal's was to be no mere military movement, imposed from the top by the rule of the few, as that of the Young Turks had become. It was to be the rule of the many, such as neither Turkey nor any other Eastern country had known in its history, a movement arising organically from the heart of the nation itself. Turkey was to have a régime chosen and backed by the whole community of Turks, a Government deriving its authority and strength from the desires and decisions of a majority of its people. A man might act no more as an individual, he must act only in the name of all. Such, from Erzurum onwards, was to be Mustafa Kemal's message, reiterated without respite across Anatolia. It was the message of a man brought up at close quarters with the Western subjects of the Empire, who had studied something of the principles of Western democracy and who sensed that, in the long run, it must provide the only political foundation on which his country could survive in the modern world.

To a trusted friend who enquired privately of Kemal at the Congress, 'Are we going towards the Republic?' he replied, 'Is there any doubt of it?' But this could not yet be divulged. He was careful at this stage to make it clear that the movement was not aimed against the monarchy and the Caliphate, but was united behind them against the threats of the foreigner. Its purpose was, on the contrary, to preserve their rights. He was also scrupulous to ensure that his movement remained ostensibly within the law, that its acts were duly recorded with the offices of the various provincial governments, in compliance with statutory Ottoman practice.

Within this framework the main fruit of the Congress was the draft version of a declaration which was later to be known as the National Pact.[1]

This document asserted by implication the principles of self-determination to which the Peace Conference pretended. It insisted on the preservation of Turkey's existing frontiers – those in effect which contained a Turkish-speaking majority; resistance against any attempt to alter them; the establishment of an elected provisional government; the denial of privileges to non-Turkish minorities. It was made clear by the Congress that if a provisional government were formed it should follow the established laws of the central Government and should, after realizing the National Pact, cease to exist.

The Pact was circulated in the form of a manifesto throughout the country, and to the representatives of foreign powers. It was with some justification that Kemal told the assembly that it had 'passed serious resolutions and had proved in the face of the whole world the existence and the unity of the nation'. History, he added, would characterize the work of the Congress as 'a wonderful performance that has seldom been equalled'.

As the Congress ended a telegram arrived at army headquarters, from the Minister of War:

As the Sublime Porte has decided to arrest Mustafa Kemal Pasha and Refet Bey immediately, on the charge that they are disobeying the orders issued by the Government, and send them both to Constantinople; and as the necessary orders have already been given to the local authorities,

[1] For full terms, as finally agreed, see Appendix.

your Army Corps is commanded to execute this order without delay and
to report that this has been done.

Kemal records laconically, 'The officer commanding the Army Corps
sent an appropriate reply.' In the course of it Kiazim protested that these
two 'enlightened and worthy citizens' were furthering the interests of the
country. In a further report to the Government on the work of the Congress,
he insisted on its national character: 'By attributing the movement to two
people only you diminish its whole scope.' It arose out of the feelings and
aspirations of the people, on whom the Government's circulars had made a
deplorable impression.

The Congress had so strengthened the hand of Kiazim that he was now
able deliberately to flout the British control officers and the terms of the
Armistice – to say nothing of the instructions of his own Government –
regarding the surrender of arms. The people themselves, he now insisted,
had taken matters into their own hands, and would no longer allow any
arms to leave the country. Shortly afterwards Colonel Rawlinson received
orders from London to move all his men out of the country, and to watch
the situation from Sarikamish and Kars, in Armenia. The British had
begun to reduce their military commitments in Anatolia, and the evacuation
of Batum was in prospect.

A copy of the Pact was now sent to Colonel Rawlinson, who had been
favourably impressed by Kemal in a long interview before the Congress
opened. He now left for London, where he tried in vain – as Admiral
Calthorpe had also done – to awaken the British Government to the
future potentialities of the Nationalist movement. Only Lord Curzon displayed some interest. He wanted to know what peace terms Kemal really
expected and would be prepared to accept – short of those of the National
Pact, which he dismissed as out of the question. He thus sent Colonel
Rawlinson back to Turkey to sound him out on these lines. But when
Rawlinson reached Erzurum the winter had set in, Kemal had moved westwards and the subsequent march of events precluded any such meeting
between them.

Meanwhile Damad Ferid's mission to the Peace Conference had ended in
failure. On behalf of his country he recited a long plea compounded of self-
abasement, self-justification and extravagant demands. He admitted that
Turkey, during the war, had committed crimes such as 'to make the conscience of mankind shudder with horror for ever'. But 'it would be fairer
to judge the Ottoman nation by its long history as a whole rather than by
a single period which shows it in the most disadvantageous light'. All these
crimes were the fault of the Committee of Union and Progress, whose
leaders had now been tried and found guilty, thus rehabilitating Turkey in

the eyes of the civilized world. Henceforward she could devote herself to 'an intensive economic and intellectual culture'. In view of these mitigating factors Damad Ferid proposed the maintenance, on the basis of the *status quo ante bellum*, of the integrity of the Ottoman Empire, which during the last forty years had been reduced to its least possible limits. In support of this claim, which went far beyond the Wilson Principles agreed at the Armistice, he invoked the pan-Islamic argument. The Empire, he pretended, formed a compact block whose disintegration would be 'detrimental to the peace and tranquillity of the East'.

The Council were not impressed by the Grand Vizier's apologia. After a few days they sent an acid reply, which agreed with his estimate of the Turkish Government's crimes. Turkey, however, could not escape the consequences simply because her affairs 'at a critical moment in her history, had fallen into the hands of men who, utterly devoid of principle or pity, could not even command success'. However excellent the qualities of the Turkish people the Council 'cannot admit that among these qualities is to be counted capacity to rule over alien races'. As to their aspirations to economic and intellectual culture, 'No change could be more startling or impressive, none could be more beneficial!' The Turkish delegation was then given permission to leave. These problems, it was explained by Mr Balfour, touched other interests besides those of Turkey, and their immediate solution was impossible. Negotiations must be suspended until the United States was in a position to say whether it could accept any form of mandate. A few days later President Wilson had a paralytic stroke, a misfortune which was to delay them for many more months.

Thus Damad Ferid returned to Constantinople with no consolation to offer his people. Abdul Mejid, the Sultan's first cousin and Heir Apparent, chose this opportune moment to write him an official memorandum on the state of the nation – a statesmanlike document which Kemal himself could hardly have bettered. The Government, he urged, was dividing the country. The Sultanate should rise above party politics and hold a neutral balance. He called for immediate elections and the formation of an all-party Cabinet, with Nationalist representation. No attention, however, was paid to this enlightened proposal by either the Sultan or his Grand Vizier.

Kemal meanwhile took advantage of Damad Ferid's humiliation in Paris to send him a telegram of condolence, laced with threats. From the point of view of the national dignity, he wrote, it was unfortunate

to be compelled to admit that the different Cabinets that have succeeded one another during the last nine months have all shown gradually increasing weakness, until, unhappily, they have now shown complete incompetence. . . . As an answer to the candour and seriousness which characterize the ideals of the nation in its struggle for life and independence, the Government prefer to maintain a passive attitude. This is most deplorable, and is liable to drive the people to take regrettable action against the Government. Permit me to insist in all sincerity that the nation is capable of enforcing its will in every way. No power can hold it back. . . . If the Government will abandon its resistance to the national movement, which is quite legitimate, and leans for support on the nation . . . it must guarantee as quickly as possible that it will convene a Parliament that shall represent the well-being of the nation and carry out its will.

It was in this mood that Kemal left, at the end of August, for Sivas, having ascertained that delegates were already on the way there from various parts of the country. Thus began the next and most crucial stage in the foundation of the Turkish Resistance movement.

CHAPTER TWENTY-TWO

THE SIVAS CONGRESS

'LOADED WITH FOLLIES, stained with crimes, rotted with misgovernment, shattered by battle, worn down by long disastrous wars, his Empire falling to pieces around him, the Turk was still alive. In his breast was beating the heart of a race that had challenged the world and for centuries had contended victoriously against all comers. In his hands was once again the equipment of a modern army, and at his head a Captain, who with all that is learned of him, ranks with the four or five outstanding figures of the cataclysm. In the tapestried and gilded chambers of Paris were assembled the law-givers of the world. In Constantinople, under the guns of the Allied fleets, there functioned a puppet Government of Turkey. But among the stern hills and valleys of "the Turkish Homelands" in Anatolia, there dwelt that company of poor men . . . who would not see it settled so; and at their bivouac fires at this moment sat in the rags of a refugee the august Spirit of Fair Play.' So wrote Winston Churchill of Mustafa Kemal.[1]

At this moment these operations of his were still on the threshold of what has been aptly called 'a twilight zone between diplomacy, planned popular rising, guerilla and open warfare'.[2] He was not yet sure of all his company, nor indeed of his modern army and its equipment. Asked by a pessimistic friend at Erzurum of what use the Nationalist troops, many of them irregulars, would be against the regular armies of the Allies, he answered, 'The Nationalist troops are like the revolver beneath an honest man's pillow. When all hope of his saving his honour is lost utterly, he can at least commit suicide with his revolver.'

At Erzurum Kemal, apart from his political tasks, had been contending with the problems of the assembly and organization of these Nationalist forces. Firstly he had to bring together his various loyal commanders with each other and with the civil authorities; secondly he had to sift and uproot

[1] *The World Crisis: The Aftermath.*

[2] Dankwart A. Rustow, *The Army and the Founding of the Turkish Republic.*

those who seemed less loyal than the rest. In this task he was helped by certain friends in the War Ministry, notably Jevad Pasha, who was still Chief of the General Staff. But he was hindered there by enemies trying to plant in Anatolia commanders inclining to the Sultan's cause.

Of the united and unqualified support of two army corps he was now sure – that of Kiazim Karabekir here in the east, and that of Ali Fuad in the west. At Angora, supplementing his regular troops, Fuad had created the nucleus of a sound irregular defence force. Moreover, on returning there from Amasya, he had seized the telegraph offices of Central Anatolia and assumed control over the civil and administrative machine.

Elsewhere the position of the Nationalists was less secure. Since the Amasya conference there had been continuous pressure on commanders to leave their posts and return to Constantinople. Mersinli Jemal, the army commander at Konya and a supporter of the Amasya Declaration, was one of those who now yielded to this pressure. Kemal thus sent out to all commanding officers a circular urging that, if obliged to vacate their posts, they should at least remain in the neighbourhood and that in any event they should disobey any orders to disband their units. No officer, in any circumstances, should return to Constantinople.

Refet, as commander of Kemal's Third Army Corps at Samsun, now found himself in a hazardous position. He had taken a truculent line with the British, who asked for his recall and, with Damad Ferid's consent, sent a destroyer to fetch him. On board was his replacement from the War Ministry, Colonel Selah-ed-Din, with a British staff major. Refet refused to embark, explaining playfully that he suffered from seasickness, hence could not stand the voyage. When the major rebuked him for so frivolous an excuse, Refet replied, 'The truth is, I'm afraid you'll take me on to Malta.' To return in a British warship would be an affront to his dignity. But he undertook to return of his own accord in a few days' time. He thus relinquished his army corps to Selah-ed-Din, a man whom he hoped to win over to the Nationalist cause. Then he sent in his resignation to the Ministry of War and prepared to leave for the Congress at Sivas, to which delegates were already on their way from various parts of the country.

The Sivas Congress was to raise the Nationalist counsels from the local to the national plane. It did not, in terms of the number and provenance of its delegates, strictly fulfil this role. Though some two hundred had been invited only thirty-nine came, and of these more than a dozen were members of Kemal's own immediate staff and entourage. None came, despite prior warning, from the plains of Thrace, where the Greeks were threatening; only a few from the valleys and mountains behind Smyrna, where they were pressing inland; none from the plateau of the salt lakes around Konya and the coastlands of Adalia beneath them, from the hot rich plains of Cilicia, beyond the Taurus, or from the arid deserts and foothills of

Mesopotamia and Kurdistan, where the Italians, the French and the British were in respective possession; none, more surprisingly, from the Black Sea coast and its mountains, from which the British were now preparing to withdraw. Constantinople, the reactionary stronghold of the Sultan and citadel of the Allies, had only one representative, though a young student claimed to represent the Sultan's Medical School.[1]

Thus Kemal had to start from small beginnings. In terms of population he seemed to have with him less than a quarter of the country. But in terms of territory he had more. He had the greater part of the plateau of Anatolia within its mountain walls, from Erzurum westwards. He had what he had initially sought, the Turkish heart-land. Here at least was the nucleus from which a new country could grow.

The Congress opened on 4th September 1919, in a cream-washed secondary school built in the classical manner. In the garden before it stood a single protective field-gun, manned by the men of Selah-ed-Din, the new army corps commander. Around it arose the graceful monuments of the thirteenth century Seljuk Turks. For Sivas had been one of their strongholds, its people imbibing throughout the centuries a certain Turkish purity of tradition and a respect for freedom which, as at Amasya, persisted still. The place was now a cattle-ranching centre, with a peasantry of sturdy Anatolian stock.

The deliberations were held in a classroom, a long rectangular chamber decorated in a provincial rococo style. Carpets had been brought by the inhabitants to cover the floors and adorn the walls. A rostrum had been contrived at one end, the carpentry of its bare planks disguised under a prayer-mat. The delegates sat in half a dozen rows on benches, at rough school desks with holes for ink-pots. There was a special table for Kemal, and a rug on the wall above it inscribed, 'Long live our Sultan'. But Kemal preferred to sit on this, removing it to cover the seat of his faded plush armchair. Often, however, he sat at a desk with the rest. The adjoining room had been furnished for him as a bedroom, with a large iron bedstead, ormulu lamps and a set of chairs on which his companions could sit when in private conference. On the bed was a silk coverlet, finely embroidered with lovers' knots and floral emblems, an item from the trousseau of a young girl who had brought it to him as a personal gift.

The delegates lived largely on school commons of *pilav* and beans, and lodged in various houses throughout the town. In the evenings they played dominoes in the cafés or strolled through the streets, wandering down to a bridge across the Red River. Here the inhabitants would converse with them, gathering news of the Congress. Rauf they found accessible and ready to talk. Kemal himself kept his distance, remaining behind in the

[1] A delegate who described himself as representing the Hakkiari, the wild mountainous frontier-land of the Kurds, came in fact from Erzurum.

Congress building, where he conferred only with the delegates and the more influential local citizens, talking incessantly to convince, to instruct, to manipulate, to reconcile, to unite. His arrival had attracted much public attention, a leading *hoja* remarking on his handsome looks, and exclaiming, '*Ma'shallah*'. God save him from the evil eye.' Behind those commanding eyes was a leader to fear and revere. Lesser men hesitated to approach him, sensing that here was a man who would sum them up at a glance, divining and respecting the truth and at once stripping them of shams and pretensions.

With an eye to the need still for acting in the name of the Caliphate, the oath taken by the delegates was sworn with a hand on the Koran. It had been drafted as follows:

> I shall follow no personal interest or ambition but the salvation and peace of my Fatherland and nation. I shall not try to revive the Union and Progress party. I shall not serve the interests of any political party. This I swear in the name of Allah.

This time it was Rauf himself who at first opposed Kemal's election as chairman. Imbued with a sense of democratic proprieties, concerned to emphasize the national and popular character of the movement, he feared that his chairmanship might give it from the outset too personal and autocratic a stamp. He was, however, elected chairman with only three dissentient votes. The Congress then proceeded to business. More aware than the delegates themselves of the precarious situation that threatened them, Kemal set to work with a sense of urgency and so managed affairs that it was over in a week.

It agreed at once to the resolutions passed by the Erzurum Congress, together with amendments which strengthened the draft National Pact. To enforce its decisions, a Representative Committee was formed. Here there was no conflict. Where it arose was over the future status of the country itself. Among these delegates at Sivas there were probably few who, for all their patriotism, sincerely believed that complete independence was likely in fact to be achieved. This involved an act of faith and of will of which only Kemal himself and a handful of others were capable. The rest were inclined to snatch at the straw which now seemed to be offered to them – the American mandate. In Constantinople this new and dignified word – the 'gilded pill of the moment', as Ismet, one of its tentative supporters, defined it – was on all lips, replacing the dirty word 'annexation'. Even patriots began to see in it a possible formula for peace without dishonour, worthy to be explored if only as the lesser of misfortunes.

At the Erzurum Congress Kemal, sounding out opinion, had raised the question of aid from some great power without territorial designs on the country. He was astute enough however to avoid mentioning the name of America. For in the east it was a name bracketed in the popular mind with the hated project of an independent Armenia. But here at Sivas it was different. To these delegates from other parts of the country the name of America carried no such sinister undertones. Thus the question of the American mandate loomed larger at the Congress than that of the National Pact, which was already agreed.

A lucid protagonist of the mandate, in relation to the international position as seen from Constantinople, was Halide Edib. A woman of intelligence, with an international political outlook, she was in close touch with Mr Charles R. Crane, whose King-Crane Commission appointed by the Big Four in Paris to study the mandate question in special relation to the Arab provinces, had reported also in favour of three mandates for Turkey itself – one over Armenia, one over Constantinople, and one over the rest of Anatolia.[1]

In a long letter to Kemal she summarized the designs of the Allies on Turkey, and referred to the feeling in Constantinople that an American mandate might be 'the least harmful solution'. It would strengthen Turkey against the pretensions of the foreign minorities; it would ensure the trans-formation of the Turkish peasantry into a modern nation, a task for which Turkey herself lacked the experience and the financial resources; it would secure her defence against European imperialism. She referred to the achievements of the United States in the Philippines, and declared that only America had the 'political efficiency . . . that could create a new Turkey within the space of twenty years'.

At her suggestion an American journalist, Mr Louis E. Browne, was sent to the Congress, ostensibly as the correspondent of the *Chicago Daily News*, but in fact rather as Mr Crane's personal emissary. The only non-Moslem to attend it, he was well received by Kemal. In a series of talks with him Kemal used the term 'American aid' rather than 'mandate' as being more acceptable to Turkish pride. It should have a social and economic as opposed to a political character. Asked whether the Congress would pass a resolution inviting America to take over such a mandate, Kemal replied, 'Yes,' but added the crucial reservation, 'Provided you can assure me that America will accept it, if offered.' Browne expressed doubts as to whether his country would do so. Kemal said that without some such assurance he could not risk an official admission that Turkey required foreign help.

Two long and confused sessions of the Congress were devoted to the discussion of the mandate. Kemal took a guarded line. Finally, with Rauf, he found a compromise which the Congress accepted. The Congress of the United States should be invited to send over a delegation to study the country and report upon its real situation. A telegram signed by Kemal, Rauf and others, was sent to the American Senate, reporting on the Congress of Sivas and conveying this request.

[1] The report was in effect to be stillborn, since the State Department suppressed it.

The despatch of this document conciliated those who favoured the mandate, without committing Kemal and his associates; it brought the standing of the Nationalist movement to the notice of the world; it might steal for it some local credit with the American Mission of General J. G. Harbord, which Kemal knew to be on its way to Armenia, on the authority of President Wilson, to examine the question of mandates in the American interest. It was a tactical move in Kemal's diplomatic offensive, which could do little harm and might do some good.

A week or so after the end of the Congress, General Harbord and his mission arrived in Sivas. Harbord found Kemal to be 'a young man of force and keen intelligence', whom he judged, from his light brown hair and high cheekbones, to have 'Circassian or other blond blood in his ancestry'. Kemal was suffering from malaria and seemed under strain. But in the course of an interview which lasted for two and a half hours he talked easily and fluently, marshalling his facts in an orderly logical fashion. He seemed to envisage a 'big brother' relationship with America, based on such advice and assistance and 'slight exercise of authority' as would not interfere with his country's internal affairs. Harbord, referring to the past record of the Turks, replied that no self-respecting nation would accept a mandatory responsibility without complete authority. He referred to the Armenian massacres. Kemal assured him that his own movement stood for just treatment of all races and religions, and that he was prepared to allay Christian fears with a declaration to this effect.

'What do you expect to do now?' Harbord asked him.

Kemal as he talked had been playing with a string of prayer-beads, drawing them through his fine-drawn hands. Now with a gesture of nervous tension he pulled the string apart, and the beads were scattered all over the floor. Picking them up one by one he remarked that here was the answer to the general's question. He meant to draw the pieces of his country together, to save it from its various enemies, to make of it an independent and civilized state. Harbord suggested that such a hope was against logic, against military facts. 'We know that individuals, now and then, commit suicide. Are we now going to see the suicide of a nation?'

Kemal replied, 'What you say, General, is true. What we want to do, in our situation, is explainable neither in military nor in any other terms. But in spite of everything we are going to do it, to save our country, to establish a free and civilized Turkish state, to live like human beings.'

Kemal put his hand on the table, palm upwards. 'If we can't succeed,' he continued, 'rather than fall into the palm of the enemy like a bird, and be condemned to a gradual, ignoble death' – he closed his fingers little by little as he talked – 'we prefer, being the sons of our forefathers, to die fighting.' His fist lay clenched before him.

Harbord was impressed by his resolution, his spirit. 'I had taken everything into account,' he said. 'But not that. Had we been in your place, we should have done the same thing.'

But to a Turkish member of Harbord's staff Kemal, indicating the people around him, said, 'Pray for me, back in Constantinople.'

CHAPTER TWENTY-THREE

FALL OF THE SULTAN'S GOVERNMENT

THE SIVAS CONGRESS meanwhile neared its end. Kemal had good reason to speed up the deliberations. He had rightly discounted the danger of which Refet had warned him, of an attempt by the British to march on Sivas and prevent the Congress, and a more specific threat by the French to occupy the area. Neither power, he judged, was likely to commit itself to so costly a military enterprise. But Kemal now knew, from a series of intercepted telegrams, that the Sultan and his Government were trying to break it up and to arrest himself and the delegates. This was the task of Ali Galib, now governor of Erzinjan, who was instructed to proceed secretly to Sivas for the purpose, with an escort of Kurdish cavalry. Concerned chiefly with the bad impression created abroad by the Erzurum Congress, Constantinople telegraphed: 'The Government is well aware that nothing of real importance can result from a meeting that comprises only five, or even ten, persons in this town; but it is impossible to make Europe understand this.'

Kemal acted quickly. He at once ordered troops to Malatya, where Ali Galib was assembling his Kurdish force. With him was a British officer, Major E. W. C. Noel who, after the capture of Mosul, had been sent to Sulimaniye to help organize the Kurds of Northern Iraq into a series of semi-autonomous provinces. He had now been sent across the frontier to Malatya by the British authorities, with the approval and backing of the Sultan's Government, to enquire into the situation of the Kurdish tribes in Turkish territory. Noel, a political officer whose unorthodox activities and contacts were sometimes a source not merely of suspicion to the Turks but of embarrassment to his own colleagues in the Allenby administration, was accompanied on his mission by two members of the Kurdish feudal Bedrikhan family, which had formerly dominated the region.

Kemal gave orders that both Ali Galib and Noel should be arrested. Ali Galib, despite the urgency of his instructions, delayed his departure for

Sivas while he bargained for a final settlement on the expenses involved in the enterprise. He delayed it too long, and had to flee ignominiously into the mountains from Malatya to avoid capture by the Nationalist troops. He left behind him incriminating documents and a large sum of money, with a receipt showing that its purpose was 'the suppression of Mustafa Kemal and his followers'.

The tribes dispersed, and Major Noel was escorted in the direction of the frontier. Meanwhile he had, a shade innocently, telegraphed in clear to the High Commission in Constantinople, complaining of his own treatment by the Nationalists. Thus, as Ryan commented in a minute on the telegram, the fat was in the fire. Kemal had been presented with evidence to incriminate not merely Damad Ferid but the British in an infamous conspiracy against him. He was to exploit this evidence to the full.

From all points of view the Ali Galib operation was a notable success for him. He had spent long hours at the telegraph, ordering and cajoling into action various commanders who were reluctant to act against an official of the Sultan, and in any case sparingly equipped with troops; and he had finally achieved his ends. He owed much to a group of telegraphists loyal to the national cause, who copied and relayed to him the Government's messages. Fully informed as he now was, he could not resist sending an abusive telegram to Adil, now the Minister of the Interior, accusing him of cowardice and treason against the nation. It was a telegram whose tone shocked Kiazim Karabekir, as unbecoming to the president of the Congress and 'a man of his social position'.

The end of the Ali Galib conspiracy coincided with that of the Congress itself. Kemal, not wishing unduly to alarm the delegates, had told them little of its course. But now he proposed to draw from it, and from the complicity of the Government which the documents concerning it revealed, the maximum public and political advantage. When the final resolution, concerning the National Pact and other matters, had been agreed he took it across to the telegraph office, a room over a shop which became his headquarters for the next few days. There he launched, amid mounting curiosity outside, into a battle of the telegraph which was to lead to the rupture of relations with the Constantinople Government.

First he called upon the Minister of the Interior in Constantinople to come to the instrument, and transmitted the resolution to him with the request that it be taken to the Sultan. The minister refused. Thereupon, in the words of Louis Browne, who was present throughout, 'for many minutes the telegraph wire sizzled with Turkish expletives. He [the minister] called Mustafa and Rauf traitors and criminals and other things besides and they responded with the accusation that Adil was nothing but a cheap skate who had sold out to the British for a pittance.'

Kemal was in his element, planning each move as though he were conducting a battle in the field, swiftly drafting telegrams, drily commenting on the replies, pacing up and down, smoking and talking and consulting with Rauf and the others, while the crowd waited outside for some announcement as to what was afoot.

They decided that it would be good tactics at this stage to avoid a frontal attack on the Sultan: 'It was wiser to concentrate our endeavours on a single point, and not scatter our forces. Therefore, we chose Ferid Pasha's Cabinet alone as our target and pretended that we knew nothing about the complicity of the Padishah. Our theory was that the Sovereign had been deceived by the Cabinet and that he himself was in total ignorance of what was really going on.'

A telegram was thus addressed to the Sultan which, 'after the usual rigmarole of expressions of our devotion, as was customary at that time', declared that his Government had 'conspired to shed the blood of Moslems in a fratricidal war, by planning a sudden attack on the Congress', and had spent public funds in an attempt 'to dismember our territory by raising Kurdistan into revolt'. It continued: 'The nation demands that immediate steps shall be taken for the pursuit of this gang of traitors; that they shall be severely punished, and that a new Government shall be formed that will be composed of men of honour.'

Kemal was soon in touch with the rest of Anatolia. Browne, in a despatch to the *Chicago Daily News*, wrote: 'I have never heard of more efficient communications than I witnessed that night. Within half an hour Erzurum, Erzinjan, Mosul, Diyarbekir, Samsun, Trebizond, Angora, Malatya, Kharput, Konya and Brusa were all in communication. Mustafa Kemal sat at one end of the wire leading to all these places, and at the other end sat the military commanders and civil authorities of the respective cities and villages. The whole situation was explained and with one exception Anatolia ordered Mustafa Kemal to use his own judgement and go to the limit. Konya responded that owing to the presence of Italian troops in the city it had to be neutral.' During that day and the night that followed, telegraph offices throughout the country were occupied by the corps commanders.

'But the Grand Vizier,' Kemal recalled, 'seemed to have disappeared. He did not reply.' The answer finally came that the message had been relayed to him by telephone. He had replied that such communications should be passed to him only through the proper channels. This provoked an ultimatum, signed in the name of the Congress:

'The nation has no confidence left in any of you other than the Sultan, to whose person alone therefore it must submit its reports and petitions. Your Cabinet . . . is coming between the nation and the Sovereign. If you persist in this obstinacy for one hour longer, the nation will consider itself free to take whatever action it thinks fit, and will break off all relations between your illegal Cabinet and the whole country. This is our last warning. . . .' The telegraph office at Constantinople refused to accept this message and was warned that, unless it did so within an hour, all telegraph lines between Anatolia and the capital would be cut.

As the battle proceeded wild reports of it were spreading around Sivas. 'Let us execute Damad Ferid,' cried the people. 'We shall drive the Greeks into the sea. If the British support them, we shall smash them too.' The crowds became jubilant at a rumour that war was about to be declared against Britain and Greece. Demonstrators paraded through the streets and surged down the alleyways, carrying torches made from oil-soaked rags, to mass before the telegraph office. Kemal appeared on the balcony amid frantic cheers. Then in dead silence the town-crier read aloud the resolutions of the Congress. The crowd remained silent for a moment, then yelled its approval.

Throughout the night Kemal and his counsellors kept vigil in the telegraph office, while at other instruments throughout the country his loyal officers did the same. At five o'clock on the morning of 12th September, since Constantinople persisted in its refusal to open communication with the Palace, a circular was sent out from all districts, breaking off all official relations and all telegraphic and postal communication with the Government 'until it is succeeded by a legal Government'. Ali Fuad was ordered to station troops across the railway at Eskishehir to prevent reinforcement of British or Government forces, and to apprehend officials of the Sultan's Government attempting to reach the interior.

The next move was to force the resignation of the Cabinet. For this purpose the General Assembly of the Sivas Congress declared that its Representative Committee would serve as a provisional Government, pledged to conduct the affairs of the nation according to the laws and in the name of the Sultan until a national Government, possessing the confidence of the people, should be formed. It guaranteed the maintenance of law and order throughout the country. It effectively confirmed the executive power of Kemal and the Nationalists over a great part of Anatolia, on what they could pretend to be a legal and constitutional basis. In effect the Committee became the first revolutionary 'Government'. But since it never in fact met as a committee, it was Kemal himself who ruled, signing documents with its seal to preserve the fiction that he did so on its behalf. Under its auspices, the legitimate Government was subjected to a barrage of thousands of telegrams from all parts of Anatolia, demanding its resignation.

Meanwhile Kemal was sifting out his enemies from his friends, persuading and threatening those districts which still held back from joining the cause, hectoring into submission or driving out officers of whose support he was doubtful. The time had come to force, throughout the country, a choice between the Sultan and the Nationalist movement. But in the process of forcing it, he was still careful not to offend religious susceptibilities or to attack the Sultan in his capacity as Caliph.

He carried on an eight-hour 'conversation' over the telegraph, in flowery Islamic language, with one Abdul Kerim Pasha, a staff officer of the old school and an intimate friend from his Salonika days, who, at Damad Ferid's instigation, tried to persuade him to agree to a joint meeting between the Sultan's representatives and his own. In the course of their exchanges of telegrams, which contained continual invocations of the Almighty and texts from the Koran, Kemal addressed him by the Islamic title of Most Exalted Excellency, while Abdul Kerim for his part referred to Kemal as 'Pole of Poles', a designation 'by which he intended to confer on me the attribute of the spiritual representative of God on earth'.

Kemal regretfully informed his 'highly honoured brother with a pure heart' that he could not accept Damad Ferid's conciliatory move: 'The questions I am urging you to answer with "yes" or "no" have unfortunately remained unanswered. Undoubtedly, my most venerable Pasha, "the hand of God is over all others", but it is none the less a fact that those who try to find a way to solve this question . . . must have a fixed aim.' The old man grew tired, and telegraphed, 'Only two more words, my Soul . . .' But Kemal insisted on having the last one, which affirmed the national strength, and suggested that it was time for the Sultan to 'deign to come to a decision and settle this question'.

It became clear that Damad Ferid could not last much longer, however confidently the British High Commission might count on his 'wonderful faculty of hanging on'. At first the Nationalist movement had been under-rated in Constantinople. What was it but a few undisciplined gangs, led by a man who had been dismissed from the army, hence had no regular forces under his command and little authority over the irregulars? But the rebel seizure of telecommunications finally awakened the Allied powers and Damad Ferid's Cabinet to the true danger which faced them. They recognized it as a 'declaration of war' against the central Government. Kemal had prepared his ground well and it was evident that the Sivas Representative Committee was a power, backed by a formidable array of army commanders and civil authorities, which must now be seriously reckoned with.

Damad Ferid, having failed in conciliation, fell back on the idea of a show of force, and pleaded to the Allies for help against the rebels. He proposed to send a large Turkish force to confront the Nationalists at Eskishehir. But the Allies refused to sanction this; nor would they provide him with Allied troops for the purpose. The threat from the Nationalists had placed them in a quandary. Only the withdrawal of the Greeks and the Italians from the region of Smyrna could appease them; and this was impossible. Resistance to them on the other hand would mean the end of the Armistice and a resumption of war – this time a civil war, of unpredictable outcome.

The British thus decided to withdraw their remaining forces from the danger-points in Anatolia. First they withdrew from the Samsun area, a departure celebrated in Sivas with torchlight processions and shouts of 'Down with the Occupation!' Two days later Ali Fuad started operations against the important junction of Eskishehir, where they had a force protecting the railway. But they were forestalled by a British withdrawal. The western rim of the Anatolian plateau was now securely in Nationalist hands.

At the instance of the Sultan, Damad Ferid now resigned. His bid to remain in the Cabinet as Minister of Foreign Affairs, and thus continue to enjoy the amenities of the official residence that went with his office, was firmly rejected. In his place Ali Riza Pasha, a former staff officer, who had served in Tevfik Pasha's Cabinet, was invited to form a 'Ministry of Conciliation'. He was instructed to hold early elections for a new Parliament, thus appearing to meet the Nationalists' demand. He established some popular confidence. The censorship was at once relaxed. The press became free, not only to attack Damad Ferid, but to publish for the first time the statements of Mustafa Kemal and full news of the Nationalist movement.

Kemal had good reason to declare in an interview to his friend Rushen Eshref, 'Now the first phase is at an end.' Within a little over four months of his landing in Samsun he had brought down the Government which had dismissed him from the army and the Grand Vizier whom the Allies were using. Thanks to astute and single-minded leadership, to an efficient and expanding organization, and to a simple and clearly defined programme, he had indicated to the Allies that they might have to deal no longer with a supine puppet government but with a positive new national force, conscious of its rights and firm in its demands, which was struggling to rise from the ashes of the Ottoman Empire.

CHAPTER TWENTY-FOUR

MOVE TO ANGORA

ALI RIZA suspected Kemal's motives. To Izzet, whom he brought into the Cabinet as one of his ministers, he exclaimed, 'You will proclaim a Republic – a Republic!' Nevertheless he had little choice but to come to terms with the Nationalists. In the exchange of telegrams which followed his accession to power, he returned the soft answer to the uncompromising demands on which Kemal thought it politic to insist. Behind his truculent façade Kemal too took a conciliatory line, announcing to his people 'the glad news that complete unity had been arrived at between the new Cabinet and the national organizations'. But he firmly refused to dissolve the Sivas Representative Committee until the promised elections had been held.

One of Ali Riza's first actions was to send emissaries to Anatolia, to report to him on the situation in the various areas. To Amasya he sent Salih Pasha, the Minister of Marine, for discussions with the Representative Committee. Kemal received him there in person amid the plaudits of those citizens who had assisted at the birth of the movement, with such imponderable prospects, only a few months before. Now they were to see it officially recognized by the Constantinople Government. On its behalf Salih and his delegation approved in effect the resolutions of the Sivas Congress. Their discussions led to agreement on all points – the principle that the new Government would send to the Peace Conference only delegates who had the confidence of the Nationalists.

The important question then arose as to where the new Parliament, due to be elected, should meet – in Constantinople or in Anatolia? Kemal nourished a deep and intuitive distrust of Constantinople and its ways. He had for long aspired to shift the centre of political gravity to Anatolia, and hoped that the moment for this might have arrived. He thus urged that Constantinople, 'being under foreign occupation, was not a very favourable spot for the deputies to carry on their legislative duties unmolested'. He quoted the precedents of the French sitting at Bordeaux in 1870, and of the

Germans lately at Weimar, as an argument that the new Assembly should sit in Anatolia until peace was signed. He succeeded in arguing Salih Pasha into personal agreement with him. He could not bind his own Cabinet but promised to do all he could to convert them to a similar view. But they were not to be converted. Nor indeed did Kemal get support from his own organizations in Constantinople, who insisted that the Parliament could very well meet there without danger – though some took the view that it would be imprudent at present for the Nationalist deputies to take their seats.

Kemal then called a conference of his army corps commanders at Sivas to discuss the question. Here he argued that Anatolia must retain its initiative, as the centre of affairs, lest the national movement lose its momentum and the people relapse into inertia. He thus urged that Parliament should meet either in Angora or Eskishehir, and that the Representative Committee should become, in effect, its Cabinet.

Kiazim, with his orthodox constitutional outlook, was cautious. Rauf was at first undecided, but eventually agreed with Ali Fuad that the Sultan and the Allies would probably suppress Parliament in any case and that this would provide ample justification for a new Assembly in Anatolia. To put the Allies in the wrong would enhance the moral position of the Nationalists in other foreign eyes.

Kemal saw that he would have to give in; the moment was not yet ripe for an Anatolian Parliament, and it was thus agreed that Parliament should meet in Constantinople. But the deputies were to meet the Representative Committee beforehand to decide on means of protection in the city and to agree on a united policy. Kemal then set to work to secure the election as deputies of those friends – not forgetting his ADCs – who would best serve his cause.

While they were conferring, an element of some discord arrived in the shape of Fevzi Pasha with a mission of investigation from Ali Riza. Fevzi was a friend of the Nationalists, who had resigned from the War Ministry on the Smyrna issue, and had supported Kemal on his departure for Anatolia. But his attitude now, and that of his colleagues, was dubious. He sought to convert the Nationalists to a moderate line, counselling them not to take too firm a stand against the Government in Constantinople.

He had hoped for co-operation from Kiazim Karabekir, whom he now found in Sivas, and to whom he even confided an idea of arresting Kemal and Ali Fuad. Kiazim, crusty and punctilious, had periodic friction with Kemal, who was apt to be off-hand with him, failing to keep him informed as to his actions and often by-passing him with orders and appointments of his own. He had misgivings moreover that, in Kemal's hands, the Nationalist movement was assuming too personal a trend and shared some of the suspicions of those around him in the east who mistrusted his ambitions and resented his arbitrary ways. In reply to Fevzi, however, he adhered loyally and sensibly to the view that for the present it was essential to support Kemal, since he was the only leader capable of accomplishing the national aims, and provided the only alternative to submission to a Government controlled by the Allies. Fevzi after a while came round to this view, and Kemal, who had himself at first talked of arresting him, bade him a polite if reserved farewell on his return to Constantinople.

Kemal, with his Representative Committee, spent four months in Sivas. But now, with the elections approaching, the time had come to move westwards – despite the misgivings of Kiazim, who feared that the east would thus be left in isolation and a prey to disorders. Kemal decided on Angora as his headquarters, a central place linked to Constantinople by rail and in touch besides with the western and southern fronts, where irregular bands, whether independently or under Nationalist orders, were engaged in guerilla warfare against the occupying troops of the Greeks, French and Italians. Thus the Nationalist deputies were invited to assemble here for indoctrination, before proceeding to take their seats in Constantinople.

Kemal and his companions left Sivas for Kayseri, *en route* for Angora, on 18th December 1919. Well received everywhere, he proceeded to Kirshehir, whose inhabitants greeted him with special enthusiasm. He conversed with the leading citizens, made a speech to the Youth Association, and at a torchlight procession launched into poetry, quoting and adapting Namik Kemal: 'A Kemal who came from the midst of this nation said:

"The foe thrusts his knife into the heart of the land.
There was none to save our ill-fated mother."

Again a Kemal coming from the heart of this nation says:

"The foe thrusts his knife into the heart of the land.
But yes, one is found to save our ill-fated mother." '

Next day he left for Angora, which he was to see for the first time. Kemal had chosen Angora as the seat of his movement because of the exceptional loyalty of its people, and those of the surrounding villages, to the Nationalist cause. The place had shown a similar spirit of patriotism at the time of the Young Turk Revolution – a spirit not shared by the people of Konya, with their fanatical Moslem spirit, or those of Eskishehir – his first choice – who were closer to Constantinople and to European influences in general. In terms of its population, Angora was one of the securest centres in Anatolia.

Kemal's choice was amply vindicated by the tumultuous welcome which the people of Angora gave him. The town-crier strode through the streets, proclaiming, 'Mustafa Kemal and his Green Army are coming.' Outlaws from the Sultan's régime, turned bandit, came out from their mountain hide-outs to greet him; crowds swarmed out of the city to intercept him on the road from Kirshehir; dervishes stood by the roadside ready to chant prayers to him.

Kemal appeared in a decrepit Benz touring-car, whose worn-out tyres he used to declare were stuffed with rags. Walking down with his friends into the city, he was welcomed by an army of irregulars – thousands of horsemen and infantrymen, swaggering by in their picturesque kilted costumes, bristling with antiquated weapons of formidable size, waving flags and breaking out of the procession to leap around in their national dances, while the beat of the drum and the clash of the cymbal and the reedy melody of the flute rang through the steep narrow streets of the citadel. A more sedate procession of the various trade-guilds brought up the rear.

Never before, within the memory of its inhabitants, had Angora seen such a gathering. The few foreigners looked on in some astonishment – the British at the station, which they had occupied a few days before, and whither the procession made a detour to demonstrate the fervour of the national feeling; the French, with their Tunisian soldiers perched on the walls around the future Parliament building, where at present the tricoloui flew. Kemal took the precaution of paying a brief visit to the Haji Bayram Mosque, with its sacred tomb. Then, from the balcony of the government building, he made a speech of thanks to the people massed below. That evening he sent out a circular telegram, announcing the arrival in Angora of the Representative Committee, which had been 'the object of sincerely patriotic and enthusiastically cordial demonstrations on the part of our great nation, not in Angora alone but along the whole of their journey'.

Not long after his arrival Kemal was joined at long last by Ismet. In Constantinople Ismet had been working in the War Ministry with Fevzi. His late arrival in the field, moreover only on an exploratory visit, won him a guarded reception. Kemal treated him at first with less than his accustomed warmth, while Ali Fuad and the rest, who had unquestioningly risked all for the sake of the Resistance, regarded him with definite coldness. Among Kemal's adherents it was the beginning of a conflict between the founders of the Revolution and its latecomers, which was to increase in intensity as time went on, and was indeed never wholly to be resolved.

The deputies now began to arrive, singly and in small groups. Day after day· Kemal set himself patiently to talk to them, working to clarify their ideas, and convince them of the need for cohesion. To unite Turkish opinion in Parliament, however, was no easy task. These deputies represented a diversity of interests. Each man was to some extent for himself. The habit of combining for a disinterested national purpose had yet to mature among them. There were many who mistrusted Kemal, many more who were irresolute. Others considered that he had served his purpose, now that their period of outlawry was over and that they were free to return to

Constantinople in the honourable guise of legislators. Many disregarded his summons. Among those who obeyed it were others whom he afterwards had cause to lash with his tongue for their lack of faith in the movement, their timidity in avowing their support of it and pressing its views, their poor fighting spirit, their inability to see that this was a moment in history at which the nation must act or perish.

As he had feared, their resolution was soon undermined by the various influences of Constantinople, and the united party for which he had urged the necessity was not to materialize. Nor, when Parliament met, did the deputies support his own candidature for the presidency of the Chamber, a position he had sought in his zeal for constitutional practice. His titular presidency would strengthen his position if the Parliament were dissolved, as was sure to happen, and the time came for him to summon a new one. But the deputies voted against it, preferring him to remain 'the power behind the Chamber'.

Ismet meanwhile returned temporarily to Constantinople, to discuss resistance measures with Fevzi and other friends in the War Ministry. For Kemal nothing remained for the moment but to consolidate his position here in Angora, and await what he saw to be the inevitable events in Constantinople. He did not have to wait for long.

CHAPTER TWENTY-FIVE

THE ALLIES RAID PARLIAMENT

THE OTTOMAN PARLIAMENT met in Constantinople on 16th January 1920. The first with a Kemalist majority, it survived for a bare two months. For the Allies at once showed their hand. They demanded the resignation of Jemal Pasha,[1] the War Minister, and his Chief of the General Staff, Jevad Pasha, on the grounds that they had been aiding the Nationalist forces. To this Ali Riza agreed, rather than resign with his Cabinet and so permit the Allies to appoint one of their own, perhaps once again under Damad Ferid. This high-handed action of theirs at least precipitated the acceptance by the Chamber of Kemal's final draft of the National Pact, which thus acquired the stamp of official recognition.

The key to the situation now lay largely in London and Paris. The illness of President Wilson, with his hopes for American intervention, had delayed the discussions of the Turkish peace treaty for a further six months – just the time needed by Kemal to build up that effective national Resistance which Lord Curzon had always predicted. Within a few months the President was to disappear altogether from the American scene, 'a broken and baffled prophet', as Lloyd George put it, 'unable to put up any further fight for his faith'. Nothing more was to be heard of American commitments to Middle Eastern affairs.

Lord Curzon thus judged that the moment had come to prepare a draft Turkish peace treaty. He remained faithful to his plan for an independent Turkey in Asia, but still sought to eject the Turks 'bag and baggage' from Europe. In this, if in little else, he had the support of Lloyd George. Both, however, were strongly opposed by Mr Edwin Montagu, the Secretary of State for India, who maintained that the expulsion of the Caliph from Constantinople would gravely offend the Moslem world and thus threaten the British position in India. His view, supported for different reasons by the War Office, ultimately prevailed in the Cabinet, which decided by a

[1] Mersinli Jemal, a supporter of the Amasya Declaration.

large majority that the Turks should remain in Constantinople, subject to international arrangements for the free passage of the Straits.

With French concurrence the decision was conveyed to the Turkish Government. Kemal, in Angora, was not impressed by such a 'gilded promise', especially as it was accompanied by a demand that all operations against Allied troops, including those of Greece, should cease forthwith. This, he judged, was an Allied threat to occupy Constantinople on the pretext that the Government could not control the national forces.

It coincided, on the other hand, with a more conciliatory policy towards the Nationalist movement on the part of the French. At Sivas Kemal had received a visit from M Georges Picot, the French High Commissioner in Syria. Though in fact his journey had the official blessing neither of Beirut nor of Constantinople, he announced himself at Sivas as 'the representative of the French Government'. Kemal received him as such, and they discussed at some length their joint desire for Franco-Turkish friendship. Picot was concerned primarily with the disturbed situation in Cilicia, where he asked Kemal to help keep the peace. But Kemal, for whom Picot's visit implied, for the first time, recognition of the Nationalist movement by an Allied power, felt himself to be in a strong position. Building it up for the benefit of the Frenchman, he talked grandiloquently of his 'national armies' – to the surprise of Rauf and the rest who knew them to consist only of a few irregular bands. Unless the French could show that they had no designs against the Turks in Cilicia, they would fight there to defend their independence. Picot was impressed by this positive attitude, comparing it favourably with that of the Government in Constantinople. Not long afterwards the Paris press began to reflect certain Nationalist sympathies.

From such signs Kemal judged that the moment had come to force the hand of the French in Cilicia. In view of 'the friendship which we have felt towards France for centuries', he protested, in the name of the Representative Committee, against the occupation of Urfa, Aintab and Marash, as contrary to the terms of the Armistice, and called upon the population to act against it.

The objective of his first attack was Marash, a place thinly held by the French, which they were thus forced to evacuate. His guerilla bands poured over the mountains to reinforce the Turkish gendarmerie and set fire to the Armenian quarter. They were well enough armed, drawing on the *caches* which Kemal had had the foresight to form at the time of the Armistice. The Turkish population fired on the Armenians from their windows and the rooftops as they fled from their own burning houses to take refuge in schools and churches. These were fired in their turn, burning hundreds, including women and children, alive. Meanwhile fanatical Moslems were slaughtering and committing atrocities against the Christians in the villages around.

It was only after nearly three weeks of bloodshed that the French could muster a column strong enough to attempt the relief of Marash. But as it approached the city orders were given to its troops, from an unexplained source and to the bewilderment and panic of the Christian inhabitants now confident of rescue, to retreat. They struggled back southwards over the mountains towards the Syrian frontier, in weather of Arctic severity, followed by thousands of Armenian fugitives, falling in the snow by the wayside. Two hundred French soldiers lost limbs, some all four of them, from frostbite alone. In the whole operation some seven or eight thousand Armenians lost their lives, a massacre which, accompanied by others in the neighbouring areas, caused consternation in the capitals of Europe.

The retreat from Marash was the first move in a reversal of French policy which was to lead to the ultimate evacuation of all Cilicia. The city of Urfa was besieged, and surrendered when its supplies were exhausted. Other places fell to irregulars, better armed than the French and raising forced levies from the villagers. Aintab was to hold out for some time longer. But the Turks had gained control of the mountain regions and were soon carrying out murderous sorties down into the wide Cilician plain to threaten the important centres of Adana, Tarsus and Mersin. Thus at the end of May 1920 the French were finally driven to seek an armistice, and sent a delegation to Angora for the purpose. Though the armistice was later broken it enabled Kemal to regroup his southern forces. More important, he had raised his prestige and won recognition for his régime by a victory against one of the great powers.

In the eyes of the British, his success simply made more urgent the execution of the policy towards which they were moving already – the suppression of the Nationalist movement. The illicit traffic of arms to Anatolia was beginning to cause them serious concern. This was well run by underground organizations, staffed largely by demobilized Turkish officers. Their task was not hard, since the guards on most of the depots were Turks and there were plenty of willing porters, boatmen and drivers to run the stolen arms into Anatolia through the gauntlet of British patrols and Greek guerillas. They concealed them in peasant carts, beneath loads of hay or sacks of coal, transporting them only by night, then burying them before dawn and reloading them at dusk for the next long slow stage of the journey. In the War Ministry itself there had been, since the Armistice, a systematic evasion of its disarmament terms with the connivance of such patriotic generals as Fevzi, who was now once more Minister of War.

The French now began to connive at the theft of arms. From a depot under their protection in the Gallipoli Peninsula the Nationalists secured a large haul, the French merely giving the excuse that their guard had been outnumbered by the raiders. The Italians, in their antagonism to the Greeks, had from the start sympathized with the Nationalists, and were now, as they prepared to withdraw their own troops, selling arms to them and helping the gun-runners to avoid the Allied control points. As for the British, they had from the start been casual over the confiscation and storage of arms. A British staff officer was heard to express the opinion in GHQ that it was unfair to disarm the Turks without also disarming the Greeks.[1] Thus the arming of the Nationalist forces continued.

With the news of the French defeat in Cilicia, and of the massacre of Armenians that went with it, a sense of the Nationalist threat had at last percolated through to the delegates in Paris. Regarding Kemal, Lloyd George admitted that 'our military intelligence had never been more thoroughly unintelligent'. Even now there seemed to be some doubt as to whether he was acting on his own or under orders from the Sultan's Government. Lord Curzon himself confessed to the Conference that he had not been aware 'that the connection between the two was as close as now appeared', and disclosed that, according to his latest information, Mustafa Kemal had recently been made 'Governor of Erzurum' – a city included in the proposed state of Armenia. Whatever his official position, it became obvious that no treaty should be framed without looking into the prospects of its enforcement.

Consulted on this point the High Commissioner, Admiral de Robeck,[2] considered that if the treaty were to be drastic, resistance to its terms should be forestalled by a strengthening of the Allied position in Constantinople. A plan thus arose in the Supreme Council for a show of force to teach the Turks a disciplinary lesson. It was to take the form, as Kemal had anticipated, of a more complete and stringent occupation of Constantinople, where the Allied forces in theory had hitherto only been 'present'. This would involve control of the War Ministry but not of the civil administration, and the establishment of a military censorship. The Supreme Council proposed also, not very realistically, the 'dismissal of Mustafa Kemal from Erzurum (sic)'. The occupation was to continue until the execution of the peace terms.

Kemal heard of the impending occupation from the French. He passed on the news to Rauf, urging that the Nationalist leaders should prepare to leave the city. Let the Chamber, by all means, continue to defy the Allied decision and carry out its duties. But it was important that Nationalist supporters should come to Anatolia in sufficient numbers and of such a

[1] An element of comedy attended the continuous raids on a large Allied depot by the shores of the Golden Horn. Each evening seals of wax were placed on the doors; each morning they were found to be broken. But all the guards protested innocence. When finally a British officer sat up one night to watch the building, he observed that a flock of goats had been let into its grassy compound. It was these bearded creatures who, in the intervals of mouthfuls of grass, approached the doors as he watched and nibbled off each of the seals. – Harold Armstrong: *Turkey in Travail*.

[2] Later Admiral of the Fleet Sir John de Robeck, Bt, GCB, GCMG, GCVO.

calibre as to form an alternative government. He telegraphed money to the Ottoman Bank to assist their escape.

Under cover of darkness in the early morning of 16th March 1920, British warships drew in to the Galata Bridge, British armoured cars rolled through the streets of Stambul and Pera, British troops occupied police stations, military posts and the main public buildings. The news came through to Angora in a series of messages from a telegraphist loyal to the Nationalist cause: 'The English have made a surprise attack this morning on a Government building at Shehzade Bashi and have had a skirmish with the soldiers. At the present moment they are beginning to occupy Constantinople. . . . We have just this moment heard that the Military School has been occupied. English soldiers are on guard outside the telegraph office at Pera, but it is not yet known whether they intend to occupy it or not.'

Kemal sat in the telegraph office in Angora, receiving the telegrams, instructing his secretaries to summarize and pass them on to all commanding officers. From the Ministry of War came a message, 'At this moment the English are patrolling the town. They are now entering the Ministry. They have occupied it. They have reached the Nizami Gate. Interrupt the connection. The English are here.'

Confirmation came from the Central Telegraph Office: 'Your Excellency, English sailors have occupied the telegraph office at the Ministry of War and have cut the wires. They have occupied Tophane, and troops are being landed from their men-of-war. The situation is getting worse. . . . Early this morning while our soldiers were still sleeping English sailors occupied the Post Office; our men, being suddenly aroused, were still half asleep when the fighting began which resulted in six of our men being killed and fifteen wounded. . . . The Telegraph Office at Pera does not reply any more. Probably it is also occupied. God grant that they will not occupy this office. . . . The director and officials of the Telegraph Office at Pera are just arriving here; they have been turned out of their office. . . . Your Excellency, I have just heard this moment that this office will be occupied within an hour.'

Kemal asked: 'Have you heard anything about the Chamber of Deputies? Is the telegraph office there in working order?' 'Yes,' the reply came, 'it is.' But from this moment the connection ceased. The Allies had occupied the office.[1]

French and Italian troops did not at first take part in the operation, but joined in later to claim their share when the city seemed securely in the hands of the British. The casualties were relatively few, but some bitterness was caused among the Turks by the killing of several musicians of a military

[1] Later Kemal paid a public tribute to the telegraphist, one Hamdi Effendi of Monastir, who had kept him informed, and brought him to Angora to take charge of the main telegraph office there.

band who had been mistaken for active soldiers. On the morning of the occupation the entire Turkish staff of the War Ministry, including Fevzi, the Minister, was seen standing in the square outside while British officers searched the building. All over the city they searched houses and dug up tombs in the graveyards where arms might be hidden.

Entering the newspaper offices, they ordered editors what to print, and introduced a strict censorship. The communiqué, explaining the occupation and blaming the Turks for it, must be printed word for word – an injunction which pleased one sub-editor, who noticed, as every reader was bound to do, that the word for battle was wrongly spelt, in the Armenian style, clearly not by a Turkish translator. Signed by 'The Army of Occupation', the communiqué reiterated the crimes of the Committee of Union and Progress, and denounced the new crimes of their partisans of the 'National Organization'. While the Allies sought peace they had embarked on a new period of war. Thus the city was to be provisionally occupied; the Turks were still not to be deprived of Constantinople, but in case of general troubles or massacres this decision would probably be modified. One newspaper ingeniously responded to the censorship by refusing to comment on the occupation at all, confining itself to daily editorials about the old public fountains in Constantinople, and thus implying to the public mind disapproval of all that was happening.

In the course of the occupation some eighty-five deputies were arrested. Those who kept away from their homes at first escaped. One of these was Rauf. Carrying out the decision he had reached at Sivas, he deliberately courted arrest in Parliament itself, thus hoping to put the foreigners in the wrong. Some others shared his view, among them Dr Adnan, the husband of Halide Edib, who confided his intention to her that evening.

'Haven't you yourself been urging,' he said to his wife, 'that the peoples are our friends and governments our enemies? Let the peoples – let the English people – see to it that their government, the oldest parliamentary government in existence, does not do injustice to a representative institution.'

Halide Edib, with her down-to-earth feminine realism 'suddenly had a vision of old Roman senators sitting tight in their seats while Rome was taken by strangers'. The more who could get clear away to Anatolia the better. Knowing Rauf's 'chivalrous and impossibly heroic nature', she could understand his point of view. But Halide 'realized with sensible clearness how painfully and irrevocably there existed in Europe two separate standards of humanity'.[1] Thus, in common with many others, she went with her husband into hiding and prepared to leave for Anatolia with the aid of the 'underground' organization.

In the Parliament building Rauf's friends tried in vain to persuade him to escape. They produced two Turkish private soldiers' uniforms, begging

[1] *The Turkish Ordeal.*

A.—8

him and Kara Vasif to disguise themselves for the purpose. But both refused. Rauf put up a show of gaiety, saying, 'Let the scoundrels come. Here we are.' Parliament, he urged, must on no account disperse of its own accord. It must be dispersed by the Allies.

The Sultan summoned a delegation from Parliament with Rauf at its head. They drove to the Yildiz Palace through streets lined with British soldiers, their bayonets fixed. The Sultan referred to the power of the foreigner, and warned them to take care what they said in Parliament. 'These people,' he said, 'are capable of anything, they will not stop at what they have done so far.' Several deputies spoke up in patriotic protest. One pointed out of the window at the Allied fleets in the Bosporus and said, 'Your Majesty, these waters are as far as these infidels can go. They cannot go beyond. Anatolia is made of steel. It will succeed in its struggle.' The Sultan repeated his warnings to be careful. 'If they wish,' he insisted, 'they can be in Angora tomorrow.'

Rauf then spoke. 'As stated in the National Pact,' he said, 'our problem is how to save the Sultanate, the Caliphate and the country. If we may interpret the nation's feelings, may we ask of you that you do not sign any international treaty without Parliament's consent?' The Sultan showed his irritation by rising to his feet. This was the signal for the rest to rise. He bade them a cold farewell.

The delegation returned to Parliament. The debate began. A detachment of British troops marched into the lobby, demanding that the Parliamentary Guard surrender Rauf and Kara Vasif. There was pandemonium in the Chamber; Rauf urged that the Guard should resist this attack on the Assembly. But the President of the Chamber instructed its commander that arms must not be used. Thus the two Nationalist leaders were arrested and led away to a British warship, where they were herded together with some hundred and fifty others, including deputies and prisoners of various and dubious kinds, to be shipped off to exile in Malta. As a reprisal for the deportations Kemal immediately ordered the arrest of all remaining British officers in Anatolia, including Colonel Rawlinson in Erzurum.

Two days later Parliament met again. A majority decided that, in view of the aggression of the foreign troops and the arrest of members by force, they could no longer perform their duty in freedom. It was thus agreed to prorogue Parliament indefinitely. Salih Pasha, who had succeeded Ali Riza as Grand Vizier, refused, in response to a note from the Allies, to disavow Kemal and the Nationalist leaders, and resigned. The post of Grand Vizier was offered once again to Tevfik. He refused it – to his subsequent regret and that of many of his compatriots. For his refusal enabled the Sultan to bring back Damad Ferid, who proceeded, in the words of Winston Churchill, 'to brew the thinnest government he had yet attempted. Its first action was to dissolve Parliament – the last in the history of the Ottoman Empire. It then proceeded to launch what proved to be a civil war against the Nationalist forces.

The British High Commission rated the occupation as a success. Admiral de Robeck reported to Lord Curzon, in *couleur de rose*, that without being a knock-out blow it had been a severe blow for the Nationalist movement. Sir Henry Wilson, the Chief of the General Staff, thought the reverse. 'The Frocks,' he wrote in his diary, 'are completely out of touch with realities. They seem to think that their writ runs in Turkey in Asia. We have never, even after the Armistice, attempted to go into the background parts.' Here indeed their occupation had been limited to a few strategic points, now evacuated. In fact, thanks to these two successive acts of aggression – the despatch of the Greeks to Asia Minor and now, ten months later, the occupation of Constantinople – the Allies ensured that the writ to run in Turkey in Asia, as eventually in Turkey in Europe, would be that of Mustafa Kemal.

CHAPTER TWENTY-SIX

THE TREK TO ANATOLIA

THE BRITISH had presented Kemal, for the second time, with a major political advantage. He lost no time in exploiting it. The occupation of Constantinople, as he saw it, and as he declared in an immediate proclamation, had 'destroyed the seven-centuries-old existence and sovereignty of the Ottoman Empire'. Throughout the consequent fight for the survival of the Turkish nation, he took care as usual to invoke Islam. 'God,' he assured his people, 'is with us in the Holy War which we have entered upon for the independence of our country.'

Kemal, good staff officer and shrewd politician as he was, forgot nothing. He remembered the rest of the Islamic world, to which he sent a similar proclamation. He remembered the foreign powers, appealing not merely to the governments but to 'the conscience of the scholars, intellectuals and civilized men of Europe and America' to take notice of action 'inconsistent with the honour and good name of the nations concerned'. By 'a criminal attempt hitherto unrecorded in history', an Armistice based on the Wilson Principles had 'resulted in a trick by which the nation has been deprived of its means of defence'.

He remembered the Christian minorities, sending out to his various local authorities a circular to stress that, as contact had been temporarily broken between Turkey and the outside world, the minorities would no longer enjoy foreign protection, hence to insist on a humane attitude towards them as 'conclusive evidence of the civilizing factors existing in the character of our race'. All these steps were taken within an hour or so of the occupation.

Kemal then went ahead as swiftly with his major task – that of summoning a new Parliament to meet, under his own auspices, at Angora. For two days he sat at the telegraph, communicating and exchanging views on this problem with all his commanding officers. Then he issued a communiqué, convening an 'Assembly with Extraordinary Powers' – in effect a Constitutional Assembly with powers to alter the system of government. It was to be attended by all available members of the previous Chamber, and by new members to be elected on a specified date by the various constituencies.

Meanwhile it became the duty of every serious patriot, every able-bodied soldier, to make his way through the Allied cordon from Constantinople into Anatolia. The British authorities plastered the city with posters, in English and Turkish, signed by the Commander-in-Chief and threatening 'DEATH', in large letters, to anyone harbouring a Nationalist. But since, in making their arrests on the eve of the occupation, they had chosen to employ uniformed troops instead of plain-clothes agents who might have known where to find them, large numbers got away, often in disguise, across the Bosporus and thence, by a number of 'underground' routes, inland.

Halide Edib disguised her husband, Dr Adnan, and herself respectively as a *hoja* and his aged wife. Crossing the Bosporus by night 'brilliantly illuminated by the lights of the warships', their guns glistening and their sailors pacing the decks, they reached the *tekke* at Scutari where they knew that the dervishes would give them sanctuary. There they found four other deputies, also escaping. Halide judged one of them to be wise, for his remark: 'What we want is a really good map and a guide'; another to be foolish for his boast, 'I have five bombs and three revolvers in my bag. Have no fear.'

Her journey to Angora with Dr Adnan was typical of innumerable others, and her description of it reflects the conditions in Anatolia at this time. The roads from Scutari eastwards down to the Izmit Peninsula, which was occupied by the Allies, were well guarded by British infantry and cavalry. The mountain paths were constantly raided by bands of Greeks whom the Allies were arming. A few Turkish bands struggled to keep them at bay, and to help the Nationalist refugees to get through. They were helped too, all along the line, by an efficient system of communications run by loyal telegraphists, who passed news secretly from one post to another of the arrival and departure of each Nationalist group, and of such movements of the Allied forces as were likely to impede them.

At the start of the journey Halide travelled by carriage while the men of the party, who were more easily identified, walked by circuitous routes. She describes her arrival one evening at a village where she ran into a detachment of English soldiers: 'Suddenly a pair of very blue and very tired eyes peered into the carriage. . . . But the soldier simply turned his head and walked on, certain that there was nothing to worry about.' After dark she reached the agreed destination. At once the news of her arrival was telephoned to the central post: 'This is Samandra. . . . Is that Guebze? Yes, she is safe, she has escaped without accident. . . . Yes, the others are walking through the fields.' Late at night they arrived safely, but all had to leave again, almost immediately, driving through the darkness on an ox-cart by side-tracks, since the British had heard of their arrival and were lighting up the fields with their searchlights for the guerillas to see them.

On the way Halide Edib had the chance to study the different types of fighting men who were forming the raw material of the Resistance. There were the Macedonian gendarmes, with 'the wildness, the enthusiasms, the emotions, the rebellious instincts under tyranny, the dominating cruel instincts when in power, common to their race. Hero-worship, desire for change, desire for some vague thing called a New Turkey prompted them.' They had fought in the mountains with Enver who, according to rumour, was now fighting the British at the Khyber Pass. He was the brave man; the Sultan the traitor. It was surely the Sultan who was selling us to the enemy – 'shame on him – a *Padishah* from the House of Osman!' Their commander led the conversation away from Enver and back to Mustafa Kemal – a great soldier too, who would beat the Greeks back to Athens.

Of a different stamp, quiet in his manner and more down-to-earth in his attitude, was a tall Anatolian with a gentle face and a round black beard. 'In him,' she writes, 'I saw the humour – quiet, sardonic, buried deep down; in him I saw this intensely practical nature. One felt with this man that he was not going to believe easily in the possibility of Mustafa Kemal Pasha's marching to Athens or Enver Pasha's fighting with the English in the Khyber Pass. However deeply he had felt injured by the Padishah's treachery, probably nothing would have induced him to swear at the Sultan. Yet for all that he would not work one particle less stoically for what he considered to be almost a lost cause.'

As they went on, every possible road seemed to be held by the British cavalry, and they had to take to the mountains, escorted over the rough paths by a local band of irregulars. To Halide, 'they seemed such boyish creatures with their personal ideas of right and wrong, mingled humanity and cruelty, all subservient to a very definite sense of the inviolability of the given word. They had an invincible resentment against the Government, considering all governments promise-breakers and capable of performing any dirty trick in the name of the law, and were very well aware that the Nationalist government, to whom they happened to be useful at the moment, would as likely as not have them all killed if it suited them to do so. Yet they would always consider themselves the faithful children of Turkey.'

Then a party of regular staff officers arrived, on their way to Angora. 'It was strange to contrast these officers, perfect in their bearing and their exquisite Old World manners, with the tiger types!' Between the two types – the regulars and the irregulars – there now arose in microcosm those elements of discord which, as the war developed, were to grow into a source of conflict on a major scale. Which was to command? The romantic bandit chief, for all his intrepidity and panache, lacked the powers of planning and organization required to confront serious risks. A regular staff officer was needed, and the choice fell on the senior of the newcomers, Colonel Kiazim. 'Oh these wretched irregulars!' was the impatient thought in his mind. But he tactfully shook the chief by the hand, and renounced any command over him and his men. Halide's own corporal and henchman, Mehmed Chavoush, was relieved. 'He never could stand these irregulars giving orders to soldiers of the Turkish army – the pride of caste.'

Thus the cavalcade, after many vicissitudes and detours, reached the last peak from which the Sea of Marmara and the waters of the Gulf of Izmit could still be seen: 'All the horses stopped and all eyes were turned towards the patch of enchanting blue-green liquid. No one looked at his neighbour; every eye was turned towards that part of his life which he was abandoning – perhaps for ever. Each and every one of us seemed entirely apart from the rest. I wrenched myself round first, and turned my horse's head downhill, down the other side of the range. The sea was shut out.' Only the wide open waterless spaces of Anatolia lay ahead of them.

Thus slowly and arduously they moved from one world to another, from the orbit of Constantinople into the orbit of Angora. A telegram came from Mustafa Kemal himself. It brought good news. Now that Ali Fuad had forced the British to retire from Eskishehir the railway was open, and they should proceed to the nearest railhead for the last stage of their journey. Here they were joined by Yunus Nadi, a well-known journalist, who had come from Constantinople by a different route. From Eskishehir the train passed on to Angora. As they approached it towards evening Yunus Nadi came up to Halide in some agitation, saying, 'Oh, Halide Hanum, the station is full of a tremendous crowd. There will be speeches. You will speak for us, won't you?'

'Don't worry,' she said, 'I will do it.'

The crowd on the platform looked sombre in the twilight. A slender grey figure emerged from it and 'moved quickly towards the train, pulling his gloves off. His face, with its large-cornered kalpak, had become indistinct and colourless in the dusk. . . . The door of our compartment opened suddenly, and Mustafa Kemal's hand reached up to help me down the step. . . . It is a narrow and faultlessly shaped hand, with very slender fingers and a skin which nothing darkens or wrinkles. Its swift and sudden movements reminded me of Mehmed Chavoush and of that new revolutionary type of whose existence I had become aware in Samandra. It seemed to me that the merciless hunting of the human tiger in Turkey had its answer in this hand. It differed from the large broad hand of the fighting Turk in its highly strung nervous tension, its readiness to spring and grip its oppressor by the throat.'

'Welcome, Hanum Effendi,' he said in a low voice.

This was Angora. This, she thought to herself, was to be the *Kaaba* – the Mecca – of the Nationalist movement.

Angora at this time was little more than a pair of twin hills, rising like nipples from the bosom of the Anatolian plateau. Crowning one of them were the half-ruined walls of a citadel which had seen and survived notable Turkish conflicts. Clambering up to it and around it and within it was a human warren of mud-brick houses and ruins of houses, huddled lattice to lattice and roof above roof amid dunghills and winding precipitous lanes. Rough with stones and, at this season when rain was frequent, awash with mud, they provided a hard climb for the horses and tne ramshackle carriages which, apart from the long peasant bullock-carts with their spokeless wailing wheels, were Angora's only means of transport.

To a Turkish war correspondent[1] who saw it for the first time after a weary journey across the mountains from Inebolu, the Nationalist port on the Black Sea, the place seemed a 'horrible hole'. The innkeepers greeted him with a cynical smile. The congestion in the town was such that accom. modation was measured by the square yard and he would be lucky to get a numbered step of a staircase on which to sleep. As it was, he slept in a cupboard.

Angora was in fact hardly more than a large village, its population reduced to a mere 20,000 by a disastrous fire which had wiped out a section of it during the war, leaving blackened remains which still scarred the lower slopes of the hillside. The citadel looked out to all points of the compass over the naked treeless plain, snowbound in winter, sun-baked in summer, waterless but for the rainfall and a few scattered wells.

From a distance a low ridge of undulating hills, rough and colourless, half-embraced the site. And 'site' it still was. The city – still to become a city – had begun to spill itself down on to the plateau, but had yet to spread far across it, obstructed largely by a stretch of waste-land which in the winter became a marsh. Here stood the railway station and a few public buildings which the Young Turks, remedying Ottoman neglect, had erected. Here was also a small and unkempt municipal garden.

This 'Mecca of the Nationalist movement' had little to offer in terms of distinction, far less of amenity. But there was, in its immeasurable skies and its clean translucent air, in the asceticism of its landscape and the contrasting softness of the violet and amber lights which bathed and transfigured it at dawn and again at dusk, a rarefied atmosphere which set it apart from other places. Even its inhabitants were a people apart, with their own individual brand of strong silent cussedness and earthy self-respect; with moreover an outlandish pronunciation of Turkish, which the men from Constantinople did not easily understand.

This sense of 'apartness', of isolation in the midst of a converging hostile world, generated in the small and still intimate band of patriots who had thrown in their lot with Kemal that strange spirit of elation and comrade-

[1] Alaeddine Haidar, *A Angora Auprès de Mustafa Kemal.*

ship which animates men in a desert. Here was a desert indeed, to which life must be given, on which order must be imposed, whose hidden scattered elements must be drawn together into a unity and an effective, positive force for the regeneration of the heart of Turkey in Asia. Such was the challenge to be faced against odds which seemed, at this moment, overwhelming.

CHAPTER TWENTY-SEVEN

PARLIAMENT IN ANGORA

THE WAR of Independence, launched as a Resistance movement against the foreigner, now developed besides into a civil war – and at that a holy war – between Turk and Turk. The Sultan declared open hostilities against the Nationalists. The Sheikh of Islam, in a *fetva* – a legal ruling – entitled 'Insurrection against the Sultan', proclaimed them to be rebels. It ended with the words: 'Is it permissible to kill these rebels? Answer: It is a duty to do so.' It was distributed throughout the country, and in places dropped by Allied aircraft. Damad Ferid as Grand Vizier further denounced the Nationalists as 'the false representatives of the nation', a corrupt group of men, ready to sacrifice the country for their own personal ambitions.

Religious leaders were sent into Anatolia to preach war against them in the name of the Sultan-Caliph. The soldiers in the Nationalist forces were incited to rebel against their officers or to desert and return to their villages. An army of the Caliphate was formed to fight the Nationalists, recruited at a good rate of pay from among men who included the unemployed riff-raff of Constantinople. Officers were hurriedly commissioned to command them and march them to a headquarters at Izmit. Very soon this army and its affiliated bands of irregulars had gained a wide measure of control over north-western Anatolia.

With such a campaign on his hands, and the consequent need to organize his army, Kemal yet realized that the organization of a Parliament must be his first concern. Only thus could his Resistance have the necessary popular backing. In a talk with Yunus Nadi he said, 'In the age in which we are living, everything has to be legitimate and legal. All actions must be based on the decisions given by the people and must interpret the general wishes of the people.' Military action must thus be based on the sanction of a legally elected Assembly.

In creating it Kemal must reply in kind to the Islamic manifestoes of Constantinople. Thus he still acted outwardly in the name of the Caliphate, whose abolition was his ultimate objective. With every appearance of deference he mobilized the *ulema*, the religious authority of Angora, which now issued a counterblast to Constantinople in the form of a *fetva* of its own. It declared that a *fetva* issued under foreign duress was invalid, and called upon Moslems to 'liberate their Caliph from captivity'. The fiction must be preserved that he was not a traitor, as he was later to be branded, but a prisoner of the enemy.

Kemal knew that the feeling among many of his supporters was hesitant. Though proscribed as rebels they shrank from the semblance of overt rebellion, clinging to their religious scruples and to the desire to preserve traditional forms. To reassure them, and to encourage such deputies as might be reluctant to come to the newly elected Assembly, he thus circulated throughout the country his own proclamation which outdid the Sultan-Caliph himself in its Islamic invocations. The opening of the Assembly, it announced, was to take place on a Friday. It was to be initiated by a solemn prayer in the Haji Bayram mosque. 'All the honourable deputies,' it instructed 'will take part in this prayer, in the course of which the light of the Koran and the call to prayer will be poured forth over all the believers.' In order to emphasize the sacred character of this day the whole of the Koran and the *Buchari*, a screed concerned with the traditions of the Prophet, were to be recited everywhere for two whole days beforehand, together with prayers for the liberation from the foreigner of the 'Sublime Person' of the Sultan-Caliph. Sermons were to be delivered on the sacred nature of the Nationalist movement. There would be prayers for the deliverance and salvation of the Caliphate, followed everywhere by a ceremony of congratulation to the Assembly, and the recital of the *Mevlud*, the hymn in verse which honoured the birthday of Mohammed.

Adhering strictly to this sacred ritual the first Nationalist Parliament opened its doors on Friday, 23rd April 1920, some five weeks after the British occupation of Constantinople, while Kemal's soldiers kept watch from the neighbouring hilltops for a possible incursion by the Sultan's irregulars. From dawn onwards the population of Angora and the surrounding countryside, flaunting such glad rags as it possessed, swarmed into the streets. By noon, the hour of the inaugural service, the congestion inside the Haji Bayram mosque was so great that all the deputies could scarcely gain entrance.

With Kemal and the rest they processed, jostled by the crowds, to the converted Parliament house, a solid structure with a mock-Oriental façade, which had formerly served as the premises of the Committee of Union and Progress. The procession was led by three Imams, bearing the green flag of the Prophet. The red flag of the Turkish state flew from the roof of the building; the green flag was draped inside, beneath a text from the Koran. After a pair of wethers had been sacrificed in the garden Kemal advanced to cut a ribbon across the door of the Chamber, and a hundred and fifteen deputies filed in to take the oath, swearing to safeguard the independence of Sultanate, Caliphate, country and people. When all had finally taken their seats, their numbers amounted to three hundred and sixty-nine.[1]

The Chamber was a long rectangular room, with balconies at either end, equipped with varnished school desks and a makeshift tribune for President and speaker. It was observed that, in the headgear of the deputies, the fez and the turban, both symbols of reaction, outnumbered the now more progressive kalpak by sixty-five to fifty. An adjoining room had been set aside as a small mosque, furnished with lecterns and prayer-rugs orientated towards Mecca. In the absence of electricity the members began their deliberations by the light of a single petrol lamp, borrowed from a café. Within a few days notices had appeared on the walls prohibiting any indulgence on the premises in backgammon or other games of chance, while the consumption of alcoholic liquors was strictly forbidden. Only in the seclusion of a dark back room, behind a neighbouring tobacconist's shop, could the more emancipated members refresh themselves with a drink.

This Grand National Assembly, as it was to be named, was the product of days and nights of exhaustive discussion between Kemal and his closer associates. With a selection of them he had taken up his headquarters four miles outside the city, in the serviceable stone building of the Agricultural School, which the Unionists had erected. It stood on a hilltop, in the midst of a model farm, an 'oasis' in the arid treeless plateau, where the acacias were now springing into bloom and the fields were lightly flushed with green. Here among others lived Dr Adnan and Halide Edib who, with Yunus Nadi, had taken in hand the organization of a new Anatolian News Agency. Ismet had returned to Angora shortly after them with a party of deputies and others, inconspicuous in his soldier's uniform until Kemal singled him out at the station, smoking quietly at the fringe of the welcoming crowd, to give him, this time, a warm and cordial embrace.

There was much work to be done. Yunus Nadi describes the scene. Rising in the morning Kemal calls his secretary, Hayati: 'Come, child, what is there in that file? Read it to us.'

There is a report from Aintab, where operations against the French still continue.

'Anything new?'

[1] The sittings of this Assembly, to which members rode on horseback, tethering their horses to a trellis outside the building, have been compared to the early meetings of the North American farmers, after the Declaration of Independence – Dagobert von Mikusch, *Mustafa Kemal*.

'The French in the American School were repulsed, but the enemy counter-attacked and fired on the city causing damage.'

'Write this down,' Kemal orders. 'The only way to solve this situation is by direct contact between Aintab and Urfa. . . .'

Another file is opened: 'The Nationalist troops in Suruch have repulsed the French. But they complain they have no weapons or ammunition. They say there is some in and near Mardin. They want it.'

'Tell Mardin to give it them.'

'The siege of Urfa continues.'

'The garrison must be strengthened. Tell them to do that, and report to me.'

'The Nationalist troops based on Adana fired on a French destroyer, near the shore.'

'That is the best way of fighting. Molest the enemy all the time. They did well to fire on the ship.'

'Demirji Mehmed Efe sends you greetings.'

'Does he still call me his brother Mustafa Kemal Pasha?'

'Yes.'

'Good for him.'

Life at headquarters was austere. 'We lived,' wrote Halide Edib, 'like members of a newly founded religious order in all the exaggerated puritanism of its inception. Mustafa Kemal Pasha shared our life, and while among us was as strictly pure as a sincere Catholic priest. But some evenings he disappeared. . . .'

Lunch at headquarters was a hurried affair. But in the evenings all relaxed for dinner around an enormous horseshoe table. Here was the atmosphere that suited Kemal. He liked, as he had done in his army mess, to preserve certain standards of ceremony, as though all were partaking not of sparse and simple rations but of a civilized Western repast. He dominated the table with his talk, sometimes amusing, sometimes boring, always astringent as he reminisced with the others of past experiences, always pointed in his anecdotes, ironic and outspoken in his assessment of enemies and friends alike. Ismet, with his gentle manners and his large thoughtful eyes, proved a contrast to Kemal. Leaning a little forward in his deafness to catch what was said, he spoke more slowly, commented less harshly, inserted his innuendoes with more caution.

In the discussion of ideas Kemal swept away pretences in a way which disconcerted and often shocked his more conservative listeners. But the next moment he might be setting up other pretences, more in line with his own purposes, to take their place. To Halide Edib he seemed 'to have no convictions whatever and he adopted now one thing and now another with the same vehemence and energy, no matter how contradictory they were, so long as he thought they would benefit him and the cause in some way'.

Kemal was no lofty idealist. He had few moral principles, only a determination to attain his ends. But, cynic though he was, these ends were none the less the country's. His was no negative cynicism, but that of the realist who seeks practicable solutions. Opportunist he might be in his means of achieving them, but once achieved they must prove inherently sound, they must work. Turkey under his aegis must not merely be saved from the foreigner; she must be rebuilt on an enduring foundation.

After dinner at headquarters came the serious business of the evening. The party would move out into the big central hall, there to talk and to work, sometimes until five o'clock in the morning, on the numerous problems which confronted them. Foremost among these was the nature of the Government which was now to be set up.

Kemal himself, and a handful of his friends, saw this as a turning-point in Turkish history. It was 'a matter of admitting that the Ottoman Sultanate and the Caliphate were finished, and of establishing a new state based on new foundations'. But here, as at Erzurum and Sivas, this ultimate goal could not then be openly specified. When in the course of their discussions Yunus Nadi tried out the suggestion that they were, in fact, being called upon to form a new Turkish state in Anatolia, the general reaction was one of dismay, and Kemal quickly silenced him. The opinion of the company, he stressed, was required only on the nature of the new Turkish Parliament.

The debates on this subject were long, now hidebound by academic pedantries, now wandering off into misty speculations. The deputies from the dissolved Ottoman Parliament in Constantinople had come with the idea that the new Government was merely temporary and should thus be a replica of the old. They envisaged no break with the principles inherent in the Sultan's régime. Jelal-ed-Din Arif, as president of the old Parliament, saw himself as thereby president of the new. Dozing a little through the nocturnal discussions, he would awake to reiterate the word, 'Continuity, continuity.' As a professor of constitutional history, with a rigidly legalistic mind, he expounded his idea of the new Government as that of a constitutional monarchy of a liberal Western kind, equipped with legislative and executive, but temporarily deprived of the monarch, who should be represented by a regent in the shape of a neutral president of the National Assembly.

Kemal and his intimates were working for something quite different. Scrupulous as he was to preserve legal forms and appearances, the last thing he in fact sought was political continuity. Anatolia must break away altogether from Constantinople, its institutions, its traditions. It must be animated by a new spirit, hence by a new system of government. Adroitly – and, in view of his ultimate Republican intentions, disingenuously – he turned Arif's argument against him by declaring, 'What you want sounds like a Republic; but the Republic is a form which will frighten the people. And why should we adopt an old form already known? We can create something for ourselves that will suit us.' What he proposed to create was something derived more literally from those theories of Jean-Jacques Rousseau which he had devoured in his student days. It should be based on the principle that power – whether legislative or executive – is indivisible, and belongs unconditionally to the people.

Kemal's mind was a compound of intuitive ideas with a smattering of such ready-made theories. Halide Edib saw it as 'two-sided, like a light-house lantern. Sometimes it flashes and shows you what it wants you to see with almost blinding clearness; sometimes it wanders and gets itself lost in the dark.' Some such confusion of thought lay behind the form of government which he now forcibly put forward as original, but which seemed to Halide and others 'merely an adapted convention', somewhat clumsy and loose, with affinities to the Soviet form in its political – as distinct from its social and economic – sense. It allowed for a National Assembly which should exercise both legislative and executive powers, to the extent even of electing each member of the Cabinet. Ministers should be com-missaries of the people, with no collective responsibility to the Cabinet as such, but only an individual responsibility to carry out the decisions of the Assembly. Nor was the president of the Assembly himself to be endowed with personal responsibility.

As, night after night, Kemal poured forth these ideas, reducing his listeners to exhaustion, some of them ventured to argue, on practical grounds, that in a country so little used to the ways of democracy the Cabinet should be appointed not by the Assembly but by the president. But Kemal had his motives in propounding the other system. Firstly he saw the vital necessity for an idea, as fuel to keep the Revolution aflame. Only this could unite the disparate elements and give positive substance to the patriotic impulse – an ultimate war aim, conceived in those more abstract terms to which the Oriental mind responds. What better than the slogan of 'The Sovereignty of the People'? The autocracy of the Sultan and the oligarchy of the Young Turks was to give place in the new Assembly to a form of popular democracy in which the people enjoyed full power, even to the extent of appointing the Cabinet.

Kemal's second consideration was tactical. He must at all costs control this Assembly. But he knew very well that its members would not be easy to handle. Professionally and socially they were a mixed crowd, many of them with a deep distrust of Kemal and his dictatorial ambitions. The need to disarm this prompted his rejection of the orthodox view that the president should appoint his own ministers. The only way to control such an Assembly was to encourage it to think it was controlling itself.

Thus Kemal assiduously lobbied not only his friends but the deputies, visiting them in the dormitories of the Teachers' Training School where they were lodged in barrack-like conditions, living on a diet of free beans and rice, armed with revolvers beneath their pillows and called to prayer five times a day from the top of the stairs.[1] He sat on their beds to answer their questions and to deliver them long and patient expositions. For the most part plain Anatolians, with little comprehension of theories of government, they were persuaded without too much trouble of the merits of his proposals. Finally Arif and his friends gave in, and agreed to accept them. Arif also agreed, with some reluctance, to concede the presidency of the Assembly to Kemal and to step down himself into the role of vice-president or Speaker.

Kemal's opening speech to the Assembly took the form of a motion, but in view of the scruples and doubts of so many members, 'a motion of which the intention remained concealed'. He proposed a Government which should not be defined as provisional, nor should its head be a regent. No power should stand above its Grand National Assembly. This should combine the legislative and executive functions and should elect a council to conduct its affairs, under the president of the Assembly. A note, in brackets, was added to this: 'As soon as the Sultan-Caliph is delivered of all pressure and coercion he will take his place within the frame of the legislative principles which will be determined by the Assembly.' Kemal had succeeded in relegating this sole reference to the Sultanate and Caliphate to an ambiguous footnote.

The Assembly greeted these resolutions with enthusiasm, and accepted them after a short debate. Kemal issued in its name a proclamation confirming them. It elected him as its president, then elected a Cabinet whose seven ministers had been previously chosen in effect by Kemal and his inner circle, and the choice afterwards canvassed among the deputies. Prompted by Kemal, they co-opted Ismet, Chief of the General Staff, as an additional member. The ministers began to work in the bare rooms of the government building, with hardly enough chairs and tables to accommodate them.

What the Grand National Assembly had done in effect was to accept, without knowing it, the prototype of a future Republic. A parliamentary committee was appointed to draft a Constitution Act, giving legal form to the Assembly and Government. Nine months were to elapse before it succeeded in doing so, thrashing out with some heat the contradictions inherent in a system by which national sovereignty lay on the one hand with the people, hence with the Assembly, and on the other with the monarchy which the Assembly was pledged not to destroy, but to liberate. But Kemal finally succeeded in pushing it through the Assembly, firmly side-tracking discussions on the future of the monarchy and Caliphate to

[1] Later, whenever there was money in the Exchequer, the deputies were paid a salary of a hundred Turkish pounds (£20) a month, and contributed to its funds by paying for their board and lodging.

pass an Act which confirmed the unconditional sovereignty of the people and must thus eventually prove incompatible with the continuance of the Sultanate.

Meanwhile, announcing the opening of the Assembly in a personal message to the Sultan, Kemal reminded him in eloquent terms of a dream of his forbear, Sultan Osman, the founder of the dynasty, which had passed into oral tradition. The sacred tree, he dreamt, which cast a shadow over three continents and sheltered a hundred million Moslems, had been deprived of its branches, and only its bare trunk remained. 'The trunk of that sacred tree,' Kemal assured the monarch, 'is in our hearts.' Loyalty to Caliph and Sultan was the first and last word of this Assembly. Printed and judiciously circulated, such sentiments had notable propaganda value in the more backward parts of Anatolia.

One evening at this time a retired officer, who smuggled arms and brought news from Constantinople, arrived at the Agricultural School with the news that seven of the Nationalist leaders had been condemned to death by a special tribunal convened in the name of the Sultan. They included Kemal himself, Ismet, Ali Fuad, Dr Adnan and Halide Edib – the first woman in Turkish history, as the officer remarked kissing her hand, to be so honoured. The sentence was confirmed by a *fetva* of the Sheikh of Islam, by which it became the religious duty of any Moslem to kill them on sight, with the certainty of a reward in heaven if they succeeded in doing so.

When the news came Kemal and Dr Adnan were sitting in the dusk near the window of the central hall, while Ismet leant against the table. Anxious to know their reactions, Halide Edib asked her husband, in a jesting tone, what he thought of the honour.

He turned towards Kemal and said, 'I feel very much upset, myself – I hate to be condemned to death. How do you feel about it?'

'I also mind it very much,' Kemal said frankly.

Halide herself argued that the sentences showed a lack of any sense of political values. 'Nothing,' she said, 'could make us more popular than this.'

Ismet, more cautious and practical, considered that, while this might apply in the occupied regions of Constantinople and Smyrna, it would operate otherwise among the large populations which had not yet decided whether to support the Sultan or the Nationalists. In the civil war areas it could win undecided minds to the other side. It was therefore necessary to keep the Constantinople newspapers out of Anatolia, and to prevent the news from spreading.

A few days later the Assembly retaliated by condemning to death Damad Ferid and the others responsible for the judgements, a sentence confirmed by the local religious authorities in a series of *fetvas* distributed throughout

Anatolia. Thus the Angora Government returned blow for blow against that of the Sultan. The Grand National Assembly then embarked on its task of governing, at least in theory, a divided country, and waging war against enemies, both from within and from without, whose numbers mounted day by day.

CHAPTER TWENTY-EIGHT

THE CIVIL WAR

KEMAL was now free to concentrate all his energies on the planning of the crucial campaigns which confronted the Nationalists. First, he needed to organize his staff. In Ismet, Ali Fuad, Kiazim Karabekir and Refet he had four loyal and seasoned commanders. An important but still doubtful quantity was Fevzi Pasha, whose somewhat equivocal attitude had been exploited to discredit the cause in the rebellious districts.

But now he arrived unexpectedly at Ali Fuad's headquarters, after an arduous journey by the 'underground' route. To Fuad he remarked, 'Mountains cannot join each other, but people can join each other.' He sat down and added frankly, 'We have joined each other, but I think it's a bit late.'

Fuad announced his arrival by telegram to Kemal, but received the reply, 'Return Fevzi Pasha to the place he has come from.' After a further exchange, however, he telegraphed, 'Send Fevzi Pasha immediately by train to Angora, under custody, but without his being aware of it.'

Kemal in fact fully appreciated the value of a man of Fevzi's calibre. He was the conservative type of Turkish officer, who had won a sound military reputation during long campaigns in the Balkans and later in the First World War. Afterwards his successive positions in the War Ministry had brought him political prestige. His character, steady and slow and industrious, his strict habits of life and his middle-class virtues were such as to earn him popular respect. He was above all a man of deep religious beliefs, the devoutest of Moslems, who never touched alcohol and recited the Koran to his troops in the heat of the battle. He was thus an especial asset to the cause at this moment.

Much was made of his arrival in Angora, where he delivered a stirring address to the Grand National Assembly. He became Minister of Defence, and head of the Cabinet – thus in effect Prime Minister. His weight helped Kemal to hold the balance between the rival commanders. Kemal had made Ismet Chief of his General Staff. A born staff officer, familiar with the workings of his master's mind, he was the obvious choice for the task, which at this stage was one primarily of organization, of planning a new army from its foundations upwards. But both Ali Fuad and Refet were hostile to Ismet, from whom they differed profoundly in temperament. They strongly opposed his appointment on the grounds that he was a late-comer, while they themselves were pioneers who had been with Kemal in Anatolia from the start. Kemal none the less confirmed it, and Ali Fuad and Refet retained their commands in the field, for which, as men of action and resource, they were more suited at this difficult time. Ali Fuad, however, remained bitter against Ismet and once, at a party given in his honour in Angora, became so angry at a guest's praise of him that he banged violently on the lid of the piano and almost broke it.

Refet had lately brought off a *coup*, in the settlement of an awkward situation at Konya. He had been organizing the irregulars on the Smyrna front, living with the guerilla warlords and building up for himself a legend, under the pseudonym of Aydin Efe, as a dashing and elusive figure who made madcap visits, at great risk, to Constantinople, to maintain contact with the revolutionary groups in the city. When he arrived in Angora in April, Halide Edib met him for the first time. He seemed to her 'to be made of nothing but nerves and muscles of steel, without an atom of flesh on them anywhere. His face was as thin and strong as his slim, wiry and rather elegant military figure. . . . Energy of an unusual quality sparkled from his face, his eyes, his movements; his head, hair and hands all talked together with dramatic gestures. His clothes were faultlessly cut, his spurs and buttons flashed, his boots were of the shiniest patent leather, his whole attire just glowed with fastidiousness.'

The holy city of Konya, some hundred and fifty miles across the bare salt plateau which stretched away southwards from Angora to the rim of the Taurus mountains, was showing signs of unrest. Instructed to hold elections its commander, backed by the leading citizens, had begun to waver in his allegiance. How could elections be held, he asked, without the author-ization of Constantinople?

This was a key city, of considerable standing throughout Anatolia, whose loss would be a damaging blow to the Nationalist cause. Urgent action was necessary, and Refet was sent to Konya to report on the situation. From a station on the railway nearby he sent a polite request to the commander and other notables to meet him for a conference. Then he sent a number of telegrams to non-existent units in the area, instructing them to march on the city. The bluff succeeded. Early next morning the delegates arrived at the station. Refet at once coupled their train to his own and set off with them to Angora.

Here, after a patriotic harangue from Kemal, the kidnapped citizens were left to make up their minds whether or not to collaborate with the

Nationalists. Finally the commander agreed to break with Constantinople and bring Konya into the Nationalist camp. This led to the withdrawal by the Italians of the detachment of troops which had moved up there from the Adalia region.

Thus Konya – though it was to rebel twice more – was for the time being quiet. But from all other directions Angora was beset by enemies. During these months of spring and early summer Kemal had to contend not merely with the threat from the foreigner but with internal upheavals, successive and often simultaneous, in no fewer than thirty-four different districts. 'The flaming fire of rebellion,' as he put it, 'raged and reduced the whole country to ashes.' It raged to the east as well as to the north and west of the city, thus obliging Kemal, while still holding the Greek front, to keep his scanty forces constantly on the move from one point of the compass to the other. Active encouragement was supplied by the British with the provision of arms for the rebels.

Typical of the leaders of this Caliph's army was an aged and illiterate Circassian bandit named Anzavur, operating in the region north of Smyrna. A fanatical Moslem, who fought under the flag of the Prophet with a Koran round his neck and hanged his enemies, likewise Moslems, on fig trees, he enjoyed the active favour of the Constantinople Government. Kemal pitted against him another of his kind, a younger, cooler-headed and not wholly illiterate Circassian named Ethem, who proved more than his match, and whom indeed the Nationalists themselves had to watch lest he gain too much personal power. Thus the south-western area was for the moment cleared of insurgents.

Now the Nationalists were faced with a more serious insurrection led also by Circassians in the north-western area, around Bolu. From their relatively isolated mountain strongholds, the revolt spread down to the plains around Angora and, gathering supporters, reached a village no more than seventeen miles from the city. When Kemal sent two deputies to parley with the villagers they were arrested and all but executed.

To control such local situations the Nationalists set up a series of emergency tribunals, somewhat on the lines of those established during the French Revolutionary 'Terror', which would administer justice of a swift and summary kind on the spot. Given the name of Independence Tribunals they were responsible not to local authorities but to the Assembly itself, thus affirming the supremacy of Parliament. Later these courts were to be used and abused for political purposes. But at this stage they were rather a military instrument, a necessary agent of rough justice for the condemnation and immediate public hanging of rebel leaders as a warning to others.

The revolt spread 'like a prairie fire', by spontaneous combustion, sparks blowing across the countryside to set alight districts far apart from one another. This could not be quenched by regular forces, tired as they were from the war and reluctant to fight their own countrymen. Kemal had to rely largely on undisciplined irregular bands whose leaders were hard to control. Ethem the Circassian was able to occupy the important centre of Bolu. On doing so, he insisted on the execution of a number of rebel leaders who had been promised their lives by Angora in return for sparing those of the two deputies previously sent to the district. The death sentences were referred to Kemal, creating tense feeling among his associates at the Agricultural School when it became clear that he was determined to sign them.

As was his habit, even when he had made up his mind in advance, he asked for the opinion of each one before announcing his decision, and it was clear that all were against the executions. Halide Edib in particular spoke with passion against what she saw as an act of deep treachery, tainting the high principles of the Nationalist movement. But she spoke in vain: 'I soon saw that Mustafa Kemal was obdurate. Occasionally his eyes flashed, then again went cold and pale; the lines of his face deepened, his eyebrows stood out, and altogether he looked extremely dangerous. He openly avowed that in our condition there was no place for mercy, pity and sentimental morality; that scruples about breaking a promise were a sign of weakness; that any who indulged in such considerations were bound never to succeed.'

The ruthless cynicism of this view shocked his hearers. But only Ismet, listening thoughtfully as Kemal spoke, rose to answer him, walking across with his light springy step to the desk where he sat, and leaning over it to engage him in earnest argument. Speaking in the simplest terms he contended that their Government, if it was to have any claims to decency, must keep its word, that there must at all costs be mutual trust between Government and people. Their discussion grew intense, and continued until the pearl-white Angora dawn began to light up the window behind Kemal's back.

Finally Kemal rose, angrily rang the bell on his desk, and sent for his secretary. Then, as Halide describes it, 'He leaned over, wrote a few lines, and signed. I see again Colonel Ismet's eyes hurriedly scanning the lines, then lifting his head with a smile of joy like a small boy. Mustafa Kemal Pasha had asked Ethem not to kill Sefer and those of his men who had been given a promise of pardon.' But the reprieve came too late. By the time it had arrived Ethem, without waiting for Kemal's signature, had executed the prisoners, as Kemal may well have known that he would do.

This was a time of tense and continuous anxiety in the offices of the Agricultural School. The Nationalist fortunes fell to a low ebb. Kemal himself, drinking endless cups of coffee, gazing silently out of the window at the bare colour-lit Angora landscape, 'looked harassed and at moments almost hopeless'. Nevertheless, 'he continued with the utmost subtlety and energy trying to keep in touch with and direct the dispersed units which were struggling for the cause.'

His secretary would come in with copies of telegrams: 'Is that Angora? This is the town of X. I am the Governor. The anti-Nationalist Caliphate army is approaching. I can hear the uproar in the town. I believe the towns-people will join them. Can you give me instructions before they cut the wires?' Then the secretary would add, with a military salute: 'The wires show earth,' meaning 'The wires are cut.'

Again: 'Is that Angora? I am the telegraph operator of the town Y. The wires are cut but I have managed to place an instrument at two hours' distance from the town and can communicate at night. I have been listening to the conversation of the Governor of Z with the anti-revolutionaries. He has come to an understanding with them. I will now repeat the conversation. . . . He is a traitor.'

Every night they found themselves cut off from more centres and shrank more into themselves, weary and haggard, working until the yellow oil lamps went pale with the light of the approaching dawn, then sleeping briefly and fitfully for fear of an attack by the enemy. Morale was low in the Assembly itself, where groups of deputies were grumbling against Kemal and his apparent inability to check the rebellion. In the Assembly building one morning Kemal, himself in a nervous mood, called a friend Kiliç Ali, who was a cavalry commander, took him to a window and showed him what appeared to be a crowd, moving down towards the city from the hills. He ordered him to take out a group of his men and reconnoitre, taking care to do so unobtrusively, without alarming the deputies. Then they looked again and saw that the 'crowd' was a herd of cattle.

Finally, after a night when nearly all the wires were cut and firing was heard quite near, the point was reached at which an emergency plan was drawn up to leave Angora for Sivas if need be, and large numbers of horses were mobilized for the evacuation. As the time ticked by it seemed more and more likely that the plan would be executed. Dr Adnan supplied himself with a phial of poison, for use in an emergency. Kemal himself began to say that the moment to leave had arrived.

When Refet reached Angora from the south-west he found an atmosphere of despondency, if not of defeatism. With his resilient optimism he laughed off all the talk about withdrawing to Sivas. He himself, for one, had every intention of staying, and if Kemal insisted on going – well then, he joked, he would shoot him. Did he not remember the vows they had taken at the outset of the campaign – either to succeed or to die? The road to Sivas was in any case threatened by hostile forces. There was, he concluded darkly, another obstacle to their journey. He had hidden the saddles of the horses. Let them instead sit down and discuss means of relieving the military position. They had still some resources available. There was, for example, his own company of faithful irregulars, his three hundred Zeybeks, whom he would summon from the mountains of Smyrna.

These wild men were soon swaggering around Angora, picturesquely caparisoned and bristling with weapons, disconcerting the citizens with their outlandish undisciplined ways. The women of the village, in the plain below their quarters, complained that they came too often near the river, staring at them and frightening them as they spread out their laundry to dry on its banks. One evening the secretary came into the central hall and announced to Kemal that the wires were cut. At that moment firing was heard outside – sometimes solitary shots, sometimes a continuous volley. 'At once,' records Halide, 'everyone was excited; Mustafa Kemal Pasha walked about and gave orders, gesticulating, his eyes gleaming, and everyone else was on foot and moving about too. Perhaps everybody thought we were living our last minutes.'

Faced with this moment of apparent danger, the two men, as she observed, reacted differently. Refet, with his natural insouciance and strong nerve born of implicit moral reserves, sat calm and apparently indifferent, continuing to smoke 'in the same peaceful and slightly sleepy way'. But Kemal, with his more highly strung temperament and more animal responses, was nervous and showed it. Outstandingly brave in battle, capable as he had proved in Gallipoli of standing up alone before his men under the fiercest fire without thought for his personal safety, he was the man of action who lacked the more restrained moral courage needed to face a mob. Here was a passive situation quite new to him, and he reacted to it 'like a powerful tiger caught in a trap, angry and afraid'. Then the telephone rang and, as Refet may well have guessed, it proved only to be his own wild mountaineers who had caused the alarm.

Refet left with them next day. Without consulting Kemal he backed his luck – and perhaps his skill in irregular diplomacy – and took the calculated risk of going out at night to parley with the rebels. Kemal rebuked him severely by telegram, but he returned and announced, 'The business is settled.' In fact the pressure of the rebels on this front was slackening. The immediate crisis was over. Angora could breathe once more. For the moment at least there was no more talk of withdrawing to Sivas.

Meanwhile, in May 1920, while the Nationalists thus struggled with the Sultan's forces, the Allies had settled on the peace terms which they intended to impose on the Ottoman Empire, embodying them in an instrument to be known as the Treaty of Sèvres. 'Like fresh fuel thrown on the smouldering fire of hatred which the Western world had provoked by its conduct in Turkey' (as Churchill wrote), it was destined wholly to vindicate the Nationalist cause. From now onwards Kemal was to have the support, not merely of a small band of patriots, but of the bulk of the Turkish people.

CHAPTER TWENTY-NINE

THE GREEK INVASION

THE TREATY OF SÈVRES was an early product of that 'circus' of Allied conferences which, with continuous rounds of entertainment, followed the signature of the Treaty of Versailles. The final draft of the Turkish peace terms was agreed by the Supreme Council at San Remo in a sumptuous villa named after that Hindu paradise where souls pass several centuries of delicious inaction between two incarnations, and provoking Lloyd George to say, 'Here we are all three in Paradise. Who is going to be the serpent?'[1]

On this issue the French and Italians, disliking the Greeks and disinclined to underrate the Turks, were not in easy accord with him. Nor was Lord Curzon, consistent to the end in his opposition to any Greek encroachment on Asia Minor. He had circulated to the Cabinet, before San Remo, a despatch from Admiral de Robeck, whose advisers saw the occupation of Smyrna and its proposed perpetuation as a 'canker for many years to come, a constant irritation which would lead to bloodshed in Asia Minor for generations'. Did the British people realize, the admiral enquired, that the proposal to dismember the Ottoman provinces of Turkey in the interest of Greece would drive the remaining Turks into the arms of the Bolsheviks?

These views were expounded in vain. At the end of the conference Lloyd George said to Vansittart, a young Foreign Office official, 'We've got all we wanted.' 'You have, sir,' Vansittart replied – a distinction which seemed to escape his Prime Minister.[2] What he wanted, and got, was a peace treaty described by Keynes as Carthaginian. It amounted, as Kemal had long foreseen, to the end of the Ottoman Empire and its break-up into a series of small states and foreign spheres of interest. All that was to remain of Turkey was a rump of an inland state, with most of its outlets to the sea under foreign control, and its sovereignty reduced to a shadow.

She was to lose all her Arab possessions – a loss to which she was already

[1] From *Le Matin*. Quoted in *The Times*, 20th April 1920.
[2] *The Mist Procession.*

resigned. But she was also to lose, to the despised and hated Greeks, the whole of Thrace, leaving Constantinople with a mere enclave of European territory a few miles wide; and she was to lose, for all practical purposes, Smyrna and its hinterland. The Greeks would also get eight Turkish islands in the Aegean, while the Dodecanese islands would go to Italy. In the east there was to be an independent Armenia and an autonomous Kurdistan. By an additional Tripartite Agreement, much of the rest of Anatolia was partitioned into French and Italian zones on the lines of the original secret treaties.

Nearer home, the Straits were to be placed under international control. Turkey's finances would be wholly directed by the Allies. The hated Capitulations would be maintained and even extended. The Turkish army would be reduced to a token force under Allied supervision, while a limited Turkish gendarmerie would be officered by foreigners. Though the Turkish delegation in Paris was given a month in which to reply to the terms, it was clear that they were those of a dictated peace.

Venizelos, on his own account, at once made them public in Athens. This premature disclosure played into the hands of Kemal by the shock which it gave to an unprepared Turkish public opinion. The Constantinople press was unanimous in its condemnation of the treaty, which amounted in effect to the end of the country's very existence. The mass of the people began at last to awaken to these realities and to the meaning of the national idea which Kemal had been preaching for a year past. The flow of recruits to Anatolia soon swelled from a trickle into a slow steady stream.

Kemal took advantage of the situation, at this moment when the Bolu revolt was under control, to despatch a force which drove the Caliphate troops out of Izmit, and advanced to the last outpost before Constantinople, which was held by a British battalion. It was a critical moment. The British army blew up depots of stores, in preparation for a retreat. Under naval fire from the Sea of Marmara the Turks wavered and retired out of range. But Kemal had once more shown his defiance of the Allies. As Winston Churchill observed, 'We were once again, this time with scanty forces, in the presence of the enemy.'

Plans for a possible evacuation of Constantinople were hurriedly drawn up. General Milne called for reinforcements. He had insufficient forces to defend Constantinople and the Izmit Peninsula against a serious Nationalist attack. Here was Venizelos's chance. He was summoned by Lloyd George to the Cabinet and, in Churchill's words, 'presented himself as the good fairy. Two divisions of the five already in Smyrna would march northward, and would fall upon the Turks menacing the Izmit Peninsula and drive them away.' Another Greek division could also be sent from eastern Thrace.

The pundits met in international conclave once more, this time informally in the elegant Italianate villa of Sir Philip Sassoon at Lympne. Here Venizelos, calm, optimistic and plausible, repeated his offer. It was strongly opposed on military grounds by Marshal Foch who was supported by General Weygand. Even if the Nationalists were at first defeated in the field, it would still be necessary, they insisted, to liquidate the irregular bands and to protect lines of communication with the coast by the sub-jugation of all western Anatolia. For such a campaign the Greek forces, of which half were required to defend Smyrna, would not be adequate. The British General Staff supported the French.

But Lloyd George, still persuaded that the Greeks were the coming power in the Eastern Mediterranean, and Venizelos, convinced that the views of these experts were animated by anti-Greek prejudice, were bent on the adventure. As Harold Nicolson put it: 'In the Attic sunlight of his serenity the Allied statesmen surrendered to optimism.' The party thus moved across the Channel, and at a more formal conference in the agree-able Villa Belle at Boulogne, with tea-parties at the *Pré Catelan* and a fête at the Casino, the Supreme Council authorized a Greek advance from Smyrna. It began on 22nd June with the crossing at four points of the Milne Line, which had been laid down in Paris as the limit of demarcation between Greeks and Turks. It was a further violation of the Armistice which Kemal compared to the German invasion of Belgium.

The Greeks, with their superiority in numbers and modern equipment, had hoped for an early battle in which they were confident of breaking up Ali Fuad's sparse and ill-equipped forces, 'mere skeletons', as Kemal described them, 'without ammunition and incapable of being reinforced'. They met with little resistance. Kemal was too shrewd a strategist to give them such a chance. 'The Greek columns,' as Churchill described the offensive, 'trailed along the country roads passing safely through many ugly defiles, and at their approach the Turks, under strong and sagacious leader-ship, vanished into the recesses of Anatolia.' For here the plateau, the natural frontier of Anatolia, rises behind tiers of mountain walls, beyond the head of two long river valleys and up over a rugged escarpment – a march of some two hundred and fifty arduous miles from the sea.

The Turks retreated in orderly fashion on Brusa, the holy city on the slopes of Mount Olympus. Every man who could hold a rifle was mobilized for its defence. But it could not be saved. Its capture led to a link-up by the Greeks with a force which had advanced along the shores of the Sea of Marmara to recapture Izmit. The main Turkish forces retired eastwards, followed by a swarm of Moslem refugees, up to Eskishehir, where Kemal at once began to regroup and reorganize them for the onslaught on Afyon Karahissar, which must inevitably follow. Concurrently another Greek force overran eastern Thrace and captured Adrianople.

These 'remarkable and unexpected manifestations of Greek power,' wrote Churchill, 'were hailed by the Ally statesmen; the Ally generals rubbed their eyes; Mr Lloyd George became enthusiastic. He was right again, it seemed, and the military men wrong.' 'They are beaten,' he boasted, in full conference (this time at Spa), 'and fleeing with their forces towards Mecca.'

'Angora,' corrected Curzon acidly.

'Lord Curzon is good enough to admonish me on a triviality,' he replied. 'Nevertheless . . .'[1]

It was in this atmosphere that Damad Ferid, with a new 'ministry of marionettes' (in Churchill's phrase) formed for the purpose, signed the Treaty of Sèvres, a document 'obsolete before it was ready. . . . At last peace with Turkey: and to ratify it, war with Turkey! However, as far as the Great Allies were concerned, the war was to be fought by proxy. Wars when fought thus by great nations are often very dangerous for the proxy.'

For the moment it was the Nationalists who seemed to be in danger. The Grand National Assembly was dismayed at the spectacle of Brusa, a symbol, both religious and historical, of the Turkish spirit, under Greek occupation. How could it have fallen to the enemy so easily?

During the past two months Kemal had devoted much time and effort to the tactical handling of this motley fraternity. 'Before reorganizing Anatolia,' he said once, 'I had to conquer its people.' He had to conquer, first, the obstinate and querulous spirit of their elected representatives. The Assembly was manifesting all the fussiness and self-importance common to newly formed public bodies. He could count on the unquestioning support of no more than a minority of its members – his own immediate entourage, the few intellectuals, most of the army officers and civilian officials. But the majority still viewed him in a critical spirit, for ever watching his actions with an eye to catching him out in a blunder or in an attempt to enhance his personal power. For the most part they were Anatolian notables tasting power for the first time on something more than a local scale, and bent on exercising it to the full. They included also a group of clericals, reactionary in spirit, who could swing the vote, one way or another.

Thus daily Kemal would go down to the Assembly. Youthful-looking, ironical, a trifle distant, handsome in his morning-coat and kalpak, he would move with his quick step into the Chamber, sitting down in his place, taking notes, then tapping with his pencil to indicate that he wished to speak. He would fix them with his cold stare, address them with a frankness and a clarity that took them aback. Determined to show no undue respect, taking advantage of that familiarity which Islam allowed, they would interrupt and heckle him. With complete self-possession and a few brief words he would silence their murmurs. In that clear resounding voice

[1] Vansittart, op. cit.

which combined the accents of persuasion and authority, he would continue
to expound his arguments, his ideas, his demands. The charm would begin to
work, their voices to acclaim him, their hands to rise in an affirmative vote.

Often, however, lacking the habit of communal deliberation or indeed of
democratic procedure, they behaved in an unruly fashion. Each man,
occupied with his own impulses and ambitions, would rush to the rostrum,
jostling his fellows aside to pour forth on the Assembly streams of fluent
but often irrelevant rhetoric. The din of conversation was continual, and
the Speaker's hand-bell did little to quell it. Fights often took place, and
the more responsible members would intervene to prevent revolvers being
brandished, faces slapped and insults exchanged. On important occasions
the deputies would be subdued by the spectacle of Kemal's own henchmen
and drinking companions, glaring around the Chamber with ugly looks
and hands straying towards holsters. Years later, when the Grand National
Assembly had become a more seemly institution, an American senator,
after a sight-seeing tour of Angora, expressed to Kemal his disappointment
that he had not seen it at work. Kemal turned to his guide and said, 'What?
Did you not show him our Zoo?'

Kemal now returned from the front to face a parliamentary crisis. The
deputies had draped the rostrum in black as a sign of mourning for the
Brusa disaster, vowing that the draperies should remain there until the
achievement of final victory. Their lamentations flowed freely. The call to
prayer would no longer be heard from the minaret of the Green Mosque.
The sacred city had been trodden underfoot by 'our worst enemies'. But the
Sultan's Government and his Sheikh of Islam came in for a healthy share
of curses: 'Do they think they can establish our religion with the help of
Greek bayonets?'

One deputy rose to speak, but burst into tears and was obliged to sit
down. Another protested that this was no time for tears. 'Gentlemen, I
pray you, put back your handkerchiefs in your pockets; don't weep. Weeping
is only fit for women. If you are men, instead of weeping roar like lions in
the face of such a tragedy. Show by your actions the sublimity of Islam.'
To save the Caliphate fiery speeches were not enough: 'We must unite and
work together night and day. Let us leave aside the wearing of elegant
clothes, drinking, pleasure and love-making.' More practically, a secret
session was called to discuss measures of defence.

Here the deputies demanded on the one hand the court-martial of the
officers responsible for the loss of the city, on the other an operation for its
immediate recapture, whatever the cost. The Chief of the General Staff
promised to furnish a report and was thus able to stall for some weeks.
But the deputies were not satisfied. Kemal waited for their indignation to
cool, then himself took the black-shrouded rostrum. Patiently, lucidly and
in factual terms, he set himself to enlighten the deputies, so unversed in

military affairs, as to the real situation. They were demanding the concentration of all available troops for the recapture of Brusa. He granted them that such an operation might indeed be possible. But its ultimate outcome would be dubious. The city would be hard to hold for any length of time. The enemy, having command of the sea, could land more troops at Mudanya, and so outflank it; he could endanger the Turkish line of retreat; he could moreover advance from the south to the vital railway line between Eskishehir and Afyon, which the Turks would thus have no troops left to defend. What mattered was not the recapture of Brusa but the defence of Anatolia itself. For this vital purpose it was essential to think realistically, act cautiously, curb the emotions, await developments and prepare coolly to meet the next stroke of the enemy, from whichever direction it might come.

Kemal turned to the question of the internal unrest in the country. To deal with this it had been necessary to withdraw four important detachments of troops from Brusa, thus doubtless facilitating the advance of the Greeks. The prime necessity was national unity. Thus it was surely more important for the present to suppress the revolts than to resist the Greek offensive. He tried to bring home to the deputies the scantiness of the Nationalist forces, which was the fault not of a Cabinet two months old but of the Sultan's Government in Constantinople:

> It is not reasonable to make a great fuss and to say that the catastrophe would not have happened if our troops had taken up a position on this or that river or in this or that village, or if the officers commanding them had stopped the enemy in his advance. . . . Fronts can be broken through, but it is necessary to fill up the gaps in the line as soon as possible. This is only possible if reserves drawn up in echelon can be held in the rear of the forces in the front line. But were our national forces facing the Greek army in such a position, and had they such reserves behind them?

The answer was no. Driving into the obstinate heads of the deputies the conception that 'facts, bitter as they might be, must never be lost sight of', he concluded on a note of optimism, trusting that the situation would soon improve and that means could be found to give the nation hope and confidence. Meanwhile there was to be a call to arms by the Cabinet of men in various categories. Thus the Assembly, for the moment, calmed down.

But there was little calm for Kemal. The need to exercise patience with this rabble of mediocrities, as they often seemed to him, tired his nerves, already tense from the anxieties of confronting a war on all fronts with inadequate resources. Through the hot summer months of 1920 his growing but still inadequate staff, at close quarters within the hermit-like bounds of the Agricultural School, found him irritable and explosive. To Halide, seeing him in part through the eyes of the disillusioned romantic:

He was by turns cynical, suspicious, unscrupulous and satanically shrewd He bullied, he indulged in cheap street-corner heroics. Possessing considerable though undistinguished histrionic ability, one moment he would pass as the perfect demagogue – a second George Washington – and the next moment fall into some Napoleonic attitude. Sometimes he would appear weak and an abject coward, sometimes exhibit strength and daring of the highest order. He would argue with all the intricacies of the old-fashioned scholastic till he had become utterly incomprehensible, and then illumine some obscure problem with a flash of inspired clarity. . . . Of course, one knew all the time that there were men around him who were greatly his superior in intellect, and far above him in culture and education. But though he excelled them in neither refinement nor originality, not one of them could possibly cope with his vitality. Whatever their qualities, they were made on a more or less normal scale. In terms of vitality he wasn't. And it was this alone that made him the dominant figure.

At this critical period Kemal needed to persuade, to consult, to seek co-operation. But at moments the mask fell, revealing a deep-seated desire only to dominate. One evening he was engaging anyone at hand in an obscure and pointless dialectical argument. He called upon Halide for her opinion. She replied that she did not grasp his point. Suddenly his tone changed and he became brutally clear and frank.

'What I mean is this: I want everyone to do as I wish and command.'

She replied, 'Have they not done so already in everything that is fundamental and for the good of the Turkish cause?'

Sweeping aside her question, he continued, 'I don't want any consideration, criticism or advice. I will have only my own way. All shall do as I command.'

'Me too, Pasha'm?'

'You too.'

'I will obey you and do as you wish as long as I believe that you are serving the cause.'

'You shall obey me and do as I wish,' was his reply.

'Is that a threat, Pasha'm?' she asked quietly but firmly.

At once his mood changed. The mask went up once again over his innermost feelings. He was eagerly apologetic.

'I am sorry,' he said. 'I would not threaten you.'

Later in the summer, while all was momentarily quiet on the Greek front, Kemal was faced with another major internal revolt. Based on Yozgat, across the plateau to the east of Angora, where the powerful feudal family of Chapanoğlu had presumed to set up an independent Government in support of the Sultan, its objective was the capture of the rich city of Kayseri.

Unless checked it could lead to the loss of a large part of Central Anatolia, and to the separation of the Nationalists in Angora from their forces in the east. To help deal with it Kemal summoned, from the Greek front at Eskishehir, the most arrogant of his warlords, Cherkess Ethem.

The Circassian swaggered into headquarters in a truculent mood. This revolt, he declared, was no business of his. Let Kemal and his generals deal with it themselves. He did not disguise his contempt for them all. But Kemal, short of troops, had to humour him. At his invitation, Ethem paid a formal visit to the Grand National Assembly, where the deputies rose solemnly to greet him. Such attentions helped to appease his vanity, and he finally agreed with an air of condescension to help Angora out of its difficulties. A special train was sent to bring his 'army' from Eskishehir.

Angora, as the heterogeneous Nationalist forces assembled from the various districts with their unorthodox equipment and their variety of ragged or picturesque uniforms, acquired the aspect of an armed camp. And indeed it was a substantial enough force which advanced to attack Yozgat, leaving Angora for a while virtually undefended. Before dawn they reached the town. All day they besieged it. After dark they swept in 'like a black cloud'.

The fighting, street by street and house by house, was venomous and brutal. The Chapanoğlu defended themselves ferociously, pouring volleys of fire from the rooftops on the invaders, who bombarded and set fire to the houses until much of the town was ablaze. With the thundering of gun-fire, the roaring of flames and the shrieking of victims, it was a 'night in hell'. The carnage continued until dawn. By now the Nationalists were in control of the town. Those caught were tried and hanged on the spot. Those who escaped tried to fight back. But they too were defeated.

Thus ended the bloodiest, the last and in a sense the most crucial of the anti-Nationalist rebellions. Kemal had been fortunate. Had the Caliphate forces proved capable of synchronizing their operations he might well have been defeated. As it was their three main revolts occurred singly, one after the other, giving the Nationalists just enough time in between to regroup and transfer their meagre forces. Hence by the narrowest of margins he was able to contain the rebellion.

He was just in time. For the autumn offensive of the Greeks was now imminent. All hinged on the ability of the Turks to hold the railway line running from north to south between Eskishehir and Afyon, thence east-wards to the vital strategic points of Angora and Konya respectively. Were they to lose it, all central and much of southern Anatolia would be open to the enemy. The Greeks held the advantage, with their regular army. The Turks had to rely largely on their irregulars. Kemal's policy was still the strategic retreat – that of the Parthians against the Roman invasion – widening the enemy's front and lengthening its lines of communication.

Forecasting the offensive Kemal remarked to a foreign correspondent, Alaeddine Haidar:

> Tomorrow, if Venizelos, obeying the orders of his dictator, Lloyd George, wants to sacrifice an army of half a million, he will perhaps succeed with difficulty in occupying Angora and even Konya. If we retire to Sivas, our guerilla campaign will redouble and our army will be able more easily to pierce their front, which will by then be six hundred miles long. M Venizelos has got himself into a scrape in Anatolia, and the Greek army will end by having to quit – after burying thousands of corpses – this country which does not belong to it.

The Greek offensive was launched in the direction of the railway. The Nationalists suffered an initial defeat all along the line. 'The Turks,' Lloyd George exulted in the House of Commons, 'are broken beyond repair.' But the French and the Italians took alarm. The imminent prospect of a Greek conquest of Anatolia did not appeal to them. They insisted that the Greeks had already achieved their objective, by freeing the Marmara coast and the zone of the Straits from the Turks. The moment had come to restrain them. This time they were able to swing the Supreme Council round to their point of view, against that of Lloyd George and Venizelos. It telegraphed instructions to the Greeks to advance no further.

They were obliged to halt and dig in at the points they had reached, halfway to the railway and the main rim of the plateau, in rough mountainous country, with a front tripled in length and inadequate railways and roads to supply their forces. Their new front was scattered in pockets over a dangerously wide area, less easy to hold than the continuous line in the lowlands which the Supreme Council had encouraged them to abandon, or than that which they might have reached had it allowed them to advance. The French and the Italians rejoiced – and Kemal won a new lease of life in which to build up regular forces sufficient to drive the Greeks back to the coast.

In the pursuit of this aim, as de Robeck had warned Curzon and Curzon had in vain warned the Cabinet, he had already turned, with serious diplomatic attention, towards Russia.

CHAPTER THIRTY

THE TURCO-RUSSIAN TREATY

'UNTIL you have crossed the bridge,' runs a Turkish proverb, 'you should call the bear your uncle.' Since the days of Peter the Great, with his expansionist designs, each generation had seen a Russo-Turkish war. Now both the Kemalists and the Bolsheviks, attacked from the west, had bridges to cross, hence at this moment in their history turned, with tentative steps, towards one another. From the moment of his landing in Anatolia Kemal began to think circumspectly of an understanding with the Soviet Union, if only for use as a threat against the Allies.

The immediate reaction of the Russians to the Turkish Revolution was favourable. Publicly it was interpreted as a counterpart and extension into the Moslem world of their own. *Izvestia* heralded it as 'the first Soviet Revolution in Asia'. Strategically Turkey was important to the Bolsheviks, who were at this moment threatened with civil war by the armies successively of Denikin and Wrangel, and with Allied intervention. Revolutionary Turkey could protect their exposed flank in Transcaucasia, where Turks and Russians had spheres of interest and where the Allies had stationed troops as a bulwark between them.

From Sivas, after the Congress, Kemal had sponsored the journey of an unofficial emissary to the Soviet Union, to explore the possibilities of securing money and arms from the Soviets. He was Halil Pasha, a former Unionist and an uncle of Enver, and it was due partly to his efforts that limited supplies of them began to trickle into Anatolia in the early days of 1920.

But it was the aggressive action of the British, in the spring of 1920, that precipitated and indeed made officially possible the first serious overtures by Kemal to the Soviets. Their occupation of Constantinople, the publication of the terms of the Treaty of Sèvres and the consequent war made Russian supplies urgently necessary.

The despatch of Kiazim Karabekir and a military delegation to Baku, in Azerbaijan, had produced negative results. The formation of the Grand

National Assembly enabled Kemal to take the more positive step of despatching an official diplomatic mission to Moscow, led by his Circassian Foreign Minister Bekir Sami, the son of a Russian general who had fallen out with the Tsarist régime and had emigrated to Turkey. He followed this up with a note to Lenin, asking for the establishment of diplomatic relations and appealing for aid to revolutionary Turkey in its struggle against imperialism.

In due course he received a letter from Chicherin, recognizing the National Pact, acknowledging the decision of the Grand National Assembly to 'co-ordinate our activities and your military operations against the imperialist governments', and proposing the immediate establishment of diplomatic and consular relations. With regard to their mutual territorial interests, Chicherin favoured a referendum in the various Turco-Russian areas, and proposed Soviet mediation in the settlement of Turco-Armenian and Turco-Persian frontier problems. Agreeing to this proposal in principle, Kemal offered a deal by which he accepted Russian claims to Azerbaijan in return for a free hand to invade Armenia. In conclusion he asked for 'money and arms in order to organize our forces for the common struggle'.

These exchanges made it necessary to postpone meanwhile the operations against Armenia for which Kiazim Karabekir had been impatiently pressing, and which Kemal had authorized for the end of June. Kiazim was thus obliged to put up with a further spell of inaction, growing increasingly irritable and consoling himself only with his Children's Army, which now amounted to seventeen regiments. To keep up the morale of his soldiers, thus thwarted of action, he organized competitions in floral arrangement, encouraging them to adorn their mess tables with bouquets of flowers in harmonious shades. 'Making bouquets,' he considered, 'has a very good influence on the souls of people, especially people of nervous, harsh temperament.'

Kiazim grew testy in his isolation, sending countless telegrams which criticized Kemal's conduct of affairs. In fact, as he failed to realize, time was working for Kemal. While he sat fretting in Erzurum at the inaction of his forces, the Supreme Council sat wrangling in Paris as to whether or not to give the city, and most of the surrounding province, to the Armenians as a 'free and independent state'. It became clear, however, that it was unprepared to reinforce the grant by any form of military action. Nor was any country prepared to undertake the necessary mandate. When President Wilson, invited to arbitrate on its frontiers, finally announced his award, it had ceased to bear any relation to realities. Together the Kemalists and the Bolsheviks were ensuring, on the spot, once and for all, that no independent state of Armenia should ever appear on the map of Asia.

The Turkish diplomatic mission had reached Moscow in July after a tortuous seventy-day journey from the Black Sea, over a Russian railway system disrupted by war and revolution. Smarting a little from its rigours and frustrations, they raised at once the urgency of opening up the route through the 'independent' Republics of Armenia and Georgia to allow the passage of arms to Anatolia. They added that they had come to seek not only aid but an alliance. The Russians hedged and prevaricated. Chicherin admitted that they were pledged to defend Turkey, but stressed the dangers that now threatened them from Wrangel's army and from the Allies in Poland – dangers that might delay any concrete arrangement. It soon became clear that the Russians were manœuvring to trade aid to Turkey for the cession of Turkish territory to Armenia, which they would later appropriate for themselves.

After some weeks of delay the delegation was received by Lenin. He showed a more conciliatory spirit over the opening of the supply route for arms and support for the Turkish cause in general. But he made little secret of impending Russian designs on Armenia and Georgia. Here, the Turks judged, was the old Tsarist policy all over again; but to be exercised by peaceful penetration rather than war. Reporting on the interview to Angora, Bekir Sami expressed his conviction that the Russians might at any time overthrow the Armenian Government. There should thus be no delay in military action from the Anatolian side.

On receipt of it, Kemal drew up for the Assembly his own cool analysis of the position. Russia's policy, as he assessed it, was governed by the present need to reassure the Moslem world as to her intentions, and to discourage the spread of Turkish influence within it; by the desire to emerge, in the eyes of the Western world, as the power behind the Turkish Revolution; by the ultimate determination to establish communism in Turkey and tie her, as a satellite, to Moscow.

On the other hand, threatened as they were by the West and by the anti-Bolshevik feeling among the Moslem peoples, the Russians could not yet do without Turkey. Thus they were probably ready to conclude an alliance. The Turks, he wrote, must make a start with a piastre and a cartridge, and transportation via the Black Sea must begin. There is no doubt that even if munitions were in short supply, they nevertheless had gold to offer. Above all, 'decisive action must be taken against Armenia, independently of Moscow's concurrence or otherwise'.

The Russians meanwhile had convoked in the month of September a Congress of Eastern Peoples in Baku, designed at once to flatter and to menace their Moslem neighbours. To this Kemal sent a large delegation. The Russians were playing, as Enver had done, with the idea of a pan-Islamic dominion extending to the frontiers of India, and indeed Enver in person aspired to assist their purpose. For both he and Jemal had reached Moscow from Germany, Enver attracting attention in the streets and in the government offices by a high black tarbush which concealed his small stature. At Baku he was a delegate among the Moslem leaders, most of them suspicious of Russia but ready to see what they could get from her.

Already he had embarked on a correspondence with Kemal, assuring him that he had come to work 'for the establishment of an organized Islamic world and the delivery of our country'. Making free use of the first person singular, he went to some pains to impress on Kemal that he was personally well in with the Soviet leaders. He might well be in a position, he indicated, to provide not merely arms but military support for Kemal. 'I have heard,' he wrote, 'from colleagues reaching here that you are in difficulties. This I had already supposed.' He was not hopeful, however, that the Russian assistance would amount to much. 'I therefore think,' he advised in tones of patronage, 'that you should take measures to diminish dissension in the country.'

Kemal replied politely enough to these various missives. Enver might have his uses. Acting as he still was in the name of the Caliphate, Kemal was ready enough to exploit Islamic influence in defeating the British and balancing the power of Turkey against that of the Soviet Union. He thus approved of Enver's basic aspiration to unify the various Eastern national movements. On the other hand he strongly discouraged him from any pan-Islamic adventures, which could only arouse Russian mistrust.

Kemal replied to a letter from Jemal in similar if more informal terms. To both he expressed confidence that an agreement with Moscow would not be long delayed. And indeed a treaty of friendship was soon initialled in Moscow and entrusted to a Turkish delegate, Yusuf Kemal, who travelled back with it to Turkey. As he was leaving Moscow, his train took on a million gold roubles (destined largely for the payment of the civil servants in Angora), together with a token instalment designed to be shipped across the Black Sea by motor-boat, of the arms, ammunition and supplies which the Turks had requested.

But a few days afterwards Chicherin raised with Bekir Sami the question of frontiers, and insisted on the cession to Armenia of territory in the Turkish provinces of Van and Bitlis. Aid to Turkey, he declared, must depend on the acceptance of this principle. On learning of this Kemal saw that the moment had come to strike. He firmly rejected Chicherin's proposal and ordered the army of the east to march against Armenia.

Thus, at last, Kiazim Karabekir's long and impatient vigil was at an end. The objective of his offensive was the recovery of those 'Armenian' districts of Turkey, including Kars, Ardahan and Batum, which had been lost to the Russians in the war of 1877, regained from them by Enver in 1918, but lost once more to the dictation of the Allies at the Armistice.

On 20th September his troops advanced and captured Sarikamish. After a pause Kiazim continued his advance to Kars, which fell without resistance. The Russian-Armenian commander was in bed at the time, and his ADC did not dare to wake him until the enemy had marched into the city, capturing his headquarters and many thousands of prisoners. The Armenian army was no match for Kiazim's and retired in disorder towards the Arpa Chai, followed in a panic by droves of civilians dreading, not wholly without reason, rape and robbery and massacre at the hands of the Turks.

The news of the fall of Kars caused rejoicing in Angora. Kemal had now removed his headquarters to a building at the railway station, and the large hall at the Agricultural School had been divided into separate compartments to accommodate the expanding staff. When Halide Edib entered it she was greeted with the news by the chief of Kemal's military cabinet, who then stood in the corridor and called out to the officers in their box-like offices, 'The Department of the East will have sweet dishes tonight. But the Department of the West will have only leeks boiled in water.' As he spoke 'thirteen doors flew open and some twenty Staff officers assembled in the narrow corridor and talked at once with suppressed emotion. This . . . was the first incident to give us confidence; and it rewarded us in some measure for those long and hopeless months.' Ismet came in overjoyed, patting her kindly on the shoulder, and together they drafted their congratulations to Kiazim Karabekir.

The Armenians, having appealed in vain to Chicherin and received empty assurances from President Wilson of mediation and 'adjustment of differences', sued for an armistice. Early in December, at Alexandropol, Turks and Russians signed the Treaty of Gümrü (its Turkish name). The first international agreement to be contracted by the Nationalist Government, it restored to Turkey her traditional eastern frontier along the banks of the Aras and the Arpa Chai.

The Russians meanwhile had defeated Wrangel's army, thus loosing on to Constantinople a flood of refugees to enrich the merchants of the bazaars with treasures exchanged for bread, to enliven the cabarets and, in the eyes of Sir Horace Rumbold, the new High Commissioner, further to debauch 'this already debauched capital'. The Russians were thus now free to annex the rest of Armenia. Their cavalry entered Erivan, their horses treading softly through the snow without a shot fired or a sound from the crowds. From the balcony of the Parliament building there were speeches with fervent quotations from Lenin and Marx, cries of, 'Long live Soviet Armenia! Long live Soviet Azerbaijan! Long live Soviet Russia! Georgia will soon be a Soviet too. Turkey will follow. Our Red Armies will sweep across Europe. . . . Long live the Third International!' The crowds in the street remained silent. An Armenian murmured 'Quelle blague!' His country thus became the Armenian Sovietic Federative Socialist Republic.[1]

During the months that followed the Turks and the Russians disposed, between them, of the rest of Transcaucasia. The Russians marched into

[1] Oliver Baldwin, *Six Prisons and Two Revolutions*.

Georgia which became another Soviet Republic. The Turks occupied Ardahan and Artvin. There was a race for Batum, which was won by the Red Army. These military gains were now to be sealed in a political form.

Kemal sent a new treaty delegation to Moscow under Yusuf Kemal. This time the delegates were able to travel by the direct route through Georgia – and incidentally to fortify themselves *en route* through the purchase of the cellar of an exiled Georgian nobleman. They had a friendly reception. They negotiated no longer with Chicherin the diplomat, but with Stalin the realist, who proved more amenable. In response to Yusuf Kemal's gesture of gratification at this, Stalin lifted up two fingers and remarked laconically of Chicherin, 'Diplo!'

On 16th March 1921, the Treaty of Moscow was signed between the Kemalist Government and that of the Soviet Union. It followed the lines of the initialled treaty with certain additions. Each party, taking note of 'the points in common between the movement of the Eastern peoples for national emancipation and the struggle of the workers of Russia for a new social order', recognized 'the right of these peoples to freedom and independence' and a free choice of government. Each undertook to refrain from subversive activities in the territories of the other.

It was thus that those two notable realists, Kemal and Stalin, settled between them by negotiation and action, not indeed all their mutual problems, but their mutual frontiers, drawing a line across the map which survives without dispute as the boundary between these hereditary enemies, Turkey and Russia, today.

CHAPTER THIRTY-ONE

END OF THE IRREGULARS

WHILE the Turkish delegation negotiated in Moscow, Kemal and his associates had been striving to guide into safe channels the consequent currents of opinion at home. Kemal himself, committed from his earliest youth to the ideas of the West, was no Bolshevik. His opposition to communism was categoric. 'For our nation,' he said while his mission was negotiating, 'there is no such problem as that of becoming Bolshevik. . . . We as a nation have principles and habits of our own to which we are faithful. . . . The Soviets have means and resources and are the enemies of our enemy. But there can be no such thing as abandoning our aim and becoming slaves of the Soviets.'

For the moment, however, political expediency made it necessary to become their friends. Kemal's task was to conciliate the bear, and yet to keep free from his greedier embraces. This involved him in intricate problems, not merely in Moscow itself but at home. Here he had to manipulate with care and adroitness the conflicting trends of Nationalist opinion, to mobilize on the one hand its pro-Russian elements, while ensuring on the other that they did not go too far.

Ever since the Young Turk Revolution there had been two main schools of thought as to the direction which Turkey should take in the future, and these now crystallized sharply. Ranged to the Right were the adherents of the Western Ideal; ranged to the Left were those of the Eastern Ideal. The Western Ideal envisaged a Government shaped on Western lines, and with Western social and economic institutions, such as the liberals of the Ottoman Empire had sought since the nineteenth century. It was, however, a bold man who would now advocate in Angora the ideals and institutions of a Europe now hated as the enemy. The 'Westerners' were thus now driven into the same camp as the 'Easterners', remaining firm however in their condemnation of the internal Soviet system, to which tradition and impulse opposed them.

The Eastern Ideal was less easily definable. It arose from a vague and confused search for a new system, derived from the feeling that Western civilization had outlived its time. It was born from among those idealists of the Party of Union and Progress who sought a solution for humanity in terms of an idea rather than in relation to facts. The fact of the Russian Revolution gave it an immediate and powerful impetus.

Its chief protagonist was Kemal's Finance Minister, Hakki Behich, who had studied Marxist philosophy and had in fact drafted the plan for the new Government which the Assembly had accepted in a modified form. Other adherents of the Eastern Ideal were to be found in the Grand National Assembly, where the nature of communism was now freely discussed, if not well understood. Some sympathizers were to be found paradoxically, among the religious classes, where some interpreted the Eastern Ideal as (in Halide Edib's words) 'a revival of the first democratic age of Mohammed'.

As paradoxically, there was a strong trend towards communism among the irregular chiefs, who chose to exploit it as a means of consolidating their power over their illiterate bands. For this purpose they made increasing use of an institution named the Green Army.[1] A secret organization of which Hakki Behich was the secretary-general, it was formed with Kemal's approval at the time of the internal rebellions. Here was a regular force sufficiently imbued with the Nationalist ideals to counteract defections among the troops and to inject new life into the national forces in general.

He had approved it to meet an immediate situation. But soon it began to develop two disturbing trends. It built up the irregular bands at the expense of the regular army on which, in the long run, the Nationalist movement would have to rely; and it became an instrument, conscious and otherwise, of the communists and in particular of Cherkess Ethem, whose arrogance, puffed up by success, took the form of an increasingly overt defiance of Kemal. The Green Army began to see itself as a Turkish counterpart of the Russian Red Army, and to spread its influence through a subversive newspaper named *Yeni Dunya* (*The New World*), springing originally from Moscow and Baku and now published in Eskishehir. Its ranks became fertile ground for Russian agents, exploiting the discontents of the Turkish peasantry and indoctrinating the irregular soldiers.

During the Greek invasion signs multiplied that the Green Army might well be used to stab Kemal in the back. The time came when he could no longer infiltrate into its ranks his own trusted supporters. Appointments were made to it without his sanction, and its activities began to pass beyond his control. When he discovered that its leaders, without consulting him, had enrolled one of his own ADCs in the army, he decided that the moment had come to suppress it.

[1] Its name was derived from that used in pre-revolutionary Russia by communist rebel organizations in Moslem provinces.

He called a conference of its leaders and commanding officers at Angora where, at a sitting which lasted far into the night, he was able to achieve this object. The meeting provided a characteristic example of his faculty for imposing his will on others, while leaving them with the impression that they had got their own way. At the end of it a list of resolutions was drafted and agreed by all. After it had broken up, Kemal turned to his henchman, Tevfik Rüştü and said, 'Look in that flower-pot.' Tevfik did so and found a paper.

'Read it out,' said Kemal.

Tevfik read it, and found that it comprised exactly those resolutions to which the meeting had just agreed as its own. They had been drafted by Kemal, with his chief of staff, that morning.

The result was the dissolution of the Green Army, and the trial and sentence by the Independence Tribunals of a number of those, including deputies, who had been involved with it. This was a setback which the Russians, who had set some store by the army, were to attribute to its 'lack of proletarian leadership'.

Concerned at this episode, and at the general growth of underground communist activities, Kemal now came out into the open and replaced the Green Army with a Communist Party of his own. By this astute move he hoped to canalize and control such elements. The editorial offices of *The New World* were removed from Eskishehir to Angora, where they could be effectively supervised, while action was taken to liquidate the more dangerous Soviet agents.

At the head of the party he placed Hakki Behich, who accordingly circularized as 'Dear Comrade' the principal Nationalist authorities. The party, he explained, was based on the principles of the Third International and directly attached to it. It had the approval of the Ministry of the Interior. Its programme would be put before the next General Congress of the Communist Party. The secret Green Army would be merged with it, and all other communist organizations engaged on communist propaganda would henceforward be invalid. To Ali Fuad, as to the other army commanders, Hakki Behich wrote, 'We are proud to have you, our Commander Comrade, included in the military sections and rely on your valuable opinions and military spirit'. Ali Fuad was taken aback by this move, which he felt could only weaken the Nationalist cause. But Hakki's circular was followed by a covering telegram from Kemal himself, which reassured him as to its motives.

Kemal intended the formation of the party as a measure of expediency, to tide over the present crisis. If the Nationalist movement succeeded it could very quickly be disbanded. If on the other hand it collapsed, at the hands of the Greeks or otherwise, Anatolia, with its capital withdrawn to Sivas or east of it, would inevitably fall into the orbit of the Russians. In this event, its own Communist Party might have to serve as its instrument of government and, as an established national institution, would be better equipped to uphold against the Soviets some degree of Turkish independence. Meanwhile, with the party behind him, he felt strong enough to liquidate the most dangerous of the Soviet agents in Turkey, a Turkish socialist named Mustafa Subhi. With sixteen of his confederates he was arrested, placed on board a boat at Trebizond – and disposed of. Chicherin's enquiries as to his whereabouts merely produced the polite answer that the party must have met with an accident in the Black Sea.

In the autumn of 1920 the Russians had sent a large embassy to Angora. The need thus arose for Kemal to send a reciprocal embassy, of a permanent kind, to Moscow. He took advantage of this to help resolve a conflict which had developed within his own ranks at home. Its focus was the commander of the western front, Ali Fuad; its essence the latent cleavage between the respective protagonists of irregular and regular forces, which the affair of the Green Army had brought out into the open. The Greek advance had made it obvious that no effective resistance was possible without a regular army to match that of the enemy. But, pending the organization of such a force, it had not proved possible to dispense with the irregulars, whose power had in consequence grown.

Kemal suspected Ali Fuad of a prejudice in favour of the irregulars. He had earned a black mark in connection with an unsuccessful attack on the Greeks before their main offensive, which was carried out in response to pressure from Ethem and against the judgement of the General Staff. Its failure was followed by demands from Ali Fuad for reinforcements and equipment for his troops, which Kemal chose to criticize, causing a meeting of the Cabinet to record that, though they would be met, they were considered 'quite unreasonable'. This incident was symptomatic of growing friction between Ali Fuad and the Angora Government, which he claimed was manufacturing difficulties for him.

Angora's quarrel with Fuad was in fact a matter of personalities as much as of principle. His enmity against Ismet had increased since the newcomer had contrived to establish himself more firmly in Kemal's favour than those who had been with him from the start. It was an enmity reciprocated by Ismet. The two men differed in outlook and temperament, and now they had become rivals for power. Kemal started an insidious campaign of propaganda against Ali Fuad's capacities. On the one hand he saw Ismet, safely under his own control, as the indispensable key to the new phase of regular warfare which was about to begin. On the other hand, he saw that Ali Fuad, in close relations with an ambitious warlord and thus with an irregular army under his virtual control, might become too independent and powerful a figure in the Nationalist hierarchy.

The time had thus come to remove him. The Russian situation provided him with the pretext he sought. Ali Fuad received a summons to Angora. He observed that his reception at the station was more ceremonious than usual and sensed from the atmosphere that something untoward was afoot. Stepping forward from the circle of ministers and the guard of honour Kemal greeted him and led him back into his compartment for a private talk. He spoke of the necessity to send an embassy to Moscow, with a leader of high calibre. Using the intimate second person singular he begged his old friend to accept the post of Ambassador to the Soviet Union.

Ali Fuad, realizing that his military career was at stake, tried to play for time. But it was clear that Kemal wanted an immediate decision. Ali Fuad promised to call upon him and give him a positive answer. Kemal's expression brightened. With a warm handshake he left him.

Sitting back in his compartment, Ali Fuad speculated as to the motives for his removal. At the front he had heard disquieting rumours of the changing trend in Angora. Kemal, it was said, was moving perceptibly towards personal rule. He had gathered around him adherents, notably Ismet, who subscribed to this trend. Gone were the days when five loyal comrades in arms launched the Revolution together in a spirit of mutual trust. Rauf was in exile, Kiazim, Refet and Ali Fuad were in the field, Kemal ruled Angora with an Assembly to bend to his will, and Fevzi and Ismet to serve as his intermediaries. Ali Fuad was no longer close to Kemal. But by quarrelling with him he would create a breach in the movement. He thus had no choice but to accept the Moscow Embassy. Soon afterwards he left, with a large staff, for Russia.

With Ali Fuad safely out of the way, it was time to come to grips with Ethem, the recalcitrant warlord. In the mountains around Kütahya he had set up what was little less than an independent feudal principality. Here he levied his own taxes, dispensed his own system of arbitrary justice and recruited his own forces, paying his soldiers three times as much as those of the regular army and indeed encouraging them to desert from its ranks. Ismet stood in the garden of the Assembly one day while a detachment of Ethem's troops marched past. As he looked at them he remarked sadly, 'The horses are mine, the weapons, the soldiers. Only the command is not mine.'

Kemal and Ismet now decreed that this force, together with all the surviving irregular bands, should be incorporated into the regular army. The decree led to a straight trial of strength between Kemal and Ethem, with his two brothers, one a deputy, behind him.

Ismet announced that Ethem's forces would now become a division, subject to regular inspection and discipline. Ethem's brother Tevfik defied him, contending, 'It is impossible to put officers or paymasters in charge of these vagabonds or induce them to agree to such a thing. At the sight of officers they will go mad as though they had seen the Angel of Death.' Already in Angora they were saying, 'Mustafa Kemal will make us all button up our tunics. And we won't. We will wear Ethem's uniform.' Tevfik spread around the report that he was about to launch an attack on Ismet's army, in the direction of Eskishehir.

In Angora it became clear that Ethem, with his other brother Reshid and their friends in the Assembly, was planning a revolt against the Government. Kemal was equal to this. The two adversaries, so alike, despite their disparity of build, in the steeliness and pallor of their looks, watched and weighed one another warily, animal craftiness pitted against human guile. One day, when Kemal was lying ill in bed, the Circassian burst without ceremony into his room. Kemal calmly put his hand under his pillow, making it clear that it clasped a revolver. Ethem had a hand on his own revolver, finely embossed and notched for each kill. His bodyguard, bristling with arms, filled the landing and staircase. An ADC went to warn Ismail Hakki, the commander of a detachment of troops outside, to surround the building and shoot Ethem's men if necessary. Ethem demanded the removal of Ismet. Kemal quietly refused. Ethem heard, through the window, the sound of rifles being loaded. He muttered to one of his guards in a Circassian dialect, 'The situation is dangerous. Let's give it up.' On the pretence that he had been paying a mere courtesy call he quietly took leave of Kemal.

Afterwards Kemal overheard the ADCs discussing the incident, laughing wrily at the fact that they had only a single revolver between them, and suggesting that he himself should have a personal bodyguard. He immediately called Ismail Hakki, and ordered him to recruit one. This was done from among the Lazes around Giresun, the Georgian warriors of the Black Sea mountains. With their ferocious demeanour and their all-black uniforms and turbans they soon became a familiar and picturesque spectacle in Angora, escorting Kemal and patrolling before the Parliament building as 'The President's Guard'.

Realizing the power of Ethem, Kemal made last patient efforts to bring his men under control. He invited the Circassian to proceed with him to Eskishehir, there to thrash out their differences with Ismet. But when the train reached the station Ethem disappeared.

Back in Angora, his brother Reshid was called to a meeting of ministers and Kemal put before him once more the need for a disciplined army with which to defend the country. After pouring contempt on the regulars, who would 'run like hares at the first noise', Reshid exclaimed, 'What does this word "country" mean? I could live anywhere just as happily. I could live with Venizelos.' Kemal reproved him with polite scorn for his foolishness, then despatched a parliamentary delegation to Kütahya, to make a last appeal to Ethem's common sense. Its members were virtually placed under arrest, to be treated as hostages. But they escaped from the hospitality of Kütahya and returned to Angora.

Ethem now sent a telegram to the Assembly, in which he questioned its legality. Declaring that the country was too tired to fight he insisted on negotiations for peace with the enemy. He signed his telegram, 'The Commander-in-Chief of all the National Forces'. Playing for the support of Constantinople he sent a copy of it to the Grand Vizier, implying in a covering message that he meant to attack the Assembly's forces and had reached an understanding with the Greeks for the purpose.

The deputies met in indignant secret session. In a subsequent open debate Kemal, exposing the intrigues of Ethem and his brothers both with the Russians and with the Greeks, still chose to refer to them with studious politeness by the title of Bey. The deputies shouted, 'God damn them!' and one of them exclaimed angrily, 'Your Excellency, don't call them Bey. These men are traitors!' Kemal proposed Reshid's expulsion from the Assembly, at which the deputies cheered and raised their hands in assent.

Kemal's troops marched on Kütahya and occupied it without resistance. They pursued Ethem south-westwards. His men showed little fight against the regular army, seeking only to save their own skins. Soon, in Kemal's words, 'Ethem Bey and his brothers with their force occupied the most suitable position for them, namely in the ranks of the enemy!'[1]

---

[1] The Greeks in fact made little use of Ethem's forces, preferring, ironically, to incorporate them into their own regular army.

CHAPTER THIRTY-TWO

THE FIRST BATTLE OF INÖNÜ

IN THE WEST and in Constantinople the political climate was changing. First Venizelos, then Damad Ferid disappeared from the scene. The change in Greece was fortuitous. Early in October 1920 the young King Alexander, while watching the antics of a pair of pet monkeys in the garden of his palace, was bitten by one of them and died. 'It is perhaps no exaggeration,' commented Churchill, 'to remark that a quarter of a million persons died of this monkey's bite.'

Venizelos, overestimating, after an almost unbroken absence of two years in Paris and London, his own prestige as a popular hero and his countrymen's capacity for political gratitude, declared a general election. In this he gave the royalists freedom to vote if they chose for the restoration to the throne of King Constantine, discredited and exiled in 1917 for complicity with the Germans. They promptly did so, defeating Venizelos and his party by a handsome majority. Lloyd George, when he received this shocking news, pulled himself together and remarked, with a grin, 'Now I am the only one left.' To Venizelos he wrote: 'It almost makes one despair of democracy.' Venizelos replied with more realism that his defeat was due rather to the war-weariness of the Greeks and to the discontent which arose from their continued mobilization.

The French, war-weary too, seized upon the change, at the Supreme Council in Paris, as an excuse to liquidate their commitments to the Greeks. The Italians followed their example. Here was a chance for the British too to withdraw, with reasonable honour, from a policy which was proving unprofitable. But Lloyd George remained true to his dreams, announcing that the King's return would make no difference to Anglo-Greek friendship, which 'is vital to us in that part of the world'. Even he, however, realized that the full implementation of the Treaty of Sèvres and its policy were doomed.

In Constantinople the Sultan could no longer maintain Damad Ferid in power. He had been discredited both by the popular rejection of the

treaty and by the failure of his civil war policy. The public saw him as a
nonentity, a weakling, a figure of fun in a tragic situation. He was reputed
to fall asleep at Cabinet meetings, and he had difficulty in finding ministers
to serve under him.[1] His own party turned against him, and the Sultan at
last intimated that his services were no longer required. Thus Damad Ferid
resigned and retired to Carlsbad, to take a long cure. His place was again
taken by Tevfik, who at once brought into his Cabinet two ministers friendly
to the Nationalists – Izzet Pasha as Minister of the Interior and Salih Pasha
as Minister of Marine.

This 'new broom' chanced to coincide with changes in personnel by the
British. They replaced General Milne by General Sir Charles Harington
and Admiral de Robeck by a professional diplomat, Sir Horace Rumbold.
There was a general feeling among the Turks in Constantinople that these
changes might lead to a shift in British policy. The Allies must surely realize
that the Treaty of Sèvres was no longer enforceable. The French had recognized that this was the moment to come to terms with the stronger Turkey
which was arising from it. Would the British do the same?

Izzet, in the hope that they might, decided to re-establish contact with
Angora. If officially the two Governments must still appear to differ, at least
unofficially they might agree to work together for peace. With the approval
of the Cabinet he sent an emissary to Kemal to propose a visit by himself
and Salih Pasha (both former Grand Viziers) to Angora, to discuss the
prospect, of which he reported signs, that the British might now be prepared
to consider some sort of settlement.

Kemal's attitude to the proposed visit was cautious. He was sceptical as
to the prospect of any such peace offer as the Nationalists could afford to
accept. In war-weary Angora, on the other hand, there was a strong feeling
in favour of peace. In this atmosphere there was a danger that any public
revelation of overtures from Constantinople might undermine the spirit of
resistance and the growth of the army. The new friendly Government might
thus prove a greater threat to the cause than the last, which could be
denounced as an enemy. Kemal could not but agree to the proposal. But
he insisted that the meeting should be secret, and should take place not in
Angora itself but in the seclusion of Bilejik, a station on the line between
Eskishehir and Constantinople.

It took place in the station waiting-room. Izzet, in his political innocence
and ignorance of the true position in Anatolia, had expected a series of
informal man-to-man chats between two former companions-in-arms.

---

[1] It was related of him that, in Cabinet-making, he called a bunch of elderly Pashas
out of retirement, stood them in a row, and appointed them according to the personal
appearance of each – the erect and martial Pasha as Minister of War, the lean and intellectual as Minister of Justice, the bearded and devout-looking as Minister of Pious Foundations, the stout and plebeian as Minister of Commerce.

What happened was different. Kemal at once created an official atmosphere
by presenting himself stiffly as the president of the Grand National Assembly.
To whom had he the honour of speaking? Salih explained that he was
Minister of Marine, while Izzet was Minister of the Interior in the Constantinople Government. Kemal replied, politely but firmly, that in his
view no such Government existed, that he could not therefore receive them
as its ministers but only unofficially as private individuals.

On this basis they talked for some hours. Izzet tried to persuade Kemal
that an out-and-out Nationalist Resistance could achieve no positive results,
and that the moment had come to seek a reasonable peace. What he evidently had in mind, as Kemal saw it, was a submission by Angora to Constantinople, followed by a joint approach to the Allies. This was out of the
question; if once Kemal compromised he knew he was lost. But to reject
Izzet's proposals outright would be impolitic. He thus decided to give him
a taste of the Nationalist atmosphere. He closed the discussion and conducted the members of the delegation to the train. At once, to their surprise
and apparent concern, it started to move towards Angora. With a glint in
his eye, Kemal explained that he would not permit them to return to Constantinople. They would continue their talks on the train and again, more
seriously, in Angora itself. 'You shall be the guest of us Anatolians for a
while,' he said.

Having thus disarmed the two Pashas, he published the news of their
arrival throughout Anatolia, but omitted to reveal that they had come to
discuss peace. To exploit their visit as a means of raising rather than lowering
the spirit of resistance, he issued a shrewdly phrased communiqué, indicating
that they had come of their own accord to meet the Government of the
Grand National Assembly and work for the country's cause.

Izzet was dismayed at this act of sharp practice. Known always as a man
given to straightforward dealings, he was now placed in a position which
could only be seen by his Government as dishonourable. A trifle ingenuously,
he had seen the Nationalist movement simply as a struggle against the
foreigner, designed to save the seat of the Sultanate and Caliphate against
Western domination. He only now realized that it was a struggle against
the Government of the Sultanate and Caliphate itself. To this he could not
subscribe.

For all his opposition to Abdul Hamid and Vahid-ed-Din, Izzet remained
a legitimist in principle. It was his genuine belief that the best solution for
his country still lay in the continuation of the Sultan's régime in collaboration
with the Nationalists. Kemal on the other hand saw that its only hope lay
with the Government of the Grand National Assembly, and that there
could be no question of peace negotiations unless it were recognized. In
his view it was Izzet's duty as a patriot to forsake Constantinople and
remain with him at Angora.

Meanwhile the two Pashas, as 'honoured but unwilling guests', were given the best available house, furnished with such rudimentary comforts as the town possessed. On the day after their arrival they called on Halide Edib, who later recalled:

> I have a vivid recollection of Salih Pasha, twice Premier and several times Cabinet Minister of the Empire, over six feet in height and beautifully dressed, nearly doubling himself in half to get through my tiny door, and then walking up the rickety stairs of what must have seemed to him to be a mere mud hut. Izzet Pasha and the rest followed in dignified but significant silence till both the Pashas involuntarily exclaimed, 'Poor Hanum Effendi! Oh, poor Hanum Effendi!' The tone of pity in their voices actually hurt me and made me feel rebellious almost to the point of wanting to be rude. . . . But they did look so fine as they came in and brought back my old world to me in my little hut with such genuine affection that I only said in a laughing tone, 'Please don't pity me; it is my choice.'

After some five or six weeks they were allowed to return to Constantinople on the understanding that they would resign from their posts in the Government. This they did. They accepted other posts later. But Izzet, still seeking co-operation, worked honourably for the Nationalist cause, supplying arms for Kemal's forces for the next phase of the fight with the Greeks.

The natural outcome of Venizelos' defeat would have been the reversal of his policy. But the supporters of the King chose to become, in this respect, more Venizelist than Venizelos. They carried out, it is true, a drastic purge of Venizelist officers from the army. But then they proceeded – in 'a mad outbreak of regal vanity', as Lloyd George, wise many years after the event, described it – with plans for a renewal of the offensive against Angora. Bereft now of Allied support, hence freed from the hampering limits which the Allies had placed on the Venizelist advance, they sought to readjust their military position.

Their present awkward line was composed of three fronts, isolated one from the other and based on inadequate communications with Smyrna. Parts of it were disturbingly vulnerable and exposed the Greek troops to unnecessary hardships in winter. Hence the strategy of the royalists was to advance to the railway and to seize its key-points, Eskishehir and Afyon Karahisar, thus uniting their forces, cutting the communications of the Turks and driving them back upon Angora and Konya respectively. A major advance must be delayed until the spring when the weather was favourable. But now on 10th January 1921, they embarked on an interim action, which was in effect a reconnaissance in force.

Kemal broke the news of it to the Assembly. Prayers were read for the success of the army. The situation was thought by all to be grave. Day after day deputies and others, their faces grey with worry, besieged Kemal's room in the Assembly, which became a bureau of information. Here, with the aid of a map, he retailed to them the daily reports from the front. He had an appearance of confidence, even of gaiety. Playing with a string of beads, he dealt with their questions, avoiding definite replies, expounding tactics, counselling patience, calming their anger at the news of the retreat of the Turkish advance-guard.

The offensive was aimed at four points between the northern and southern sectors of the front, the weight of it falling in the north, where Kemal had concentrated the bulk of his forces. The main thrust came from Brusa. Aimed upwards over layers of steep but broken ridges in the direction of Eskishehir, it reached within sight of the plateau before it. Ismet met the Greeks in a valley at Inönü, a position which had been partially fortified to cover the city.

His troops put up a resistance which surprised and disconcerted the Greeks. In the light of the earlier campaign, they had expected an easy walk-over against undisciplined and ill-equipped men. Instead they found themselves, for the first time, faced with a resolute and disciplined force, greatly inferior in numbers and equipment but not in leadership and fighting spirit to their own regular divisions, whose troops were in any case now commanded by unfamiliar and often inexperienced royalist officers. Knee-deep in mud and snow the Turks stubbornly defended their own territory. After an all-day battle they counter-attacked with success. Next day the Greeks, fearing that they had fallen into a trap, accepted failure and retired, as speedily as they had come, towards Brusa, there to prepare, with the new lessons thus learnt, for a major campaign in the spring.

The Nationalists chose to play up this first Battle of Inönü for the benefit both of local morale and of Russian opinion, as their first major victory against the foreigner, and it was celebrated in Angora with unbounded rejoicing. In the Assembly thanks were expressed to the army. Kemal flattered the deputies by praising their own behaviour in the face of the threat. Their serenity had given the soldiers a feeling of confidence.

After the battle Halide Edib was sent to Eskishehir to visit the wounded in hospital. She was struck, as she travelled down the railway, with the change in the atmosphere:

Gone were the good-humoured, 'swanky' Irregulars who used to fire from the train windows to display their marksmanship. The station no longer echoed with the din of their wild songs and their live, lively repartee. All seemed under an iron discipline, and if the Regulars who were there instead were priding themselves on their recent achievements, they certainly repressed any expression of it under their quiet manners. . . . Everybody moved as though by machinery; there was an occasional chink of spurs, a single voice here and there commanding – nothing more.

Such was the spirit of the new army with which the Greeks, as they now began to realize, would have to contend.

CHAPTER THIRTY-THREE

THE LONDON CONFERENCE

AS THE Nationalist organization grew, so did the atmosphere of Angora change. Much of its intimacy disappeared. The small 'band of brothers' had grown into a large general staff, divided and sub-divided into various departments. Kemal moreover was more aloof than before. No longer did he sit around at headquarters of an evening, working and talking and sharing problems with the rest. First he had moved his own office to a building near the station where he could be near to the telegraph office. For this was a war of wires, and Kemal, with his modern outlook, realized the paramount importance of communications.

Then he had changed his place of residence. He had moved to a large stone villa on a hillside at Chankaya, some five miles away. Built by a Levantine merchant, it flaunted pinnacles and a pentagonal turret, while its interior was heavily ornate. But the rooms were spacious and light, such as appealed to Kemal, with many windows looking down over the plain to the twin hills of the city beyond it. Here he now lived what might well be described as a marital life.

The strain of the previous autumn had told on Kemal's health, and Dr Adnan felt that he needed feminine care. At this moment, as though in answer to the need, Fikriye announced her impending arrival from Constantinople. She had contrived, to the strong disapproval of Zübeyde his mother, and Makbule, his sister, to follow him to Anatolia. She travelled alone on one of the rough tramp-steamers which plied along the Black Sea coast, carrying discreet and anonymous male passengers who, on arrival at the small port of Inebolu, would put on Kemalist kalpaks and reveal themselves as officers and others come to serve the Nationalist cause. A small boat took her ashore from the roadstead, to be warmly greeted by the local Director of Posts and Telegraphs, all too unused to seeing a young and attractive girl disembark with the rest. The pretext for her journey was to nurse the wounded, but she indiscreetly confided to him that she had come to marry Mustafa Kemal.

She was sent on her way by carriage over the rough mountain road which at this time was almost the only supply-line for the national forces, conveyed like the rest in one of the 'covered wagons' of Anatolia, where she was able at will either to squat cross-legged or to lie, not too uncomfortably despite the jolts of the road, at full length. On arrival in Angora she settled into the house at Chankaya.

Kemal was a man wedded to his career and his country and the society of other men, to whom women meant little save as a source of distraction, an outlet for his appetites, and a stimulus to his masculine vanity. For all his refinements, he was in this respect still the rough soldier. Asked once what qualities he admired most in a woman, he replied, 'Availability.' Fikriye fulfilled this specification, and gave him something more. Restless and sporadic in his sexual appetites, he had had to be content through years of campaigning with such *femmes faciles* or other promiscuous companions as garrison cities provided. Fikriye's arrival provided him with a regular outlet in which affection and intimacy played their part. He was fond of her and flattered by her love; he enjoyed her feminine ways; she was a woman who, at this stage of his life, suited him well.

Dark and slender, Fikriye was receptive and gentle in manner. She had a natural intelligence, with just enough education to make a show of responding to Kemal's ideas. She was tactful, never seeking to interfere with his work, but holding her own by her charms at his table. She put his friends at their ease, she spoke their language, and they came to appreciate the domestic atmosphere which she had brought to the house. They could drink in her presence, but she would always know when to leave them alone with Kemal for more serious drinking. To Kemal Fikriye gave, without family ties, that sense of familiarity and ease which marriage afforded. But he did not contemplate marrying her. Were he ever to marry he would seek a wife who could take her place beside him, as a Western wife should do. The place of Fikriye, still the Oriental woman, would always be behind him.

The unveiled young Fikriye became familiar to the people of Angora, as she drove through the streets in Kemal's open carriage or rode over the hills above the city. No hot-house plant, she liked open-air pursuits, and could not only ride but shoot. It was on horseback that Halide Edib first saw her, 'someone with a very pretty face, though she looked very tired and very cold – the tip of her nose was almost blue and the lips had no colour. Framed in black the delicate lines of the oval face were at their most effective. Her eyes were grave and dark, and with long brown and curling lashes. . . . She looked at me with something of a smile on her wan face, and when she had passed I was haunted by the ineffable sadness of her look.' It was the look, Dr Adnan revealed to her, of the incipient consumptive. The sadness was due in part to the intuitive feeling that Kemal would not marry her. She must live for the moment – and this was a moment at which she could provide him with an environment in which to relax and calm his nerves.

His other method of seeking to calm them was through alcohol. Kemal had been drinking freely all his life. In his early youth, less sure of himself than he liked to appear, he had drunk to gain confidence, to impose himself the better on others. As his brain developed, he drank to relax it. At night his thoughts denied him peace; in the daytime they drove him like a dynamo. In the evening – but seldom before sundown – he would drink to release nervous tension.[1] Kemal drank not from weakness but deliberately, because he enjoyed alcohol and needed it. He made no secret of the practice, preferring to flaunt it without hypocrisy.

When foreigners wrote of his drinking habits he expressed his approval' 'If those things are not written,' he argued, 'people can't understand me.. When the governor of Smyrna once ordered the curtains in the restaurant where he was at table to be drawn, that the people in the street should not see him drinking, he protested, 'If you do that they'll think we're going to make women dance on the table. At least let them see that we're only drinking!' A French journalist wrote that Turkey was governed by one drunkard, one deaf man (Ismet), and three hundred deaf-mutes (the deputies). At this Kemal commented, 'This man is mistaken. Turkey is governed by one drunkard.'

Kemal seldom drank when in action, when a situation was serious. At Erzurum during the Congress he had drunk only black coffee. In the Agricultural School, when the Sultan's armies threatened, he had remained – thanks perhaps to the influence of such fellow-workers as Dr Adnan and Halide Edib – relatively abstemious. But the present period was one of inaction, of improvisation, of suspense. So he drank once more.

It was a habit which did not endear him to his more strict Moslem deputies. One of the Assembly's first actions had been the passage of a bill against the import and general sale of spirituous liquors. The consumption of alcohol, contrary to the laws of Islam, was alleged to be paralysing the armed forces, ravaging the population with illness, dragging the country to the edge of an abyss. It was now punishable by heavy fines, flogging or imprisonment. When, however, an emissary was sent to Kemal in his office, begging him to abstain from the practice, he was laughed out of the door.

The drinking-table had always been Kemal's natural orbit: the café tables of Salonika, with the torrents of talk which he could never translate into action; the mess tables of his various headquarters, where the talk ran

[1] The release was not only mental but physical, for he was chronically constipated, and maintained that the alcohol loosened his bowels.

on war. And now, in the dining-room of Chankaya, he returned to it surrounding himself night after night, over bottles of *raki*, with colleagues and cronies for whom his words could at last become deeds.

Often the sessions were rough and convivial, leading to a casual game of poker which might last until dawn. But as time went on they came to play a more constructive role. 'The Table' was to become something of a national institution. Around it, as much as in Parliament or at Cabinet meetings, was policy formed. It became Kemal's indirect instrument of government. It became also a school in which he trained and modelled in his own image a new ruling class for a country whose government was indeed to be for, but not by the people. State secrets, it is true, were not bandied about. The discussion – usually a one-way discussion – was at this time on the general principles, political, social and economic, on which the state was to be based.

Few men in Angora could afford to be excluded from the table, though some shunned it – and begged the secretary to strike them off the list – on account of the long drinking hours it entailed, while others, like Ismet, with his sober domestic habits, graced it as seldom as possible. Many, on the other hand, yearned to be invited, and became unabashed sycophants when their yearnings were realized. The 'regulars' were the henchmen, the ex-brother officers and *aides* (become deputies), and now a young 'court' of journalist-intellectuals to whom, though they held their own in conversation, Kemal always remained a hero. As Falih Rifki wrote later in a starry-eyed mood: 'All the things that died within us all the dreary lifelong day, by degrees and one by one came alive again. It was there . . . that we understood, more vividly than ever again, how the will of a believer can become the creator of miracles.'

But the miracles had yet to be performed. For the next Greek offensive was looming. Before it could open, the Allied powers joined in a move towards peace. The Supreme Council invited delegates of the Turkish and Greek Governments to attend a conference in London in February 1921, under the presidency of Lloyd George, to consider a new solution of the Eastern question – in other words, a revision of the Treaty of Sèvres. It insisted moreover that delegates from the Angora Government should form part of the Turkish delegation. This invitation was relayed by Tevfik, the Grand Vizier, to Kemal over the direct telegraph line between Constantinople and Angora which, after a lapse of nine months, was reconnected for the purpose.

Kemal was quick to exploit this *de facto* recognition of his Government. Manœuvring tactically with a view to strengthening his ultimate strategic position, he replied that the invitation was a matter not for himself but for the Grand National Assembly, 'the only lawful and independent sovereign power', which had lately been given constitutional form. The Angora

Government should thus be officially recognized, not merely by the Allied powers but by the Sultan himself. Tevfik replied that this was a constitutional, hence a domestic matter, appropriate for settlement after an agreement had been reached with the Allies. Insistence upon it at this stage could lead to a refusal of all Turkish representation at the conference.

Having made his point against the Sultan, Kemal called upon the Assembly to pass a resolution for despatch to Tevfik. In this, after a lengthy preamble in which appropriate feelings were vented against the Sultan's Government – 'nothing but a discarded authority no longer wielding any power in the country' – it declared its refusal to be involved in any delegation formed in Constantinople. Instead it would send a separate and independent delegation of its own, which alone represented the Turkish people, together with that of Tevfik. Bekir Sami, who had resumed his duties as Foreign Secretary on returning from Russia, was appointed its leader. The delegation left for London, not via Constantinople, but via Adalia and Rome, where it was greeted by Count Sforza, the Foreign Minister and chief Italian delegate to the conference.

The two delegations stayed at the Savoy Hotel. They occupied separate floors, and at first preserved an official aloofness. Bekir Sami seemed, to *The Times*, unwilling to ask to see Tevfik. As the representative of a 'bandit government', their reporter found him disappointing. 'He might have been tailored in Bond Street. Well groomed, dressed in a morning coat and smart striped trousers, he does not even wear a fez.' Tevfik, who looked unwell and sat with a rug over his knees, set all divergences at rest from the outset by deferring to the Angora delegation as the legal representatives of the Turkish nation. Bekir Sami was thus left to present the Turkish case, and acted as spokesman throughout the conference, continually irritating Lloyd George by his failure to make clear what he really wanted.

'The conference,' observed Aubrey Herbert in *The Times*, 'need not necessarily break the crockery of the Treaty of Sèvres; with a different glaze it may become tolerable porcelain.' No such metamorphosis occurred. The Turks opened with a demand for the restoration, in Europe, of Turkey's 1913 frontiers, a proposition which the Allied statesmen received with smiles and, from one quarter, a murmured, *'C'est ridicule.'* Otherwise they demanded the evacuation of Smyrna, full Turkish control of the Straits and the withdrawal of foreign troops from Constantinople – demands 'so extravagant', remarked *The Times*, 'that to grant a tittle of them would be tantamount to tearing up the Treaty of Sèvres'. The Greeks, who refused to sit down with the Angora delegation, were heard separately. They were content to reiterate the claims already made at other conferences by Venizelos, amplifying them with a well-selected flow of population statistics.

After hearing these statements the Allies proposed the appointment of an International Commission, to investigate on the spot the distribution of the population in eastern Thrace and the province of Smyrna. They laid down the prior condition that both Greeks and Turks should accept the results of such arbitration. The Turks, confident that it would produce statistics in their favour, accepted the proposal on certain conditions. The Greeks, for the same reason, rejected it. The two delegations then had tea together 'in apparent amity'.

Thinking again, the Allies proposed a series of modifications of the Treaty of Sèvres, allowing concessions to the Turks on the Straits, Constantinople and Kurdistan, with a League of Nations Commission to examine the now academic question of Armenia. Over Thrace there was no further mention of a count of populations. Over Smyrna there was to be an 'equitable compromise'. This amounted to a form of Greek autonomy which, as the Turks knew only too well from past experience, was likely in the long run to lead to the severance of the province from Turkey. Far from ensuring peace, Bekir Sami insisted that it would become a 'source of permanent conflict'. Expressing, none the less, qualified approval of the other proposals, he left for Angora to consult his Government. The Greeks, likewise, left for Athens.

The Greeks left with the impression that Lloyd George, whatever the attitude of the French and Italians, was still on their side. Not wholly satisfied, however, with his modification of their original claims, they weighed in the balance against acceptance the more tempting solution of a renewed military offensive, whose success might well strengthen their bargaining position. Whatever the official attitude of his Government, Mr Lloyd George, they felt confident, would not disapprove of such a step. They thought, 'the great man is with us, and in his own way and in his own time and by his own wizardry he will bring us the vital aid we need'.

Their psychology was not far wrong. 'The Prime Minister,' Lord Curzon wrote to his wife, 'is as convinced a Venizelist and phil-Hellene as ever, and uses all the advantage of his position as Chairman in that direction.' Mr Churchill, his adversary and Minister of War, urged upon him in a memorandum the need for a peace with Turkey. 'The alternative of the renewal of war,' he wrote, 'causes me the deepest misgivings. I dare say the Greeks may scatter the Turkish Nationalists on their immediate front, and may penetrate some distance into Turkey; but the more country they hold, and the longer they remain in it, the more costly to them. . . .' After outlining the unfavourable effects of such an action he added, 'In these circumstances it seems to me a fearful responsibility to let loose the Greeks and to reopen the war'.

But Lloyd George was in no mood to heed such warnings. On 23rd March, the Greeks launched an offensive from Brusa and Ushak. At a Cabinet meeting Lloyd George explained that there was 'a great concentration' of Turkish troops in front of them, and that it was impossible to pre-

vent the Greeks from attacking in self-defence. According to War Office
information there was, wrote Sir Henry Wilson, 'no concentration of Turks
on that railway, and therefore this coming attack is entirely uncalled for
and wholly unprovoked. And Lloyd George knows this. The whole thing
is a ramp, and a disgusting ramp. Because the Turks are at this moment
considering the terms offered to them a fortnight ago here in London, the
Greeks, with the full knowledge of Lloyd George, attack the Turks.'

The London negotiations had at least given the Turks time to complete
the grouping of their forces, to bring up more arms and to strengthen the
defences of Eskishehir. The two-pronged attack of the Greeks was aimed
against Eskishehir in the north and against Afyon Karahisar in the south.
Their forces captured Afyon without too much difficulty, then established
themselves to the east of it on the road towards Konya, obliging Kemal to
withdraw forces from the north to hold them. This attack he later criticized
as a strategical error. They should rather have moved northwards to support
and ensure the success of the attack on Eskishehir.

As it was, following the same line of advance as before, they now met
with a stout resistance from the Turks, well entrenched and well supplied
with artillery on the escarpment before Eskishehir. It was only after several
days of fighting that they broke through the Turkish positions at Inönü to
look down once more over the plain before the city. But the Turks brought
up reinforcements, of which the Greeks had none, and in a counter-attack
drove them back once more from the escarpment.

An American correspondent with the Greeks, named Ernest Hemingway,
proceeded to 'where they had made the attack with the newly arrived Constantine officers that did not know a god-damned thing, and the artillery
had fired into troops and the British observer had cried like a child'. It was
the first time he had seen 'dead men wearing white ballet skirts and upturned
shoes with pompoms on them. The Turks had come steadily and lumpily,
and running there themselves, and he and the British observer had run too
until his lungs ached and his mouth was full of the taste of pennies and
they stopped behind some rocks and there were the Turks coming as lumpily
as ever'.[1] This necessitated a retreat of the Greek southern force from
Afyon, the strategy of whose advance Kemal had justly criticized.

The Greek losses were heavy, but their forces had escaped destruction.
Professor A. J. Toynbee, retreating with one of their divisions towards
Brusa – 'an interminable procession of troops, mules, ox-carts and lorries
crawling along a foundered road' – was puzzled that no enemy attacked
them from the mountains commanding their southern flank.[2] In fact the
Turks had despatched all their available forces to cut the railway and the
line of retreat of the southern force. But this they failed to do.

[1] The Snows of Kilimanjaro.
[2] The Western Question in Greece and Turkey.

It was a failure blamed by Kemal on the faulty tactics and judgement of Refet whom, after an enquiry on the spot with Fevzi, he moved to Angora, offering him the post of Minister of Defence, and placing both the armies on the western front under Ismet's command. Refet irked Kemal by an insouciant disrespect for his authority and a free-lance spirit in the field which amounted on occasion to irresponsibility. In Angora he could keep him under his vigilant eye, while Ismet could be trusted to carry out his intentions at the front.

Such was the second Battle of Inönü, a place from which Ismet was later to take his name. Kemal telegraphed to him in the name of the Assembly: 'The greed of the enemy has foundered and broken up on the rugged rocks of your resolution and zeal.' Congratulating him on this great 'Holy War' and victory, he declared that few commanders in the history of the world had been entrusted with a task so difficult as these two battles.

The victory was far from being final, but it was, as Kemal recognized, a turning-point in the Nationalist fortunes. The Nationalists, still inferior in numbers and equipment, had shown themselves superior in staff-work and strategy to the Greeks. It was hard for the Greeks to admit this. Taken by surprise, despite their preliminary reconnaissance, by the transformation of irregulars into regulars, they sought, in their disrespect for the Turk, to explain it, as Professor Toynbee recalls, by the myth of the hidden hand: 'The Turkish artillery must have been served by Russian or German gunners to make such good shooting, Italian sappers must be traced in the trenches, French officers have kept the infantry steady. I convinced myself to my own satisfaction that this was a hallucination.'

The old military spirit of the Turk had revived. A new army had been created, and it was led by young officers well trained in the art of modern warfare. From now onwards Kemal could see ahead of him, however remotely and faintly, the prospect of possible victory.

CHAPTER THIRTY-FOUR

FALL OF ESKISHEHIR

THE ALLIES, following the breakdown of the London Conference, declared their neutrality in the Greco-Turkish conflict. Neither this nor the Greek defeat at Inönü had any effect on King Constantine, who preferred to believe that Lloyd George, if not his Government, would still give him backing. He might yet reign, as his namesake had done, in Byzantium.

Early in June 1921, he proclaimed himself Supreme Commander of the Greek forces in Asia, and left for Smyrna – the first Christian king to set foot on Anatolian soil since the Crusades. Symbolically he stayed in the seaside suburb across the gulf, where Richard Coeur de Lion was supposed to have landed. In an interview with *The Times* he spoke of his forthcoming offensive and of his confidence that the Greek troops would finally break the Kemalist power. Then he left to inspect the front and to decide on the date of the offensive.

It was, as Churchill wrote, 'the worst of all possible situations. The Greeks deserved at least either to be backed up through thick and thin with the moral, diplomatic and financial support of a united British Government, or to be chilled to the bone with repeated douches of cold water.' Lord Curzon made yet another attempt at a settlement. Obtaining agreement from Briand in Paris, he repeated the former proposal for the autonomy of Smyrna, but with the withdrawal of Greek troops. If the Greeks would agree to this the Allies would approach the Turks for a suspension of hostilities. They refused on the grounds that only military considerations now counted.

Thus the Greek army, in Churchill's words, was soon 'marching steadily forward through harsh and difficult country to engage in the greatest campaign undertaken by Greece since Classic times'. It had a slight superiority in arms, aircraft and supplies. The initial objective once more was the railway. This time, however, the main attack came in the south instead of the north, and was aimed at Afyon Karahisar and Kütahya instead of Eskishehir.

It was planned to take Eskishehir, the key to western Anatolia, not by a frontal attack but by a turning movement from the south.

The plan was successful. From Brusa the Greeks sent one column eastwards to hold the Turkish northern forces, and another south-eastwards, by a march through the mountains, to attack Kütahya; from Ushak, which had the advantage of a direct railway link with Smyrna, they sent a third and stronger column to attack Afyon Karahisar. They captured it, then moved northwards up the railway to converge with the second force and capture Kütahya. Eskishehir and its communications with Angora were immediately threatened with encirclement.

Ismet, from his headquarters in a village on the outskirts of the city, was faced with the responsibility of deciding on its evacuation. He was anxious, discouraged, indecisive. Halide Edib, retreating with a party of wounded, found him seated in a bare low-ceilinged Anatolian room. He wore, as he always did during a campaign, the khaki uniform of a private soldier. Behind his cordial manner 'his face was haggard and his eyes feverish, and the lines about his mouth and eyes had multiplied'. Here, for the first time in his career, was a crisis which might well prove a catastrophe. He was called upon to order a retreat whose results for his country would be incalculable and which would inevitably be criticized as a major national failure.

Halide tried to tell him that the heroic efforts of his army outweighed any failure. 'But he did not agree with me. He told me with bitterness that it was only success that mattered. The world never considered sacrifice, however sublime and great it might be, if it was not crowned with success.' But later, as they dined together off grilled tomatoes in the open air of the hot summer night, Ismet told her with an air of relief, 'Pasha is coming.' The decision would be his.

Halide proceeded on her journey. At the station in Eskishehir

the lamps glared like so many wicked eyes. Women sat on the open trucks, near their goods, nursing their babies. Women swarmed over the station, trailing their household goods and holding the hands of their bewildered children. . . . Women looked up at the sky, frightened; the station lights were brilliant; the aeroplanes might come. Mustafa Kemal Pasha stood on the platform and talked with the high officers. His face was greyer than his kalpak, a kind of rigid mask which hid the man behind. They all looked unconcerned, while the women squatted in rows with their kitchen utensils scattered around them. They stared at the group with infinite bitterness, but with the inexhaustible patience which belongs only to Anatolians.

Beneath the grey mask Kemal was resolute. None of this was wholly unexpected. Had he not himself criticized the strategy of the Greeks three months before, in storming Eskishehir by a frontal attack from the west instead of a flank attack from the south? This time, as though answering his criticism, they had done just that. They had reached the city, whose loss thus became inevitable. Unlike Ismet, Kemal, as his military career had shown, had no fear of making ruthless or unpopular decisions. As soon as he reached Ismet's headquarters, he surveyed maps and telegrams, summed up the position, and without hesitation, on his responsibility as head of the Government, ordered a general retreat. Rearguard actions must be fought to cover the withdrawal and to allow time for the dismantlement and removal of the munition works, arsenals and training camps which had been assembled in the city. But its fortifications, strong and laboriously constructed as they were, would have to be scrapped. Having arrived at this drastic and courageous conclusion, Kemal returned by train to Angora.

Here, from his headquarters, he followed the retreat. Halide Edib found him 'discomposed and sullen'. Ismet, with his rearguard, was still fighting before Eskishehir. Kemal invited her to stay to hear the result. As they sat over cups of coffee he incessantly nagged at his staff for news.

As his aide-de-camp came in to tell him the whereabouts of this or that regiment he grew restive, and his language became more and more realistic; the men in command at that unfortunate battle would have been aghast at the names he called them. Again the morning came, the lamp paled out, and he said with a tone which was almost a groan, 'Ismet has lost the battle for Eskishehir. Let us have another cup of coffee.' Then he leaned against the desk, his face greyer and more discomposed as he smoked. Dr Adnan came in, with a smile on his face. He had been with Fevzi, who he declared to be 'the most hopeful sight in the universe; he believes that all this is tending to the final defeat of the Greeks'. Pasha laughed and called Fevzi Pasha a name which is not usually complimentary, though one saw that he was well pleased at Fevzi Pasha's optimism. He was always most superstitious at the critical moments.

Halide and his intimates saw him with the mask down. For others whose morale needed boosting, he put on another mask and assumed another mood. To one of his close journalist friends, he proclaimed with defiance as though to the world, 'Whatever happens we are going to remain in this country. We are going to defend every hill of our sacred Fatherland. We are going to die under our flag in the furthermost frontiers.' Together they sat, looking out into the moonlit August night and down over the plateau which spread nakedly away to the west. Now the enemy had reached its outer rim, and the future, to many at headquarters, seemed ominous. But Kemal spoke as coolly as though he were expounding a routine manœuvre.

A map lay before them, and with his fine long-fingered hands, surely created, as it seemed to the journalist, 'only for handling the most delicate works of art', he traced the position. Drawing a line with his finger-tips he said, 'Here we are now. Our forces are retiring in a half circle from the north and south of Eskishehir. The night is bright and suitable for marching. But after the exhaustion and heat of the day this weather may lead to sleep. I have seen soldiers asleep while marching and especially while riding on horseback. I have a friend, a cavalry officer, who told me he only slept comfortably on horseback. When he got to bed he could not sleep.'

The moonlight poured in through the curtainless window, merging with the harsh glow of the single petrol lamp to give Kemal's face the colourless aspect of death. But as he mused and joked he seemed to the journalist to radiate vitality and power.

'They say drink is a touchstone among men,' he continued, 'but I say the real touchstone is a field of battle. At this moment, when I close my eyes, I can see just how all my friends are behaving. For instance, I know that the commander of this division has reached this village' – he pointed to the map – 'that he has got himself the most comfortable house in the village and that he must be in a deep sleep of oblivion on his camp-bed. Would you like me to prove this to you?'

He rang the bell for the duty officer and instructed him, 'My child, get me at once the commander of the X. Division.' His friend could hear the telegraphist tapping away downstairs as Kemal continued, 'By tomorrow we must have put a distance of at least a hundred miles between ourselves and the enemy. The most suitable place to stand is here, north of the Sakarya River. We shall fight a big battle only after we have reached it. The Greek army, of course, will follow us. They will cross the plain here, and advance towards here. This means . . .'

He was interrupted by the duty officer, who saluted and said, 'Sir. The divisional commander has reached the village and is resting. Shall we wake him up?'

Kemal chuckled at his own psychological perception: 'Didn't I tell you so? Now let's look at this man. Find me,' he ordered, 'the commander of the Y. Division.' He turned to the journalist and winked: 'He is not going to find him, because this man is marching very quickly to reach his appointed place as quickly as possible.' The telegraphist returned to report that he had been unable to contact the divisional commander.

Kemal changed his tone: 'The really important thing is to know what the enemy is going to do and how he is going to do it. Is he going to follow us now, while we are withdrawing in this systematic way?' Continuing to talk, he gave a feeling of confidence. Kemal knew in the calmer recesses of his mind that there was reason for optimism, as Fevzi had said. He knew that the enemy was superior in arms. His own army was still an incomplete fighting force. Lack of transport hampered its mobility; arms still came only slowly from Russia. There could be no question yet of risking the reserves – behind Angora, in Cilicia, around Amasya – which gave him on paper a

1 & 2 Bust of
Kemal Atatürk

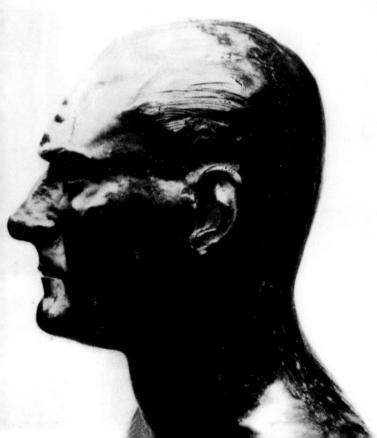

3 Major Mustafa Kemal,
General Staff, Salonika

4 His mother, Zübeyde

5 Mustafa Kemal at the Sivas Congress, 1919, with (left to right) Refet and Rauf

6 In Smyrna after his victory, 1922, with Fevzi

7 Mustafa Kemal as Commander-in-Chief, with Ismet, on a visit to the front at Akshehir, 19

8 A pause on the Western front, 1921

9–12 Mustafa Kemal in various roles: (*above left*) as
an Arab Sheikh in Egypt, on the way to the Tripolitanian front, 1912; (*above right*) the man of the world;
(*below left*) the countryman; (*below right*) as a
Janissary at a masked ball in Sofia, 1913

13, 14 & 15 Mustafa Kemal: (*above*) receiving a petition in the train between Ankara and Istanbul, 1930; (*below left*) with Latife, his wife, on a journey in 1924; (*below right*) teaching the new alphabet in the park at Gülhane (Istanbul), 1928

16 Kemal Atatürk, President
of the Turkish Republic

17 Mustafa Kemal, victor in
the War of Independence

18 Kemal Atatürk in his last years at Florya, with his adopted daughter, Ülkü

numerical superiority over the Greeks. Confronted by this major offensive Kemal, with these various factors in mind, judged that the moment had not yet come to risk a stand. Territory must still be sacrificed in the interests of time. His plan of campaign remained as he had laid it down in a general directive after his visit to Ismet's headquarters:

> After the army has been concentrated north and south of Eskishehir, we must establish a large area between it and the enemy's forces, so that we shall be able to carry on our reconstitution, reorganization and reinforcement. For this purpose we should be able to retire even to the north of the Sakarya. If the enemy should pursue us without coming to a halt, he would be getting farther away from his base of operations and would be obliged to take up new positions. In any case, he would find that there were many difficulties in front of him which he would have to provide for. Taking this into account, our army will be able to rally and meet the enemy under more favourable conditions. The disadvantage of such tactics would be the moral shock which might be produced in public opinion by the fact that a wide territory and places so important as Eskishehir would be abandoned to the enemy. But these disadvantages will automatically disappear in a short time as a result of the successes which we shall achieve.

As Churchill summed up the position: 'The Greeks had gained a strategic and tactical success; they had gained possession of the railway for the further advance; but they had not destroyed the Turkish army or any part of it.' That army had soon vanished from sight. It was trekking across the long weary wastes of the plateau towards Angora and the heart of the Anatolian homeland. Soon, essentially intact after casualties no greater than those of the Greeks, it had reached a point within fifty miles of Angora, behind the great bend in the Sakarya River on which Kemal had decided to stand.

All this had to be convincingly explained to the Turkish people. Their 'moral shock', which Kemal had predicted, now fell upon him with full force. The Assembly was aghast at the catastrophe. The deputies bayed, first for the blood of Ismet, then for the appointment of Kemal himself as Supreme Commander-in-Chief. Some sought by this to discredit him finally, to shift on to his personal shoulders the responsibility for what they took to be the irretrievable defeat of the army and the collapse of the Nationalist cause. Others, more loyal and less pessimistic, sought it from confidence that he could still save the situation. Others again opposed the appointment on the grounds that his personal implication in a further retreat would damage the cause irremediably. He should be held in reserve, they argued, only as a last resource, for which the moment had not yet arrived.

But by an ironical chance Kemal in this crisis had for the first time the

A.—10

support of the bulk of the Assembly – from his friends for the right reasons, from his enemies for the wrong ones. He would thus obtain the supreme command. But he must obtain it on his own terms. While the storm raged within and without the Assembly, he kept a wary silence, showing no disposition to accept the command, and thus turning into a positive conviction the general fear that disaster was inevitable. As soon as he judged that feeling had reached this point he called a secret session and mounted the rostrum. He agreed to accept the supreme command, provided he was given the full powers of the Assembly. Only thus could he prepare the army with sufficient speed for the next round in the struggle. But, in view of his respect for the principle of national sovereignty, he requested that these powers be granted him only for a period of three months.

At this his opponents came out into the open. Some objected to his investment with such comprehensive powers. Others objected to the title of Commander-in-Chief, as being one inherent in the Assembly itself. Kemal insisted that they were passing through extraordinary conditions, which called for extraordinary actions and decisions. He must be able to act energetically and swiftly, freed from the delays which would result from an appeal to the Cabinet or to the Assembly's authority. He must be able to give orders unconditionally, and this could be done only with full powers. Finally he overcame their objections and put before them an Act, conferring on him the functions of Commander-in-Chief: 'In order to develop the forces of the army materially and morally to the fullest extent, so as to secure and consolidate the leadership and administration of these forces, the Commander-in-Chief will be authorised to exercise full powers in the name of the Assembly in these matters.' The Act was passed, and Kemal undertook 'to prove myself worthy in a short time of the confidence that you have reposed in me'.

For the next three months Kemal was thus military dictator. He made immediate use of his powers by a drastic series of requisitions throughout the country, to obtain equipment for the forces. He commandeered, against ultimate compensation, forty per cent. of all stocks of cloth, leather, foodstuffs, oil and a variety of specified articles. The public were ordered to hand in all arms and ammunition suitable for military purposes. Ten per cent. of their ox and horse-carts were confiscated, and twenty per cent. of their riding and draught animals. A census was made of all smithies and workshops. To bring home to all the gravity of the threat to their homes Kemal demanded from each household a contribution for the forces of a parcel of linen, a pair of socks and a pair of shoes.

This, as Kemal saw it ahead of his time, was total war. It was not 'two armies fighting against one another but two nations who are both risking their existence and who summon for the fight all their resources, all their possessions and all their material and moral forces. For this reason, I had to inteiest the Turkish nation in the war in all their actions, their sentiments and their conceptions, in the same way as the army at the front. Every single individual in the village, in his home, in the fields, had to consider himself in the same way as those fighting at the front.' He added prophetically, 'In future wars also the decisive element of victory will be found in this conception.'

Churchill, who was to find it so many years later, describes how Kemal now 'called upon the wives and daughters of his soldiers to do the work of the camels and oxen which he lacked'. This mobilization of the women played a key part in Kemal's plan to rouse national sentiment, to point the need for a total effort, from civilians and soldiers alike. The arms and supplies, brought from centres as scattered as Erzurum and Diyarbekir, Sivas and Trebizond, were loaded on to the long peasant ox-carts beneath loads of hay for the oxen. The women, jacketed and pantalooned, with their feet in rope-bound woollens, drove the carts over mountain and plateau, covering hundreds of miles to the front at a mere three miles per hour, the solid wooden wheels creaking and sighing over the tracks as they had done since Sumerian times. Many of the women carried babies, lashed securely to their backs, as they loaded and unloaded the artillery shells and the rope-handled boxes of ammunition, carrying a shell on each shoulder and carefully covering it with a shawl, often at the expense of the baby, to protect the delicate fuses from dust or rain. When the carts broke down they hoisted the loads on to their backs and carried them thus for miles. To those who stayed at home fell the task of ploughing and sowing and gathering in the harvest, despite the requisitioning of animals and implements, to produce foodstuffs for the fighting forces.

Refet was now an energetic and resourceful Minister of War. He speeded up the ox-cart convoys by a system of relays, no longer changing the carts at each village as the peasants had preferred, but changing the oxen instead at fixed staging-points, to draw them right through to the battlefield. He had carpets cut up to make tunics for the soldiers, and petrol-tins converted into medicine canteens. In the absence of flour he instructed the peasants to boil up their raw grain or to grind it with pestle and mortar, until a single disused flour-mill could be put back into commission. In the absence of timber, on this plateau denuded of trees, wooden houses were demolished to fire the trains.

Ploughshares were almost literally beaten into swords. The railway workshops in Angora were turned over to the forging of daggers and bayonets. Everywhere maintenance workshops were improvised, so that no weapon might go unrepaired. Refet was searching for recruits for the army from the remotest corners of the country. Recruiting appeals were broadcast from the tops of the minarets. Those who responded might have to travel on foot for hundreds of miles, often through country harassed by bandits. They might find, when they arrived, that there were no arms to equip them. On leaving for the front they would be instructed to pick up those of the dead and wounded – and those of the enemy. Meanwhile deserters were rounded up and rigorously punished, new classes were called up, and reinforcements drafted from Cilicia, the eastern provinces, the Black Sea coast and other outlying parts of Anatolia.

The Turks had a respite of a bare three weeks in which to complete these preparations for the crucial battle. In Angora they were anxious weeks. Civilian morale fell to a low ebb. Many of the richer beys and merchants left the city with their families and possessions for the security of Kayseri. Others, even men in responsible positions, prepared to do so. Infected by their example, the peasant classes began to waver. The city was full of stragglers and deserters from the army; the Greeks were said to be near; nothing seemed safe. Their women sat patiently waiting, veiled and dressed for the journey. Should they too abandon their lands and go?

Kemal himself left for the front with Fevzi, now his Chief of the General Staff, on 12th August, and took up his headquarters at Polatlı, on the railway some fifty miles to the south-west of Angora. On arrival he rode to the top of a commanding hill, Kara Dağ, and dismounted to survey the probable line of the enemy advance. As he was remounting he lit a cigarette. Taking fright at the flash of the match, the horse reared away and threw him violently on to his side. A rib was broken, and pressed on his lung, momentarily affecting his breathing and speech. A doctor warned him, 'You will die if you go on.'

'I shall be all right when the battle is over,' he answered.

He returned to Angora for treatment but was back at the front after twenty-four hours. The injury continued to trouble him; he walked with difficulty, and had often to rest, leaning against a table. Rumour exaggerated the accident: it was a bad omen that the Commander-in-Chief should be put out of action before the battle had begun. But even such an incident as this could be turned to propagandist advantage. Among the soldiers he was quoted as saying, 'It is a sign from Allah. On the spot where one of my bones has been broken the resistance of the enemy will also be broken.'

CHAPTER THIRTY-FIVE

THE BATTLE OF THE SAKARYA

THE GREEKS resumed their advance on 13th August 1921. Constantine's battle-cry was, 'To Angora!' and the British liaison officers were invited, in anticipation, to a victory dinner in the city of Kemal. The Athens press drew a parallel with the noble conquests of Alexander the Great. The Greek armies were to cut once again the 'Gordian Knot' as he had done, and thus to found an Empire in Asia. For Gordion was on the direct line of advance. They forgot, as Professor Toynbee observed, that Alexander had not after all outwitted the oracle, since he had cut, not untied, the knot, thus failing permanently to annex western Anatolia to his kingdom, as Constantine now aspired to do.

In fact he did not intend permanently to occupy Angora itself. The object of the advance was predominantly political: to drive the Nationalist Government out of the city to Kayseri or Sivas, and so fatally to undermine its authority and precipitate its fall, with the aid of risings in Konya and other disaffected areas. The campaign was in fact the product of divided counsels, for there were two general staffs, those of the King and of General Papoulas. There were officers on the general's staff who preferred, thinking in military terms, to dig in at Eskishehir, thus ultimately luring the Turks into a hazardous counter-offensive.

But the King's will prevailed, and now the Greek troops moved forward across the stern unending steppe, marching and halting and marching again for ten long days before they could see their enemy, getting farther and farther away from the gentler valleys and coasts they knew. The drought and the heat of the sun were more merciless than the blizzards and frosts of the earlier campaign. They carried no tanks for the storage of water hence suffered from thirst. Their modern lorry transport broke down on the rough tracks, hence they depended on ox-carts, camels and the normal regimental pack transport for supplies. Often they had little to eat but fried maize. When taken prisoner in the subsequent battle they would beg bread from their Turkish captives. The dust choked them and the malignant malaria of the plateau thinned their ranks as they marched towards the valley of the Sakarya River – a ribbon of green in the tawny threadbare landscape.

Here the Sakarya, one of the three great rivers which carve their way across the Anatolian plateau into the Black Sea, throws out a loop before Angora. Flowing from the west it coils suddenly northwards, over a fifty-mile reach, then, as suddenly turns back on its tracks to the west. It was beyond this reach, in a bare primitive region of plains patched with stubble and of hills rearing up from them, broken by outcrops of rock, that Kemal and his army awaited them. Their front was flanked north and south by two tributaries of the Sakarya, completing as it were a loop in reverse, while the main channel of the river protected its centre. Narrow, and at this season shallow, the stream ran through a series of gorges with precipitous banks, and was bridged at only two places, north and south. Altogether the Turks had a good defensive position, with the advantage of an accessible railway and a well enough watered country to the rear of them.

Kemal's headquarters were at first on the railway, at Polatli, then on the hill of Alagöz which surveyed all the region, in a half-built mud-walled house with cobwebs festooned from the beams. Around him at all times was his black-clad Black Sea bodyguard, who had increased sufficiently in strength to fight in the battle as a separate unit. He wore the uniform of an ordinary soldier, without badges of rank, for the Assembly had given him no official military status and he had had none since his dismissal from the Ottoman army. With his injured rib still in bandages he directed the battle from a seat brought from the train, unable – perhaps fortunately – to hurry on horseback from one sector of the front or another, and thus always on the spot to conduct its general course.

With him as he welcomed Halide Edib – now an acting-corporal – was Colonel Arif, a boon companion of his drinking and wenching life, whom he had known from his cadet days, who had been at his side since the start of the Revolution, and whom, in his recent dismissal from a divisional staff post on account of his drinking habits, Kemal had attached to his military Cabinet. Arif resembled him closely, with 'the same stern elegant figure, the same lines of the head, the same cynical curve on the thin-lipped and tightly closed mouth. . . . The same blue eyes, but they protruded slightly and were not so pale.' Arif at this time was his most intimate confidant.

To Halide there was something about Kemal, here at the Sakarya, 'which he never had before or after. He was less cynical; he was not quite sure that this would lead to victory, and he saw that he had to die with the rest if the disaster took place. He was feeling almost as a condemned man would feel towards his comrades who will die with him.' Leaning painfully over a map on the table he treated her to a lucid survey of the military position.[1]

[1] See map, page 509.

There, as she saw it, 'was the Sakarya traced out "like a magic coil" on the paper'. To her feminine imagination 'the Greek army was a long black dragon coiling towards Angora to devour it. The Turkish army was another long coil stretching out in a parallel line on the east of the Sakarya in order to reach Angora first and prevent the black dragon from swallowing it.' What would happen, she asked, if the Greek dragon, 'so much thicker and so much bigger than ours', reached Angora first and left the Turks behind. Kemal 'chuckled in his dangerous, tiger-like way' and replied: 'I will say, "*Bon voyage, messieurs!*" And I will attack them behind and they will perish in the wilds.'

This was, in fact, the first Greek plan of attack. Their intention was to turn the enemy's left flank and so open the road to Angora from the south. They made an exhausting detour through the desert to do so, their long marches hampered by shortage of water and lengthened by the use of inaccurate maps. On 23rd August they engaged a division on the Turkish left, south of the stream, and forced its withdrawal after an all-night battle from the hilltop of Mangal Dağ. This initial setback brought a ruthless order from Kemal, dismissing the divisional commander for retiring without orders, and stressing that any such failure in future would be as drastically punished. For it was the task of the army to prevent any Greek soldier from setting foot in the centre of Turkey. On hearing afterwards that the commander had in fact been acting under superior orders Kemal reinstated him. But the order had served as an example to the rest, putting them on their mettle for the battle to come.

Then suddenly General Papoulas changed his tactics. An error in air reconnaissance contributed to the change. This showed substantial Turkish concentrations on the left flank, and suggested that the Turks were shifting their forces in that direction. The outflanking movement thus seemed to him too hazardous, extending too far a line of communication already harassed by the Turkish cavalry. Thus he switched his main force northwards to make a frontal attack nearer the centre, where in fact the Turks were more strongly entrenched. For the purpose he threw bridges across the river.

The ensuing battle lasted for twenty-two days and nights. Kemal afterwards claimed that it was, by one day, the longest pitched battle in history. The fighting was fierce and murderous. The Turkish positions were centred on a series of heights, and the Greeks had to storm and occupy them, one after the other, against the stubborn infantry defence at which the Turkish soldier excelled. The Turks held certain hilltops and lost others, while some were lost and recaptured several times over, in assaults which wiped out unit after unit. Yet they had to conserve men, for the Greeks held the numerical advantage. Thus circumstances taught Kemal a new tactical lesson: this was no longer the Gallipoli Peninsula, where he had thousands of fully armed reserves to throw recklessly into the battle. He talked once or twice of possible failure and withdrawal to Sivas. But Arif twitted him ironically: 'You will always find enough men in this country to send to death with or without reason. No one ever asks questions about the waste of human life.'[1]

Kemal kept in his head every detail of the forces at his disposal – the strength of each unit, its disposition in the field, the qualities of its commanding officer. Perusing each evening the Order of Battle, he would pounce on any error, however minute. Arif, who had been trained by the Germans, complemented him with his knowledge of the lie of the land and of the other officers and men. As Halide describes them: 'He leaned over the Pasha's shoulder, his face looking like that of a twin brother and saying in his low voice, "The village X lies ten kilometres to the north; there are two mounds on the left." "Excellent – the commander of the regiment?" "Like wood – stupid – but what a soldier! – and the men are veterans. No fear of artillery panic in that quarter: when they exhaust their ammunition, they will fight with bayonets, commander and all." '

Sometimes at these sessions Kemal reminded her of a novelist working out a plot, as she herself might have done. The battle was the theme, the pins in the map were the characters. The characteristics of each must be considered in fitting together the general pattern and prompting the story's development. Kemal studied the forces of the enemy as minutely as his own. At one crucial moment during the battle his Intelligence reported that the position was lost, because the Greek concentrations were too strong for the Turkish defences. Kemal instructed, 'Bring me all last week's reports on the placing of the Greek units.' He studied them, then said, 'The Intelligence Branch is mistaken. We have the enemy beaten.'

The front which Kemal had to control was some sixty miles long. His tactics were defined in an order to his officers, issued at a critical stage in the battle: 'You will no longer have a line of defence, but a surface of defence. Retiring groups will halt when they can, but the whole line will not retire to form a new front. All of Turkey shall be our surface of defence, upon which our units will resist everywhere and all the time.' Not an inch of the country should be abandoned until it was 'drenched with the blood of the citizens. Every unit, dislodged from its position, but every unit, large or small, re-establishes itself in face of the enemy at the first spot where it can hold its ground, and goes on fighting. Units which observe the neighbouring ones forced to retire must not link their own fate to theirs; they must hold their positions to the end.'

Section after section of his front was pierced by the Greeks, but the gap was filled by reinforcements for as long as they lasted, in as short a time as possible. Thus, though the Greeks advanced, their progress was slow.

[1] Arif was executed following the Smyrna trials, in 1926.

In ten days' dogged fighting they gained ten miles. In attack, Papoulas could not apply the same principle as Kemal in defence. Units which had broken through would have to halt until their neighbours caught up with them, thus giving the enemy time to reinforce and recover.

The Turkish situation, none the less, was acute. Though the attack had come virtually in the centre, it shifted round once more to the left. The outflanking of the Turkish armies and the advance on Angora was still the main Greek objective. Here gradual progress was made, and the Turks had to abandon several positions. Their line had swivelled round until its axis was rather from east to west than north to south, and at the eastern end of it the Greeks were now nearer to Angora than the Turks themselves at the western.

The central key to the defence – and thus to the salvation of Angora – was a long broad broken ridge named Chal Dağ, rising a thousand feet from the plain between the two principal Turkish positions, to command the railway to Angora and the whole battlefield. Flatly scored with a pattern of vertebrae like the hide of a reptile, it offered little cover and was hard to defend. 'Until they occupy the Mount of Chal,' Kemal would say, 'there is nothing serious to worry about; but if they do that, we had better look out – they could easily occupy Haymana, and after that they have us in a trap.' The people of Angora might console themselves with the heroic thought that there were still several more hills between Chal Dağ and the city and, as one of them put it, 'if we leave so many dead on the summit of each one of them, the enemy, on arriving here, will be reduced to about fifty. And those we shall beat to death with sticks.' But at the front the position was known to be critical.

One evening the news came that Chal Dağ had fallen, and that the Greeks were advancing towards Haymana. Halide recounted the scene at headquarters:

> There was grim silence everywhere, and the ugliest sort of fate seemed to hang over everyone in the headquarters. Mustafa Kemal Pasha was most affected. He fumed, swore, walked up and down, talked loudly, summed up the situation with the rare lucidity of a delirium, and tormented himself with indecision as to whether he should order the retreat or not. And I sat opposite him feeling as if the iron curtain of doom, something like the fire curtain of a theatre, was coming down, ever so slowly but surely.

The fight for Chal Dağ had raged for four days. First the Greeks, exploiting a gap in the Turkish line, drove back the cavalry unit which held it, but were that night driven back in a counter-attack by the infantry. They maintained their pressure, at the same time now reinforcing it with an attack on Haymana, which the Turks resisted with the loss of as many as eighty-two officers and nine hundred men, until lieutenants were commanding battalions and a division of artillery was reduced to seventeen shells. Next day the Greeks captured the mountain in an engagement so confused that at one moment two soldiers, drinking from a spring beneath it, looked up at one another and ran off in different directions – for one was a Turk and the other a Greek. Having taken it the Greeks advanced towards the village beyond.

But in Kemal's headquarters, at two o'clock in the morning, the telephone rang. Fevzi Pasha was on the line. He had been in the field throughout the battle, coming little to headquarters. He still maintained the serenity and certainty of success which had sustained him and those around him. He had a strange light in his eyes and 'the air of a man who has a great secret conviction'. This came in part from his religious faith. At the front he moved from trench to trench, reciting passages from the Koran to strengthen the morale of his men. On one occasion, when Kemal sent for him urgently, he could not be found. Finally an officer came upon him behind a large rock, out of sight of headquarters. He was tranquilly performing his devotions.

Now, at this critical moment, Kemal's voice is heard speaking to him over the telephone: 'Mustafa Kemal speaking. Is that you, Pasha Hazretleri? What? Did you say that the day is in our favour? Did I understand right? Haymana is nearly occupied – do you say that the Greeks are at the end of their strength? What? A coming retreat of the Greeks?'

As he returns to the group, 'there is a strange chuckle in his throat, half amused, half pleased. Will the division he is sending to close the gap be there before the Greeks make another move? He calculates, writes, the red and blue flags are moved higher and thither. There are enormous blue circles around his eyes, he looks like a face in Dante's inferno, tortured beyond words.'

'Hadn't you better rest, Pasha?' Halide says.

'No, I cannot,' he says hoarsely. 'Let us have another coffee. Is that rascal Ali asleep?'

This was the turning-point of the battle. The two armies had momentarily fought themselves to a standstill. Each was ready to retreat. But it was the Turks who held on the longest. The Greeks were too exhausted to follow up their attack on Haymana, and the Turks brought up reserves to close the gap in their line. It looked as though the force of the Greeks was spent. Their shortage of food and water had begun to tell. Their artillery had so squandered its ammunition in the early days of the battle that few shells remained. Their casualties were such that, according to prisoners in Turkish hands, their companies were reduced from a hundred and fifty to thirty men.

The Turks were now in a position to strike back. But there was more hard fighting to be done. Kemal had checked the Greeks on his left, and had so saved Angora, but he still had to drive them out of central Anatolia. He switched troops to the right and the centre for a counter-offensive. Here they confronted Greek units which outnumbered and outgunned them. For three days they fought stubbornly. More effective, however, in defence than in attack they were repulsed on three fronts, with heavy losses on both sides. They, too, were expending their last reserves of ammunition. A group commander warned Kemal that only one counter-attack would be possible. Kemal decided on the point at which to make it, and called for reinforcements. He insisted on commanding one of the artillery units in person. When the engagement was over, Kemal saluted and reported to him, 'Commander, the position is taken. We have no more ammunition.'

Units were clamouring for it everywhere. Kemal-ed-Din Sami, an army group commander, demanded shells from the General Inspector of Artillery, and on his refusal raged and threatened him with death, receiving only a smile in return. In the middle of the night he telephoned to plead with Kemal personally, but with no more success. The officers at headquarters talked in awed tones of the group's grave losses. But Kemal, who knew his commanders, merely grinned and remarked, 'It is not as bad as he says.'

Despite Fevzi's insistence it could not yet be certain that the Greeks would retreat. In a brief reversion to positional warfare they were digging in at points east of the Sakarya. Then the fighting was resumed. Halide Edib watched the scene from a hill overlooking the wide Sakarya valley, where clouds of earth and smoke rose into the air. Kemal's sergeant, Ali, came to her. 'Your left spur is put on the wrong side. Pasha sent me to put it right,' he said with a grin. And over his shoulder she saw Kemal's face peering from a trench and laughing at her. He called her into the trench, saying, 'We are fighting . . .' with the delighted voice of a boy who is at his favourite game.

'We are attacking Dua Tepe,' Kemal explained, 'the highest hill on the left.' The hills surrounding the valley below were 'lively with the lugubrious intonation of artillery and the nervous *tic-tac* of machine guns. Through the field-glass . . . I could see men coming nearer and nearer and even the fall of the men in the front line, leaving it indented and broken, and the final onslaught with bayonets. Thus the ants take their exercises around the small yellow mounds of their nests.'

Then Kemal said to her, 'Do you see that black pyramid, very pointed? It is called Kara Dağ. Look there through the opening and you will see the Greek retreat.'

She looked and saw 'a mighty cloud of dust rising from the ground to the sunlit sky, and a dark mass flowing ceaselessly like a flood.'

Kemal went on: 'The Greeks are fighting gallantly, their artillery is doing its utmost, and sacrificing itself to cover the retreat of the main forces.'

Kara Dağ, the summit on which Kemal had broken his rib and which had been the centre of some of the fiercest fighting, was recaptured, at the cost of half a division. On 9th September Kemal moved his headquarters forward. Corporal Halide was with them. They established temporary offices on a train near Polatli, loading the horses on to trucks.[1]

Would the retreat become general? Would the Greeks face the hazards of a last defensive battle with the Sakarya River at their backs? The Turkish cavalry was continuing to harass their supply lines, beyond the river. Farther still to their rear the guerillas came to life once more, sweeping down from the mountains to harry their transport, raid stations, destroy stretches of railway. The Greek troops, many of them Turkish subjects who, if captured, stood to be court-martialled and shot for treason, were growing discouraged. A young prisoner had said, 'They tell us that Angora is behind every mountain we attack; but sixteen days have passed and no Angora. They tell us that if we fall into the hands of the Turks, we'll be killed, and they drive us on with machine-guns.' Now the Turkish net threatened to close around the Greeks as, a few days earlier, the Greek net had threatened to close around the Turks.

Then the order for a final retreat came from Athens. By 12th September no Greek unit remained east of the Sakarya. The Greeks were trailing back to their starting-point on the rim of the plateau, scorching the earth as they went, evading the pursuit of the Turks, who were too exhausted to press it home but for a spectacular cavalry sweep on the town of Sivrihisar. King Constantine had attempted, for political motives, a task beyond his military powers. Geography had defeated him. The Gordion of Alexander, with its bridge across the Sakarya River, had been abandoned, the knot still untied. As Professor Toynbee enquired: 'Would a Greek army ever penetrate that distance into Anatolia again?'

Kemal, in praising his troops, ascribed their salvation of 'our sacred country' to the grace of God, but later credited it to their sense of a new ideal, that of national independence. After the battle he changed into civilian clothes, with a pair of smart white suède gloves, and returned unannounced, in his decrepit staff car, to Angora. Walking into the Assembly he received an ovation, which the people of Angora, who had lived for three weeks with the sound of the guns, then had heard it recede, carried on through the night amid a blaze of torches. With the aid of maps Kemal gave the deputies a precise review of the battle and the lessons to be drawn from it. Jesting to a friend, he remarked, 'I think that what I do best is my job as a *soldier*.'

---

[1] Here Halide met Captain Fazil, the hero of the Turkish air force and a man of French education, who with a single reconnaissance aircraft claimed to have achieved more important results than the Greeks with a squadron. When she had asked his liaison officer what she could do to help Fazil, he replied, 'Please send *Le Temps*. Fazil wants only that.' And thenceforward he got it.

Simultaneously *Te Deums* of thanksgiving were being sung in the churches of Athens. The battle had been, in a sense, a drawn one, since both armies remained in being to fight another day. But as Churchill summed it up: 'The Greeks had involved themselves in a politico-strategic situation where anything short of decisive victory was defeat: and the Turks were in a position where anything short of overwhelming defeat was victory. No aspect of this was hidden from the warrior-chief who led the Turks.' He was now promoted by the Assembly, on the motion of Fevzi and Ismet, to the rank of Marshal, and endowed with the honorific Moslem title of Gazi, meaning 'Conqueror', or traditionally 'Destroyer of Christians'.

Years later Kemal was presented by an artist with a large picture of the Battle of the Sakarya, in the foreground of which he was shown prancing across the battlefield on a magnificent charger. The painter, awaiting his congratulations, was taken aback when he ordered sternly, 'That picture must never be exhibited.' There was an embarrassed silence. 'All those who took part in the battle,' he explained, 'know very well that our horses were all skin and bone and that we were hardly any better ourselves. Skeletons all of us. In painting those fine warriors and sleek horses, you dishonour Sakarya, my friend.'

CHAPTER THIRTY-SIX

THE TURCO-FRENCH TREATY

THE REPULSE of the Greeks at the Sakarya was swiftly followed by a strengthening of Kemal's international position. Secret negotiations with the French, which had been dragging on throughout the hot Angora summer, now reached their conclusion with the signature of a Franco-Turkish Agreement. It was an agreement which aroused the intense indignation of the British.

It clinched a policy which the French had been pursuing for some time past – that of opposition to the Greek offensive and support for Kemal. This was based on three main considerations – economic, political and military. Firstly the French enjoyed comfortable financial and cultural assets in Turkey, with which the extension of Greek rule into Asia Minor might well interfere. Secondly they were jealous of British political power in the Middle East, and saw Lloyd George's support of the Greeks as a design to perpetuate it. Finally the French, looking more realistically than the British at the Anatolian scene, soon saw that the Allies would not be able to enforce drastic peace terms on a Turkey which was prepared to resist them, and that the Greeks would not be able to enforce them without a degree of aid which the Allies were not prepared to give. Their own military experts had declared that the Greek invasion of Anatolia was not a practicable operation; and this was a view which the Battle of the Sakarya now seemed to have vindicated.

At the London Conference they had come to a separate agreement with Bekir Sami by which hostilities in Cilicia, which had continued sporadically since the breakdown of the local armistice, would end. The French would evacuate the territory north of the agreed Syrian frontier and receive in return economic concessions, covering mines, railways and other development projects on a fifty-fifty Franco-Turkish basis. The Italians had reached a parallel agreement by which Italy would support Turkey's territorial claims in return for similar economic privileges over a wide area of southern and western Anatolia.

On Bekir Sami's return to Angora both these agreements were repudiated by Kemal, without even consulting the Assembly, on the grounds that they simply acknowledged the division of Anatolia into Allied spheres of interest. He wanted peace in Cilicia, if only to release troops much needed for his western front. But he wanted it and, with the evident deepening of the rift between France and Britain, now knew that he was likely to get it, on his own terms. He had not long to wait. In June 1921 the French sent a semi-official emissary to Angora, in the corpulent form of M Franklin-Bouillon, an ambitious ex-deputy of jovial demeanour and unorthodox outlook, whose mission could be explained away in terms of his journalistic and business interests.

Franklin-Bouillon was soon on close terms with Kemal. He presented him with a consignment of French brandy, which lent a convivial air to their initial conversations. They talked freely and at length, with much frank disagreement on either side. One night, when deadlock seemed to have been reached, Kemal's Foreign Ministry adviser turned to him and whispered, 'It's no good. Let's stop for tonight.' 'No,' Kemal replied firmly, 'They'll stop' – and after another round or so of brandy the French delegates proposed an adjournment until the morning. Kemal had talked and drunk them to a standstill.

The two sides started from opposite poles, Kemal insisting on the National Pact, Franklin-Bouillon on the Treaty of Sèvres. But the gap was gradually narrowed, and in due course Franklin-Bouillon was able to return home with an optimistic report for the French Government. Kemal's concrete proof of power at the Sakarya, soon afterwards, resolved any doubts in Paris as to his capacity to win. It was swiftly followed by Franklin-Bouillon's reappearance in Angora. Here, on 20th October, he signed an agreement with Kemal which amounted to little less than a separate peace between France and Turkey.

It gave the Turks all they needed. It allowed for the evacuation of Cilicia, an adjustment of frontiers to Turkey's advantage between Cilicia and Syria, and the establishment of a special régime in Alexandretta to safeguard the interests of the Turkish population. In return the French obtained the concession they sought covering rights over certain stretches of the Baghdad Railway. But no other economic concessions were incorporated in the treaty.

On the French side the agreement represented a realistic move to reduce unpopular military commitments and to strengthen their position in Syria, where their true Middle Eastern interests lay. They now handed over to the Nationalists large stocks of arms, including Creusot guns, munitions and other war materials, with the implication that more might well be available. This went far to redress the military balance between Turks and Greeks.

The Angora Agreement following and seeming to confirm his victory at the Sakarya, secured Kemal's prestige in the eyes of the world at large. For the first time, thanks to his determined and patient diplomacy, Nationalist Turkey had won official recognition from a Western power. She had won it, moreover, on terms wholly favourable to her national interests.

In London the agreement inspired Lord Curzon with feelings of 'astonishment and almost of dismay'. Here was an end to all mediation. Rumbold wrote to him from Constantinople that the 'dishonourable' action of the French had compromised the whole Allied position: 'The Nationalists are more uppish now than they have been for a long time past.' Curzon, after a series of interviews in London with M Gounaris, the Greek Prime Minister, sought to retrieve the position by arranging a meeting of the Allied Foreign Ministers, to agree upon new peace terms, and subsequently a meeting of the Supreme Council in Constantinople, to place them before the belligerents. But early in January 1922, following a meeting of the Supreme Council at Cannes, Briand fell from power. He was succeeded as Premier by Poincaré, who refused to agree to any such conference. He had his way, and received support from the fact that the Italian Government too had fallen. Thus the Anatolian winter wore on, the campaigning season approached – and the Allies did nothing.

It was not only the French who made peace overtures to Mustafa Kemal in the course of 1921. The British War Office – though not the Foreign Office – was thinking on similar if more tentative lines. Ever since the Allied entry into the city, the British authorities in Constantinople had been inclined to divide into two camps, one supporting the Greeks and the other the Turks.

The diplomats were generally pro-Greek, imbued as they were with Hellenophil ideals and the Gladstonian conception of the 'unspeakable Turk'; unfamiliar as they were with the interior of the country and indeed with any Turks beyond a limited circle in Constantinople. The soldiers were generally pro-Turk, respecting 'Johnny Turk' for his fighting qualities; regarding him, despite certain appearances, as a 'gentleman'; in closer personal touch with him in the course of their duties; moreover, more aware of the strategical realities which underlay the position of Kemal and his forces. As the Resistance proved more and more effective, the rift deepened and there were now in effect two policies in Constantinople: that of GHQ, which thought one thing, and of the British Embassy, which thought another.

Presiding over GHQ was Lieutenant-General Sir Charles Harington, General Officer Commanding the Allied Forces of Occupation in Turkey. Summoned to London after the failure of the London Conference, Harington addressed a meeting of the Cabinet at which Churchill urged some arrangement with Kemal. The Cabinet was as divided as ever and no decision was reached. But the idea gained ground among the soldiers in Constantinople of a direct personal approach to Angora.

A convenient pretext arose in the form of a specific need – that of negotiating for the return of British prisoners still in Nationalist hands, in return for Turkish prisoners in Malta, which had been agreed in principle at the London Conference. The general now sent an emissary to Anatolia to expedite the exchange and at the same time to sound out the Nationalist political attitude. The officers he chose for the mission were Major J. Douglas Henry, who had business interests in Turkey, and Major Stourton.

They arrived early in June and were received at Inebolu, the Black Sea port, by Refet. Kemal had arranged for a car to convey them to Angora, but the state of the road, due to recent storms, made the journey impossible. He thus authorized Refet to speak for him, and through him expressed his readiness to release all the prisoners.

Major Henry gathered from Refet that Kemal wished to make contact with General Harington, to discuss broader issues. Refet claimed to reflect Kemal's general views – his antagonism to the French, but not to the British; his mistrust of the Bolsheviks; his readiness for a plebiscite in Smyrna and Thrace. His remarks were interpreted by the major, and in due course by the general, back at GHQ, as a move towards peace talks. A meeting with Kemal was suggested, either at the general's villa on the Bosporus or at Inebolu. The British Government, still hoping at this stage that the Greeks would agree to mediation, opposed any definite negotiations with Angora. But it favoured an unofficial preliminary contact to exchange views with Kemal. With the prior agreement of the French and Italians it thus authorized Harington to proceed with his plan.

Major Henry was sent back to Anatolia, this time with a representative from the British Embassy, bearing a letter from General Harington to Kemal. He had been informed, he wrote, by Major Henry, that Kemal wished to put certain views before him as one soldier to another. If this were so, he was authorized by the British Government to proceed on board the battleship *Ajax* either to Inebolu or Izmit to discuss the situation with him openly and frankly. He was empowered to listen to any views which Kemal might express and to report them to his Government, but not to negotiate or to speak on its behalf. He proposed that the interview should take place on board the British warship, and assured Kemal that he would be appropriately received and would enjoy full freedom until he landed.

Harington's letter implied that it was Kemal who had asked for the interview. Kemal, in a polite but uncompromising reply, made it clear that this was not so. It was Harington, through Major Henry, who had asked for it. Kemal was prepared to negotiate on the basis of those complete national demands with which the general was familiar. If this were recognized in advance he was ready for a meeting on land at Inebolu, where 'the most agreeable reception' would be prepared for the general. But if he merely wanted to exchange views Kemal would send one of his colleagues instead.

Harington made no reply to this intransigent note. Talks on such a basis were out of the question. It was clear that Major Henry had exceeded his instructions, giving Refet the false impression that it was the British themselves who sought peace talks. Clearly, in the present confused state of British policy, no such man-to-man approach as the general envisaged was feasible. Kemal had thus negotiated instead with Franklin-Bouillon, on the basis that he had suggested to Harington. Hence the Angora Agreement.

But the soldiers in the War Office and in Constantinople were obstinate. The fact that the French had stolen a march on them rankled. They were determined to have one more try. A few months later General Harington sent Major Henry to Inebolu again, but this time without Foreign Office approval. Sir Horace Rumbold knew nothing of his mission until the day after his departure from Constantinople. As before its ostensible pretext was the exchange of the British prisoners.

In fact Major Henry had a week of talks with Refet, as one officer to another, on quite other matters. In the course of them he stressed the dangers to the British Empire from Soviet Russia. Refet did the same. He referred to the pre-war threat of pan-Slav expansion from Imperial Russia which had prompted Britain to uphold Turkey's integrity, and the even more dangerous threat of it from Soviet Russia today, which called for a similar policy. To meet this, Britain should withdraw the Greeks from Asia Minor and Thrace, and let the Turks defend the Straits on her behalf. He impressed Major Henry with the idea that Turkey was an altogether new nation, with which the British should negotiate. Refet remarked that in this respect he would sooner deal with Harington than with the Embassy. Major Henry returned home to the War Office with a document in his pocket recording their talks.

Kemal, in the hope of driving a wedge for his own purposes between the two British departments of state, had briefed Refet astutely enough. But the wedge was not to be driven. The Foreign Office did not share the confidence of the War Office in Kemal's reliability, and moreover deplored such 'escapades of amateur diplomatists'. The military were thus firmly requested to keep out of politics. Rumbold was glad to hear from the head of his department that Henry had been given a 'flea in the ear'; but the affair, as he confessed to Sir Horace, had been 'the very devil'.

The ostensible purpose of Major Henry's missions – the release of the British prisoners – had now been achieved. Arrangements were tied up for the final exchange. The most important of them was Colonel Rawlinson, who had for eighteen months been imprisoned in Erzurum, growing sick and weak and near to starvation as time went by. The colonel and his men were now escorted to the coast. The exchange took place in the open roadstead of Inebolu, where a British cruiser awaited them with Rauf and other Turks from Malta on board. Here, as Rawlinson recalled, the British sailors, observing their pitiful condition, 'came forward to assist us with the utmost gentleness and care to climb on board the launch'.

On arrival in Constantinople Rawlinson was embarrassed to learn that there had been indignant questions in Parliament and reports in the press about his treatment in Turkish hands. Still, despite his experiences, a staunch believer in Anglo-Turkish friendship, he resented their exploitation for anti-Turk propaganda: 'I considered our treatment to be due to the ignorance and neglect of duty of subordinate officers, and under these circumstances it appeared to me that a much larger view should be taken of the whole question.'

Thus Rawlinson returned to London and Rauf to Angora. Fethi was there already. With the exception of Ali Fuad, still in Moscow, Kemal was surrounded by his old colleagues once more. They were to find many changes.

CHAPTER THIRTY-SEVEN

SUPPORT FROM THE EAST

DURING the eighteen months that Rauf and Fethi had spent in exile the face of their country had been transformed. Mustafa Kemal had set up a Parliament in Angora; he had laid down a Constitution; he had established, for all practical purposes, a new Turkish state. He had reduced the Government of Constantinople to impotence; he had broken the unity and weakened the resolve of the Allies; he had all but defeated the Greeks. All this had followed directly on the actions of the Allies themselves – the occupation of Smyrna and of Constantinople, the Treaty of Sèvres, the Civil War, the Greek invasion. But none of it could· have been achieved without the blinding conviction and driving will-power of Kemal. The Allies had furnished the spark for the smouldering national pride of the Turks. But no other living Turk could so have lit and enflamed it as to confound altogether the Allied designs.

On the other hand he could hardly have done so without the initial help of his friends. From the start it had been in essence a joint and concerted effort by Kemal, Rauf, Ali Fuad, Refet and Kiazim Karabekir, the five who, from Amasya, had issued its 'Declaration of Independence'. Kemal was their leader, but it was the rest in a sense who had chosen him as such. His actions were based on their support and common counsel. He needed at this stage, their ideas, their co-operation, their encouragement, the free expression of their views. He needed Kiazim for the backing of his army, Rauf for his sage advice, Ali Fuad and Refet for their competence and influence in the field. Thanks to the four, he had progressed step by step from Amasya to Erzurum, to Sivas, to Angora. Thanks to the foundations which they had enabled him to lay, he was now the commander of a strong army, and the head of a united state which was becoming recognized by the world at large. He was the Gazi.

But Kemal was not born for co-operation, except in so far as necessity demanded it. He was born to dominate. Aware of this, the early founders of the Revolution, while following him loyally, had watched him warily. They accepted his leadership, but remained on their guard against the personal ambition that conditioned his patriotism. This was growing with every step in the country's resurgence. Had he not exclaimed unguardedly to Halide Edib, 'I want everyone to do as I wish'? Was the original band of brothers to be supplanted by one Big Brother?

Already Ali Fuad, a possible military rival, had been moved out of the way, to Moscow. Kiazim Karabekir, petulantly voicing complaints and suspicions and criticisms, was conveniently out of the way as it was, on an eastern front where the battle had already been won. The position of Refet, outspoken, irreverent, fully aware of Kemal's failings, was productive of continual friction. The pattern had changed. Kemal's inner circle now consisted of Ismet and Fevzi, latecomers to the Revolution, men, for all their qualities, to be commanded rather than consulted, men who would 'do as he wished'. And on the periphery were yes-men of a lesser order – unscrupulous henchmen, unquestioning younger officers, admiring intellectuals and journalists.

It was into this atmosphere that Rauf, preceded by Fethi, returned at the end of 1921. In Angora he was given an ovation by the Assembly, and was offered the Ministry of Public Works. There were insufficient votes to secure his election to the post: after all, despite his high reputation, he was personally unknown to most of the deputies. His opponents withdrew and he reluctantly accepted it. But he resigned some weeks later on the pretext of ill-health. He had by now had time to study the parliamentary situation, and judged that he could play a more useful role in opposition.

Of all Kemal's early associates Rauf, though there was at this time no quarrel between them, was the most opposed to him in outlook and character. Rauf was not a man to be commanded, as in his frank sailorly way he would tell Kemal; he was one to be consulted, to share, to discuss. Rauf was a democrat by conviction and temperament; Kemal was a democrat by conviction but an autocrat by temperament.

Rauf believed profoundly in the liberal principles of government by consent, and lived up to them with the democratic virtues of tolerance, moderation, a sense of political balance and compromise. His experiences in Malta had done nothing to shake his deep respect for the British parliamentary system and for its constitutional monarchy – no more than Colonel Rawlinson's experiences as a prisoner in Turkey had shaken his belief in Anglo-Turkish friendship.

Kemal believed in these ideas less from theoretical principle than from a sense of their practical necessity for the conversion of his country from an Eastern empire into a Western state. Outwardly he lived up to them. He was assiduous in his respect for constitutional practice and in his observance of democratic forms. He made a habit of open discussion, seeming to consult his friends, seeking their opinions and using them, claiming to act with their agreement. But in fact, as a rule, he bore down their resistance by the weight of his words. It was his own rather than the general will that prevailed – though it might well be to the general advantage.

Within himself he was an amalgam of East and West. Western he was in his respect for the power of reason as opposed to that of emotion. Oriental he was still in his habit of overriding the principle of consent by the practice of authority. By contrast with Rauf, his were the autocratic vices of ruthlessness, intrigue, jealousy of rivals and a demeanour towards his associates in which good fellowship alternated with suspicion and barely disguised contempt. For at the root of his attitude lay a profound belief, not altogether unjustified, in the superiority of his own ideas and capacities. Who but he could prescribe the national aims and achieve them?

Rauf, looking at the Assembly through Western eyes, saw that if it was to function as a healthy body it needed an organized Opposition. This balancing factor was all the more essential at this time when Kemal held full powers, as Commander-in-Chief and president of the Assembly in one. Granted originally for three months, they were now renewed, despite some grumbling from the deputies, at three-monthly intervals, on the grounds that the military situation still called for a strong centralized control. Kemal had already strengthened his ascendancy over the Assembly through the formation of a Defence of Rights Group – a party in embryo, with himself as chairman. Now, under the Commander-in-Chief law, it was redoubled through his personal control over the Cabinet itself.

When Rauf resigned from his Cabinet post, Refet resigned from the Ministry of Defence, objecting ostensibly to the separation of its functions from those of Fevzi as Chief of the General Staff, but actually to the Gazi's increasing arrogation of power to himself. Refet, according to his periodic habit with Kemal, temporarily withdrew from the scene. But Rauf, with Kara Vasif, a fellow exile from Malta, became the nucleus of an organized Second Group in the Assembly, designed to draw together the various elements of opposition and thus balance Kemal's First Group. He chose to work for it largely in the background, maintaining his good relations with Kemal and thus serving as a go-between, endeavouring to act among the rest as a calming and conciliatory influence.

To all these manœuvres Kemal acceded with a good enough grace. He approved of an Opposition in theory – was not this the Western way? Moreover its leaders now were his friends and thus open to his influence. But in practice he mistrusted it. As he commanded in the battlefield of war, so he must command in the battlefield of politics. The ends of both were after all the same, the salvation and regeneration of the country, and to his military mind the means too should be similar. But this battle with his Opposition was not yet to be joined. Latent it was, but latent it must for the present remain. Rauf hoped, by the encouragement of a moderate and responsible Opposition, to hold the balance against the Gazi's extremists, and the Gazi did not openly discourage him.

This was a further period of waiting, of outward satisfaction fraught with inward tension. Many months must elapse before the fight with the Greeks could be resumed; and they were months to be devoted to the strengthening and arming of the Nationalist forces, this time up to the hilt. But now that the sound of the guns was momentarily stilled, Angora, for all its sense of discipline and dedication to the labours of the cause, permitted itself a mood of relaxation and even of gaiety, which was their natural complement.

The Gazi, well guarded by his turbaned Black Sea bodyguard, surveyed and dominated the expanding city from his house on the hillside at Chankaya, which had grown in size and where he was now able to live in reasonable comfort. A community of satellite chalets and villas was springing up among the vineyards around it, and his staff officers, now joined by wives unveiled in the Nationalist fashion and by families, were moving in to be at hand when required. During his walks he would drop in to call on them, impressing them by his informality. From mid-morning onwards there was a continual coming and going of visitors toiling up the hillside on horseback or in carriages from the city below, to whom he was always accessible.

Kemal had furnished the rooms of the house in a comfortable if ponderous style. Leather armchairs were disposed among pieces of furniture of a noticeably Germanic origin. Turkish carpets covered the floors and a collection of arms, including a jewelled sword from the Grand Senussi, hung on the walls. The two principal rooms were greatly enlarged by a wide pentagonal alcove, with high double windows around it. One of these was Kemal's office, the large modernistic desk so placed that he sat with his back to the windows, his eyes fixing a visitor already dazed by the light, whichever way he turned his head, and thus placing him at some disadvantage. The dining-room, where each day visitors remained to meals, resembled an interior courtyard, reflecting Ottoman taste with its pots of flowers, marble fountain and table of blue Kütahya faience.

Kemal liked to walk in the gardens, starting to grow green with the shrubs and the trees he had planted, thrusting his hands in his pockets as he strode up the paths through the vineyards, smelling the freshness around him and watching the cloudscapes which played over the infinite expanses of the plateau. Over the crest of the hill a long track of dust betokened the ox-drawn convoys, winding towards the horizon, with the peasant women still in command as they bore arms to the front and returned for more.

At the end of the garden was a pink-washed kiosk, which Kemal used as a guest-house, and where for some months Madame Berthe Georges-Gaulis stayed. A Frenchwoman and a journalist, he could talk with her, as he could not with Turkish women, of international affairs and of his plans for the country, while she could play a useful part in making the cause of the Nationalists known and understood among his new French allies.

One evening, suddenly relaxing after a heated diatribe against his British enemies – which Madame Gaulis, who had fiery political prejudices, was only too ready to echo – he called for music. The officers in the neighbouring houses were invited in with their wives, who came in evening dresses, their heads – but not their faces – covered with veils of the same material. Each of them carried a lute, which they played at his request and to which they soon began, in low voices at first, to sing traditional Turkish songs, tales of love and death and military glory. This was music which Kemal had loved from his childhood, and as they sang he took pleasure in translating and explaining the songs to his guests, humming them in time with the solemn and often melancholy rhythm.

'Then,' she recorded later, 'forgetting for a moment the bitterness of conflict, he relaxed for the first time; his past came back to his mind. He described his first childhood; his mother who loved him passionately, his youth, his first troubles, his first successes, and he relived all this with the intensity, the fullness of impressions which he brought to everything. He became once more the man of the early days, the young officer surprised himself by the abundance of his gifts.'

Zübeyde, his mother, had now come to live at Chankaya. Sick and ageing, bent with rheumatism, she had never recovered from the loss of her native Salonika. Anatolia meant nothing to her, but she fretted and pined to see Mustafa and finally, sensing that she had not very long to live, he fetched her to Angora. Presenting her to his friends, he made a move to kiss her hand, as he had always done, but she stopped him. He might be her son, but he was also now effectively head of the state, so it was for her to kiss his hand instead, and this she did. At Chankaya she had a house of her own, furnished in the old Turkish style to which she was accustomed. Here she would sit cross-legged on the floor before a brazier of charcoal. He treated her with the ceremony and respect due from a Turk to his mother. Each day he visited her formally, always sending to ask permission to do so, and thus giving her time to prepare for him. This, even if she were sick, she did with care. She grew harassed by the restless life of Chankaya and liked to pay visits to a tree-shaded spring near the Agricultural School, named Nectar of Willows, where Kemal arranged for her a one-roomed cottage, mud-walled and roughly timbered in the old peasant style.

She was like Mustafa in looks but, as Halide Edib recalls, 'without the sinister expression of the face and the tiger-like agility of his slim body. She was built on a majestic scale. Although she was seventy, her big round face was hardly lined at all, and it still retained its milk-white and pink complexion. The eyes were of a darker blue, warm and affectionate, and the mouth was benevolent, although she had a temper equal to his in her own way.'

She disliked Fikriye, largely from feminine jealousy, partly from a feeling that she was not good enough for her son. When Fikriye came into the room she 'would bristle all over with resentment and boom out hints at young people in general which were meant to be for Fikriye Hanum in particular. The young woman sat opposite her, respectful but cool, and very conscious of the old lady's animosity.'

She scolded Kemal and spoke of him as though he were still a schoolboy, calling him 'little Mustafa'. Once at a circumcision party the Azerbaijan Minister asked to meet her. Kemal had her fetched from the women's tent, and made her sit down beside them. After they had talked for some minutes, Zübeyde turned to Kemal and said with a frown, 'Listen to what he is saying. He says you should be Sultan, that would be suitable for you.' She added, 'You must not be Sultan.'

Kemal reassured her. 'Don't worry. I'm not going to be Sultan, but I'm certainly going to be the head of this country. That's what the Ambassador meant.'

The social life of Angora at this time had more of an Eastern than a Western flavour. This followed inevitably from the close relations now established with the Soviet Union and its satellite Republics. The Treaty of Moscow, preceded by a treaty with Afghanistan, had been followed by the Treaty of Kars, which confirmed it in respect of relations with Armenia, Azerbaijan and Georgia. This was followed in its turn by an economic and military agreement with the Ukraine and the arrival of a Ukrainian mission. A Turkish mission was sent to Tiflis, in Georgia, while diplomatic feelers had come from Bokhara, in Turkestan.

These small Turco-Slav countries, precariously placed as they were, saw Nationalist Turkey, with its aspirations so akin to their own and its independence now so evidently assured, as a potential bulwark against Russian domination. They thus sent embassies to Angora so large as to cause embarrassment in a city still short of accommodation. Their influx brought a convivial spirit to the austere city of the plateau. They entertained lavishly, with vodka and caviar, providing Kemal with an outlet for those festive proclivities which had been starved in him since his departure from Constantinople. They furnished him also with feminine company of a free and unconventional kind, soon giving rise in the strait-laced Moslem circles of Angora to lurid rumours of his carousals among the loose-living Slavs.

The Azerbaijanis were the most hospitable. At one of their dinners, when Ukrainians and Soviet Russians sat grouped around the table, the Soviet Ambassador, Aralov, rose to his feet and, speaking for the benefit of Madame Georges-Gaulis in French, launched a strong attack on France as the oppressor of the oppressed in her policy towards the Russian Revolution.

The Gazi, speaking in Turkish, dexterously retorted with a counterblast on the theme that 'there are neither oppressors nor oppressed. There are only those who allow themselves to be oppressed. The Turks are not among these. The Turks can look after themselves; let others do the same.'

One night at the Soviet Embassy – described by Angora as '*Chez les Bolshéviks*' – the Gazi was in mischievous mood, and began to tease the Ambassador. Looking around at the rich carpets and the laden table, above which the portraits of Karl Marx and Lenin struck a bleak and unfamiliar note, Kemal, after some glasses of vodka, turned to his host and said, 'I don't see among us any of the men who prepared this feast. Will you not invite them to join us?'

Aralov looked embarrassed, but after a moment's hesitation sent for the cook and the other servants, who crowded in to join the guests at what the Gazi now described as a 'classless' table. Warming to the theme with more vodka, he delivered a homily on the principles of equality which underlay the Russian Revolution. 'Off duty,' he said, 'men are equal with each other. . . . Your Revolution does not acknowledge differences of class. It is the same in Islam, where rich and poor are equal.' He turned to a porter who sat drinking by himself:

'*Tovarich!*' he exclaimed. 'You can't drink alone. Come, let's all fill our glasses and drink together. They have a Turkish saying, "Some drink, and some only watch, and the result of this is Doomsday." ' Toasts were drunk and then all the company danced. 'What do you think of that?' Kemal remarked to his friends as they left. 'They talk of equality, but as soon as it comes to eating and drinking, class differences begin.'

An important delegation from the orbit of the Soviets was that of the Ukraine, under General Frunze, who promised substantial shipments of munitions, but went too far in offering to draft a plan of campaign against the Greeks, in which Red Army officers might participate. Kemal had not been best pleased when Aralov, on a visit to the front, delivered harangues to the troops on the glories of Bolshevik Russia and the brotherly generosity of its aid to Turkey; nor by the flood of congratulations from the Red Army which followed each stage in the subsequent campaign.

In Constantinople, on the other hand, isolated from realities behind the double Iron Curtain of Anatolia and Russia, it was widely assumed that Kemal in his financial and military embarrassment would call in the Red Army to his aid. General Frunze's mission was interpreted as an attempt 'by Bolos and Enverists' to get control; Sir Horace Rumbold himself had an idea, which he mentioned to Curzon, that it might be the intention of the Bolsheviks to instal Enver as their 'Viceroy at Angora'.

Enver, while the war was going badly for the Nationalists, had indeed organized revolutionary groups among the Turkish-speaking Moslems, and had planned to raise a Caucasian force which would march into Anatolia and overthrow Kemal's régime by a *coup d'état*. He tried through an agent to form a battalion in Trebizond, ostensibly in support of Kemal but in fact for this purpose. He received some support from dissident deputies in the Assembly, mostly former members of the Union and Progress party.

But Kemal's success at the Sakarya put an end to such dreams and conspiracies. Enver had been disappointed in his contacts with the Russians, who had not been inclined to trust him or take him too seriously. Thus, still in pursuit of pan-Turanian visions, he turned eastwards. Collecting a few followers, he proceeded to Turkestan, where he helped to launch a war against the Bolsheviks with irregular forces of Turkish race. For a while he reigned as Emir of Bokhara. But the Russians sent strong forces against him and one morning, in the summer of 1922, he died fighting them, hit by a salvo of machine-gun fire.

Meanwhile Jemal, who had similarly fallen out with the Russians, sent an officer to Angora with a letter to Kemal, requesting permission to return to Turkey. Kemal refused; and soon afterwards Jemal was assassinated in Tiflis. Thus Transcaucasia became a graveyard of the Young Turk leaders.

In the new diplomatic circles of Angora, the Indian Moslems created around them a sterner atmosphere than that of the Slavs. At the Friday receptions of the Ambassador of Afghanistan, there was an abundance of turbans, flowing robes, pelisses trimmed with fur. He was struck, as were the other visitors from the East, by the order, the discipline, the upright bearing of Angora, where even the ill-dressed crowds had a martial air. Pan-Islamic in sympathy, he said to Madame Georges-Gaulis, 'Islam is a large body of which Turkey is the head, Azerbaijan the neck, Persia the chest, Afghanistan the heart, India the abdomen. Egypt and Palestine, Irak and Turkestan are its arms and legs. When you deliver rough blows at the head, how can the rest of the body not feel it? England has hit our head too hard, and we have protested.'

The East, with its dawning Nationalist movements, had indeed begun to look to Nationalist Turkey for example and leadership. Here was the first Oriental country to make a stand against Western imperialism and fight to throw off its yoke. The name of Mustafa Kemal spread throughout Asia, as that of Garibaldi had once spread throughout Europe, firing the imagination of all those peoples in whom the First World War had kindled a spark of national consciousness and awakened the desire for freedom. The news of his struggle had its repercussions throughout Syria and Egypt, as far as Persia, India and even China. Here surely was the prototype, for others to emulate, of the Eastern Nationalist Revolution.[1]

[1] Early in 1920 two emissaries from Syria had reached a tentative agreement with the Kemalists in Istanbul for Turco-Syrian co-operation against the Western powers. This

Kemal was far from aspiring to Asiatic leadership. His eyes were stead-fastly fixed on the West. But at this time, with half Europe still ranged against him, he had need of the moral and material support of the East. Watching him at work at Chankaya, Madame Georges-Gaulis observed 'this constant communication with two poles: Asia, Europe; this facility of assimilating, without ever allowing himself to be submerged, of turning the helm some-times to the right, sometimes to the left, to maintain equilibrium; of rallying to himself all the reasonable and conscious elements of the Islamic world'. Publicly in his speeches he built up the idea of Anatolia as a 'kind of fortress against all the aggressions directed to the East'. The struggle was not that of Turkey alone. 'It is the cause of the East. And until this purpose is achieved, Turkey is sure that all the nations of the East will stand by her.'

Materially, his strongest support came from the Indians, who saw Nationalist Turkey as the only independent Moslem nation. The Khilafat Committee in Bombay started a fund to help the Turkish Nationalist struggle, establishing contact with a representative of Kemal in Con-stantinople who received constant letters of encouragement:

> Mustafa Kemal Pasha has done wonders and you have no idea how people in India adore his name. The honour of the Turkish nation has been once again vindicated. We are all waiting to know the terms on which Angora offers peace to the Greeks. . . .
> The Musulmans of India – particularly the poor and middle-classes, are doing their very best in subscribing to the Angora fund. . . . May the Great Allah grant victory to the Armies of Gazi Mustafa Kemal and save Turkey from her enemies and the enemies of Islam.

Part of the Indian fund, which eventually amounted to some £125,000, was used to pay the army. But most of it was husbanded and later devoted to the construction of a new parliament building in Angora and the founda-tion of the first Nationalist bank.

Roubles meanwhile were now coming from Russia, not indeed to the extent that the Russians had promised but in sufficient instalments to make up for the deficiencies in the promised supply of Russian arms. Much of the money was used for their purchase elsewhere, mainly in Italy, which had become, like France, a steady source of supply through the Medi-terranean ports of southern Turkey. For Italy too was now an ally. She had withdrawn her troops from Anatolia, and not long afterwards signed an agreement with Angora, comparable to that of the French, promising to upport Nationalist claims at the peace conference and asking for no economic benefits in return.

---

envisaged a unified command and ultimately a close treaty relationship between an inde-pendent Turkey and Syria on the lines of the former Austro-Hungarian Empire. But it was rejected by Feisal, as King of Syria. – Zeine, *The Struggle for Arab Independence*.

Thus the Gazi was in a strong position. He had allies, he had arms, he had a recognized Government and an army which was growing in strength from day to day. But he was in no hurry to resume operations. Time was on his side. His troops were defending their own homeland, and their morale was high. Those of the Greeks were in a strange land, drawn into an escapade for which they had no great enthusiasm, and their morale was slowly deteriorating. Kemal would strike at them when his forces were entirely ready, when he felt certain of victory – but not a moment before.

Before he did so, a last effort was made by the Allies for peace. The resources of the Greek Treasury were dwindling. Monsieur Gounaris, the Greek Premier, having tried without success to raise either arms or a loan in London, warned Lord Curzon that the Greek command might be obliged to withdraw its forces from Anatolia. Curzon immediately proposed a meeting of the powers in Paris, with a view to securing an armistice, followed by a Greek evacuation on equitable terms for both sides. In anticipation of it, the Gazi sent his Foreign Minister, Yusuf Kemal, to Constantinople, *en route* for London. As the first Nationalist minister to visit the capital, he found himself an object of some curiosity, being greeted with marked affability by the French and with polite reserve by the British.

The Constantinople Government was now little more than a shadow of a Cabinet, with a puppet Sultan at its head. Nevertheless it was now, as before, to send its own representative to Europe in uneasy harness with Kemal's. Though Rumbold had long since recognized that no settlement could be reached without Kemal, he was still working for some kind of fusion between the two Governments, but with the emphasis rather on Constantinople than on Angora. He favoured the policy of strengthening the Sultan by offering him a reasonable treaty. The Sultan's delegate was Izzet Pasha, with whom Yusuf Kemal was instructed by Angora to make common cause. Both however left separately for London, and were received separately, at Yusuf's insistence, by Curzon. Both stood firm in their interviews on the principles of the National Pact. Both were disappointed by his insistence that the Greeks should retain eastern Thrace, with Adrianople. Curzon told them that he would try, in Paris, to secure an evacuation of Anatolia by the Greeks. But as a condition the Turks must accept an armistice first.

Curzon led the conference in Paris, wrestling with Poincaré throughout four exhausting days. To Austen Chamberlain he wrote, 'I shall come back with a plan which I think it quite likely the Turks may ultimately refuse, but which will approve itself to the public opinion of the world as a just and generous solution.' It was put to the Turks and the Greeks in two successive notes. The first proposed an immediate armistice. The armies were to stand on their present lines, with a neutral zone of six miles between them. The second proposed a basis for the discussion of peace terms of which the first provision would be a Greek evacuation of Anatolia. The Greeks accepted the armistice and expressed no views on the peace terms. The Turks accepted the armistice, but only on condition that the Greek withdrawal should follow it immediately, regardless of peace discussions. The Allies rejected this condition.

Passing through Paris on his way home to Angora, Yusuf Kemal explained to Poincaré that if a single Greek soldier remained on Turkish soil the Gazi risked being hanged before the Assembly's doors – at which Poincaré seemed suitably impressed. On Yusuf's arrival in Angora, Kemal remarked to him, 'So you'll have what you wanted.' As on his return from Russia, a year earlier, his report on the negotiations was in effect to give Kemal the all-clear for an offensive.

In reaching this decision, he was prompted by the conviction that it would be fatal to accept anything short of the National Pact. He had little faith in the British, far less in Lloyd George, hence no guarantee that the evacuation would in fact take place. As to the proposed peace terms, they were still linked, if in a greatly modified form, to the Treaty of Sèvres, the total rejection of whose very name was a fundamental article of the Nationalist faith.

Thus the four months that might have been devoted to the evacuation were in fact devoted to a further period of watching and waiting by the two armies, while the snows melted in the mountains, the crops sprouted on the plateau, and the sun hardened the ground to a point at which a successful advance of the Nationalists became a practicable venture.

CHAPTER THIRTY-EIGHT

PREPARATIONS FOR BATTLE

KEMAL, during these months, had been faced with the task of stiffening his own home front. His intransigence in face of the peace offer had not been wholly popular. In Angora there was an element ready enough to accept peace at any reasonable price, even if it fell short of the National Pact. There was a disposition to trust the Allies, to contend that a settlement was possible without further bloodshed. Let the army stand on its present line and seek the national aims by negotiation.

Kemal was mainly concerned with the effects of such an attitude on the army itself. He thus toured the front to boost morale, and found some of his fears confirmed. On announcing to one of his army corps commanders that he had rejected the armistice proposals, he received the reply, 'How could you do that? To refuse such proposals was wrong.' In the course of his tour he encountered the view that, since the Allies had clearly abandoned the Treaty of Sèvres, there was no reason to endure new and questionable sacrifices.

The deputies, in their ignorance of military matters, adopted a variety of attitudes. On the one hand there were the hot-heads who called for an immediate if only a partial attack. On the other, there were those who believed that the army was incapable of attacking at all, and that Kemal was merely exploiting his continued position as Commander-in-Chief to strengthen his personal hold over the nation. Kemal's problem was that he could not, for security reasons, disclose the actual strength of the army or the extent of the arms which were coming in, mainly from secret sources.

In a secret session of the Assembly he tried patiently to explain to them that a half-prepared attack would be worse than no attack at all. He taunted deputies for their defeatism. There were, he stressed, two fronts: the outward and the inward, the foreign and the home. The outward front was that of the army, opposing the enemy directly. The inward front was formed by the whole nation. Neither could be shaken unless the Assembly encouraged the enemy and discouraged the army by pessimistic orations.

The Gazi's powers as Commander-in-Chief had been renewed, with many grumbles, for two further periods of three months. But in May its renewal for a third term had been rejected by the Assembly, taking advantage of his absence through illness. The army was thus left without a leader. The Cabinet proposed to resign. But the Gazi rose from his bed and came down to the Assembly to answer his critics. After lecturing it on the way in which such bodies normally conducted their affairs in wartime, he declared that he had no intention of abandoning the army, which had been for two days without a Commander-in-Chief. The debate became heated, and there was a moment when both Kemal and one of his more irresponsible enemies, Ziya Hurshid, were seen to have hands on their revolvers. But when the question was put to the vote he was confirmed in the command.

None the less, many of Kemal's own friends remained uneasy. They feared a drift from parliamentary government to a form of personal rule by a strong man, comparable to that which was developing in the South American republics. With this in mind they now worked on another tack to redress the balance of power. At present Kemal was not merely president of the Assembly – hence in effect head of state – but Prime Minister as well, controlling a Cabinet of ministers who were in practice his own nominees. Though in theory the Assembly elected the ministers, in fact it accepted those candidates whom it was the president's privilege to put forward: Kemal could thus effectively impose his will both on the Assembly and the Cabinet. The opposition now sought to divide his responsibility. They secured the passage of an Act providing for the effective election by secret ballot not merely of the ministers but of the Prime Minister himself. This meant that Kemal not merely ceased to be his own Prime Minister but had to accept in his Government ministers who might be opposed to his views. The move had been initiated largely by Rauf who, since he had not actively joined the opposition, now became the obvious choice for Prime Minister.

At first, despite Kemal's efforts at persuasion, he was reluctant to accept the post. Asked why, he replied frankly, 'If I do, you will continue to interfere in my conduct of affairs. I shall be unable to accept this and find myself forced to resign. I firmly believe that you are the one person who, at the head of the armies, can save the country, and I will not be placed in a position of having to disagree with you.'

Kemal replied sincerely, 'I give you my word of honour. Agree to become head of the Government. Form a Cabinet, and I shall not interfere in any of your decisions.'

It was a promise which Kemal faithfully kept, henceforward accepting the principle that he did not attend Cabinet meetings unless specifically invited. In fact he was invited when any major issue came up for discussion. But the Cabinet retained its separate and corporate identity.

Kemal however was still head of the Group for the Defence of Rights, which formed the majority in the Assembly. Here too he compromised. He brought Ali Fuad back from Moscow, where an ambassador of his status was no longer needed, and made him its active president, while remaining its supposedly neutral patron. The differences between them had never been personal, and now Fuad stayed with him at Chankaya, where the two old friends sat up together at nights over the *raki*, talking of the problems that had developed at home in his absence and particularly of the growing divisions in the Assembly. The rift, as Ali Fuad saw it, seemed likely to grow into an eventual struggle between republicans and constitutional monarchists. Kemal recognized this, but stressed the need to postpone the issue until the war was won. The problem was, as he put it, to reconcile this phase of the political struggle with the need for authority and discipline for the final military struggle. In reply to Fuad's contention that Kemal should elevate himself to a neutral position, mediating from above the political arena, Kemal expressed serious misgivings as to the threat from the forces of religious reaction and doubted whether any such neutrality were possible. Meanwhile he counted on Fuad to do all he could to maintain unity on the home front.

The time now approached when it would be necessary to review Kemal's powers as Commander-in-Chief yet again. This would perhaps be the last term of renewal. For it was clear that the final offensive was near. A Turkish success seemed assured. But to make it doubly sure, it was essential, in the eyes of Rauf and Ali Fuad, that the Commander-in-Chief law should this time pass the Assembly without such opposition as might suggest Turkish disunity and revive the flagging hopes of the Greeks. At the same time, whole-hearted in their support for Kemal until victory was won, they were becoming concerned as to what might happen afterwards. The Gazi must be given his powers. But it must be ensured that he did not retain and exploit them once peace had been achieved. The new Turkey must be a democratic Turkey. For the future their ambitious and victorious friend must be curbed in his dictatorial designs.

They went to consult Refet, who had been living in virtual seclusion in his house at Kechiören, a suburb of Angora, since the dispute with Kemal which had led to his retirement from the Ministry of Defence. He echoed their views, and Rauf proposed that the three friends should put them frankly before Kemal. Refet agreed to invite him to a dinner at his house, which would also serve as a gesture of reconciliation. The dinner was arranged for the eve of the relevant debate in the Assembly.

The house had a welcoming atmosphere, for Refet appreciated the refinements of life and knew well how to make himself comfortable. The four

A.—11

founders of the Revolution sat down on a hot July evening to an ample meal in a hall where a fountain played. The drink flowed. The atmosphere soon became relaxed. The conversation was free. They reminisced of old times and speculated on times to come.

Kemal spoke critically of the opposition group: 'I know well how to carry on a fight,' he said, 'but this is neither the time nor place for it. And later no fight should be necessary.'

The others stressed that the majority, though they might oppose him in Parliament, trusted him personally, and believed in his success. They were only concerned with one question. After the cause had been won, what line did he mean to pursue? His future intentions were the subject of rumour. Even his supporters feared some *fait accompli* in terms of his personal power. Doubts on this score created divisions in the Assembly. They hoped that he would resolve them, restoring confidence and a spirit of unity.

Kemal fenced with his friends, answering their outspoken criticisms with reserve and circumspection. Touching on the new arrangements for a Cabinet with an elected Prime Minister, he repeated his assurances that he would respect Rauf's position as such. But on the question of his own ultimate powers he was not to be drawn.

They talked and drank until daybreak, only Rauf, who was a moderate drinker, abstaining. Unfortunately, Refet, as the drink took effect, went too far. Never able, in his disrespectful way, to resist scolding and needling and teasing Kemal, he pricked at his pride with home truths about his unpopularity, dragging up faults from the past, girding at his personal life in the present. Angora – or so Refet declared – was ringing with scandals about his 'debauches' at the Azerbaijan Embassy; his reputed affair with a diplomat's wife; the seduction, with Arif's connivance, of an innocent nurse at the front; the installation at Chankaya of a barber's boy, picked up during a visit to Izmit. Kemal stiffened as he drank. His eyes gleamed pale with resentment.

Rauf and Ali Fuad tried to soothe him, to laugh off Refet's indiscreet charges. But on the issue of the future they had no intention of sparing him. They urged that, when the war was over and his main duty done, he should retire from the fray and accept an elevated presidential status, acting as an arbiter and consultant and letting others run the country on democratic lines. Good-humouredly enough, they promised that they would obtain for him a handsome grant from the Assembly, and even produced for him the design of a projected medal, which they would have cast for himself alone as a reward for his salvation of the country.

Kemal brushed this lightly aside, but reassured them: 'Don't worry. I shall consider your advice. I shall make a statement to calm all this fuss about myself and the country's future.'

His friends expressed satisfaction. Kemal drank to their health. 'Friends,' he said, 'it is morning. I think I've pleased all of you. Now let's go home and rest for a while before we get down to business.'

Refet showed them to the door. Dropping Rauf at his house, Kemal and Ali Fuad drove up to Chankaya. Fuad slept for a few hours. Kemal took a hot bath, shaved and dressed. Then he sat down to work on his speech. Fuad appeared in time for luncheon, to find the Gazi, in full field-marshal's uniform, standing in a habitual pose, erect with one hand behind his back. His hair was sprucely combed, his eyes were clear, and he showed no trace of fatigue after his sleepless night. They ate briefly and after a quick cup of coffee went down to the Assembly, where he mounted the rostrum.

The Gazi, who normally appeared in civilian clothes, cut an impressive figure in his uniform. He spoke of the Commander-in-Chief law: no Parliament in the world would grant such authority to a single person, except on two conditions – that the situation was exceptional and that the person was above all suspicion. The Assembly had shown great trust in him, for which he expressed gratitude. But the time had now come when it was no longer necessary to maintain these extraordinary powers. The moral and material forces of the army had reached such a degree of perfection that the national effort could be realized without them. He continued:

Then I, like the rest of you, will only be an individual in the nation, and, of course, this will be, for me, the greatest happiness. When that day comes, gentlemen, I shall have two kinds of happiness. The second will be that I shall then be able to withdraw to my former post – the post I had three years ago before we began our sacred fight. (Cheers) Indeed, there is no happiness comparable to that of being a free individual in the bosom of the nation. For those who realize this truth, and for those who have moral and sacred joys within their souls and their conscience rank, however high, has no value whatsoever.

Disarmed by his tactics, dissolved by his rhetoric, the deputies forgot their misgivings. Had the Gazi not offered to renounce his privileges? Had he not made it clear that, when victory was won, he would become once more a private citizen, dependent on the nation's will? What greatness, what nobility of character! They reinvested him with the powers of Commander-in-Chief. But this time they imposed no time limit. He was to retain them, subject only to the Assembly's right to withdraw them, until the national aims had been finally realized. Kemal stepped down from the rostrum well satisfied with his night's vigil and his afternoon's work.

The Turkish offensive could not now be long delayed. It was in fact hastened by a last desperate gamble on the part of the Greeks. Foiled in their designs on Angora, Gounaris and Constantine now switched their attention to Constantinople. They swiftly removed two divisions from Asia Minor and transferred them across the Sea of Marmara to reinforce their troops in Thrace. With a strong force thus threatening the lines of Chatalja, they demanded the permission of the Allies to enter Constantinople.

By this threat they sought to put pressure on the Allies, who were once again contemplating peace discussions – this time at Venice – to resolve the conflict in their favour, or at least to save their faces. Constantinople was now so lightly held that the Allied troops had been compared to the 'jam in a sandwich', of which the Greeks on the one side and the Turks on the other represented thick slices of bread. An entry into the city would be a simple enough operation. It would restore the prestige in Greece of Constantine's régime, revive the confidence of his army, and provide him with a valuable bargaining asset.

'It is quite possible,' as Churchill afterwards analysed the move, 'that under cover of a temporary Greek occupation of Constantinople with Allied approval, the escape of the Greek armies from Asia Minor might have been honourably and comparatively painlessly merged in negotiations for peace. . . . At least it could be argued against the Allies that if they would not help the Greeks in their military operations they ought not to hamper them; and if on general grounds they felt compelled to hamper, they ought at least loyally and actively to help them to their ships.'

Thus once again, as in the Balkan War ten years before, all eyes in Constantinople were turned anxiously towards the Chatalja Lines. Harington entrusted their defence to a French general, with French and British troops which at once started to entrench. He issued a statement, on his own responsibility, that the troops of both powers would combine to resist any attack on the occupation forces. Rumbold returned hurriedly from leave and an Allied meeting at the British Embassy confirmed this. British warships made a demonstration in the Marmara. The Greeks withdrew a short distance, but continued to land troops. Lloyd George upheld the decision, and the Greeks agreed to advance no further without Allied approval. The British warships turned to the more peaceable pastime of holding their annual regatta. The Greeks had lost their last chance. Moreover, in taking it they had weakened their defences on the Anatolian front.

Lloyd George, however, in his incorrigible philhellenism, elected to give them a final gleam of hope. 'In the dying hours,' as The Times put it, 'of a weary session of the House of Commons,' he made a speech which could only be interpreted by both sides as an encouragement to the Greeks still to seek a decision by force. The Prime Minister permitted himself a eulogy on the gallant Greek army in their 'daring and reckless military enterprise'. They had been compelled to 'march through impenetrable defiles hundreds of miles into the country'. They had established their military superiority in every pitched battle. They had been beaten only by the conformation of the country and by the long lines of communication 'which no other army in Europe would ever have dreamed of taking the risk of allowing'.

Then he said, with apparent significance, 'Peace the Kemalists will not accept, because they say we will not give them satisfactory armistice terms; but we are not allowing the Greeks to wage the war with their full strength. We cannot allow that sort of thing to go on indefinitely in the hope that the Kemalists entertain that they will at last exhaust this little country, whose men have been in arms for ten or twelve years with one war after another, and which has not indefinite resources.'

The speech was received with enthusiasm throughout Greece. The newspapers headlined its more laudatory passages. Extracts from it were published in an Order of the Day to the Greek forces, who became filled with a new hope that the British would, at this eleventh hour, help them to defeat the enemy. The stratagem of the threat to Constantinople had surely achieved its object. There was no more talk of peace.

All these events favoured Kemal's plans. As soon as he got wind of the Greek troop movements he decided to put forward the date of his offensive. For the transfer to Thrace would equalize the Turkish and Greek forces in Anatolia. Now was the moment to strike. He had sent Fethi, his Minister of the Interior, to Rome, Paris and London, on the off-chance of a peace still in terms of a Greek evacuation; otherwise as an emissary for the peace which must follow a victory. Then he left for the headquarters of the western front at Akshehir.

CHAPTER THIRTY-NINE

FINAL VICTORY

WHILE THE ALLIED High Commissioners in Constantinople were discussing the Greek threat to the city, Kemal and his General Staff were watching a football match at Akshehir. This was the security cover he had chosen for a secret staff conference, to settle the date and the final arrangements for the Turkish offensive against Smyrna. The plan of campaign had been drawn up in secrecy nine months before, between Kemal, Fevzi and Ismet. Fevzi now explained it on a map. Then Kemal asked his generals for their opinion. Several were critical, less of the plan itself than of the timing of its execution. Ismet, irresolute as ever, was not convinced that it could lead at this moment to a decisive victory. He favoured a sound policy of defence, with the object of wearing down the Greeks. If there were to be an attack, then he wanted more time to complete preparations.

The defensive psychology had become deeply engrained. Others echoed Ismet's doubts. Now that there was an army in being, they shrank from the risk of losing it. It was not, they maintained, really ready. The Second Army commander, who had been one of Kemal's instructors at the War School, protested that the country's very existence would be jeopardized by this risking of a force which was all it possessed. Kemal, enquiring of Fevzi whether it was in fact all, and receiving a positive reply, turned to him and said, 'All right, my dear instructor. We are not playing the war game at Harbiye now. We shall throw *all* into the effort of securing a definite result for the country.'

Though he had gone through the motions of consulting the generals, Kemal's mind was already made up. With that extra dimension, which his lesser commanders lacked, of decisiveness, flair, political judgement and psychological knowledge of his enemy, he was as confident of victory as it was prudent to be. He ordered that the armies should be ready for the offensive by the middle of August. Ismet rose to his feet, stood at attention and, speaking as the commander of the front on behalf of the rest, said,

'You wanted to know our opinion. We expressed it freely. But if what you have told us is an order, we shall obey it.'

Kemal returned to Angora, where he had the Cabinet – to say nothing of the Opposition – to deal with. He informed the ministers of his decision and of his belief in success. Fevzi considered that there was an eighty per cent chance of it – allowing twenty per cent. for the hazards of war. The two Opposition ministers became less pessimistic. The Cabinet agreed to the attack. There remained the Opposition itself, whose propaganda implied that the troops were demoralized and incapable of action. This, as Kemal admitted to Ali Fuad, had its advantages, since it put the enemy off the scent as to the imminence of an attack. But he took steps to reassure those whose influence counted.

As a modern security-minded officer, Kemal fully appreciated the need for secrecy concerning the date of the attack. For the success of his strategical plan depended essentially on surprise. Only a few people knew of his departure for the front, and they were instructed to talk and behave as though he were still in Angora. Ali Fuad was to pretend to the deputies that he had dined with him that night. Rumours were assiduously spread among the agents of the foreigners that the army was not yet ready for an offensive. At Chankaya the sentries were instructed to admit no one: the Gazi was busy. When he was already at his headquarters in the field, it was announced in the press that he was giving a reception next day at Chankaya.

Saying goodbye to his mother he said, as he kissed her hand, that he was going to a tea-party. She looked at his field dress and boots and said, 'This uniform is not for a tea-party.' He soothed her and left. Later she rang the area commander to ask where he was, and was again told, 'He has gone to a tea-party.'

'No,' she replied. 'I know. He has gone to the war.' She sent him a note:

My Son, I waited for you. You did not come back. You told me that you were going to a tea-party. But I know that you have gone to the front. Know that I pray for you, and do not come back before the war is won.[1]

That night he supped with a few of his henchmen in a suburb of Angora. He drank freely, in anticipation of the relative abstinence which was his rule at the front. As he said goodbye, with his hands around their shoulders, he remarked, 'I'm going straight away to the front, to start the offensive.'

Taken aback, one of them asked him, 'Pasha'm, what if you don't succeed?'

'What do you mean? Within fourteen days of the start I shall have destroyed the Greeks and thrown them into the sea.'

[1] Perihan Naci Eldeniz. In *Belleten*.

Instead of taking the train, he drove by car through the night across the salt desert to Konya. There he took over the telegraph office so that his arrival should not be announced. Fethi had telegraphed from London that Lord Curzon had refused to see him. The moment had come for the offensive. Kemal moved from Konya to Akshehir, where he was soon giving final orders to his two army commanders.

The Greek front stretched over some three hundred miles from the Sea of Marmara to the Menderes valley. Its strong points were at Eskishehir in the north, and at Afyon in the south. The forces on either side were roughly equal, with a slight Greek advantage in arms and a slight Turkish advantage in cavalry. The Greeks expected the attack to come against Eskishehir, in the north, where the Turks had large concentrations, and where Intelligence sources – which included the British employees of the liquorice industry – reported lively activity. Kemal encouraged them in this expectation, but in fact planned to attack in the south, against Afyon, since it commanded the direct supply line by the railway to Smyrna. This was the stronger defensive position, moreover so fortified that British engineers judged it impregnable and likely to prove 'the Turkish Verdun'. But to Kemal it had the greater strategic importance. He thus laid plans for its reduction.

The keynote of his plan was surprise, first strategical then tactical. Profiting by the methods of his enemy, Allenby, in the Palestine campaign, Kemal withdrew the necessary forces from north to south over a period of a month and with the greatest possible secrecy. All troop movements were made at night, while the men rested by day in the villages and under the shade of trees, invisible to air reconnaissance. Where roads had to be made they were made also in the inessential areas, to mislead the enemy further. Meanwhile, though only a small force remained before Eskishehir, camp fires were lit at night to suggest a concentration of several divisions, and dust raised on the roads by day to suggest troops moving north to reinforce them. Thus he sought to achieve strategical surprise.

His objective was to turn the Greek right flank. This was concentrated over a front of some fifty miles, around the town of Afyon Karahisar and the supporting region of Dumlupinar, facing in two directions, east and south. To the south it was defended by an irregular range of mountains, rising dramatically to a height of two thousand feet from the plain. It was this bastion of nature that Kemal, in pursuit of tactical surprise, proposed to attack with his First Army, its main force of infantry and artillery supporting a secondary thrust from the east. His cavalry would then sweep westwards to cut the retreat of the Greek armies with a swift enveloping movement, such as Allenby had employed against the Turkish armies in Palestine.

To confuse the enemy, he ordered a northward feint attack towards Brusa on his right flank and a southward cavalry move towards Aydin, in the

Menderes valley, farther to the rear. He anticipated a quick success. To a cavalry commander suggesting postponement because of a lack of fodder for his horses, he remarked, 'In two days' time you will have food in plenty for men and horses alike.' He had calculated the date for the attack on the basis that the grain in the Greek fields would be ripe but not yet harvested; moreover the streams would be dry, thus facilitating swiftness of movement.

On the evening of 25th August Kemal gave orders to cut all communications between Anatolia and the outside world. He had moved his headquarters up from the plain into the mountain region next to the village of Shuhud, then to a camp behind the crest of Koja Tepe. His troops had marched up by night into position on the slopes, often as close to the enemy as a few hundred yards, taking cover and camouflaging themselves against air observation by day. As zero hour approached Kemal issued a battle order to the troops which had been drafted by Ismet. It read: 'Soldiers, your goal is the Mediterranean.' The first major offensive of a nation committed, for twelve years past, to defence, was about to begin.[1]

In the hour before dawn on 26th August, the Gazi rode slowly up the dark rounded hill of Koja Tepe, from which he was to direct the battle. A file of soldiers with lanterns lit the way, as they were lighting it for the horses and pack animals on the slopes around. He was silent and evidently wrapped in thought. Continually he looked eastwards towards the horizon, where presently a slight red glow announced the rising of the sun above the Anatolian plateau. Then with a thunderous roar the artillery barrage began – and the Greeks woke up. Many of them had been out at a dance in Afyon until an hour or so earlier.

Kemal had ordered that all generals should direct their troops from the front line. Now, with Fevzi and Ismet, he surveyed from his hilltop the first line of the general attack which was developing a mile or so off. A broad irregular amphitheatre of other hilltops, steeper and rockier, straggled in echelon across the horizon before them. Each was fortified by the Greeks. Each was the objective of a Turkish division, to be stormed in an uphill attack until the summit was reached. The fighting was bloody but brief. All but two of these objectives were in Turkish hands by 9.30 in the morning. The surprise was complete. The Greeks had no inkling of the presence of those forces which had crept up on them overnight under cover of the opposite slopes. Air reconnaissance had shown a mere three Turkish divisions, easy enough to contain. Instead, here was a force that overwhelmed them by a local superiority of three to one.

Some time moreover elapsed before they grasped that this was the main attack. Expecting it to come from the east, they kept a strong force here in the plain to meet what proved only to be a holding attack. By the time their mistake became clear the battle was already as good as lost. For in

[1] See map, page 509.

the meantime the Turkish cavalry had swept round to their rear, harrying them from the west and cutting the railway to Smyrna at a point to be known henceforward by the name of Yildirim Kemal – appropriately enough, since this was indeed at last a 'lightning' offensive.

At two key points only, one on the left flank and the other on the right, did the Turks meet with an effective resistance and thus fail at first to take their objectives. At Chigil Tepe, on the left, the young officer in command committed suicide on account of his failure to do so. Kemal, ruthless in the heat of the battle, cursed him for dying in vain. His unit had in fact done what he had expected of it, and the position was captured later in the day. It was not until the evening that he relented so far as to remark, 'What a pity for this child!'

On the right was an equally formidable strong-point, a precipitous slope on which the Greeks, fighting fiercely, repulsed several Turkish assaults. Then Kemal, with the army corps commander, Kemal-ed-Din Sami – a man nicknamed in the army 'the Lightning Conductor' from his propensity to draw the enemy's fire – appeared on the scene. 'I'd sooner see the sky fall than the Greeks win,' he said. He harangued the front-line troops. He called for volunteers, but only for men who wanted to die. Every man came forward. Then, know as he did the psychology of the Turkish soldier, he taunted and cursed them for their cowardice. They were unworthy of their wives, who should have the right to divorce them.

Bewildered and furious they asked why? Had they not volunteered to die? Having thus summoned up their blood to boiling-point, he ordered them over the barbed wire and up the slope. The Greek fire mowed them down. Soon there were pyramids of Turkish dead before the wire and the earth was red with blood, lying in pools on the hard ground. But more came on, clambering over the bodies of their comrades. Kemal-ed-Din Sami looked away, overwhelmed by the spectacle of slaughter and bloodshed. Then he heard an Imam chanting from the top of the rock, and knew that the position was captured.

Thus the first line of defence of the Greeks was no more, its hillsides criss-crossed with abandoned fortifications like a huddle of giant deserted ant-heaps. They had barely time to man their second and third lines of defence beyond the hills, which fell as quickly to the Turks. During the next two days the main Turkish forces soon reached the road through the valley before Dumlupinar, which led down towards Smyrna, while the cavalry and mobile infantry, now covering up to thirty-five miles a day, wheeled round even farther to the west of them in an endeavour to close the line of retreat. The holding force from the east now moved forward to aid in the pursuit, capturing Afyon itself, which the Greeks had been forced to evacuate with barely a shot fired.

Here, in the municipal building beneath Afyon's 'Karahisar', the black fortress perched on its towering rock, Kemal now installed his headquarters, resuming telegraphic contact once more with the whole of his force and the rest of the country. Here Halide Edib – whom with a touch of superstition he had summoned back to his side as a kind of female mascot – first saw him gesticulating and poring over a map with Fevzi by the light of two lamps. As he came to greet her he had, to her eyes, so exalted and radiant a look that he seemed to be 'blinking at a hundred suns all rising over his head. The ring of his voice and the shake of the hand made you feel his excitement – the man with the will-power which is like a self-fed machine of perpetual motion.' To her congratulations he responded with a mighty chuckle, like the purr of a royal tiger. 'Yes, we are doing it at last.'

Fevzi was patting his own right shoulder, as in moments of satisfaction, and sucking his teeth. Ismet was himself. There was an excess of cordiality. Halide, recalling the hard times, was touched by Kemal's exuberant joy: 'After you take Smyrna, Pasha, you will rest, you have struggled so hard.'

'Rest? What rest? After the Greeks, we will fight each other, we will eat each other.'

'Why should we?' she said. 'There will be an enormous amount to do in the way of reconstruction.'

'What about the men who have opposed me?'

'Well, it was natural in a National Assembly.'

He spoke in a bantering tone, making fun of her feminine squeamishness; but there was a revengeful look in his eye as he mentioned two of his political enemies. 'I will have those lynched by the people. No, we will not rest, we will kill each other. . . . When the struggle ends it will be dull; we must find some other excitement, Hanum Effendi.'

On the morning of 30th August he moved his headquarters forward to the region of Dumlupinar. Here the bulk of the Greek forces, endeavouring to retreat, were contained in a wide oval basin by a ridge of scrubby hills whence the Second Army was converging to join the First; by the broad mountain of Murad Dağ, to the west, which no force could surmount; and by the troops of the First Army closing in from the east and south, to draw the noose tighter around them. But for a single escape route down the road to the west, through the long narrow valley of Kiziljidere, the Greeks were surrounded.

That day, four days after the initial attack, half their army was annihilated or taken prisoner, with the loss of all its war material. A large column of troops, including the Greek army corps commander, General Tricoupis, and his staff, found itself trapped in the valley between two Turkish divisions at its entrance and a third which had moved swiftly ahead to block its exit. The scene of the consequent slaughter looked to Halide afterwards 'like a disordered dream. . . . Forsaken batteries glistened in the sun; rifles and ammunition in huge piles, endless material of all descriptions lay huddled in a great mass all over the valley. And amidst it all corpses – of men and animals – lay as they had fallen.'

The other half of the Greek army was in headlong flight to the coast, out of range of its pursuers, a fighting force no longer, burning villages and crops, slaughtering men, women and children as it fled. For this, according to the Greek soldiers' orders, was a 'war of extermination'.

Such was the victory which, lest the credit for it be disputed between Kemal and Nur-ed-Din Pasha, his ambitious First Army commander, was dubbed by Ismet 'The Battle of the Generalissimo'.[1] It was the fruit of meticulous planning and a masterly concept of strategical and tactical surprise. The 'Verdun' of the Greeks had crumbled before an overwhelming force, directed unexpectedly at a single point, and to a swift exploitation of its undefended flank.

In a ruined village by the battlefield, Kemal's tent was pitched on the roof of a stable. The peasant women gathered around, staring at him, begging him to avenge the sufferings which they had endured at the hands of the Greeks. His exuberance turned to a mood of depression. He came down to sit silently on a chair by the roadside, watching the droves of Greek prisoners as they filed back, dusty and ragged and bloodstained. The scene of devastation shocked him, inured though he was to the carnage of war. To an ADC he confessed to his hatred of it, philosophizing on the failings of mankind – and those of the Greeks in particular. Then, seeing a Greek flag lying on the ground, he ordered him to pick it up and drape it over one of the Greek guns.

Among the prisoners brought before him he recognized an officer he had known in Salonika. The prisoner, puzzled to see no badge on his shoulder, asked him his rank. Was he now major, colonel, general, what? Kemal replied that he was marshal, Commander-in-Chief. The Greek exclaimed in Turkish, 'Whoever heard of a Commander-in-Chief being near the front line of a battle?' Kemal said to him jovially, 'We are soon going to take back Salonika, and to create an autonomous Macedonia. I shall make you a commander there.'

In fact the Turkish victory owed much to deficient Greek generalship. The Commander-in-Chief, General Hajianestis, who had been appointed for political reasons, directed the battle from a yacht in the harbour of Smyrna, lying in bed or frequenting the coffee-shops ashore, alternately terrorizing his commanders and confusing them with irresponsible or unconfirmed orders. He developed signs of insanity, believing sometimes that he was dead, sometimes that his body was made of glass and that, if he rose to his feet, his legs would break. General Tricoupis had received a general order that, in the event of a Turkish attack on Afyon, he was to move southeastwards on the village of Chobanlar, with a view to outflanking and thus

---

[1] Later Nur-ed-Din had visiting-cards printed with the title 'Conqueror of Smyrna'.

checking the enemy. But when the attack came he feared, in the absence of specific confirmation of the order, to do so. Instead he held on until forced to retreat. He tried to mount a counter-attack, but his men would not follow him. Hence his capture in the fatal valley by a Turkish cavalry squadron. Only afterwards did he learn that Hajianestis had been dismissed from his post, and that he had been appointed Commander-in-Chief in his place.

A day or so later, with a fellow army corps commander, General Dionis, he was brought to Kemal's headquarters, which had moved forward by this time to Ushak. Here Kemal received them, standing between Fevzi and Ismet. Halide Edib describes how he did so:

> As a soldier one recognized at once in him the supreme artist and the supreme sportsman. He kept the rules of his game with dignity, with tact, and with exactitude. He thought neither of the appearance nor of the misdeeds of the Greek generals. Tricoupis, especially, was the man with whom he had played a real game. Now that his military opponent was on the ground, he showed that military art and military courtesy he possessed to his fingers' ends. He gripped General Tricoupis's hand heartily and held it imperceptibly longer than for an ordinary handshake. 'Sit down, General,' he said, 'you must be tired.' Then he offered his cigarette case and ordered coffee.

Tricoupis was looking at him with surprise. 'I did not know you were such a young man, General,' he said. They sat down around the table, Kemal fixing him with his pale steely gaze. He was eager to talk about the battle. The conversation began, through an interpreter, in Greek, but continued in halting French. Kemal asked Tricoupis, as one soldier to another, why he had not foreseen that the attack was likely to take the course it did. Tricoupis confessed that he had been taken by surprise. He was impressed to hear that Kemal had conducted the campaign from the front line itself. He pointed out his own difficulties to Kemal, sounding to Halide's ears 'like an amateur speaking to a professional': his absentee Commander-in-Chief, who knew little of the situation; the refusal of his commanders to obey him; the break in the Greek communications, thanks to the Turkish cavalry, who cut the telephone lines and destroyed the transport; the political squabbles between Venizelists and Constantinists, destroying cohesion and discipline.

They talked of tactics. Why, Kemal asked, had he not done this or that? Tricoupis spoke of his proposed move on Chobanlar, in defence of Afyon. Kemal explained just how he would have countered it. He had allowed in his calculations for every potential move of his enemy. The two Greek generals started to dispute with each other. The Turks looked a trifle contemptuous at this lack of decorum, this contrast between highly strung

Greek volubility and Turkish restraint. Finally Kemal asked Tricoupis if there were anything he could do for him. The general asked that his wife, who was on the island of Prinkipo off Constantinople, should be told of his capture.

Kemal gave the promise, gripped and held Tricoupis's hand, and said sincerely but with a twinkle in his cold blue eyes, 'War is a game of chance, General. The very best is sometimes worsted. You have done your best as a soldier and as an honourable man; the responsibility rests with chance. Do not be distressed.'

But Tricoupis made a theatrical gesture. 'Oh, General,' he exclaimed, 'I have not done the last thing I ought to have done.' He had not had the courage to commit suicide. At this emotional outburst Kemal narrowed his eyes and gave him a cynical look. 'That,' he said tersely, 'is a thing which concerns you personally.'

Two months later Hajianestis was impeached and executed, together with Gounaris and four of his Cabinet ministers, by a Greek revolutionary tribunal. Many years later Tricoupis confessed to the view that the campaign in Anatolia, where the Greeks had no real interests of their own as distinct from those of the European powers, had been a disastrous mistake for his country.

In Angora and Constantinople little was known of the progress of the battle until it was virtually won. Kemal, still intent on security, issued only brief daily communiqués, which announced a series of forward movements without revealing their scale. 'Our object,' he explained, 'was to conceal the situation as much as possible from the eyes of the world.' And indeed, ten days from the start of the battle, Rauf had to seek instructions from Kemal on an Allied note, carrying a stage further the old negotiations for an armistice. Kemal was able to reply that the question of Anatolia no longer arose, and that he was prepared to discuss an armistice only in relation to that of Thrace.

Angora, closer to the situation than Constantinople, did indeed get some inkling from the communiqués as to the true nature of the advance. When it was realized that operations had started, anxious crowds moved to and fro between the Ministry of War and the Assembly, seeking news and speculating on the laconic reports which were read out to the deputies in secret session. On the second day, when the battle had been virtually won, there was no communiqué. Then, belatedly, came the news of the capture of Afyon. It drew great crowds into the streets, demonstrating for the Gazi and the army and the Turkish people, firing joyful salvoes into the air. From then onwards Angora felt that all would be well. When the news of the triumphant capture of Smyrna was sure, the black flag was removed from the rostrum of the Grand National Assembly. (Brusa itself, for which it was a token of mourning, was to be liberated on the same day as Smyrna.) But Kemal still had his enemies, one of whom grumbled, 'Why all this fuss? The Allies would have given us Smyrna anyhow.'

Constantinople was less confident of the outcome. Talk was still of an armistice, of a conference in Venice. Eyes were still on the Greek troops threatening the city from the lines of Chatalja. There was a general atmosphere of doubt and defeatism. To many the Anatolian offensive seemed a foolhardy enterprise. News of it came only from the Greek communiqués, which belittled the Turkish successes and hinted at a Turkish retreat. The Greeks drank champagne in the clubs of the city, to the destruction of Mustafa Kemal. A rumour got around that he was taken prisoner. There were long Turkish faces in the streets and on the boats taking the commuters each evening to their homes across the water.

When the first authentic news of the Turkish successes came through, the newspapers printed it guardedly for fear they would not be believed. Then the day came when it was evident that the truth far exceeded their most optimistic reports. It was not Kemal but the Greek general who had been captured. The Greek armies were defeated and in full retreat. Falih Rifki, the journalist, was laughing that night on the boat back to Prinkipo, sharing with a friend the good news which could not be released till the morning. Used to his anxious expression, the Greeks looked at him oddly and with an evident twinge of foreboding. 'Let's pretend we are defeated,' his friend said, 'and that the Gazi is a prisoner in Ushak.' But their smiles could not be disguised. Next day, when the news was printed in triumphant headlines, the crowd before the newspaper offices was such that it blocked the doors and the papers had to be thrown from the windows.

In Smyrna, right up to the last moment, the Levantines clung to the belief that a conference would solve the problem, that the Allied warships, reassuringly anchored in the gulf, would prevent the Turks from entering the city. And even if they came, surely business would carry on as it had done before they went, with all Anatolia opened up to trade. The export season approached; the warehouses were filling up with raisins and figs; the sacks were being sewn up, the packing-cases closed; the merchant ships from Italy, Germany, Holland, were standing by to take on board their autumn cargoes.

It took much to shake this mood of false optimism. But doubts began to creep in. The radio bulletins from the Allied warships, pinned on the board of the *Cercle Européen*, brought increasingly ominous news. A Greek hospital ship dropped anchor in the harbour. The wounded and the refugees began to trickle into the city, with lurid tales of bloodshed. The merchants in the coffee shops exchanged rumours from the interior, debated anxiously whether they could meet their commitments, whether the Turks, if they arrived, would requisition all stocks. Then suddenly the Bourse was at a

standstill. No more waggon-loads of raisins and figs came from the interior.
The merchant ships sailed hurriedly away, with empty holds. Distractions
continued. There were *diners-dansants* in the moonlight, on the terrace of
the Hotel Naim; at the Sporting Club an Italian opera troupe played *Traviata*
and *Rigoletto*: the guitarists sang in the cafés until curfew, while the waiters
brought *sorbets* and replenished the *narghiles* with charcoal. But beneath it
all was a sense of deep foreboding.

The retreat lasted a week. The Turkish forces hurried on towards the city,
striving to overtake the Greeks before they could decimate all western
Anatolia 'by fire and sword'. The cavalry followed close on the enemy's
heels; the infantry, geared over the two hundred miles of winding roads
between the plateau and the sea to the pace of its ox-carts and mule trains,
moved more slowly. In three days its main body contrived to march a hundred miles. But it still failed to catch up with the enemy. Already most of
the towns in its path were in ruins. One third of Ushak no longer existed.
Alashehir was no more than a dark scorched cavity, defacing the hillside.
Village after village had been reduced to an ash-heap. Out of the eighteen
thousand buildings in the historic holy city of Manisa, only five hundred
remained.

Everywhere the Greek troops, especially those from Anatolia, revenging
themselves in desperation and in obedience to orders for generations of
Ottoman oppression and persecution, carried off Christian families that
their quarters too might be burned and not a roof left for the advancing
Turks. They tore up the railway between Smyrna and Aydin. They pillaged
and destroyed and raped and butchered. 'They went to pieces altogether,'
as Rumbold recounted to Curzon on the basis of reports from his consul
in Smyrna. It was 'a sickening record of bestiality and barbarity'. There was
little, he added, to choose between the two races, Greek and Turk. Per-
meating the atmosphere, as the Turks advanced down the valleys, was the
stench of unburied bodies, of charred human and animal flesh.

Kemal moved his headquarters swiftly forward in the wake of his army –
from Ushak to Salihli, to Nif, on the hills above Smyrna. At Salihli he
made his military dispositions in case of a final Greek stand before the city
itself. But a personal telegram arrived from the Allied powers, relayed
through the French cruiser *Edgar Quinet* in the harbour of Smyrna. They
had instructed their consuls to negotiate with a view to handing over the
city to the Turkish army, and asked him to fix a time and place for a meeting.
They added a hope that he would protect the Christian population.

Kemal thumped on the table. 'Whose city are they giving to whom?' he
enquired. But he now knew that the fight was over, the victory won. He
knew also that, from now onwards, the Allies would have to deal with him
in person. He replied that he would be ready to receive them at Nif, on

9th September. Someone brought and read him extracts from an English newspaper. 'Poor Lloyd George!' he exclaimed. 'What's going to happen to him tomorrow? He'll be destroyed.' Already the Greek women, borne away from their villages, were crying prophetic maledictions: 'Bad times for George!'

Punctually Kemal arrived at Nif. His car was at once surrounded by peasants. He took off his goggles and lit a cigarette. As he did so a man walked slowly towards him, looked him in the eye, took a crumpled photograph from his pocket, scrutinized it, and looked at him again. 'It's you,' he exclaimed. He turned to the crowd and said, 'This is the Gazi, Mustafa Kemal.' He entered the headquarters prepared for him, contemptuously ignoring a portrait of Venizelos which still hung on the wall. There was no sign of the foreign consuls. His message, relayed through Angora and Constantinople, had not reached them in time. Already his advance guard was entering Smyrna. The Turkish army had fulfilled his orders. It had reached the Mediterranean.

Next day Kemal would follow his army into the city. That evening, at Nif – soon to be renamed Kemalpasha – he was relaxed and gay.

'What's this?' he exclaimed. 'We've taken Smyrna today. Are we going to be so quiet? At least let us sing.'

A drink was brought to him. He refused it. Drink and duty, he declared, did not go together. He had not had a drink since the attack began, and would not have another till the goal was reached. Stimulated only by coffee, he and his officers sang together around the table, beneath the portrait of Venizelos, to celebrate their victory.

He had won it in fifteen days. When he eventually returned to Angora he apologized to his friends: 'Forgive me. One can sometimes make mathematical errors. I was one day out in my estimate.'

CHAPTER FORTY

THE BURNING OF SMYRNA

THE FIRST Turkish soldier to reach the Mediterranean was a young cavalry
lieutenant. On the deserted quay of Smyrna he was greeted by a French
colonel, who delivered to him a long speech, advising him to see to the
protection of the Christians. The lieutenant advised him, for his own protection, to keep clear of the quay – and as he spoke a Christian bomb fell
from a window and a Christian rifle fired, wounding the lieutenant.

The last of the Greek troops, but for a few stragglers, had left the day
before – forty thousand of them in a convoy of Greek warships, together
with all the Greek civil servants and police. They left behind them fifty
thousand prisoners in the hands of the Turks. Filling the vacuum until the
Turkish troops should arrive, the Allied warships landed armed patrols,
to keep order, prevent arson and looting, and calm the fears of the
population.

In command of a detachment of British marines and bluejackets – who
formed the bulk of the force, since the French and the Italians contributed
little – was Captain Bertram Thesiger of HMS *King George V*.[1] Guards had
been posted at the Consulate and at the gasworks, and were now needed at
the stores of the railway station, where he could see, as he later recalled,
'about three thousand Greeks, some armed, cheerfully looting everything.
At this moment there was a general scream and a rush. Shots were being
fired, and there were yells of "the Turks are coming". ' They came in his
direction – a unit of Turkish cavalry, advancing in extended formation
across open ground. They galloped towards the captain with drawn swords
and a swashbuckling air.

Foreseeing unnecessary bloodshed, he determined to halt them. Getting
between Greeks and Turks, he held up his hand, looking, as a British eye-
witness put it, 'for all the world like a London policeman', feeling none too
confident since his white uniform was like that of a Greek naval officer.

---

[1] Now Admiral Sir Bertram Thesiger, KBE, CB, CMG.

The Turkish commander, however, halted his men and dismounted. Captain Thesiger went up to him. In awkward French he explained to him that the Allies had landed troops to keep order and that if he would refrain from firing there was little danger of trouble. The Turkish officer, who bore the rank of colonel, replied that he did not intend to fire but wished to enter the city. He suggested doing so by a side street, but the captain advised him to follow the sea-front. He agreed to do this, and also to place a cavalry guard on the gasworks and station.

Captain Thesiger was struck by the discipline of the Turkish forces. Nevertheless soldiers were demanding money from the Greeks and he saw one of them shoot a Greek dead, presumably because he had refused to comply. Presently the listless hordes of refugees, squatting on the pavements, saw the Turkish cavalry general make his entry into the city, riding the white horse of General Tricoupis, and soon long outlandish files of baggage camels were lumbering slowly along the sea-front.

Next day Mustafa Kemal, still unadorned by badges of rank, drove down into Smyrna at the head of a procession of open cars, decked with olive branches. It was 10th September – three years, almost to a day, since the proclamation of the National Pact at the Sivas Congress. At the entrance to the city the procession was met by a regiment of cavalry, which was to act as escort. The soldiers had been in the saddle, fighting almost without respite, in and behind the Greek lines, for nine days past. When Kemal promised his cavalry food in plenty, once the advance had begun, he did not reckon with the enemy's 'scorched earth' tactics.

At this moment of triumph, witnessed by Halide Edib, 'men and horses looked spectral. Not one ounce of flesh was visible on either; dresses and gears were worn out, faces and heads of both men and beasts burned by some devastating fever; the eyes of men glistened strangely in emaciated and haggard faces.' At the order to march, 'in a single lightning flash two long lines of horsemen drew their swords, and the sun gleamed on their steel as they galloped past us on either side. The clash of steel and the beat of the iron hooves became deafening as we crossed the closed bazaars. . . . Along the smooth marble pavement reeled the moving walls of men and steel, horses sliding and rising, and the steel curving like swift flashes of lightning in the sombre air of the arches. Behind the cavalry one saw thousands of mouths as though transformed into an eternal shout – roaring and shouting applause.' So Mustafa Kemal reached the Mediterranean.

He drove to the *konak*, the government building on the quay, which had been the Greek headquarters. A large Greek flag had been spread like a carpet on the steps of it, as a Turkish flag – so it was said – had been spread for the reception of King Constantine. Kemal refused to walk on it and ordered its removal. 'That is the symbol,' he protested 'of a country's independence.' From the balcony he looked down on the cheering crowds, on the Allied warships lying at anchor opposite. Three years earlier, in Constantinople, he had looked across at these warships, speculating as to what the Allies would do. Now the initiative had shifted. Their crews looked across at him, speculating as to what he, Kemal, would do.

He was presented with a car by the people of Smyrna. They were preparing to slaughter and sacrifice an ox, in his honour. Wincing at such Islamic barbarities, he sent orders to stop the ceremony. But he was too late; the beast was already roasting. He withdrew from the balcony, passed inside through the mirrored hall where dusty khaki-clad figures sat silently awaiting him, and retired to a smaller room, where he sat down with Nured-din, the commander of his occupying troops. Order had still to be established. Street fighting continued. There was work to be done.

Later he strolled into the lounge of a hotel, which the foreigners frequented. The merchants sat over their drinks, discussing the news, wondering anxiously what was to happen. Despite his compelling appearance, they did not at first recognize the young Turkish officer. Nor did the waiter, who regretted that no table was free. Then a customer identified him and he sat down among them, begging them to be at their ease. The Greeks gazed at him curiously as, faithful to last night's promise, he raised his glass to his friends and downed his first victory drink. He turned to the Greeks and asked, 'Did King Constantine ever come here to drink a glass of *raki*?' On receiving a negative reply, he asked, 'Why did he bother to take Smyrna, then?' That evening he moved his headquarters to the district of Karshiyaka, where two houses had been prepared for him and two elderly Turkish ladies treated him with motherly hospitality.

The situation in Smyrna was tense. Some thousands of refugees had embarked with the Greek forces, but more were still pouring in, standing all along the footplates and swarming on the roofs of the trains, passing their dead out at the stations over the heads of the living. They camped in the streets, hungry and hopeless and often sick, with their possessions in bundles around them. Thanks to the burning of the crops there was danger of starvation. With no Greek troops left to protect them, the people of the city, their minds still dwelling on an Ottoman past, had become obsessed with fears of a massacre of Christians. Reprisals were feared for this devastation of the countryside, and for the maltreatment of Turks by Greeks on the occupation of the city three years before. The foreign consuls were anxious for the safety of their nationals. Thus one of Kemal's first actions was to issue a proclamation, sentencing to death any Turkish soldier who molested non-combatants.

The British representatives in Smyrna had been instructed from London not to call on Kemal in person, as the French had done. Kemal's own first instinct was to ask the British warships to leave, within a stated time. Then he chanced to meet Sir Harry Lamb, the British Consul-

General, in the street, and had an unofficial talk with him. Kemal asked him what were his functions since the change of government in Turkey. Lamb said that he represented the British High Commissioner in Constantinople. Kemal retorted that his Government did not recognize any such authority. 'Technically,' he said, 'Turkey is still at war with Britain. I should be justified in interning all British subjects in Smyrna. But I do not intend to do so.' He added, 'Are you not the people who landed the Greek army in Anatolia? We are the people who defeated the Greek army, and threw them out of our territory. In such a situation it is for you to decide what to do, not us.'

This attitude created a flurry on board the *Iron Duke*, the British flagship. Already Turkish sentries had prevented Admiral Brock,[1] the British Commander-in-Chief, from coming ashore, and the Turks observed that his guns were trained on the city. Later, however, he called upon Nur-ed-din, who apologized for the incident and, in response to the admiral's assurances of British neutrality in terms of the Armistice, declared that no state of war existed.

The admiral sent a note to Kemal asking for official confirmation of this contradictory statement. He instructed Commander Barry Domvile to be prepared to go ashore and call on the Gazi for an answer. The question arose as to the appropriate dress for the interview. Should he, for example, wear a sword? The captain disposed of the problem in summary fashion: 'A sword for that fellow? I should think not. I shall carry a walking-stick.'

Kemal had spoken in heat. He replied, confirming Nur-ed-din's statement. His own remark had been made unofficially and not as the representative of the Grand National Assembly. There was no state of war. On the other hand, diplomatic relations between the two countries did not exist. Formalities would be necessary before these were established. Unofficially he suggested that this should be done, and for the purpose telegraphed to Angora for his Minister of Foreign Affairs.

Thus the incident was closed. But Kemal remarked humorously to Halide, 'In the name of all common sense tell me how, Hanum Effendi, could the Greeks have landed in Smyrna without the strong help and desire of the British Government? Could anything have happened in the Near East without their express desire? Of course we were at war with them, not with the Greeks – a thousand times so.' Meanwhile the British authorities were taking no chances. On instructions from London, Lamb arranged for the evacuation of all remaining British subjects who wished to go. Already a party had left of their own accord some days before.

With the French and especially the Italian representatives Kemal was more cordial. He raised no such question of official recognition. In an interview, conducted in French, with Admiral Dumesnil, at which Ismet was

[1] Later Admiral of the Fleet Sir Osmond de Beauvoir Brock, GCB, KCMG, KCVO.

present, he gave assurances as to the protection of the Christian population.[1]
The gendarmerie was on its way, and would restore order within twenty-
four or at the most forty-eight hours. Serious measures were being taken, in
liaison with Constantinople, to feed the refugees.

The admiral then referred to the arrest and internment by the Turks of
all the able-bodied male Christian population, and their threatened deporta-
tion to the interior as indicated by Nur-ed-din. This had caused panic throughout the Greek and Armenian communities, and would create a bad impression
abroad, as recent deportations from the Samsun area had done. Kemal
replied in a conciliatory spirit. Nur-ed-din had spoken in military terms, at
the moment of victory, concerned to prevent the passage of potential Greek
recruits to continue the war in Thrace. In fact the Turkish intentions were
not so drastic, and he undertook to reassure the population accordingly.
None the less deportations continued.

As events turned out it was not massacre but fire that made a tragedy of
the Turkish reoccupation of Smyrna. The excesses committed by the Turkish
soldiery against the local Greeks were brutal indeed, but of a sporadic and
individual kind. There was no repetition of the organized massacres which
had occurred elsewhere and which the Christians feared. An official American
observer, contradicting lurid reports in the American press, afterwards
estimated the total deaths, from various causes, at about two thousand.

Nevertheless feelings ran high between the Turks and Armenians, and
for several nights there was bloodshed, with knives and bayonets, in the
streets of the Armenian quarter, where the Turkish troops were ostensibly
rounding up suspected traitors and confiscating arms. Typical of such
skirmishes was one described, with true British understatement, in the diary
of a midshipman on board the *King George V*: 'Looking out of the window
I saw an Armenian throw a bomb at some Turks. They chased him and he
jumped into the sea. They got a boat and chased the Armenian and brought
him on shore. He then died unpleasantly.'

This internecine violence led, more or less by accident, to the outbreak
of a catastrophic fire. Its origins were never satisfactorily explained. Kemal
maintained to Admiral Dumesnil that it had been deliberately planned by
an Armenian incendiary organization, and that before the arrival of the
Turks speeches had been made in the churches, calling for the burning of
the city as a sacred duty. Fuel for the purpose had been found in the houses
of Armenian women, and several incendiaries had been arrested. Others
accused the Turks themselves of deliberately starting the fire under the
orders or at least with the connivance of Nur-ed-Din Pasha, who had a
reputation for fanaticism and cruelty.

More probably it started when the Turks, rounding up the Armenians to
confiscate their arms, besieged a band of them in a building in which they

[1] Benoist-Mechin, *Mustapha Kemal, ou La Mort d'un Empire*.

had taken refuge. Deciding to burn them out, they set it alight with petrol, placing a cordon of sentries around to arrest or shoot them as they escaped. Meanwhile the Armenians started other fires nearby to divert the Turks from their main objective. The quarter was on the outskirts of the city. But a strong wind, for which they had not allowed, quickly carried the flames towards it. By the early evening several other quarters were on fire, and a thousand houses, built flimsily of lath and plaster, had been reduced to ashes. The flames were being spread by looters, and doubtless also by Turkish soldiers, paying off scores. The fire brigade was powerless to cope with such a conflagration, and at Ismet's headquarters the Turks alleged that its hose-pipes had been deliberately severed. He himself chose to declare that the Greeks had planned to burn the city.

By nightfall all of it was ablaze, and the flames were spreading down to the water-front, driving the inhabitants and the refugees towards the sea, until tens of thousands were huddled there in bemused and helpless swarms. The sick and the aged were brought down from the hospitals on improvised stretchers. After midnight almost the whole line of houses along the front caught fire simultaneously. There was, as Captain Thesiger described it, 'the most awful scream one could ever imagine'. The crowds surged away from the houses towards the sea, and many jumped or were pushed into the water. Had they stayed still, the danger would not have been great, since the houses burned out quickly; but panic took hold of them. Had they moved along the quay away from the fire, they would have been safe; but a false rumour circulated that pickets of Turkish machine-gunners were blocking it at either end. Instead they ran around aimlessly, clutching bundles which were often already on fire.

The roar of the flames was deafening, but the wail of the crowds could be heard above it. Soon the fire along the front was some two miles long. 'The surface of the sea,' wrote Ward Price, a correspondent on board the British flagship, 'shone like burning copper. . . . Twenty distinct volcanoes of raging flame were throwing up jagged, writhing tongues to a height of a hundred feet. The towers of the Greek churches, the domes of the mosques, the flat roofs of the houses, were silhouetted against a curtain of flame.' The commanders of the warships were concerned largely to save their own nationals and, as neutrals, refused at first to take refugees on board. But women threw their children into boats to save them; men plunged into the water and swam out to the ships; families crowded into *caiques*, which capsized, so that many were drowned.

On the crowds squatting ashore a paralysis descended. 'Starving, dazed and exhausted, they had lost even the capacity for panic,' said an eye-witness. 'They sat herded together, often in the way of the flames, and if ordered to move, obeyed almost with an animal docility, their eyes only expressing their despair and fatigue.' Within their hearing, faithful to Service routine at this hour, the naval band of the British flagship played while Smyrna burned, adding the strains of light music to the roar of the flames and the shouts and cries of the victims.

In the early hours of the morning the British admiral reversed his orders and sent all his boats ashore, to save as many foreign civilians as possible, regardless of nationality. The foreign warships did the same. The scene changed instantly. On the quay there was an orderly blowing of Allied whistles, a shouting of orders, a tramping of booted feet. The refugees stampeded towards the fleet of small boats, a torrent of terrified humanity pouring over their bows, disregarding the officers' shouts of 'Women and children only!' until the crews had to fight back the men with their fists and with sticks. Some two thousand of them were taken on board the *Iron Duke* alone.

In the morning the wind changed and the fire gradually died down. But it smouldered for several days more, punctuated by explosions as the Greek hoards of explosives went up. The European city of Smyrna was no more, and tens of thousands of homeless citizens now shared the plight of the refugees. Whose fault was it? To the question 'Who started the fire?' an American observer returned the pertinent query: 'Who started the San Francisco earthquake?'

Kemal, hardened to the disasters of war and its inevitable bloodshed, was not unduly perturbed by the fire – in which, after all, though the loss of property had been vast, the loss of human life had been comparatively small. To Admiral Dumesnil he described it as a 'disagreeable incident', and when rebuked for his understatement insisted that, compared to other questions, it was an episode of secondary importance.

For the Nationalists indeed, callous as such an attitude was, it had a certain symbolic justice. For Smyrna was a foreign city, and as such represented all that they had been fighting against. The Smyrna that rose from its ashes would be a Western city – but it would be wholly Turkish. Much of the destruction wrought by Turks, both in the First World War and after it, had arisen from no mere wanton impulse, but from that sense of inferiority which sought to eliminate the visible signs of European occupation. Thus, whether or not the Turks had a major hand in the burning of Smyrna, it represented in their hearts a fitting culmination to the Nationalist victory.

Throughout the fire Kemal had remained at his headquarters, his harsh sun-tanned face lit up by the glow of it. A party of Turkish journalists had arrived by boat from Constantinople, not knowing whether Smyrna had yet fallen until they saw the Turkish flag flying proudly from the citadel. Falih Rifki found the Gazi with two British naval officers standing at attention beside him – a sign of respect, he reflected with pleasure, which he had never witnessed in Constantinople. Kemal greeted him jovially:

'You don't know what things we have seen. We have become history.' He asked for news of Constantinople, and added drily, 'Do they really believe we are now victorious?'

As the flames came closer his ADCs and friends grew worried, and begged him to move. Taking his own time, he did so in his open car, a lorry preceding him to force a way through the crowds. Slowly and imperturbably he drove between thousands of suffering Greeks and Armenians, who exclaimed with fear and wailed, 'Oh! ... Oh! ... Oh! ...' at the sight of the conqueror.

Kemal had now moved to the suburb of Göztepe, which lies on the south side of the Bay. Soon after his arrival in Smyrna a young woman had come to his headquarters and asked to see him. Impatiently he refused, telling the orderly to send her away. But as he was doing so she walked into his office. Taking a look at her, he dismissed the orderly and asked her to sit down. This was no peasant woman, but a lady of evident breeding, unveiled and wearing, with her Turkish headdress, sober but elegant clothes. She was short, round-faced and stocky in figure, with a fair olive skin, large dark eyes that showed intelligence, and a tight-drawn mouth that showed character. She combined the liveliness of youth with the self-assurance of maturity.

Kemal was intrigued by her forwardness, her frank way of talking, her directness of gaze. Her name was Latife; her father a well-to-do Smyrniot, Ushakizade Muammer, who had interests in commerce and shipping and connections abroad. She had studied law in Europe and spoke French like a Frenchwoman. Her parents were spending the summer in Biarritz, but she had insisted on returning to Smyrna on her own when the offensive seemed imminent, determined to work for the Kemalist cause. She had made a hero of Kemal and sought him out as soon as he entered Smyrna with his liberating army. As she now revealed to him, she wore a locket round her neck, with his picture inside. 'Do you mind?' she asked him.

'Why should I mind?' he replied with a chuckle, recounting the interview later, with schoolboyish delight, to Halide Edib. Already, Halide guessed, he was imagining her in love with him – though in fact she must be one of thousands of Turkish women who wore his picture in a locket. Nothing better, she thought, could have happened. Latife would have 'a humanizing effect on him and keep him out of mischief'.

She now invited him to move with his staff to her parents' house. It lay outside the city, away from its confusion and noise and smouldering fires, calm amid the luxuriant gardens of Göztepe, where the wealthier Levantines had made their homes. It was large, it was comfortable, it was well-staffed with servants. She would look after him and help him in any way he required. She offered him in effect the stimulus of a new feminine attachment in a relaxed Western atmosphere. He accepted the offer. Here surely was the

appropriate setting for the conquering hero. From here he issued a highly
coloured report to the 'great and noble Turkish nation' on the victorious
liberation of Smyrna and Brusa by armies which sprang from its 'national
conscience'.

One hot summer evening the Gazi gave a party at the Göztepe villa for
the journalists from Constantinople and others. Latife, 'a very little lady in
black' with a black scarf over her head, received the guests with a pleasing
dignity, at the top of the steps of a verandah, festooned at this season with
wistaria, jasmine and a casual profusion of roses. Kemal stood beside her,
slim and elegant in a white belted shirt of Caucasian style, his fair hair neatly
brushed backwards, his fair eyebrows bristling upwards, his eyes responding
with a glint of good-humour to the glow of dawning adoration in those of
Latife. Introducing her to Halide, he said, 'We are celebrating Smyrna –
you must drink with us.'

Halide refused to touch *raki* and asked for champagne, raising her glass
to wish him happiness. Kemal stuck to *raki*, and remarked that it was the
first time he had dared to drink it in Halide's stern presence. He seemed
ruffled when Latife too chose champagne, reminding her that she had drunk
raki on previous occasions. She at least, he implied, was no Puritan.

Throughout the evening he talked, going over the past and the present,
restraining for Latife's benefit his usual ironical comments, conceding an
unfamiliar measure of praise to his friends in the Nationalist movement,
impressing the journalists with conversational talents at once eloquent, gay
and profound. Later there was music. He broke into the Rumeli folk-songs
he cherished, with a hint of nostalgia in his soft resonant voice, conjuring
up in the guests poignant visions of the lost Macedonian mountains. Then
he swept them into the *zeybek*, the vigorous masculine dance of the reclaimed
Aegean coast-lands, in the performance of which his Caucasian shirt became
him well.

Ismet, through round eyes, beamed upon the company. He approved of
Latife, as Rauf on his arrival was also to approve of her. Himself a marrying
man, he saw marriage as the proper state for others, and now especially for
Kemal. A good wife at this moment was just what he needed, to soften his
hard edges, curb his excesses, present to the nation an image of respectable
marital stability. It was time for him to settle down – and with whom better
than Latife, clearly an intelligent woman, moreover of Turkish race but
Western background?

He took Halide aside and asked, 'What do you think of Latife Hanum?'

'She is very charming,' Halide replied. She was thinking of Fikriye, of
the suffering that awaited her on hearing of Kemal's new attachment.

Latife became in effect Kemal's secretary; she soon emerged from the
background which she had at first tactfully chosen to help him in all kinds
of practical ways. In her forceful style she looked after his health and

domestic comfort. But she gave him something more besides. With her knowledge of English and French she became an efficient translator of his diplomatic correspondence. She stimulated his mind with her fluent talk, her arguments, her advice, her ideas born of a wide European culture. Here was a woman to whom he could talk as to few of the men around him. It was a relationship he had tasted before, never with Fikriye, but with such European women as Corinne Lütfü and Berthe Georges-Gaulis. But Latife was of his own race, and stirred his blood as the others had done only perfunctorily. With a lively masculine mind she combined a desirable feminine body. She excited him physically. Used to women who were 'available', who yielded easily, he made vigorous advances.

But she firmly resisted him. She might become his wife, but she would not become his mistress. She was an emancipated modern woman. Such were her principles. They conflicted with his. He was a soldier; he had work to do; he could not and would not marry until this work was completed. The Oriental male thus met his match in the Western female. For the first time Kemal could not have the woman he wanted. There was deadlock between them. It was still unbroken when he left Smyrna for Angora at the end of the month.

CHAPTER FORTY-ONE

CRISIS AT CHANAK

THE WESTERN POWERS waited, with some concern, to see what the victorious Kemal would do next. 'It was,' wrote Vansittart, 'as if a boxer, after being counted out, had risen from the ring, stunned his opponent, knocked the referee through the ropes and levanted with the purse.' Churchill put it more sonorously:

> The catastrophe which Greek recklessness and Allied procrastination, division and intrigue had long prepared now broke upon Europe. The signatories of the Treaty of Sèvres had only been preserved in their world of illusion by the shield of Greece. That shield was now shattered. Nothing but a dozen battalions of disunited British, French and Italian troops stood between the returning war and Europe. . . . The re-entry of the Turks into Europe, as conquerors untrammelled and untamed, reeking with the blood of helpless Christian populations must, after all that had happened in the war, signalize the worst humiliation of the Allies. Nowhere had their victory been more complete than over Turkey; nowhere had the conqueror's power been flaunted more arrogantly than in Turkey; and now, in the end, all the fruits of successful war, all the laurels for which so many thousands had died on the Gallipoli Peninsula, in the deserts of Palestine and Mesopotamia, in the marshes of the Salonika front, in the ships which fed these vast expeditions; all the divisions of Allied resources in men, in arms, in treasure which they had required; all was to end in shame.

What was to be done? Kemal had no intention of halting his operations in Smyrna. His objectives were Constantinople and Adrianople, in eastern Thrace – no more but no less than the frontiers of the National Pact. In a series of press interviews in Smyrna he made it clear that he was ready to seek them by immediate negotiation. To an American journalist he chose to declare that he would be in Constantinople within eight days and would thence proceed to occupy eastern Thrace. He claimed also Mosul, but renounced any designs on Mesopotamia. His quarrel, he declared, was not with Britain but only with Greece. He had his peace plans as well as war plans, and they included guarantees for the security of the Straits. But if the Allies would not accept them he was ready to pursue the Greeks into Europe.

Meanwhile he was moving his troops up the coast towards Chanak, on the Asiatic shores of the Dardanelles. Here was the frontier of the Neutral Zone, the Allied ring around Constantinople, which extended from the lines of Chatalja in the west to the Izmit Peninsula in the east, from the Black Sea in the north to the Dardanelles in the south, which the Sultan's Government was committed to respect and the Allies to defend. When the Greeks had threatened it two months before, at Chatalja, the French and the Italians had joined the British in its defence. Would they do so again, now that the Kemalists were threatening it at Chanak?

The choice confronting the Allies lay between resisting Kemal or placating him. Before his entry into Smyrna Lloyd George's Cabinet, insisting upon the control of the waters of the Straits as a cardinal British interest, had decided that any attempt by the Turks to cross over to the European shore should be resisted by force. London had few illusions as to the probable reaction of Paris and Rome, where public opinion rejoiced at the defeat of the Greeks and mistrusted any intervention which might lead to war. The Cabinet hoped for French and Italian support in defending at least this European shore. Without them, however, the British would defend it alone. But the Asiatic shore was less essential to the control of the Straits, hence should not be defended without such support. Since the French and the Italians seemed unlikely to provide this, General Harington was authorized to withdraw his troops from Chanak.

The general, however, was a man of determined spirit. At a meeting of the High Commission in Constantinople he succeeded in obtaining a promise of support from his French and Italian colleagues. They would join with the British in 'showing the flag' by the despatch of token contingents to Chanak and the Izmit Peninsula. Their respective Governments agreed and General Harington did not withdraw. Instead Kemal's representative in the city was warned that the three Allies were united in opposition to any attempt to violate the Neutral Zone. The French and Italian troops arrived, to be given a cheerful welcome by a British military band. Three flags flew at Chanak – for the moment at least.

Co-operation among the Allies persisted in the High Commission, where it was appreciated, at a meeting on 15th September, that Kemal might soon force the issue, probably by transporting troops across the Straits. To forestall him they urged the calling of a peace conference, without delay. London shared these views. On the same day the Cabinet held a meeting at which, acting still on the assumption of French and Italian support, they agreed to send a division to reinforce Harington, and moreover drafted an appeal to the Dominions and to the Balkan states for aid, if need be, in resisting a Kemalist advance. It was hoped thus to show that the British Empire was in earnest, to stiffen the French, and to sober Kemal until arrangements could be made for a conference in Venice or Paris.

The decision was much influenced by Churchill, smouldering as he was with shame at his country's humiliation. For three years he had championed the Turks against Lloyd George's championship of the Greeks. But now that this policy had failed he threw his weight on to the side of Lloyd George in resisting the consequences. An invasion of the Straits, Constantinople and Thrace by the Turks was a danger to Europe and to the Christian population of Turkey – moreover an affront not to be borne. 'Defeat is a nauseating draught; and that the victors in the greatest of all wars should gulp it down, was not readily to be accepted.' Kemal must be stopped. 'The press might howl, the Allies might bolt. We intended to force the Turk to a negotiated peace before he should set foot in Europe.' Lloyd George's secretary, Miss Stevenson, overhearing a discussion on this Cabinet decision between her master and Churchill, was horrified, seeing in it the prospect of another Great War. She was tempted to send in a note of her fears to the Cabinet meeting, but forbore from doing so. These fears were soon to be shared by others.

Harington now prepared, in Constantinople, to put pressure on the French to reinforce in their turn. At this juncture, however, the French High Commissioner, General Pellé, suddenly left Constantinople in a warship for Smyrna, without informing his Allied colleagues. He hoped to extricate France from her predicament by persuading Kemal to respect the Neutral Zone, in return for implied French support at a conference. But the Gazi could afford to take a belligerent line. Playing the victorious general at the expense of the wise statesman, he protested that he and his government recognized no such Neutral Zone. The purpose of military action, he instructed the general, was to follow an enemy rapidly and defeat him. In pursuit of this aim it would be impossible to hold back his troops until they had liberated eastern Thrace. They were already on the move and were preparing to march on Constantinople. He was ready to come to a conference, but refused meanwhile to halt his operations, which must be finished by the winter.

Meanwhile Churchill, obtaining Lloyd George's approval but omitting to consult the Foreign Office, issued a communiqué which Curzon, who was spending the weekend in the country and read it for the first time in the Sunday newspapers, angrily condemned as a 'flamboyant manifesto'. It confirmed, for public consumption and in provocative tones, the decision of the Cabinet, in concert with the Dominions, to resist any Turkish encroachment by force. As Kemal uttered his threats to Pellé, this defiant pronouncement rang around the world. It evoked grumbles about 'colonial rule' from the Dominions, whose ministers read it in the press before they had seen Curzon's official telegrams. They gave qualified promises of military support. It awoke Britain to the gravity of the crisis and aroused fears of an imminent war against the Turks, with the *Daily Mail* thundering: 'STOP THIS NEW WAR.' In France it enraged Poincaré and precipitated the change in French policy towards which he had been moving. The French Government ordered their forces to withdraw from Chanak and the Izmit Peninsula. The Italians, who had already made promises of neutrality to Kemal, followed their example. Only one flag now flew at Chanak. There could no longer be any question of a British withdrawal from Chanak, whose retention had thus acquired a moral significance greater than that of Constantinople itself. Harington indeed received authorization from the War Office to withdraw if he thought fit from the capital. But he was instructed at all costs to hold Chanak.

Curzon hurried over to Paris to confront and reproach Poincaré. After a long and acrimonious dispute at the Quai d'Orsay, it was finally agreed to send a joint invitation to Kemal – or a representative of the Grand National Assembly – to attend a meeting at Mudanya, on the Sea of Marmara, to discuss with the Allied military chiefs lines of demarcation beyond which the Turks would not advance. This was to precede a conference, at Venice or elsewhere, to decide upon conditions of peace between the Allies and Turkey and Greece.

Kemal did not at once reply to this invitation. While Curzon, back in London, was graciously acknowledging the plaudits of his Cabinet colleagues, a Revolution took place in Greece. King Constantine was deposed, and hurried into exile. A military Government was installed, and Venizelos hurried to London as its ambassador. The hopes of the pro-Greek party in the Cabinet revived. Lloyd George and Venizelos between them might once again throw the Greeks into the field or at least press for a settlement in their favour.[1]

Kemal, sensing this danger – or at least the advantage to be gained from exploiting it – and encouraged by the defection of France and Italy, at once intensified his pressure against Britain. On 23rd September, disregarding a warning from Harington that the British proposed to defend the Neutral Zone, he sent a detachment of cavalry across its frontier to Ezine, south-east of Chanak.

The Turkish patrols, advancing through rough hilly country, encountered those of the Third Hussars, under the command of Captain J. C. Petherick.

[1] Lloyd George was still reluctant to believe in their total defeat and, when Kemal was advancing on Smyrna, had strongly advised them – without consulting the Foreign Office – not to sue for an armistice, as the Germans had mistakenly done in 1918, but to hold the Turkish advance before the city, with a view to obtaining better terms.

The British officers had orders not to fire unless fired upon. It soon became evident from their tentative attitude that the Turks had received similar orders. There followed a strange mock skirmish, consisting, as Captain Petherick described it, of 'tactics in reverse'. Each side sought to reveal rather than to conceal its forces, stationing them prominently on the crests of the hills instead of taking cover behind them. The British squadron – which the Turks thus took to be a regiment of cavalry – withdrew, in this way, to a series of positions around the battlefield of Troy, while the perimeter of Chanak itself was entrenched within barbed wire defences.

Soon the Turks were facing the British through the wire, often with no more than twenty yards between them. Many of them marched in with rifles reversed, as a disclaimer of hostile intentions. Good humour and restraint prevailed on both sides. The British officers were happy to confirm that, as they had always suspected, the Turkish officer was also a gentleman. The opposing troops fraternized with the exchange of pots and pans and camp equipment.

One day an agitated Turkish infantry officer asked the British detachment confronting him for a loan of barbed wire. A general was coming to inspect his defences, which were not yet wired. He would faithfully return it after the general had gone. He started to put up the wire, but with little success. So the British troops did it for him.

All this time Harington and Kemal were exchanging polite but firm telegrams. Kemal was warned, through the British admiral at Smyrna, that sooner or later Harington would be obliged to drive his troops out. Kemal reiterated that he did not recognize the Neutral Zone and that his troops were in pursuit of the Greek army. Later he insisted to the French in Smyrna that he could not withdraw them, but confirmed that he had ordered them not to attack the British. It was shadow-boxing, a game of bluff on both sides, and Harington was convinced that a conference could be reached without the loss of a single life. It had to be admitted that a stray shot or a misunderstood order might at any moment cause an involuntary explosion. But among the men on the spot there was little anxiety. It was in London that the danger seemed to lie. As a French officer had remarked to Captain Petherick, Lloyd George was *peu stable*.

It was evident that Kemal's show of force was building up to substantial proportions, and this was duly reported to London. Five days after the initial incursion, Harington estimated that a force of 40,000 now threatened Chanak, while another 50,000 threatened Izmit. This took no account of a general reserve of 40,000 in Constantinople, and 20,000 more troops in eastern Thrace.

London, on receiving these reports, became thoroughly alarmed. This must not continue. On 29th September the Cabinet took note of the fact that Kemal had not replied to the Allied invitation to a conference. They drew up an ultimatum for delivery by Harington to the Turkish commander, threatening war unless the Kemalists withdrew.

The moment for this was oddly chosen. British reinforcements were now arriving in Chanak, from Aldershot, Gibraltar, Malta, Egypt. The British were in a well-entrenched, well-wired position, with air supremacy and strong artillery support from Gallipoli. From this only a major operation could now dislodge them. It was hardly likely that Kemal, having refrained from attacking them when they were weak, would elect to do so now that they were strong. It would have been in a sense the Gallipoli campaign all over again, but in reverse, with the British and their fleet defending Constantinople and the Turks attacking it. On the other hand, he could not afford to lose face by a withdrawal in response to such a threat as the ultimatum implied.

The ultimatum had its opponents in the Cabinet, notably Curzon, who had always judged the danger to be exaggerated, and was now more than ever convinced that a solution could be found by diplomacy rather than force. Seeking to delay it for twenty-four hours, he sought around for contact with the Kemalists. Learning that Fethi, whom he had refused to receive as their representative a month before, had left Paris for Rome, he sent urgently for his deputy, Dr Nihad Reshad, who hurried over from Vichy and was immediately shown into his presence. Curzon urged him to impress upon Kemal the danger of the situation. The atmosphere at Chanak, he said, was explosive and might well give rise to an incident. But if a Turkish soldier opened fire, this would still not be regarded as a *casus belli* unless an order to do so had been given by Kemal himself.

The Cabinet was divided between those, like himself, who still counselled patience, and those who thought that its limit had been reached and that any idea of a conference at Mudanya must now be abandoned. There were even some ministers who, as a day passed without a reply from Harington, wished to send the ultimatum to Angora at once, without waiting for it. Theirs was the mentality that still saw Kemal as a blustering bandit chief, ready to collapse at the first serious threat. They remained obstinately blind to his emergence as the responsible and calculating founder of a nation, a soldier of genius, with an army behind him strong enough to involve Britain in a major war.[1]

The French meanwhile sent an 'unofficial' emissary to Smyrna in the shape of Franklin-Bouillon, who urged restraint on Kemal. In fact he

[1] Criticizing this attitude, and that of the Government in general, Lord Derby had written to Sir Austen Chamberlain: 'It is all very well to call Mustafa Kemal a rebel; but transpose England and Turkey; such a man would nòt have been looked upon as a rebel, but as a true patriot fighting for his country and determined not to see it divided up and given to that wretched Greek nation which is incapable of fighting for or of administrating a great Empire.' – Randolph Churchill: *Lord Derby*.

A.—12

needed no such injunction. He had assessed the position shrewdly enough. There were hot-heads in his entourage who urged him to exploit the victory by advancing, regardless of the Allies, not only into eastern but into western Thrace, and thence into Macedonia. Thus a great part of Rumeli could be regained. To one of them he said sharply, 'Certainly not. The cry would go up again, "The Turks are coming!" and every state in the Balkans would be appealing to the powers for assistance against us.' Another, dreaming of a reconquest of Salonika, earned the rebuke: 'Do you want to make sure that Lloyd George stays in power?' Calling a conference of his generals and his ministers from Angora, he had found the majority in favour of such an advance. But he overruled them, insisting that Turkey, for the sake of her future international reputation, must on no account go a step beyond the initial demands of the National Pact.

The promise of eastern Thrace, with Adrianople, was his already without a shot being fired. The conflict between the Allies, which he had been quick to exploit from the start, had at the end solved his problems. There was nothing to be gained by attacking the British, who were now committed to retaliation, and for whose power, if they chose to demonstrate it as Churchill had done through his call to the Dominions, he had in any case too much respect. He knew Harington, initially from his conciliatory approach to Angora the year before, and in the last few days from their exchange of telegrams and from intercepts of others, as a man who was not anti-Turkish and who was working for peace. This was one of those occasions, not unusual in history, when the generals were the peacemongers and the politicians the warmongers.

Interviewed in Smyrna by Clare Sheridan, a war correspondent and cousin of Churchill, Kemal said of her compatriots, 'I am acting with such patience, in order to give them every chance of retiring with dignity from the attitude they have adopted.' It was his policy to tighten his pressure on Chanak and strengthen his forces around Constantinople until the last possible moment, thus gaining the maximum advantage from the conference which would follow. Only such an ultimatum as the British Cabinet had drafted could cause him to revise this policy and fight.

Fortunately the ultimatum was not to be delivered. Harington who, in Churchill's words, 'knew how to combine a cool and tactful diplomacy with military firmness', had the courage and patience to delay its delivery, to ignore his instructions and gain just the time needed, at this eleventh hour, for peace. He was supported by Admiral Brock and above all by Rumbold, convinced of 'the absolute necessity of avoiding any action which might lead to war'. Thus national pride on both sides was to be satisfied without it.

Kemal was now drafting his acceptance, in the name of the Grand National Assembly, of the Allied invitation to a peace conference. In agreeing to the conference he insisted on the immediate restoration of eastern Thrace. The preliminary meeting at Mudanya was announced for 3rd October. Kemal appointed Ismet as his delegate. He then left Smyrna for Angora to receive a conqueror's welcome. From the station a group of his more devout subjects bore him off to give thanks at the Haji Bayram Mosque. But he adroitly turned aside into the Parliament building, and gave thanks from one of its balconies to no dead saint but to the Turkish soldier himself.

In the Chamber a grateful delegation of both groups received him. In a stirring oration he expressed the hope that 'the sweet sun of peace will not delay in shining on the horizon of our country . . . watered with the blood of her children'. He presided over a great military parade and accepted the freedom of the city. Then he settled down to follow the proceedings of the conference, in continuous contact, by telegraph and telephone, with Ismet, and in attendance at all Cabinet meetings with Rauf and his ministers.

Mudanya was a shabby mosquito-ridden port, with cobbled streets and timbered houses, serving Brusa and the interior from the southern shore of the Marmara. The conference, which opened in teeming rain and a boisterous wind from across its waters, was held in the former Russian Consulate, a small house whose shabbiness was hurriedly screened by the hanging of carpets on the whitewashed walls. Since space was limited, only the heads of the four delegations – British, French, Italian and Turkish – sat down at a table to confer, with interpreters between them. Among the 'observers', Franklin-Bouillon – 'Boiling Frankie' to the General Staff, 'that Prince of Levantines' to Rumbold – was ubiquitous. The British saw him as the arch-enemy of the Allied cause, and Harington curtly refused his offer of help and advice.

The success of the conference was by no means assured. After two days of discussions some twenty-eight points, mostly of detail, were still not agreed. Ismet, negotiating stubbornly with the evident encouragement of the French, was insisting on an immediate take-over from the Greeks in eastern Thrace, the departure of all Allied missions, and the right to recruit an unlimited gendarmerie.

Eventually a protocol was drafted, covering the essential points, and Harington informed Ismet that this was his Government's last word. He was returning in the *Iron Duke* that evening to Constantinople, and would come back next day for a final reply. In Constantinople he reported to Rumbold that the situation seemed grave. He made military dispositions for the defence of the city. Seeing that only a restoration of Allied unity could save the situation, Lord Curzon hurried over to Paris once more. He persuaded Poincaré to agree to a compromise by which an Allied detachment would occupy eastern Thrace for a limited period; the gendarmerie would be unlimited; and the Turks would respect the Neutral Zones. This decision was telegraphed to Constantinople, and conveyed to Mudanya in a British destroyer.

Two anxious days followed, while Ismet sought instruction by telegram and telephone from Angora, first on the concessions, then on a draft convention agreed by the Allies. Just before the conference reassembled Harington was handed a telegram from his Government, followed later by another, authorizing him, in the event of rejection, to issue an ultimatum to the Turks and, if necessary, to start operations. He put them both in his pocket. But he authorized his army commander at Chanak to open fire at a fixed hour unless otherwise instructed.

The atmosphere however was now noticeably different. Only six points remained to be settled, and Ismet's manner seemed friendlier. Agreement was reached on the first four points. On the fifth Harington was obliged to insist on the retention of certain areas in the Neutral Zone from which the Turks must withdraw. As he afterwards described it: 'Ismet Pasha said that he could not agree, and that there was a deadlock . . . the scene is before me now – that awful room – only an oil lamp. I can see Ismet's Chief of Staff – he never took his eyes off me. I paced up one side of the room saying that I must have that area and would agree to nothing else. Ismet paced up the other side saying he would not agree. Then quite suddenly he said, "J'accepte!" I was never so surprised in my life!'

The sixth point was easily settled, and Harington realized that agreement had been reached. But he trusted no Turk and was taking no chances. Thus, despite French and Italian remonstrances, he insisted on signature that very night. The conference sat for fifteen more hours, while the agreement – with the aid of inexperienced typists – was recorded in five different languages. The Turkish military band played periodic tunes to keep everyone awake. Finally it was completed and signed.

In the cold blue light of the morning the text was handed to the press. General Harington made a brief nervous speech: 'We met as strangers, but we part as friends.' The compliment escaped Ismet, deaf as he was, but he replied that this day would be among his happiest memories. To Franklin-Bouillon, who had been in touch with Kemal from the outset, he remarked, 'It is your day of triumph, my friend.' At last peace was assured.

The Kemalists were now free to occupy eastern Thrace. Here the Greek population was trekking westwards across the plains, whole families tramping, laden with trunks, beside ox-drawn waggons piled with household goods, while their flocks trooped before them and at night their camp-fires dotted the earth like stars in the sky. It was a spectacle which recalled to Ward Price the migrations of the Thirty Years War. Such was the culmination of Lloyd George's attempt to create a new Greek Empire; such, in a few days time, the valediction to his political career.

For some months past the Conservatives had been fretting uneasily at his policies and at the constrictions of the Coalition Government. Now at Chanak he and Churchill had brought the country – or so they saw it – to the brink of war. As one of them remarked: 'We cannot afford to keep him any longer. It is too expensive.' They sought a return to Conservative Party rule. They found a leader in Bonar Law who wrote in a historic letter to *The Times* that Britain could no longer maintain other than her own direct interests without Allied support. 'We cannot act alone,' he wrote, 'as the policeman of the world.'

The reply of his Conservative opponents in the Cabinet was a decision, confirmed at a dinner in Churchill's house, to dissolve Parliament and go to the country as a Coalition. This meant continued support of Lloyd George. He followed up his apparent victory with a speech, in his birthplace of Manchester, in the course of which he chose to launch a last diatribe against the barbarous Turks, and 'the scenes of intolerable horror' which they had been perpetrating in Asia Minor over the past years. But five days later, at a meeting at the Carlton Club, Bonar Law, with the last-minute support of Lord Curzon, inspired a majority of Conservative MPs to break with the Coalition and go to the country on a party basis.

Thus Lloyd George resigned, remarking to his secretaries as he bade them farewell that he would not be returning 'unless I come back as head of a deputation to see Mr Bonar Law (and Lord Curzon) to ask for a grant for Welsh education'.[1] Bonar Law became Prime Minister. Kemal had won his battle. After three years of fighting the despised Turkish rebel had helped to bring down a British Government and a renowned Prime Minister. The romantic had fallen to the realist. The Macedonian had defeated the Celt.

[1] Frank Owen, *Tempestuous Journey: Lloyd George, His Life and Times.*

CHAPTER FORTY-TWO

END OF THE SULTANATE

WHAT, MEANWHILE, was to become of Constantinople? Here the position, pending the peace conference, was anomalous. The Allies still occupied the capital. Tevfik Pasha's Government still exercised nominal authority. Above all, the Sultan-Caliph still sat on his throne. As Caliph he kept his spiritual powers. All that was now left of his temporal Empire, however, was the city itself. The rest of the country was controlled by the Government of the Grand National Assembly, whose leaders he had proscribed as rebels, excommunicated and condemned to death. But in Constantinople it still had no status.

Both in Smyrna and afterwards, back in Angora, Kemal had discussed at length with his ministers and friends how the problem of the Sultanate and its Government should be solved. He had long ago made up his mind to abolish the Sultanate when the moment was ripe. The Assembly shrewdly suspected that this was his intention, and grew agitated at the prospect. To discuss the next step to be taken, Kemal, Rauf, Ali Fuad and Refet, the four founders of the Revolution, met once again for an all-night session around the drink-table. Kemal cautiously invited his three friends in turn to express their views on the question.

Rauf replied that he was bound by conscience, sentiment and tradition to the Sultanate and the Caliphate. He made it clear, however, that he held no brief for Vahid-ed-Din in person, who had played the traitor and must be replaced by another. Refet considered that the Sultanate should become a constitutional monarchy, under which the monarch would merely confirm ministerial appointments, made by a Prime Minister responsible to Parliament. This view was shared by Rauf, with his respect for British institutions, and by others in the country. The Angora Government, it was being suggested, should move to Constantinople, where the Sultan would be its nominal head, serving as an element of national stability. But effective power would be in the hands of Kemal, as Prime Minister – on the analogy of Mussolini in Italy. Ali Fuad, when asked for his opinion, hedged with the reply that, having only lately returned from Moscow, he had not yet had time to study public sentiment and so to form a concrete view.

Kemal saw that he could not yet force this issue. He replied to his friends that for the present the question of the Sultanate did not arise. He made a statement to this effect in the Assembly, thus reassuring the deputies. The Nationalists, none the less, must be represented in Constantinople. Kemal thus decided to appoint a military governor of eastern Thrace, with his headquarters provisionally in the capital, and chose Refet for the post.

Meanwhile, a chief delegate must be chosen for the peace conference which was to be held at Lausanne. Kemal favoured Ismet. Feeling in the lobbies of the Assembly however preferred Rauf. Ismet, the deputies argued, was a mere soldier, who knew little of politics and would be worsted by the cunning foreign diplomats. Let him go, by all means, but as deputy and military adviser to Rauf. Kemal in reply championed Ismet's intelligence, foresight and other qualities which, owing to his long absence in the field, were not properly appreciated in Angora. 'Take this table at which I am sitting,' he said in illustration. 'If I ask any of you to knock it down, you will be able to knock it down in two ways, or in three ways, or at the most in four ways. But Ismet Pasha is so clever that he could knock it down in eight, nine or even ten different ways.' He side-tracked a claim for Kiazim Karabekir on the pretext that he was not on good terms with the Russians, who were expected to be present. Finally the question of protocol was raised. Rauf was Prime Minister. The other powers would be represented by their Foreign Ministers and Turkey, it was argued, should conform to their choice.

This argument suited Kemal, who judged that Rauf, with his independent spirit, his experience of Europe and his conciliatory ways, might not prove easy to handle. He knew how to control Ismet. His will thus prevailed and Ismet was chosen, Yusuf Kemal agreeing to relinquish the Foreign Ministry in his favour. Ismet was thus faced with a *fait accompli*. He was dismayed and reluctant to accept the post. He saw himself, as the deputies saw him, as a military man, not a diplomat. He had little aptitude for negotiation. He had found even the Mudanya Conference a strain. But he had no choice. When he hesitated Kemal, once more the commander instructing his chief of staff, made it clear that his proposal was an order.

Soon afterwards Kemal left for Brusa, the holy Ottoman city on the slopes of Mount Olympus, whose loss to the Greeks had caused such mourning and recrimination among the delegates to the Grand National Assembly. Alone among the burned towns and villages around, it had chanced to escape destruction. Its inhabitants now hoped that, among other celebrations, he would pay suitable tributes of thanksgiving at the tombs of his Ottoman predecessors. Kemal, however, was more concerned to regroup his forces, which now amounted to some 140,000 men, encircling the neutral zones. This he did, leaving one group south of Chanak, from which its advance guard had now retired, and another opposite the Izmit Peninsula, while the reserve was concentrated at Brusa itself, ready to reinforce either wing in the event of a breakdown in the peace negotiations.

Ismet and Fevzi were already in Brusa, Kiazim Karabekir, now Minister of War, and Refet came with Kemal. Thus he had his commanders around him. The liberated citizens gazed upon the victorious pashas with rapt admiration. There was an air of suppressed excitement. The cars of the generals, the carriages of staff officers thronged the streets, which had been hurriedly decked with triumphal arches. Military bands played. Kemal, spruce in his kalpak, held the centre of the stage.

At a victory dinner he announced Ismet's appointment to Lausanne. Ismet remained silent. He did not smile, as was his habit. He had a sombre, distracted look in his eyes. In a rhetorical discourse, rich with high-flown sentiment, Kemal spoke of him as, 'the best, the most perfect among us all – the surest counsellor, the most faithful support, the best of comrades, the most ardent of patriots, revered not only by all Turks but by all Moslem peoples, as the defender of their honour, virtue and probity.' Now he carried the nation's mandate to Europe: 'Her treatment of him will be for us the touchstone of her feelings towards us.' The nation sought peace, but if forced would know how to make war right to the end.

Kemal did not forget to give Kiazim Karabekir his share of praise – his intelligence, his hardihood, his powers of organization, his military valour. Kiazim, while many still hesitated, had created an army, with which he had secured and stabilized the eastern frontiers, giving the Nationalist Government its first proof of strength. Kemal recapitulated the past – the early struggles, the comrades who had come to him at the start, asking for nothing and hoping for nothing, conscious of the folly of their sacrifice; the three long years that had led to the liberation of Anatolia and the emergence of the Turkish nation aware of itself, its rights and its strength. Now the most difficult task of all remained – that of using victory to the full.

How he intended to use it was implied one evening at a large victory rally in a cinema. War orphans in uniform represented the generation of the future; school teachers, the generation of the present. The pashas were ranged on the platform, posed against an outsize Turkish flag. All were in uniform with the exception of Kemal himself, who wore with his usual elegance the civilian costume of Angora, with an astrakhan kalpak.

To the women, who outnumbered the men, he declaimed, 'Win for us the battle of education and you will do yet more for your country than we have been able to do. It is to you that I appeal.' To the men he said, 'If henceforward the women do not share in the social life of the nation, we shall never attain to our full development. We shall remain irremediably backward, incapable of treating on equal terms with the civilizations of the West.' To all, with a sweeping gesture, he concluded, 'And all that will still be nothing if you refuse to enter resolutely into modern life, if you reject the obligations which it imposes. You will be lepers, pariahs, alone in your obstinacy, with your customs of another age. Remain yourselves, but learn how to take from the West what is indispensable to an evolved people. Admit science and new ideas into your lives. If you do not, they will devour you.'

There was prolonged applause. The women were in tears. It was a foretaste of the future, that future of which Kemal had remarked to Falih Rifki as they looked down over the smouldering embers of Smyrna, 'They think that this is the end, that I have reached my goal. But it is only after this that we shall really begin to do something. It is only now that our real work is beginning.'

Kemal had brought Fikriye with him from Angora to Brusa. On the road outside the city Halide Edib chanced to meet them as they arrived. Getting out of the car, Kemal explained that he was sending her to a sanatorium in Munich. Her consumptive condition had gradually worsened and the doctors in Angora had been urging specialist treatment. There were thus good medical reasons for her departure – though Kemal had other reasons in mind.

It was an appropriate moment to end the affair. Fikriye had become wearisome to him. He was impatient of illness in others. She clung to him in an irritating fashion. She was the Oriental mistress, who had distracted him and suited his needs for a while. But no woman could hold his affections for long, and Fikriye now represented a period of his life that was over. For the life that lay ahead she had nothing to offer him. To Halide, though she could not but approve the decision, 'coming as it did immediately after Smyrna, it looked as if she were being hurriedly put out of the way'.

Halide asked to say goodbye to her and Kemal opened the door of her car. Of their meeting she wrote:

> She stretched out her hand and caught mine rather convulsively, and I was struck by its resemblance to another hand. Though emaciated to an extraordinary degree, the form was exactly like that of the plump hand of the plump girl from Smyrna – broad palms of a man, thick finger-tips and square small nails. . . . She looked extraordinarily fragile. The pretty little chin was a sharp blade-edge, the small nose almost transparent in its thinness and squeezed, tortured air. . . . But the thing that hurt most was the eyes – out of this devastated mask of pain they looked, the lower and the upper lashes curled and intermingled more than ever; tears falling through their webby edges on the sunken and drawn cheeks. . . . The grave and rather disturbing contralto voice spoke with composure in spite of the tears, but there was some anxiety hidden in the tones.

She had not wanted to go, 'but Pasha insisted'. She was going to Constantinople. She said, 'I will stay a few days in Paris and get myself some beautiful clothes.' Scrutinizing Halide's face, she tried to read the conviction, 'not so much in her recovery as in her return, decked in beautiful clothes and once more restored to love'.

Halide kissed her tenderly and said, 'You will be well and you will come back, my dear.'

'*Insh'allah*,' she said fervently, clinging to the other woman and kissing her.

Fikriye was entrusted to the care of Refet, and was thus ironically to witness, sick and in despair as she was, the celebration of Kemal's final triumph in Constantinople. Refet's own instructions were left purposely vague. In theory his jurisdiction was to extend over eastern Thrace alone. The evening before he left he sought out Kemal in the hope of obtaining a more explicit directive as to how he should proceed in Constantinople. But all he could extract from him, as he sat drinking with some press correspondents in Brusa, was a convivial greeting, followed by the airy assurance, 'My old friend, you have been with us from the start. We both think alike.'

Refet's reception was tumultuous. As his steamer approached the Golden Horn, thousands of small boats sailed out from either bank to greet her, all decked with flags – red and white for Turkey, green for Islam – and with fluttering streamers. The Galata Bridge itself was festooned with garlands. The Turkish flag flew from each roof, each dome, each minaret. Each house was draped with Turkish carpets. Triumphal arches bridged the streets, crowned with portraits of Kemal and his generals, and with inscriptions lauding the heroes of the War of Independence and the power and the glory of the Turkish people. The people themselves, in tens of thousands, expectantly thronged the streets. On the big square by the bridge, hundreds of Turkish women, many of them unveiled, stood massed in groups in the Moslem style. Spectators clustered on the roofs of the houses, on the domes and the minarets of the mosques, even on the masts of the boats in the harbour.

As Refet's ship drew alongside the air was rent by a deafening chorus of sirens from every ship at anchor in the Bosporus and the Golden Horn, and a full-throated roar from every man, woman and child on shore. The ADC of Abdul Mejid, the Heir Apparent, came to welcome him on board, expressing his master's satisfaction at the happy victory and conviction that his arrival would bring justice, security and welfare to Thrace. In expressing his thanks Refet referred to the fact that Abdul Mejid was heir to the Caliphate, whose preservation was one of his Government's objectives. When he was received on shore by a deputation including an ADC of the Sultan himself, welcoming him in His Majesty's name, he made a significant reply, expressing his sentiments of religious devotion to the 'high office of the Caliphate' but making no mention of the Sultanate or of His Majesty in person. There were knowing looks from those present, and the ADC turned a trifle pale.

His attitude to the rest of the delegation was similar. In accepting a message of welcome from Tevfik Pasha, the Grand Vizier, he made it clear that he did so only from his personal respect for him, but that Anatolia did not acknowledge his Government's existence. Later, replying to a speech delivered in the name of the Minister of the Interior, he expressed his cordial thanks, but added that he recognized no such minister.

When Refet passed through the barrier the crowds broke the police cordon and mobbed him, carrying him shoulder-high to his car. Along the route of his procession they waved flags and brandished portraits of the Gazi, framed in laurel and pine. Standing up in his car, a small dapper figure at the salute, he was visibly moved by the passionate plaudits of the crowd. He drove straight to the tomb of Sultan Fatih – Mehmed I, the Ottoman conqueror. Here, after performing his devotions, he made a brief speech to a group of students, assuring them that only youth, through the sacrifices of its fathers, had made the victory possible. To a large popular concourse he lauded the occupant of the tomb. This great Turkish commander had given them the city, and no Turk would allow it to be torn from them.

The pent-up emotions of three years were released as the various Nationalist organizations, which had hitherto languished underground, came out into the open and rejoiced and proclaimed their loyalty to the cause. The festivities continued for several days, culminating in the Friday prayer in Santa Sophia, when Refet addressed a huge concourse from the preacher's pulpit, reducing many to tears. Dashing, energetic, loquacious, ubiquitous, he was well-cast for his role of popular hero. As the people jostled around him to kiss his garments and abstract objects from his person as souvenirs, he exclaimed, 'They will kill me, they will break me, they love me so much.'

A detachment of Nationalist gendarmerie arrived *en route* for Thrace, and were cheered as they marched through the streets. The foreigners, the Levantines, kept out of sight, comforting themselves with the hope that all this Nationalist bravado was no more than a flash in the pan which would subside, leaving things much as they were before. The Sultan meanwhile seemed forgotten, save by a band of students who shouted, 'Down with the rascal in Yildiz!' He was said however to have voiced some alarm at Refet's continual references to the sovereignty of the people.

Refet swiftly established relations with the Allied authorities. With Harington he was soon on easy terms over a whisky and soda. He was quick to sense the reluctance of the British, now that the Mudanya Convention was signed, to maintain their former firm control over the city. Taking full advantage of this attitude, he spared no effort to make the power of the Nationalists felt. Fencing with the Occupation forces, he made courteous demands of the Allied authorities which were for the most part courteously met. When he grew more truculent the demeanour of the British was passive; their protests were mild; their officers were instructed to avoid trouble. Slowly the machinery of the once-powerful Occupation was being whittled away.

In the administration Nationalists asserted themselves above the heads of the Sultan's supporters. Vengeance was taken upon traitors to the Nationalist cause. Ali Kemal, a hostile journalist, who as Minister of the Interior had outlawed Mustafa Kemal, and who had since campaigned for the Allies and against the Resistance, was singled out as a victim. One evening, in a barber's shop in Pera, he was arrested 'in the name of the Grand National Assembly' by members of the Nationalist secret police. They gagged him and took him on board a motor-boat, with its lights dimmed to avoid the British patrols, to Izmit, which the Nationalist troops had now entered. Here at dawn he was taken to the *konak* for interrogation by the Turkish army commander. But at midday, as he was being escorted back to the gaol, a large crowd set upon him, overpowered his escort and brutally stoned him to death.

His end caused serious alarm in the Yildiz Palace. Since the fall of Smyrna, the Sultan had been wavering irresolutely between one course of action and another. With the fate of Abdul Hamid for ever in mind, he planned at one moment to withdraw from Constantinople, at the next to make a show of clemency to the Nationalists. Now his staff began to desert him, and he appealed to General Harington to reinforce his guard.

Thus protected, still hoping to cling to his throne, he received Refet in audience. Refet saw before him a demoralized old man in a frock coat, without decorations, attended by a single ADC – the last symbol of a fallen Empire. Refet, the young general of the new age, stood before him, brisk in his uniform with a revolver at his hip. He took the initiative. 'Sir,' he said, without further protocol, 'the present situation cannot be prolonged much longer. We cannot have in Turkey two Governments, one in Constantinople and the other in Angora. I come to beg you to bow before the force of events, and to put an end to this dualism, which is contrary to the interests of the nation, by demanding the resignation of your Government.'

Vahid-ed-Din played for time. He replied that he was ready to consider a fusion between the two Governments. He demanded to know the intentions of Angora. Refet, now talking on his own responsibility, put forward the view, which he had already expressed to Kemal, that the Sultan should be a constitutional monarch, appointing the ministers approved by his Assembly, with the right to confirm but not to veto legislation. Meanwhile, however, he must dismiss his present ministers, men of a past age who no longer represented the nation.

Vahid-ed-Din prevaricated. To the dismissal of the ministers he objected that, as a constitutional monarch already, he was obliged to consult them first. Refet replied that the decision must be reached now or never. If the Sultan would agree to his proposal, he would put it before the Angora Government and try to gain their consent. But Vahid-ed-Din would not admit himself beaten. He still clung to the hope that something would happen to save him and his throne. He put an end to the audience. Refet telegraphed to Kemal that the Sultan was 'far from our way of thinking'.

At this juncture the Allies took a maladroit step, which gave Kemal just the chance he awaited to pass into action. Still adhering to protocol and invoking the precedent of past conferences, they sent joint invitations to Lausanne both to the Government of the Sublime Porte and to that of the Grand National Assembly.

At this the deputies exploded in wrath. Sixteen orators in succession denounced it as a manœuvre of the Sultan to divide the country in the eyes of the foreigner. They rehearsed at length the crimes of his Government. The despatch of its delegates to Lausanne would be regarded as an act of high treason. Ismet, speaking for the first time as Minister of Foreign Affairs, con- tended that the double invitation was a breach of the Mudanya Convention.

The psychological moment for the abolition of the Sultanate had arrived. Kemal, faithful to his pragmatic methods, decided on an immediate com- promise. The Sultanate would be separated from the Caliphate. The former, representing the temporal power, would be abolished; the latter, repre- senting the spiritual, would remain. It would be transferred to a prince whose office would be religious but in no way political. A motion was drafted, recording the breakdown of the Ottoman Empire and the birth of the new Turkish state, whose sovereign rights belonged constitutionally to the people.

It was hoped by this compromise to dispose of the Sultan, while at the same time placating the religious elements in Parliament. But these, reinforced by Kemal's personal enemies, were strong and vociferous. Kemal tackled the Opposition on their own ground. Briefing himself well, with the aid of his Minister of Justice, on the history and laws of Islam, he pointed out that the Sultanate and the Caliphate had been separated in the past and could very well be separated again. His speech created turmoil in the Chamber, which rang with alternate shouts of 'Vahid-ed-Din! Vahid-ed-Din!' and 'God damn him!' followed by cheers. The various motions were then discussed in committee, with a learned *hoja* in the chair and Kemal in a corner listening patiently to a flow of hair-splitting arguments. The Opposition sought to prove that the two institutions were inseparable. 'They relied,' he said later, 'on the well-known fallacies and absurdities.'

A breath of realism was needed. The problem, from Kemal's point of view, was to find a formula linking the power of the Caliphate with that of the Assembly. When he saw that his own supporters were hesitant he asked the chairman for permission to speak. Standing on a bench in front of him, he said loudly:

> Gentlemen, sovereignty and Sultanate are not given to anyone by anyone because scholarship proves that they should be; or through discussion and debate. Sovereignty and Sultanate are taken by strength, by power and by force. It was by force that the sons of Osman seized the sovereignty and Sultanate of the Turkish nation; they have maintained this usurpation for six centuries. Now the Turkish nation has rebelled and has put a stop to these usurpers, and has effectively taken sovereignty and Sultanate into its own hands. This is an accomplished fact. . . . The question is merely how to give expression to it. If those gathered here, the Assembly and everyone else could look at this question in a natural way, I think they would agree. Even if they do not, the truth will soon find expression, but some heads may roll in the process.

This implied threat of force, which was followed by a theological disquisition, brought forth, from one of the *hojas* from Angora, the admission, 'I beg your pardon, sir, we were looking at the matter from another point of view. We have been enlightened by your explanation.'

Thus, by a combination of persuasion and menace, characteristic of his political tactics, Kemal achieved a settlement in committee. The draft law now submitted to the Assembly was composed of two articles. The first declared that the form of the Government in Constantinople, resting on the sovereignty of an individual, had ceased on 16th March 1920 – the date of the British occupation of the city. The second declared that, though the Caliphate belonged to the Ottoman Empire, it rested on the Turkish state, and that the Assembly would choose as Caliph 'that member of the Ottoman house who was in learning and character most worthy and fitting'. It proposed, for the first time in the history of Islam, the legal separation of the temporal and spiritual powers.

On a proposal for a nominal vote Kemal rose and said, 'There is no need for this. I believe that the Assembly will unanimously adopt the principles which will for ever preserve the independence of the country and the nation.' The chairman, putting the law to the vote, announced its acceptance by acclamation. One opposing voice only was heard to exclaim, 'I am against it.' But it was drowned by cries of 'Silence!' The session ended with prayers, recited no longer in Arabic but in Turkish.

'In this way, gentlemen,' Kemal was to record, 'the final obsequies of the decline and fall of the Ottoman Sultanate were completed!'

As soon as the news of the Assembly's decision reached Constantinople, Refet informed the Allied High Commissioners that he had taken over the

Government of the Sublime Porte in the name of the Grand National Assembly. On 4th November 1922, Tevfik delivered up to the Sultan at the Yildiz Palace the seals of office of the last Government of the Ottoman Empire. The Allies declared their neutrality in the internal affairs of Turkey. The city authorities called on Refet and placed themselves under the orders of Angora, accepting a régime which was provisionally described as a 'national monarchy'. Constantinople gave itself over once more to celebrations, with cries of 'Long live the monarchy of the nation! Long live Parliament!'

The Sultan meanwhile stayed where he was, now deserted by most of his entourage. Kemal, reluctant to risk the popular resentment which would follow his deposition by force, preferred to await events. Presently the Sultan summoned Rumbold to an audience which was painful and long. He sought reassurance but in vain. Rumbold informed him that the British could now deal only with the Angora Government. Otherwise he confined himself to a promise of personal protection in case the Sultan found himself in imminent danger and felt obliged either to abdicate or to leave without doing so. Soon afterwards Rumbold left for Lausanne. Before doing so he made Harington responsible for the life of the Sultan who, if his situation became serious, would communicate with him through his bandmaster, a man on whose loyalty he could count until the end.

Still searching about for some means to escape his fate, Vahid-ed-Din, sent his chamberlain to Refet, with a message that he was anxious to contact the Gazi. He was ready to receive an emissary from Angora and would openly telegraph or write to Kemal in this sense. Kemal and Rauf requested him to write. But no letter materialized, and Refet suspected that the Sultan would soon try to leave. He thus enlisted the Sultan's naval ADC to spy on his movements, promising him future employment if he was discovered and dismissed.

At midday on 10th November the Sultan, as though nothing unusual was afoot, proceeded to the ceremony of the *Selamlik* – the Friday prayer. He emerged from the Palace sunk back in his carriage, arrayed only in the ordinary uniform of a Turkish officer, without decorations and with a kalpak on his head. His features were ravaged, his face so pale as to suggest the mere ghost of a monarch. Behind him were his black eunuchs and a few ADCs, but no one else – no dignitaries, no generals, no ministers, since his Cabinet no longer existed. He drove in a funereal silence. When the meagre cortège reached the mosque, the *muezzin* recited the call to prayer, no longer in the name of the great and victorious Padishah and of the illustrious Imperial family, but simply in that of Commander of the Faithful and Caliph. Dull and lifeless as an automaton, the last of the Sultans stepped down from his carriage and entered the mosque for his last *Selamlik*.

Soon the bandmaster called upon General Harington to say that the

Sultan believed himself in imminent danger and requested the British to remove him at once. Reluctant to act without a direct request, Harington secured it from the Sultan in writing. Harington was now faced with the problem, as he put it, of getting 'the last Sultan of Turkey out of his palace alive'. Since the palace was well guarded and the spies of the Nationalists were active, this was no easy task. Confiding only in a few of his officers, he devised a plan for the purpose.

On instructions, the Sultan announced to his staff his intention of spending the night in the kiosk of Merasim, at the far end of the garden, conveniently adjoining the Malta Gate, which led to the British barrack square. This aroused no suspicion. In the kiosk he was joined by his son and by those who were to accompany them: his First Chamberlain, the bandmaster, his doctor, two confidential secretaries, a valet, a barber and two eunuchs – a suite of nine in all. Throughout the night, with revolvers on the ormolu tables around, he supervised the packaging in trunks of his jewels, precious stones and other valuables, including a small gold table which had belonged to Sultan Selim.

At six o'clock in the morning the little group left the kiosk. The gate was opened by a eunuch. Two British ambulances with Red Cross markings had been parked outside, while a Guards detachment drilled on the parade ground beyond. Steps were let down to enable the party to enter them. The rain was pouring down in torrents and the Sultan's umbrella got caught in the door. But finally they were off, unobserved by those around.

Harington, looking out at the rain from his house at Therapia over an early breakfast of eggs and bacon, reflected that his troops must think their officers mad to hold a parade on such a morning. As he drove to the naval dockyard at Tophane, where he was to meet the Sultan, he saw the officers he had placed at various posts, strolling with a forced look of casualness in the rain. On the quay he found Nevile Henderson, Chargé d'Affaires at the Embassy since Rumbold's departure. The second ambulance soon arrived but not the first, though it had started ten minutes earlier. Both looked anxiously at their watches. Had there been a hitch in the operation?

It was only a small hitch. The ambulance containing the Sultan developed a puncture, and the wheel had hurriedly to be changed. But it duly arrived. The general and Henderson greeted the Sultan and escorted him with his party aboard a naval launch. It conveyed them across the water to the British battleship HMS *Malaya*. On the launch General Harington half hoped that the Sultan would present him with his cigarette case as a souvenir of this historic occasion. Instead Vahid-ed-Din turned to him and confided to him the care of his five wives, with a request that they be sent after him. Then he walked up the ladder on to the deck of the warship.

On board Henderson told him that he was now safe on British territory, and asked him where he wished to go. The Sultan expressed no preference, and agreed to the proposed destination of Malta. He dictated a message to his doctor for his wives and daughters, to be delivered by one of the eunuchs. The doctor, flustered as he was, made a mistake in the draft. Only then did the Sultan, for a moment, lose his equanimity. He turned angrily on the doctor and reproached his suite for losing their heads at a moment when he might have been justified in losing his own.

Formal farewells were exchanged and HMS *Malaya* steamed away around the point of the Seraglio, the old palace of the Ottoman sultans, into the Sea of Marmara. Henderson, on his return to the Embassy scribbled a postscript to a letter he had written to Rumbold: 'All is well. H.I.M. was on board *Malaya* by 8.45 and all proceedings went without a hitch. I am glad he is off.'

The operation had been effectively concluded without the interference and apparently without the knowledge of the Turks. Refet had sensed that the Sultan's departure was imminent. Lying in bed in the Sublime Porte, awaiting a report from his agent, the naval ADC, he could not sleep. After dawn had broken, the ADC burst into his room, distraught and dishevelled in carpet slippers. The Sultan, he revealed, had left. From a window in the kiosk he had seen him step into an ambulance, escorted by a detachment of British soldiers. There had been no previous warning. Such was the measure of the success of his stratagem in moving to the kiosk and thus warding off suspicion.

In a fever of guilt and anxiety the ADC dashed out of the palace, ran for more than a mile in his slippers before finding a carriage, then drove as fast as the mud and the rain would allow over the two and a half remaining miles to the Sublime Porte. Now what was to become of him? He had failed in his duty. He flung himself hysterically on Refet's mercy.

Refet reassured him with a pat on the back: 'Go to bed and get some sleep. I am going to do the same.' Before doing so he telegraphed Kemal, announcing the Sultan's departure. When he awoke an hour or so later he was handed a reply, enquiring who was responsible for letting him go. He would have liked to reply, 'I was.' Instead he replied in effect, 'No one.' It was a happy solution. The Nationalists had avoided the odium of his arrest and exile. He had fled of his own accord with the aid of the infidel and, far from becoming a martyr, would surely incur the contempt of the Moslem world.

Refet now called, on instructions, on Prince Abdul Mejid, the Sultan's cousin and Heir Apparent, and invited him to accept the position of Caliph on conditions to be laid down by the Grand National Assembly. A robust upstanding man of fifty-four, Abdul Mejid had been excluded from politics by Abdul Hamid, for his enlightened liberal views, and had devoted his leisure to the arts, designing and embellishing the gardens of his palace, becoming learned in music, dabbling in painting to the extent (after Abdul

Hamid's death) of having a picture exhibited in the *Salon* in Paris.[1] A devout Moslem, he was none the less modern in outlook and had shown sympathy with the Nationalists. He now accepted the Caliphate, signing a document which bound him to abide by the Assembly's decisions.

The deputies met next day in secret session. Rauf recalled the various treacheries of Vahid-ed-Din to the Moslem world and called upon the deputies to elect a new representative on earth of the Prophet. A high Islamic dignitary supported him. First the Sultan, who had chosen not to abdicate, was formally deposed. Then the candidature of Abdul Mejid was proposed for the Caliphate.

There was excitement among the *hojas*, who poured forth views in wearisome detail as to the character and powers of the Caliph's office. Kemal allowed them to wrangle on for a while, then pulled them up sharply. The matter, he explained to them, was really quite simple. It was no concern of the Moslem world, as certain speakers had insisted, but only of the Turkish nation, which was now in full possession of its sovereignty. In this the Caliphate could have no part. All that was required was the deposition of the fugitive Caliph and the election of a new religious head in his place. Thus finally, by a majority vote, the appointment of Abdul Mejid was agreed.

He was to be bound by the terms of a manifesto, which the Government must approve before its publication to the Moslem world. This was to be strictly non-political in character. It was to record his satisfaction at the Assembly's choice of him and condemn the conduct of Vahid-ed-Din.

His formal installation took place on a Friday in a ceremony carefully curtailed by the Nationalists. In place of the traditional cloak and turban as worn by Fatih the Conqueror, he wore frock-coat and fez. At the Old Seraglio he was received by a delegation from the Grand National Assembly, who handed to him a document in which the terms of his office were suitably inscribed on parchment. After appropriate speeches, he took over the custody of the sacred relics of the Prophet. But the sword, symbolizing the temporal power, was withheld from him.

Finally the new Caliph drove, accompanied by Refet and followed by a procession of carriages so long and so reminiscent of a Sultan's parade that it displeased the more radical deputies, to the Fatih Mosque, where he celebrated his first Selamlik. First a band played the new Independence Anthem. Then the Friday prayer was recited – in Turkish. Finally a telegram of thanks was sent by the Caliph to the Grand National Assembly. On the insistence of the more conservative deputies, the house rose to its feet to receive it.

The ex-Sultan was soon on his way from Malta to San Remo, where he settled down in a villa of moderate size. The British Embassy, after Rum-

---

[1] He painted a portrait of Refet himself, which he presented to him.

bold's last audience with him, had arranged the transfer abroad of his cash and securities. He thus had enough money to live on. A month or so after his departure, one of his eunuchs came to Constantinople to arrange for the transfer of his wives and family. The news of this brought a telegram to the British Embassy from a certain American impresario. It read: 'Hippodrome New York could use wives of ex-Sultan kindly put me in touch with party who could procure them.' When this message was shown to King George V he was greatly amused.

Such was the last act in the Decline and Fall of the Ottoman Empire.

CHAPTER FORTY-THREE

NEGOTIATIONS AT LAUSANNE

ISMET left for Lausanne with a sense of deep misgiving. A new and grave responsibility lay unsought on his shoulders, involving not merely his own career but his country's future. He was venturing, reluctantly and with an acute sense of his unfitness for the task which Kemal, always his master, had imposed on him, into territory unfamiliar and in all probability unfriendly. He knew how to contend with a military adversary. But he knew nothing of the field of European diplomacy, with its artful commanders and its armoury of unknown and insidious weapons. He had never before set foot in Europe, but for a few weeks in Austria and Germany for the sake of his health. Ismet was all too well aware that he had big guns against him. Lloyd George had been deposed, but Lord Curzon still ruled – with a determination moreover to restore at all costs, and at the expense of the Turks, the prestige of his country in the Near Eastern world.

Here was a conflict of psychology. The Allies saw the Turks as a vanquished people; the Turks saw themselves as victors. Turkey was the first of the defeated central powers to be in a position to negotiate peace. But she was to negotiate at a disadvantage. For the Allies aspired to impose a treaty upon her, as the Treaty of Versailles had been imposed on the rest. Ismet came to Lausanne hoping to gain for his country respect as an equal. Instead he found himself treated as a suppliant.

Curzon dominated the conference. It was, as Ismet remarked to Madame Georges-Gaulis, who had come to report on it, 'always the English voice, and the English fist banging on the table'. The English he could accept as his enemies. But the French disillusioned him bitterly. With Franklin-Bouillon in mind, he had counted upon them to support the Turkish cause. But Curzon, on his way through Paris, had succeeded with Poincaré in re-establishing the Entente Cordiale, and Ismet found himself faced with a united front between Britain, France and Italy. If Curzon seemed to look upon him as 'one of his subjects in India', Bompard, the French representative, behaved to him, so he said, with the haughtiness of a Grand Vizier of some early Ottoman sultan. Small wonder that Ismet was touchy, quick to suspect affronts to his country's dignity and threats to her sovereignty, hence the more assertive in manner and obstructive in tactics.

Unable to compete with his adversaries in the thrust and parry of extempore debate, he soon evolved his own methods of fighting. He dug himself in. He contested every point, however small; he pleaded deafness, consulted interminably with his colleagues; he read out long prepared statements. He would demand time to consult Angora and defer his replies until subsequent sittings. He would make a concession and withdraw it the next day. At first he exasperated Curzon and the rest, but as time went on his doggedness, his restraint, his straightforwardness, his evident sincerity, began to earn him some respect. Perhaps after all his war of attrition would succeed in wearing them down, or even in winning them round.

Slowly it dawned upon some of the Allied delegates that they were dealing with a new type of Turk. As Sir William Tyrrell, one of Rumbold's deputies, expressed it to Madame Georges-Gaulis, 'We used to know two sorts of Turk: the Old Turk, he is dead: the Young Turk, he exists no longer. We see today the third, quite different from the other two: Ismet Pasha. For us he is the incarnation of the Third Turk. His personality, his attitude have strongly impressed the conference, of which he is today the great figure. Well, it's with that Turk we want to make peace.'

Rumbold himself, though one of the old school and still secretly hankering to give these pig-headed people 'a real good blow on the head', was familiar enough with the Angora psychology, as reflected by the Turkish delegation. 'I do not see,' he wrote to London, 'how they can abandon any demand included in the National Pact without exposing themselves to disapproval or even a trial by court martial.' On the other hand, it seemed clear that they wanted an agreement with Britain. 'I am inclined to think,' he wrote to Henderson in Constantinople, 'that if they could absolutely count on Britain being the friend of Turkey after the peace, they would not make such bones about getting out of the Russian friendship.' These were shrewd enough assessments. The Angora-Moscow axis had been a measure of expediency, arising out of British hostility. Kemal now sought British friendship. But there was much stony ground to be covered. There was the problem of the Straits, the problem of Mosul, the problem of the Capitulations.

The question of the Straits was discussed early in December, after the arrival of Chicherin. Ismet, gaining time to sound the views of the conference, at first deferred to him as protagonist of the Turkish case. Chicherin, in his high-pitched rasping voice, stated it with an air of protective patronage, basing it on the principles laid down in the Turco-Soviet Treaty and the National Pact. These were essentially defensive. Both countries sought to keep all warships, apart from those of Turkey, out of the Straits, which the Turks should have the right to defend. The view of the Allies, on the other hand, was that the Straits should be internationalized and open to the warships of all powers.

While listening to the Russian delegate's discourse, Curzon 'thought M Chicherin must have mistaken his role and assumed the kalpak of Ismet Pasha'. He pressed Ismet to say whether the views of the Turks were identical with those of the Russians. Ismet replied that he was willing to consider alternative Allied proposals. Chicherin looked startled. Eventually Ismet agreed, with a few modifications, to an Allied Straits Convention, which Chicherin shrilly declared to be 'primarily directed against Russia'. He refused to sign it and the rift between Russians and Turks seemed complete.

The convention allowed for an international commission to protect the Straits, with freedom of passage for the ships of all nations. The Turks sought a joint guarantee against aggression from the Lausanne powers. They were obligated instead to accept a guarantee in terms of the Covenant of the League of Nations – an institution repugnant to Soviet Russia. This afforded them a more nebulous degree of security and was to call for a revision at Montreux thirteen years later, before the Second World War. Its acceptance now was a measure of Kemal's realistic statesmanship, and of his desire for Turkey's admission, on a basis of mutual trust, into the Western community of nations.

This spirit was further displayed when the time came to discuss the Christian minorities, mainly the Greeks and Armenians in Turkey. The Allies demanded measures for their adequate protection, once more under an international commission. Ismet insisted that they be subject to the Turkish courts, which exemplified the new liberal laws of his country. Curzon rejected this plea with some sarcasm. But he offered Ismet a loophole in the form of a suggestion that Turkey should join the League of Nations, accepting its provisions for minorities as the European member states had done. To this Ismet, to his surprise and relief, agreed. Thus over two issues the future international position of Turkey was strengthened, through the need of the Allies to maintain a balance of power against the Soviet Union.

It was strengthened once again over the issue which had caused all the trouble – that of relations between Turkey and Greece. Venizelos, though he had strayed with Lloyd George into romanticist paths, was a realist at heart. Kemal was a realist too. Venizelos knew that his policy had failed; Kemal knew that his had succeeded. But both knew that Turkey and Greece must live together as neighbours, hence must quickly forget their mutual grievances. The conference was thus treated to the spectacle of the two main protagonists settling their differences in relative harmony.

The frontiers of eastern Thrace and of Adrianople were agreed in a manner consistent with the National Pact. Over the other main problem, that of the large Greek minorities in Turkey and Turkish minorities in Greece, the League was invoked once again. It was to supervise a compulsory exchange of populations between the two countries. Thus within a few years, apart from a Turkish minority in western Thrace and a Greek minority in eastern Thrace, virtually no Greeks remained in Turkey and no Turks in Greece. Such, ethnologically, was the final end to that fusion of races which had symbolized the Byzantine and Ottoman Empires.

Much as the Grand National Assembly might grumble, the Turks had reason, so far, to be satisfied with the progress of the Lausanne Conference. But more formidable problems still lay ahead, notably that of the province of Mosul. Here lay a fundamental conflict between the respective interests of Turkey and Britain. The British had occupied Mosul 'as a point of strategical importance' some days after the cease-fire, hence in violation of the terms of the Armistice, in 1918. Its occupation had aroused strong protests from Kemal, then in command of the neighbouring army in Syria, to Izzet Pasha, then Grand Vizier.

Strategically it was important to the British for the defence of the frontiers of Irak[1] and the route to India. Economically it was important to them on account of its oil-fields, to which France had abandoned her claims in favour of Britain. To the Turks it was important, or so they claimed, for the defence of their frontiers, and as an integral part of Anatolia, whose ports provided the province with its natural outlet to the sea. Ethnologically, however, its inclusion within the frontiers of the National Pact was debatable. For it contained a large population not only of Turks but of Arabs and Kurds, with a mind to their own independence.

The Grand National Assembly felt strongly on the subject of Mosul. The House of Commons, as it happened, felt less strongly. Bonar Law, committed as he was to a policy of peace, was anxious to clear out of Irak 'bag and baggage'. To Curzon he expressed two convictions: 'The first is that we should not go to war for the sake of Mosul; and secondly that, if the French, as we know to be the case, will not join us, we shall not by ourselves fight the Turks to impose what is left of the Treaty of Sèvres.' The Prime Minister's views were echoed by the popular press; 'Mosul,' wrote Lord Beaverbrook's *Daily Express*, 'is not worth the bones of one single British soldier.' Mespot was merely a wastepot, a miserable wilderness of swamp and desert: its proposed evacuation became indeed a paramount issue in the 1922 election.

Curzon, however, was determined to assert British interests in Mosul to the utmost limit – short of war. He had the advantage of knowing more about Mosul than Ismet, who delivered, in support of the Turkish claim, a long, monotonous and often inaccurate lecture of a historical and statistical

[1] Mesopotamia.

kind. Curzon made havoc of his facts. The Turkish population of the province, he asserted, was a mere one-twelfth of the whole. Moreover, a majority of it had voted, in a plebiscite, for inclusion in the Kingdom of Irak. As for Mosul itself, it was a wholly Arab city, built and inhabited by Arabs. When it came to the Kurdish areas, he replied with some sarcasm to Ismet, 'It was reserved for the Turkish delegation to discover for the first time in history that the Kurds were Turks. Nobody has ever found it out before.' Curzon concluded with the proposal that the entire question of the frontier should be referred to the League of Nations.

Ismet hedged for a while, his eye cocked nervously on the Grand National Assembly, his voice, as Curzon put it irritably, reiterating 'the same old tune.... Sovereignty, sovereignty, sovereignty.' He proposed first a plebiscite in the area, then independent negotiations outside the conference between Britain and Turkey. But he had in the end to agree that if these were to fail the question, like that of the minorities, should be submitted to the League of Nations.

Now that there seemed no danger of a break over Mosul, Curzon impatiently resolved, after many delays, to force the conference to a swift conclusion. Calling for the French and Italian delegates, he proposed that a draft treaty should be presented to the Turks for signature in six days' time. If they could not agree to it within the following four days, the conference would be dissolved. He himself proposed to leave Lausanne for London on 4th February 1923.

While Curzon had confined himself to the territorial problems now approaching solution, he had left to the French and the Italians the thornier problems of finance, economics and the status of foreigners which concerned their interests more directly than those of Britain. In his preoccupation with a political settlement, he had underrated the obstacles likely to arise in these fields. They were, as the French had found, formidable.

To the patriotic Turk, the expulsion of the foreigner from his doorstep availed little without his expulsion from within his house. The Capitulations, those privileges which had in effect created a series of foreign states within his state, rankled with him more directly, and more personally, than any foreign encroachments on his farthermost frontiers. The banks, the railways, the mines, the forests, the public utilities – all were controlled by foreigners. They were exempt from taxes and customs dues. They were subject only to the laws of their own courts. It was largely to put an end to all this that the Turks had been fighting so obstinately.

In the negotiations, the Allies, and especially the French, insisted on their maximum safeguards; the Turks on their independence from all restrictions. In the domain of justice the Allies proposed foreign legal advisers, or observers, to replace the foreign judges. The Turks rejected all such proposals. The domain of finance, economics and commerce embraced such thorny problems as reparations and indemnities, the distribution of the Ottoman Debt, Turkish property rights abroad and Allied property rights in Turkey, communications, taxation of foreigners, company law, insurance policies, contracts and concessions. In general the French accepted the replacement of former privileges by agreements on equal terms between foreigners and Turks. The discussions, however, raised intricate problems in which questions of detail, which did not appear important, involved issues of principle, which were. Time and patience were needed, as Ismet insisted, to resolve their complexity.

But Lord Curzon was in a hurry. Moreover, by looking as though he were in a hurry, he judged that he would the better achieve his ends. Still thinking, unlike some of his colleagues, in terms of the old Ottoman Turk, he believed that Ismet was holding out until the last possible moment, bargaining like a carpet merchant to get the best deal he could, but would yield in the end. In his dealings with Orientals, he was used to the old and often corrupt régimes where interests overrode principles and the flexibility of personal rule made for compromise.

But here, as he failed to realize, was something new: a patriotic Nationalist movement, unprecedented in an Oriental country, in which principles were paramount. Curzon allowed too little for the national pride of the new Turk, for the fact that he had laid down a programme from which his ruler could little afford to deviate. He underrated the Assembly and the power of its extremists; he misjudged the psychology of Ismet himself, who was no bargainer by training and moreover unsure of his position at home.

'What are they going to say in Angora?' was Ismet's eternal refrain to his friends. On the Capitulations he declared to Madame Georges-Gaulis, 'On this point we will never yield. If we did, our personal power at home would not be worth more than a straw.' Thus the danger of a breakdown loomed ahead.

On 31st January the draft treaty was presented to Ismet as planned. He asked for eight days' grace in which to formulate the Turkish reply. Curzon, despite the entreaties of the French and the Italians, refused his request. The Turks were informed that he would leave Lausanne on the evening of 4th February as arranged.

On 3rd February Ismet was presented by the Allies with a few last-minute concessions. Early that afternoon he delivered to them his own last counter-proposals. In these he accepted eighty per cent of the terms. They reflected, in his view, 'sufficient unanimity on fundamental points' for the signature of a treaty of peace. Let it therefore be signed on this basis, and let the remaining terms, reflecting only 'small differences' on certain judicial and economic matters, be held over for later negotiation. Lord Curzon rejected this proposal. In the evening he summoned Ismet to a meeting in his room at the Beau Rivage Hotel. Here he informed him that the treaty as it now stood 'must be signed here and now'. Bompard, the French delegate, supported him. But Ismet remained obdurate. He had gone as far as he could towards judicial guarantees, with a promise to accept foreign assistance in general. He had accepted a number of economic clauses. But the acceptance of those which remained would place Turkey in a position of 'economic servitude'. Bombarded by the Allied delegates with appeals and menaces, he could only murmur wretchedly, '*Je ne peux pas.*'

The meeting broke up. Curzon prepared for his departure. The hall of the hotel was crowded with delegates waiting to assist, as they confidently expected, at the signature of the treaty. Ismet came down the main stairs, took off his bowler hat, bowed right and left to the crowd, forced a smile and walked out of the hotel. He was closely followed by the French and Italian delegates. It became known that the treaty had not been signed.

The American observers made a last-minute bid for a compromise. They called upon Curzon, but found him pacing up and down in his room, 'like an angry bull', wringing his hands and declaring that there was nothing to be done. Leaving him, they went across to Ismet's hotel. 'Ismet,' wrote Admiral Bristol, 'was evidently greatly perturbed and several times rubbed his face in a truly Turkish manner, and used a Turkish expression which means, "My heart is being squeezed. . . . I am wrung with anguish!" ' He agreed confidentially to concede a point on the Capitulations. But this must be contingent on concessions by the Allies on the economic clauses, which he could not accept as they stood. For one thing, he was not entirely sure what they meant. How could he sign unless he knew what he was signing? The Americans hurried to the station to propose a compromise on these lines. But Curzon's train had gone. Next day the world learnt that the Lausanne Conference had broken up, without agreement being reached.

Ismet returned in trepidation to Angora, faced with the ordeal of a vote of confidence to be debated by the Grand National Assembly.

Kemal's victory against the powers of Europe had not made this obstreperous body any easier to handle. The reverse was the case; for it had relaxed some of the pressure towards national unity. The Opposition continued in devious forms their moves against him. In December 1922 they had proposed a change in the law for the election of deputies, confining candidature to those born or five years domiciled within the present frontiers of Turkey. This was aimed at the exclusion of Kemal, who had been born in Salonika and thanks to his military duties had not since lived continuously in any electoral district.

Had he done so, he drily reminded the Assembly, he could not have fought the invader and 'the country of these gentlemen who have given their signatures would likewise be outside the frontiers, which may God prevent'.

He continued, 'I believed and still believe that our enemies would perhaps have even tried to deprive me of the possibility of serving my country by an attempt on my life. But not for a single moment could I have imagined that there were people, be it only two or three, in the High Assembly who shared the same mode of thinking.'

Now, on the occasion of the breakdown at Lausanne, the Opposition deputies chose to vent against Ismet in particular and the Government in general their growing mistrust of the Gazi himself. Day after day in a series of stormy secret sessions, they poured forth their grievances. A victory had been won by the bayonet of Mehmedjik, the Turkish soldier. But now, through the ineptitude of Ismet's diplomacy, the fruits were being sacrificed to the tricks and intrigues of Lord Curzon. The Turkish delegation was a toy in the hands of the British. Procedure was disregarded while deputies interrupted the debates, leaping up from their seats to fire protests at random. 'Why do you cheer instead of weeping?' one cried, while another reiterated at intervals, 'There won't be any peace.' Kemal and Rauf sat through these unseemly proceedings with patience, Kemal intervening with authority at well-chosen moments.

Though the conference had broken down on the economic clauses, these were beyond the comprehension of most of the deputies – including indeed Ismet himself – and were soon referred to committees under the Ministry of Finance, for an expert analysis and report. It was chiefly the prospect of a direct threat to Turkish territory, to the sacred principles of the National Pact, that inflamed them. 'They are selling Mosul to the enemy!' was the loudest cry. The Opposition called for war rather than a peace which ceded an inch of its precious soil to the enemy.

Rauf admitted the importance of Mosul, and confirmed that it lay within the frontiers of the National Pact. But at Lausanne the delegates were trying to liquidate a past of six centuries. The problems were complex and must be seriously and responsibly weighed. People must ask themselves, would the resumption of war be to the country's advantage? How long might it last? What might be its results?

At this a member interjected, 'Only God can know that!'

Rauf replied, 'No doubt. But God has given us a mind that we should think with it. Thus we have thought. . . . We want to negotiate further on the economic problems. We are ready to fight if necessary. But meanwhile we shall do all we can to secure peace.'

Kemal followed Rauf, calling for a cool logical approach to these problems. If they insisted now on the retention of Mosul the result would be war, with not only Britain but the whole world against them. If they postponed the issue for a year, Mosul might be secured by diplomacy. If not, the country would be in a stronger position to fight. The warmongers however were not easily silenced. Their nucleus was a small but vociferous group of

Kemal's personal enemies, who had backing from a section of the press. Their ringleader was one Ali Shükrü, the member for Trebizond, a man of fanatical temperament who had long waged a feud against Kemal and was now systematically stirring up trouble.

After a week of these polemics Kemal determined to bring the debate to a close. He reaffirmed the Government's peaceful intentions and called upon the Assembly to sanction a new general directive to the Cabinet for the resumption of the Lausanne talks. These would not, he explained, cover the position of Mosul, which had already been dealt with. They would mainly concern the country's right to administrative, political, economic and financial freedom. Ali Shükrü's repeated objections brought an outburst from Kemal, 'You have been speaking for a whole week in a way harmful to the country. What is your purpose?' Ali Shükrü protested, 'You have no right to accuse anyone.' Another deputy shouted, 'Is there no security in the Parliament?'

This created a turmoil. Ali Fuad, who was presiding, tried to restore order, but the deputies were uncontrollable. Members of the two groups stood face to face before the rostrum, hurling accusations and threats at each other, with Kemal in the midst of them. At any moment revolvers or other weapons might be drawn. Ali Fuad, in a moment of inspiration, flung the presidential bell between the opposing groups and the clangour was followed by a momentary silence. Of this he took immediate advantage to adjourn the session.

After an interval the members returned to their places and the vote of confidence was taken. It showed less than a two to one majority for Kemal, while a large number of abstentions showed the great gulf which now existed between Parliament and Government. It was virtually a vote of no confidence.

The Lausanne debate touched off a crisis in Angora which was to shake Kemal's position. Ali Shükrü, the principal trouble-maker, continued to rail against Kemal, not only in the Assembly but in the cafés and streets of the town. He denounced his drinking habits; he declared that he was plotting to make himself Sultan. One day Ali Shükrü disappeared in mysterious circumstances. After two days of wild gossip and worried enquiries from his family, the question of his whereabouts was raised in the Assembly.

The deputies at once assumed that Ali Shükrü had been murdered. How otherwise could a man vanish without trace, in a place hardly bigger than a village, for two whole days? Insinuations were made against the Government and against Kemal's own entourage. No country was civilized in which certain men chose to place themselves above the law! Let them be damned a thousand times! Let those treacherous hidden heads be broken! The

Government must take instant steps to solve the mystery and punish the guilty men.

After some days Rauf was able to report to the Assembly that the corpse of Ali Shükrü had been found. Suspicion had fallen on Topal Osman the Laz, the leader of Kemal's Black Sea bodyguard. Investigations now proved his complicity. Ali Shükrü was last seen alive walking away from a café in the market-place, arm-in-arm with a captain in Osman's guard. Later screams and other strange noises were heard from Osman's house. Osman reassured the scared neighbours with the explanation that he had merely been beating up two of his insubordinate soldiers. But early next morning a car arrived at the house and drove away with a load of 'furniture'. The police grew suspicious. Osman disappeared. Not long afterwards a mound of fresh earth was discovered outside the city, with flies swarming over it. The police dug – and only a few feet down found the body of Ali Shükrü, wrapped in sailcloth.

Osman, it later emerged, had in his fierce protective loyalty to his master convinced himself that Ali Shükrü was plotting to kill him. He had thus had him strangled by two of his guard. It was an awkward situation for Kemal, which his enemies readily turned to his discredit. Taking immediate action, he sent emissaries to Osman to give him a chance to confess his guilt. But Osman forcibly denied it. He must thus be disposed of.

Fearing for his own security, Kemal moved down secretly after dark from Chankaya to his former office, near the railway station. Feeling himself once more trapped and surrounded by enemies he was in a highly nervous state. Meanwhile orders were given to round up Osman's force in the morning. The Laz refused to surrender, preferring to fight to the death. Kemal could hear the sounds of the shots on the hill, from the station below. A number of deputies went up to watch the engagement. It ended in the capture of Osman, mortally wounded. He died while being carried away on a stretcher. A dozen of his men had died fighting.

In the Assembly, when Rauf made his statement, the Opposition made the most of the incident. A deputy who had inspected his friend's 'sacred remains' called for curses, which were willingly voiced, against 'these brutes, these monsters' who had crushed him and cut him to pieces. Ali Shükrü was a martyr to the freedom of the nation, to the supremacy of the people. But Ali Shükrü was not dead, for there is life in every death. 'His soul is with us.' The Assembly adjourned for five minutes that the members might pray for his soul. Two of them were granted leave of absence to carry his body to Trebizond. That of Osman, meanwhile, was hanged and exhibited at the gates of the Parliament.

CHAPTER FORTY-FOUR

SIGNATURE OF THE TREATY

CLEARLY, Kemal realized, the moment had come to dissolve his recalcitrant Parliament. This first Grand National Assembly, elected for the conduct of the war, had outlived its purpose. To achieve peace, to vote the sweeping internal reforms which Kemal had in mind for the future, a new Assembly was needed, a body more adult than the old, more moderate, more responsible – and more manageable.

Kemal called upon Rauf to summon an extraordinary meeting of the Cabinet. It took place in his house and continued all night. It was agreed to dissolve Parliament and to hold elections. The First Grand National Assembly met for the last time on 16th April 1923. As a final precaution before the elections it passed, despite some opposition, a new law extending the penalty for high treason, already covering the misuse of religion for political purposes, to the refusal to recognize Parliament and the abolition of the Sultanate. The country then entered upon new elections with party candidates carefully vetted and chosen by Kemal, and Opposition candidates effectively discouraged.

Already, earlier in the year, Kemal had taken two steps to this end. His chief need was for a reliable political instrument. Thus he announced to the press his intention to form a new party, the People's Republican Party, to replace his Parliamentary group, and called upon the educated men of the country to help him in drafting its programme. In due course it published a manifesto. Its programme, which was studiously vague, confined itself to a restatement of the principles on which the new state was founded, together with limited proposals for reform. Kemal, with his empirical approach, did not care in this election to come out into the open with more specific principles, or with any hint of the more fundamental reforms which the new party would be called upon to sponsor.

Next Kemal needed to establish close touch with the people themselves, both to indoctrinate them with his views and to ascertain their own. Thus he went to the country in person, covering, in a month's tour of western Anatolia, much of the ground over which the armies had fought.

Until now, primarily engaged in the business of fighting, he had made few speeches to the general public. But in the course of this month he treated them to thirty-four major orations – some of them lasting as long as six or seven hours – of a patriotic and instructive kind. This was the first of many tours whose routine recalled, in its meetings with officials and notables, that of his early progress through the country to Sivas and Erzurum. But now all was in the open, with personal appearances before crowds thronging around him to hear and to question him. Never before had a Turkish head of state left his capital to address his subjects directly. Thus the Gazi was breaking with precedent to forge a new and personal bond between ruler and ruled.[1]

From now onwards the Turks were to be encouraged to believe that they had a practical say in the government of their country, that its sovereignty did indeed lie in the hands of the people. His was to be, at least in appearance, a 'grass-roots' régime, built not from the top but from the bottom. His task was in its way harder than either the military campaign he had just won or the diplomatic campaign he was waging at Lausanne. It involved the preparation of a conservative and obstinate people for a fundamental revolution in their habits and thought, moreover at a moment when they were tired and inclined to relapse, now that the threat from the enemy was removed, into their traditional apathy.

The chief obstacle that Kemal had to face lay in the forces of religion. To counteract its more reactionary influences became his main concern, as he now talked his way around the country. At the same time he must still pose as the champion of Islam. From the pulpit of a mosque in the bigoted centre of Balikesir, he declared that Islam was the last and greatest of all religious revelations, and moreover one which conformed with logic and reason. After complimenting his audience for their piety and heroism, he instructed them that henceforward the Friday sermon should not be in Arabic but in Turkish, so that all might understand it. Pointing out to them that the Prophet himself had set the precedent of discussing public affairs in the House of God, he then preached not only of the Caliphate but of the negotiations at Lausanne and the principles of the new People's Party – 'a school to give our people political training'.

[1] Some confusion as to his identity persisted, however, for some years to come. Inspecting some soldiers in Anatolia, Kemal once asked, 'Who is God and where does He live?'

The soldier, anxious to please, replied, 'God is Mustafa Kemal Pasha. He lives in Angora.'

'And where is Angora?' Kemal asked.

'Angora is in Istanbul,' was the reply.

Farther down the line he asked another soldier, 'Who is Mustafa Kemal?' The reply was, 'Our Sultan.'

– Irfan Orga: *Phoenix Ascendant.*

In Smyrna, a more advanced centre, he took a different line, speaking more openly of the way in which the Caliphate had deprived the people of their rightful sovereignty, of the religious propaganda which had incited them to fight for the Caliph's army. It was thanks to a belief in 'selfish and ignorant people like these that the Turkish people had for centuries lived in huts made out of mud and rushes, with their bare feet exposed to the merciless attacks of snow and rain'. It was now necessary for them to renounce such fanaticism and regain a proper perspective.

This was where the People's Party came in. It would work for the common welfare of all, regardless of any one class. It would teach them modern methods and so augment the fruits of their labours. Help would be given to farmers and producers, and a forthcoming economic congress in Smyrna would show the world that the new Turkish state was to be formed not with bayonets but with the tools of industry. In a later tour he showed his respect for the peasant as the backbone of the country, declaiming in a speech to the farmers of Tarsus:

> In the past you were allowed all the work and suffering but none of the rewards. And the reason for this? There were few who thought about you. When they thought, it was for one of two reasons: either there was a war in process and they needed you to fight in the army, or the Treasury was empty and your money was needed. All this will be different in the future. We shall be better farmers, better soldiers.

It was a far cry from such places as Tarsus and Balikesir to Lausanne, but Kemal found in such small Anatolian towns a public opinion responsive to news of the peace negotiations – the fruits of the war he had inspired them to fight. At Lausanne, as he later put it:

> centuries-old accounts were being regulated. It was surely neither a simple nor convenient task to find our way through such a mass of old, confused and rubbishy accounts. . . . The Ottoman Empire, whose heirs we were, had no value, no merit. . . . But we were not guilty of the neglect and sins of the past and, in reality, it was not ourselves from whom they ought to have demanded the settlement of accounts that had accumulated during past centuries. It was, however, our duty to bear the responsibility for them before the world. . . . What we demanded from the conference was nothing more than the confirmation in a proper manner of what we had already gained. . . . Our greatest strength and our surest point of support was the fact that we had realized our material sovereignty, had actually placed it in the hands of the nation and had proved by the facts that we were capable of maintaining it.

Such was the general theme. At Smyrna, where the press had come from Constantinople to listen to him, he spoke more specifically. He stressed the sincere desire of the Turkish people for peace. But if the powers at Lausanne failed to appreciate this and allowed the talks to break down once again, Turkey would not hesitate to resume the struggle for the recognition of her claims. The Allies must not mistake her desire for peace as a sign of weakness. Suiting actions to words he called up new classes for military training and recalled others already demobilized. He declared Eskishehir a military zone and let it be known that important troop movements were afoot.

Before starting on his tour Kemal had received news of the death of his mother Zübeyde at Smyrna, where she had gone for the sake of her failing health. On arrival he made a speech over her grave:

> We are leaving my poor mother in the sacred earth of Smyrna. She has been a victim of a period of tyranny and oppression. . . . While I was in Anatolia, I sent a close friend to see her. When she saw him alone, she thought I had been executed. She had a stroke. In three years she wept every night. She almost lost her eyesight. After the war, when I rejoined her, she was barely alive any longer. I suffer a lot at her death. One thing gives me comfort – the fact that the country has been saved from the rule which destroyed it and dragged it to calamity. I swear on my mother's grave and in the presence of God that, in order to protect the supremacy of the people, for which so much blood has been shed, I shall not hesitate to join her in this grave.

Zübeyde, in Smyrna, had met and approved of Latife, with whom Kemal had been corresponding since his return to Angora. It was an exchange of letters which revealed both her love for him and her concern with his affairs. To this he readily responded. Kemal had loved Fikriye after his fashion and had enjoyed her companionship. But she could never have been more than a mistress. What he now needed as head of a Western state was a wife – a woman capable of fulfilling, in the eyes of the people, the image of educated and emancipated womanhood to which he now sought to convert them.

Latife, he saw, could fulfil this role. A few days after the death of his mother, whom Latife had visited during her illness, he went to her house and insisted that they marry at once, without ceremony or publicity. She asked for a few hours' delay. Next day, not a Thursday, the day normally consecrated to Islamic marriages, but a Monday, Kemal went with her to find a *kadi* and asked him to marry them at once. Mastering his surprise and confusion he agreed. The ceremony took place in the European style, at her father's house. In defiance of the Islamic tradition that bride and bridegroom should not see one another until after the ceremony, they took their vows sitting together at a table, he with Kiazim Karabekir as his witness.

After she had had time to settle down in Angora, Kemal took Latife on

A.—13

a 'honeymoon tour', this time covering the main cities of southern Anatolia. He showed her off without the veil as a living symbol of those social reforms which he now intended to introduce, with her help, throughout the country. The women of Turkey henceforward were to be free of this encumbrance and of the state of servitude to the male which it symbolized. They were to have a status of their own, complementary to that of the male. They were to be respected in modern civilized terms, as his own wife was respected. Symbolically she stood at his side, wearing breeches as he did, her white face defiantly revealed beneath a tight black headkerchief. At a parade she would sit astride on horseback beside him, as though, he remarked with satisfaction, she were one of his ADCs.

Kemal at once made it clear how he expected his wife to be treated. On arrival at Adana a group of ladies invited Latife to stay in their house. But Kemal firmly refused, insisting, 'My wife has to stay with me.' There was to be an end to the harem, to the separation of women from men. He took pleasure in showing her off as an educated woman, persuading her to read aloud a poem by Byron which none understood, then another by Victor Hugo, of which a few got the gist. When she interpreted for him with a group of Greek prisoners of war, Kemal looked proudly around as though to say, 'You see what an accomplished wife I have.'

Everywhere besides he was at pains to emphasize the democratic nature of his tour. There was to be an end to those formal ceremonial functions, with exchanges of gifts and elaborate compliments, so beloved of Oriental officials. He wanted to mix with the people, to seem approachable to all. At Mersin he lost his temper with the mayor, who at a dinner insisted on waiting upon him in person, doing so moreover ineptly and provoking him to the irritated comment, 'For God's sake, sit down! Are you a waiter, or the mayor of this city?' Later at a firework display he refused to sit with Latife in the golden thrones provided, and called for a pair of ordinary chairs, on which they sat with the rest of the crowd.

But his overt display of Latife was not wholly popular. It was shock tactics for a traditionalist country, where segregation between the sexes died hard. Sometimes the shock was effective; more often it provided fuel for propaganda against him, the reactionaries assiduously circulating press photographs of the pair to show how 'he exhibits his wife all *décolletée*'.

For all their outward marital harmony, there was soon some friction between Kemal and Latife. This arose over his drinking. As the tour went on he drank more, to relieve the strain of it, but Latife planned subterfuges to prevent him from doing so. On their last evening at Konya a news agency correspondent came to check with him a report of one of his speeches. Kemal approved of it, boasted of the excellence of the speech, then turning to Latife said, 'Ask them to bring a glass of *raki* for this child.' The correspondent realized that Kemal too wanted a drink. But Latife replied that all the bottles had been sent to the train with their baggage. Kemal became furious and shouted at her, 'This is our guest and you don't even offer him a glass of *raki*!' Latife gave in and ordered the drinks to be brought.

With the Assembly now safely dissolved, the time had come for 'little Ismet' to return to Lausanne. The scale and composition of the conference had changed. Here gathered around the table was no majestic assembly of international statesmen. Curzon had disappeared, handing over to Rumbold; the French too were represented by their man-on-the-spot, General Pellé. The conference, deprived of its great figures, was, as Rumbold described it, a 'deflated Zeppelin'. In fact its composition was dictated by the nature of its outstanding problems. The political clauses had been settled; there remained only those which involved economic, financial and judicial matters. These, intricate and crucial in their bearing on the Capitulations, required the attention of technical experts rather than statesmen.

This time 'the backwoodsmen from Angora' had come to the conference table better prepared than before. The Assembly had got through their work quicker than Rumbold expected, and Ismet arrived with a counter-proposal in business-like form, covering the whole system of foreign controls. These concerned chiefly the vested interests of the French, who were thus intransigent from the start, bargaining tenaciously for reparations, for the payment in gold of the interest on the Ottoman Public Debt, for the ratification of concessions obtained before the war from the Ottoman Government.

Their attitude was hardened by a fresh incursion into the economic field – that of the Americans, with whom, on the principle of the 'Open Door', Angora was now starting to do business on favourable terms. With the encouragement of Rauf the Grand National Assembly had granted a concession to the American Chester Group, for railway and harbour construction and other development projects, and its representatives were firmly entrenched in Angora, to the acute suspicion of their European rivals.

Ismet, in standing firm against the French, thus had the encouragement of Ambassador Grew, the American observer, who relieved his fears that the Allies would go to war on these issues. He recorded a seven-hour meeting at which Ismet, until two o'clock in the morning, received treatment at their hands 'which would make the third degree in Harlem police station seem like a club dinner'. Ismet, as Rumbold wrote to Constantinople, was 'between hammer and anvil'. His experience at the hands of the Grand National Assembly had unnerved him. He was for ever aware of the Opposition deputies at home, temporarily silenced by the elections but still lying in wait to discredit him; and now, to crown all, of Rauf, goading and flustering him with an impatient bombardment of telegrams.

Loyal as Rauf had been in his defence of Ismet before the Assembly, he had no great belief in his powers of diplomacy, and now his reports from

Lausanne to the Cabinet suggested a spirit of compromise so disquieting as to prompt a move for his recall. Rauf himself in his sailorly way would have handled things differently. 'Take it or leave it', was the line to adopt with the Allies. The Cabinet had briefed Ismet with specific proposals. Let him now insist upon them as a whole and refuse to be drawn into piecemeal concessions. Ismet complained that Angora allowed him too little latitude, dictating to him not merely the matter of the negotiations but the manner of carrying them out. His deputy compared Rauf's instructions to a series of commands from quarter-deck of the old *Hamidiye*.

Ismet in his growing mistrust gained the impression that they did not reflect Kemal's own views, and thus appealed to him over Rauf's head for an assurance that he would follow the negotiations in person. This Kemal now did, attending meetings of the Cabinet as, out of deference to Rauf, he had not in principle been doing, and sometimes drafting its decisions in person. He became the arbiter between the partisans of Ismet and Rauf by (as he expressed it) 'agreeing with one party and imposing silence on the other'.

The conference dragged on week after week. Nerves grew strained. Once Rumbold lost patience so far as to exclaim in French, that the attitude of the Turkish delegation '*m'écœure*', at which Ismet broke into smiles, taking the word to mean its opposite, 'hearten'. He confessed that he had 'never been so tired in his life'. He took to drinking Green Chartreuse, and developed, into the bargain, 'a dreadful cough'. His irritation with Rauf flared up periodically, goading him to compare Angora's interference with that of the Palace in its direction of the fatal campaign against the Russians in 1877. Once he demanded that Rauf himself should come to the conference in his place, and thus earned a sharp rebuke from Kemal.

Since neither Allies nor Turks wanted war, the issue over each clause was that of finding a formula, and in the end, thanks largely to British conciliatory efforts, formulæ were found which saved all faces. The question of the Debt was reserved for subsequent settlement. Reparations were waived. Economic concessions became subject to negotiation under Turkish law, according to the merits of each. A few foreign legal advisers were accepted for a limited period. Kemal could with justice claim, of the treaty now ready for signature, that 'Capitulations of any description are completely and for ever abolished'.

Rumbold, writing to King George V, described it as 'not a glorious instrument but the least unsatisfactory terms possible'. *The Times* described it as 'a model of generosity and justice', and remarked, in a tribute to the conduct of the Turks at the conference, 'Has Turkey become, by some miracle, a civilized power?' It was signed, in a brightly caparisoned hall of the University of Lausanne, on 24th July 1923, by Rumbold, who alone wore a grey top-hat to the ceremony – 'as if', commented the *Daily Express*, 'it were Ascot'.

Kemal telegraphed his congratulations to Ismet: 'You have thus crowned with a historic success a life which consists of a series of eminent services rendered to your country.' Rauf's congratulations, delayed for a day longer, had a more reluctant ring. He had toned down the draft, prepared for him, with the remark that it gave too much credit to Ismet: 'Have we done nothing here?'

Together he and Ali Fuad brought the news of the signature to Kemal at Chankaya. The Gazi, who had just risen, received his two friends in an Arab burnous, worn as a dressing-gown. He gazed at the historic telegram with evident signs of emotion. Pulling himself together he admitted, 'In these last days I have been hoping that peace would be signed, but I have had constant doubts and hesitations. I always had the fear that these people would change their minds at the last moment. You have given me great joy. I thank you.'

Rauf made an emotional little speech, attributing the success of the day firstly to Kemal himself, then to Kiazim Karabekir, Ali Fuad and Refet. He was happy to have worked in their midst. Ever since Amasya, he confessed, 'I have felt like kissing your hand. But I could never reveal this desire. Now let me express this feeling, which has always been with me, by kissing your hand.'

Kemal brushed the gesture aside as unnecessary. 'Your services to the country,' he said, 'are no less than ours.'

All were in an emotional mood. They drank coffee to steady themselves. They were entertained to dinner by Latife. Kemal remarked that Ismet had left Lausanne for Angora. Rauf, to his surprise, said, 'Yes, he has. And with your permission I too intend to leave.' He announced his intention, now that peace was signed, to relinquish the premiership, before the second Assembly met, and pay a visit to his former constituency, Sivas. He was overtired and having trouble with his stomach. But he made his real reason clear – Ismet's attitude at Lausanne, not only to himself but to the rest of the Cabinet: 'I personally do not wish ever again to come face to face with Ismet Pasha. It is impossible for me to continue to work with him. Since he has signed the peace treaty it seems to me that he should carry out its promises.'

Kemal asked, 'You mean that you won't even greet him when he comes?' Rauf replied, 'No. Please forgive me. But after so many unjust attacks I do not wish to see Ismet Pasha again.'

Kemal tried to soothe him. But Rauf adhered to his resolve to resign. There was more behind it than his disagreement with Ismet. There were his fears for the future. He remembered that evening at Refet's house, before the final offensive, when Kemal had undertaken to relinquish his extraordinary powers once peace was signed. It was now signed; but he showed no disposition to do so. On the contrary, he planned to reinforce these powers by becoming head of the new People's Party, and thus, in Rauf's view, prejudicing from the outset the democratic development of the new Turkish state. In his usual frank manner he spoke to Kemal of his misgivings. He said that he envisaged the Gazi's position as that of an impartial arbiter, a head of state above all parties and individuals. But now he was involving himself in day-to-day politics.

Ali Fuad shared these views, which he had voiced at the time of the party's formation, arguing that Kemal's association with it would prevent the free growth of political parties in a country committed to popular sovereignty. So indeed it had proved in the recent elections, when Kemal had intervened actively, using his commanding position as both head of the party and Commander-in-Chief of the army to preclude the emergence of any Opposition group.

This was to be the dominating issue in the new political phase which now followed the peace. It was the struggle for power between the Gazi in person and the forces of democracy as seen by Rauf and others. Kemal was not at this stage to be drawn into discussing it. He expressed his regret to Rauf at his resignation, to which he replied, 'Do not be sorry, Pasha. You can govern this country with twelve honest men.' He left for Sivas, seen off by his fellow-ministers and a large concourse of friends. Kemal appointed Fethi Prime Minister. Asked why he had not chosen Ismet, he replied, 'I'm keeping him for later.'

Ali Fuad consented to remain for the present vice-president of the Assembly. But three months later he too resigned, to resume his military career, consistent in his mistrust of Kemal's one-party rule. To Kemal he had said, 'Who are now your "Apostles" may we know?' To this he received the airy reply: 'I have no apostles. Those who serve the country and the nation and show merit and ability for service, those are apostles.'

Some days after Rauf's departure, Ismet reached Angora with his fellow-delegates, to be granted an official ovation. Kemal gave a party in his honour at Chankaya. As the conference was being discussed before dinner, Ismet could not in his bitterness forbear from referring to the obstructions he had endured from Rauf and the Cabinet. To Kemal he said, 'You, *you* settled all my difficulties. You saved me by coming to my help. Without you my coffin would have come back from Lausanne. My coffin!'

Fethi reminded him, with some irritation, 'I too was a member of the Cabinet you criticize.' Ismet gave him a curt answer. Both rose to their feet in anger. The ladies grew alarmed, but the gentlemen restrained the combatants. Kemal ordered dinner to be served. But throughout the meal he talked little. A cloud had descended on the guests. It was an awkward homecoming.

In submitting the treaty to the new Assembly for ratification, the Government stressed that no territory within the bounds of the National Pact had been sacrificed, and that there was no thought of conquering or reconquering lands beyond them. Ismet described the treaty as 'the product of the struggles of a whole epoch'. Turkey was no longer an empire, as she had been to her loss for half a century past; she was a sovereign state, like any other in the international field, conscious of her strength and jealous of her independence.

Assessing the treaty years later, in historical perspective, he described it as an instrument of durable peace, because 'both sides were thoroughly tired of fighting, and the sacrifices were confined within bearable and justifiable limits'. It was indeed the only peace settlement signed after the First World War in which one of the central powers was able to demand her own terms from the Allies, and the only one to survive the second as an instrument of peace for the future. For it was a treaty based not on artificial theories but on existing facts. It did credit at once to Kemal's restraint, in renouncing any form of expansion, and to Ismet's obstinacy in pursuing his limited objective. Both had proved adroit in exploiting differences between the Allied powers, both patient in reserving for negotiations such questions as Mosul and the Straits which, as they understood, raised complex international issues, hence could not at once be solved.

Ten weeks after the signature the Allied forces evacuated Constantinople. It was a great day for Harington, whom the Turkish crowds could not help cheering as he drove along the Bosporus with a colour party of guardsmen, none under 6 feet 1 inch tall, as an escort. At the quay guards of honour of the other Allied and Turkish forces met the general, with a huge crowd of Turks pressing behind. When he saluted the Turkish flag the crowd broke, and, 'Before I knew where I was, there were fifteen thousand Turks between me and my wife.' He embarked in the *Arabic*, which blew all her sirens. The *Marlborough* escorted her out, playing 'Auld Lang Syne'. Such was the end of an occupation which had lasted longer than the whole of the First World War.

Not long afterwards the Gazi decided that Turkey should seal the integrity of her territory by fixing her capital in Angora instead of Constantinople, and a draft bill for the purpose was introduced into the Assembly. There was strong opposition from the press and the die-hards of Constantinople. They urged that their city, the seat of the Caliphate, should remain also the capital, as it had been for four hundred and seventy years past – to say nothing of the eleven hundred years of Byzantium before that.

Angora, they argued, was inappropriate on account of its remoteness, its harsh climate, its primitive character, its lack of water and the other amenities of a civilized city. Against this was set its geographical and strategic position, secure against the inroads of the foreigner and above all the fact that, as the symbol of the Nationalist struggle, it had acquired a mystique of its own. Moreover, Kemal himself had a deep mistrust of Constantinople, with its age-old corruption, its insidious traditions and habits of intrigue. Had he not in his youth dated the doom of the Ottoman Empire from the day the House of Osman moved to the Bosporus from the austere spaces of the Anatolian plateau?

Since the bulk of his deputies were Anatolians, Kemal had little difficulty in passing the bill through the Assembly. 'The Seat of the Turkish State,' it read, 'is the town of Angora.' Constantinople would remain the home of the Caliphate; Angora the home of the Parliament, hence the capital of Turkey. It was to become known instead, to the rest of the world, as Ankara, while Constantinople as such was no longer to exist. There was to be left to it none among its various names but Istanbul.

PART THREE

THE RISE OF THE TURKISH REPUBLIC

CHAPTER FORTY-FIVE

PROCLAMATION OF THE REPUBLIC

'THE WAR IS OVER,' it was said in Angora after Lausanne. 'Long live the war.' Mustafa Kemal the Macedonian had reached his first objective. He had saved and revived Turkey; he had transformed a crumbling, straggling empire, beset by enemies, into a compact homogeneous state, recognized by potential friends. Urgency of purpose, tempered by deliberation of method and galvanized by the flame of a fierce vitality had achieved this. A realist in an unrealistic age, he had seen what was possible and had pursued it, with singleness of aim, against friends who doubted him and enemies pursuing what was not. The task had called for a high degree of foresight; a patience which conflicted with his temperament and could be attained only by a rigid self-discipline; an intuitive sense of essentials and an understanding of the psychology of people, friend and enemy alike; an urge to grasp responsibility and use it decisively. Thanks to these qualities the power which Kemal had passionately craved since his youth was now his. He had boasted, 'I'm going to be somebody' – and now, after years of frustration, he was, at the age of forty-two, somebody.

Basically, the work he had done was, for all its political overtones, the work of a soldier, of a man skilled in planning, in organization, in improvisation, in action. What he had to do now called for something more – for the talents of a reformer, a prophet, a statesman. Having saved his country, his next objective was to create a new country. His ambition was nothing less than to transform Turkish society – to sweep away a medieval social system, based for centuries on Islam, and replace it by a new one based on modern, Western civilization.

It was still in the spirit of the soldier that he now faced the new task. There was to be no resting on victory; no relaxing before the new campaign, with the Gazi still in command, was launched. This time it was to be a war with moral, not material, armaments. But its dynamic and its tactics would be similar. As before, it was to be achieved by gradual stages. But the momentum, now that the initiative was his, would be swifter. Far-sighted in planning but pragmatic in execution, Kemal had decided as far back as 1920 that 'the great capacity for evolution that he sensed in the conscience and future of the nation should be kept as a national secret in his conscience and when the time came should be applied to the whole of society'. The time had now come. Turkey was to enter a new phase of her development.

But she was still, as Falih Rifki put it, like a ship which had left harbour for the open sea, and of which only the captain knew the course. What course was he to take? Kemal had made up his mind. Throughout his patient voyage towards victory from Samsun to Erzurum, Sivas, Angora, Smyrna and now Lausanne, his objective had been clear to him. Turkey, he was resolved, must become a Republic.

He was now in a strong position to achieve his design. Victory and an honourable treaty had sealed his prestige. A new Parliament, packed by himself, and a new party, of which he was the founder and leader, had opened up new channels of power. The launching of this drastic reform was now only a matter of timing and tactical handling.

The idea of the Republic had taken concrete shape in his mind during the summer, while the Lausanne conference still sat. Devising a draft formula for its Constitution, he sent it confidentially to Seyyid, the Minister of Justice, who had advised him on the abolition of the Sultanate and previous constitutional matters. Seyyid approved the principle of the draft, from the legal standpoint, and returned it to him with a few proposed changes of detail. It was then laid aside, until peace should be signed.

Kemal now began to try out the idea on his closer associates. At a dinner at Chankaya, at which Falih Rifki and a few trusted journalists were present, he remarked that he had been reading the history of the French Revolution, and had made a few notes on the name Republic and its equivalent in Turkish – *Cumhuriyet*. A dictionary was sent for, and the translation found to be *Chose Publique*. A discussion was held on the exact meaning. Kemal then divulged his plan, which was still incomplete and on which further work remained to be done. His friends must discuss it among themselves, and in good time it would be put to the party. Someone asked him, 'Will you still remain president of the party after you become President of the Republic?' Kemal replied, with a twinkle, 'Between ourselves, yes.' But he protested curtly when another, referring to the duration of the presidential term, suggested, 'For the rest of your life?'

The news spread. For the local press it was still 'off the record'. But Kemal, flying a kite, revealed his intentions to the world in an interview to the *Neue Freie Presse*, a Viennese newspaper. He took the line that the Turkish state was a Republic already, in all but name. The first article of the law which defined it declared that its sovereignty belonged to the people;

the second that the sole representative of the people was the Grand National Assembly.

The two phrases [he continued] may be summarized in a single word: *Republic*. . . . Within a short period of time the form which Turkey has now actually assumed will be confirmed by law. . . . Just as, basically, there is no difference between all the Republics of Europe and America . . . so also Turkey's difference from these Republics is merely a matter of form.

The interview electrified Ankara. The concept of a Republic was one wholly at odds with that of the traditional Moslem state, and this was the first time the ugly word had been uttered in a Turkish context. The threat of the change caused commotion, both in the press of Istanbul and in the lobbies of Parliament, where no serious republican movement had yet existed. Kemal realized that a debate on it might be fatal. The Republic must be forced through by other means before the Opposition had time to unite.

Hitherto the new Assembly had proved responsive enough to his assiduous direction. In its crucial early weeks he seldom missed a sitting, expounding measures before they were debated, making his own views clear, for or against acceptance. Once when the ayes had it, he said, 'Please, will you put down your hands. I see I have failed to explain this point to you.' He did so, making it clear that he wanted rejection – and on the next vote the noes had it. All the time he was patiently instructing the deputies on the nature of a modern Western state. Once a *hoja*, in the course of an oration, asked angrily, 'What does this word "modern" mean?'; to which the Gazi replied, 'It means being a human being, *hoja*. It means being a human being.'

For all this it was a soberer body than the first Parliament, younger, more level-headed and aspiring to live up to Kemal's definition of it as an 'Assembly of Intellectuals'. The wilder backwoodsmen were no longer in their places, to bedevil serious discussion, and the balance had been redressed by a group of writers, journalists and professional men, maturer in mind and with some comprehension of Western ideas.

The Republic was nevertheless such an issue as to stir strong currents of opposition, both from Right and from Left. The die-hards, opposed to any radical changes, sought at all costs to preserve the power of the Caliphate, and some argued that if there were to be a Republic, then the Caliph should be its President. The progressives sought to preserve a balance of power. Some played with the idea of a constitutional monarchy, with the Caliph as sovereign; others favoured the Republic, provided it were a real democratic republic on the Western model – that of France, for example, or America. But they feared lest, in the hands of Kemal, it should become in effect a dictatorship, like the republics of South America or the Soviet Union. Such were the views of Rauf and Ali Fuad – at heart constitutional

monarchists both – whose disappearance at this moment from the parliamentary scene thus suited Kemal's designs. In either case there was resentment at his apparent intention to spring the Republic on Parliament as a
fait accompli.

This was in fact what he planned. As a pretext he engineered a ministerial
crisis. The Assembly was still responsible for the election of ministers, a
privilege which impaired its cohesion by encouraging factional and personal
manœuvres for power. A faction within the party, which Kemal proscribed
as a 'secret Opposition', now put forward two candidates for vacant posts
in the Government – one of them Rauf, for the vice-presidency of the
Assembly, which Ali Fuad had vacated. Kemal objected to these nomina-
tions. Deciding to call the Opposition's bluff, he instructed Fethi and the
other ministers to resign, and to refuse posts in a new Cabinet if chosen.
The Opposition was then left to draw up its own list of ministers.

This was a challenge to Parliament to come out into the open and fight
him – which he knew very well it would be unable to do. He let it be rumoured
that, in the event of a showdown, he was prepared to fight back, with his
Presidential Guard, confident of the support of the army and of his prestige
with the people. The Opposition groups, in the absence of Rauf, tried to
compose their differences and produce a list of ministers acceptable to all –
but in vain. This created a situation in Parliament which Kemal chose to
interpret as anarchy. After the country had been without a Government for
two days he took action. He invited a few friends, including Ismet and
Fethi, to dinner at Chankaya. During the meal he announced, 'Tomorrow
we shall proclaim the Republic.' There was no disagreement. He briefed
Fethi and his colleagues on the tactics to be followed, and the party
broke up.

Kemal was then left alone with Ismet. Together they completed the draft
of the Republic, in the form of changes in the existing Constitutional Law.
To this the sentence was added, 'The form of the Government of the Turkish
state is a Republic.' Its President would be head of state and would be
elected by the Grand National Assembly. He would appoint the Prime
Minister, who would then appoint the other ministers, with the approval
but no longer on the initiative of the Assembly. This assured to him the
power he needed.

Next day the new provisions were put before the People's Party caucus,
the body that now counted in terms of political power. By prior arrangement with Fethi he was called in to 'arbitrate'. He spoke briefly, if only for
the fortuitous reason that he had had a new set of dentures fitted that day,
which shifted insecurely and gave a whistling sound to his voice. But he
spoke coherently. The present form of government was based on a radical
fault. It required each member of the Assembly to participate in the choice
and by implication control of each minister. The disadvantages of this

system had now been proved. They must be resolved in the way he had decided. The draft of the amended Constitutional Law was then read out by Ismet. It aroused murmurs of dismay among members of the party, who resented so sudden a move to change the Constitution. But Kemal's ally, the Minister of Justice, argued that its formula involved no innovation, but sought only to clarify the existing law.

Despite a number of protests the meeting could do little but accept the new Constitution. Its acceptance by the Assembly itself, that evening, was hardly more than a formality. The *hojas* were stunned into silence, while the poet Mehmed Emin ventured to compare the Ankara Republic to the government founded by the Prophet in Mecca, fourteen hundred years before. Kemal was elected its President by 158 unanimous votes. But there were more than a hundred abstentions. The session was closed with prayers for the Republic's future welfare. The news of the proclamation was celebrated throughout the country with a salute of a hundred and one guns. The date of it was 29th October 1923.

Thanking his 'comrades' for their support on this 'historic occasion', Kemal, his eye always on the West (and his dentures now secured) stressed the effect of it abroad. 'Thanks to the new title of its Government, our nation will better succeed in manifesting before the eyes of the civilized world the qualities and merits with which it is endowed. The Turkish Republic will know how to demonstrate by deeds that it is worthy of the position it occupies among the nations.'

He made Ismet his Prime Minister. He knew he could count on him to carry out his intentions in Parliament, as he had done in the field. Of Fethi, with his more liberal outlook, he felt less sure. One evening at Chankaya, when Fethi was announced in the midst of some talk of a 'revolutionary' kind, he had silenced the guests with the words, 'Hush, children, the Government is coming.' He made him president of the Assembly instead. By a masterly technique of timing, surprise tactics and veiled intimidation, Kemal had assumed paramount power over the country. He was a President in triplicate – head of the state, effective head of the Cabinet and of Parliament, head of the only party. When Tevfik Rüştü, his admiring comrade of the Salonika days, compared him to the Holy Trinity itself, 'Father, Son and Holy Ghost', Kemal admitted with a glint in his eye, 'It is true, but don't tell anyone.'

Rauf, in Istanbul, was awoken by the sound of the hundred and one guns. So the Republic, he concluded, was a fact. Its abrupt proclamation, without reference to himself, Ali Fuad or Refet, was to widen the rift between Kemal and his old associates to the point of overt opposition. It aroused outspoken criticism from the Istanbul press, which was freer than that of Ankara – its master's voice. Even an article under the heading of 'Long live the Republic!'

defined the manner of its introduction as 'putting a pistol to the head of the nation'. The powers granted to the Gazi, it was written, were such as had never been granted even to a Sultan. How different from the example of George Washington, who had retired to his farm while his Parliament, before electing him President, spent six years working out a Constitution!

These views reflected in principle those of Rauf and his adherents. In view of the failure of the attempt at constitutional monarchy, Rauf now favoured a Republic. But its constitution should have been carefully studied and debated in the Assembly before it was proclaimed. As to the new method of choosing the Cabinet, which had been rejected by the previous Assembly, he said, 'You speak of having a strong Government. What I understand by a strong Government is an experienced Cabinet which knows its duties and its rights and which is based on the supremacy of the people. I was astonished to hear that some people see a strong Government as one which rules the country with the fist.' Rauf's words to the press were wilfully misinterpreted in Ankara. Kemal, seeing Rauf and his group as a potential Opposition, sought to discredit him, and for the purpose used the smear of reaction. Rauf had paid a courtesy visit to the Caliph and from this it was easy to impute to him a plot that the Caliphate should now play a political role.

Such was the atmosphere in which Rauf now left for Ankara, seen off by Ali Fuad, Refet, Kiazim Karabekir, an ADC of the Caliph, and a crowd of followers who included naval personnel and medical students. Kiazim Karabekir had supported Rauf and the rest with a statement, 'I am in favour of the Republic, but I am against personal rule.' Thus the four other fathers of the Revolution were now ranged openly against Kemal.

At this juncture Kemal, while walking in his garden, collapsed with a heart attack. It proved to be slight, but he was unconscious for long enough to feel, as he put it to Ali Fuad, that he had visited the other world for a while. Now his doctors had cut him down to two or three cigarettes a day and prescribed a diet which Latife was imposing with strictness. Fuad urged him to take care of his health from now onwards. At his age he had after all completed only half of his natural span. Kemal reassured him. The doctors had forbidden him *raki* but allowed him an occasional glass of whisky – as they had allowed it to Abdul Hamid when he too was forbidden *raki*.

On account of his condition, Rauf had only a brief talk with Kemal at Chankaya, in which he forbore from raising political issues. He found himself cold-shouldered in the Assembly. He was summoned to appear before a meeting of the party, to justify his statements to the press. These, it was alleged, were calculated to weaken the Republic, and implied his intention to form a party in opposition to it. Ismet, who presided over the meeting, took an uncompromising line. In disciplinarian tones, drawing parallels from wartime events, he stressed the need for unity of opinion at this second vital stage in the national struggle. Rauf, by these statements of his, was threatening the country with anarchy. He implied support by him of the Caliph, declaiming, 'If at any time the Caliph takes it into his head to interfere with the destiny of this country, we shall not fail to execute him!' Finally he enquired whether Rauf meant to withdraw his hostile statements and remain within the party, or adhere to them and leave it to form a party on his own.

Rauf replied to this with frankness and dignity, reiterating his belief in the sovereignty of the people, and insisting (as indeed he had done to the press) that there was no conflict between himself and the Government. His statement had been made from the conviction that the only honest policy was to express freely his own ideas and opinions. He had no intention of forming an Opposition party. But if his fellow-members chose to dismiss him from the People's Party, he would accept their verdict. To allow them to decide freely, he left the meeting, uttering the words, 'Personalities are not eternal. Ideas are eternal.'

His speech was greeted with cheers, and Ismet, sensing the feeling of the meeting in his favour, did not press his demands. Next day it was stated in a communiqué that Rauf had made it clear that he was in favour of the Republic and against the monarchy. He would remain in the party, which was satisfied that a false interpretation had been placed on his statement to the press.

Ali Fuad, before leaving to take up an army inspectorship at Konya, tried to reassure Kemal as to Rauf's views. He was in favour of the Republic, 'provided it does not sacrifice the principles of popular supremacy and you yourself remain above the whole organization'. Knowing of Rauf's predilection for British institutions, Kemal commented sceptically, 'The Kingdom of England is based on the supremacy of the people. But the head of it is a King.' It did not yet suit him to quarrel openly with Rauf and Ali Fuad. But later, seeking to discredit Rauf's motives, he declared that the decision in his favour 'gave to Rauf Bey and his friends the opportunity of still working for some time in the party to accomplish its overthrow'.

CHAPTER FORTY-SIX

ABOLITION OF THE CALIPHATE

KEMAL'S SECOND and more radical move followed a few months later.
Like a general following up an advantage, with a secure base behind him,
he proceeded swiftly towards his next planned objective. This was nothing
less than the complete disestablishment of Islam, the final separation between
the spiritual and the temporal power.

Always careful, until the military victory was won, to imply in public
the orthodoxy of his religious views, Kemal had over the past years been
speaking more freely and critically on the subject of religion. He still professed himself a believer, but a rational believer, for whom Islam was a
'natural religion', in harmony with reason, science, knowledge and logic.
He was strongly opposed to fanaticism, 'a poisonous dagger which is
directed at the heart of my people'. He took to task those who pretended
that a modern outlook was against the Moslem religion. The Friday sermons
in the mosques should be in harmony with the truths of science and knowledge; the preachers should follow closely the political and social conditions
of the civilized world. That the people might understand them, the sermons
in future must be delivered in Turkish, not in an ancient dead language.

For centuries the Turks had 'always walked from the East in the direction
of the West'. They would continue to do so, but this meant that the 'moral
treasure' of the Caliphate must finally go. Was it not both a symbol and a
rallying-point for those dark forces of 'religious reaction'? Here, as at
certain previous stages in his campaign, Kemal's task was made easier by
an ill-judged foreign intervention. The Aga Khan and Ameer Ali, another
distinguished Moslem leader, wrote a letter to Ismet, pointing out that the
separation of the Caliphate from the Sultanate had increased its significance
for Moslems in general, begging the Turkish Government to place it 'on a
basis which would command the confidence and esteem of the Moslem
natives, and thus impart to the Turkish state unique strength and dignity'.
This letter was published by three Istanbul newspapers before it reached

Ankara. It led to the summoning of a secret session of Parliament, where it caused a tumult of indignation. In Kemal's adroit hands its contention that the Caliphate was a link with the past and with Islam was alone sufficient to ensure its immediate end.

The way thus became clear for him to go ahead, and 'cut out this tumour of the Middle Ages' – the Caliphate. The news of the abolition of the Caliphate was foreshadowed, as that of the foundation of the Republic had been, by a foreign periodical, this time the *Revue des Deux Mondes*. Here in an interview (given, in fact, some months before) Kemal, playing on two meanings of the word, declared that inherently Caliphate meant no more than administration or government. With the existence of another administration and Government it became, he implied, redundant. The Caliphate had never enjoyed universal jurisdiction over the Moslem world, as had the Papacy over the Catholic world. The office was an Arab institution adopted by a former Turkish Sultan, whom millions of Moslems had never acknowledged as their spiritual ruler. The new Turkey was not irreligious, but needed a religion stripped of artificiality, which implied nothing contrary to reason or hostile to progress. The Turkish press was carefully briefed on similar lines.

Kemal chose the fourth anniversary of the Grand National Assembly as an appropriate occasion on which to introduce his proposal. He did so with the words: 'It has now become a plainly evident truth that it is necessary to liberate and to elevate the Islamic religion ... from its position of being a tool of politics, in the way that has been traditional for centuries.' He then put forward three main points: the Republic must be protected from every attack; the principle of unity in instruction and education must be applied to it; and 'in order to secure the revival (*sic*) of the Islamic Faith' religion must cease to be a political instrument. According to a routine which had now become common practice, these points were discussed at a meeting of the party, which drafted the necessary laws. Thus, as Falih Rifki expressed it, were 'the bridges attaching Turkey to the Middle Ages to be blown up'. The resulting scenes in the Assembly itself were so fiery as to recall to him etchings of the French Revolution. At one moment, during a brief suspension of the debate, orators were climbing on to chairs and tables in the lobbies, and shouting themselves hoarse for the expulsion of the Ottoman family; at another, turbaned *hojas* were running in and out of the Gazi's room, declaring themselves ready to abolish the sacred Book itself rather than listen to the terrible pleas being made in the Chamber for the abolition of that religious instruction on which their power depended. But in this relatively sober new body the debate was easily enough managed by Kemal and Ismet, with the aid once more of the Minister of Justice.

The Caliph was deposed and his office abolished; the members of his dynasty were for ever forbidden to reside within the frontiers of the Turkish

Republic; the Ministry of Religious Affairs was disbanded, the historic office of Sheikh of Islam ceased to exist, the revenues of the Pious Foundations were confiscated; and all religious schools were transferred to the secular arm. By a further decree a month later the religious courts of the *Sheriat*, which still administered the laws relating to such matters of family and personal status as marriage, divorce and inheritance, were closed, and a Civil Code based on that of the Swiss planned to prevail over all.[1]

On the night of the Assembly's decision the Caliph, Abdul Mejid, was awoken in the Dolma Bahche Palace by the Chief of Police and a party of officials, who instructed him to leave Turkey at five o'clock in the morning. He was overcome with emotion, but soon recovered his dignity so far as to request that he be allowed to pack some personal possessions, and that provision be made for the women of his seraglio. With indecent haste – since the Government was taking no chances with public opinion – he was hurried off by car to Chatalja, whence he took the train in the evening to Switzerland. Here he was held up at the frontier on the grounds that polygamists were not allowed into the country. But after a delay he was provisionally admitted, pending a later enquiry into his marital situation.

In Istanbul the superstitious noted that this last head of the Ottoman family had left Turkey on a Tuesday, the same day of the week as his forbears had chosen to enter Constantinople. On the following Friday the prayer at Santa Sophia contained for the first time no mention of the Caliph. It read, 'Oh God, grant Thy protecting aid to our Republican Government and the Moslem nation. Make eternal the glory of the Moslems and raise the flag of Islam, which rests upon the Republic of Turkey, above all other flags and make them live by the spiritual Prophet!'

In a few hours Kemal had swept away an epoch of history. He had done so through an unsurpassed faculty for imposing his ideas upon others – Parliament, party, or the press – and an uncanny sense of the psychological moment at which to impose them. He was proved right in anticipating that the abolition of the Caliphate would cause little disturbance, whether at home or abroad. With the abolition of the Sultanate, achieved on a wave of popular indignation against the actions of the Sultan in person, the Caliphate had become little more than a vestigial survival. In the Moslem world, its abolition created a certain initial dismay, especially in India where the Turkish Revolution had been seen as a fight by a Moslem state for its freedom, with Kemal as the 'Sword of Islam'. But this soon subsided as the truth became clear. The Caliphate, deprived of its temporal, hence

---

[1] A last-minute attempt to rescue the Caliphate was made through an emissary, claiming to represent Indian and Egyptian Moslems, who suggested to Kemal that he himself should become Caliph. He refused, pointing out realistically that the various Moslem sovereigns would be unlikely to execute his orders as Caliph, hence the role would be illusory.

its political power, no longer had any reality. A prominent Turkish journalist might well enquire, 'What is that which has been abolished?'

For a century past Turkish secular reformers had been waging a slow battle against religious conservatism. Kemal, abruptly accelerating it and bringing it to its logical end, became the first ruler openly to assault and to vanquish the entrenched forces of an orthodox Moslem state. But though he might, by a single act of his Grand National Assembly, abolish the political power of the Islamic religion, he could not neutralize its spiritual and social influences, and indeed did not pretend to interfere with freedom of religious conscience. Islam was more than a code of belief; it was a system of living. God still ruled over the minds and the souls and directed the lives of the bulk of the Turkish people, and would continue to do so. The Caliphate itself might be forgotten. The replacement of religious by secular schools, with a scientific positivist curriculum, was to have profound effects on the intellectual development of future Turkish generations. But this in its turn was to have its counterpart in the survival of an 'underground' Moslem force, widespread in its influence, which was often to erupt to the surface, facing Kemal with a recurrent and radical problem during the years of reform which lay ahead.

CHAPTER FORTY-SEVEN

THE PROGRESSIVE PARTY

ANKARA, the capital of the Republic, grew slowly. The new deputies to the second Grand National Assembly, many of them used to the civilization of Istanbul and other Westernized cities, the civil servants who came in their hundreds now that Istanbul was no longer the seat of government, were disconcerted by its primitive character. Furniture and other household utensils were unobtainable, since the Armenians, who once manufactured and sold them, had fled, leaving Ankara without shopkeepers or artisans. There was little or no electric light. 'Rooms to let with electricity' was an infrequent advertisement.

Men still slept ten or twelve to a room. Women were scarce, fearing to brave such discomforts and leaving their husbands grass widowers. A deputy, seen one day with his wife unveiled in the street, caused unfavourable gossip in Parliament. The local inhabitants, loyal as they were to the cause, tended to hold aloof from the intruders. They spoke a different dialect, making it hard to negotiate for the purchase of building land, of which, however, they were too ignorant to appreciate the value.

In the summer the land was a dust-bowl; at other seasons a muddy morass. The mayor wrung his hands: 'You clamour for roads to be built, but at the same time you don't want dust.' The landscape, once green with vineyards and forests, had succumbed through the centuries to neglect and erosion. A single pine tree grew before the Parliament building, and deputies reassured one another, 'Look, it is growing quite well.' In the winter the snows were such that dinner guests might have to stay for two or three nights. Rooms were heated by primitive stoves, which often had to be moved out to make room for the guests. As one of them drily remarked, 'There can be no civilization with a temperature below zero.'[1]

[1] In the wintry weather there were often rumours of wolves roaming the town. Once after an official reception at Ismet's house, no cars could drive away on account of a heavy fall of snow. The British Ambassador (by then Sir George Clerk), as he set off light-heartedly to walk, threw out the macabre observation, 'If we are torn to pieces, it will at least be the first time that tail-coats and opera-hats have been left behind by wolves.'

There were a few rough eating-houses. But since prohibition still reigned it was hard to get a drink, and a drink in this atmosphere was needed. It was served only in one of them, in discreet doses, with the connivance of a henchman of the Director of Public Security. Some members were lucky enough to possess vineyards, where they distilled their own liquor illegally and were even known to drink it before it had cooled. But up at Chankaya the drink flowed without interruption.

An innovation now on these evenings around the Table was the presence of Latife. Not a wife to remain in the background, she made her personality felt. From the start of the marriage, Kemal had drawn from her companionship a stimulus such as no woman had yet given him; moreover, practical help and advice in his work, for she still acted to some extent as his 'secretary'. She was intelligent and well educated; she was self-confident, with ideas of her own; they could hold serious discussions together. Here, as he saw it, was a relationship between man and wife on equal terms, such as prevailed in the West. He discussed with her especially his plans for the emancipation of women.

At home Latife, as their living embodiment, did him credit enough at his table. But she was not always tactful. She tended to run the house as her own and showed ominous signs of trying to run Kemal as well. She behaved rather as the wife of any army officer, seeing it as her role to tame and civilize the confirmed bachelor she had married, to cure his rough ways, to introduce order and refinement into a home which, in her eyes, derived too much from casual garrison habits. She sought to model it rather on that of her own family in Izmir (as Smyrna was now to be called), with its more correct – and as she was inclined to imply, more civilized – social standards.

She tried to order his dinner-parties, demanding to know in advance just how many guests were expected, and objecting to those she disliked; she insisted that wives should be invited with their husbands as in respectable Westernized households. For a while she even introduced evening-dress, causing many to decline the invitation who, in this backwoods 'capital', did not possess it. One evening the guests, arriving in dinner-jackets, were disconcerted to find a palm court orchestra playing in the hall, and amused to see Kemal coming downstairs to greet them, likewise dressed, with a shrug of the shoulders and a mock-martyred smile on his face. Kemal disliked all social pretensions, and this was not the way he cared to entertain his friends, unless on a formal occasion. He was a natural host, polite in his manner and assiduous in his attention to guests, but he liked to do things in his own easy way.

Latife was omnipresent, a short stocky figure sitting at the head of the table, even on a bachelor evening when he drank with his cronies. She would try to lead the conversation. For, as the favourite spoiled child of her father, she liked to be listened to – and Kemal did not take easily to the listener's role. Receiving foreign visitors, she would presume to speak for Kemal. To Ward Price of the *Daily Mail* she said in excellent English, 'If I tell you anything you may consider it just as authoritative as if you had it from the Gazi himself.' She passed on information to Kemal, which was not always reliable and sometimes made mischief.

But where Latife most erred in her psychology was in seeking too obviously to moderate his drinking habits. She tried to cut down the drink at the table. She would come into the room and exclaim before his friends, 'What's this, Kemal, drinking again?' She would move to break up the party at a reasonable hour. She was even known to bang on the floor above, as a hint that it was time for him to come up to bed. A clash of strong wills, of high-strung temperaments loomed ahead of them.

Kemal found a frequent refuge on the model farm which he was developing on the slopes around his former headquarters at the Agricultural School – an easy ride from Chankaya. Since his boyhood there had grown in him a feeling for nature. Partly it was the love for growing things of a man who had spent much of his life in harsh barren places. He liked to see and with his creative spirit to make the desert bloom. The sight of a pine tree gave him a sense of almost pagan veneration. Once, while riding with Ismet, then his chief of staff, near Diyarbekir, he had exclaimed, 'Find me a new religion.' 'Let it be a religion,' Ismet answered, 'whose form of worship is to plant trees.' He admired the old trees of Istanbul, but liked better to see a tree growing day by day before his eyes.

He planned and supervised in person the planting of the orchards at his farm. But the older trees must not be sacrificed. Once, while driving through it, he stopped his car and exclaimed, 'There was a gum tree there. What has become of it?' Nobody knew, but he remembered it as the one living green thing in the days of the war, when the farm was still almost a desert. 'It was a puny old tree,' he said, 'but it was alive. It smelled good in the spring.' He gave orders for the preservation of all old trees in future.

The farm was eventually to become an experimental station for the nation's forestry and agriculture. But at first it was his own personal play-ground, where his mood was always relaxed. Here he smiled at the world and at himself, at the fact that this 'estate' of his would never pay its way. Tapping new sources of water, he created two pools amid the trees, one small and shaped like the Sea of Marmara, one large and shaped like the Black Sea. In one he installed a fountain, which his manager turned on one evening after fitting fairy lights around it. At the sight of the coloured water, Kemal joked in a peasant idiom, 'Oh you, Kemal, did you ever study agriculture? No. Are you a farmer? No. Was your father? No. There is reason for even the waters to mock you for poking your nose into things you know nothing about.'

Kemal still thought of Fikriye. He had corresponded with her intermittently during her spell in a sanatorium in Munich, and later when her health had improved in Paris. There she had heard the news of his marriage. Pining away from her love for him and now tormented by jealousy, she returned to Turkey. She wrote to him from Istanbul to announce her arrival. Kemal, whose affection for Fikriye survived, although he did not reciprocate her love, hoped in some way to reconcile her with Latife. But she came to Ankara and appeared at Chankaya one day without warning. Here she was told that the Gazi was still asleep. She said she would wait, and retired to the lavatory.

She stayed there so long that the two *aides* who had received her grew worried. For they had noticed her distraught appearance. One of them tried the door and, receiving no response, broke it open. He saw Fikriye putting a revolver into her bag. He pretended not to notice, but for Kemal's safety explained to her that the Gazi could not see her just now, and asked her to leave. He escorted her to the gates, where she got into her carriage. She drove to a neighbouring house, where a cousin was staying. But he was not at home. She then took the revolver from her bag and shot herself dead, there in the carriage. In her desperation she had perhaps come to shoot Kemal, or Latife, or both of them – or to shoot herself before him, as a reproach for his treatment of her. More probably, she had no clear idea of what she meant to do.

Kemal was troubled by her death, and remained taciturn and morose for some time afterwards. It would not occur to him to feel guilty – no more than he felt guilty for the thousands of men he had sent to their deaths in battle. But Fikriye was the woman to whom his affection had come nearest to love.

Kemal liked, in his vanity, to be loved, and throughout his life chose women who took the initiative in showing their feelings. But he could not endure to be loved too much, to become tied by a woman's emotions, whatever form they might take. In each of these two women in his life they took the form of possessiveness. Fikriye's fault lay in clinging to Kemal, her misfortune in becoming sick, hence unable to disguise her dependence upon him. Latife's fault lay in seeking to lead him. Kemal would not marry Fikriye because he wanted a wife who would stand beside, not behind him. On the other hand, the last thing he wanted was a wife who, like Latife, might seek to stand before him.

The issue between Kemal and his old friends had now to be joined. Bent as he was on full powers, in the operations for reform as in the field of battle, it had become clear, after the proclamation of the Republic, that his four co-founders of the Revolution – Rauf, Refet, Ali Fuad and Kiazim Karabekir – were to be denied a fair share in its fruits. The latent differences between them, kept under control before victory was won, now erupted to the surface. With the possible exception of Ali Fuad, they were not personally his kind, nor he theirs. Socially, they had roots which he lacked. Morally, they were imbued with a loftier spirit of idealism. Kemal's own ideals were tempered by expediency and above all by his ruthless sense of realities. His head ruled his heart. He had a colder, more penetrating intelligence than they.

Their differences now proved fundamental. Kemal was embarking on a social revolution. Rauf and his friends, at this stage, preferred social evolution. What need was there for hurry, for sudden and radical change? Give the people time to settle down after their ten-year upheaval. Give them security from brigandage and aid in recultivating their lands. Let social reforms come gradually in response to their needs and demands. Sovereignty was theirs. Let them exercise it through their own representative institutions, as it was exercised in the democratic countries of Europe. They had an honourable peace. Let them now have two or three years of good government and after that decide, through a referendum, what kind of régime they would prefer. Thus spoke the voice of the liberal Turkish gentleman.

Kemal's mind worked in a more practical way. To bring his country into line with the West he had set up a democratic system in which, on a long-term view, he believed. He stood by his Occidental Assembly. But it needed, on the short-term view, a President exercising some degree of autocracy – a power which, though he would not himself have admitted it, was in character Oriental.

Kemal knew his people too well to have any illusions as to their political maturity. They were still an Oriental people culturally backward and temperamentally unfitted for the literal application of Western democracy. They could not yet rule; they required to be ruled. The strong religious authority of the Sultan-Caliph needed to be replaced by an equally strong secular authority; and this for the present only Kemal himself, by his personal manipulation of Parliament, could provide. Rauf and the rest, by the integrity of their principles and the moderation of their outlook, threatened to undermine it and thus to prejudice that process of reform which no one else but he, as he saw it, had the foresight to plan and the capacity to execute. Here was a struggle for power, with his friends as with his enemies which, in alliance with Ismet and Fevzi – the two latecomers to the Revolution – and his less scrupulous henchmen, must soon be fought out. It was a struggle between the forces of a liberal democracy, literally interpreted, and those of a democratic structure conditioned by one-party government and personal rule.

It brought out the Oriental in Kemal. An atmosphere of intrigue now permeated the ante-rooms of Chankaya and the lobbies of the Assembly. Schemers and informers flourished, feeding him with mischievous gossip. He grew cold, sly, suspicious of the motives of all who might stand in his way. He launched whispering campaigns to make mischief against Refet and Rauf, minimizing their services to the country and insinuating that they favoured reaction. A useful instrument to him in his various stratagems was Rejep (Peker), his Minister of the Interior, a petty despot of ruthless character and Germanic aspect, who issued a press statement in Istanbul that activities aimed against reform would be punished by the same methods as in the War of Independence.

In this atmosphere Rauf, Ali Fuad and Kiazim Karabekir met together in Rauf's house in Shishli in the autumn of 1924, to decide on a course of action. They agreed on support for Kemal's reforms, but insisted that these should benefit national, not sectional interests; they would strive to prevent the Republic from becoming an instrument for the rule of any one person or group; they would take their seats in the Assembly and work through its machinery to these ends, with other friends who might share their opinions.

While they conferred, Kemal was on tour with Latife. He returned to Ankara in time for the reassembly of Parliament. A few days before it Kiazim Karabekir, according to a plan prearranged with the rest, resigned his army inspectorship on the grounds that his recommendations were ignored by the War Ministry, and that he wished to resume his functions as a deputy. Ali Fuad meanwhile had come to Ankara. He did not see Kemal, who claimed that he had asked him to dinner at Chankaya on his arrival, but could not locate him – a claim which Fuad attributed to deliberate ill-will on the part of his entourage. Next day he handed his own resignation to Fevzi, the Chief of the General Staff, who showed some dismay.

The two resignations touched off a crisis, which Kemal chose to see as a 'great plot' by the generals, in concert with Rauf to overthrow him in the Assembly with military backing. Reviving, for different motives, the argument he had used fifteen years earlier against Enver, he decreed that the army must at all costs be eliminated from politics. Obtaining, for the sake of consistency, the resignation of Fevzi from Parliament, he requested those of his six army corps commanders stationed in different parts of the country. Only two of them refused, preferring to retain their seats and thus losing their commands.

Rauf publicly reaffirmed his support of the Republic and ridiculed the implication that he and his friends were planning a military coup. He had been one of the first to deplore any interference of the army in politics. Was it likely that, at his time of life, having done his duty to his country, he would retire into the mountains like a Chinese general to form a Government of his own? All he sought was to prevent any one group from monopolizing the power that rightly belonged to the Assembly.

It was on this ground that the Opposition planned to force an issue. The occasion for the crucial debate was what Rauf described as the 'tremendous scandal' of the resettlement of the Turkish immigrants from Greece, under the Lausanne Treaty, of whom an alarming percentage had died from neglect and maltreatment. The Opposition criticism was outspoken. The debate was stormy, with many bitter exchanges between Rauf, who pressed for a commission of enquiry, and Rejep, who accused him of treachery against the Republic. At one moment Rauf was interrupted with the taunt that he should 'go back to the country from which your father and your ancestors came' – a reference to his Caucasian origins. Ismet, however, evaded a division on the issue by turning it into a vote of confidence in the Government, which he easily won.

This was more than Rauf and his fellow-critics could stomach. Feeling unable to remain in the People's Party, they resigned from it in a body and came out into open opposition by forming a party of their own. Rauf in his letter of resignation protested that the form of the debate had destroyed all chance of unity and that he preferred to work independently. Thus Kemal's new Republic was to taste for a spell the methods of Western two-party democracy.

The new party thus founded in November 1924 was at first named the Progressive Party. When its rival became the People's Republican Party, it stressed its own republicanism by becoming the Progressive Republican Party. From the start it aspired not to oust Kemal and to form an alternative Government, but merely – as Rauf defined its aims to an American journalist – to curb and limit his authority. It was to be in a sense a permanent minority pressure-group, standing up for the rights of free speech and discussion and criticism, and hoping thus to influence the Government from within. The party contained some thirty members, all of whom had resigned from the People's Party. Kiazim Karabekir was its president, thus giving it high prestige, for hitherto he had kept relatively clear of politics, confining himself to his military duties and refusing all Government appointments. The party did not intend at first to go to the country and put up its own candidates for vacant seats in the Assembly; it would simply support Independent candidates. But it set up party organizations in Istanbul and three other provincial centres, with a view to intervention at a later stage. Had it chosen to admit the more conservative deputies to membership, it might have obtained on occasion a majority. But it did not, despite the accusations of its enemies, care to be linked with reactionary forces or to create a serious split in the Assembly.

It claimed to be Turkey's first political party conceived on Western lines. In the past the Turkish 'parties', including that of the Union and Progress, had been little more than personal power-groups of no consistent political colour. The People's Party itself was based on no specific programme, but only on a series of general principles, such as all might accept. The Progressives, on the other hand, drew up a full programme and a party constitution of their own. This they submitted to the Minister of the Interior for official recognition, which was formally granted.

In its declaration, it stressed that its function was to maintain equilibrium and guard against autocracy within the constitutional framework. It stood for national unity and individual liberty, free from oligarchic or personal pressure. It affirmed its respect for religious opinions and beliefs, thus following a formula used in the West to stress the dissociation of religion from politics, but here in the East laying itself open, as it proved, to the reverse interpretation.

The various points in its programme differed from the principles of the People's Party in several important respects. The President of the Republic must remain above party, obliged on election to resign his seat in the Assembly. There must be no modification of the Constitution without a mandate from the electorate. There should be first degree in place of second degree elections, bringing democracy closer to the people through direct representation in smaller and more local constituencies. Further, the law alone should reign, nor should judges be removed or transferred without their consent; and administration should be decentralized, with the election in place of the appointment of mayors and the granting of more powers to local authorities, especially in the field of education. The party produced also an economic programme, which differed from that of the Government in giving more scope to free enterprise and encouraging foreign capital investment. The press was to be free, and so was discussion within the party itself. Its meetings were to be open, like those of the parties in Europe, whereas those of the People's Party were secret.

Initially the attitude of the People's Party to its Progressive renegades was to treat them as suspects, endangering the security of the Republic. But within two months Kemal found it expedient to appease the new Opposition by removing their main enemy, Ismet, from the premiership, on the grounds of illness, and replacing him with Fethi, with his more liberal views. For a time the Progressives nourished a hope that this change of personalities might lead to a change of mentality. The extremists in the People's Party, seeking power for themselves by encouraging the arbitrary power of Kemal, tried but failed at a party meeting to induce Fethi to hold aloof from the Opposition. Thus the position of the moderates was strengthened.

For the next few months the Progressives played an active and not wholly ineffective part in the Assembly. They had constructive contributions to make in the budget debates, on such issues as economic policy and administrative reform. On defence policy they strongly opposed – but without success – a manœuvre of Kemal further to strengthen his power through a Supreme Military Council, with a Chief of the General Staff independent of ministerial and thus of parliamentary control. But Fethi, steering a course between the two parties, was often, for all his good intentions, in a quandary. Under pressure, he found it necessary to close down an Opposition newspaper for likening the People's Party to a parasite, and thus provoked fierce attacks from the Progressives.

The atmosphere was not improved by a brawl in Parliament, fatally injuring an Opposition supporter, Halid Pasha. Halid had unearthed the story of a corrupt deal by which a group of Kemal's henchmen – including Arif, his old comrade-in-arms – were drawing money from a state industrial enterprise to finance a secret political campaign against his opponents. He taxed them with this in the lobby of the Assembly, and a violent dispute followed, in which revolvers were drawn. Halid, a man of hot temper, flung an adversary to the ground and might have killed him but for the restraint of his friends. Emerging from the Chamber to see the fight, another deputy, with the apparent encouragement of those who stood by, then drew his revolver on Halid, and shot him in the back.

He died five days later. Despite strong protests in the Assembly, no action was taken against the culprit, who was declared to have acted in self-defence. The incident, however, could not easily be hushed up, and caused general disquiet. But now a disturbance of graver and more national import occurred. An insurrection flared up among the Kurds, in the remote highlands of south-eastern Turkey.

CHAPTER FORTY-EIGHT

THE KURDISH REVOLT

THE KURDS, a feudal people of separate race and language to the Turks, were a dissident minority of combative temperament and extreme religious beliefs, who had given periodic trouble to a succession of Ottoman Governments. After the war their aspirations to freedom were encouraged by the Allied move, at the Peace Conference, to create an independent Kurdistan, and they were now adroitly playing off the British, in the region of Mosul and beyond the frontiers of Irak, against the Turkish central Government.

The leader of the revolt, which broke out in the Dersim region of the upper Euphrates, was one Sheikh Said of Palu, the rich hereditary chieftain or 'abbot' of the local Nakshibendi dervishes. He was a picturesque and illiterate overlord who lived on – and largely for – the vast herds of sheep which he bred and grazed on the pastures of his tribesmen and increased at their expense by the exploitation of his religious prestige and authority. His influence extended, through a series of judicious dynastic marriages, over the powerful sheep-owning families of the neighbouring mountains. These feudal powers seemed now to be threatened by the new 'Turkified' Government of Ankara.

Bent on their retention in an autonomous Kurdistan, the sheikh now stirred up his tribesmen against the abolition of the Caliphate and the godless policy of the Kemalist Government. On 13th February 1925 'charged by God' after some weeks of assiduous propaganda, he proclaimed the revolt. Rising beneath the green Islamic banner, in the name of the restoration of the Holy Law, his forces roamed through the country, seized government offices, imprisoned gendarmes and marched on the important cities of Elaziğ and Diyarbekir.

At first Parliament made little of the affair, treating it as a local outbreak of brigandage. The situation, so Fethi maintained, could be brought under control by martial law in the region, and a plan of military action was prepared by Fevzi. The success of his operations could not be seriously in doubt, with the army still mobilized and only a few bands of wild Kurdish irregulars to contend with.

But the People's Party extremists took an opposite view. They preferred to see the rebellion as an attempt at a counter-revolution, which could spread from Kurdistan to other parts of Turkey in an attempt to overthrow the régime. Martial law should thus be declared not only locally but throughout the country, including Istanbul. Fethi rejected the proposal. His opponents then turned their fire against the Progressive Party, claiming that it was they who, by inflammatory religious propaganda, had helped to stimulate the revolt. Fethi became worried and summoned to him Kiazim Karabekir, Rauf and Ali Fuad – who sent Dr Adnan in his place. He asked them, in order to avoid bloodshed, to dissolve their organization and collaborate with the People's Party.

Kiazim Karabekir protested with vigour. His party had a legal right to exist, and no Government was entitled to dissolve it.

Fethi said, 'You know I am always against the use of force. But I fear that I may be in a minority.'

Kiazim compromised. He and his friends realized the dangers of the revolt, and were unanimously resolved on its suppression. They would not dissolve their party. But they would support the Government, wholeheartedly, over this particular issue. Fethi thanked them, and added that the operations were going according to plan. There should be no need for new measures, since peace and calm reigned everywhere outside the area of the rebellion. Next day in the Assembly, after Kiazim had denounced the rebels and promised support to the Government, a law was passed, pronouncing as guilty of high treason those who used religion as an instrument to destroy the public order of the country.

But this moderate policy was not to prevail for long. At the news of the revolt, Ismet had hurried back to Ankara from the island in the Marmara where he had been recovering from an indisposition. He was soon in touch with the Gazi, who summoned a Cabinet meeting. Kemal's reaction to the revolt was twofold. Firstly he saw it in terms of his chronic dread of religious reaction. 'If we can manage to keep the right wing under control,' he once said, 'we do not need to fear the left. . . . One should not wait before crushing a reactionary movement. . . . One should act at once.' Such, during the War of Independence, had been his response to the widespread rebellion of the Caliph's army. Such now was his response to this localized revolt, in which he chose to detect once more the hidden hand of his enemies in Istanbul. Secondly, he saw in it a useful pretext for silencing the Progressives in Parliament. He thus supported Ismet's view of the emergency, and rejected that of Fethi, who agreed to accept the arbitration of the People's Party.

A party caucus was thus convoked, in which Ismet and Rejep condemned the Government's handling of the revolt and demanded the adoption of more radical measures throughout the country. They put forward a bill to provide for Independence Tribunals, censorship of the press and other stringent regulations directed against sedition. Fethi, backed by a majority of his ministers, opposed it. He persisted in his view that action should only be taken against those who had caused the trouble. When the extremists struck at the moderates by flinging their religious beliefs in their faces, he replied that Islam, after all, was constitutionally the religion of the Turkish Republic. 'Is there a single one among you who feels no respect for religious beliefs?'

In the furore which followed the question, a party member drew his revolver, but was deprived of it before he could shoot. The moment had come for Kemal's well-rehearsed formula. A member rose to remind the meeting, 'Gentlemen, this party has a leader. Let us listen to him'; and Kemal was called in from the president's room, where he had been awaiting the summons. Arbitrating in favour of the extremists, he made a long speech in which he reached the conclusion: 'It is necessary to take the nation by the hand. Those who started the Revolution will complete it.' A motion of no-confidence in the Government was put to the vote and carried – though only by a one-third majority. Rather than appeal to the Assembly over the head of the party, Fethi chose the line of least resistance, and announced to the deputies the resignation of his Government. Thus Ismet became once more Prime Minister, this time with Rejep as his Minister of Defence.

Meanwhile Sheikh Said and his followers swept through the Kurdish highlands 'on the road to God', waving green flags and clutching Korans to their breasts, raiding banks and plundering shops and houses, calling in the name of the Almighty for all Turks to surrender. The preachers inflamed them with promises of heavenly rewards. Leaflets were distributed and scattered from the air, declaring that the Caliph demanded their sacrifice, that Islam was not Islam without a Caliphate. Let them restore the Holy Law, let them destroy this Government, which taught atheism in its schools and allowed its women to go about naked.

The rebels hoped by a swift campaign to gain control of the region before reinforcements from Ankara could arrive. Gathering the support of the tribes as they marched, they drove back the scanty Government militia. They occupied village after village. They captured Elâziğ and surrounded Diyarbekir. They mustered a large force outside the walls of the city and, with the aid of a fifth column within, succeeded in reaching the Kurdish quarter by means of trenches dug for sewers. But support from the inhabitants failed to materialize, and the Government forces drove them out after twenty-four hours of street-fighting, in which Kurds shot at Turks from the

A.—14

minarets. They refrained meanwhile from pursuit of the rebels. For Fevzi, in consultation with Kemal and Ismet, had ordered the local militia to avoid major engagements until the regular forces arrived.

They planned gradually to surround the whole area, then to close in on the rebels in a large-scale offensive, with an army on a war footing of eight divisions, and air force support. This would take time, since Kurdistan was a country without roads and so mountainous that, in the words of von Moltke, there was nothing flat in it but the roofs of the houses. At this season it was lashed by blizzards, and its passes often blocked with snow-drifts. The reinforcements must march hundreds of miles to reach the front. But the French gave permission for the use of the Baghdad railway through Northern Syria, on the understanding that the operations were not to be aimed against the British in Irak.

While the army completed its preparations, Ismet clinched his hold over the country with the introduction into the Assembly of a drastic Law for the Maintenance of Public Order. This was to give the Government wide dictatorial powers. For a period of two years (in the event to be extended for a further such period) the Cabinet was accorded the right to forbid and suppress any organization, any attempt, or any publication which might encourage 'reaction and rebellion'. The law was to be enforced through Independence Tribunals. Most of these would be in the region of the military operations, where they would replace the courts martial and have the power to carry out death sentences instantly, without seeking the Assembly's approval. There was to be one additional tribunal in Ankara, with jurisdiction over the rest of the country to suppress reactionary propaganda and punish actions threatening to disturb the peace, but requiring the Assembly's approval for death sentences.

The law aroused fierce opposition from the Progressives, who condemned it as unconstitutional, destructive of all liberties and contrary to the Rights of Man. But Ismet remained adamant. 'National rostrums,' he declared, 'where every member of the Opposition is allowed to express his opinion are rare in the world.' Ignoring shouts of dissent, he defended the law in terms of the overriding need to maintain order and security. Only on such a basis could the national reforms be carried out. He won his two motions by a large majority, and the judges and prosecutors of the Independence Tribunals were appointed by the Assembly from among members unlikely to prove too tolerant of a Progressive Opposition. In a presidential statement, Kemal explained that these extraordinary measures had 'given to all government officials the task of preventing an incident before it happens rather than repressing it after it has happened.' The state must have the power to suppress speedily 'the aggressive actions of drunkards in the streets, bandits in the mountains, rebels who dare oppose the armed forces of the Republic, and those who create confusion in the innocent mind of the nation.'

By the end of March 1925 the necessary troop movements were completed, and the whole area of the rebellion was quietly encircled. Sheikh Said was blockaded within his own territory, and all routes of escape across the frontiers of Persia, Syria and the province of Mosul were stopped. It now only remained to close in and exterminate the rebel forces, who were devoid of artillery and moreover known to be averse to bayonet-fighting. Sheikh Said had not been wholly successful in rallying his neighbouring tribes, since he had chosen to emphasize the issue of religion above that of Kurdish independence, and they were disinclined to accept the spiritual authority of a Nakshibendi dervish. He had moreover failed to capture Diyarbekir, the obvious capital for any Kurdish state.

The victory of the Government was thus mathematically certain. Its progress however must inevitably be slow, since the Kurds scattered into their mountains in small mobile groups, incapable of serious resistance, but harassing the enemy by ambushes, fusillades from the hill-tops and surprise attacks from his rear. One by one however these forces were rounded up and their strongholds captured. Finally, in the middle of April, Sheikh Said himself was surrounded, with a number of chiefs and a small force of followers. He accepted defeat and surrendered freely. Incriminating documents were found on him, and a large sum of money in gold. His rebellion had lasted just two months.

Sheikh Said's arrival in Diyarbekir, with a cavalcade of some thirty other rebels preceded and followed by detachments of Government infantry and cavalry, attracted the attention of the whole population. Tall, slim and sunburned, he rode with a swagger. Aircraft flew overhead showering fireworks on the crowd. The authorities received him with studious politeness. Had his journey been tiresome? All campaigns, he replied were tiresome. He had been ill. How was his health now? It was better, but he still could not eat. He was promised good treatment. The doctors would look after him. Amid a whirring of cameras he was taken away.

A month later he and his various confederates were tried by an Independence Tribunal. Apart from the Public Prosecutor, it was composed of members of the Assembly, who sat ostentatiously beneath a large red Turkish flag, in emphatic and symbolic protest against the green Moslem flag of the Kurds.

Sheikh Said at his trial behaved calmly and even joked with the judges. But he objected as a Moslem to the film cameras in court, pursing his lips and mumbling prayers against them. He declared that he had rebelled because religion was losing its hold on the people. He refused to admit that he had been wrong in drawing his sword against other Moslems, arguing that they had ceased to be faithful to their religion. Had he succeeded, he would have reopened the religious schools, restored the Holy Law, and reimposed the traditional law, cutting off the tongue of the liar and the hand of the thief. Thus Kurdistan would have been once more as happy as in the days of the Prophet.

On these grounds he and his fellow-accused pleaded not guilty. They were none the less condemned to death as traitors. Sheikh Said and some forty others, of whom nine were sheikhs, were hanged before the big mosque in Diyarbekir. They died for the most part courageously. The sheikh kept up his panache to the end. Before mounting the scaffold, he remarked with a smile to the president of the tribunal, 'I like you well, but we shall settle our accounts at the Last Judgement.' Teasing the military commander, he said, 'Come, General, say goodbye to your enemy.' He stood quietly while the shirt was put over his head, and without another word was hanged.

Thus ended the rebellion of the Kurds. The public reaction to it throughout the new Turkey had been hostile. There had been little or no sign, despite the expressed fears of the Government, of a sympathetic reaction in other parts of the country. In the neighbouring provinces and elsewhere, the peasants had organized their own defence. In Istanbul the students and the porters – the intelligentsia and the proletariat – had come out strongly against these manifestations of religious reaction. As Ismet himself admitted to Parliament, the 'children of the Republic' had responded willingly to the order for mobilization. They were angry at this attempt to disrupt the peace which had just been so hardly won. They resented this use of religion for political motives. In this first crisis since the War of Independence, the Gazi's new national front had come reassuringly to the fore.

But Kemal was taking no chances. It was not at present his intention to guide it into the channels of too liberal a sytem of government. The power of his Opposition in Parliament and the press must now be vanquished as the rebels had been. During the revolt, at a moment when victory had become certain, Ismet had remarked to Ali Fuad that an Opposition was unnecessary. To Admiral Bristol, the American representative, he expressed his view even more frankly with the words, 'Opposition in this country means Revolution.'

In this spirit the forces of the Government, with its newly won powers, were first turned upon the press. Immediately after the passage of the law, five leading newspapers in Istanbul were suppressed. Within a few weeks a mere half-dozen of the fourteen newspapers in the city survived, and their circulation dropped low, since they no longer had the power to publish accurate news or to criticize. Hussein Jahid's influential *Tanin* remained circumspect, and thus survived until the Government turned its forces against the Progressive Party by raiding its premises in Istanbul. Jahid was then apprehended for using the word 'raid' in his report. With three of his sub-editors he was called before the Independence Tribunal in Ankara, and sentenced to 'perpetual exile' in Chorum, where he remained for some years.

The police found no evidence to incriminate the party itself, and the tribunal had to content itself with prosecuting two of its members on a charge of exploiting religion for political purposes. It chose to regard their conviction as a pretext for closing down the party. This 'nest of reaction' was thus eliminated. Its suppression was followed by the arrest and trial, on various pretexts, of certain members of the Opposition in the previous Assembly.

It led also to further arrests of journalists, some of whom, to their alarm, were transported as far afield as Elaziğ and Diyarbekir for their trials. But the Government, well versed in the arts of propaganda, was careful to treat them well. They were formally and politely received by the local authorities; they were given comfortable accommodation; they had long and informative interviews with the governors; they were free to talk to the local inhabitants, to see the sights, to send souvenirs home to their families. This treatment impressed the city-bred journalists, most of whom were setting foot for the first time in the Anatolian wastes. It served to emphasize, by shock of contrast, the general backwardness of the country and the diversity of its social conditions, and to rub in the need for a united effort to cope with its problems. The tribunal dismissed the case against them, and they returned to Istanbul, chastened and potentially converted to the policy of Mustafa Kemal.

This policy was championed by the Ankara press with the reiteration of such words as Law, Order, Unity, and above all, Strength. It was illustrated in terms which were often macabre. One night, staying in the ramshackle inn on the main square which was still Ankara's sole apology for an hotel, the Bulgarian Minister, Simeon Radev, was awakened from sleep by a commotion outside. Going to the window, he saw three sides of the square lined with scaffolds, eleven in number. Lighted up by the flares of torches and the first streaks of dawn, several men were already hanging from them, while others were about to be hanged, crying and protesting their innocence, as soldiers ran hither and thither and officers shouted their orders.

A Secretary of the American Embassy, Howland Shaw, came upon the scene at eight o'clock in the morning, and thus described it:

> Each man was hung down from a tripod and had on a sort of white smock with a placard pinned to him on which was scrawled his name and some account of his crime. There were groups of spectators in front of each tripod and others, intent I suppose upon a more careful inspection, were seated on the steps of nearby houses. Children were scurrying about and nobody seemed particularly concerned. It was a sight like any other.

Such was the reign of the Independence Tribunal in Ankara, now sitting in the hall of the Turkish Hearth organization, where concerts of Turkish music and other such functions had helped to disseminate Turkish culture throughout the previous winter. Its judges were respected citizens, whose departure to enact similar scenes in other parts of the country were attended at the station by ceremonious official farewells. Thanks to their labours, the new Turkish Republic was able, within eighteen months of its proclamation, to boast that it had effectively silenced all political opposition.

CHAPTER FORTY-NINE

THE MOSUL SETTLEMENT

THE KURDISH REVOLT had been well enough timed. It coincided with the examination by the League of Nations of the Mosul dispute, and with the peregrinations in the area of a League Commission of Enquiry, whose members the rebel sheikhs hoped in vain to impress. The question of Mosul, outstanding from Lausanne, still remained to be settled. For the past year it had seriously occupied the attention of Kemal and his ministers in Ankara, in periodic conference with the diplomatic representatives of Britain.

When Ankara became officially the capital of Turkey in 1924, the foreign diplomats had begun to trickle into the city from Istanbul. But it was not yet equipped to provide a full Diplomatic Corps with such amenities as befitted its station. King George V, for one, roundly refused to inflict such a place of residence on any Ambassador of his; while the other Western powers took a similar line. It was thus several years before the principal embassies moved to the capital. This was not an arrangement which altogether pleased the Gazi. Once, meeting a junior British Secretary and learning that his Ambassador was in Istanbul, he commented with some acerbity, 'Istanbul is such a pretty place!' But in the absence of accommodation in Ankara there was still no alternative.

The Mosul negotiations were to be handled by Sir Ronald Lindsay, Rumbold's successor as British Ambassador. When he came for a day or so from Istanbul to present his credentials to the Gazi, Sir Ronald was obliged to live in a railway coach, shunted into a siding near the station. In common with his foreign colleagues he left behind him in Ankara a Second Secretary. This was Knox Helm,[1] who thus became the effective representative of his country with the Turkish Republic – a pillar of the young and informal Diplomatic Corps which came to animate Ankara in these early days, mixing well enough with the young entourage of Kemal.

On behalf of the British Government Helm took steps to acquire a piece

[1] Later Sir Knox Helm, GBE, KCMG, British Ambassador to Turkey 1951–54.

of land, as near as possible to Chankaya – the property, indeed the per-quisite, of one of the Gazi's principal *aides*. Here a few sheds were erected as a provisional Chancery, pending the construction of a permanent British Embassy. The French had their Embassy in the station and gave their receptions in a former warehouse of the Ottoman Bank, while the Americans had to be content with a very small flat. Only the Russians, well established with their satellites since the early days of the Revolution, yet possessed a full-grown Embassy, well furnished and fitted with electric light, where they maintained a complete diplomatic staff.

Here they continued to entertain hospitably, concerned at this stage to further their commercial relations with Turkey. Kemal enjoyed their enter-tainments, as did his officials and friends. A complaint reached him from a disapproving source that some of them had been seen rolling insecurely down the stairs at the end of a Russian party. But one of the Gazi's *aides* protested in their defence that this was due, not to an excess of vodka, but to the fact that they were used only to narrow stairs and that these were so wide as to cause them to lose their balance.

Such parties were none the less infrequent in Ankara, where the main relaxation in the evening was cards. The favourite resort for this pastime, as for occasional dances, was the Anatolian Club, which Kemal visited often. The British representative was well placed, up at Chankaya, to know when the Gazi was embarking on one of these late night excursions, and thus to follow him if he felt in the mood. For the Presidential guard would turn out within earshot to line the road for his descent – and remain lining it until his return, often in daylight.[1] The club was small, hence enabled its few foreign habitués to meet at close quarters, if not always on intimate terms.

The members fell into two groups – the more sedate gathering around Ismet, who played bridge (the game he had learned while on duty in the wilds of the Yemen) usually with a minister or two, at one end of the card room; the more convivial at the other end around Kemal, who played only poker, maintaining that bridge was a game with too many rules. He enjoyed the excitement of poker but never took the game seriously, liking to win, but often, to the annoyance of others who had done so, sweeping the chips together and cancelling all debts at the end of the session. The young diplo-mats, in furtherance of such informal contacts, were ready to stay up playing at the club all night, but were still often outstayed by Kemal, who continued to play until the sun was well up in the sky.

Kemal adhered strictly enough to protocol in his relations with diplomats. Officially, as head of state, he received them only in the presence of his

---

[1] Kemal liked to joke, in a rough Turkish way, with his sentries. Going out early one morning, he asked one of them what he was doing. 'Watching over the President,' was his reply. 'You fool!' Kemal exclaimed, 'it's I who am watching over *you*!'

Foreign Secretary, who now and for some years to come was Dr Tevfik Rüştü. Tevfik was the old adherent whom he had prophetically designated for the post over the café tables of Salonika in his youth. He was at home in Europe; he spoke several languages; he had a supple enough mind and above all knew that of his master; he was convivial in his habits, with an affable garrulity which endeared him to the foreigners, though it disinclined them to take him too seriously. They saw him often, finding him always communicative, if not always consistent, though sometimes fatigued by an all-night session of politics, poker and drinking with his master. 'Poor man,' an American Ambassador remarked after keeping an appointment with him at 4.30 p.m., 'how he must have hated me for breaking into his night's rest!' Tevfik's staff was well trained in preparing elaborate briefs for Kemal on the various countries, so that when he received a foreign ambassador he would surprise and often disconcert him with a barrage of well-informed questions.

Kemal in his lighter moments enjoyed making a buffoon of Tevfik Rüştü, who responded happily enough to the treatment. One evening at Chankaya he had to receive a foreign ambassador after dinner. The interview was important, and as Kemal's mood was already festive his friends employed various stratagems to dissuade him from drinking further. Seeing through them, he looked crossly around him and said, 'Look here, I don't see why you're making such a fuss. If you're thinking of my interview after dinner, you don't need to worry. Whatever my condition is, however drunk I may be, I can never commit blunders as dreadful as those committed by Tevfik Rüştü when he is as sober as a judge.'

In the post-Lausanne atmosphere of Ankara, Britons and Turks were soon on amicable terms. Kemal's entourage took to dropping in on its British neighbours at Chankaya for a drink or a game of bridge – so much so that their master at the club one evening remarked to Helm, with an expression of mock severity, 'You are taking my friends away from me.' Helm asked whether this did not meet with the Gazi's approval, and received the reply that it did.

Kemal had always respected the moral and political qualities of Britain. The very fact that she had been his enemy intensified his resolve that she should now become his friend. 'Once an enemy, always an enemy' had been the principle, typical of the Oriental mentality, which had for centuries underlain and bedevilled the foreign policy of the Ottoman Empire. Under the Republic there was to be an end to such hereditary grudges and feuds. Already Kemal had shown this spirit by his swift reconciliation at Lausanne with the Greeks, and by his patient attitude to the demands of the British, then and at Chanak beforehand. To maintain it was now especially important, in view of the need to solve the problem of Mosul.

At Lausanne it had been agreed to refer the question firstly to direct negotiations between Turkey and Britain and subsequently, in the event of their failure, to the League. The point at issue was the delimitation of the frontier between Turkey and the new British mandated territory of Irak. It led firstly, in May 1924, to an Anglo-Turkish conference in Istanbul, at which Turkey was represented by Fethi, and Britain by Sir Percy Cox, the High Commissioner in Irak.

The atmosphere of the conference was studiously friendly. But it soon became clear that a wide gulf divided the two parties. Fethi insisted on the restoration of the pre-war frontiers of the Mosul province, which the British now occupied, using the ethnical argument that the majority of its inhabitants were Turks and Kurds, two 'sister nations' which had 'united their destinies in perpetuity'. Sir Percy on the other hand saw them as two separate races, hence argued that the Turks were in fact in a minority, and that the Kurdish majority were satisfied with the local autonomy which the British had given them in Irak.

The British, however, were no longer content with the former Mosul frontier. They were now claiming a line further north, drawn to include the Christian Assyrian minority, who sought their protection. They maintained that this was a 'no man's land' without effective Turkish authority. The Turks refused to accept this line and the negotiations broke down. The dispute was then referred to the League Council, which agreed on a provisional line, corresponding roughly with the original boundary. A League Commission was thus enabled to tour the area in reasonable security interviewing representatives of the different inhabitants.

The Commission presented its report to the League Council in September 1925. It held that a plebiscite was impracticable. It found on balance a feeling among the population in favour of Irak rather than Turkey, influenced largely by considerations of security and economic advantage. It proposed union with Irak of the former Mosul province, now excluding the 'no man's land' to the north of it, subject to a twenty-five-year mandate of the League, and guarantees for Kurdish rights. The British had undertaken to accept in advance any decision by the League Council. The Turks now refused to do so. On 16th December 1925 they withdrew their delegation from Geneva, leaving the Council to grant a mandate to Britain without their consent.

Kemal countered this diplomatic reverse by producing, the very next day, a non-aggression pact with Soviet Russia. As soon as it became clear that the League decision would go against Turkey, Tevfik Rüştü, who had been handling the negotiations at Geneva, proceeded on instructions to Paris. Here he intercepted Chicherin, then *en route* from the South of France to Berlin, who proved ready enough to retrieve the set-back to his diplomacy at Lausanne. They spent four hours together, in the course of which, without the aid of relevant documents, they drafted and signed a three-year treaty. It disregarded for the moment the economic problems which were at the time the main bone of contention between Russia and Turkey, and confined itself to a re-affirmation of their political harmony, each agreeing to refrain from aggression and participation in alliances against the other. With this document in his pocket, he returned to Ankara.

The signature of the pact helped to mitigate the storm of indignation which greeted the League award. The press were foreshadowing war. The British became once more the treacherous hereditary foe, continuing in a new guise the policy of the Treaty of Sèvres and the occupation of Smyrna. This time Mosul was their breach in the wall of Turkish national security, while Irak was a spearhead directed straight at the Turkish heart. Their headquarters for this sinister operation was the League of Nations, 'the plaything of the imperialist powers'.

Kemal did nothing for the moment to discourage such polemics, which provided a serviceable safety-valve. If a show of warmongering could scare public opinion in Britain and thus hamper the task of her negotiators, well and good; and in fact the British opposition to the Mosul award both by the Labour Party and by the popular press was vociferous enough, if more subdued than in 1922, when the question first arose. Neither Mosul nor Mespot was worth a war, and the *Manchester Guardian* suggested that the next six months might be profitably employed in negotiation with the Turk, 'who is by no means so terrible a fellow as he is sometimes regarded'.

This reflected Kemal's own attitude. He had no intention either of becoming entangled in a Russian embrace or of fighting the British. Friendship with Britain remained the corner-stone of his foreign policy, and the British themselves, following the decision of the League, showed every disposition to help him out of his difficulty. Sir Ronald Lindsay, the British Ambassador, went on instructions to Ankara, where he negotiated with tact and ability, his task made easier by a threat from Mussolini to land troops at Adalia (now Antalya) if Kemal marched against Irak. The Turkish press calmed down and the Turkish public was reassured as to Britain's pacific intentions.

The Gazi, in a bantering mood, coached Tevfik Rüştü for the negotiations, bidding him rehearse his words to the British before him. Tevfik in doing so put on his smoothest and most conciliatory manner. 'Not strong enough,' interrupted Kemal. 'No conviction.' Tevfik tried a belligerent attitude, thumped the table and implied a threat to attack. Kemal mocked, 'What are you going to attack with?' The strong line was no good either. What mattered was to bury the hatchet with Britain. The province of Mosul, unlike those of Adana and Alexandretta (Cilicia and Hatay) contained, quite apart from its Kurdish population, a strong Arab element. Thus its inclusion within the National Pact could be regarded as a borderline case. Kemal the soldier had voiced his indignation in 1918 at the British occupation of Mosul. Kemal the statesman was not one, at this late stage, to prejudice the entry of his country into the western comity of nations for the sake of any part-Arab *terra irredenta* of the Ottoman Empire. Tevfik Rüştü must obtain the best terms he could from the British.

The terms he was offered involved in effect Turkish acceptance of the British claim to the Mosul province, together with arrangements between Turks and Irakis for co-operation in keeping the peace on their mutual frontier. The Gazi, before agreeing to them, had to contend with stormy opposition from the People's Party, whose members at a five-hour meeting argued the *pros* and *cons* of war. Some favoured it now, since it was bound to come eventually from the threatening presence of British forces in Irak. But when it came to a vote, the members resignedly agreed that Mosul must go the way of other lost provinces of the Ottoman Empire. With the second Assembly well under his thumb, Kemal was now strong enough to climb down, as he could not have done while the first Assembly yapped away at his heels. Thus on 5th June 1926 the treaty was signed at Ankara between Turkey, Great Britain and Irak. It was followed six years later by Turkey's admission to membership of the League of Nations.[1]

[1] Curiously enough, the question of oil, which underlay the dispute, scarcely rose to the surface of the Mosul negotiations. The British Government was zealous to keep its record unsullied by the taint of oil politics. The Turkish Government thought in territorial rather than economic terms, and seemed unaware of the full relevance of oil to the future welfare of the country. In the treaty Turkey not only ceded the territory but waived her claims to the oil, in return for a ten per cent payment on royalties which she later compounded for a lump sum of a mere £500,000.

CHAPTER FIFTY

REVOLUTION IN HEADGEAR

THE KURDISH REVOLT helped Kemal not merely to stifle his Opposition but to push through the rest of his religious reforms. The Caliphate, the religious schools, the Holy Law had been swept away. Now, since the revolt had been inspired by a dervish order of fanatical traditions, the Nakshibendis, it was a good moment to sweep away all the dervish orders, regardless of complexion.

These brotherhoods had played an important part in the religious life of the Turks, and had, with some exceptions, prevented them from becoming as fanatical as some of their Moslem neighbours. They represented a break-away, still within the framework of Islam, from the aloof orthodox hierarchy. It was in the brotherhoods that the ordinary people of the country found the warm human outlet they sought for their intuitive faith.

In so far as they were political the brotherhoods were traditionally opposed to the central authority. The Ottoman state had countered this by adroitly playing them off one against the other. The most enlightened of them, the Bektashis, had given support to the Nationalists following the Sultan's *fetva* against Kemal. Such elements among them might well have continued to act in his interests, as a solvent, diluting religious extremism, furthering a policy of a reformation of Islam and its conversion into a constructive social force from within. But this was not Kemal's policy. No Moslem him-self, he saw the brotherhoods less as a help than as a danger. Independent in spirit and used to opposition, they could as likely oppose his own Govern-ment as that of the Sultan – doubly so since it was a secular régime. More-over, they had power over the masses, and it was the masses that Kemal, having disarmed the formal religious hierarchy, now feared. To him the brotherhoods were 'secret societies', such as he had learnt to mistrust since his early days in Salonika.[1] Thus they must go.

In August 1925 he pronounced their doom in a speech at Kastamonu.

[1] In his youth, nevertheless, he had himself attended Bektashi gatherings in Salonika.

The Turkish Republic was to be 'a state of society entirely modern and completely civilized in spirit and form'. Hence all superstitions must be crushed:

> To seek help from the dead is a disgrace to a civilized community. . . . I flatly refuse to believe that today, in the luminous presence of science, knowledge and civilization in all its aspects, there exist, in the civilized community of Turkey, men so primitive as to seek their material and moral well-being from the guidance of one or another Sheikh. Gentlemen, you and the whole nation must know, and know well, that the Republic of Turkey cannot be the land of sheikhs, dervishes, disciples and lay brothers. . . . The heads of the brotherhoods will . . . at once close their monasteries, and accept the fact that their disciples have at last come of age.

A series of decrees clinched his decision. Henceforth Turkey, at least in theory, was to be free not only from sheikhs and dervishes but from 'fortune-tellers, magicians, witch-doctors, writers of amulets for the recovery of lost property or the fulfilment of wishes, as well as the services, dues and costumes pertaining to these titles and qualities'.

At the same time all sacred tombs were closed as places of worship and religious resort. When this closure aroused opposition in the Assembly – for some of whose members they involved vested interests in the form of their own defunct ancestors – a friend of Kemal,[1] who had been speaking against it, was taken aside by him, and enjoined in an undertone, 'Don't oppose the motion. In ten years' time you'll be able to open them all up again.' For all his agnosticism it was not Kemal's policy to attempt the eradication of religion. What he sought, as he once put it, was 'to disengage it from the condition of being a political instrument, which it had been for centuries of habit'. His policy was to break this habit by depriving the people, through a series of abrupt shocks, of such influences as might rival that of the centralized state, and especially of their outward and visible symbols. Today the dead in their tombs were such a symbol, exploited as a living and menacing force to be crushed without scruple. But in ten years' time they might truly be dead and could be resurrected without danger.

On his journey through the region of Kastamonu Kemal struck at another such outward and visible symbol. Its disappearance was to uproot a habit deeply engrained in every male individual in Turkey. For it involved what he wore each day of his life on his head. This was the fez.

Costume, in the Islamic religion, had a deep symbolic significance. The fez itself, so it happened, was a mere century old as a form of Moslem headgear. Ironically it was a Greek Christian fashion, prevalent in the

[1] Hamdullah Suphi Tanriöver.

islands and initially derived from the Barbary corsairs. Manufactured for
the Ottoman market in Austria, its introduction was the climax of a sartorial
revolution aimed, early in the nineteenth century, at the ultra-conservative
turban, and had led to riots in many parts of the Empire. But the fez in its
turn soon became a symbol of Ottoman and Islamic orthodoxy as the
turban had been, and as such was fiercely defended and as fiercely attacked.

Kemal's plan to replace this symbol with that of the hat was thus a
daring revolutionary gesture. It was one which had been quietly simmering
in his mind since the days of his youth, when he had been humiliated abroad
by the stigma of inferiority conferred by his national headgear. Now at
Chankaya in the evenings he had been discussing the change with his friends,
consulting those who had travelled abroad as to which form of hat was
most suitable.

In his own costume he had been making experiments. He was photo-
graphed on a tractor on his model farm wearing a Panama – without a
black ribbon. An old friend came upon him one day in a train wearing a
cloth cap with his brown tweed suit. 'Does this become me?' Kemal asked,
as though seeking assurance. He revealed that in recent months he had
three times dreamed of the fez. 'And whenever I did so Ismet knocked at
my door in the morning to report a reactionary movement somewhere in
the country.' The idea of a reform was unobtrusively canvassed in the press,
but still no newspaper dared use the ugly word *shapka*, or hat. They preferred such euphemisms as 'civilized headgear', 'protector from sunshine',
or 'head-cover with a brim'.

Kemal deliberately chose, for the disclosure of these various religious
reforms, a province known for its reactionary sentiments. Boldly he was
striking at the enemy at a strong point where, if his shock tactics succeeded,
their impact would be twice as effective as elsewhere. Shrewdly calculating
the effect of his public image, he explained to Falih Rifki that in such a
city as Izmir, where he was already known, the people would look not at
him but at the hat. In Kastamonu they would be seeing him for the first
time, and would see him 'as a whole, hat and all'. Kastamonu moreover,
for all its backwardness, was in a sense a symbol of the Revolution itself.
Bestriding as it did the direct line of the army supply route from Istanbul,
through Inebolu, the Black Sea port, to Ankara, it had played a loyal part
in the War of Independence, and its loyalty should survive the jolts which
it was now to receive.

Nevertheless Kemal, in that distaste for the darker forces of religion
which had haunted him since youth, approached his tour with unusual
nervousness, asking for water when he first spoke and finding that his
hands, as he raised it to his lips, were trembling. He had left Ankara bare-
headed, in an open car. The people, swarming down to the main road from
their mountain villages, hardly knew what to expect from this first sight of

their national hero. In one village an artist had drawn on a wall an imaginative portrait of the Gazi, the slayer of infidels, as a formidable warrior with sweeping moustaches and a sword seven feet long. The villagers had spread carpets on the streets for him to walk on. One of them, a young student, recalled the scene years later: 'When the President walked slowly down the street, greeting the crowds, there was not a sound. The clean-shaven Gazi was wearing a white, European-style summer suit, a sports shirt open at the neck, and a Panama hat. The few officials applauded frantically, urging on those near them, but a flutter of hand-clapping was all they would muster, so great had been the shock.'[1] For the conqueror was wearing the costume of the infidel.

But the shock was slowly absorbed. Outside Kastamonu itself the Gazi got out of his car and walked into the town ahead of his entourage, first carrying the Panama hat in his hand, then putting it on his head. His *aides* did the same. Had they done so a generation earlier, they might well have been stoned or manhandled by the crowd. But now they were greeted merely with silent curiosity. Throughout his tour Kemal's interest in costume and especially in headgear was made evident to all. Sometimes he remained hatless, in which case a few people out of politeness removed their own fezes. Inspecting a military detachment, he took off the cap of each soldier and examined it with attention. A few months earlier a narrow peak had been added to it, ostensibly for the protection of the soldier's eyes against the sun. For had not the Prophet enjoined his followers always to fight with their faces towards it?

His approach to the sartorial question was practical. At one meeting he turned to a tailor in the audience and asked him, pointing to a man in baggy Turkish trousers and a robe, which was the cheaper – this outfit or the modern, international type of suit. The tailor replied, 'The international kind.' Pointing the moral, Kemal said to the audience, 'There, you see? Out of every costume such as this man is wearing you could make an extra suit.'

All this was a mere foretaste of what was to come – an open declaration of national policy in which civilization was equated with costume. For this he chose the port of Inebolu itself. To symbolize their part in the War of Independence, its townspeople had decorated and placed in the square a boat and an ox-cart of the type that had carried the munitions. Kemal was pelted with flowers as he drove into the town, which was bedecked with flags and branches. Later, wearing his Panama, he walked through the streets while the people crowded around to kiss his hands and his garments. He conversed with all sections of the population, questioning them personally on their problems and enlightening them on his plans for their future.

[1] Quoted by Latimer.

For two days he took part in organized festivities. Sheep were sacrificed in his honour in barbarous fashion, but out of his sight at his request – a scruple which they ascribed to his deep devotion to animals. Bushels of apples were heaped upon him, products of the annual harvest. School-children processed before him, singing the march he had sung on the road from Samsun and crying, 'Long live our Father!' Boatmen organized a regatta for his entertainment, danced their traditional dances and sang their traditional songs. All these compliments he returned with appropriate speeches of praise to the inhabitants for the richness of their province and the enlightenment of its people.

The climax was reached on the third day, when he delivered a long oration to a dazed and respectful audience, variously clad, in the club-room of the Turkish Hearth.

'Gentlemen [he said] the Turkish people, who founded the Turkish Republic, are civilized; they are civilized in history and reality. But I tell you . . . that the people of the Turkish Republic, who claim to be civilized, must prove that they are civilized, by their ideas and their mentality, by their family life and their way of living. . . . They must prove in fact that they are civilized and advanced persons in their outward aspect also. . . . I shall put my explanation to you in the form of a question.

Is our dress national? (Cries of no!)

Is it civilized and international? (Cries of no, no!)

I agree with you. This grotesque mixture of styles is neither national nor international. . . . A civilized, international dress is worthy and appro-priate for our nation, and we will wear it. Boots or shoes on our feet, trousers on our legs, shirt and tie, jacket and waistcoat – and of course, to complete these, a cover with a brim on our heads. I want to make this clear. This head-covering is called "hat".'

The word was out. There was to be an end to all euphemisms. This and his other pronouncements were relayed by the news agencies to all parts of Turkey. In Kastamonu not a murmur was raised at the heresies they con-tained. He had brought off a daring operation by the shock of his ideas, which at first dazed his hearers, by the rough intimacy of his approach which then won their confidence, by the commanding impact of his per-sonality, which inspired the reverence of a people given to the worship of heroes but hitherto denied any contact with the remote being who ruled them. Now he had materialized, and they readily submitted their wills to his, as formerly to the will of the Padishah.

On his return to Ankara the Gazi was received, outside the city, by a group of hatted officials and friends. He liked the look of the model worn by Yunus Nadi and exchanged his own for it before proceeding on his way. Thereafter the change in fashion among the upper crust was swift. It must now be extended by legal means to the people as a whole. First a decree banned the wearing of religious vestments or insignia by all not holding a recognized office, and imposed instead the costume 'common to the civilized nations of the world' – in other words, the Western suit and hat. At first it was confined to officials only. But the deputies, most of the professional classes and many students adopted it.

Towards the end of November, when Kemal judged that public opinion was ripe, a new bill was passed by the Assembly which obliged all men to wear hats and made the wearing of the fez a criminal offence. For the present there were not enough hats to go round, and thousands went hatless or crowned with an odd diversity of headgear dumped on the market by the hatters of Europe. It was not until local hat factories came into full production that all were appropriately hatted. For the masses they produced cloth caps with a peak designed to prevent them from touching the ground with their heads as they prayed, but easily reversible and often reversed.[1]

The Hat Law, however, caused widespread riots in the East. They were inflamed by placards in the name of religion on the walls of public buildings, which led to mass demonstrations beneath the green flag of Islam. They had been anticipated by the Government, who sent Tribunals of Independence in advance to the danger spots. They were suppressed by ruthless means.

Of the abolition of the fez Kemal remarked later:

We did it while the Law for the Maintenance of Order was still in force. Had it not been, we could have done it all the same, but it certainly is true that the existence of the Law made it much easier for us. Indeed the existence of the Law for the Maintenance of Order prevented the large-scale poisoning of the nation by certain reactionaries.[2]

By these various reforms the Gazi translated into action those plans which, in the days of the Young Turk intellectuals, had been confined to the realm of ideas. Abdullah Jevdet, an early influence on Kemal and his friends, wrote in 1912 that there could be no civilization but Western civilization. His periodical *Ichtihad*, published at that time a vision of the future westernization of Turkey entitled 'A Very Wakeful Sleep'. It envisaged, among other changes, the replacement of the fez by a new form of headgear; the limitation of the turban and cloak to professional men of religion; the closing of the religious schools and brotherhoods and the use of their

---

[1] In a village near Izmir men wore women's feathered hats from the shop of a deported Armenian. Articles appeared in the newspapers on 'How to wear the Hat'. Officials were instructed to greet their superiors no longer with a salute but with a slight inclination of the head and a bow from the waist. But the habit of saluting died hard, and men would knock off their hats in attempting to do so.

[2] The Moslem world as a whole took the reform quietly. When Kemal sent a delegate to an Islamic Congress at Mecca, wearing a hat and a lounge suit, the other robed and turbaned delegates treated his gesture with normal politeness.

funds to assist a modern educational programme; the suppression of vows and offerings to the saints and of the activities of witch-doctors and exorcists; and a reform of the whole legal system.

The dream, then considered a fantasy, had now become a reality. It only remained for the Gazi to fulfil its prophecies regarding the freedom of women. According to Abdullah Jevdet, they were to be free to dress as they pleased, to choose their own husbands, without family dictation. Here Kemal had to tread circumspectly. It was one thing in Turkey to clap a hat on the head of a man. It was quite another to tear the veil off a woman. No Law for the Maintenance of Order, no Independence Tribunals would enforce such a metamorphosis. He had begun, none the less, in the course of his tour to Kastamonu, to prepare the way for its gradual enforcement.

CHAPTER FIFTY-ONE

EMANCIPATION OF WOMEN

THE WOMAN'S position in Turkey had changed relatively little since the days of the Prophet. Despite growing discussion of her predicament, both before and after the reign of Abdul Hamid, she still lived subject to the letter of the laws of Islam, in a seclusion which amounted at its worst to personal slavery and at its best to conventual segregation from a predatory world.

The average Ottoman Turk, in his masculine pride and possessiveness, chose still to see women as an inferior species, a female animal deficient in morality and self-respect, who required protection by the male against her own weaker instincts. It had become a collective as well as a personal duty to supervise her behaviour. Not merely the husband and father and brother but the whole street, the whole neighbourhood, was concerned to watch over her, to see that her limbs were totally and decently covered, to catch her out if she seemed to stray for an instant from the narrow path which society laid down for her.

In Constantinople no woman might be seen walking in the street or driving in a carriage with a man, even if he were her husband. If they went out together he was obliged to walk ahead, disregarding her. Never did she appear with him at social gatherings; thus there was in effect no mixed Moslem society. On trams and boats there was a curtain, to divide women from men. In girls' schools, when feminine education was introduced, the only male teachers were eunuchs. In the theatre the female parts were played by men, as in Elizabethan England, or by Christian women. When women were eventually allowed into the audience it was on certain 'ladies' days' set aside for them. Only in parts of Anatolia, among the peasantry, were women freer, and indeed often unveiled before all but strangers. For (thanks sometimes to the influence of the brotherhoods) the peasants were often less orthodox in their customs, and moreover their women had, for economic reasons, to work in the fields and perform other outdoor tasks for the family living.

Such taboos prevailed right into the twentieth century. The Young Turks were unable to make much headway against the prevailing prejudice, reinforced as it was by the clerical interest. But they were persistent in their efforts to do so and zealous in their championship of women's rights. It was too soon to talk openly of abolishing the veil, but a pamphlet was secretly distributed, insisting that it had nothing to do with religion, but was a more primitive pagan survival.

The Young Turks however made progress with the education of women, opening the middle and secondary schools and finally the universities to girl students, and thus preparing the way for their entry into the professions. During the war they replaced men in certain jobs, in factories, offices and public services, and were even recruited into a labour battalion, of a para-military kind, in which they cleaned the streets of Constantinople. Here the veil became an obvious encumbrance and, though it survived in theory, it tended to develop into the long *charshaf*, a headkerchief which did not cover the face unless drawn across it. Towards the end of the war a Family Law was passed, introducing a form of secular marriage which gave women monogamous rights. It was the principles of this law that Kemal had just made general, with the abolition of the religious courts and the preparation of the Swiss Legal Code.

The road had thus been prepared. Kemal was now to carry it towards its final destination – but more tentatively than the other religious reforms. He was quick to remind the public of the part played by women in the War of Independence, declaring once that no other country in the world could show a heroism comparable to that of 'these sublime, these self-sacrificing, these divine women of Anatolia'. But there was still much ground to be covered. Early in 1923 an uproar arose in the Assembly over the suggestion of a deputy that women should be included in the census for representation under the new electoral law. Nor did it abate when he hastily explained that this would not involve giving them the right to vote. The mere mention of such a possibility caused him to be howled down, and prevented him from finishing his speech.

Kemal, however, was already sowing the seeds of a new outlook, deliberately choosing reactionary soil for the purpose. At a congress of teachers in Ankara both sexes were represented; but the women sat apart, separated from the men by several rows of seats. On hearing of the meeting a shocked deputation of *hojas* called upon the Gazi to protest. He sent for the president of the Teachers' Association and loudly berated him: 'What have you done in the teachers' meeting? How dare you do it? This is a shame!' The *hojas* looked jubilant. But Kemal continued, 'You called the women teachers to the meeting. But why did you make them sit apart from the men? Don't you trust yourselves, or have you no faith in the virtue of these ladies? Let me never hear again of this segregation of women.' The deputation stood paralysed, then slunk out of the room, too astonished to speak.

From now onwards Kemal in his speeches referred frequently to the topic of women. Women must have the same education as men – indeed a better education, for were they not destined to be the mothers of men? 'We need men who have better minds, more perfect men. And the mothers of the future will know how to bring up such men.' He could not at this stage go so far as to suggest that women should abandon the veil. Let them continue to be veiled, but only slightly – so slightly as no longer to give the impression that they were blindfolded and embarrassed in their movements.

In Kastamonu he had spoken out plainly. A social body consisted of 'two kinds of human beings, called men and women'. It could not advance without both:

> Is it possible that, while one half of a community stays chained to the ground, the other half can rise to the skies? There is no question – the steps of progress must be taken . . . by the two sexes together, as friends, and together they must accomplish the various stages of the journey into the land of progress and renovation. If this is done, our Revolution will be successful.

Recounting what he had observed on his tour, he continued:

> In some places I have seen women who put a piece of cloth or a towel or something like it over their heads to hide their faces, and who turn their backs or huddle themselves on the ground when a man passes by. What is the meaning and sense of this behaviour? Gentlemen, can the mothers and daughters of a civilized nation adopt this strange manner, this barbarous posture? It is a spectacle that makes the nation an object of ridicule. It must be remedied at once.

It was remedied gradually over the next decade. The women of the towns were to set the example; but many years were to pass before it percolated down to the more bigoted villages.

Soon after his visit to Kastamonu Kemal proceeded in 1925 to the more sophisticated city of Izmir (Smyrna). Here he presided over an entertainment which was in effect the first Turkish ball. Only Moslems and their ladies were invited. An orchestra played Western music, and they were expected to dance together – an ordeal which they faced with reluctance, even after the Gazi himself had opened the ball by performing a correct foxtrot with the governor's daughter. Never until this moment had a Turkish woman, in her own country, danced with a man in public.

In Istanbul the habit soon caught on. Elsewhere Kemal had to use all his talents of persuasion to make dances an accepted social function. At first there was little mixing, the ladies remaining in one corner, the men in the other, reluctant to introduce their wives to their friends. On one typical occasion, in the clubroom of the Turkish Hearth in Ankara, Kemal noticed a few bold ladies who stood awkwardly in the middle of the room, imprisoned by masculine eyes. Kemal rallied the men like children at a party, 'Go and talk to the ladies standing up. Offer them things. Be nice to them. Let's make the sitting ones jealous. If so, they will get up one by one.' And so in the end it was to prove.

In Ankara he gave a ball in honour of the foundation of the Republic. It went well enough. But late in the evening the Gazi noticed a group of young officers, none of whom was dancing. They explained that the ladies had refused their requests for a dance. Kemal immediately addressed them for all the guests to hear: 'My friends, I cannot conceive that any woman in the world can refuse to dance with a Turk wearing an officer's uniform. I now give you an order. Disperse through the ballroom. Quick march! Dance!' Sensitive to the taunt, the ladies rose at the approach of the officers, and soon all were fox-trotting stiffly away. Club dances on Fridays became a habit in Ankara and the main provincial centres, and a new profession, that of the dancing-master, began to flourish.

The social ice slowly melted of its own accord as women were admitted to the various professions and finally to politics. Kemal did not hurry this process. But within five years women were given the vote at the municipal level; within ten they were permitted to vote in parliamentary elections; and in 1935, with Kemal's support, seventeen women were elected deputies to the Grand National Assembly.

Ironically Latife, the spearhead of his social campaign, his own outward and visible symbol of emancipated Turkish womanhood, was not with him to witness these manifestations. Asked once why he had married, in the teeth of his often-quoted Turkish proverb, 'To be a bachelor is to be a Sultan', he had answered in terms of this very reform. How could he persuade the people to unveil their wives if he himself had no wife to unveil? He had married indeed as much for sociological as for personal reasons. Through a paradox in his nature, that clash between mind and temperament which caused him to think like an Occidental and act like an Oriental, his marriage had turned out badly.

In Latife, too, there existed this conflict between East and West. By upbringing and education she was an Occidental. She held serious views on such subjects as education and the position of women in a modern society. She could hold her own in discussion with any man, Kemal included. She saw marriage, as he claimed in his speeches to see it, as an institution in which the two sexes should progress together 'as friends', each helping and influencing the other.

But in practice Kemal did not want to be influenced or helped, least of all by any woman. His house, his habits of life were his own, and he did not want them changed, as she tried to change them. For all his advanced theories, the conception of the equality of the sexes was in practice against his nature. Women, apart from their physical charms, interested him little as such. Their role was to serve man, as in the harem. What drew him to Latife was not the feminine side of her character, but the masculine side of her mind. Here they had something to share. Otherwise he must always be master – and Latife, as befitted a Western wife, would not be mastered. Nor had she the feminine tact with which to dissemble, to manage him without seeming to do so, as he, with his more subtle approach, had always been able to manage others. Intelligent though she was, she lacked the gift for handling human beings. Thus increasingly there were frontal clashes between them.

They alternated none the less with periods of harmony. Kemal was for a while faithful to Latife. Fikriye was dead; no other woman especially interested him; and he had too much finesse to introduce loose women into the nuptial home. Often he found himself living what was in effect a family life. The family was hers, not his: her father and mother, her sisters and brothers, who made long stays at Chankaya. They were to become in the end an encumbrance. But Kemal meanwhile treated them with patient politeness, and developed in particular an affection for one of her young cousins, a sensitive youth in his teens.

Latife nevertheless was frustrated. Her early hero-worship had developed into passionate love. But his own feeling for her was not rooted in passion, and his initial desires cooled as time went by. She grew jealous; and here the Oriental side of her nature emerged, for hers became at times a jealousy which she became unable, like any woman of the harem, to conceal or control. She was jealous of any woman to whom he might pay a compliment; jealous of his friends and of their influence upon him; jealous even of his dog and the attention he paid to it. One evening she made a scene when, in a gesture of congratulation, he patted the head of her young cousin, as he was playing the piano.

Such outbursts grew more frequent. She nagged at him and criticized him when others were present. She taunted him with his social inferiority and the superior position and wealth of her own family. He drank more, he became angry and brutal, humiliating her in front of his friends, some of whom were only too ready to fan his feelings against her.

The situation came to a head during a visit to Erzinjan in the eastern provinces, where there had been a serious earthquake, and then to Erzurum. Here a luncheon was given to which, at the Gazi's request, officers and officials were bidden with their wives. It was the first time men and women had sat down at table together in this conservative city – hence a social occasion of a symbolic and somewhat stilted kind. Few of the guests were at their ease, and Kemal, breaking the ice, chose to rally his hostess, the handsome wife of the military commander, with expressions of gallantry and admiring glances across the table. Latife showed her displeasure, then lost control and exclaimed, 'Be careful of your feet, Kemal. They are reaching as far as me.'

Kemal went rigid with anger. The guests became silent with embarrassment. The social experiment had ended in disaster. After it Kemal refused to speak to Latife. Instead he telegraphed instructions to the Cabinet, in Ankara, to arrange on his behalf for an immediate divorce. Latife was sent off by train next day, with two officers for escort. Kemal did not bid her farewell; nor did the wife of the commander with whom they were staying.

From Erzinjan, the scene of the earthquake, she wrote a letter to Kemal at Erzurum, admitting herself to have been at fault, and begging that her mistakes might be buried amid the ruins of Erzinjan. She sent it through Kiliç Ali. But Kemal refused to look at it. Kiliç Ali put it in his pocket, awaiting a more favourable moment. Later he remarked to Kemal that the commander's wife had refused to say goodbye to Latife on the grounds that she was now divorced. Kemal, as he had foreseen, was indignant at this clumsy slight. He asked for the letter, and read it. Appreciating its wit, he announced his forgiveness, and joined her in Erzinjan. They returned to Ankara together.

But the reconciliation could hardly endure. The same quarrels arose once more. One night at Chankaya she again lost her temper. She turned on the friends with whom he had been drinking and tore their characters to pieces before him, one by one. This was more than Kemal could tolerate. The end had come. He declared Latife divorced, and instructed his Cabinet accordingly. Latife's mother came from Izmir to fetch her away. Kemal did not see her before her departure. His ministers saw her off at the station – Ismet urging her to remain, for he saw her presence as a last restraining influence on Kemal. It was given out that she was leaving for Izmir for the sake of her health. The official news of the divorce was announced when she had gone. Both behaved with dignity afterwards – Latife leading a strictly private life and refraining from demands and reproaches; Kemal treating her family with open politeness whenever they came his way.

If there was an irony in the failure of the marriage – the failure of two headstrong Oriental natures to come to terms with the give-and-take problems of a Western relationship – there was an irony too in the manner of its end. On marrying her Kemal had been at pains to break with Moslem tradition, adapting the ceremony to Western principles; in divorcing her he reverted to the letter of the Moslem law, which allowed a man to repudiate his wife without question. All he had to say was, 'Leave the house,' or, 'I do not want to see you any more.' This was in effect what he did, seeking however to soften the harshness of his decision with an announcement that it had been reached in agreement between them.

A few months later his action would not have been possible. For the new Civil Code, which lay at the root of his major reforms, framed on the lines of the Swiss, was then finally passed by the Assembly. Repudiation of a wife by a husband was abolished, with polygamy, and was replaced by civil marriage and divorce, with equal rights for both parties. Henceforward women enjoyed, at least in the eyes of the law, a new freedom and dignity.

In terms of this series of legal reforms, all citizens of the foreign minorities in Turkey became subject to the law of the land, thus finally putting into practice the agreements which had been agreed at Lausanne. Meanwhile, a new law school had been established in Ankara, to train new lawyers. It was opened by the Gazi with the words: 'The greatest and at the same time the most insidious enemies of the revolutionaries are rotten laws and their decrepit upholders. . . . It is our purpose to create completely new laws and thus to tear up the very foundations of the old legal system.'

It was indeed one of Kemal's most significant achievements that he gave his country, for the first time, an independent judiciary.

CHAPTER FIFTY-TWO

TRIALS FOR TREASON

KEMAL was now alone at Chankaya, with his drinking companions, his casual women, his court of journalist intellectuals, his amenable ministers – and Ismet. Since his assumption of dictatorial powers and his smothering of the Opposition, his old friends appeared seldom at the Table. This was not a healthy seclusion. It made him a prey to suspicions, and to the influence of those who sought, by encouraging them, to strengthen their own position against that of their personal enemies. It left him out of touch with the feeling of the country, where the Independence Tribunals spread fear and resentment. It drove the Opposition underground and led to the exploitation of its more reputable leaders by unscrupulous adventurers. It created an atmosphere in which plots must inevitably thrive.

The initial plotters were men of scant account – small fry with personal grudges against Kemal. One of their ringleaders was Ziya Hurshid, a swash-buckling adventurer from Trebizond, seeking vengeance for the murder of his friend Ali Shükrü by the leader of Kemal's bodyguard. He had led the attack on the Government, with strong innuendoes against Kemal himself, during the debate in the Assembly which followed it. This was the culmination of a feud of long standing. When, on Kemal's return to Ankara as the conquering hero of the Sakarya, the deputies crowded on to the terrace of the Assembly to applaud him, Ziya Hurshid alone had remained inside, where he wrote on a blackboard: 'The nation creates its own idol and then worships it.'

His hatred and jealousy of Kemal had grown by the end of 1925 into a determination to kill him. Mobilizing a pair of desperadoes, a Laz and a Georgian from the Black Sea mountains, he started to explore means of doing so. He reconnoitred the Parliament building and speculated as to the chance of throwing a bomb from the stranger's gallery across to the President's box. He opened a hole in the roof from which to shoot at him. He contemplated a raid on a Cabinet meeting, but found the security measures too strict. He considered an ambush outside the Anatolian Club, and chose for the purpose a neighbouring cemetery, where the assassins could hide among the trees and the tombstones. But the chief brigand pointed out that the trees at this season were leafless and afforded no cover, and when they lay in wait there one night the Gazi, inconsiderately, failed to emerge before daybreak.

Among Ziya's confederates was Colonel Arif, the boon companion of Kemal throughout the War of Independence, whom he had afterwards made deputy for Eskishehir. He had since grown disgruntled through his failure to make good in politics and through an instance of corruption which had turned the Gazi against him. A further conspirator was Abdulkadir, a former Governor of Ankara. But the most influential was another, Shükrü, a former Minister of the Union and Progress Party, who had been notorious for his *komitaji* methods and his association with a secret terrorist committee during the Young Turk period. Shükrü had quarrelled openly with Kemal, whose henchmen had been treating him roughly. In a brawl in a restaurant one evening they threw plates at him, thus provoking him the more as, by their behaviour in the lobbies of Parliament, they were provoking other opponents of their master. Shükrü was in league with dissident elements in Istanbul, notably with a former Union and Progress party boss, Kara Kemal. Here, where the party still survived 'underground' and the press had outspoken habits, Kemal had many old enemies, and the arbitrary acts of his Independence Tribunals had brought him renewed unpopularity. Shükrü hoped also, as a member of their party, to get support from the more disgruntled Progressives.

One evening in Ankara when the execution of the plot was imminent Shükrü, under the influence of drink, dropped hints about it to a third person, a Progressive Party deputy, who at once told Rauf. Rauf obtained indignant denials of the story from Ziya Hurshid and Shükrü, who protested, 'How can you take seriously the words of that foolish drunken man?' He advised his original informant that if he really believed in the plot, he should, as a responsible deputy, tell the Government. Meanwhile Arif had hurriedly called off the Laz hired assassin.

Rauf, with Ali Fuad and Refet, were inclined to underrate the incident, seeing it as a reversion to the atmosphere of intrigue and conspiracy which they knew all too well from the Young Turk period. But they agreed that if ever again such a rumour arose, the Government must instantly be warned, however unlikely it seemed. What chiefly concerned them was the risk that the Progressive Party might be used as cover for any such future conspiracy. They took steps accordingly, warning their members to be discreet in their contacts, to remain on the alert and report any suspect, and tightening up security precautions within their own premises.

Hence the attempt was postponed for six months. But it was not abandoned. The conspirators transferred their operations from Ankara to Izmir, which Kemal was due to visit in June 1926 at the end of two long tours through Anatolia. A group of them travelled by boat from Istanbul, supplied with funds by Shükrü and with weapons concealed in valises exempt from police inspection by his deputy's visiting card on the labels. Thus the gang assembled in Izmir.

Here the scene for the crime was chosen at a point between the station and the hotel where three narrow streets met, and where the Gazi's procession would thus be forced to drive slowly. The two hired assassins, the Laz and the Georgian, were reinforced by a third, named Pock-marked Hilmi. All three, followed if necessary by Ziya, were to fire at Kemal with revolvers, and throw hand-grenades at him hidden in bouquets of flowers. Having killed him they were to escape through the crowd, jump into a waiting car, and drive to the harbour, where a new confederate, a Cretan, would be ready with a motor-boat to take them to one of the offshore islands. When the plan was complete two of the conspirators, prudently seeking an alibi, returned to Istanbul.

Their abrupt departure however led the Cretan confederate to suspect that the Government had learnt of the plot. The date of Kemal's arrival was postponed for twenty-four hours and this seemed to confirm his suspicions. To save his own skin – and perhaps also his conscience – he went to a police inspector and divulged the whole story. The Governor acted at once. Ziya Hurshid was arrested at midnight in his hotel, the Georgian and the Laz in a hotel nearby and the pock-marked assassin at his house. Ziya made no attempt to evade arrest, nonchalantly handing to the police a revolver from beneath his pillow and two bombs from beneath his bed.

Kemal himself reached Izmir next day and behaved as though nothing had happened. He had delayed his arrival from Balikesir – and thus perhaps saved his life – for no reason other than an instinct which may well have been a presentiment. For suspicions of some such plot were for ever in his mind, reinforced by the reports of his secret police, who had been shadowing Ziya Hurshid for some time past. He was received enthusiastically by the people of Izmir, who had read of the plot and the arrests from an official communiqué and were crying for the blood of the miscreants. Crowds surged around his hotel, where he deplored to the journalists that this should occur in the proud city of Izmir, of all places, which he had delivered from the enemy. But such ignoble attempts could not extinguish the fire of the Revolution.

The Gazi then summoned Ziya Hurshid under guard to the hotel where, coldly polite, he reminded him of their collaboration in the revolutionary struggle and asked why he had now plotted against him. Ziya admitted his guilt as the ringleader of the plot, and next day made a fuller confession.

He pleaded for mercy, but Kemal replied that the law must take its course, without his own interference.

Kemal summoned also one of Ziya's hired assassins, who was brought before him unaware of his identity. The man admitted that he had intended to kill Mustafa Kemal. He had been paid to do so; he had been told that he was a bad man, who did harm to the country; he did not know him personally. 'But how,' asked Kemal, 'could you kill a person you had never seen? You might have picked the wrong man.' He explained that Kemal was to be pointed out to him before he fired. Kemal then drew his revolver and handed it over to him saying, 'Well, I am Mustafa Kemal. Come on, take this revolver and shoot me now.' The man looked at him in amazement, then sank to his knees and sobbed.

It was clear that the plot had been the work of some dozen conspirators, led by Shükrü, and including Ziya and Arif – who declared afterwards that he had not seriously believed it would materialize. It was largely personal in character and could easily have been handled by an ordinary criminal prosecution. The culprits were, after all, men of the familiar *komitaji* type, against several of whom there had been previous charges. None showed any clear idea as to their political intentions once they had disposed of their enemy, while the ringleaders were politicians of no reputable standing. Their sentence should have been enough to uphold public security and act as a deterrent to any future attempts on the Gazi's person.

But Kemal preferred to treat the affair as a major political conspiracy. The chance which it offered of implicating and eliminating at one stroke all his opponents was, in his current mood of suspicion and impatience for complete power, too good to be missed. The Independence Tribunal was at once summoned by special train from Ankara to Izmir. Its president, as in the Kurdish trials, was 'Bald' Ali, a 'hanging judge' concealing a merciless disposition beneath a kindly and even distinguished exterior which Sir Ronald Lindsay – a Scotsman – had likened to that of an elder of the kirk. His chief confederate was his namesake, Kiliç or 'Sword' Ali, Kemal's own most ruthless henchman, a man who disarmed by his bonhomie, knew his master's mind and stopped at nothing to do his bidding.

Between them they began to order arrests which, in the next few days amounted to a formidable total. Those accused of complicity in the attempt consisted not merely of the obvious conspirators, including Shükrü and Arif but, regardless of parliamentary immunity, some twenty-five deputies. They included, as might have been expected, such former associates of the Union and Progress Party as Javid, the financier, and Dr Nazim, against whom Kemal had long-standing grudges; also Abdulkadir, who was caught at the frontier trying to escape in an ox-cart, and Kara Kemal, who evaded arrest for a while, but when the police tracked him down ran away into a hen-coop and shot himself. But they included also the leading members of the essentially moderate Progressive Party, among them Kiazim Karabekir, Refet, Ali Fuad and two other generals; also Rauf and Dr Adnan, who were in Europe and thus had to be charged in their absence.

Kiazim Karabekir was arrested in Ankara on the tribunal's instructions. But Ismet objected and on his own responsibility ordered his friend's release. He insisted moreover that none of the generals could have played a part in the conspiracy. This meant an open clash between the Government and the tribunal, which thereupon threatened to arrest Ismet himself. Acting as it claimed to do in the name of the Assembly, its members insisted that the Government had no authority over it and no right to interfere with its decision. Kiazim's re-arrest was ordered and Kemal at once summoned Ismet to Izmir. He arrived and, after attending a session of the tribunal, withdrew his objections, thus according it the Government's blessing and leaving the field clear to the two Alis. To the people of Izmir he wept crocodile tears: 'My heart is full of sorrow and I shudder with horror. I had hoped that most of those friends of mine in Parliament, with whom I take pleasure in exchanging ideas, would be incapable of seizing power by means of conspiracy.'

After individual interrogation the accused were all conveyed to the Alhambra Cinema, which had been transformed into a court-room. There, seated in two rows of chairs with an armed guard beside them, amid a subdued hum of voices from the boxes around, they awaited the members of the tribunal who, in a sudden silence from the audience, marched solemnly on to the stage.

From their indictment and from a statement to the press by Ali, the line of the prosecution became evident: the Progressives were to be nailed with the responsibility for the plot. The Unionists, in the person of Shükrü, Javid and Kara Kemal, had linked up with them to pursue their counter-revolutionary aims – to assassinate the Gazi and bring a Government of their own to power. The Progressives, in a 'sleep of ignorance', had allowed their party to be exploited as a cloak for these secret terrorist activities. Had their generals seen what was really happening, they would hardly now be in this plight. As it was they had shown no foresight, they had turned a blind eye to the conspiracy, they had failed to report it to the Government, hence they were guilty of the crime of sowing anarchy and disorder in the country.

For this they were to be tried by a tribunal which placed itself above the law of the country and above such constitutional trifles as the privilege of members of the Assembly, to which it was in theory responsible. They had neither counsel for defence nor the right of appeal. They were assumed guilty unless they proved themselves innocent. They were at the mercy of flimsy and arbitrary evidence, obtained by methods akin to those of Abdul Hamid and the Young Turk *komitajis* which Kemal had always so outspokenly deplored. Witnesses were largely dispensed with, and the accused were treated simply to an interrogation and an arraignment by the judge. Faced with this mockery of justice, the generals and other Progressive leaders took the only course consistent with their honour. They refused to plead. Asked if they had anything to say in their defence, they replied, 'No.'

Interrogation of the real culprits, Ziya Hurshid and Shükrü and their gang, failed to provide any evidence against the generals. Ziya admitted that 'of course' his attempt had had a political purpose. But neither Rauf nor Ali Fuad nor any of the Progressives had any knowledge of it. They were 'all timorous people'. Knowing that they could never defeat the People's Party, he and Abdulkadir, who shared his contempt for them, had formed a group of their own, unconnected with any party, to achieve a *coup d'état*. Throughout his interrogation Ziya, knowing his inevitable fate, admitted his guilt with a *sang-froid* amounting to insolence.

The Izmir trials lasted for three weeks. After they had started the Gazi retired to a villa in the neighbouring seaside resort of Cheshme. Here he was able to preserve an appearance of impartiality, pretending that justice must be allowed to run its course and that its outcome was not his concern, but receiving members of the tribunal and other influential persons. The verdicts were thus such as to meet with his approval. Ziya Hurshid, Shükrü, Arif, Abdulkadir (still at large) and eleven others were condemned to death; Rauf and seven others to various periods of imprisonment and of exile. Javid, Dr Nazim and the group of Unionists were committed for subsequent trial at Ankara. But Kiazim Karabekir, Ali Fuad, Refet, the two remaining generals and ten others, mostly of a Progressive persuasion, were acquitted. The arrest of the generals, heroes of the Revolution all, had been unpopular with the crowd, and open sympathy had been shown to them from the well of the court. Though Kemal may well have intended rather to teach his former associates a lesson than to hang them, their acquittal was ascribed to the influence of Ismet.[1]

Most of those sentenced to death were hanged that night in various parts of Izmir. Kemal signed their death warrants, including that of Arif, automatically, smoking as he did so and displaying no sign of emotion on his grey mask of a face. For him this was war – against the enemy from within. It was Arif who had taunted him at the Sakarya, 'You will always find enough men in Turkey to send to their death, with or without reason.' Arif was sure until the last minute that his old friend would reprieve him. After his sentence he wrote him a letter, recalling their long-standing friendship and pleading for a pardon. On reaching the scaffold he asked whether the Pasha had answered his note. 'He surely will,' he insisted. 'Can't we wait for five more minutes?' But no answer came.

[1] Kemal himself later declared to Ali Fuad that he had spared him as a friend and the rest for his sake.

Ziya Hurshid prepared himself for the scaffold in dandyish fashion, dressing slowly and with care, sprinkling *eau-de-Cologne* over his person, and arranging a silk handkerchief tidily in his breast-pocket. Learning the names of the ten others to be hanged, he remarked, 'There must be a mistake somewhere. Some of those, I think, do not deserve hanging.' (One of them was in fact a Government informer who pleaded without success that his services as such should be taken into consideration.) Ziya then gave the money in his wallet to the governor of the prison for his brother, as the price of a decent grave. 'If you don't carry out this wish of mine,' he jested, 'I shan't let you alone in the next world. I shall try to murder you there and this time I shall certainly succeed.'

The scaffold had been erected on the spot where he had planned to shoot Kemal. 'What a wonderful contrivance it is!' he remarked. 'It reminds me of a cradle. And it is high, too. All of you will remain down here and I shall be looking at you from on high.' He insisted on passing the cord around his own neck. It was the hangman who seemed nervous, insisting, 'Hurry up, sir, time is passing!' Ziya Hurshid laughed: 'What is your hurry? I am the one to die. So don't get worried. . . . In a few minutes I'll be in the other world. Tell me, can I do anything for you? Can I give any message to your kith and kin over there?' So he died, still with a smile on his lips. Next day eleven corpses were seen hanging by the crowd, each with a paper attached to its shirt with the verdict inscribed on it.

Ali Fuad and his companions were not immediately released on acquittal. They were taken to a store beneath the cinema. They waited in apprehension as a night and a day and a second night dragged by. Still unable to believe in their release, they asked each other anxiously what this added humiliation, this continued implication of guilt, might mean. Fuad and Kazim Karabekir tried to reassure their comrades. Among them were those sentenced to terms of imprisonment. Two of them, deputies respectively for Istanbul and Sivas, bewailed the injustice of their sentences, in tones of indignant despair. They began to clamour for a re-trial. Ali Fuad, who knew them both well, urged them to do nothing rashly. Such political condemnations were often revised with time. But they would not listen to him. They could not live under this stigma. They must appeal. A warden came to the door and announced, 'Those who want to appeal, come this way.' Both rushed to the door, which closed behind them. The hours went by and they did not return. Later that night they were seen handcuffed, being led to the general prison. Their sentences were changed, and that night, together with Rüştü, one of the generals, they were hanged.

In the morning the acquitted prisoners were finally released. The generals were mobbed by the crowd outside crying, 'Thank God, who has returned our Pashas to us!' Concerned at the demonstration, the governor sent an official car to take them wherever they wanted to go. At first they refused

A.—15

it, preferring to walk. But since this became impossible, the crowd led them
to the car, many clambering in beside them and insisting that it drive
slowly that the rest might follow. Their release thus became a triumphal
progress.

The Izmir trials had liquidated all criminal conspirators and silenced the
Progressive opposition to Kemal – for the generals and their friends would
henceforward be effectively excluded from political life. The Ankara trials,
which followed a fortnight later, were intended to dispose, once and for all,
of his remaining enemies, the members of the former Union and Progress
Party. Some fifty were accused, of whom the most prominent were Javid
and Dr Nazim. Here the indictment concerned not a criminal attempt on
Kemal's life, but a political attempt to overthrow his régime. It was the
final culmination of that feud between Unionists and Nationalists, between
the followers of Enver and those of Kemal, which had divided the Turkish
revolutionary movement. Kemal judged the remnants of the Union and
Progress group partly in personal terms, through his own obsessive memories
of past rivalries, slights and intrigues, but partly also in political terms, as
the survivors of a régime bounded by individual interests with no radical
national programme. What remained of the party, armed as it still was
with funds and animated by leaders well versed in underground political
intrigue, must thus inevitably be the enemy of his own. Until the Unionists
were finally eliminated Kemal could enjoy no sense of security.

The tribunal dragged up the association of the Unionist leaders with
Enver, after his flight and during his subsequent attempt to return to Anatolia.
It accused them of manœuvres to change the Government during the period
of the first Grand National Assembly; of agitations during the elections for
the second; of the formation of an Opposition through the Progressive
Party; of secret meetings for such purposes in the house of Javid and the
office of Kara Kemal; and of the inspiration of press articles which supported
an anti-Government programme.

As at Izmir the accused were assumed guilty unless able to prove themselves innocent, and the negative fact that they did not support the Government became, in the eyes of the judges, sufficient proof of their guilt. The
absence of any damning revelations against them led to a general public
belief that there would be no capital sentences. But Kemal's personal hatred
and suspicion of the Unionist leaders was now reinforced by disquiet at
reports of economic unrest in the interior, and a show of strength seemed
desirable – more especially as the release of the generals might have been
interpreted in some circles as weakness. Moreover, continuous pressure for
Javid's acquittal had come from Jewish and other organizations abroad,
and these sinister implications of the hidden foreign hand did little to weaken
his resolve to be rid of him. The last-minute evidence of Abdulkadir, sen-

tenced to death for his complicity in the plot but only now apprehended, proved sufficient to turn the scale against him.

The announcement was thus made that thirty-seven of the accused were acquitted – including Hussein Jahid, the editor of *Tanin*, whose earlier sentence of exile was, however, still in force; six of them, besides Rauf, were sentenced to ten years' exile; and Javid, Nazim and two other former Unionist leaders were sentenced to death. Thus the old scores were paid off, the old words translated into deeds. Of both Javid and Nazim, Kemal had exclaimed in the early days of the war, 'A man like that deserves to be hanged' – Javid for turning down his deal for supplies from Bulgaria, Nazim for blocking his promotion with Enver; and lately Nazim had been taunting him openly as 'Gazöz Pasha',[1] the 'little Napoleon' who built himself up by imprisoning his friends. Ismet too had his grudges against both Javid and Jahid, for their obstruction to his policy at Lausanne – though, in response to pressure from the press, he had achieved the release of the latter.

The executions took place that night in the centre of Ankara. Javid approached the ordeal with a nonchalant dignity. Reaching the foot of the gallows, he requested the prison doctor to convey his felicitations to Jahid on his release, to embrace his wife and child on his behalf, to transmit his greetings to the Gazi and the tribunal judges with the comment that his condemnation was against all the principles of justice. He recited two lines concerning the punishment of tyrants, from the Turkish poet, Ziya Pasha. Then he turned to the executioner and said, 'Do your duty.' He climbed nimbly on to the platform and asked what he should do, where he should stand, apologizing for the fact that he had no practice in such a procedure. He assisted the executioner by leaning forward to place his head in the noose. And thus, gallantly, he died. Kemal, when told afterwards that Javid's widow had, in a vindictive moment, threatened to strangle him, commented quietly, 'She could hardly do otherwise.'

The Gazi was not at Chankaya on the night of the executions. He had spent the day out of reach, on his farm, celebrating its usual anniversary at midday with draughts of *ayran* (the sour milk of the peasant) and in the evening with an informal dinner to some of his ministers, members of the tribunal and friends in the kiosk which he had built by his 'Sea of Marmara'. In the course of the evening the trials were not discussed.

Among those not present was Tevfik Rüştü, his Foreign Minister, the brother-in-law and lifelong boon companion of Nazim, who had preferred to decline the invitation. A day or so later Kemal came to lunch with him alone. He expressed sympathy for his loss, and explained the reason for the trials, which Tevfik had missed through his absence abroad. The point had been reached at which one or other of the two groups in Parliament

---

[1] *Gazöz*: fizzy lemonade.

must go. The matter had been placed in the hands of the tribunal, hence was not on his conscience. But, as he had confessed to Kiliç Ali with a gesture of distaste as he read its reports, the whole affair had been 'very disagreeable'.

Its instrument was not to survive for long. The power of the Independence Tribunal, thus misused for political purposes, had become such that it threatened to create a dual authority within the state – its judges on the one hand, Kemal's ministers on the other. This so irked and impeded Ismet in the business of government that he persuaded Kemal after a while that the moment had come to disband it. One evening at a party at Chankaya the Gazi remarked casually to Bald Ali, 'I have decided to abolish your tribunal. It is no longer required.'

Ali replied that he would study the question and furnish his master with a report.

'Report!' Kemal exclaimed. 'Report! I have studied the question myself and from tomorrow your tribunal will no longer exist.'

Its abolition was confirmed next day by the party caucus. The members of the tribunal, who for two years had tasted irresponsible power, reverted to the status of ordinary deputies. The 'reign of terror' was no longer necessary. Kemal's dirty work was done.

CHAPTER FIFTY-THREE

RETURN TO ISTANBUL

'IT WAS THE PEOPLE that I was afraid of.' Thus did Kemal, in a remark to a friend, seek to justify afterwards the liquidation of his opponents and his assumption of supreme dictatorial powers. It was the people, he was for ever telling them, who had saved Turkey. Yet ironically it was for fear of them that he now pursued a policy contrary to all his professed democratic principles. In fact his prestige with the people had never been higher than in the first years of the Republic. They were more securely under his control than they had been under that of any Sultan. Moreover, theirs was now a personal loyalty, based on the fact that he had led them personally in war, saving their lands from the enemy, making his capital in their midst, and as no Sultan had done, moving continuously among them as though he were one of them. His hold over the army was unchallenged. Communications, to say nothing of secret service techniques, were now so developed that no centralized administration need fear serious local unrest. Kemal knew better than most the congenital inertia of the Turkish people, whom he alone, at Gallipoli and later in the War of Independence, had known how to galvanize into action; and now, throughout Anatolia, there was no other potential national leader able to do so and thus to threaten his power.

Paradoxically Kemal had become a dictator not in order to obtain power but after he had done so already. In the early days he had had to work democratically – if only because his prestige was not yet sufficiently established to enable him to do otherwise. As a result he had won a resounding victory against the foreigner and had secured an honourable peace, which for the first time admitted Turkey into the family of respected Western nations; he had eliminated the old concept of Sultanate and Caliphate with their well-entrenched political power, and had swept away the institutions of an obsolete medieval society. The main foundations of a new Turkey were now complete – and their last stages had been completed against scant opposition.

This might well have been the moment for an experiment in some kind of liberal democracy, whose principles were after all inherent in the new Turkish Republic. This would have been a fitting culmination to that movement of reform which had been born in the Ottoman Empire a century earlier. The Young Turks, giving it a new brief lease of life, had lapsed from parliamentary democracy into a dictatorial triumvirate at a time of crisis when the foreigner was threatening the Empire from every side, and when a parliamentary Opposition had showed signs of endangering the unity of the country. But Kemal had surmounted these very obstacles; he had no need for a dictatorship – for the duumvirate which, with Ismet as his reliable factotum, he had now set up. Extraordinary measures might have been necessary to deal with such local outbursts as the Kurdish rebellion and the subsequent hat riots. But there was no need to extend these over the whole country, and above all no need to use them for the suppression of a parliamentary Opposition of an essentially moderate kind.

But he had decided otherwise. His decision was firstly a matter of temperament. By nature and training a soldier, he might delegate his authority, but he could not tolerate the idea of any threat to it; he might plan his campaigns in co-operation with others, but he must have sole control of their execution. And what was the transformation of Turkish society but another campaign in which, as he saw it, a rapid decision must be reached?

For his former associates, the Progressives, the problem had a remoter and more complex perspective. Turkish society for them was a deep-rooted organism which could only be transformed by slow and patient stages, and by a process of co-operation, both in planning and execution, with which all must be involved from the bottom upwards. Nevertheless, once Kemal's reforms were decreed, they were prepared to back their implementation in principle, reserving the right only to criticize their administration in detail. They sought not to rival his authority, but merely to counterbalance it. They could have served for him as a window on the country, widening the perspective and range of his Government's view. They could have furnished him with much-needed governing talent, the lack of which was to retard the growth of the state. Where they erred, somewhat naïvely, was in allowing their prestige and their party organization to be exploited by malcontents as cover for subversive purposes of which they wholly disapproved. This was the error used to justify the fatal 'purge'.

Psychologically, Kemal's emergence as a 'hanging dictator' was rooted in two other factors. The first was an obsessive suspicion of all who had spurned and obstructed him. The iron had been entering deeper into his soul from his fatherless lone-wolf childhood onwards; his cold-shouldering by the members of the Committee of Union and Progress, as a young man who knew that he knew better than they; the obstruction of his military career by rivals jealous of his worth and success. All these rebuffs had built up in his imagination a host of powerful enemies who still aspired to drag him down from his pinnacle. Such was the legacy of a past fraught with frustration and nourishing restless revengeful hates; such the reason, in particular, for the execution of Javid, which not only antagonized Western opinion, but deprived Turkey of a shrewd financial counsellor.

The second impulse behind his drastic actions was a fear of what he did not understand – the forces of religion. Agnosticism was born in him early and grew in him with time – through reaction against his mother's devoutness; through his secular education and his reading of the rationalist philosophers; through his horror, as a young man, at the Arab fanaticism of Damascus and his growing awareness of its hold, in a different degree, on his country as a whole; finally through his open proscription and condemnation to death by the powers of Islam, followed by a 'holy war' against him which he all but lost.

In his rationalism he understood little of the spiritual concept of Islam, which represented an inner need for the mass of his people and which a mere social philosophy, however enlightened, could not easily replace. He saw it as mere superstition of a dark and primitive kind. But he did not underrate its force. It was a secret weapon liable to be used against him by the peasants and the 'priests' who controlled them, a 'hidden hand' wider in its reach and stronger in its grip than that of any mere rival political party. He understood little – whatever he might say in his speeches – of the social and political principles of Islam as the Prophet had seen them, and as the liberal reformers of the past century had been striving to regenerate them. For Kemal, Islam and civilization were a contradiction in terms. 'If only,' he once said of the Turks, with a flash of cynical insight, 'we could make them Christians!' His was not to be the reformed Islamic state for which the Faithful were waiting: it was to be a strictly lay state, with a centralized Government as strong as the Sultan's, backed by the army and run by his own intellectual bureaucracy.

On a short-term view, this attitude seemed at first justified by results. With the dirty work done, there could now be an end to the policy of force and repression. The period that followed was one of stability and peace in which life and personal liberties were reasonably secure. It was a time of respite from fifteen years of war and revolution, a time of gestation in which the social reforms imposed during the past three years might have a chance to mature in the minds of the Turkish people.

There was a rest from political activity. The press was controlled. But there was reasonable freedom of speech among the people in general. Kemal was no ideologist; he was pragmatic in his ideas and did not attempt to impose on them a rigid conformity. To a group of school-teachers who asked him whether, as certain European writers maintained, he was really a dictator, he returned the soft answer, 'If I were, you would not be allowed to ask me that question.' As Bernard Lewis defines it, Kemal's was 'a dictatorship without the uneasy over-the-shoulder glance, the terror of the door-bell, the dark menace of the concentration camp',[1] so soon to arise in the West. Admitting once that he was a dictator, he qualified the admission: 'But I have not had pyramids built in my honour like the Pharaohs of Egypt. I did not make people work for my sake, threatening them with whips when I wanted an idea to be accepted by the country. I first called a congress, I debated the situation with the people, I carried out my plans only after taking authority from the people. The congresses of Erzurum and Sivas and the Grand National Assembly are living proofs of this.'

His was a dictatorship based on democratic forms, within a legal and constitutional framework which he scrupulously observed. For he was building, as his fellow-dictators of the period were not, for his own disappearance, trying to lay down a system of government which could survive his time. Into this the true spirit of democracy, which it lacked for the present, could be infused when the time became ripe. It could perhaps have been encouraged to ripen more quickly. But as Ismet, a generation later, explained the delay,[2] 'At that time we were on fire.'

With his enemies safely out of the way and his capital securely established at Ankara, the time had now come for the Gazi to revisit Istanbul, where he had not set foot since his departure for Anatolia eight years before. His sister Makbule and a group of ladies prepared accommodation for him in the Dolma Bahche Palace – now proclaimed, with the other palaces, the property, no longer of the shadow of God, but of the Turkish people. The Gazi, arriving there in his yacht, received a rapturous welcome, the steamers blowing their sirens while thousands of small boats, dangerously overloaded with passengers, sped out across the Bosporus to cluster around her and escort her ashore. Many had paid as much as a month's salary for the hire of a motor-boat. At night illuminations blazed, and a torchlight procession paraded through the streets to gather before the palace, where the Gazi, amid frantic cheers, came out on to a marble balcony to salute the crowds. To the people of Istanbul his arrival, after all these years, was a glorious reconciliation. They had been sulking at his neglect, but now they sulked no longer.

The Dolma Bahche Palace, with its ornate nineteenth-century halls of marble and crystal and ormulu, was an incongruous setting for Kemal. He felt caged by its restrictions. But at least, unlike Abdul Hamid's Yildiz behind its high walls, it looked out on the world. The broad terraces spreading along its encrusted façade confronted the Bosporus, and here he could

---

[1] *The Emergence of Modern Turkey.*
[2] In an interview with the author in 1960.

sit drinking and watching the life on its waters – the small boats scurrying across them and the big ships sailing past from the Golden Horn to seas and worlds beyond. When he grew restless, he would take a boat and cruise on the waters himself; or he would go up to Pera and pace the streets on foot, revisiting familiar haunts, dropping into some *patisserie* at the tea-hour amid unabashed looks of admiration from its feminine clientèle.

But it was to Ankara, the cradle of his Revolution and the seat of his Government, that his heart, and as time went on the hearts of the Turkish people, belonged. A serious start was now made with the replanning and rebuilding of the capital. A German and an Austrian town-planner were called in to furnish designs. Here, on virgin land, almost devoid of buildings, it should be possible to create the world's most up-to-date city. The plan envisaged wide radiating boulevards in the European manner, with a central *étoile* to be graced by an equestrian statue of the Gazi, and handsome public buildings disposed on a variety of well-chosen sites. Thousands of trees were to be planted across the bare arid plateau, leading up to Kemal's official residence at Chankaya and around it. The marsh beneath the citadel was to be drained and transformed into a People's Park. Already Ankara boasted a new Parliament building and, conveniently opposite, a modern luxury hotel. These had been designed in an Oriental manner; but the predominant style of the city's architecture was to be, rather, Germanic in character. A high priority was given to the construction of an opera house, such as had impressed Kemal, the young military attaché, above all the civilized Western blessings of Sofia. In time a city was to arise, provincial perhaps in its atmosphere but Western in character and amenity, which did credit enough to the new Turkish Republic.

The Gazi was due back in Ankara in the autumn for the opening of the third Grand National Assembly. In Istanbul he had been working on the speech which was in effect to be his own documented history of the War of Independence and of the Revolution to date. One of the longest speeches in history – just as the Sakarya had been one of its longest battles – it took him three months to write and six days to deliver. He dictated it in advance, sometimes for more than twenty-four hours at a stretch, to his secretaries, who for months past had been collating the necessary documents. As he did so he would reduce them to exhaustion, one by one, so that they had to be reinforced at their desks like soldiers on a battlefield. After dictating all day he would take a bath, then try out what he had written on his friends, then retire with the intention of sleeping but, such was the throbbing energy of his brain, often resume dictation and continue right through until morning. Delivered to the Congress of the People's Party, it was essentially a political speech, hence often tendentious – notably in its attempts to discredit Rauf and the rest. But it remains the classic account of the Kemalist revolution.[1]

---

[1] Comparable, it has been suggested, to Julius Caesar's '*De Bello Gallico*'.

The opening of the third Assembly in 1927 signalized the end of the 'foundation period'. The deputies were housed for the first time in the new building, purged of the stormy associations of the first and second Assemblies. Comprising only a single well-disciplined party, it relieved Kemal of all parliamentary worries, and indeed of the necessity to concern himself any longer with the details of politics. He likened his Parliament this time to an 'Assembly of Philosophers', as Napoleon's Five Hundred had been. For a new phase lay before the Republic. Political independence had been won; cultural independence must now be achieved – with the Gazi's 'philosophers' as its automatic instrument, and a growing generation of Republican Turks as its fervent adherents.

CHAPTER FIFTY-FOUR

REFORM OF THE ALPHABET

THE FIRST ACT of the third Grand National Assembly was to round off the religious reforms by deleting from the Constitution the formula that 'the religion of the Turkish State is Islam'. Turkey thus became, legally and constitutionally, a secular state, in line with those of the West. Religious belief became a matter of individual conscience. There remained, however, one tie with the East and Islam – the Arabic script, in which Turkish had been written. It thus became the first task of the new Assembly to reform the Turkish alphabet.

The simplification of the script had been discussed at intervals, against strong opposition from the Islamic authorities, for a hundred years past. The alphabet was that of Islam, as used by the Arabs and Persians, and was originally adopted by the Turks for religious reasons, despite the fact that it did not fit the sounds of their language. With its complexity of characters and accents, its paucity of vowels and its ambiguity of sounds in differing contexts, it was hard for an ordinary person to read, and even the educated Ottoman Turk would often make mistakes in its spelling. This led to the growth of two separate languages, that of the Ottoman mandarin class, which was written but largely unspoken, and that of the people, which was unwritten but spoken. This excluded the bulk of the population from most written literature. How could popular sovereignty thrive without an alphabet which all the people could learn and read?

At the time of the Triumvirate, Enver had made a half-hearted attempt at a change in the offices of his War Ministry, by separating the Arabic letters instead of running them together into the normal script. But this was abandoned on the outbreak of war. For fear of religious opposition he had not dared introduce the Latin script. Nor did Kemal, until the people had grown used to his other more radical religious reforms. In 1926 however, at a congress in Baku, the Latin alphabet was adopted for all the Turco-Tartar republics in the Soviet Union. This meant that two large groups of

Turkish people would no longer be able to read one another's language, and it provided an argument for a change. In the following year the Latin script was used on a new issue of postage stamps.[1] Ismet, however, was at first strongly opposed to a general change. With his methodical staff officer's mind he was dismayed at the prospect of the consequent confusion in government offices, in the army, in the universities and the schools and in the press, while the people learnt the new letters.

Kemal, though he was determined on the reform and had been discussing it with intellectuals for some years past, did not intend to implement it without unanimous backing. Thus it was not until 1928 that, after a few preliminary fanfares, he launched his campaign. He appointed an Alphabet Commission to prepare a new script. Knowing that, left to itself, the Commission might take years to accomplish its task, he attended its meetings in person and gave it the benefit of his forceful views. Early in the proceedings he asked Falih Rifki, his own principal nominee on the Commission, how long the change was likely to take. The consensus of opinion, said Falih Rifki, was five years. This allowed for a period in which both scripts would be taught in the schools and printed side by side in the newspapers. Kemal protested that in this case people would continue to read the old script, disregarding the new, and decreed, 'The change will happen in three months or it will not happen at all.'

Thus within six weeks the new alphabet was ready. Kemal was always shrewd in his choice of an audience. For his introduction of the hat he had chosen a reactionary part of the country. For the introduction of the new letters he chose the more advanced centre of Istanbul. He picked, moreover, on a popular audience, assembled one August evening in the Sarayburnu Park, below the Sultan's Old Seraglio, for a People's Party fête. It was in this park that, in defiance of Moslem taboos against the portrayal of the human figure, a statue of the Gazi had been unveiled two years earlier. The Gazi took his place on a platform amid plaudits from the crowd, many of whom had not set eyes on their hero before. On a rival platform a modern jazz band played, and alternately a troupe of Egyptian entertainers sang in a mournful Arabic wail. After listening to this impatiently for a while, Kemal called for a notebook and started to scribble in it. As he did so he tore out the sheets and passed them over to Falih Rifki, remarking, 'Take a look at this.' Falih Rifki saw and approved it as the draft of a speech, written in the Latin script.

When he had done so the Gazi rose to his feet, said a few introductory words, then brandished the papers in his hand and called for someone who could read Turkish to come up to the platform and recite their contents.

[1] The Americans were first in the field with Latin numberplates on their diplomatic cars, but when they wrote out a Customs declaration in Latin characters, it was politely returned to them with a request that they re-submit it in Turkish.

A youth ran up, but on seeing that they were in the Latin script, was silent. Kemal explained: 'This young man is puzzled because he does not know the true Turkish alphabet. I will therefore have one of my comrades read it to you.' He handed it to Falih Rifki, who read it aloud:

Our rich and harmonious language will now be able to display itself with new Turkish letters. We must free ourselves from these incomprehensible signs that for centuries have held our minds in an iron vice. You must learn the new Turkish letters quickly. Teach them to your compatriots, to women and to men, to porters and to boatmen. Regard it as a patriotic and national duty . . . and when you perform that duty, bear in mind that for a nation to consist of ten or twenty per cent of literates and eighty or ninety per cent of illiterates is shameful. . . . We shall repair these errors, and in doing so I want the participation of all our compatriots. . . . Our nation will show, with its script and with its mind, that its place is with the civilized world.

A pandemonium of applause followed his words. The jazz band and the Arabic singers were silenced. Here was a far more unusual entertainment, with the Gazi himself as its star, a fascinating new game which all, whether or not they could yet read, must now learn, to please their hero. Kemal rose to his feet to drink a toast to the crowd with – to Ismet's consternation – a glass of *raki* in his hand. Raising it to his lips, he said, 'Sultans drank this. Kings have drunk it. I want to drink it with my people.' His people showed no signs of disapproval. On his way out of the park he noticed an attractive woman, wearing a *charshaf*,[1] with her husband. He asked her to lift it and reveal her beautiful face. She did so eagerly and gave him an embrace. From that August evening onwards the populace of Istanbul were at his feet.

With the literate classes he knew that he had a harder task before him. A few days later he summoned a conference of scholars, men of letters, journalists, deputies and others to discuss the reform in the Dolma Bahche Palace. Determined to have his way, but expecting certain members of his audience to be critical, he encouraged them to express their views from the platform, but conveyed to them privately a hint that their criticism, if too strongly worded, would not be welcome.

Opposition thus effectively stifled, he announced that passages in the new alphabet would be inserted from now onwards in the newspapers, and that within three months it would entirely supersede the old. He ordered that, from the autumn onwards, all teaching in the schools should be done with the new alphabet – an order which caused consternation among schoolmasters, who did not themselves know it. They had neither the necessary text-books nor the means of having them printed. The presses had no Latin

[1] A form of veil.

characters until they could be procured by air from abroad, and no compositors to set the type until they themselves could learn them.

Kemal then instructed all the deputies to proceed to their constituencies, to organize the teaching of the new alphabet and to make propaganda in its favour. Ismet himself was sent for this purpose to his own constituency of Malatya. Expounding the new alphabet to his constituents, as the means of raising Turkey to the level of the literate nations of the West, he remarked, 'Today the whole country has been transformed into a class-room, and the headmaster in that class-room is the Gazi himself. The Turkish people are going to work hard until they pass the exam of that school.'

This was a role that suited Kemal nicely. He had once declared that, after winning his victory, he would like to become Minister of Education and really educate the people of Turkey. And now he had achieved this ambition. Blackboards were disposed around the Dolma Bahche Palace, an article of furniture to which its marble halls had not before been accustomed, and Kemal as he moved through the rooms gave lessons to visitors who came for an audience, to officials, to friends, to guests, to his personal servants. The blackboard became the symbol of the new Turkish Republic.

He became so carried away by these educational activities that he even composed an Alphabet March for the people to sing and so master their letters more quickly. He called the leader of the Presidential band, and recited the march to him with instructions that it should be orchestrated and played back to him early next morning. The musicians worked on it the whole night through. But when they played it he listened morosely and said, 'Children, though I composed this march I don't like it a bit.' Thus the Alphabet March was abandoned.

In November 1928 the new script became law. Introducing it into the Assembly as the 'key which would enable the people of Turkey to read and write easily,' he artfully referred to it not as the Latin but as the Turkish script, thus pointing its distinction from the Arabic, whose use was prohibited from the end of the year onwards. For the first time his speech was broadcast over the rudimentary Turkish radio. As 'a token of the gratitude of the Turkish people', the Assembly presented him with a golden board, on which the letters of the new alphabet were carved in relief. That evening they were displayed, in coloured lights, on the main buildings in Ankara.

A few days later civil servants throughout the country sat for an examination in the script, and a 'School of the Nation' was founded, whose 'chief instructor' was to be 'His Excellency the President of the Republic, Gazi Mustafa Kemal'. Its object was to create a literate population – from those who could not read and write at all to those who could do so only in the old characters. Within a year more than a million citizens had received its diploma. Inevitably the children and the illiterates were those who learnt the quickest, their minds unencumbered with knowledge of a previous alphabet, and they were soon giving lessons to their parents and grand-parents. For the older generation some effort and strain was involved in the change, and many continued in private to use the old script. But for the younger generation it was the reform above all which appealed to their imagination and aroused their patriotic enthusiasm. It liberated them effec-tively from the Ottoman past, and made them feel that they had a stake in the new Turkey of the Republic.

For the youth of Turkey henceforward, as one dramatic change followed another with the promise of new and expanding horizons, this was an exciting time to be alive.

CHAPTER FIFTY-FIVE

EXPERIMENT IN DEMOCRACY

WHILE THE GAZI busied himself with his country's cultural future, its present economic situation was growing acute. Kemal was no economist. Money and all that it involved was never a matter to preoccupy his thoughts. His attitude towards it was careless. He would laugh at his ineptitude for business, telling against himself a story of how it had led him to lose his war savings to an unscrupulous Smyrna merchant. Personally incorrupt, he tended to be casual in his attitude to corruption in his friends, provided it did not go too far.[1]

For his country he had, from his early days in Anatolia, scorned the notion that lack of funds could make the War of Independence impossible. Not indeed God but circumstances would provide – and so it proved. The war was won by improvisation. The new state was founded on less capital than any small business corporation. Kemal arrived at Ankara to find the equivalent of a mere few shillings in the Treasury. When he sent Yunus Nadi to collect five hundred Turkish liras (£100) to start a newspaper, the Treasurer replied cheerfully, 'The safe is open. Help yourself!' for it was empty.

Kemal had to depend largely on local levies and on gifts which, ironically, came oftener than not from the 'clergy'. The first hard funds of the Executive Committee were three hundred Turkish liras (£60) which a man of

---

[1] He seldom carried money on his person. One day, walking on the hills around Chankaya with a rich friend, he fell into conversation with a poor young peasant. After interrogating him on various subjects he asked whether he had any money. The boy shyly said no. Atatürk, finding that he had none with him, said, 'Do you see this man with me? He is stinking rich. Knock him down and take his money.' Hesitantly the boy, obeying orders, began to wrestle with the man in Turkish fashion, threw him and took his wallet. But it contained only 52 liras. Atatürk then ordered him to take his friend's watch. At this the man protested. Atatürk then said to him, 'Very well. Take this child's address, send him a hundred liras and he will send the watch back to you.' To the boy he said, 'Keep the watch until you get the money. You can't trust these stinking rich people.'

religion had collected from his flock and brought to Kemal wrapped in a handkerchief. The day-to-day expenses of the first Grand National Assembly were covered largely by the conversion of public buildings into dormitories and canteens, where the deputies paid for their board and lodging – though the arrears in their parliamentary salaries often prevented them from doing so. After the break with Istanbul Kemal, taking over the civil administration, could draw on the revenues of Anatolia. But the financial situation of the Nationalists and their armies was always precarious.

When victory was won – a victory which followed ten years of continuous warfare – many economic problems had to be faced. Devastation was widespread. Houses and farms were in ruins. Livestock was decimated, fields had become wildernesses, food and clothing and money were scarce. Turkey had emerged from the war much reduced in size, but uncomfortably large in relation to her population and means. She needed capital to develop her natural resources, but feared to borrow it abroad lest she fall once more into the foreigner's grip, while the foreigner himself was chary of investing until he felt more confidence in the new régime. Trade, which he had previously handled, was paralysed. The country lacked not only artisans but bankers and business men.[1] For it was largely the Greeks and other foreigners who had fulfilled these roles, and they had departed. Turkey thus found herself in an economic vacuum at a time when it was necessary to raise the standard of living and replace the gospel of religious reaction with that of material progress.

With a view to filling the vacuum Kemal had called an economic congress at Izmir in 1923. Here he voiced once more the doctrine that the masters of the nation were the people, this time carrying it from the political into the economic field. In his opening speech he sought to shake the Anatolian peasantry out of their submission, in the name of Islamic fatalism, to life at a bare subsistence level. The people's era, in his opinion, could be called the era of economic ideals,

> the sort of era in which we say, 'Let our country be prosperous! Let our people live in plenty! Let them be rich!' And on this point let me remind you of a philosophical saying: 'Being satisfied (with what you have) is an indestructible treasure.' I say, let this era of economic ideals put an end to the idea that being satisfied is an indestructible treasure and that poverty is a virtue! . . . If what we call our land had been made up of bone-dry mountains, of stones, swamps and naked plains . . . there could have been absolutely no difference between it and a prison. . . . But this country of ours is one that is not only fit but most suitable to be made

[1] It was a moment at which Javid, one of the few Turks with an international status in the world of finance, might have been helpful, had Kemal chosen to admit him to the fold instead of executing him. Javid had offered his services to the Nationalists at the time of the Sivas Congress, but Kemal had rejected them.

into a paradise for our children and grandchildren. . . . The arm that wields the sword grows weary and in the end puts it back in the scabbard, when perhaps it is doomed to rust and moulder; but the arm that holds the plough grows daily stronger, and in growing stronger becomes yet more the master and owner of the soil.

There must, in brief, be economic self-reliance. In pursuit of this, agriculture must be mechanized, industries developed, communications improved. To achieve this all classes of Turks – farmers, artisans, merchants, workers – must unite, for each needed the other. Such principles were enshrined, at the end of the conference, in an economic counterpart of the National Pact, allowing for control by the state from the point at which private enterprise ended.

During the next few years certain measures were taken to translate them into practice. The burden of the tithe, by which the peasant had been virtually enslaved, was abolished. State monopolies, in such basic commodities as sugar, salt, matches, tobacco, alcohol, petrol and shipping were established, transferring the fiscal burden to the landlords and townspeople who were their principal customers. They covered so many products that a facetious deputy enquired, 'When are we going to have a monopoly of *kebab*?' A start was made with land reform, by changes in the system of tenure and by redistribution of parts of the big estates to landless peasants and immigrants – a policy leading in the former Greek districts to the emergence of a new class of small Turkish landowner. The People's Party aspired to take over the role of the former magnates through its own local organizations, 'advising' the peasantry. For the country, if it was to feed itself and leave an exportable surplus with which to buy other necessities from abroad, must cultivate more land and grow more produce.

Nevertheless the peasantry and their production languished throughout these years, owing to the preference given to industrial before agricultural development. The economic argument for this was that Turkey could not now afford to buy all the manufactured goods she needed, hence must make them. But there was a political and psychological argument too. Turkey, bent on coming into line with the West, did not wish to be regarded as a nation of peasants. Western countries were industrialized; therefore Turkey must be industrialized. Hence the expenditure of capital, not on the improvement of the soil, but on the creation of factories, blast furnaces, steel-works, mines.

The capital was provided at this stage predominantly by the state, but with a leavening of private enterprise. Four state banks were established. Kemal drew the money subscribed by the Moslems of India for the national struggle, handed it to Mahmud Jelal (Celal Bayar), one of his few associates who knew anything of such matters, and told him to open a bank with it –

the first Turkish bank. In a derelict shop in the old town of Ankara he did so. It became the İş Bank (Work Bank) and was followed by three others: the Sumer (Sumerian) Bank, the Central Bank and later the Eti (Hittite) Bank. The state banks and industries would help to create a new Turkish middle-class, filling the gap left by the foreigner. Private enterprise too had its chance, with the granting of lesser industrial concessions to individuals – mainly prominent members of the party and of Kemal's own entourage. Ismet, beyond favouring a rigid system of state control, concerned himself little with economic policy as such. His mind ran primarily on politics – but also on military strategy. Throughout the war and the Revolution he had been brooding on the lack of communications. Thus his main concern was the construction of railways.

Despite these various measures, the country's economy hung fire during the first six years of the Republic, and with the crash on the New York Stock Exchange in October 1929 and the consequent world depression it slowed down to the point of stagnation. The depression aggravated a general feeling of discontent which had been growing for some years past. Harvests had lately been bad, partly from droughts, partly from the lack of seed to plant, and there were cases of famine. Dislike of Westernization was thus reinforced by fear of starvation. God was not providing, and this was seen as a punishment for godlessness, for the breakaway from religion, so that in the Ramadan fast people flocked back to the mosques to make amends.

There was too little incentive to the peasants themselves to provide, and reassurances that conditions would improve were disbelieved. Government officials were underpaid and thus subject to corruption. Banditry again became rife in the Black Sea mountains, where troops had to be mobilized to round up the gangs. There was a more serious disturbance, once again, in Kurdistan. All these operations cost money. There was resentment at the high prices and other hardships arising from the state monopolies, at the funds spent on the building of railways while the peasants lacked roads to take their produce to market. Ismet's policy was generally disparaged, and from the early months of 1930 it was openly attacked in a new newspaper named *Yarin* (Tomorrow). This was the first time for five years that any organ of the press had dared thus freely to criticize the Government. Moreover it was clear that the Gazi condoned the criticism, and Ismet was goaded into promising a new economic programme.

But Kemal's intentions went further than this. Late in the summer he announced the formation of a new party, in opposition to his own Government. The economic crisis was at last bringing home to him the disadvantages of one-party rule. It brought him unpopularity, since the mistakes of the Government were blamed on him personally; it left him in the dark as to trends of public opinion, and created an explosive situation by blocking the normal channels of public discontent. His censored press told him little; he could not always be in the Assembly to feel its pulse; the ministers revealed to him only the rosiest of pictures and he was thus hampered in assessing the effects of his Government's policy and in guiding it effectively. Some form of parliamentary criticism, he had begun to see, was desirable.

Speaking of such matters, he drew a parallel between himself and the enlightened Augustus, the first Caesar, who under the Roman Republic was endowed by the Senate with absolute powers, with the result that at the time of his death the Republic was forgotten and his successors crowned emperors thereafter. This must not happen here. Kemal still disapproved of dictatorship in theory, and it was his genuine desire to create a system which would outlast him and evolve, to the benefit of his country, into a replica of a Western-style democracy.

Foreign opinion moreover meant much to him. Abroad, in the democratic countries, Turkey's one-party system was seen as a sign of her inferiority to the West. He had been stung by the criticism of European writers that the Turkish system, though Western in form, was Eastern in practice. He now saw a chance of countering such criticism, of furthering his ultimate aim, and of providing a safety valve for the present discontents in a more democratic form, but still without prejudice to his own authority.

The Progressive Party he had suppressed because of its 'unwelcome spontaneity' (as a foreign diplomat put it), because of his mistrust of the popularity of Rauf and the generals. Instead he would form a new Opposition party, not independent, as Rauf's had been, but under his own indirect control. He would ride two party horses at once, gaining credit for the successes and evading blame for the failures of either. As the rival leader to Ismet he picked upon Fethi, who since his resignation from the Premiership, five years before, had been Ambassador in Paris, and whom he knew he could manage and trust. The new party would be called the Free Republican as opposed to the People's Republican Party.

The proposition was discussed at the Table throughout the summer of 1930, and in effect agreed before Fethi's return on leave from Paris towards the end of July. A few days after his arrival in Istanbul Kemal called upon him and invited him to lead the new party. The burden of his thesis was, 'I do not want to die without bringing the régime of personal rule in Turkey to a close. I want to create a liberal Republic.' He alluded to Fethi's well-known sympathy for the British parliamentary system, and suggested that here was a chance for him to put it into practice at home. He had also, in recent years, become familiar with the workings of French parliamentary institutions. What better man than he thus to complete the democratization of his own country?

Fethi hesitated, largely because of the personal conflicts in which the venture was sure to involve him. On the other hand he was a convinced liberal. Sitting day after day in the gallery of the *Chambre des Députés*, he had pondered regretfully on the limitations of his own country's one-party Assembly. Above all, he had from his youth made a serious study of economics: during his exile in Malta he had translated into Turkish a work by Maynard Keynes. He believed profoundly in the principles of a free economy, disapproved of Ismet's rigid statist methods, and had strong views of his own as to the causes of the present economic crisis. Largely on these grounds he responded to pressure not only from Kemal but from Ismet himself, and agreed, on reflection, to accept the proposal.

Discussions followed at Yalova, a watering-place on the Marmara which Kemal had created, and where he was now spending much of his time, free from the constrictions of the Dolma Bahche Palace. He made it clear that, though Fethi was to be the leader of the party, he himself would take a hand in its management, as in that of the People's Party. He promised Fethi some seventy or eighty seats in the Assembly, at the next election, and asked him to submit a list of candidates. Meanwhile members of the People's Party would be encouraged to transfer their allegiance.

Having chosen the leader of his Opposition it now remained for Kemal to choose its other chief members. But the deputies proved reluctant to join. After five years of one-party rule, the idea of Opposition had grown so unfamiliar that prospective members needed reassurance from Kemal that they would not be victimized for opposing him. He gave it emphatically, declaring that he looked forward to watching the fight. However heated it became, both sides would be invited to his Table, where they would be expected to speak freely and give him the chance to judge between their respective views. For a start, to help establish confidence, he instructed Nuri (Conker) his closest *aide* and friend, to act as secretary-general of the party. He enrolled also his sister, Makbule, a woman who shared his obstinacy and his high-strung temperament, but little of his intelligence and none of his education. Quarrelsome and frank in her speech, she was now, as a member of the Free Party, to have a chance to deprecate him in public, which she used to the full. Thus did the Turkish Republic embark on its second experiment in democracy.

After a mere three months it was to end in failure. Trouble very soon arose when Fethi visited Izmir, to inaugurate a new branch of the Free Party. He did so against the advice of his wiser counsellors, who urged that the party should move slowly and should not yet seek electoral representation, but in response to promptings from Kemal, who took the opposite view. It was none the less arranged that Fethi's arrival in Izmir should be as unobtrusive as possible. The police feared disturbances against him. In fact the exact reverse happened. Despite these precautions a huge crowd swarmed down to the harbour to greet him as a popular hero. Fethi did his best to calm his over-enthusiastic admirers. But so open a demonstration against the Government thoroughly alarmed the local authorities, who requested him in the interests of law and order to postpone the party meeting he had planned to address.

Meanwhile the People's Party hurriedly organized a rally of their own. They found difficulty in mobilizing sufficient supporters, and their speakers were howled down by a crowd calling for Fethi. The crowd swarmed through the streets to demonstrate before his hotel and before the People's Party headquarters and newspaper office. Here windows were broken and the police opened fire, killing a boy of fourteen. A detachment of troops was called in to restore order. When Fethi, on telegraphed instructions from the Gazi, finally made his speech, he did so flanked by police, in a voice growing hoarse and in any case insufficiently powerful to reach the large crowd which had assembled.

He revealed the somewhat nebulous programme of the Free Party, and praised the Gazi, 'the spiritual guide of the people', who had welcomed its formation. He argued against Ismet in favour of a liberal system, giving scope to private enterprise while leaving certain spheres to the state. He was greeted with tumultuous enthusiasm, except by a member of the crowd who withdrew on learning that he had failed to promise the restoration of the fez and the Arabic script.

He then left for Manisa and Balikesir, where he was treated to similar ovations. Everywhere the peasantry seized the chance to ventilate their wrongs. In one place, when he unwisely raised his hat, the crowd removed their own and flung them to the ground with cheers; in another he was greeted with Islamic banners as the defender of the Faith against the godless Republic.

'The new party,' as Grew, the American Ambassador, expressed it, 'had become a clinical thermometer for taking the political temperature of the country and there could be no doubt of the fever which it registered.' The press of the People's Party raised it further in articles against Fethi, while in Ankara its alarmed bosses brought pressure to bear on Kemal. As a result he went back on his policy of benevolent neutrality and affirmed, in a press statement, his 'historical' allegiance to the People's Party, disclaiming any intention to sever his ties with it. He then tilted the scales against the Free Party by deploring the attack on the People's Party offices at Izmir, and the insults directed against the Government by 'a few irresponsible persons'. These various acts of aggression would be punished by the laws of the Republic.

It was thus a distinctly aggrieved Fethi who now returned to Ankara. Here the two-party struggle was continued within the walls of the Assembly. Kemal, in opening the debate, encouraged both sides by reiterating that he favoured neither at the expense of the other. As Ambassador Grew, quoting the report of his commercial attaché, recorded the scene:

The Gazi sat in his private box watching the tilting between the Government and the Opposition from the tribune – beaming when a telling point was scored, frowning when a point was awkwardly handled. Gillespie says it reminded him of nothing so much as a proud father watching his sons competing in two opposing debating teams. . . . The whole outlook of the Assembly has changed and whereas formerly the measures of the Government were accepted and voted in an automatic and apathetic fashion, now everyone is full of zest, important points are freely debated, and constructive criticism formulated and a real parliamentary atmosphere prevails.

But this first glow of enthusiasm was soon to fade. Neither of the two parties showed notable signs of leadership or of a new and positive policy. Tensions between them mounted to a climax during the municipal elections – a dress rehearsal, as it were, for the general election to come – which were held under police supervision, with ruthless discrimination against the Free Party.

On 15th November Fethi launched a forcible attack in the Assembly on the Ministry of the Interior for these fraudulent practices. The debate grew so heated that it began to recall, in its atmosphere of personal abuse, those of the first Grand National Assembly. The Gazi in his President's box listened in silence throughout, with a look of some depression on his face. Were his people, after ten years of his tuition, still as ignorant of the decencies of democratic debate? He displayed however a clear determination not to become involved in the discomfiture he had brought upon his friend; and at the end of the session the Government received a vote of confidence by 225 votes to 10.

Fethi thus decided to dissolve the Free Party. With Nuri, his Secretary-General, he proceeded to Chankaya with a draft of the terms of its dissolution. It reiterated that the party had been sponsored by the Gazi and that this had ruled out any possibility of opposing him in person. But now that the prospect of doing so arose, its existence must be brought to an end.

Its failure was due partly to mismanagement. Fethi was not the ideal choice for the role which Kemal thrust upon him. Convinced democrat though he was, he lacked the gift of effective political leadership. He was neither a forceful speaker nor an astute debater. He had too few supporters of standing, and could make little headway in the Assembly against the well-trained, well-entrenched professional legions of the People's Party. For five years he had been out of the country, thus out of touch with the political and personal currents which underlay this Assembly, and with public opinion in general. His tactics moreover had been faulty. He would have had a better chance of success had he built up his party more gradually, trying it out tentatively as a small pressure group in the Assembly to act as a corrective to the party in power, as Rauf had at first done with the Progressives, instead of springing it suddenly on the country as a whole. His local organizations had been hastily and casually planned, becoming rallying points for a mixed collection of extremists and malcontents, and thus endangering public security.

But the main fault was in essence Kemal's. Unlike his previous adventures, that of a licensed Opposition had been inadequately thought out and prepared in advance. Instead of being allowed to grow organically, as the Republic itself had done – or had been made to seem to do – it had been abruptly, even capriciously launched upon an unsuspecting country. Such shock tactics as had served well enough for the abolition of the fez were inappropriate to so radical an operation as the introduction of parliamentary democracy, so soon after its deliberate suppression. Kemal had rejected the two-party system five years before, at a time when the momentum of the Revolution and the calibre of his Opposition leaders might have carried it through. He had tried to reimpose it when the momentum had waned, at a time, not of military and political victory, but of social and economic depression. Only two factors could have given substance to the democratic form which he had thus failed to achieve: his own willingness to subscribe to it wholeheartedly and readiness to relinquish some degree of his own power; and the capacity of the Turkish people, retarded as they had been by centuries of autocratic rule, to adapt themselves to so adult and responsible a system. Neither of these factors existed.

The debâcle, however, had one good result. It showed that Ankara knew all too little of what was happening in the rest of Turkey. This, at least, could now be remedied. Immediately after the valedictory debate, the Gazi set off on a three-month tour of the country, to find things out for himself.

He took with him a large personal staff, including officials from the various ministries. They made a detailed study of social and economic conditions, while Kemal himself conferred with local officials, inspected institutions of all kinds, questioned the people and encouraged them to talk to him of their problems in person. His objective was to translate the letter of reform into its spirit, to probe beneath such superficial symbols as changes in headgear and script at the fundamental mentality of his people.

Always the teacher, he examined quantities of pupils in the schools. He would stride into a classroom, often petrifying the teacher into silence by his presence, and wander around the class, questioning the students and scrutinizing their text-books. In one of these, written by a young official of the Ministry of Education on his staff, Hassan Ali (Yücel), he detected some Arabic words, and summoned him to dinner for a discussion on the reform of the language. He fired at him a number of questions on mathematics which, as the young man was careful to explain, was only incidentally his subject. 'What is a point? What is a line?' the Gazi asked him. Then, 'What is zero?'

Hassan Ali, with his wits about him, replied, 'It may best be defined, Pasha, as "myself in your presence".'

'But zero,' Kemal insisted, 'is important.'

'So must I be, Pasha, if I am here in your presence.'

Kemal filled Hassan Ali's glass with *raki*, and said aloud before the rest of the table, 'You have passed your exam.' He was later to be rewarded by many years' service as Minister of Education.

The Gazi made speeches in which he endeavoured to explain to the people the meaning of that incomprehensible word, democracy, and the responsibilities attached to it. In Izmir he said, 'When a citizen says, "I want this, I want that," it should mean, "I must do this or do that." ' Everywhere he took direct action on the spot, changing government and party officials, dismissing the executive committee of the People's Party at Samsun, ordering seed for the farmers of Havza, calling for increased sugar production at Ushak, opening banks in various places.

His enquiries had revealed widespread discontent with living conditions in general – moreover a discontent no longer accepted with the fatalism of the past. On the return of Kemal and his staff to Istanbul a report was prepared, summarizing their conclusions and recommending improvements in various fields. This helped to point the moral that any political reform, such as the Free Party had embodied, must first be rooted in a policy of basic reforms in the social and economic lives of the people.

Another moral was pointed, six weeks after the dissolution of the Free Party, by an ugly religious disturbance at Menemen, in the region of Izmir. It was staged, as the Kurdish Revolt had been, by the fanatical Nakshibendi sect. A group of its extremists, led by a dervish chief, arrived in the town on a pilgrimage from Manisa. Exalted by a preparatory period of religious exercises and fasting, on a diminishing diet of figs and water – but with the occasional stimulus of drugs – they held forth as they marched to the peasantry, urging them to join their ranks and provide them with arms. They gathered in the main square of the town where, in frenzied rhetorical tones, their leaders preached open sedition, demanding the return of the Holy Law, the veil, the fez, the Arabic script, prophesying the overthrow of the godless Republic by the militant forces of Islam, calling for an Army of the Faithful to march upon Ankara and thereafter to conquer the world.

The temper of the crowd, which soon massed around the marchers, was uncertain. Some were apathetic, some curious. The dormant fanaticism of others was roused by the words of the speakers. A young officer happened to pass through the square with a small group of soldiers. In an attempt to disperse the rioters, he ordered his men to fire a few rounds of blank ammunition. But when no one was wounded a *hoja* cried out, 'You see, they have not been hit. They are saints.' The officer then rashly tried to parley with the ringleader, Mehmed the Dervish. The dervish instantly shot him; then, as he lay bleeding to death on the ground, sent for a saw, with which he cut off his head. This was tied to a flag-pole and carried bleeding through the streets, while his followers ran wild with fanatical invocations.

The gendarmerie, unable to handle the mob, called in the military. When they arrived the men stood by, reluctant to fire on the holy men. But the officers, without any such scruples, turned their machine-guns on the crowd. Several dervishes fell, and the outbreak was quelled without further serious trouble. Martial law was at once introduced, and arrests made over a wide area, including the city of Izmir. Over a hundred persons were tried for inciting the population to sedition in an attempt to 'alter the Constitution by force'. Some were sentenced to death and some to spells of imprisonment.

The incident was given wide and lurid publicity in the newspapers. They found it convenient to imply that it was the fault of the Free Party, which had in fact been disbanded six weeks before. They made a martyr of the murdered officer, extolling his heroism as an inspiration to Turkish Youth and reporting demonstrations in his honour.

The riot showed that the brotherhoods, which had for centuries underlain not merely the religious but the social and political life of the country, had not been eliminated by a mere stroke of the Assembly's pen. Because the people needed them, they still survived beneath the surface, ready to erupt at the least provocation. For Kemal's religious reforms had not been allowed to grow organically, as new habits of life; they were ideas imposed artificially, from the top downwards. A generation or more must elapse before the people could be awakened to the true meaning of the Revolution which had been achieved in their name.

Meanwhile, if it was to be saved, there must be no further talk of democracy. Instead there must be a strengthening but at the same time a broadening of one-party rule. The 'strong man' of the People's Party henceforward was to be Rejep Peker, now appointed its secretary-general. A ruthless but intelligent autocrat, his political philosophy envisaged a policy of change by 'force and coercion', contrasting with Kemal's earlier 'step by step' approach.

At the same time the party, which as Ismet publicly admitted had lost touch with the people, was reorganized to become a more flexible instrument, with an extension of responsible leadership at the top and a wider delegation of control lower down. A means of achieving closer touch was devised through the adaptation to a new form of the old 'Turkish Hearth'. Once a cultural institution, it was now converted into a network of 'People's Houses', which soon proliferated throughout the country, serving also political purposes and helping to fulfil the role, imposed upon the party by Kemal, of 'tutor to the nation'.

The ideological message now preached to it was symbolized by the 'Six Arrows' of what came to be called Kemalism, with the addition in 1931 of Statism and Revolutionism (or Reformism) to the four previous principles of Nationalism, Secularism, Republicanism and Populism. Each was interlocked with the other – statism insuring through populism against exploitation; populism guaranteed against it by secularism; all protected by nationalism against foreign aggression, and kept alive by the revolutionary dynamic.

Kemal had consistently opposed ideologies as limiting freedom of action. But, with the complexity of the problems which now lay ahead, defined doctrines were needed. With Fascism arising on one front and Communism on the other, it was important for the Turks to show the world that they wanted neither of them. Hence the more flexible ideology of Kemalism, whose principles at least had the merit of being forged not from preconceived theories but from the hard school of ten years' practical experience.

In terms of statism the Government now embarked on a Five Year Plan for the increased development of state-financed industries. This was inspired by the precedent of Soviet Russia and aided by Russian machinery and an interest-free loan. But Kemal was zealous to point out that it was based on no socialist theory. Communism, he maintained, had failed to achieve its aims and promises. Liberalism too was dead. Turkish statism was to be something different from either, leavening state control with a certain element of personal enterprise.

Whether it achieved the best or the worst of both worlds, it at least gave the country useful industrial enterprises. Where it still failed was in its persistent neglect of agriculture, the country's most valuable natural asset. It was not until a second World War began to cloud the horizon that the urgent need was expressed for an agricultural policy 'based on serious studies', moreover within the grasp of all peasants, none of whom must now be left without land.

The new economic policy brought to the fore a new political figure. He was Celal (Bayar),[1] a former Unionist with a crafty mind, who had become a respectful adherent of Kemal. Once a bank clerk in Smyrna, he had been employed by the Gazi to organize the banking system of the Republic. 'I gave him a bag of gold,' Kemal would say of him, 'and he gave me a bank.' He was now to become his Minister of Economy. Henceforward Kemal left economic policy, in which he had never been seriously interested, to Bayar. It was to foreign policy that he now devoted his principal personal attention.

[1] Mahmud Jelal.

CHAPTER FIFTY-SIX

TURKEY'S PLACE IN THE WORLD

FRUSTRATED in his hope of presenting to the Western world a new Turkey shaped in its own democratic image, Kemal was none the less determined on her acceptance within it as a free and responsible sovereign power. There must be concrete proofs of his own international statesmanship. The conception of the one-party dictatorship was nothing new to the Europe of the nineteen-thirties. What was new, and what Turkey must now manifest to her neighbours, was the existence in the world of a one-party 'dictatorship' which, unlike those of Hitler and Mussolini and Stalin, was essentially pacific, nourishing no territorial or political ambitions at any other country's expense.

Peaceful co-existence, 'Peace at home and peace abroad', were Kemal's watchwords. The Turks were the friends of all civilized nations. The hatchets of the past, with its lust for conquest, were buried. The Turkish mind harboured no thoughts of reconquest or revision of frontiers.[1] As Kemal's Foreign Minister defined his country's policy, 'Turkey does not desire an inch of foreign territory, but will not give up an inch of what she holds.'[2]

Of all the dictatorial régimes that of Turkey had been alone in basing itself on a policy not of expansion but of retraction. As far back as 1921 Kemal had been saying, 'Let us recognize our own limits.' By keeping Turkey small he would make her great. The Turkish Republic desired only its territorial integrity and freedom. As long as the West would respect this, Turkey in return offered the West a zone of peace in an explosive corner of the East. The new sovereign Republic, geographically poised between East and West, was to be a stabilizing element.

[1] Once, to a Hungarian diplomat bemoaning the fate of his former Empire, Kemal showed marked lack of sympathy. 'But *you* have no children,' the Hungarian protested. 'All the Turkish people are my children,' Kemal replied. Then he said, 'Listen to me.' 'Yes, sir.' 'I am a Macedonian. But I make no territorial claims.'

[2] J. Walter Collins, *The Times* correspondent. *Contemporary Review.*

Thus there were to be pacts both with Russia and her neighbours and with the European powers, both with the Arab and with the Balkan worlds, the former provinces of the Ottoman Empire. Above all there was to be loyal and unquestioning co-operation with the League of Nations. As a revolutionary power, Turkey would be doubly scrupulous in honouring her engagements, seeking a name for giving never less but sometimes more than she promised. Reconciliation with Britain had been achieved with the Mosul agreement. It now remained to complete the reconciliation with Greece.

The surgical operation of the exchange of populations agreed between Turkey and Greece at Lausanne led to a pact of friendship between the two countries, which settled its outstanding problems in a common-sense fashion. It was followed, in October 1930, by an official visit by Venizelos to Turkey on board a Greek warship. His welcome in Ankara was well organized, with Greek flags flying and inscribed Greek banners stretched across the street. But it was not quite spontaneous enough for the exuberant Greek Premier, who could not help remarking to Ismet that a Turkish athletic team had been more warmly received in Athens. To this Ismet replied amicably that the Greeks were the more effervescent people. Moreover, their territory had not been invaded, like that of the Turks.

There was, however, a grand ball at the Ankara Palace Hotel, to celebrate the happy coincidence of his visit with the anniversary of the Turkish Republic, a banquet at the Ministry of Foreign Affairs at which the Gazi showed evident enjoyment, and a military parade which they attended together. In their political talks, official and otherwise, Kemal and Venizelos understood one another, and Venizelos went so far as to throw out the imaginative idea of some kind of union between the two countries, which was discussed at some length. It was not long afterwards that Kemal, burying religious with political hatchets, authorized the conversion of Santa Sophia, which had been a mosque for five hundred years, not indeed back into a church, hung again with bells as the Greeks had for long hoped, but into a museum and a symbol of cultural affinity between Turkey and Europe.

The Turco-Greek Pact had been preceded by a Turco-Italian Pact which, as the 'thirties wore on and the imperialist aims of Mussolini became clearer, acquired the character of a defensive alignment against him. The Gazi, who had discarded military uniform to become a civilian dictator, had no great respect for the Duce, whom he saw as a civilian strutting about in uniform like an actor pretending to be a soldier. Mussolini, he judged, would sooner or later be unable to resist playing the role of a conquering Caesar. To a friend he predicted, 'He will be hanged by his people, one of these days.' Once at Chankaya, where Mussolini's Ambassador was pressing the renewed claims of his country to the Antalya (Adalia) region, Kemal listened to him in silence, then excused himself for a few minutes and left the room.

He returned wearing, for the first time since the proclamation of the Republic, full-dress field marshal's uniform. Without comment he sat down and said, 'Now go ahead, please.' But this time it was the Ambassador who was silent. Rejep Peker, on the other hand, Kemal's party boss, submitted a report to him after a visit to Italy, in which he praised the Fascist system and proposed, in some detail, a similar form of government for Turkey. Kemal glanced at the report and handed it back with the remark, 'You'll do all that after I die.'

On the Hitler régime Kemal approved the dictum of an anti-Nazi German friend that, whereas his own dictatorship had freed an enslaved people, Hitler's had enslaved a free people. Kemal described the German dictator as a tin-peddler, and after reading *Mein Kampf* expressed horror at 'the meanness of his language and the madness of his thoughts'. Thus the Germans got no political change out of a long-term financial credit and the supply of railway materials under the Turkish Five Year Plan.

But of Stalin, the supreme realist, Kemal declared that in a hundred years' time, 'when the fame of all other dictators will have vanished', history would single him out as the most important international statesman of the twentieth century. This respect for Stalin made him the more vigilant in his relations with Soviet Russia – signing agreements which were essentially commercial, resisting all Russian blandishments of a political kind, maintaining a polite friendship but refusing to be weaned away by it from his closer relations with the West.

The rise of Mussolini and Hitler drew Turkey together not merely with Greece but with the other Balkan countries. Already she had agreements with Yugoslavia, Hungary and Bulgaria. What she now sought was a Balkan Entente, as a counterweight to Italian and German imperialism. With this object meetings were held between Turkey and the five Balkan states in their various capitals, until a Balkan Pact was signed early in 1934. It was an incomplete and precarious combination, affording its member states guarantees rather within their own ranks than against the aggression of a great power. But it helped to give Turkey a reputation for international leadership. The Comte de Chambrun, the French Ambassador, when the Gazi talked to him of his plans for thus uniting his neighbours, remarked, 'You talk just as Monsieur Briand does.'

'That's because I think as Monsieur Briand does,' was Kemal's reply. What he was trying to do was to set up, as it were, his own regional 'League of Nations'.

One evening, after dining officially at a Western embassy for the first time as the guest of the British, in honour of Princess Alice and Lord Athlone, Kemal gathered around him a circle of foreign representatives and lectured them on the need for peace between nations. Of the Russian, the Rumanian and the Czech he demanded, 'Why can't you gentlemen settle your differences amicably instead of always quarrelling about territorial and other questions?' There was an embarrassed silence, which was broken after a moment by Lord Athlone, 'Your Excellency,' he suggested, 'the trouble is that nations still distrust each other.' At this observation the Gazi exclaimed, 'Bravo! Bravo!' The party then proceeded to the poker-table.

King Alexander of Yugoslavia, in the course of an informal visit to Istanbul, developed a hero-worship for the Gazi and expressed his readiness as a soldier to obey him in the event of a war. After dining with him he voiced an ardent desire for his friendship, and confided to him that, had he believed the promises of certain European countries, it would have been the Yugoslavs, instead of the Greeks, who would have landed in Anatolia. To this the Gazi replied, 'Then you had a narrow escape, your Majesty. Instead of the Greeks it would have been the Yugoslav Army which would have been thrown back into the Mediterranean.' He despatched a decorative symbol of goodwill to the Balkans in the shape of his adopted daughter Sabiha, who had graduated as the first woman pilot in Turkey, and who flew a new American bomber on a Balkan tour.

The former enemies of Turkey in the Balkan Wars were now, ostensibly, her friends. Her western frontiers were reasonably secure. So were her frontiers with Russia. It now remained to secure those other eastern frontiers, with Russia's neighbours and with the former Arab provinces of the Ottoman Empire. The Balkan Pact must be supplemented by an Eastern Pact. A start had been made ten years before, with the aid of Soviet diplomacy, by a treaty with Afghanistan. A treaty with Persia proved harder to negotiate, on account of frontier disagreements in the Kurdish areas, and of religious hostility in Persia to the abolition of the Caliphate. These differences however were now forgotten, and a treaty of friendship with Persia was followed, in 1934, by an official visit of the Shah to Turkey.

Riza Shah had a personal admiration for Kemal, as a soldier and statesman, which overrode their marked differences of temperament. He shared his views as to the vital need for a good neighbour policy between their two countries. The negotiations for the settlement of the Turco-Persian frontier, along the foot of Mount Ararat, had threatened to break down over a small but vital hill, which each side claimed was essential to its own strategic security. But the goodwill of the two rulers broke the deadlock. Tevfik Rüştü, negotiating in Tehran, bewildered the Persians by calling, on the Gazi's instructions, for the arbitration of the Shah himself. A senior staff officer brought maps to the Shah and spread them out before him, to put the Persian case. Presently however he realized that his master was not paying attention and was looking, not at the maps, but at himself. He interrupted him saying, 'There is only one thing I am interested in. That is friendly relations with Turkey.' The result was a face-saving agreement, to the advantage of the Turks, which drew the frontier along the ridge of the hill.

In his personality the Shah was the antithesis of the Gazi – a strait-laced, taciturn man. But he was familiar with the Turkish dialect of Azerbaijan, where he had served as a soldier, and brushed it up to talk the better with his host. He greeted the Gazi as 'My Brother'. His first evening at Chankaya ran true to Kemal's late habits. The guests did not sit down to dinner till 9.30. At ten o'clock precisely, after finishing only his first course, the Shah, liking to retire and to rise early, took his leave. It was his bedtime. Kemal escorted him back to the house where he was staying, then rejoined his guests, whose dinner had cooled in the meantime. The evening soon took on a more convivial air.

The Shah preferred poker to polite conversation. One evening he played a game at the Persian Embassy with the Gazi and Sir Percy Loraine, the new British Ambassador, to whom Kemal had taken a strong fancy. He and Sir Percy had played together before. On that occasion, when the game finished in the small hours, they had talked together frankly and intimately until long after dawn, about all outstanding Turco-British and Mediterranean problems, thus establishing a personal relationship which was greatly to benefit the two countries and indeed their allies as well.

Now Kemal, after taking a hand, left the poker-table to wander around the room, but returned to stand behind the Shah and to give him advice as to how to bid against Sir Percy, while guests stood around, surveying the scene with some curiosity. They took especial notice when the Gazi remarked to Loraine, with a twinkle, upon the blessings of such close international co-operation. 'We are good adversaries,' he said. 'How much better shall we be as allies!'

During his visit the Shah made a tour of Western Anatolia with the Gazi, visiting the air base at Eskishehir and the battlefields and forts of the Dardanelles. As soldiers the two found much in common. In other respects their differing habits led to some awkward moments. On the presidential train Kemal drank freely. When they reached Ushak, on the line to Izmir, a large crowd swarmed around the train, kissing the hands of the two heads of state. Among them was a *hoja*, in turban and robes. On seeing him the Gazi started to growl insults at Islam.[1] The *hoja* deftly removed his turban, dived into the crowd, and escaped. But Kemal, before proceeding, ordered the imprisonment of the local governor, and instructed that the town of

[1] The Gazi, in such moods, was inclined to 'see red' when confronted with a fez or a turban. At a reception in Ankara one evening his eye lighted on the fez of the Egyptian Ambassador. The Gazi sent a waiter to him with a salver for the fez, remarking, 'Tell your King I don't like his uniform.' To avoid an incident the Ambassador removed it himself, and took his leave. When the news of the episode reached Cairo, King Fuad was furious, and a break in relations with Turkey was only avoided by tactful diplomacy on both sides.

Ushak be bombarded and razed to the ground the next day. Next day, when the order was submitted to him for confirmation, he shamefacedly cancelled it.

Before the Shah left for Persia the Gazi, taking him on a farewell visit to the army, paid him a compliment. 'If ever,' he said, 'I cease to be head of the Turkish state, I trust that your Majesty will permit me to serve, with these other officers, as a member of your staff.'

The remaining link still to be forged in the chain of eastern defence was with Irak. Britain granted her self-government in 1930, and soon afterwards King Feisal paid a visit to Ankara, in which Turco-Arab differences were settled, with the benediction of the British, in a round of diplomatic entertainments. During a talk at a reception in which the King lowered his voice lest others should hear, Kemal interrupted him and said with an amicable nod towards the British Ambassador, 'There is no need to whisper. The Ambassador will know it all in any case tomorrow.'

When similar relations had been achieved between Irak and Persia, Kemal at last had his Saadabad Pact in the East to balance his Balkan Pact in the West. Neither pact was to amount in effect to much more than a pious expression of goodwill. But both at least advertised, to the rest of the world, the change from aggressive to pacific intentions inherent in the demise of the Ottoman Empire and the rise of the Turkish Republic.

Kemal, surveying the world around him with his perceptive international vision, saw clearly the way it was heading. With General Douglas MacArthur, who visited him in 1934, he had several conversations in which he prophesied its course with uncanny insight. The period in which they were living, he believed, was no more than an armistice. For the Allies had made a conqueror's peace, without regard for the root causes of the war or the characteristics and problems of the nations defeated; the Americans had withdrawn from Europe, abandoning the Wilson policy and so preventing the armistice from becoming a peace; the Germans thus held the fate of Europe in their hands, as before. 'The moment these seventy million people,' he said, 'who are industrious and disciplined and have extraordinary dynamism, get caught by a new political element which will stir up their nationalist ambitions, they will have recourse to the liquidation of the Versailles Treaty.'

The war, he predicted, would break out between 1940 and 1945. The French no longer had the qualities which made for a strong army, and the British would be unable to rely on them for the defence of their island. The Italians, if they kept out of the war, could play an important part in the peace which followed it. But Mussolini's ambitions would prevent them from doing so. Thus the Germans would occupy all Europe except Russia and Britain. The Americans would be unable to remain neutral, and their intervention would cause Germany's defeat. But the real victors would be the Bolsheviks, with their use of new political methods unknown to the

A.—16

Europeans and Americans, and their capacity for taking advantage of the slightest mistakes made by their rivals:

> We Turks, as Russia's close neighbour and the nation which has fought more wars against her than any other country, are following closely the course of events there, and see the danger stripped of all camouflage. The Bolsheviks are exploiting with marvellous skill the minds of the awakening nations of the East, and know how to caress and to flatter their nationalistic ambitions and to stir up their masses. The Bolsheviks have now reached a point at which they constitute the greatest threat not only to Europe but to all Asia.[1]

Kemal was a nationalist; but there was nothing parochial in his nationalism. He saw that the day of empires was done and that the day of nations had arrived. But with his global sense he saw beyond this conception towards that of a federation of nations, an amalgamation of sovereignties such as Wells envisaged in his United States of the World. He was attracted by the idea that a number of individual federations might precede something of the kind. He was too much of a realist to believe that such an apotheosis could readily be achieved. But he saw that Russia would seek to achieve it in terms of the communist ideology, and that the principle of internationalism would animate the second half of the twentieth century as that of nationalism was animating its first half. Meanwhile the welfare of nations was inter-dependent:

> We must think of the whole of mankind as being a single body and of each nation as constituting a part of that body. . . . We must not say, 'If there is sickness in a certain place in the world, what does that matter to me?' . . . If there is such sickness, we must be just as much concerned with it as though it happened right in our midst.

[1] Washington correspondent of *Cumhuriyet*, Ankara; 8th November 1951.

CHAPTER FIFTY-SEVEN

A NEW LANGUAGE AND HISTORY

WHEN THE Balkan powers first conferred in Ankara to seek a basis of unity between themselves, the Gazi assured the delegates, in an opening discourse, that their various ancestors derived from Central Asia: 'Coming by routes to the north and to the south of the Black Sea, following one after the other, like the waves of the ocean, for thousands of years, these streams of humanity which settled in the Balkans – in spite of the fact that their groups carried quite different names – are in reality kindred peoples who come from a common cradle and in whose veins circulates the same blood.'

These words were but one manifestation of the new theories which were obtaining a strong hold over Kemal's mind – if not always to the exclusion then sometimes to the distortion of other and more important problems. His reform of the Turkish alphabet was leading, logically enough, to a reform of the Turkish language, in terms of the elimination of Persian and Arabic forms. Less logically, this was accompanied by researches designed to discover a new version of Turkish history. For these two purposes Kemal founded two learned bodies, the Turkish Linguistic and the Turkish Historical Society.

Kemal's own cultural background was scrappy. He had studied subjects *ad hoc*, in periodic bursts of concentration – skimming through them, on occasion, to rationalize some intuitive preconceived notion. But he had never acquired the habit of systematic reading. He knew much of the military and a little of the political sciences. The science of linguistics, to which he now turned his restless attention, was distinctly beyond his range. But with his quick impatient mind he was adept at picking the brains of others, and this he now did voraciously. Summoning around him all the linguistic specialists he could muster, he soon had forcible views of his own to express on a reform of the Turkish language designed to bring out its 'general beauty and richness' and 'elevate it to the high rank it deserves among world languages'.[1]

[1] The object, as Dr Adnan defined it, was to free the Turkish language from the 'linguistic capitulations of Arabic and Persian'.

The views of these experts reflected two schools of thought. There were those who favoured merely the simplification of the language, as mooted twenty years earlier – the elimination only of those Persian and Arabic words for which a Turkish equivalent could be found. There were those on the other hand who favoured its purification – the elimination of all Persian and Arabic words and the coining of new Turkish words to replace them. Kemal himself was a purifier.

The seat of the annual deliberations of the Linguistic Society was the ornate throne room of the Dolma Bahche Palace. Those present at the inaugural meeting numbered a thousand, the hall was wired for radio, and Kemal's speech was broadcast through loud-speakers to the public squares of all the main towns in the country. The delegates ranged from lexicographers of international reputation to a village school-teacher who had prepared a dictionary of a remote Anatolian dialect, and an Armenian from Sofia, whose articles on language had caught the Gazi's attention.

From now onwards Kemal spent much of his time surrounded by piles of dictionaries, old and new, searching for 'pure Turkish words' or trying to trace some philological link between Turkish and foreign words. In pursuit of purification the whole public was invited to co-operate in the suggestion of Turkish equivalents for them, through lists of words published daily in the press. The Gazi would try out in his speeches new and incomprehensible words, to the bewilderment of his audience, while Falih Rifki, hero-worshipper though he was, would 'writhe with fury' at the sound of them and 'helplessly ask myself how he could possibly bring himself to perpetrate so heinous a crime'. Those anxious to gain favour found themselves avoiding in his presence the use of essential everyday terms simply because their origin was Arabic or Persian, while others tried to please him by learning up new words and dragging them into their conversation.

At one moment he was seduced by the theory of the 'Sun Language', thrown out by a Viennese philologist. According to this, primitive man uttered his first sounds, which evolved into words, in response to the awe induced in him by the sun. Attempts to link them to Aryan and Semitic roots had failed. But now the link was discernible in the Turkish language, which might thus be the 'mother of all languages'. Kemal at once ordered the Sun Language theory to be taught in the new Faculty of Letters in Ankara, and sponsored the publication of a quantity of literature on the subject. It had the obvious advantage, for the linguistic reformers, that all Arabic, Persian, Latin and other words in the Turkish language could now be ascribed to a Turkish source, hence might continue to be used with impunity. But the theory came in for sharp criticism from more serious scholars and was eventually dropped, to the discredit in Kemal's eyes of those experts whom he had encouraged to develop it.

In time he realized that his linguistic operations were leading the Turkish language into a blind alley. It threatened to become a mandarin language as artificial and incomprehensible to the ordinary Turk as that of the old Ottoman ruling class. A halt was finally called when he was presented with the draft of a speech for his delivery at the annual opening of the Grand National Assembly, and realized that it would seem to the deputies to be couched in a foreign tongue. Thus the policy of purification was abandoned and the principle adopted that words need no longer be sacrificed simply because their origins appeared to be foreign. Henceforward, if no Turkish equivalent for a foreign word could be found it was 'naturalized' and permitted to remain in the language. The Turks thus found themselves with a reformed language which closed the gap between the written and the spoken word, and was comprehensible to any Turk who had learnt his ABC. This, more perhaps than any of Kemal's other reforms, made them conscious of their 'Turkishness'.[1]

These researches ran parallel with those designed to investigate the history of Turkey and the Turks. One morning the Gazi's private secretary, Hassan Riza, returned to Chankaya from Istanbul, expecting to find his master still asleep. For he knew his habits – late to bed and late to rise. Usually when Kemal awoke, sitting cross-legged in his nightshirt in the Oriental posture, drinking a cup of black Turkish coffee and smoking his first cigarette, he would send for his secretary and discuss with him the business of the day, confirming or more often countermanding the orders he had given the night before. For he subscribed to the Sultan's old adage, 'A *firman* issued while drinking must never be executed in sobriety.' Then he would be shaved by his barber, who lived on the premises, take his bath and perhaps a massage, dress fastidiously and sit down to work, at which he seldom followed a regular routine.

But this morning was different. The secretary was told that the Gazi had not been to bed at all for two nights. For forty hours at a stretch he had been reading, drinking only black coffee and taking hot baths at intervals. Hassan Riza found him in his library, wearing a dressing-gown over the habitual nightshirt, as he pored over a book. He was wide awake, he insisted. But his eyes looked tired, and he was dabbing them at intervals with strips of fine linen. The book he was reading was H. G. Wells's *Outline of History*.

It was to become for him a book of revelation. As soon as he had finished

---

[1] On the other hand, a number of new European words were clumsily and often unnecessarily inflicted upon the language, so that today the Information Bureau at the Izmir International Fair becomes the Enternasyonal Fuari Enformasyon Bürosu, while the Turkish betting man goes to a *konkuripik* in the hope of becoming a *ganyan*. The phraseology, however, was so simplified that the Republican Civil Servant will now write, 'I have been thinking about your suggestion,' where his imperial predecessor would have written, 'Your slave has been engaged in the exercise of cogitation in respect of the proposals vouchsafed by your exalted person.' – G. L. Lewis, *Turkey*.

it he gave orders for its translation into Turkish, and its publication by the Turkish Government a year or so later was followed by that of an *Outline of Turkish History*, on similar lines. Wells became his principal hero, and he was soon quoting long passages from his work at the table. He was a great historian and prophet; he was Britain's 'master thinker'. He opened Kemal's eyes to a new view of history.

What he was seeking to do, in making a nation of Turkey, was to wean his people away from their old sense of identity with the supra-national 'fatherland' of Islam and to create for them a new allegiance to their own national fatherland. One of his problems was to link this in their minds with a past which fitted the history of Turkey into that of the world as a whole, thus eliminating the conflict, which for ever possessed him, between East and West, and lead them towards that 'civilization' to which in his own mind only the West belonged. Wells, with his theories of the common origins of mankind, showed him the way, and it remained to fit the history of the Turkish race into some such universal context.

Thus in 1932 he convened, under the auspices of his society, a Turkish Historical Congress in Ankara. It was attended by professors and teachers of history from all parts of Turkey, and by scholars and other delegates from abroad. Its task was to carry out research with a view to 'proving' the theory that the Turks were a white Aryan race, originating in Central Asia, the cradle of human civilization. As their lands progressively dried up they moved westwards, migrating in waves to various parts of Asia and Africa and carrying their civilization with them. Anatolia had thus been a Turkish land since remote antiquity. By teaching the Turks this he hoped to give them that sense of unity between land and race which creates a spirit of patriotism in the Western sense.

Such was his objective political aim. But there was behind it also a subjective personal impulse. Kemal, as he grew older and his work neared its end, needed a mystique of his own. One side of him was the man of action, the saviour and reformer of his country – a concrete image, visible and comprehensible to all. But there was another, inner side of him, that of the solitary, turning from action to speculation as he rode over the hills of Chankaya or strode through the groves of his farm before sundown, his dog following behind him, his shoulders stooping and his hands in his pockets. This was the more nebulous image of a man alone with his thoughts. There were times when the frontiers of Anatolia and the confines of his daily life, now so inactive, seemed to imprison his spirit. As food for his imagination he needed something more than the mundane tasks of government; the brutish nature of his people, bound to their arid somnolent steppes; the limited company of his own entourage – the yes-men who were his slaves, the so-called intellectuals who none the less heeded no one but him.

A man without human ties, he found love only in an atavistic feeling for the land that had nourished him. A man without spiritual beliefs, he nevertheless felt the need to identify himself with something outside and beyond himself. Who was he and whence did he come? The answer was perhaps to be found in the history, stretching back to an age before man was troubled by religions, of a race – *his* race – spreading its various branches from the homeland of humanity itself over all parts of the world.

Turks as depicted by Kemal to the American Ambassador Sherrill, 'early gained the qualities of the eagle – far of vision, swift of flight and strong of body to house that spirit. Restless within any restricting environment, whether of things physical or mental, it revolted against the isolation of that high central birthplace.' It caused them to speed over the earth, creating conflict and crisis, fighting and mingling with other racial groups – all from the same root – but for ever bestowing upon them the benefits of their own special civilization. They were, in short, the fathers of the civilized world.[1]

Such, paradoxically, were the day-dreams of a mind hitherto remarkable in its attention to objective truth, whether it was assessing the facts of a military or of a political situation; a mind highly sceptical of such unrealistic concepts as racial expansion and the wishful-thinking emotions which prompted them. Turning as it now did from action to speculation, in fields unfamiliar to it, governed by an obstinate need to believe what it wanted to believe, Kemal's mind began to lose itself in a labyrinth of those truths tangled with errors and half-truths which beset the untrained intellect. More and more did he now surround himself with a court of experts, so-called experts, charlatans and cranks in the sciences of history, archæology, anthropology, phrenology, etymology and philology, all propounding their pet theories and trotting out their pet works for his edification.

The Table at Chankaya became a seminar, a 'brains-trust' for the study and discussion of these problems of language and history – with occasional excursions into music and poetry. On the more formal occasions, when women were present, a European orchestra often played. For this spelled progress, civilization. He had banned from Ankara Radio the 'whining and wailing' of Turkish music, which he personally preferred – calling on less formal evenings for a Turkish orchestra and often singing to it himself in an undertone, with an adequate grasp of the quarter-tone scale of those Rumeli folk tunes of his childhood. When a foreign gramophone company presented him with a recording machine for his speeches, he often sang into

---

[1] Ambassador Grew was once asked whether there did not exist some book, showing the influence of Turkish civilization on the American Indians. A British diplomat was once startled by Kemal's statement that Kent was a Turkish name, and its existence in the country a proof that the Turks had conquered Britain, while one of his colleagues. an Irishman, was dubbed a Turk on the grounds that all words with the prefix 'ir' were of Turkish origin.

it, listening afterwards with pleasure to the sound of his voice and expecting his friends to do the same.[1]

When an evening was devoted to poetry, some famous poet like Yahya Kemal would read his poems aloud – with perhaps those of Victor Hugo thrown in for good measure. He liked to supplement these recitals himself with remembered quotations from the nineteenth-century Turkish poets. His respect for poets survived even a scene one evening when one of the moderns, Nazim Hikmet, on being asked to recite, replied rebelliously, 'I am not a cabaret singer,' and left the table. At this Kemal expressed a regret without rancour, since he had genuinely wanted to talk to the young man of his art.

Whatever the company there was a certain ritual about these evenings at Chankaya. Meticulous in his habits, the Gazi liked the table to be properly set, and would often adjust cloth or cutlery before sitting down. The guests sat where they chose, only the most important being allotted their places. When they had done so the drink began to circulate. It was usually *raki*, with a roughage of nuts to help digest the alcohol, and appetizers of chick-peas, olives and white sheep's cheese. Unless the occasion was formal the drinking often continued for an hour or so before any solid food was served; and even then the host, if he were not yet hungry, might send it away, so that when it came back re-heated, perhaps around midnight, it had lost much of its savour. Kemal took no interest in food, eating what came, with a preference for such plain peasant dishes as dried beans and *pilav*, to which he had grown used in his campaigns but which disagreed with his stomach. He ate little during the day, but liked eggs at all times. All he needed of life, he liked to say, was 'a piece of bread and to be able to eat and drink with friends'. With these friends, old and new, most evenings were now devoted to serious debate. The proverbial blackboard, with its chalk and its mop, stood permanently at the end of the room and was in frequent use, both by the Gazi himself, never wearying, and by guests trying hard to disguise their weariness as the night wore on.

Kemal, the dictator turned educator, treated his guests like a class, interrogating them one after the other around the table – and learning from them as much as he taught them. All were expected to express their views, which some did with more circumspection than others. He disliked blind agreement, and preferred guests who argued with him, if only for the satisfaction of battling with them and battering them into submission. He enjoyed

[1] The cleavage in his musical tastes emerged in Istanbul, where he once had two orchestras, one Turkish and one European, brought to the Park Hotel. He listened with constant interruptions, commanding one to stop and the other to play in turn. Finally, as the *raki* took effect, he lost patience and rose to leave the restaurant, saying, 'Now if you like you can both play together.' Another evening, incensed by the sound of the *muezzin* from a mosque opposite, which clashed with the dance-band, he ordered its minaret to be felled – one of those orders which was countermanded next morning.

dialectic, however tedious and pedantic it might become, and would persevere until dawn, despite the entreaties of an *aide* to spare himself the trouble, to convince by his powers of logic an obstinate if negligible adversary. Nor, if the talk got out of hand and Kemal out of temper, would he bear a grudge against a man who disagreed with him at table. He was too confident in his own superiority to mind the lapses of lesser creatures.

One of his methods was to set a guest an essay at dinner, and make him read it aloud the following week. A historian was once interrupted in the midst of his recital and afterwards kept back when the 'class' was dispersed. Kemal took him to his study, and dictated the essay as he wanted it to be. At the next session the guest read it out, to receive praise from the Gazi and applause from the rest of the company.

His gift was for synthesis. Looking around his table with those cold appraising eyes that saw two ways at once, he could listen, even when talking, to several conversations at once, suddenly intervening to pounce on some point he had overheard. He plucked at ideas, pieced them together and summed them up to propound a thesis which all must accept. But now, leaving the field of politics for the deeper waters of scholarship, he found the synthesis less easy to achieve. In the historical domain it was eventually to be achieved by others, providing the Turks with a history which at once fed their natural pride and approximated, so far as it could be known, to the truth.

Of his feminist reforms the personal symbol had been Latife. For his cultural reforms he found a new personal symbol. What the country needed above all at this time was teachers. It was thus to their recruitment and training that, in his tours throughout the country, he devoted his main efforts of persuasion. On one such visit to Izmir, he met a young woman named Afet, who had completed her schooling and had since begun to work as a teacher. She was fresh-looking, with a pleasing expression, and Kemal took a fancy to her responsive ways and to her nicely rounded feminine form. He owed a debt of gratitude to her father. He thus offered to adopt her, accepting responsibility for the completion of her education and her subsequent professional career. The offer was gratefully accepted.

For Kemal there was nothing unusual in such a step. Once or twice before he had adopted children – usually war orphans encountered on his campaigns, who were handed over to his mother to bring up and educate. Two small girls, named respectively Zehra and Rukiye, already lived in his house at Chankaya, one adopted from an orphanage and the other from an impoverished family, at the time of his childless marriage to Latife. A third was Sabiha, a fair, lively and intelligent child who was to become the first woman air pilot. These three were now joined by Afet and a little later by a fifth, Nebile, a slim dark girl with blue-green eyes who had once been a maid in his house.

Adolescents attracted and interested him, and when the girls reached the age when they sat regularly at table he began to take notice both of their charms and their talents. None of them was exceptionally pretty; nor had they the graces of women of the world. But they provided him with the ideal 'harem'. They were in his power, thanks to their youth and their dependence on him. He could groom them and mould them and guide them in the direction he wanted them to follow. He could use them as he chose – and when he no longer chose, could 'wean' them and launch them into marriage or into a career. For the girls themselves, so ambivalent a father-lover-schoolmaster relationship might create certain psychological stresses. But for Kemal it provided the family background he needed, one from which irksome ties of blood were missing, and in which wife and children became in effect one.[1]

The position of Afet, who was to become a professor of history, was different from that of the rest. She was no longer a child when Kemal first 'adopted' her, but a girl on the threshold of maturity. Gradually, from then onwards, she became what a wife might have been to him. She was homely, good-natured, undemanding, serious-minded. She kept house for him. She sat at the head of his table. She appeared with him in public causing problems of protocol to foreign ambassadors. As 'Her Master's Voice' she assiduously recorded his ideas, taking pains to interpret them in the counsels of the Turkish Historical Society and of the various organizations for social reform. Above all she gave him restful companionship.[2] Thus the domestic hiatus which had prevailed at Chankaya since Latife's departure was closed, and Kemal entered on his fifties still a bachelor, but not wholly deprived of a private life.

[1] On several occasions he adopted young boys, paying for their education and installing them in jobs. But they did not live with him at Chankaya, as the girls did. Rukiye and Nebile married respectively an officer and a diplomat, with Kemal's blessing. Zehra was unhappily killed, falling from a train in France, while on her studies abroad.

[2] She remained with him till his death, not herself marrying until afterwards, and is known today as Dr Afetinan. (See Bibliography.)

CHAPTER FIFTY-EIGHT

FATHER OF THE TURKS

EARLY IN 1935, while economic problems multiplied at home and the threat of Axis aggression darkened the horizon abroad, Kemal introduced two last measures of Westernization. Already the old Turkish calendar, based on Christian months and an Islamic year, had given place to the complete Gregorian calendar of the Christian era. From this it was a natural step to the abolition of the Moslem Friday and its replacement as a day of rest by the Christian Sunday. Thus the Western week-end, regardless of its infidel implications, became an integral feature of the life of the ordinary Turk.[1]

More important, he was now instructed by law to follow Western practice by adopting a surname. Hitherto the Turks, like the Arabs and other Moslems, had not used family names. A man was known by his birth name and perhaps that of his father – Ahmed son of Mehmed, for example, was a normal designation, despite the confusion caused everywhere by its multiplication. But from now onwards all must have family names, and Kemal amused himself at the Table by conferring suitable patronymics on his friends. Ismet became Inönü, after the site of his victory; Tevfik Rüştü added Aras, the name of the river defining the frontier which he had negotiated between Turkey and Persia; Celal (Mahmud Jelal), the Minister of Economics, was dubbed Bayar, or 'Sublime'. Fethi had chosen a name in consultation with his family, but was obliged by Kemal to abandon it for Okyar, a 'spiritual companion'. Sabiha, his adopted daughter, the air pilot, was given the name Gökçen – 'of the skies'. At the same time the old titles of Pasha, Effendi, Bey and Hanim (Lady), following the name, were officially abolished and replaced by plain Bay and Bayan (Mr and Mrs) preceding it. The President of the Republic himself renounced the titles of Gazi and Pasha,[2] and chose a name, as no ruler of his race had done before

---

[1] This measure was combined with the adoption of the twenty-four-hour international clock.

[2] The title of Pasha, however, died hard. One evening Atatürk rounded on a minister and scolded him for using it. 'You will please not call me Pasha any more. Is that clear?' To which the minister replied, 'I promise not to do it again, Pasha.'

him, which displayed pride in his Turkish origins. He became Atatürk, or Father Turk, dropping the Arab name of Mustafa and signing himself Kemal Atatürk.

Atatürk was indeed the father of the Turks. The Turkey which now existed on the map, a compact whole salvaged from the wide-strewn fragments of the Ottoman Empire, was his creation. But for him it might have been reduced to a mere fragment itself, enclosed by the empires of others and perhaps eventually absorbed as a satellite by one of them. He had made of it a nation, reviving its patriotism and restoring its self-respect. He had given it a durable political system. From among its people he was moulding a new type of Turk, fitting him by education and example to rank with the peoples of Europe, releasing him from a dead past to seek a place for his country in contemporary civilization.

Atatürk had above all created a legend. In a land needing heroes his mystique was such that a child, blessed by his handshake, would for weeks leave his hand unwashed, lest the virtue depart from it; that an old peasant woman, once asked what her age was, replied, 'Seventeen', for her life had begun only when she first saw him with her eyes during the War of Independence. For the youth of his country his words were to become a gospel and his deeds a mythology, destined to point and illuminate the national ideal for perhaps generations to come. Meanwhile both inspired youth with the sense of a new, challenging life in the present and new foundations on which to build for the future. All this, within little more than a decade, had this modern 'Cromwell of the Near East' (as an English writer[1] was to describe him) achieved – through a fanatical personal ambition directed into patriotic channels, phenomenal energy and will-power, and a rare combination within him of an Eastern temperament with a Western mind.

But was it enough? It was Atatürk's task, as he once put it, to form men, much as a gardener cultivates plants. He had thus formed a new élite, with new values. But it must take longer to form a new Turkish people; the mass of the Anatolian Turks still remained as of old. To succeed in his Revolution, as he had seen from the start, he must first conquer the people. For a while he had conquered them – their inertia, their fatalism, their conservative prejudice. He had followed up his conquest by suppressing at least the outward symbols of their more backward traditions.

But in so doing he had in a sense left a vacuum; and it was a vacuum which only time could fill. Many more decades were needed before his work was complete, and inevitably he would not himself be there to complete it. Atatürk was like a successful commander forced to leave the field of battle before he knows the final result. For a man so used to the swift tempo of war it was hard to accept the slower tempo of peaceful evolution, to admit to himself that there was little more he could now do to assist the growth

[1] *The Times*, 11th November 1938.

of the people he had fathered; hard to bequeath to his successors the task of transforming his country into a civilized Western state.

A rationalist without a rationalist philosophy, he fell into moods of disillusion and despondency. A man of action with no actions left to perform, he fell back on the familiar substitute, alcohol; and this began to undermine his physical and mental condition. Atatürk saw no reason to fuss about his health. Ever since his heart attack in 1923, repeated in a mild form a few years later, he had assumed this to be the danger to which he was prone. If his heart was all right, as it had been since, then nothing need trouble him. His principal doctor, a heart specialist, had encouraged him accordingly. Hence oblivious of the fact that he might be taxing not his heart but other organs in his body, he continued to drink; and his doctors did all too little to discourage him.

His friends however noticed with growing concern that Kemal Atatürk was not the man Mustafa Kemal had been. His mind was deteriorating. Losing himself in the maze of linguistics and historiography, he would say one thing one moment, another the next. His memory was failing. Talking of everyday affairs, he would forget altogether what he had said the day before. His nerves were no longer under control. He lost his temper more easily, the tiger now for ever caged, snarling abruptly at friends and enemies alike.

As a rule, he had vented his rages only on adversaries tough enough to take the assault. But now no man was safe. Spoiling for trouble one evening at the club, he picked on a harmless professor of history. In his usual schoolmasterly style Atatürk examined a group of young people around him on their historical knowledge. Dissatisfied with their answers he rounded on the professor, who was the author of one of their text-books, and treated him to a long and contemptuous diatribe on his methods of training the young. The professor, too paralysed with alarm to answer back, sought to mollify him by eulogies and rose to drink his health. Disgusted at such lack of spirit, Atatürk shouted, in tones audible to all, 'You are an ass. Go and dance' – and the professor slunk hurriedly away.

Such scenes caused general gossip. Often however, as his adherents knew well, Atatürk's bark was worse than his bite, and his explosions amounted to mere horseplay. One evening, in the Dolma Bahche Palace, he took exception to an attack made by one Reshid Galib on the Minister of Education, and ordered him to leave the table. But Galib refused on the grounds that it was the People's Table, not the President's, and that in a Republic any citizen had the right to criticize another. In reply Atatürk said, 'Very well, we'll leave you with the people,' and himself left the table, taking his other guests with him. A few months later he had his revenge on Reshid Galib. One evening he invited him to Chankaya. Reshid took his place with some apprehension, fearing a scene. He had hardly done so when Atatürk called in a pair of sentries and ordered them, 'Lift that gentleman from his seat and take him away.' Reshid was removed and Atatürk said with a grin, 'That's how we get rid of people in this Republic.' Afterwards Reshid Galib was appointed Minister of Education in place of the man he had criticized.

Atatürk's moods were capricious. How would he be tonight, his friends would ask each other? Sometimes he was Satan personified; at other times a toreador, restlessly seeking a bull. More and more often at Chankaya, when there were women at the table, he would send them home early and sit drinking without restraint until dawn with his masculine cronies. Once, still sitting there at five o'clock in the morning, he felt like going for a ride. His two *aides*, to discourage so rash an enterprise, told him that his horse was lame. Next day he learnt that this was a lie, and in the evening instructed Hassan Riza, his secretary, to terminate the appointments of the two officers. The secretary, as usual, took no action, but next morning submitted the note to his master, who smiled sheepishly and instructed him, 'Forget it.'

Restlessness gnawed and devoured him, especially at nights, Often he would disappear all of a sudden, leaving his ministers in the dark as to where he had gone. Sending for Ismet one night, he learnt that he was on his way from Istanbul by the night express. On a sudden impulse he ordered a special train, that he might go to meet him. Only a shunting engine was available, but a train was made up and he set off. When the two trains met early in the morning Atatürk was asleep. Ismet, rather than wake him, ordered the presidential train to be shunted into a siding, that the express might proceed. The President woke up later in the morning, asking his entourage where he was. He did not get back to Ankara until the evening. The press meanwhile had announced that he had left on a visit to Eskishehir.

Reluctant to sleep, he would call on friends or even strangers in the middle of the night, often dragging them from their beds to receive him. One evening at the Table he was told that a certain rich merchant had compared his aloofness with that of the Sultan. No one, he said, ever saw either of them. The remark nagged at Atatürk and he continually reverted to it: 'Did he really say that?' Finally, around three o'clock in the morning he rose from the table and said, 'Come on, we'll go and ask him.' To the alarm of his companions, he strode into the man's house, unannounced. To their relief he embraced him, had his children brought from their beds that he might embrace them too, spread his charm all around and won a lasting adherent.

Atatürk in his mid-fifties was a man alone – without wife, family or loves. Afet was at hand, to look after him and give him some comfort. Otherwise his home life remained essentially the mess life of the bachelor officer. When his guests left him at night he was lonely and often self-pitying. Marriage, apart from the brief episode with Latife, he had renounced; it was a state for which neither his career nor his temperament fitted him. But the subject of marriage was often on his mind, if only for others. As 'father of his people' he enjoyed playing the matchmaker's role. Often young persons, prevented by their parents from marrying, would come to him for advice and assistance and he would send for the father and secure his agreement. He discouraged divorce, and would mischievously invite divorced couples to his table together. When his friends married he liked to visit their houses, often unannounced, and to inspect each room with an appraising eye, criticizing the arrangement of the furniture here, straightening a curtain there, and paying especial attention to bedroom furnishings and sanitary arrangements.

As Atatürk grew older he became fonder of children and liked to collect them around him. He did not regret his own lack of a son, remarking once that the sons of great men were too often degenerate. A son moreover might have been inconvenient politically, abhorring as Atatürk did all dynastic conceptions. But he took an interest in the children of others, playing games with them and singing Rumeli songs to them. Once, at a children's party at lzmit, a small boy, after gazing at Atatürk for a while with rapt adoration, suddenly rushed upon him and started to kiss him. The other children instantly broke away from their teachers and were soon clinging to him and showering him with kisses. Atatürk turned to a group of grown-ups and said, 'You see, these children are of my own generation.'

But it was when children reached school age that they interested him most. He would seat a child by his side at table and examine it. He had a series of stock questions, of which his favourite was, 'What is the difference in French between revolution, rebellion, reform, revolt, insurrection?' Some were subjected to a more searching examination. The intelligent student daughter of one of his ambassadors was interrogated at the dinner-table for several hours on historical subjects, principally that of Napoleon. She remarked that he had been in love with Josephine. Atatürk became angry. It was impossible for such a man to fall in love, with all he had to do. 'You're boring me,' he said to the girl. He changed the subject to that of Caesar. Was he greater than Napoleon? She replied that he was. Caesar did not need to take a title, since his name became one. Napoleon had to make himself Emperor.

Atatürk commended her, and summed up: 'Napoleon started with his country and ended with himself.' For Napoleon as a general he had great admiration, though he was not flattered at the comparison of his own victory at the Sakarya to that of Austerlitz. But he was a man, he maintained, without a sound political idea, more concerned with his ambition for world conquest than with the national interest of France. He liked to compare his advance to Moscow with the Ottoman advance to Vienna, at the expense of the country's internal welfare. Napoleon, asked what was his programme, had once replied, 'I just go ahead and my progress is the result of my movements.' Atatürk commented, 'Those who "just go ahead" finally knock their heads against the rock of St Helena.' Napoleon, he believed, had been carried away by events which he thought he could control. Thus 'democracy was delayed for sixty years'.

Another hero of history to whom Kemal used to give qualified praise was his fellow-Macedonian, Alexander the Great. Once, comparing Alexander unfavourably with himself he remarked, 'He forgot about his country and went far away.' It was a mistake he himself never made.

As Atatürk aged the myth which had been woven around him by the foreign communities of Ankara and Istanbul assumed a yet more fanciful shape. They had for long magnified him, in their imagination, into a debauchee of Roman proportions, ruthless and insatiable in his appetite for women, with whom he was said to indulge up at Chankaya in licentious and disreputable 'orgies'. It was a picture of him, deriving initially from the gossip of his political enemies in Istanbul and from the strictures of his more puritanical Moslem supporters in Ankara, which shocked agreeably the conventional susceptibilities of foreign writers and the *Corps Diplomatique*.

By their standards Atatürk was indeed a loose-liver. Like many an army officer he had used women fitfully and casually, taking them when he wanted them and throwing them aside when he did not. He had made no more secret of these proclivities than he had made of his drinking habits, preaching frankness as a virtue, liking to outrage the bourgeoisie and the men of religion, and moreover judging that a reputation for virility in a ruler was not distasteful to the mass of his people. Such was the image of himself that he liked to encourage. In fact it reflected a side of his life which meant relatively little to him. Just as work, when he was young, left him no time for marriage, so as he grew older did drink cool his lusts. In his youth and in the prime of his manhood he had enjoyed women freely when opportunity allowed. But from his mid-forties onwards his desires and with them his powers declined; and now the less potent he became the more he chose to advertise his potency.

Thus the dining-rooms of the embassies and the clubs and the Ankara Palace Hotel hummed with the latest gossip about Atatürk's public behaviour. No woman was held to be safe at his hands. Turkish mothers might indee thrust their daughters at him (and Turkish husbands their wives), but Diplomatic mothers would hurry their daughters away from a party for fear he would invite them to his table. When he did so he would often merely subject them to a *viva voce* exam. Taking a fancy to a young Polish girl at an Embassy party, he was heard asking her for proof of the existence of God. With a married woman the interrogation might be on the more intimate subject of her relations with her husband. He had always sensed just how far to go with women, and was a good judge of husbands, never flirting with the wife of one likely to be jealous, and continually warning his less discerning friends against blunders of this kind. Occasionally, however, a scandal arose when the wife of some diplomat allowed herself to become emotionally too much involved with the President, while once Ankara was diverted by the tales of an American lady who, in pursuit of him, lay down across the road by which he drove through his farm and was invited to stay for some days at Chankaya.

But for all his vagaries and the scandal concerning him, Atatürk was still seriously respected by the *Corps Diplomatique* for his unimpaired faculties in the field of foreign affairs. On such matters as history and language his mind might wander; on the problems of the actual world, now increasingly threatened by the European dictators, it remained as acute as ever. Ambassadors to whom he talked beyond the bounds of protocol might be subjected, however late the hour and convivial the atmosphere, to examinations as searching as those to which he had accustomed his countrymen. 'Sometimes,' wrote Sir Percy Loraine, 'it was a drumfire of questions: at others a long statement of his own views: then an interrogative pause, marked by a piercing look from those ice-blue eyes from beneath contracted eyebrows. One came to be able to translate that look. It meant, don't shilly-shally: we speak as man to man. You are right: you are on the mat a bit: but I detest yes-men and I want to hear what *you* think. Maybe you've got something. Let's get at it.'

His main attention was now given to those questions remaining to be settled between Turkey and the West before the Second World War, which he confidently predicted, began. In the preparatory war of nerves it was Mussolini who first threatened Turkey. In a speech in the spring of 1934 he defined his historical objectives as Asia and Africa – a clear threat of war and annexation. The Turks retorted with ostentatious manœuvres on the coasts of the Aegean. When Mussolini began to fortify the island of Leros, off the Turkish coast – in fact as a prelude to the invasion of Abyssinia – Atatürk chose his own method of making his attitude clear.

Dining one evening with a party at the Ankara Palace Hotel, he observed the Italian Ambassador at an adjoining table. The Albanian envoy was also present. As it happened, the Gazi was sober. But it suited him to pretend that he was not. Leaning towards the Albanian he said, 'Asaf Bey, I see lots of funny pictures in the newspapers. What's going on in Albania? Are you performing an operetta?' He was alluding to the photographs of King Zog, with his gaudy uniforms. 'Anyway,' he continued, 'what was wrong with the Republic? Why did you think it necessary to have a King? And what is more you are following a dangerous policy. The Italians will use you in order to infiltrate into the Balkans.'

The Italian Ambassador tried to intervene. Turning to address him through an interpreter, who repeated his remarks loudly for all to hear, Atatürk protested at the fact that in Rome Italian students had been demonstrating in front of the Turkish Embassy with demands for Antalya (Adalia). 'Antalya,' he explained to him, 'is not in the pocket of our Ambassador in Italy. It is right here. Why don't you try to come and get it? I have a proposition to make to His Excellency the Duce. We'll allow him to land Italian soldiers in Antalya. When the landing is completed, we'll have a battle, and the side which wins will have Antalya.'

The Ambassador asked, 'Is this a declaration of war, Your Excellency?'

'No,' replied Atatürk. 'I am speaking here as a mere citizen. Only the Grand National Assembly can declare war in the name of Turkey. But try to remember that, when the time comes, the Grand National Assembly will take into consideration the feelings of mere citizens like myself.'

Atatürk, satisfied with the effects of his calculated indiscretion, then left the hotel. When the war broke out Turkey voted, as a member of the League, in favour of sanctions against Italy, thus emphasizing Atatürk's policy of co-operation with the community of nations. It was emphasized more strongly in the spring of 1936, by an official request from Turkey for a revision of the régime for the Straits as laid down by the Lausanne Treaty. This no longer emphasized the issue of their freedom, as at Lausanne, but the issue of their security, invoking an article in the League Covenant which allowed for joint consultation in the event of a threat to the Straits.

Both the manner and the timing of Atatürk's request were faultless. They owed much to his close relations with Sir Percy Loraine, whom he had once described over the poker-table as the holder of the only ace in the Mediterranean, and who had emphasized to him the necessity of avoiding any hint of an ultimatum or of a threat to march troops into the zone. The request came at a moment when Britain was greatly concerned as to the security of the Straits. It had been feared at Geneva, following the German occupation of the Rhineland and the Italian invasion of Abyssinia, that the Turks might march into their demilitarized zones and so present the world with another *fait accompli*. Atatürk's choice of the correct juridical approach to the issue thus favourably impressed the Western powers, and the British – fearing rapprochement between the Turks and the Germans as in 1914 – were ready to make important concessions for the sake of an Anglo-Turkish understanding.

The resulting conference was held at Montreux. It was boycotted by the Italians, and the matter was speedily settled. Turkey obtained all she needed. She was allowed to remilitarize the Straits; the former International Commission was abolished; she regained absolute control over the waterway, such as the Ottoman Empire had enjoyed in the past; she now had the right to control the passage of warships in time of war and, if she believed herself threatened by war, in time of peace as well. Thus at midnight on

20th July thirty thousand Turkish troops marched into the demilitarized zone of the Straits, where the whole of the Turkish fleet, led appropriately by the *Yavuz* – the *Goeben* in Turkish guise – awaited them. Here was a triumphant reversal of the historical precedent of 1914, against which he had protested so strongly but with so little effect.

Neither Italy nor Germany were pleased at this outcome. But they could afford less than ever to quarrel with Turkey. Early in 1937, at a meeting in Milan, Count Ciano tried to bargain with Tevfik Rüştü with the offer of a trade agreement and to draw Turkey into some form of alignment with the Rome-Berlin Axis. But her Government publicly clarified its allegiance 'only to the *bloc* of peace and to no other *bloc*'. To the Germans a veiled snub was administered by the granting of the contract for the refortification of the Straits not to Krupp's, with whom Turkey was in commercial relations, but to Vickers, who had offered less favourable terms. When the Germans objected to certain clauses of the Montreux Convention, they received from the Turks the sharp reply that this matter, since Germany was neither a signatory of Montreux nor a Mediterranean power, was no concern of theirs.

Russia too was displeased by the Convention. It had given her advantages but not all she had hoped for – in essence the closing of the Straits to foreign warships in time of war. Since it was a cardinal point of Atatürk's foreign policy to remain on good terms with her nearest great sea power, Britain, and with her nearest great land power, Soviet Russia, he sent Tevfik Rüştü with a delegation to Moscow, to reassure the Russians both on the Montreux Convention and on the Saadabad Pact.

A chance publicly to display his friendship with Britain arose in September 1936, when King Edward VIII paid an informal visit to Turkey in the course of a Mediterranean cruise in the *Nahlin*. Sir Percy Loraine had encouraged the visit as a gesture of goodwill at a time when Britain was competing in the economic war against Germany for a loan to the Turks. It was the first visit in history by a British sovereign to Turkey, and the first by a European sovereign since the Kaiser's reception by Abdul Hamid forty years earlier. Thus Sir Percy urged that the visit should be official, and that the King should come to pay his respects to the President in Ankara. But the King, being on a holiday cruise, preferred to treat it as unofficial. Atatürk, momentarily disconcerted but no servant to protocol, thus proceeded to Istanbul to meet him.

The King's yacht anchored off the Dolma Bahche Palace. With Atatürk he drove to the British Embassy, through the streets of Istanbul, in an open car. This, Sir Percy explained to him, was a compliment from a head of state used to traversing them in a bullet-proof limousine. Thousands had spent the night by the banks of the Bosporus to await the King's arrival. The Union Jack and the Star and Crescent flew from the rooftops, and after dark flood-lights shone from the minarets, with streamers inscribed,

'Welcome, Eduarde Rex.' The entertainments provided for the King and his party – of which Mrs Simpson was an honoured member – included a 'Venetian night', in which Turkish warships took part, on the moonlit waters of the Bosporus, and a regatta on the Sea of Marmara. At one of several dinners a waiter dropped a large dish of food on the floor, prompting an apology by Atatürk to his guest, 'I could teach everything to this nation but I couldn't teach them to be good lackeys.'

In the course of their talks, which were conducted in German, the King and the President established friendly relations. The visit was indeed, on King Edward's part, an exercise in cordial diplomacy to rank with the foreign excursions of his grandfather, King Edward VII. Psychologically, it transformed the attitude of the Turkish people towards Britain, to whom they had grown used, from the outbreak of the First World War, as an enemy. King Edward VIII helped to create a new climate of Turkish public opinion. For many years afterwards the walls of coffee-houses in Istanbul and throughout Anatolia were adorned with a bright coloured picture of the two rulers, seated together beneath their respective national flags, a symbol, not to be forgotten, of the Anglo-Turkish *Entente Cordiale*.

It still remained for the Turks to establish a similar entente with the French. The question of the sanjak of Alexandretta, or Hatay, outstanding from the Franco-Turkish agreement with Franklin-Bouillon, remained to be settled. It concerned the future of a province which marched with Syria, which contained – or so it was claimed – a majority of Turkish inhabitants, and which in Iskenderun (Alexandretta) provided Turkey at that time with her only effective Mediterranean port. The matter had been amicably shelved by the creation, under French mandate, of a special régime for the province which safeguarded Turkish interests. But in the summer of 1936, France proposed to grant independence to Syria and to include Hatay within its new frontiers. The question was put before the Council of the League of Nations, which debated a Turkish request for the withdrawal from the province of French troops and their replacement by a detachment of neutral gendarmerie. But the League at this stage would only agree to the despatch of three neutral observers to report, pending further discussion.

Atatürk now took a personal hand in the dispute. Backed by a party meeting which protested against the slowness of the proceedings, he decided on a show of force against the French. Shrewdly timing his movements to coincide with the return of their Ambassador, M Ponsot, from Paris, he proceeded by special train to Konya, the headquarters of his Southern Command, with the apparent intention of moving troops towards the frontier. The cautious Ismet dissuaded him from going beyond the Taurus. But Atatürk's action served its purpose. The French grew alarmed by a rumour that Turkish troops were concentrating on the borders of Hatay, and by subsequent clashes, between Turks and Arabs, within the province itself. Negotiations followed between Paris and Ankara in an atmosphere favourable to the Turks.

When a settlement was ultimately reached it was largely through Atatürk's favourite methods of ballroom diplomacy. Its foundations were laid at a ball at the Ankara Palace Hotel. To the table in the alcove where he normally sat, and where he was now sitting with Sir Percy Loraine and a few others, Atatürk summoned Ponsot, the French Ambassador, and his wife. After they had conversed for a while, he ordered the music and dancing to stop, and broached to him the subject of Hatay. Stressing his fervent desire for Franco-Turkish friendship, he assured the Ambassador, that, none the less, he had promised the Grand National Assembly to take back the province, and could not break this promise. Hatay was for him a personal issue.

On this basis he now discussed the problem with Ponsot, calling in a French-speaking lady from among the guests to interpret, and instructing her, lest any mistake should be made, to write down his own words in Turkish before translating them into French. Sir Percy Loraine, who had promised Atatürk his help with the French when the time for it should come, was brought into the discussions. They conversed on the problem until the light of dawn filtered in through the mock-Oriental windows of the Ankara Palace Hotel and Atatürk, in a moment of inspiration, suggested the lines of a feasible solution.[1]

Ponsot himself was ready enough for a compromise. Hatay, he had to admit, was not essentially Arab; moreover Iskenderun, wide open to the Cilician plain, was a natural harbour for Turkey, and would be hard for the Syrians to defend. But the Quai d'Orsay was slow to accept such a 'dismemberment' of Syria, involving as it would the stigma of a military withdrawal. Atatürk, for his part, realized that a country which had refused to fight for the Rhineland was unlikely to fight for Hatay, but he realized also the need to safeguard French *amour propre*. Hence, while keeping up the pressure on the spot, he acted with patience at the conference table.

Finally the intricate quadrangular negotiations between Paris, Geneva, Ankara and Syria led, early in 1937, to a settlement by which Hatay became a separate political entity, enjoying full independence in its internal affairs but linked by a customs and monetary union with the state of Syria, which would be responsible for the conduct of its foreign affairs. Both Turkish and Arabic were to rank as its official languages. It only remained to be seen how this arrangement would work out in practice.

[1] On another informal occasion, at the Russian restaurant of Karpich, Atatürk applied a more eccentric form of pressure. Seeing the French Ambassador, he called upon the ladies at his table to raise their hands and shout, 'We want Hatay!' One of his adopted daughters chanced to have a toy revolver in her bag and he made her fire it off. The explosion took M Ponsot aback and Atatürk playfully sent for the police and had her arrested for the illegal use of firearms. He then informed Ismet that the women of Turkey must have Hatay and instructed him to make representations on their behalf to the French.

CHAPTER FIFTY-NINE

A SERIOUS ILLNESS

THROUGHOUT the summer in Istanbul Atatürk was increasingly restless. He fretted with impatience at the 'prison' restrictions of the Sultan's vast gloomy palace which so incongruously housed him. He was always plotting to escape from it and played with the idea of building himself a kiosk on the hillside above it, close to a popular café. Occasionally he succeeded in escaping without being observed. One evening, like a schoolboy playing truant, he rose from the table on the pretext of going to bed early, eluded his guards by a ruse, slipped out of the palace and disappeared into the night. He was found eventually in a Greek fishermen's *taverna* on the shores of the Bosporus, drinking and dancing a Greek dance with his arms around the fisherman's shoulders, to the music of a lute-player from Trebizond.

On another such night a group of military cadets were amazed to see a taxi draw up beside them, with Atatürk seated alone in it. He sat down with them by the roadside and talked of military matters. Soon the noise of cars and motor-bicycles was heard in the distance, and he exclaimed, 'Oh, I am done for. They're coming after me.' The cars drew up and a worried group of officials led the President of the Republic away.

He liked, in these long summer days and nights, to sail up and down the Bosporus, across the Marmara and around the islands in his motor-yacht the *Ertuğrul*, which became a familiar sight to the people. One night, when the boat reached the last station on the Bosporus, he suddenly ordered the captain to turn into the Black Sea and head for the mining port of Zonguldak. Then he retired to his cabin and slept. His guests were worried. The *Ertuğrul* was a long slim boat, ill-equipped to face the storms which could suddenly sweep down on these treacherous waters. She reached Zonguldak safely, however, and Atatürk spent the morning ashore inspecting mines and factories. But on the way back the ship ran into a sudden storm, and began to roll in a dangerous fashion, so that the crew had to rip the auxiliary sails with their knives. Atatürk only laughed at their anxiety and, in boyish high spirits, put a *zeybek* record on the gramophone, to which he insisted on dancing until the *Ertuğrul* sailed back into the calmer waters of the Bosporus.

To escape from the palace Atatürk spent many of his days, not only at Yalova, which had now developed into a large thermal resort, but at Florya, a place which he had revived as a bathing resort, with a presidential villa built right on the beach. Here he liked to mix with the people, rowing boats and teaching himself to swim. Here and in the palace his constant companion was a young child, the last of his adopted daughters, whom he had named Ülkü, the Ideal. A lively little girl, with Tartar features and slanting Mongol eyes, he became much attached to her, and used to say that, of all his entourage, she was the only person upon whom he could count always to tell him the truth.

In the entourage, undertones of conflict were now rumbling uncomfortably beneath the surface. The theme of them was Ismet, now Inönü. Atatürk's friends had never been Ismet's friends. Ismet, the respectable family man, had little in common with those dissolute and often unscrupulous henchmen at Chankaya and in the Dolma Bahche Palace. These men sought two things, power and money, and Ismet was an obstacle to the acquisition of both. He was hardly likely to further their ambitions for influential posts. Nor indeed was Atatürk himself. He knew his friends well enough to keep them in their places, and would never appoint a man to a responsible place who lacked the capacity to fill it. To quieten them, he gave them latitude in business dealings, allowing them pickings from the industrial enterprises, and refraining, unless public scandal threatened, from too close an enquiry into their methods of seeking their fortunes. But this outlet too was often obstructed by the scrupulous Ismet.

At 'court' there was thus a perennial atmosphere of personal intrigue, of which the principal *motif* was mischief against Inönü. Atatürk managed this situation astutely enough by division and rule, now pitting the contestants against one another, now forcing them in his presence to make up their differences. He liked to bring his enemies to his table and confront them with the remarks they had made against one another, and this treatment was applied alike to the friends and the enemies of Ismet. Sometimes he would put up an *aide* to criticize the Cabinet in Ismet's presence; once, in his absence, he banged the table and exclaimed of him, 'I can take a man and raise him up. But if he can't understand this and thinks he has risen by his own worth, I can fling him away, like a rag.'

This now was his prevalent mood. As Atatürk's health deteriorated, so did the mutual irritation which arose from their basic differences of temperament grow. The pinpricks on both sides multiplied and festered. Ismet resented Atatürk's caprices, his criticisms of his ministers, his habit of giving orders to them over the Cabinet's head. As time went on, he found it harder to bear his taunts and outbursts, and in unguarded moments expressed his annoyance to others, who repeated his words back to Atatürk. For years he had taken in his stride Ismet's fussiness, his pedantry, his slowness in reaching decisions. But now these shortcomings, combined with a growing presumptuousness, got on his nerves.

The restrictive trend of Ismet Inönü's economic policy had ranged many opponents against him. But it was over foreign policy that his relations with Atatürk became especially strained. When Italian submarines, masquerading as Spanish, started to sink merchant shipping in the Mediterranean, Turkey, on Atatürk's instructions, co-operated fully in the international patrol set up by a League Committee conference at Nyon to counter these piratical acts. But Ismet showed timidity over the agreement, fearing war with the Italians and favouring a submarine patrol in which each country remained in its own territorial waters. Atatürk, resenting this, took more and more to by-passing Ismet and dealing direct with Tevfik Rüştü. He resented also Ismet's restraining hand over Hatay. Telephoning to him from Istanbul, he overrode in strong terms a Cabinet proposal not to press for the use of Turkish as the official language of the province.

The tension between them came to a head one evening at Chankaya ironically enough on a minor issue – a matter of economic policy concerning a beer factory. Ismet lost his temper and blurted out, 'How much longer is this country going to be governed from a drunkard's table?' Atatürk coldly replied, 'You seem to forget that it was a drunkard who appointed you to your post,' and the conversation jolted awkwardly on to less explosive topics. After Ismet had left, Atatürk gave way to his anger, and threatened to denounce him in Parliament. He was dissuaded from this. But clearly the moment had come for him to change his Prime Minister. He broke the news to Ismet next day, summoning him to his private compartment on the presidential train, in which he was starting on an official tour. He proposed that Ismet should officially take a few weeks' 'sick-leave', during which a deputy Prime Minister would serve in his place.

Ismet Inönü, for whom this had simply been one among a number of recent disagreements, was dismayed, after fourteen years in the office, at so abrupt a dismissal. Throughout the journey he wrote notes of contrition to Atatürk, imploring him to reconsider his verdict. But they remained unanswered; Atatürk's mind was made up.

As Ismet Inönü's successor he chose Celal Bayar, whose power had been growing and whose economic ideas were less rigidly statist than Ismet's. Bayar initiated his Premiership with an economic programme which involved more equitable taxation and a second Five-Year Plan. But Bayar was not the competent 'chief of staff' that Ismet had been, and Atatürk was soon missing his old Prime Minister. He could not delegate to Bayar as confidently. To a woman friend who remarked on his look of fatigue after Bayar had been a few weeks in office, he complained, 'With my new Prime Minister I can no longer sleep calmly at nights.' He remained on friendly personal terms with Ismet, who continued on occasion to dine at Chankaya.

During that winter of 1937 it became evident that Atatürk was seriously unwell. His mind, preoccupied with the war to come, still showed flashes of insight. He expressed a low opinion of General Gamelin, saying, 'As long as such men are at the head of things in France, France is doomed to be destroyed.' He compared the Maginot Line to the tomb of Nasreddin Hoja, the Turkish story-teller: it had a single façade, with a huge lock, but the rest of it was open so that anyone could go round the edge of it. Of the customary reception for the anniversary of the Republic, at the end of October, Sir Percy Loraine, after sitting at his side for hours, could still write: 'It was a first-class opportunity for observing Atatürk's fantastic power of concentration. He had something to say to, or learn from each newcomer to the circle; everything he said was leading somewhere, and one could sense the unflickering purpose and the tireless spirit of enquiry that lay behind it. An inquest, as you will; but not an inquisition.'

Nevertheless, for a year or so past he had shown signs of fatigue, both in body and mind. He had headaches and suffered from the cold, as he had not done before. He had aged in appearance; the skin had grown pale, the lines in the face had deepened, the hair was thinning, he had developed a paunch. He was becoming listless in his movements. His energy declined and he slept until late in the afternoon, with the aid of sedatives. Still tired on waking, he began to drink earlier than before, but by the end of dinner his vitality had waned once more. He walked seldom and had a lift installed for him in the Dolma Bahche Palace. He was always seeking a pretext to sit down, sometimes cross-legged on the floor. He had two bouts of influenza, and feared pneumonia. His doctor one day warned him to be careful, and to drink less.

Early in 1938 he went from Ankara to Yalova, where he was examined by the doctor of the spa. He complained of itching on his legs and thought that the baths would do him good. The doctor told him that his liver was enlarged and hardened, and that the itching was due to his diet and especially to alcohol. His own doctor now made the same diagnosis. The remedy was to rest, to take care what he ate, to drink only in moderation. *Raki*, with its aniseed flavour, was especially bad for his complaint. For a while he drank a little less. After ten days the itching had stopped, and he went, as he had previously planned, to Bursa (as Brusa was now spelt).

Ali Fuad went with him. Of the old friends whom Atatürk had tried for their lives he alone, more easy-going than the rest, had returned to the fold. With Refet he had been reconciled, but their former relations were never resumed. A reconciliation with Rauf had been prevented, after his return from exile, by the People's Party bosses. Kiazim Karabekir had come, on his invitation, to a meeting of the Historical Congress in Istanbul. But, owing to a misunderstanding, the two did not meet. Thus, of these friends of his youth, only Ali Fuad was now at his side.

At Bursa Atatürk delivered an exhortation to the youth of the country which was to become a text for a generation or more to come. In effect it appointed them guardians of the future. If ever the Revolution were in danger,

the young man of Turkey is not going to say, 'There is a police force in this country . . . there is a gendarmerie . . . there is an army . . . there is the machinery of justice in this country.' The young man of Turkey is going to intervene himself, to protect his work. The police will come, and instead of catching the real guilty man, will arrest the young man. The young man will say, 'This means that the police is not yet the police of the Revolution and the Republic!' A tribunal will sentence the young man. Again he will think, 'This means that the justice of the country has still to be adapted to the régime.' He will be thrown into prison. He will defend himself legally. But he will not try to get out of prison by begging for mercy or by asking for special treatment. The young man will say, 'I have acted according to my convictions and beliefs. I am right to intervene and act thus. Since it was unjust that I should be put into prison, it is my duty to correct the reasons and motives which caused this injustice.' This, according to my ideas [concluded Atatürk] is how a Turkish young man, and the youth of Turkey should behave.

These injunctions echoed the even more prophetic peroration of his six-day speech, in which he put forward the hypothesis

that those who hold the power of the Government within the country have fallen into error, that they are fools and traitors, yes, even that these leading persons identify their personal interests with the enemy's political goals, it might happen that the nation came into complete privation, into the most extreme distress; that it found itself in a condition of ruin and complete exhaustion. Even under those circumstances, O Turkish child of future generations, it is your duty to save the independence of the Turkish Republic. The strength that you will need for this is mighty in the noble blood which flows in your veins.[1]

On leaving Mudanya for Istanbul by boat after his visit to Bursa, Atatürk

[1] The words of both these exhortations were widely quoted in 1960, as an inspiration to the youth of the country which had been largely responsible for the overthrow of the Democrat Government of Celal Bayar and Menderes, and its replacement by a provisional military régime.

became suddenly unwell during dinner. He was pale and in pain. Ali Fuad persuaded him to retire. He did so on condition that the party continued with Fuad as host. But no one was now in the mood for it. Soon after midnight, Atatürk called Ali Fuad into his cabin. The doctor had given him drugs and the pain had decreased. Atatürk hoped that he would now be able to sleep. But it looked, he added, as though his illness might take a long time. 'And if I have to stay in bed, I shall be terribly bored. I shall be able to bear it only with the help of friends like yourself.'

When the boat arrived at Dolma Bahche early in the morning, Atatürk looked better. In the evening he went with Kiliç Ali to dinner at the Park Hotel. They stayed there until four o'clock in the morning, sitting at a table in the window where they began to feel the cold. Next day Atatürk had a high fever and developed a touch of pneumonia. He was in bed for more than a week. He insisted on leaving for Ankara before he had fully recovered, and his friends there were shocked at his appearance. He looked exhausted. He could stand only with difficulty. He complained of eruptions on his legs and stomach. At a dinner in honour of the Yugoslav and Greek Premiers he arrived late, owing to a hæmorrhage from the nose which he had been unable to stop. If this arose from his liver condition, it was an ominous symptom.

The Turkish doctors examined him and recommended an outside opinion. Atatürk was reluctant to call in any foreign specialist. The news of his illness would thus become known abroad, and might prejudice the solution of the Hatay problem, where a hitch had arisen. But finally Celal Bayar persuaded him to summon Dr Fissinger, a specialist from France. He came to Ankara and at once diagnosed cirrhosis of the liver. It was a disease of which the Turks say of its victims, 'He has swallowed a monster.' This, his friends now realized, was the monster that had been gnawing away at him all these months.

If he listened to his doctors the illness could still pass. Fissinger was reasonably optimistic. 'I am going to cure you,' he said to Atatürk, 'but you will have to cure yourself first. You may be a great commander, who has won great victories. But now I am your commander, and you have to help me.' The simile appealed to him, and he promised to do what he was told. Hitherto he had been truculent with his doctors, refusing a blood test, lying as to the number of cigarettes he smoked a day. (If he said fifty, they would cut him down to ten, so he said two hundred.) But now, aware of the gravity of his condition, he was ready to compromise. He must lie down for three months, rising only for an hour each day. After that he must lead a restful life for a year. He must follow a special diet and drink no alcohol. If this were only for three months, he replied, he could endure it.

A special *chaise longue* was brought from England, in which he could lie at full length, and in this he was able to read and write and deal with state papers. But the prone position irked him, and he would often rise and sit cross-legged, which was bad for the circulation in his liver. Most evenings he would dine in his chair, with a few friends around him, and retire to bed reasonably early. After a month or so of this treatment he looked better and seemed less tired. He had regained some appetite; his energy and spirits were slowly returning. Over-confident in his strength, he became restless for action once more.

For his mind was never at rest. As in his youth he had lain awake at nights, grappling with problems of military and afterwards political science, so now, in the spring of 1938, he lay awake grappling with the problems of a world on the brink of war, and with the need to round off his own life's work against its outbreak. For the incorporation of Hatay within the frontiers of Turkey had still to be finally clinched.

CHAPTER SIXTY

DEATH OF ATATÜRK

TURKEY had secured the autonomy of Hatay. But elections had still to be held to decide who should control it. The International Commission, sent by the League to organize the elections, devised a system of registration which revealed the Turks to be in a slight minority, with the Arabs and Armenians in the majority. A Turkish mass-meeting was staged in Antakya (Antioch), which led to the suspension of the registers. If the Turks were to get their way, direct pressure must be turned once more on the French. As before, there must be a show of force, and in this Atatürk, despite his illness, insisted on taking a personal hand.

He rose from his invalid chair and, after a tiring day at a youth festival in the stadium at Ankara, took the train with his doctor to Mersin, the Turkish port near the frontier of Hatay. As the train moved south the heat grew oppressive, and Atatürk confessed to a friend, 'This illness is something different, something I have never known before.' Looking down at his stomach he remarked, 'I am putting on weight. My trousers are getting too small. I shall have to have them let out.'

At Mersin he faced an exhausting programme. For forty minutes he stood in the damp torrid heat, taking the salute at a military parade. He had diffi-culty in standing, and Kılıç Ali and Salih, his *aide*, standing behind him, murmured, 'Lean on us.' But he proudly refused, only giving the order 'Quick march!' that the troops should move less slowly. There followed visits to railway yards and to the classical sites nearby. Finally, in the relative cool of the evening, he had a few hours' relaxation in a motor-boat out in the harbour. Next day he was able to rest. He played Turkish music on the gramophone, listening absently as though lost in thought, and sometimes quoting with philosophic melancholy some line from the song. On the third day he stood through another and longer parade, at Tarsus. He proceeded to Adana, to help celebrate the anniversary of its liberation from the French. Then he took the night train back to Ankara, fretting in the heat for it to start amid the ritual of unending goodbyes, devouring a basket of fresh oranges and sighing with relief as he lay down for a feverish sleep.

After two days in the dry heat of Ankara, he left for Istanbul. Normally, at Haydar Pasha station, he would walk down the strip of red carpet from the train to the motor-boat. This morning he knew he would have difficulty in walking, so to shorten the distance his compartment had been hitched to the front of the train. But he refused help, and even stood by the boat with an outward attempt at gaiety to watch the transfer of his baggage. He could not, however, hide his true condition, which was noticed by the crowd with concern.

That day he spent in the relative coolness of Florya. Driving back to the palace in the evening, he had a sudden acute pain at the heart. The car was stopped, and Salih gave him his heart medicine.[1] Back at the palace the doctor explained that this was no ordinary heart trouble, but a symptom of the liver complaint.

Atatürk knew by now that his disease was cirrhosis. He had looked it up in a French medical dictionary and had remarked, 'It looks as though my days are numbered.' The Yalova doctor examined him again, and diagnosed that he had reached the secondary stage of the disease, when the liver, having previously expanded, contracts. His increase in weight was due to an accumulation of water and gas in his belly, a consequent dropsical condition. He must go to bed and lie prone, moving as little as possible. Fissinger was called in again, without Atatürk's knowledge, from Paris, and confirmed the diagnosis. He found his patient's condition worse than he expected. He had risen too soon, and his trip to Mersin had neutralized the effects of his period of rest.

Fatal as it might prove to him personally, his journey, coinciding with Tevfik Rüştü's strong protests at French interference in Hatay, was to have the political effect he had hoped for. For it had helped to create an impression in Paris, as his similar tactics over the Straits had done in Geneva, that Atatürk was preparing an *anschluss* in the familiar style of the other dictators. His own diagnosis of the international situation was proved correct. The French were far too preoccupied with Hitler's activities in Europe to bother themselves about a portion of a Syrian state which would in any case cease, sooner or later, to be theirs. Nor was this the moment to quarrel with a friendly Turkey, which controlled the Straits and could thus, if she chose, bar French access to Soviet Russia, a potential ally in the forthcoming struggle.

The French Government thus opened talks with the Turkish Ambassador in Paris. They led to an agreement by which a Turkish military mission was admitted to Hatay, to keep order in the elections. Early in July a treaty of

---

[1] Salih (Bozok), unwilling to live without his master, was to shoot himself through the heart on the day of Atatürk's death.

friendship was agreed between the two nations, which allowed for the policing of Hatay by French and Turkish forces, and amounted to their effective control in the form of a joint Franco-Turkish guarantee of its autonomy.

Impatiently Atatürk, as he lay on his sick-bed in Istanbul, sent a telephone message to Tevfik Rüştü in Ankara, demanding its immediate implementation. The preliminary detachment of Turkish troops must march into the territory the following Wednesday, at the latest. Tevfik Rüştü realized the reason for his impatience – the fear that there might be further delays and that he would not live to see Hatay within the frontiers of his National Pact. But it was now Saturday, and the final details of the take-over had yet to be settled. Tevfik explained the urgency of the matter to Ponsot who, respecting Atatürk as he did, showed his sympathy, but explained that Paris must first agree, and that the Quai d'Orsay did not function over the weekend. He promised, however, to do his best.

Tevfik Rüştü, with the aid of his son-in-law, a Foreign Office official named Zorlu, typed out in person a draft agreement, completing the treaty, and despatched it to Paris for signature. The Turkish Ambassador contacted the Foreign Minister, who was away in the country. To carry out such a formality on a Sunday was unprecedented. It involved disturbing the weekend rest of several responsible officials. But when Atatürk's condition was explained to him, the minister came up to Paris and in the evening the treaty was formally signed. The Turkish troops marched into Hatay on the day appointed. Conveniently the electoral register, published in the following month, showed a majority of Turks, who occupied twenty-two out of the forty seats in the subsequent Assembly. Its deliberations were to open the way, a year later, to the complete incorporation of Hatay within the Turkish Republic. Thus Atatürk's last work for his country was done.

The year before he had ordered a sea-going yacht. She was named the *Savarona*; she had been built for an American millionairess; and Hitler had made an offer for her but withdrawn it when he learned that the Turks had been first in the field. She chanced to arrive just at this moment when Atatürk's last illness began. He remarked ironically, 'I waited for this yacht like a child expecting a toy. Is she then to become my grave?' In the stifling heat of Istanbul he was moved from the palace to the *Savarona*, which at least caught the breezes, and which became in effect his hospital-ship.

Fissinger now seldom left his bedside. Atatürk treated their daily consultations like staff conferences for a battle, whose issue was now his own life, with himself no longer in command but a mere private soldier, submitting to orders. Hearing that Ismet too was ill, hence unable to come to Istanbul to see him, he asked Fissinger to visit and examine him in Ankara. Reluctant to leave him for long, Fissinger went to Ankara for only twenty-four hours, and on his return told Atatürk that Ismet had diabetes, but that he had advised against an operation. Finally, Fissinger had to return to Paris. When Atatürk urged him to stay, the doctor remarked to an *aide*, 'If I stayed one day longer, I should find myself obeying *him*, his will is so strong.'

Atatürk in his *chaise longue* settled down to the monotonous routine of the invalid. In the morning the sign that he was awake was the sound of the gramophone in his cabin. Then Ülkü, the little girl, would go in to him, keeping him amused, as she did for most of the day, with her games and her prattle. Usually on emerging on deck he remained in his nightshirt, sitting thus among his friends – Kiliç Ali and Ismail Hakki, the former captain of his bodyguard, his two or three *aides*, and often Afet or Sabiha, his other 'daughters'. But when official visitors came he would dress carefully, donning a white yachting-cap with a blazer and perhaps a flower in his buttonhole. While they discussed state business, Ülkü would sit on his lap and he would fondle her affectionately.

One of his more illustrious visitors was King Carol of Rumania. The visit, however, was not a success. The King said to him, 'The Sudeten affair is of primary importance in Europe today. The President of the Czecho-slovakian Republic, Dr Benes, is complicating the situation by his obstinacy, and the result is that there may be a war in Europe.' Atatürk stiffened in his armchair and with a flash of the old fire turned to Tevfik Rüştü, saying, 'Ask His Majesty this. What sort of attitude does he expect from a President of the Republic who is the person mainly responsible for the independence of his country?' The King went pale, and switched to the safer subject of Rumania's adherence to the Balkan Pact.

Presently Atatürk began to find even the *Savarona*, with the low ceilings of her cabins and saloons, unendurably hot. Blocks of ice were placed around his cabin to cool it. But Atatürk, in his pain and his fever complained, 'My belly is swimming in water. Can such a man go on living?'

Once or twice he sailed down into the Marmara and back, seeking fresh air. One day, in a motor-boat, he paid a visit to Florya – his last. The people on the beaches, seeing him thus, well-dressed as always in the yachting-cap which so suited him, went wild with enthusiasm and broke into cheers. He rose awkwardly to his feet, walked to the prow of the boat, and waved back to them. Reluctant to return to the *Savarona*, he cruised up the Bos-porus. From the streets and from the houses by the shore the people cheered him.

Back on board the yacht, he had a high temperature, which lasted for several days. One night, distraught by his fever and the pain of the water in his belly, he cried out, 'I'm being strangled,' and staggered out on deck, flinging himself on the *chaise longue*. His friends begged him to go in, out of the damp heat, but he said with resignation, 'Whatever is destined to happen will happen.' He had difficulty in walking back to his cabin. There he sank into an armchair and said to Kiliç Ali, 'Telephone your mother and ask if she has not some household remedy for this temperature and pain.' Kiliç Ali did so, and his mother sent over a bottle of rose vinegar, which she had treasured for years. Cloths were dipped in it and placed on his forehead and wrists, giving him a certain relief.

As the fever mounted it was decided to transfer him back to the palace, where it might be cooler. The move was made at midnight with the lights on the quay extinguished that no one might see. The doctor ordered that he should be carried ashore on a stretcher, since it was dangerous for him to walk. But he refused angrily. Instead an armchair was brought, and in this he was carried ashore and into the lift of the palace. On reaching the first floor he pushed his helpers aside and, despite their protests, walked to his bedroom.

It was a high room with a carved walnut bed and other furniture in a Frenchified style. The three windows were elaborately draped with brocade curtains. The floor was of parquet, and the room was illuminated by a crystal chandelier. Atatürk sank down with relief on the bed, which was draped with a mosquito-net, and exclaimed, 'How wonderful! This place really *is* cooler than the yacht.' But the rooms of the palace proved almost as hot, and every day firemen came to spray water on the outside walls of his bedroom. He looked often with a sigh towards a picture on the wall, portraying a cool Alpine scene with fruit blossom in the foreground and forest trees above. With the pressure of the fluid and the gas his pains grew worse. His belly continued to swell, he found it hard to lie down and to breathe. He was ivory pale, and his eyes seemed to have grown larger. He begged his doctors to draw off the fluid, but they wished to postpone the operation for as long as possible.

Realizing its dangers, Atatürk sent for Hassan Riza, his secretary, to make his will. At first they talked of the world situation. Hassan Riza read him the news summary, to which he listened with interest. It confirmed his own opinion. There would be no war this year. Neither the Germans nor the Italians were ready for it. It would break out either in 1939 or in 1940. Showing some signs of emotion, he then stretched out a hand to Hassan Riza and with his aid sat up cross-legged in bed. Looking out through the long windows at the Asiatic shore of the Bosporus he instructed him to make a list of all he possessed. A typewritten draft of the will was prepared, and Atatürk transcribed it in his own handwriting, making a few changes of detail and phrase.

A notary was summoned. To receive him, Atatürk rose from his bed, had himself shaved and changed his nightshirt for a pair of silk pyjamas and a red brocade dressing-gown, with a red silk scarf around his neck. They sat by the window overlooking the Bosporus, drinking coffee and discussing the new law which governed the duties of notaries. Then Atatürk

A.—17

handed him the will. By its provisions, signed and dated 5th September 1938, he left all his estate, including Chankaya and its contents, to the People's Party, to be administered as hitherto by the Iş Bank. The income was to go, in specified sums, to his sister Makbule and his five adopted daughters. Sabiha Gökçen was to receive in addition money sufficient to buy herself a house, while Makbule was to retain her house at Chankaya for her lifetime. Funds were to be set aside for the higher education of the children of Ismet İnönü.[1] The residue of the income was to be divided equally between the Linguistic and Historical Societies.

Fissinger returned from France and examined him carefully. He could hardly sit up in bed, and the time had come for a puncture to draw off some fluid. To Kiliç Ali he murmured afterwards, 'Did you see the water they took out? How could one bear it if so much water were put in a container and laid on one's belly.' He seemed to his friend to have suddenly become very thin, as though he were shrinking in bed from hour to hour. He was weak, but still signed documents, read the newspapers or had them read to him by Afet, listened to the gramophone and radio.

He saw few visitors, partly because the doctors discouraged them, partly because it suited the entourage to keep away those they mistrusted. Ali Fuad, after several unsuccessful attempts, finally succeeded in gaining admission. Atatürk pulled up the coverlet on his bed to conceal his swollen belly. He complained of his difficulty in breathing. Then, frowning and fixing his steel-blue eyes on Fuad, he took a long breath and launched into a discussion of the future. The present situation was far more critical than any they had faced together at the time of the Armistice. A pair of adventurers was trying to conquer and rule the world by force, and there were no statesmen strong enough to stand up to them. Soviet Russia would know how to profit from the errors of both sides, and the whole international balance would change.

'If we commit the slightest mistake,' he said, 'we may possibly be faced with a catastrophe. . . . I *have* to be well enough to take the state in hand at that time. You know that here, in this country, one can never control anything from one's bed. I've *got* to be at the head of affairs.' He talked of his illness, and Ali Fuad spoke words of reassurance. But Atatürk said, 'Fuad Pasha, you're trying to soothe me in vain. One has to see the truth exactly as it is.' They embraced one another goodbye. Despite further attempts, Ali Fuad was not admitted to see him again.

The fifteenth anniversary of the Republic was approaching – 29th October 1938. Some weeks before the celebration he called Kiliç Ali and Salih. Pointing to the bandages and the long woollen socks on his bedside table

---

[1] Ismet himself had adequate means to support and educate his family. But Atatürk believed him, at this time, to be iller than he was, and was providing for his possible early death.

he said, 'Which shall I put on when I go to Ankara?' Humouring him, Salih said, 'Pasha, I have some stockings at home made for varicose veins. They will support your legs better.' When they came, Atatürk said, 'I will put these on my feet and a scarf round my neck. We can leave the train at the Gazi station, and go straight to Chankaya. We must do this quickly.'

But a few days after the puncture he fell into a coma. This lasted for more than forty-eight hours. The doctors moved him into a narrower bed. Occasionally he opened his eyes, which were lifeless and dull. Intermittently he muttered, 'Ah no, Effendim. No, no!' This might, it was feared, be the end. But he regained consciousness. By his bedside he found Celal Bayar, summoned fron Ankara. 'What happened to me?' he asked.

'You have slept deeply,' Bayar replied. 'A few hours longer than usual.' Lest he suspect, Ülkü was told to tell him that he had slept for twelve hours. Instead, she said, 'You have slept a long time.' As usual, he had the truth from her. He asked why his bed had been changed, and was told, 'This one was cleaner.' 'Well,' was his comment, 'let me not ask too many questions.' He started to talk once more of going to Ankara. His speech must be prepared for the Assembly. Let the various ministers provide notes, let Bayar prepare a draft which he could then write, in his own style, in Ankara. If he felt too tired, he could shorten it. For the ceremonies a special lift was installed in the stadium, to take him up to his box; a special rostrum constructed in the Assembly, in which he could lean back, half sitting but apparently standing.

But the doctors pronounced the journey impossible. The vibration of the train alone might be fatal. Rebelliously he insisted, 'Let us go to Ankara. Whatever is going to happen to me, let it happen there.' But, realistic to the last, he accepted their verdict. 'All right,' he concluded, 'there is no sense in my going.' He must at least be able to walk from the train to his car and from the car into the Assembly, and this he now knew he was too weak to do.

The speech must be read to the Assembly by Bayar. He received his Prime Minister in a dressing-gown, and insisted on hearing the whole of it. His mind was as lucid as ever, and to occupy it with politics, far from tiring him, seemed to give him renewed life. He made Bayar repeat paragraphs, corrected errors, redrafted with him the beginning and the end. To this he added the words, 'I wish the Grand National Assembly success in all the business they undertake.' These were the last of his words to be spoken in public.

The day of the fifteenth anniversary of the Republic arrived. A group of cadets from the Kuleli Military School passed in a ferry-boat before the Dolma Bahche Palace. They shouted in unison, 'We want to see Atatürk!' He heard them and insisted, despite efforts to restrain him, on going to the window. He was helped to a chair and looked out on the cadets. When they saw him they broke into a roar of welcome. Some of them jumped into the water in their uniforms and swam towards the palace to see him more closely. That night there were illuminations in the Sarayburnu Park. Celal Bayar returned from Ankara and gave Atatürk a detailed account of the parade there, and the people's enthusiasm.

There now remained only one problem to decide – that of the succession. Atatürk wanted Inönü to succeed him as President of the Republic, and had sent an emissary to Ankara to ask him to come to his bedside. He was told that he was too ill to travel. He suspected, however, that Ismet's enemies among his entourage might be keeping him away. At one moment he even had the delusion that Ismet was dead and that the news was being kept from him. He thus secretly sent a second emissary in the shape of his dentist, Dr Gunzberg, to report to him on the position.

In Ankara, the city of rumour, there were indeed some who believed that Celal Bayar and his friends were plotting to seize power on Atatürk's death. Inönü was thus strongly advised by responsible persons not to go to Istanbul, lest he be assassinated. These fears proved groundless. Bayar, much as he may have hoped for the succession, realized that the weight of opinion was in favour of Inönü. Fevzi (now Çakmak), the only other possible candidate, renounced his claims. Fethi (Okyar) went to Istanbul to clinch the matter of Ismet's succession with Bayar. When the end seemed near both Ismet and Fevzi were summoned to a Cabinet meeting in Ankara, at which one of Atatürk's doctors reported on his condition and the transference of the Presidency was settled.

On 6th November, Atatürk got up for the last time. Afet and his attendants helped him to his feet. His shoulders were thin and bony. Only his hands had not lost their shapeliness. He held out a hand to them and they kissed it, one by one, sure that they would never do so again. Next day the doctors gave him another puncture, drawing off a large quantity of fluid. Afterwards he had a craving for an artichoke. They were out of season, and a consignment of them had been ordered from Hatay. But when the artichoke came he could not eat it. Not long afterwards, after a painful paroxysm he murmured, 'Goodbye.' He fell into his last coma, still and apparently peaceful.

Next day towards midnight the climax approached. It became clear that he was dying. One of the doctors was weeping. The two others were massaging his feet. Hassan Riza, Kiliç Ali and Ismail Hakki stood at attention by the bedside, like soldiers. Hassan said to Kiliç Ali, 'Look. A piece of history is passing away.' His face was drained of all colour. Soon after nine o'clock on the morning of 10th November 1938, he opened his eyes, which for a moment gleamed blue as ever, without recognition, at those around him. Then he closed them. His head fell back on the pillow. Kemal Atatürk was dead.

Istanbul was stunned into a poignant silence. Children tore ribbons and bows from their heads; women wept and muttered prayers in the streets before his photographs, now swathed in crêpe. His embalmed body lay in state beneath the painted dome of the throne room, its chandeliers extinguished, in the Dolma Bahche Palace. The Turkish flag covered the ebony coffin. Six torches illuminated it; four officers of the land, sea and air forces, with drawn swords, watched over the catafalque in shifts. For three days and nights he lay thus, while the people of Istanbul in their hundreds of thousands filed endlessly, reverently past him, bowing silently, whispering prayers, intoning softly, '*Ata, ata,*' for their father who was dead.

On the last night, they stayed out in the streets until morning. They thronged the pavements, perched in the branches of the trees, clambered on to the domes and minarets of the mosques to see the long funeral cortège pass by. After a few brief prayers (on which his sister Makbule had insisted) the coffin was borne on a gun-carriage, drawn by soldiers, in a slow procession to the quay below the Old Seraglio. Behind it an officer marched, carrying on a velvet cushion a solitary medal, that of the War of Independence. The procession crossed the Galata Bridge to the strains, unfamiliar to Turks, of Chopin's Funeral March. The coffin was conveyed to a torpedo-boat, then out to the *Yavuz*, which lay off Seraglio Point. Flanking her were the ships of all the nations so soon to be at war, among them HMS *Malaya*, which had carried the last of the Sultans into exile. After salutes had been fired they slowly escorted the *Yavuz* out of the Bosporus and into the Marmara, where they bade her farewell.

At Izmit, in the evening, the coffin was placed in Atatürk's private saloon on the white presidential train, for burial in Ankara. The six torches surrounded it, the four officers carrying naked swords kept watch. As the darkened train steamed off into the night, his compartment alone formed a rectangle of light, moving slowly over the infinite Anatolian landscape. Peasants in their thousands crowded down to the track to await the train and see the last of their 'father'. They waved torches and poured their scant rations of petrol on the ground, setting a light to it to blaze his way back into that homeland which he had made into a new Turkish nation.

EPILOGUE

EPILOGUE

KEMAL ATATÜRK had created a new Turkey. He had left it in the hands of an experienced leader, an efficient administration, and a flexible parliamentary system, capable of evolution in more liberal terms when the time became ripe.[1] He had transported his country from the Middle Ages to the threshold of the modern era and a stage beyond. It was now the task of his successors, covering new ground and filling in ground behind him, to carry it on a stage further.

The progress had been rapid – too rapid for some. In a mere half generation Atatürk had sought to build a new Turkish society. He had abruptly uprooted the traditions of centuries, but had not yet evolved a new culture in place of them. This had caused some dislocation in the mind and the life of the ordinary Turk, whom a leader more sympathetic to Islam might well have weaned more gradually from one civilization to the other. As it was, some twenty years after Atatürk's death, a successor was to imperil his Revolution by reviving and exploiting dormant forces of religion for political purposes.[2]

Socially, before Turkey could consolidate the unity which Atatürk had given her, a gap remained to be closed between the 'two nations' of her illiterate peasantry and her literate bourgeoisie. It was this class, essentially urban in character, which was for the present the true beneficiary of the Turkish Revolution. Formed by Atatürk as a Westernized élite for the support and direction of a centralized Government, it still needed to achieve close touch with the mass of the rural population, to whom the full benefits had not yet been able to percolate. Only the spread of education could close this gap, together with an effective grasp of economic problems which the generation of Atatürk lacked. Twenty-five years after his death his successors were engaged on a fresh national struggle to establish the country as a whole on a productive economic basis.

These however are hardly more than the growing pains of any new

[1] This happened in 1950, when free elections returned an Opposition party, that of the Democrats, to power, with Celal Bayar as President of the Republic.

[2] This was Adnan Menderes, the Democrat Prime Minister. His autocratic tendencies, suffused with an aura of 'divine right', provoked, in 1960, a revolution which overthrew his régime and, after an interval of military government, established a new Constitution.

country. What Atatürk left to the Turkey he had freed was strong foundations and a clear objective for her future growth. He gave her not merely durable institutions but a national ideal, rooted in patriotism, nourished by a new self-respect, and promising fruitful rewards for new energies. He created, by his deeds and his words, a personal myth, to feed the imagination of a people given to the worship of heroes. He infused them with a belief in the values of Western democracy, which they learnt sincerely to respect, differing only as to the means of achieving it. All that he gave them survives as a living force in the Turk of today.

The logical outcome has been the emergence of the Turkish Republic as a reliable ally of the West. The soldier in Atatürk saved his country, confounding, as no other man at that time could have done, the designs of the European powers against it, and thus changing the face of its history. The statesman in him then won their acceptance of his country on equal terms, and ultimately its incorporation into the Atlantic Alliance, as a bulwark against Russia – its hereditary enemy – and an element of stability in the shifting Middle Eastern world.

Such was the life's achievement of Mustafa Kemal, 'Father of the Turks'.

LONDON – ISTANBUL – ANKARA – LONDON
1960–64

MAPS

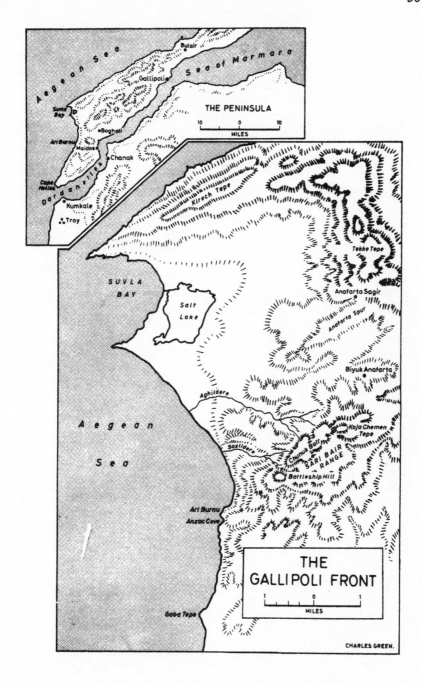

THE PENINSULA

Aegean Sea

Sea of Marmara

Bulair

Gallipoli

Suvla Bay

Boghali

Ari Burnu

Maidos

Chanak

Cape Helles

Dardanelles

Kumkale

Troy

10   0   10
MILES

Kirech Tepe

Tekke Tepe

SUVLA BAY

Salt Lake

Anafarta Sagir

Anafarta Spur

Biyuk Anafarta

Aghildere

Aegean Sea

Sazlidere

Koja Chemen Tepe

Chunuk Bair

SARI BAIR RANGE

Battleship Hill

Ari Burnu

Anzac Cove

Gaba Tepe

THE
GALLIPOLI FRONT

1   0   1
MILES

CHARLES GREEN.

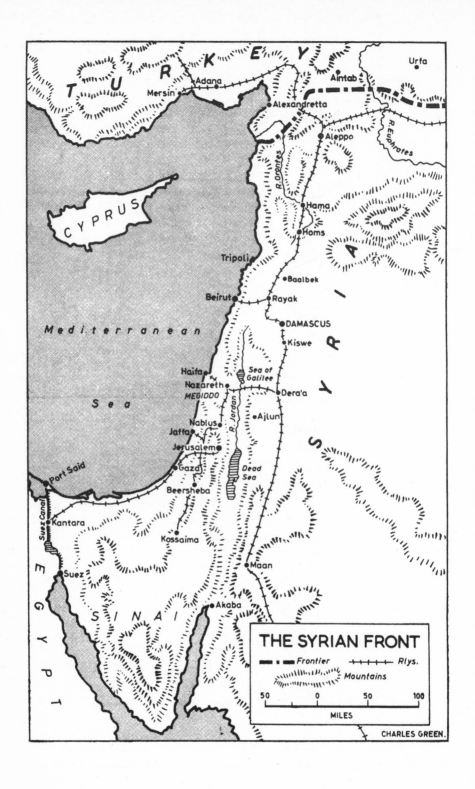

THE SYRIAN FRONT

Frontier ·—·—· | Rlys. +++++

Mountains

50   0   50   100

MILES

CHARLES GREEN.

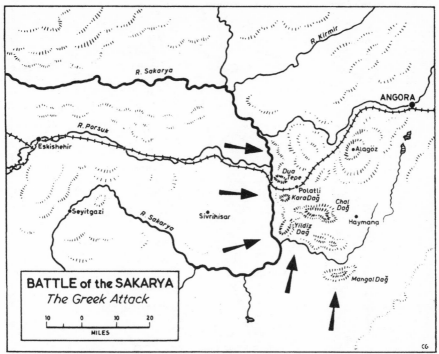

BATTLE of the SAKARYA
The Greek Attack

10 0 10 20
MILES

R. Kirmir
R. Sakarya
ANGORA
R. Porsuk
Eskishehir
•Alagöz
Dua Tepe
•Polatli
KaraDağ
Chal Dağ
Seyitgazi
R. Sakarya
Sivrihisar
•Haymana
Yildiz Dağ
Mangal Dağ

CG

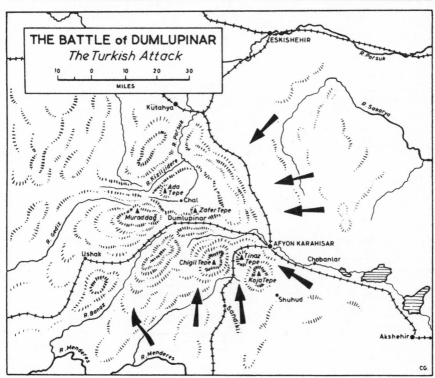

THE BATTLE of DUMLUPINAR
The Turkish Attack

10 0 10 20 30
MILES

ESKISHEHIR
R. Porsuk
R. Sakarya
Kütahya•
R.Kizilijidere
Ada Tepe
•Chat
Zafer Tepe
Muraddağ
Dumlupinar
R. Gediz
AFYON KARAHISAR
Chobanlar
Ushak
Chigil Tepe
Tinaz Tepe
KojaTepe
•Shuhud
R. Banaz
Sandikli
Akshehir•
R. Menderes
R. Menderes

CG.

THE OTTOMAN EMPIRE
at the time
of its greatest extent

| 100 | 0 | 100 | 200 | 300 |
MILES

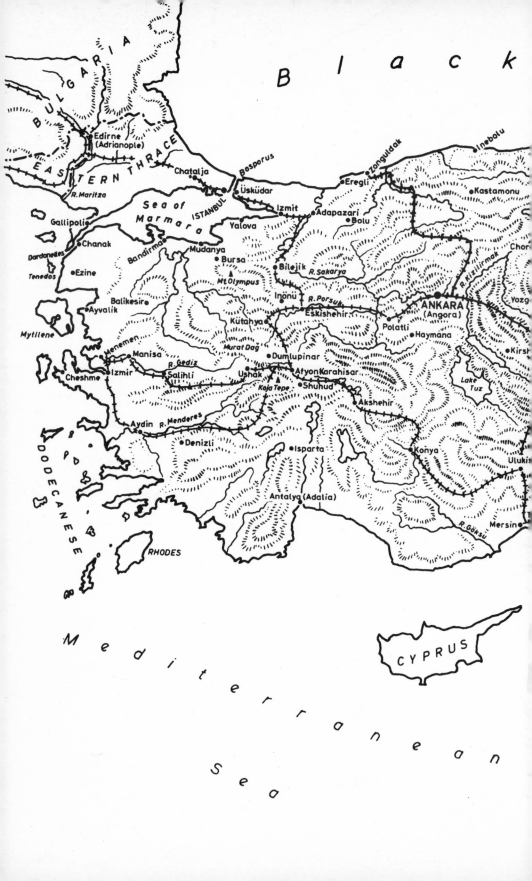

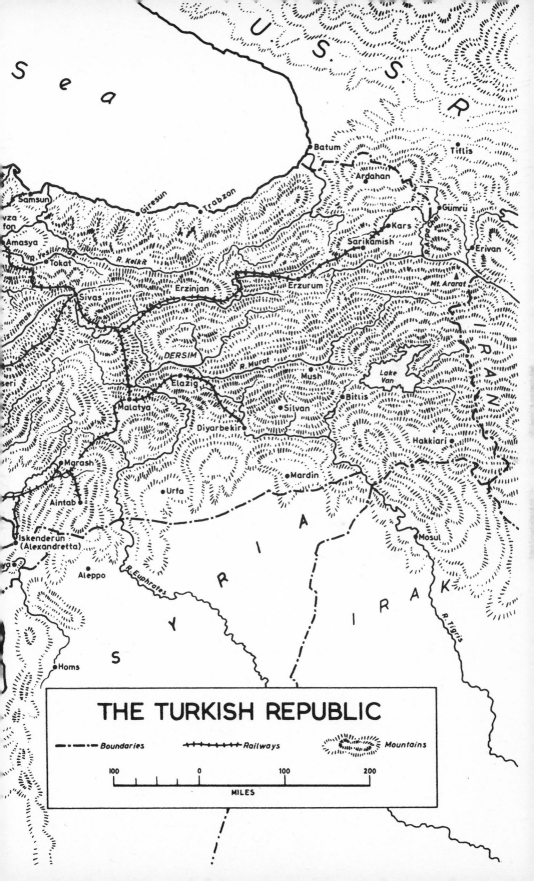

THE TURKISH REPUBLIC

- — ·· — ·· — Boundaries
- —+—+—+—+— Railways
- Mountains

100   0   100   200
MILES

SELECTED BIBLIOGRAPHY

Unpublished Sources

Presidential Archives, Çankaya, Ankara.
Papers on the History of the Revolution. Ankara University.
National Archives. Washington.
Papers of Louis E. Browne. Stanford University, California.
Papers of Admiral Bristol. Library of Congress, Washington.
Papers of Ambassador Joseph C. Grew. Harvard University.
Papers of Sir Horace Rumbold. Private.
Naval Memoirs of Admiral Sir Bertram Thesiger, 1875–94. Private.
Frederick P. Latimer, *The Political Philosophy of Mustapha Kemal Atatürk*.
　Doctoral Dissertation (Princeton, 1960)
Walter F. Weiker, *The Free Party of* 1930 *in Turkey*. Doctoral Dissertation
　(Princeton, 1962)

Books: Turkish

Dr Afetinan, *Atatürk Hakkinda Hatiralar ve Belgeler* (Memoirs and
　Documents on Atatürk) (Ankara, 1959)
Samet Ağaoğlu, *Babamin Arkadaşlari* (My Father's Friends) (Istanbul, n.d.)
Kiliç Ali, *Atatürk'ün Hususiyetleri* (The Characteristics of Atatürk)
　(Istanbul, 1955)
　Hatiralarini Anlatiyor (Recollections) (Istanbul, 1955)
　Istiklal Mahkemesi Hatiralari (Recollections of the Independence
　Tribunals (Istanbul, 1955)
　Son Günleri (The Last Days) (Istanbul, 1955)
Asim Arar, *Son Günlerinde Atatürk* (Atatürk in his Last Days) (Istanbul,
　1958)
Mehmet Arif, *Anadolu Inkilabi* (The Anatolian Revolution) (Istanbul, 1924)
Falih Rifki Atay, *Mustafa Kemal'in Mütareke Defteri* (Atatürk's Armistice
　Note-book) (Istanbul, 1955)
　Babamiz Atatürk (Our Father Atatürk) (Istanbul, 1955)
　Atatürk'ün Bana Anlattiklari (What Atatürk told me) (Istanbul, 1955)
　Çankaya (Istanbul, 1958)
Kemal Atatürk. Edited by Uluğ Iğdemir. *Anafartalar Hatiralari* (Recol-
　lections of Gallipoli) (Istanbul, 1955)
　Edited by Enver Ziya Karal. *Atatürk'ün Söylev ve Demeçleri* (The Speeches
　and Statements of Atatürk). 3 Vols. (Istanbul, 1945 ; Ankara, 1954–59)
Kemal Atatürk. *Atatürk'den Düsünceler* (Thoughts from Atatürk) (Ankara,
　1956)

Şevket Süreyya Aydemir, *Suyu Arayan Adam* (The Man who Searched for Water) (Ankara, 1959)

Niyazi Ahmet Banoğlu, *Fikra, Nükte ve Çizgilerle Atatürk* (Anecdotes concerning Atatürk). 3 Vols. (Istanbul, 1954–55)

Celal Bayar, *Atatürk'ten Hatiralar* (Recollections of Atatürk) (Istanbul 1955)

Mustafa Baydar, *Atatürk ile Konuşmalar* (Interviews of Atatürk with Journalists) (Istanbul, 1960)

Mevlut Baysal, *Çankaya'da Gazinin Hizmetinde* (At Çankaya: In the Service of Atatürk) (Istanbul, 1954)

Ahmet Hamdi Başar, *Atatürk'le Üc Ay* (Three Months with Atatürk) (Istanbul, 1945)

Tevfik Biyiklioğlu, *Atatürk Anadolu'da* (Atatürk in Anatolia) (Ankara, 1959)

Behçet Kemal Cağlar, *Dolmabahçe'den Anit-Kabir'e* (From Dolmabahche to the Mausoleum) (Istanbul, 1955)

Ali Fuat Cebesoy, *Milli Mücadele Hatiralari* (Recollections of the National Struggle) (Istanbul, 1953)

Moskova Hatiralari (Moscow Recollections) (Istanbul, 1955)

Siyasi Hatiralar (Political Recollections). 2 Vols. (Istanbul, 1957–60)

Behcet Cemal, *Seyh Sait Isyani* (The Sheikh Said Rebellion) (Istanbul, 1955)

Cevat Dursunoğlu, *Milli Mücadelede Erzurum* (Erzurum during the National Struggle) (Ankara, 1946)

Ahmet Cevat Emre, *Iki Neslin Tarihi: Mustafa Kemal*) (History of Two Generations: Mustafa Kemal) (Istanbul, 1960)

Tayyip Gökbilgin, *Milli Mücadele Başlarken* (The Beginning of the National Struggle) (Ankara, 1959)

Mustafa Selim Imece, *Atatürk'ün Şapka Devriminde Kastamonu ve Inebolu Seyahatleri* (Atatürk's Journeys to Kastamonu and Inebolu during the Hat Reform) (Ankara, 1959)

Mahmut Kemal Inal, *Osmanli Devrinde Son Sadriazamlar* (Last Grand Viziers of the Ottoman Empire) (Istanbul, 1940–53)

Feridun Kandemir, *Siyasi Darginliklar* (Political Quarrels) (Istanbul, 1955)

Izmir Suikastinin Ic Yüzü (The Inside Story of the Izmir Conspiracy) (Istanbul, 1955)

Serbest Firka Nasil Kuruldu Nasil Kapatildi (How the Free Party was formed and suppressed) (Istanbul, 1955)

Kâzim Karabekir, *Istiklal Harbimiz* (Our War of Independence) (Istanbul, 1960)

Yakup Kadri Karaosmanoğlu, *Atatürk* (Istanbul, 1946)

Macide Vildan Kunter, *Atatürk'ün Hayati ve Basarilari* (The Life and Achievement of Atatürk) (Istanbul, 1953)

Yunus Nadi, *Ali Galip Hadisesi* (The Ali Galib Incident) (Istanbul, 1955)

Mustafa Kemal Paşa Samsun'da (Mustafa Kemal in Samsun) (Istanbul, 1955)

Ankara'nin Ilk Günleri (Early Days in Ankara) (Istanbul, 1955)

Birinci Büyük Millet Meclisi Açilişi ve Isyanlar (The First Grand National Assembly and the Insurrections) (Istanbul, 1955)

Çerkes Etem (Istanbul, 1955)

E. Behnan Şapolyo, *Kemal Atatürk ve Milli Mücadele Tarihi* (Kemal Atatürk and the History of the National Struggle) (Istanbul, 1958)

Ismail Habib Sevük, *Atatürk Için* (For Atatürk) (Istanbul, 1939)

Feridun Fazil Tülbentci, *Cumhuriyet Nasil Kuruldu?* (How the Republic was Founded) (Istanbul, 1955)

Ali Fuat Türkgeldi, *Görüp Işittiklerim* (What I saw and heard) (Istanbul, 1949)

Ruşen Eşref Ünaydin, *Anafartalar Kumandani Mustafa Kemal ile Mülakat* (Interview with the Commander of Gallipoli) (Istanbul, 1954)

Atatürk'ü Özleyiş (Longing for Atatürk) (Ankara, 1957)

Atatürk ve Miʿli Tesanüt (Atatürk and National Solidarity) (Istanbul, 1954)

Türk Dili Tetkik Cemiyeti Kurulduğundan Ilk Kurultaya Kadar Hatiralar (Recollections of the Turkish Language Society) (Ankara, 1933)

Tarih ve Dil Kurumlari Hatiralari (Recollections of the Language and Historical Societies) (Ankara, 1959)

Atatürk'ün Hastaliği (Atatürk's Illness) (Istanbul, 1959)

Atatürk'e Ait Hatiralar (Recollections of Atatürk) (Istanbul, 1949)

30 *Agustos Hatiralari* (Recollections of the Victory of 30th August) (Istanbul, 1955)

Atatürk'ün Yakinlarindan Hatiralar (Recollections of Atatürk by his friends) (Istanbul, 1955)

Atatürk'ün Nöbet Defteri 1931–38 (Atatürk's Appointments Book) (Ankara, 1955)

Minutes of the Grand National Assembly, 1920–23

Periodicals and Newspapers: Turkish

Makbule Atadan, *Recollections of her brother, Atatürk*. Milliyet, Istanbul. November, 1955

Kemal Atatürk, *Letters to Corinne Lütfü*. Milliyet, Istanbul. November, 1955.

Ömer Sami Coşar, *The Change in the Alphabet*. Milliyet, Istanbul. November, 1960.

Necmeddin Deliorman, *Recollections of Atatürk in Sofia*. Her Gün. Istanbul. September–October, 1955.

Perihan Naci Eldeniz, *Recollection of Atatürk*. Belleten LXXX. Ankara. October, 1956.

Çerkes Etem, *Recollections*. Dünya, Istanbul. May–June, 1962.

Ismet Inönü, *Recollections*. Akis, Istanbul. January–September, 1959.

Rauf Orbay, *Recollections*. Yakin Tarikhimiz. Istanbul. March, 1962–January, 1963.

Military History Commission, Turkish General Staff. *Askeri Mecmua* (Military Journal) (Istanbul, 1939)

Books: Other Languages

Allen, W. E. D., and Muratoff, Paul, *Caucasian Battlefields* (Cambridge, 1953)

Alp, Tekin, *Le Kémalisme* (Paris, 1937)

Armstrong, Harold, *Turkey in Travail* (London, 1925)

Atatürk, Kemal, *A Speech*. Delivered at Angora, 15th–20th October, 1927. English translation (Leipzig, 1929)

Aspinall-Oglander, Brig.-Gen. C. F., *Military Operations: Gallipoli*. 2 Vols. (London, 1929–32). 1

Baldwin, Oliver, *Six Prisons and Two Revolutions* (London, 1925)

Bean, C. E. W., *The Story of Anzac*. 2 Vols. (Sydney, 1921, 1924)

Beaverbrook, Lord, *Politicians and the Press* (London, 1935)
  The Decline and Fall of Lloyd George (London, 1963)

Benett, J. G., *Witness* (London, 1962)

Bennett, Ernest N., *With the Turks in Tripoli* (London, 1912)

Bischoff, Norbert de, *La Turquie dans le Monde* (Paris, 1936)

Brémond, E., *La Cilicie en 1919–20* (Paris, 1921)

Buxton, C. Roden, *Turkey in Revolution* (London, 1909)

Callwell, Major-General Sir C. E., *Field-Marshal Sir Henry Wilson: His Life and Diaries* (London, 1927). 2

Child, Richard Washburn, *A Diplomat Looks at Europe* (New York, 1925)

Churchill, Randolph, *Lord Derby* (London, 1959)

Churchill, Winston, *The World Crisis: The Aftermath* (London, 1929). 3

Davison, Roderic H., *Turkish Diplomacy from Mudros to Lausanne* (in *The Diplomats, 1919–39*) (Princeton, 1953)

Deny, Jean, *Souvenirs du Gazi Moustafa Kemal Pasha* (Paris, 1927)

Edib, Halide, *Memoirs* (London, 1926)
  The Turkish Ordeal (London, 1926). 4

Edmonds, C. J., *Kurds, Turks and Arabs* (Oxford, 1957)

Ellison, Grace, *An Englishwoman in Angora* (London, 1924)
  Turkey Today (London, 1928)

Evans-Pritchard, E. E., *The Sanusi of Cyrenaica* (Oxford, 1949)

Eversley, Lord, *The Turkish Empire* (London, 1917)

Fischer, Louis, *The Soviets in World Affairs*. Vol. 1 (London, 1930)

Georges-Gaulis, Berthe, *Angora, Constantinople, Londres* (Paris, 1922)
  Le Nationalisme Turque (Paris, 1921)
  La Nouvelle Turquie (Paris, 1924)

Gentizon, Paul, *Mustapha Kemal, où L'Orient en Marche* (Paris, 1929)

Gibbs, Sir Philip, *Adventures in Journalism* (London, 1923)

Graves, Philip P., *Briton and Turk* (London, 1941)

Graves, Sir R. W., *Storm Centres in the Near East* (London, 1933)

Grew, Joseph Clark, *Turbulent Era* (Boston, 1952)

Hamilton, General Sir Ian, *Gallipoli Diary* (London, 1920). 5

Harington, General Sir Charles, *Tim Harington Looks Back* (London, 1940). 6

Haidar, Alaeddine, *A Angora Auprès de Mustapha Kemal* (Paris, 1921)

Hemingway, Ernest, *The Snows of Kilimanjaro* (London, 1963). 7

Henderson, Sir Nevile, *Water Under the Bridges* (London, 1945)

Herbert, Aubrey, *Ben Kendim* (London, 1924)

Haslip, Joan, *The Sultan* (London, 1958)

Heyd, Uriel, *Foundations of Turkish Nationalism: The Life and Teachings of Ziya Gökalp* (London, 1950)
  Language Reform in Modern Turkey (Jerusalem, 1954)

Hodge, E. R. Vere, *Turkish Foreign Policy, 1918–48* (Geneva, 1950)

House, E. M., and Seymour, C., *What Really Happened at Paris* (London, 1921)

Howard, Harry N., *Partition of Turkey* (Oklahoma, 1931)
Inönü, Ismet, *Negotiation and National Interest* (in *Perspectives on Peace, 1910–60*) (New York, 1960)
Islamic Encyclopædia (Islam Ansiklopedisi), *The Life of Atatürk*. English Translation (Ankara, 1961)
Jäckh, Ernest, *The Rising Crescent* (New York, 1944)
Jäschke, Gotthard (with Erich Pritsch), *Die Turkei seit dem Weltkriege* (Berlin, 1929)
  Mustafa Kemals Sendung nach Anatolien (in *Aus der Geschichte des Islamischen Orients*) (Tübingen, 1949)
Jemal, Ahmed, *Memoirs of a Turkish Statesman* (London, 1922)
Karpat, Kemal H., *Turkey's Politics: The Transition to a Multi-Party System* (Princeton, 1959)
Kannengiesser, Hans, *The Campaign in Gallipoli* (London, 1928)
Ismail Kemal Bey, *Memoirs* (London, 1920)
Knight, E. F., *The Awakening of Turkey* (London, 1909)
Larcher, Commandant M., *La Guerre Turque dans la Guerre Mondiale* (Paris, 1926)
Lawrence, T. E., *Seven Pillars of Wisdom* (London, 1935)
Lewis, Bernard, *The Emergence of Modern Turkey* (London, 1961)
Lewis, G. L., *Turkey* (London, 1955)
Lloyd George, D., *The Truth About the Peace Treaties* (London, 1938)
Loti, Pierre, *Disenchanted* (London, 1906)
Mears, E. G., *Modern Turkey* (New York, 1924)
Benoist-Méchin, *Mustapha Kemal, ou La Mort d'un Empire* (Paris, 1954)
Mikusch, Dagobert von, *Mustapha Kemal* (London, 1931)
Moorehead, Alan, *Gallipoli* (London, 1956)
Morgenthau, H., *Secrets of the Bosporus* (London, 1918)
Nicolson, Harold, *Sweet Waters* (London, 1928)
  Lord Carnock (London, 1930)
  Peacemaking 1919 (London, 1933)
  Curzon: The Last Phase (London, 1934)
Orga, Irfan, *Phœnix Ascendant* (London, 1958)
Orga, Irfan and Margarete, *Atatürk* (London, 1962)
Ostrorog, L., *The Angora Reform* (London, 1927)
Owen, Frank, *Tempestuous Journey: Lloyd George, His Life and Times* (London, 1955)
Paillarès, Michel, *Le Kémalisme devant les Alliés* (Paris, 1922)
Pallis, A. A., *Greece's Anatolian Venture – and After* (London, 1937)
Papen, Franz von, *Memoirs* (London, 1953)
Pears, Sir Edwin, *Forty Years in Constantinople* (London, 1916)
Petroff, Sultane, *Trente Ans à la Cour de Bulgarie* (Paris, 1927)
Presland, John, *Deedes Bey* (London, 1942)
Price, G. Ward, *Extra-Special Correspondent* (London, 1957). 8
Ramsaur, E. E., *The Young Turks* (Princeton, 1957)
Rawlinson, A., *Adventures in the Near East* (London, 1923). 9
Robinson, Richard D., *The First Turkish Republic* (Harvard, 1963)
Ronaldshay, Earl of, *Life of Lord Curzon*. 3 Vols. (London, 1928)
Ryan, Sir Andrew, *The Last of the Dragomans* (London, 1951)

Sanders, Liman von, *Five Years in Turkey* (London, 1927). 10
Sciaky, Leon, *Farewell to Salonika* (London, 1946)
Sforza, Count Carlo, *Makers of Modern Europe* (London, 1930)
  European Dictatorships (London, 1932)
Sheridan, Clare, *Nuda Veritas* (London, 1927)
Sherrill, C. H., *A Year's Embassy to Mustafa Kemal* (New York, 1934)
Smith, Elaine Diana, *Turkey: Origins of the Kemalist Movement and the
    Government of the Grand National Assembly*, 1919–23 (Washington,
    1959)
Sperco, Willy, *Mustapha Kemal Atatürk* (Paris, 1950)
Spector, Ivan, *The Soviet Union and the Moslem World* (Washington, 1956)
Temperley, H. M. V., *A History of the Peace Conference of Paris*. Vol. 6
    (London, 1924)
Townshend, Maj.-Gen. Sir Charles, *My Mesopotamian Campaign* (London,
    1920)
Toynbee, Arnold J., *The Western Question in Greece and Turkey* (London,
    1922). 11
Vansittart, Sir Robert, *The Mist Procession* (London, 1958)
Waugh, Sir Telford, *Turkey: Yesterday, Today and Tomorrow* (London, 1930)
Wavell, A. P., *The Palestine Campaigns* (London, 1929)
  Allenby, Soldier and Statesman (London, 1946)
Webster, Donald Everett, *The Turkey of Atatürk* (Philadelphia, 1939)
Windsor, The Duke of, *A King's Story* (London, 1951)
Yalman, Ahmed Emin, *Turkey in the World War* (Yale, 1930)
  Turkey in My Time (Oklahoma, 1956)
Yeats-Brown, Francis, *Golden Horn* (London, 1932)
Zeine, Zeine N., *The Struggle for Arab Independence* (Beirut, 1960)

Lausanne Conference on Near Eastern Affairs, 1922–23 (H.M.S.O., London,
    1923)
Papers Relating to the Foreign Relations of the United States, 1919
    (Washington, 1934)
Survey of International Affairs. 1925 Vol. I; 1936, 1938 Vol. I (Oxford,
    1927, 1931, 1941)

Thanks are due to authors and to the following publishers for permission to quote from
works indicated above:

  1   William Heinemann Ltd
  2   Cassell & Co. Ltd
  3   Odhams Books Ltd
  4   John Murray Ltd
  5   Edward Arnold Ltd
  6   John Murray Ltd
  7   Jonathan Cape Ltd and the Executors of the Hemingway Estate
  8   George G. Harrap & Co. Ltd
  9   Hutchinson & Co. Ltd
10   Baillière, Tindall & Cox Ltd
11   Constable & Co. Ltd

Newspapers, Periodicals, etc.: Other Languages

A. Adnan. *Ten Years of Republic in Turkey*. Political Quarterly VI. London 1935.

Anon. *Turkish Facts and Fantasies,* Foreign Affairs III. New York. July, 1925.

J. Walter Collins. Article in Contemporary Review XIV. London, 1933.

Sister Ethel Curry (E. McLeod Smith), *A Prisoner in Aleppo*. Nurses' League Journal VII. Kensington, London. December, 1919.

Maj.-Gen. James Harbord, *American Military Mission to Armenia*. Inter national Conciliation CLI. New York. June, 1920.

Investigating Turkey and Trans-Caucasia, and *Mustapha Kemal Pasha and his Party*, World's Work XL. New York. May–June, 1920.

Enver Ziya Karal, *History-writing in Turkey*. Middle Eastern Affairs. New York. October, 1959.

King-Crane Report. Editor and Publisher. New York. December, 1922.

Sir Percy Loraine, *Kemal Atatürk: An Appreciation*. Reprint from broadcast delivered 10th November 1948, B.B.C., London.

Clair Price, *Kemal Pasha: Creator of a New Turkey*. Current History XVI (New York, 1922)

Dankwart A. Rustow, *The Army and the Founding of the Turkish Republic*. World Politics XI (Yale, 1959)

Foreign Policy of the Turkish Republic. (In *Foreign Policy in World Politics*) (Englewood Cuffs, N.J., 1958)

Talat Pasha, *Posthumous Memoirs*. Current History XV (New York, 1921)

The Chicago Daily News
Daily Express
Daily Mail
The Manchester Guardian
The Times

Oral Sources

As listed in Acknowledgements.

CHRONOLOGY

1876

31st August. Abdul Hamid II proclaimed Sultan of Turkey.

22nd December. Abdul Hamid proclaims Parliamentary Constitution.

1877

24th April. Russia invades Turkey.

May. Abdul Hamid suspends Constitution and dissolves Parliament.

1878

31st January. Turkey sues for an Armistice.

3rd March. Treaty of San Stephano.

13th June – 13th July. Congress and Treaty of Berlin.

1881

Birth of Mustafa to Ali Riza and Zübeyde at Salonika.

1883

German military mission established in Turkey.

1893

Mustafa enters Military Secondary School at Salonika, where he is given the additional name of Kemal.

1895

Mustafa Kemal enters Military Training School at Monastir.

1896

Revolt by students of Military Medical School in Constantinople suppressed.

1897

17th April. Turkey declares war on Greece, following a Greek threat to annex Crete. Peace settlement by intervention of the European Powers.

1898

State visit of Kaiser Wilhelm II to Turkey.

1899

13th March. Kemal enters War College in Constantinople.

1902

Kemal graduates as Lieutenant to Staff College in Constantinople.

1905

11th January. Kemal passes out of Staff College with rank of Staff Captain and is afterwards posted to Fifth Army in Damascus.

1906

October. Kemal helps to found Fatherland (*Vatan*) Society in Damascus.

1907

20th June. Kemal promoted Adjutant-Major.
September. Kemal posted to Third Army at Salonika.

1908

24th July. 'Young Turk' Revolution in Salonika. Committee of Union and Progress forces Abdul Hamid to restore Constitution of 1876 and recall Parliament.
5th October. Bulgaria proclaims independence.
7th October. Austria-Hungary annexes Bosnia and Herzegovina.
12th October. Crete votes for Union with Greece.
Kemal sent to Tripolitania on mission for Committee of Union and Progress.

1909

13th April. Counter-revolution in Constantinople. Union and Progress striking force, with Kemal as divisional chief of staff, marches on the city from Salonika.
27th April. Deposition and exile of Abdul Hamid. Succession of Mehmed V as Sultan.
Kemal attends Congress of Union and Progress Party in Salonika.
6th September. Kemal appointed Commander of Third Army training course and later Commander of Thirty-eighth Infantry Regiment.

1910

Kemal serves as chief of staff in suppression of revolt in Albania.
Kemal sent to Paris with military mission to attend French army manœuvres.

1911

13th September. Kemal posted to General Staff in Constantinople.
5th October. Italian invasion of Tripoli.
Kemal with Turkish Forces at Tobruk and Derna.
27th November. Kemal promoted to Major.

1912

8th October – 3rd December. First Balkan War. Montenegro, Serbia, Bulgaria and Greece invade Turkey. Severe Turkish defeats. Loss of

Salonika. Armistice agreed before Constantinople. Kemal returns home. *Coup d'état* against Government by Union and Progress officers.

25th November. Kemal appointed Director of Operations for relief of Adrianople.

Fall of Adrianople.

1913

30th May. Treaty of London between Turkey and Balkan states.

30th June – 20th July. Second Balkan War. Bulgaria attacks Greece, Serbia and Rumania. Turkey recovers Adrianople.

27th September. Treaty of Bucharest restores territory to Turkey.

27th October. Kemal appointed Military Attaché in Sofia.

1914

1st March. Kemal promoted Lieutenant-Colonel.

28th June. Assassination of Archduke Franz Ferdinand at Sarajevo.

16th July. Kemal sends despatch to War Minister from Sofia, urging a policy of Turkish neutrality in the event of war, with a view to possible later intervention against Bulgaria and Central Powers.

28th July. Austria declares war on Serbia, with support of Germany.

2nd August. Turkey signs secret alliance with Germany.

11th August. Turkey purchases German warships *Goeben* and *Breslau* on arrival in the Bosporus.

28th October. Turkey shells Russian Black Sea ports.

3rd November. Russia declares war on Turkey.

5th November. Britain and France declare war on Turkey.

1915

2nd February. Kemal appointed to reorganize and command Nineteenth Division, in Thrace.

19th February. Unsuccessful Allied naval attack on Dardanelles.

25th February. Kemal establishes Headquarters of Nineteenth Division at Maidos, on Gallipoli Peninsula.

25th April. Allied military landings at Ariburnu (Anzac). Advance checked by Kemal, with Nineteenth Division.

1st June. Kemal promoted Colonel.

8th–9th August. Kemal appointed to command of Sixteenth Army Corps. Checks second Allied advance.

1916

9th January. Allied evacuation of Gallipoli Peninsula.

14th January. Kemal posted to Adrianople in command of Sixteenth Army Corps. Transfer to Caucasus front.

1st April. Kemal promoted General and Pasha.

27th June. Sherif of Mecca proclaims independence of Arabia.

6th–7th August. Kemal recaptures Bitlis and Mush from Russians.

1917

5th March. Kemal appointed second-in-command – effective Com mander – of Second Army.

11th March. British forces capture Baghdad.

5th July. Kemal appointed Commander of Seventh Army in Syria.

20th September. Kemal sends report to Government on the poor state of the army and the country, and relinquishes his command.

October. Kemal returns to Constantinople.

11th December. British forces capture Jerusalem.

15th December – 5th January 1918. Kemal visits Germany with Crown Prince Vahid-ed-Din.

1918

3rd July. Death of Sultan Mehmed V. Vahid-ed-Din succeeds him as Mehmed VI.

7th August. Kemal reappointed Commander of Seventh Army, in Palestine.

19th–30th September. British forces, under General Allenby, drive Turkish forces out of Palestine and Syria. Kemal defends frontier north of Aleppo.

30th October. Armistice signed between Turkey and Britain at Mudros.

31st October. Kemal takes over command of Army Group at Adana.

7th November. Dissolution of Army Group.

13th November. Kemal returns to Constantinople. Allied fleets enter Constantinople.

21st November. Dissolution of Parliament.

1919

18th January. Opening of Peace Conference at Versailles.

30th April. Kemal appointed Inspector-General of Ninth (later Third) Army in Anatolia.

15th May. Greek forces land in Smyrna, with Allied approval.

19th May. Kemal lands in Samsun.

21st June. Kemal issues 'Declaration of Independence' at Amasya. Summons Nationalist Congress at Sivas.

23rd June. Kemal ordered by Government to return to Constantinople.

8th July. Kemal resigns from the army and is dismissed by Government.

23rd July–6th August. Nationalist Congress at Erzurum, under presidency of Kemal. Issue of National Pact.

4th–13th September. Nationalist Congress at Sivas under presidency of Kemal. Confirmation of National Pact. Establishment of Representative Committee.

5th October. Resignation of Government.

7th November. New Parliament elected in Constantinople with Nationalist representation.

27th December. Kemal establishes headquarters at Angora, with Representative Committee.

1920

28th January. National Pact adopted by Constantinople Parliament.

9th February. Evacuation of French garrison from Marash and start of general withdrawal from Cilicia.

16th March. Military occupation of Constantinople by Allies.

11th April. Dissolution of Constantinople Parliament.

23rd April. First Grand National Assembly meets at Angora.

11th May. Kemal condemned to death by Sultan's Government.

10th June. Treaty of Sèvres presented by Allies to Sultan's Government.

22nd June – 9th July. Greek army advances into Anatolia and captures Brusa.

10th August. Treaty of Sèvres signed by Sultan's Government.

24th August. Draft treaty initialled in Moscow between Soviet Union and Nationalist Government.

28th September – 2nd November. Nationalist forces invade Armenia and capture Kars.

2nd December. Soviet Union establishes Armenian Republic at Erivan.

3rd December. Treaty of Gümrü settles Turco-Armenian frontiers.

1921

6th–10th January. Greek advance checked at First Battle of Inönü.

20th January. Grand National Assembly at Angora adopts Constitution Act, based on popular sovereignty.

23rd February – 12th March. London Conference fails to reach agreement with Nationalists on modifications to Treaty of Sèvres.

16th March. Treaty of Moscow between Nationalist Government and Soviet Union.

23rd March – 1st April. Greeks resume offensive in Anatolia, and are checked at Second Battle of Inönü.

10th July. Greeks resume offensive and capture Eskishehir.

5th August. Kemal given full powers as Commander-in-Chief by Grand National Assembly.

23rd August – 13th September. Battle of the Sakarya. Turks check Greek advance before Angora.

19th September. Kemal given title of Gazi and rank of Marshal by Grand National Assembly.

13th October. Treaty of Kars between Nationalist Government and Transcaucasian Soviet Republics.

20th October. Treaty of Angora between Nationalist Government and France.

1922

26th August – 9th September. Nationalist forces defeat Greeks in counter-offensive and capture Smyrna, which is destroyed by fire.

23rd September. Nationalist forces enter Neutral Zone at Chanak, threatening Constantinople.

3rd–11th October. Conference at Mudanya agrees on Armistice between Allies and Nationalist Government.

19th October. Resignation of Lloyd George and his Government.

1st November. Kemal proclaims abolition of Sultanate.

17th November. Flight of Sultan Mehmed VI from Constantinople.

20th November. Opening of Peace Conference at Lausanne.

1923

14th January. Death of Zübeyde, Kemal's mother, in Smyrna.

29th January. Kemal marries Latife in Smyrna.

4th February. Breakdown of Lausanne Conference.

17th February. Kemal opens Economic Congress in Smyrna.

23rd April. Resumption of Lausanne Conference.

24th July. Treaty of Lausanne.

9th August. Foundation of People's Party.

11th August. Second Grand National Assembly.

2nd October. Turkish forces occupy Constantinople, following Allied evacuation.

9th October. Angora (Ankara) becomes capital of Turkey.

29th October. Proclamation of the Turkish Republic, with Kemal as President.

1924

3rd March. Abolition of the Caliphate, Ministry of Religious Affairs, and religious schools.

8th April. Abolition of religious courts.

17th November. Foundation of Progressive Party.

1925

11th February – 12th April. Revolt in Kurdistan.

4th March. Law for Maintenance of Public Order gives Government exceptional powers.

3rd June. Suppression of Progressive Party.

5th August. Kemal divorces Latife.

30th August – 2nd September. Kemal tours Kastamonu province, announcing abolition of fez, suppression of religious brotherhoods, and closing of sacred tombs as places of worship.

1926

17th February. Adoption of new Civil Law code.

5th June. Agreement on Mosul. Treaty of Angora between Turkey, Britain and Irak.

15th June – 13th July. Plot against life of Kemal in Izmir (Smyrna). Trial and execution of ringleaders.

1st–26th August. Trial and execution of 'Young Turk' leaders and others in Ankara.

1927

1st July. Kemal revisits Istanbul (Constantinople).

15th–20th October. Kemal makes historic speech to Congress of People's Party.

1st November. Third Grand National Assembly. Kemal re-elected President of the Republic.

1928

3rd November. Introduction of Latin alphabet.

1930

12th August. Foundation of Free Party.

17th November. Dissolution of Free Party.

23rd December. Religious riot at Menemen. Trials and executions.

1931

15th April. Foundation of Turkish Historical Society.

4th May. Fourth Grand National Assembly. Kemal re-elected President of the Republic.

1932

12th July. Foundation of Turkish Linguistic Society.

12th August. Turkey becomes member of League of Nations.

1934

9th January. First Five-Year Plan for industrial development.

9th February. Balkan Pact concluded between Turkey, Greece, Rumania and Yugoslavia.

29th November. Kemal takes name of Atatürk, in terms of new law requiring Turks to adopt surnames.

8th December. Women made eligible to vote in Parliamentary elections and to become members of Parliament.

1935

1st March. Fifth Grand National Assembly. Atatürk re-elected President of the Republic.

1936

29th May. Dispute regarding future status of Hatay (Alexandretta) referred to the League of Nations.

20th July. Montreux Convention signed, regulating future Turkish régime for the Straits.

4th September. Visit of King Edward VIII to Atatürk in Istanbul.

1937

27th January. Autonomy of Hatay agreed between Turkey, France and Syria.

9th July. Saadabad Pact signed, between Turkey, Irak, Persıa and Afghanistan.

1938

11th March. Illness of Atatürk officially announced.

3rd July. Franco-Turkish agreement to send French and Turkish troops into Hatay, to supervise elections.

2nd September. Grand National Assembly votes nominal Republic of Hatay, with Turks in effective control.

18th September. Second Five Year Plan for industrial development.

10th November. Death of Atatürk

11th November. Succession of Ismet Inönü as President of the Republic.

APPENDIX

THE NATIONAL PACT

CLOSE translation from the Turkish, made independently of the French version, of the text of The National Pact, as printed in the PROCEEDINGS OF THE TURKISH CHAMBER OF DEPUTIES of the 17th February 1920.

The Members of the Ottoman Chamber of Deputies recognize and affirm that the independence of the State and the future of the Nation can be assured by complete respect for the following principles, which represent the maximum of sacrifice which can be undertaken in order to achieve a just and lasting peace, and that the continued existence of a stable Ottoman Sultanate and society is impossible outside of the said principles:

First Article – Inasmuch as it is necessary that the destinies of the portions of the Turkish Empıre which are populated exclusively by an Arab majority, and which on the conclusion of the armistice of the 30th October 1918 were in the occupation of enemy forces, should be determined in accordance with the votes which shall be freely given by the inhabitants, the whole of those parts whether within or outside the said armistice line which are inhabited by an Ottoman Moslem majority, united in religion, in race and in aim, imbued with sentiments of mutual respect for each other and of sacrifice, and wholly respectful of each other's racial and social rights and surrounding conditions, form a whole which does not admit of division for any reason in truth or in ordinance.

Second Article – We accept that, in the case of the three Sanjaks which united themselves by a general vote to the mother country when they first were free, recourse should again be had, if necessary, to a free popular vote.

Third Article – The determination of the juridical status of western Thrace also, which has been made dependent on the Turkish peace, must be effected in accordance with the votes which shall be given by the inhabitants in complete freedom.

Fourth Article – The security of the city of Constantinople, which is the seat of the Caliphate of Islam, the capital of the Sultanate, and the headquarters of the Ottoman Government, and of the Sea of Marmara must be protected from every danger. Provided this principle is maintained, whatever decision may be arrived at jointly by us and all other Governments concerned, regarding the opening of the Bosporus to the commerce and traffic of the world, is valid.

Fifth Article – The rights of minorities as defined in the treaties concluded between the Entente Powers and their enemies and certain of their associates shall be confirmed and assured by us – in reliance on the belief that the Moslem minorities in neighbouring countries also will have the benefit of the same rights.

Sixth Article – It is a fundamental condition of our life and continued existence that we, like every country, should enjoy complete independence and liberty in the matter of assuring the means of our development, in order that our national and economic development should be rendered possible and that it should be possible to conduct affairs in the form of a more up-to-date regular administration.

For this reason we are opposed to restrictions inimical to our development in political, judicial, financial and other matters.

The conditions of settlement of our proved debts shall likewise not be contrary to these principles.

From *The Western Question in Greece and Turkey*,
by Arnold J. Toynbee, op. cit.

INDEX